# Thomas Jefferson
# and the Rhetoric of Virtue

# Thomas Jefferson
# and the Rhetoric of Virtue

JAMES L. GOLDEN

AND

ALAN L. GOLDEN

ROWMAN & LITTLEFIELD PUBLISHERS, INC.
Lanham • Boulder • New York • Oxford

ROWMAN & LITTLEFIELD PUBLISHERS, INC.
Published in the United States of America

Rowman & Littlefield Publishers, Inc.
4720 Boston Way, Lanham, Maryland 20706
www.rowmanlittlefield.com

12 Hid's Copse Road
Cumnor Hill, Oxford OX2 9JJ, England

British Library Cataloguing in Publication Information Available

**Library of Congress Cataloging-in-Publication Data**

Golden, James L.
   Thomas Jefferson and the rhetoric of virtue / James L. Golden, Alan L. Golden.
      p. cm.
   Includes bibliographical references and index.
   ISBN 0-7425-2080-3 (alk. paper)
      1. Jefferson, Thomas, 1743–1826—Views on virtue. 2. Jefferson, Thomas,
1743–1826—Philosophy. 3. Jefferson, Thomas, 1743–1826—Language.
4. Virtue—Political aspects—United States—History—18th century.
5. Rhetoric—Political aspects—United States—History—18th century.
6. Discourse analysis—United States. 7. United States—Politics and
government—1775–1783. 8. United States—Politics and government—1783–1809.
9. Liberalism—United States—History—18th century. I. Golden, Alan L., 1956–2001
II. Title.
   E332.2 .G65 2002
   973.4'6'092—dc21

2001008730

Printed in the United States of America

♾™ The paper used in this publication meets the minimum requirements of
American National Standard for Information Sciences—Permanence of Paper for
Printed Library Materials, ANSI/NISO Z39.48–1992.

# In memory of Alan L. Golden, 1956–2001

On December 8, 2001, Alan L. Golden died in an automobile accident as he drove home from the college where he taught—Lock Haven University of Pennsylvania. He was an associate professor of history and a student of the life and career of Thomas Jefferson. As coauthor of this ten-year study, Alan was a conscientious collaborator, comforting counselor, thorough researcher, and meticulous editor.

One of the major themes of this volume—the discourse of virtue—is an apt description of Alan's worldview and his professional career. He sought to incorporate the traditional cardinal virtues of courage, temperance, wisdom, and justice into his communication practices. These virtues were visibly present during the past decade as we labored together on this project. He always recommended that we show courage in taking a stand on the side of virtue when dealing with a sensitive or highly controversial issue. Moreover, on those rare occasions when he and I had different opinions on a particular question, he never attempted to defend his position in an intemperate way; but, like one of his heroes Benjamin Franklin, he phrased his sentiments in a conciliatory question such as this: "Do you feel that the following argument would help solve the problem?"; or, "Is this a point worth considering?" Similarly, he consistently showed wisdom in choices made and sources used throughout this volume. For this reason, he spent many days checking every sentence and footnote in his effort to increase the accuracy of the final draft. Finally, he was fully committed to upholding the moral concept of justice, the noblest virtue of all. For it is this integrating virtue which maintains the principle that "all people in the same essential category must be treated in the same way." It was he, for example, who first recognized the need to add a new chapter (16) focusing on Jefferson's attitudes and actions on African Americans and slavery.

By working as equal partners on this book, we both profited. I gained a greater understanding of and appreciation for the discipline of history. Alan, in turn, learned more about rhetoric and political communication. In the end, together we came to realize, as did Jefferson, why the Greek and Roman historians and their counterparts in rhetoric and public address recognized the strong relationship that exists between these fields of study.

In all, the collaboration experience with a loving son represents the most unforgettable and enduring moment in my personal and professional life. Whenever I examine this work in the future, I not only will think of Mr. Jefferson, as well as the powerful theme of virtue, but of the dedicated co-author who helped make this volume possible.

James L. Golden
December 20, 2001

# Contents

~

# Preface

~

At the midpoint of the twentieth century, at the height of Cold War tensions, Henry Steele Commager described Thomas Jefferson as "the most philosophical" and "contemporary" Founding Father, whose commitment to freedom and virtue, as expressed in his voluminous writings and memorable actions, had made him "the central figure in American history." He then added that "if freedom and democracy survive in our generation—he may yet prove to be the central figure in modern history."[1] More than four decades later, thirteen thousand students, faculty, administrators, guests, and members of the general public assembled on the grounds of the University of Virginia in 1992 to hear Mikhail Gorbachev, the former president of the Soviet Union, deliver the principal address of what was to be the official beginning of a year-long celebration of the 250th anniversary of Jefferson's birth. In an unforgettable, and perhaps ironic, statement, Gorbachev declared that "having started a dialogue with Jefferson, one continues the conversation forever."[2]

That Jeffersonian ideals have had relevance both to Americans during the early struggles of the Cold War and to a later president of the Soviet Union provides an interesting commentary on his historically broad appeal. If anything, the fascination with Jefferson—evident from the time of the dramatic moment of his death on July 4, 1826—has grown in recent years, both nationally and internationally.[3] We have come to expect the constant scrutiny of his life and career in a seemingly endless number of books, articles, convention programs, and seminars. As evidence of the vitality of the scholarly debate over the public and private Jefferson, the University of Virginia hosted a conference as a prelude to its commemoration of the 250th anniversary of his birth. Building on the theme of Jefferson's continuing relevance and influence, the conference's sessions, along with its companion volume of published essays, were dedicated to Jefferson's legacy as it related to the 1990s.[4] In addition to the intensifying scrutiny from scholars, in recent years Jefferson has received widespread popular attention in the form of newspaper articles, television documentaries, and even a major Hollywood movie and television miniseries. Most dramatically, recent scientific tests proving that he had an intimate relationship with one of his slaves created a media frenzy and forced more than a few notable Jefferson scholars to reevaluate their earlier assessments.

As we enter into the twenty-first century, Thomas Jefferson stands as the most compelling, controversial, and enigmatic of the Founding Fathers. Because it seems as though virtually every aspect of Jefferson's life and career has been carefully dissected and scrutinized again and again, it is necessary for those undertaking research on the third president to consider whether their work is breaking new ground, or at least shedding new light on a previously considered theme.

## Jefferson, Discourse, and the Rhetoric of Virtue

The idea for this study first began more than a decade ago when one of the authors—a rhetorician—visited Monticello. During the tour, he noticed the works of Ossian, regarded by some in the mid-eighteenth century as the "Scottish Homer," on the shelves of Jefferson's library. The inclusion of Ossian among Jefferson's now legendary library holdings indicated his probable knowledge of Hugh Blair, the most popular and influential British rhetorician of the era and primary advocate of the legitimacy of Ossian. Although the existence of the mythical Ossian was being questioned by many scholars during the late eighteenth century, Blair continued to embrace him. The familiarity of Jefferson with Ossian, and quite probably with Blair, was compelling. In the weeks and months following the tour of Monticello, closer inspection of Jefferson's diverse library holdings and preliminary work in his voluminous writings confirmed that he was a careful student of classical and modern scholars of rhetoric. So great was his interest, as it turned out, that during his long career he even developed a clearly defined program for the study of discourse. (Throughout this study, we use the words "rhetoric" and "discourse" interchangeably.) Because of the enormous volume of work on Jefferson's life and career, it seemed likely that work had been done in the area of his interest in rhetoric. But although Jefferson scholars had noted his interest in this field, surprisingly no one had conducted a careful and systematic examination of his rhetorical philosophy and practice as a whole.

Despite the initial enthusiasm of discovering a new perspective on Jefferson, it eventually became clear that merely establishing his interest in discourse was not enough. A single synthesizing theme was necessary to make sense of his wide-ranging writings on the subject. The one concept that emerged from further research as a constant theme throughout Jefferson's writings on the subject of rhetoric appeared to be, not surprisingly to students of the early American republic, virtue. Rhetoric, to Jefferson, was a vehicle for upholding virtue. With this realization, we came to understand why he was so keenly interested in rhetoric. This study argues that, because Jefferson's philosophy of rhetoric or discourse set the parameters for how he felt virtue should be studied and how it could be expressed, it is necessary to examine his rhetorical philosophy to understand more fully his commitment to virtue.

The title we have chosen for this volume—*Thomas Jefferson and the Rhetoric of Virtue*—captures the overarching theme we emphasize throughout the study. A quest for virtue was the guiding principle of his life, and the crucial duty of discourse, he believed, was to move individuals and society as a whole upwards on the scale of good.

With virtue as the underlying theme of our study, we understood that our work would be drawn into the long-standing debate over the major ideological influences on Jefferson and the other leading figures of the early American republic. For generations, historians and other commentators on the Founding era of American history stressed liberalism as the dominant ideological influence. Especially when viewing the Revolutionary period, they argued, the influence of liberal ideas could not be disputed. Many older scholars were less than subtle in declaring, for example, that not to begin with John Locke was not to understand the ideological orientation of Jefferson. In recent decades, however, reinterpretation has provided an alternative view. In a series of pathbreaking studies published in the 1940s, 1950s, 1960s, and 1970s, scholars such as Douglass Adair, Bernard Bailyn, Gordon Wood, and J. G. A. Pocock began to focus on what they believed was a striking, and largely ignored, ideological influence on the Founding generation: preliberal or classical republicanism. Advancing the ideas first presented by these eminent scholars, other historians have provided what they consider to be convincing evidence to support this view.[5] Although the debate over the ideological influences on the Founding era continues to be a lively one, what can be defined as a republican synthesis has long dominated the discussion.

In view of this reorientation of historical interpretation, certain questions now need to be raised when studying any topic that in one way or another focuses on the ideology of the early American republic. If we stress the influence of republican ideals, as has been the trend, do we reject the conclusions drawn by those earlier historians who focused on the liberal nature of the ideology of the Founding era? Conversely, if we choose to stress the influence of Locke and others who promoted individual liberty, are we automatically discounting classical republican ideology? Specifically in regard to our topic, in uncovering virtue as the dominant theme in Jefferson's philosophy of discourse, are we taking a strong republican position? Viewed another way, does his clear passion for establishing a model for public and private discourse based on the ideal of virtue reduce his desire to promote individual freedom? Finally, have some historians gone too far in assuming that, in the unique environment of the early American republic, these two ideological strains were incompatible? Could both liberal and republican ideas have been evident, or must they be viewed as being at odds, or at least inherently independent of each other? In recent years, scholars building on previous research have been addressing many of these questions more effectively. For example, in her *Liberalism and Republicanism in the Historical Imagination*, Joyce Appleby questions whether our application of modern definitions of republicanism on the late eighteenth century, most especially on the political ideas of Thomas Jefferson, is too restrictive. Meanwhile, Lance Banning and others have argued that, at least when considering the years of the early American republic, republican and liberal ideologies should not necessarily be considered mutually exclusive.[6]

In our study, we do not intend to analyze the broader ideological influences on the early American republic. In fact, in considering his philosophy of discourse, we do not even hope to provide definitive answers to all questions regarding the ideological influences on Jefferson. We are not, after all, focusing our attention on political ideology. In addressing his fairly sophisticated discourse philosophy, however, we have made a significant effort in our volume to identify those ideas that most influenced his rhetoric of virtue.

# Ideological Orientation of Jefferson's Rhetoric of Virtue

Close examination of Jefferson's extensive writings on rhetoric, we believe, reveals that he drew his ideological inspiration from a variety of sources. This study contends that Jefferson's ideological influences, at least in certain areas, were more diverse than has been believed. If true, this doubtless was the result of several factors. It is probable that he found no one philosophy that suited the unique rhetorical environment of the early American republic. Whereas it goes without saying that Jefferson was a product of his time, we must always remember that he was concerned—virtually obsessed—with constructing a worldview that rose to meet the peculiar exigencies of his cherished republic. Further, while Jefferson was constructing his philosophy of discourse—a lifelong process—he also was a participant in the creation and development of political institutions; thus, his philosophy had to have the potential for real, practical application. Since he was in many ways a pragmatic politician, he felt compelled to construct a model for effective public as well as private discourse.

Because most recent analyses of Jefferson's ideology primarily have been concerned with political philosophy, it is understandable that, since the pathbreaking studies of Bailyn and others, they have focused on the influence of a certain strain of republican thought. In attacking corrupt political institutions, ideas of the classical period as adopted by certain Renaissance and later seventeenth- and eighteenth-century writers provided an attractive model for leaders of the Revolutionary era. But even if true for political ideas, as Jefferson established his philosophy of discourse such refraction was not necessary. We see Jefferson's rhetorical principles as grounded not only in seventeenth- and eighteenth-century thought, but also directly tied to the Classical era itself. There is no question that he went to the original sources, especially Greek and Roman, for his philosophy of discourse. Although some have questioned the extent of the Founding Fathers' firsthand knowledge of Classical texts,[7] we find compelling evidence that Jefferson knew many of these sources intimately. In not focusing exclusively on political ideology, we have identified a purely classical inspiration perhaps heretofore underappreciated.

In sum, it is argued in this study that in constructing his rhetoric of virtue, Jefferson sampled from a wide variety of classical and modern sources. Jefferson's taste in previous rhetorical thought was, for no better word, eclectic. This drawing from diverse ideological inspirations is in keeping with what one historian has determined to be his "great gift . . . as a synthesizer."[8] For this reason, Jefferson's views on discourse—perhaps even more than with his political philosophy—defy traditional classifications. In developing our thesis, we argue that in regard to his philosophy of discourse, certain ideological strains, thought by some to be in conflict, may not be incompatible. At least in this one area, Jefferson seemed to fit well into both liberal and republican traditions. Readers may draw whatever conclusions they feel appropriate as to broader applications of our thesis.

## Plan of the Volume

The main body of our study is divided into two parts, the first dealing with Jefferson's principles of moral philosophical discourse and the second with an analysis of select samples of his rhetorical practice. The eight chapters in part 1 seek to put his perspectives on discourse in clear focus. Chapter 1 outlines Jefferson's basic views on the importance and value of discourse. Chapter 2 lays the groundwork for his philosophy by describing how he came to believe that virtue constitutes the primary subject matter of discourse. Given that appeals to virtue are closely allied to the quality of reason, chapter 3 strives to show how argumentation is designed to promote morality and societal values. Chapter 4, building upon the nature of informal or practical reasoning, explains how personal and emotional appeals arouse the social affections, thereby creating a desire for virtuous conduct and actions. Chapter 5 depicts the part that language control and delivery play in the channeling of a message. These five chapters center their attention on discourse in general. The final chapters in part 1, 6 through 8, concentrate on specific forms of oral and written communication, all of which have special challenges in stressing various aspects of virtue.

The chapters in part 1 show that in constructing his rhetoric of virtue, Jefferson found inspiration in sources that focused on the public and private actions of the individual. As we see in part 2, during his long career Jefferson's principles of moral philosophical discourse very often were challenged. Attempting to assess how his principles stood up to these challenges, the eight chapters in part two offer critiques of representative samples of Jefferson's rhetorical practice. Chapters 9 through 13 describe his discourse performance as a conversationalist and letter-writer, a polemicist during the Revolutionary War era, a special occasional speaker, a legal advocate, and a historical writer and social commentator. His role as a rhetorical critic is the subject of chapters 14 and 15. Chapter 16 focuses on Jefferson's verbal and nonverbal communication on the subjects of African Americans and slavery. We believe that this chapter, added as a response to recent revelations regarding Sally Hemings, helps to synthesize key issues relating to his rhetorical philosophy and practice. The purpose of the postscript is twofold: (1) to summarize the essence of Jefferson's rhetorical ideas and practice; and (2) to draw several major implications of the study.

The organizational structure adopted for this study, we feel, is necessary in order for readers to understand and appreciate Jefferson's rhetoric of virtue. Because he came to believe that one of his principal missions in life was to acquaint and inspire his countrymen with leading principles of Enlightenment thought, he knew that the medium for achieving this end was to develop a discourse philosophy based on virtue, and then attempt to implement its essential elements on the regional, national, and international stage. This he sought to do, as our analysis attempts to show, by taking advantage of his extensive readings, note-taking procedures, keen observational and critical powers, and rich personal experiences at home and abroad.

For the purpose of this study, the term rhetoric is defined, as one of the authors suggested in an earlier work, in the following way: "Genuine rhetoric occurs when a communicator presents an informative or suasory ethical verbal (written or oral) or nonverbal message specifically designed to create a persuasive effect in an audience comprised of readers or listeners who have a choice or perceived choice and the power to modify the exigencies upon which the discourse is constructed."[9] Since the written are included with the oral messages, rhetoric, from our perspective and that of Jefferson, is combined with belles lettres.

## Note on Sources

Preferring to allow Jefferson to speak in his own words, we made extensive use of direct quotations throughout our study. In doing so, we relied on various editions of his collected writings. In most cases, we allowed his spelling, punctuation, grammar, and syntax to stand as published. For example, we allowed his tendency to write "it's" when using the possessive pronoun to remain. But in certain cases, we made some changes for the sake of clarity. We begin sentences with capital letters, for instance, when he often began in the small case. We feel, however, that such minor editing in no way changes the meaning of the ideas Jefferson wished to express.

## Notes

1. "Thomas Jefferson Still Survives," *New York Times*, 1950. Reprinted in Francis Coleman Rosenberger, ed., *Jefferson Reader: A Treasury of Writings About Thomas Jefferson* (New York: Dutton, 1953), 23 and 25.
2. *Charlottesville Daily Progress*, April 14, 1993.

3. Merrill D. Peterson chronicled the ongoing fascination with Jefferson through the mid-twentieth century in his volume, *The Jefferson Image in the American Mind* (New York: Oxford University Press, 1960).

4. The essays commissioned for this conference were published in Peter S. Onuf, ed., *Jeffersonian Legacies* (Charlottesville: University Press of Virginia, 1993).

5. See Bernard Bailyn, *The Ideological Origins of the American Revolution* (Cambridge, Mass.: Harvard University Press, 1967); Trevor Colbourn, ed., *Fame and the Founding Fathers: Essays of Douglass Adair* (New York: Norton, 1974); J. G. A. Pocock, *The Machiavellian Moment: Florentine Political Thought and the Atlantic Republican Tradition* (Princeton: Princeton University Press, 1975); Gordon S. Wood, *The Creation of the American Republic, 1776–1787* (New York: Norton, 1972). Almost any study of this general topic includes what apparently has become an obligatory historiographical summary of this debate. One of the better analyses is found in Joyce Appleby, *Liberalism and Republicanism in the Historical Imagination* (Cambridge: Harvard University Press, 1992).

6. See Appleby, *Liberalism and Republicanism*, 1–33; and Lance Banning, *The Jeffersonian Persuasion: Evolution of a Party Ideology* (Ithaca: Cornell University Press, 1978).

7. For an analysis of this debate, see Carl J. Richard, *The Founders and the Classics: Greece, Rome, and the American Enlightenment* (Cambridge: Harvard University Press, 1994), 1–11.

8. Joyce Appleby, "Jefferson and His Complex Legacy," published in Onuf, ed., *Jeffersonian Legacies*, 7.

9. James L. Golden, et al., *The Rhetoric of Western Thought*, 1st ed. (Dubuque, Iowa: Kendall/Hunt, 1976), 3.

# Acknowledgments

~

We are indebted to numerous groups and individuals in the creation of this book. First and foremost, we wish to express our thanks to the library staffs of the University of Virginia and the College of William and Mary. In their main libraries and in their rare book and special collections rooms we were treated in a cooperative and friendly manner. Our special thanks also are extended to all those who offered readings and critiques during the manuscript phase, including the late Edward P. J. Corbett, a long-time professor of English and rhetoric at The Ohio State University. Although we sought to implement many valuable suggestions for improving the study, we are responsible for the final interpretations that appear.

We are similarly appreciative for the support of Madison House and Rowman & Littlefield. In particular, we wish to acknowledge the assistance and support of John Kaminski, a Jefferson scholar, Director of the Center for the Study of the American Constitution at the University of Wisconsin, Madison, and a guiding force at Madison House. We are indebted to the editorial staff at Rowman & Littlefield, particularly Mary Carpenter, Terry Fischer, and Lynn Gemmell, for the enthusiasm they exhibited while working with an inherited project.

Also of importance to this study is the nomination by Senator Robert Dole and appointment by President Clinton of one the authors to serve as a member of the Presidential Commission in Honor of the 250th Anniversary of Thomas Jefferson's Birth. In particular, we are grateful for the assistance of the late John Diamiantakiou in helping to make this appointment possible. Under the leadership of Merrill D. Peterson, this commission provided informative and inspirational dialogues on Jefferson's life and legacies.

We are further thankful for the help and encouragement from Daniel Jordan, president of the Thomas Jefferson Memorial Foundation. Throughout the many years required for this study, he provided us with important materials—and also participated in an interview regarding Jefferson's views and actions on the slavery issue. We appreciate the interviews granted to us by Eugene Foster on the nature, findings, and importance of the DNA study that he conducted in his effort to add to the knowledge of Jefferson's lineage. Finally, we wish to acknowledge the assistance of Mrs. Gale Spangler in the preparation of this manuscript and express our appreciation to family and friends, who showed great patience during this lengthy process. We are especially indebted to our wives, Ruth and Kimberly, for the help and inspiration they have given us the past ten years.

# PART ONE

# Jefferson's Philosophy of the Rhetoric of Virtue

# CHAPTER ONE

~

# Introduction of Jefferson to the World of Rhetoric

According to historian Gordon S. Wood, early in his life Thomas Jefferson had a compelling "desire to become the most cosmopolitan, the most liberal, the most genteel, and the most enlightened gentleman in all of America." This desire prompted him to learn to play the violin, study the classics and the French language, and acquire "the tastes and refinements of the larger world." Possessing "perfect self-control and serenity of spirit," adds Wood, "he came to see himself as a kind of impresario for America, rescuing his countrymen from their 'deplorable barbarism' by introducing them to the finest and most enlightened aspects of European culture."[1]

Upon his arrival at the College of William and Mary in 1760, following his extensive pre-college learning in the classics,[2] Jefferson already knew that he could not strengthen his interest in becoming an arbiter of taste and as a participant in the Enlightenment movement unless he became well versed in the principles of discourse and developed skills as a practitioner of the art of persuasion. For it was through discourse, he believed, that knowledge could be disseminated to the American people. Moreover, he also was convinced that if the citizens of the colonies could gain competence in discourse, they could enhance their communication competence and taste, and their appreciation of the concept of virtue that permeated the Enlightenment. William and Mary proved to be an ideal institution for the study of discourse; and Jefferson took advantage of the opportunity.

# The Making of Jefferson's Ideas on Discourse

## Rhetorical Training in Williamsburg

In the two years he spent at the College of William and Mary pursuing his undergraduate training, Jefferson worked closely with Dr. William Small, a native of Scotland and a graduate of Marischal College in Aberdeen. Appointed to the faculty of William and Mary in 1758, Small had an educational background that enabled him to teach a variety of courses both in the sciences and in the arts and humanities. One of his mentors had been the well-known Scottish philosopher and logician William Duncan.[3] Moreover, as an alumnus of Marischal College, Small doubtless knew the rhetorician George Campbell who, after graduating from Marischal, became principal of the institution in 1759. It is also highly likely that Small was fully aware of the interest in rhetoric and belles lettres that was developing in Edinburgh and in other parts of Scotland.[4]

When he joined the faculty, Small's specific title was professor of natural philosophy—a position that required him to teach mathematics and the laboratory sciences. One observer noted: "Under his instructions the sciences struck deep root in Virginia and were the parents of Revolution in Church and State."[5] But, fortunately for Jefferson, circumstances forced Small to take on an additional assignment that was to have a profound effect on Jefferson's scholarly pursuits throughout the rest of his life. Soon after the dismissal of professor Jacob Rowe,[6] who had been responsible for the subject area of discourse, Small became "the first who ever gave in that college regular lectures in Ethics, Rhetoric, and Belles Lettres."[7] In using the lecture format, Small was credited with introducing a new method of instruction at William and Mary.[8]

But Small's influence on Jefferson did not end with the completion of Jefferson's undergraduate work in 1762. He continued to meet with his former student, almost daily, for the next two years before his return to Birmingham, England, in 1764. These conversations, Jefferson later noted, broadened his knowledge of the arts and sciences, and helped him choose a profession. It seems clear, moreover, that Small, during his Williamsburg years, had come down hard on the side of freedom of thought and expression, and in favor of the natural rights of man. For this reason, Jefferson felt free to write to his former professor and friend in 1775, expressing his dismay that British troops had attacked "our brethren of Boston"—an unwarranted action that "has cut off our last hope of reconciliation. . . ."[9]

Although we have been unable to discover any written documents by Small in America, his name abroad, according to Edmund Randolph, "was not concealed among the literati of Europe."[10] Moreover, his influence on his students at the College of William and Mary was deep and enduring. John Page, a classmate of Jefferson's and later a governor of Virginia, used such superlatives as "beloved," "illustrious," and "great" to describe his favorite professor.[11] Jefferson's tribute was equally memorable. "Dr. William Small," he said in his "Autobiography," "fixed the destinies of my life. . . ."[12] He did so, first of all, by including in his classroom lectures and in his informal dialogues an emphasis on the latest developments in European culture, such as consideration of emerging thought in the arts and sciences. This message was warmly received by the youthful Jefferson who, observed Edmund Randolph, "panted after the arts, and discovered a taste in them, not easily satisfied with such scanty means, as existed" in the colony of Virginia.[13] Small, in short, succeeded in helping to strengthen Jefferson's wish to acquaint his fellow citizens with the essence of the Enlightenment. Small's second great contribution in helping his student fix the "destinies" of his life was his decision to persuade his friend George Wythe to accept Jefferson as a student of law.

Wythe was a largely self-educated man who shared Jefferson's interests in all matters of the law. He directed the attention of his students to the leading works in English law, and to the value of discourse for everyone seeking to become an attorney. After joining the faculty of William and Mary following the departure of Jefferson, Wythe continued to trumpet the advantages to be gained by aspiring legal students if they became highly proficient in oral and written discourse. By 1780, Jefferson proclaimed to James Madison:

> Wythe's school is numerous. They hold weekly courts and assemblies in the capitol. The professors join in it; and the young men dispute with elegance, method and learning.[14]

In making this positive assessment, Jefferson was taking pleasure in knowing that both Wythe and the College of William and Mary had endorsed a form of innovative discourse designed to elevate the students' taste and strengthen their speaking effectiveness, thereby placing themselves in an important part of the mainstream of Enlightenment thought and practices.

Wythe went on to become the teacher of such well-known judicial and political leaders as John Marshall, James Monroe, and Henry Clay. He

also became a member of the House of Burgesses; "a signer of the Declaration of Independence; designer of the seal of Virginia; and Chancellor
of the Commonwealth of Virginia."[15] One of his most remarkable
achievements, however, was the contribution he made to Jefferson.
Through his teachings and example, he demonstrated the power of ethos
that emanates from an exemplary life committed to virtue; the significant
role that argumentation based on reasonableness must play in discourse;
the usefulness that conversational ability and writing effectiveness have
as a means of conveying knowledge and virtue; and the potential that
parliamentary law holds for maintaining order and decorum in a legislative assembly. With such an influence, Wythe became the model whom
Jefferson most wished to emulate. In 1788, Jefferson called him "one of
the greatest men of the age. . . ."[16] Twenty-two years later, in 1810, he described Wythe as his "second father."[17] By the time he wrote his brief
"Autobiography" near the end of his life, Jefferson looked back with nos-
talgia, saying: "Mr. Wythe continued to be my faithful and beloved mentor in youth, and my most affectionate friend through life."[18]

But Jefferson's rhetorical training in Williamsburg went beyond the
tutelage of Small and Wythe. It also included his observation of discourse
practices in the House of Burgesses which featured the oratory of men
who were to become dominant political leaders in the colonial period and
beyond. Not the least of these persuasive spokesmen was Patrick Henry
who, with Jefferson present at the entry of the assembly hall, delivered his
celebrated speech on the Stamp Act. Henry's eloquence on this occasion
made a lasting impression on Jefferson which he enjoyed recounting.[19]

## Library Holdings

To reinforce what he had learned as a college student and young lawyer,
Jefferson developed a practice that was to have an unusually strong impact on his evolving ideas on discourse. Stemming from his love of books
and of reading in general, he began accumulating a personal library un-
surpassed in size and scope by any of his contemporaries. Reading was to
him the "greatest of all amusements," and an enormous "delight"; as an
old man, he observed that he could not "live without books. . . ."[20]

This urge to read became the driving force in his purchase of books. An
analysis of his letters, account books, and other documents reveals the
care he took in ordering volumes, often calling for specific editions and
particular sizes.[21] When, in 1814, pressing financial exigencies and his patriotic desire to replace the nation's library, which had been destroyed by

a British-set fire in the War of 1812, forced him to begin negotiations with the Library of Congress for the sale of most of his books, he explained how he had put together a collection ranging from nine to ten thousand volumes.[22]

If we were to visit Jefferson's library as he had developed it, we would find many volumes embracing the classical and modern periods that focused on discourse theory and practice. Among the classical Greek rhetorical works to be seen would be Plato's *Dialogues*; Aristotle's *Ethics, Logic,* and *Rhetoric*; Isocrates' *Complete Works*; the *Complete Works of Demosthenes and Aeschines*; and Longinus's *On the Sublime*. Additionally, we would note that Jefferson did not limit himself to the most celebrated Greek rhetoricians and orators; indeed, he also had copies of the volumes on discourse produced by Demetrius of Phalerum and Dionysius of Halicarnassus.

As we proceed through the stacks, the writings of the Roman scholars Cicero and Quintilian come into view. Cicero's rhetorical works included his *De Oratore, The Orations, Letters, Epistles to Atticus, de Fato,* and *de legibus*. Moreover, we would observe the presence of Quintilian's *Institutio Oratoria* and his *Declamations*.

Similarly important, we would discern numerous holdings on British theories of discourse. These would include representative works from the psychological-epistemological authors (Francis Bacon, John Locke, Lord Kames, David Hume, William Duncan, Thomas Reid, etc.); from the belletristic scholars (especially Lord Shaftesbury and Hugh Blair); and the elocutionists (John Mason, Thomas Sheridan, John Walker, and John Rice).

In continuing our library tour, we would become aware that the traditional rhetorical works cited in the previous paragraphs were buttressed by hundreds of volumes dealing with belles lettres or polite literature. In this category, we would find extensive classical and British/Continental holdings on poetical and dramatistic productions, and on historical and philosophical writing. These books would range from Homer and Virgil to Milton and Pope in poetry; from Herodotus, Thucydides, Tacitus, and Livy to Voltaire, Hume, and Robertson in history; from the Epicureans and Stoics to Bacon and Locke in philosophy; and from Euripides to Shakespeare in dramatic literature.[23]

Not a few scholars have suggested that Jefferson could not possibly have read all the works in his library. That this premise is sound there can be little question. Subsequent chapters, however, demonstrate Jefferson's familiarity with a large portion of the works on discourse that he had obtained for his vast library, as well as the degree of influence these studies exerted in shaping his ideas and practices on discourse.

## Commonplace Books

A valuable addendum to Jefferson's library was his use of commonplace books. This method of recording excerpts from materials he had read for eventual use in a rhetorical situation found its roots in Bacon's *Advancement of Learning*. Bacon regarded a commonplace book as a productive means of increasing a rhetor's inventive process. Beginning this Baconian practice in the 1760s while he was in Williamsburg, Jefferson devised a category system that permitted him to file the passages he copied under the headings of law and government, the Bible, and literature.[24] He explained this procedure to Dr. Thomas Cooper in a letter written in 1814:

> In my letter of Jan. 16, I promised you a sample of my Common-place book, of the pious disposition of the English judges. . . . When I was a student of the law, now half a century ago, after getting through Coke Littleton, whose matter cannot be abridged, I was in the habit of abridging and common-placing what I read meriting it, and of sometimes mixing my own reflections on the subject. I now enclose you the extract from these entries which I promised. These were written at a time of life when I was bold in the pursuit of knowledge, never fearing to follow truth and reason to whatever results they led, and bearding every authority which stood in their way.[25]

By far the most important of these books for students wishing to know more about the roots of Jefferson's philosophy of discourse was the *Literary Commonplace Book*. This work contains 407 excerpts, some short and others extended, from the writings of thirty-five classical and modern scholars.[26] Taken in their entirety, the commonplace books demonstrate clearly that Jefferson had created a memory system that would be of inestimable value to him in the formation of his philosophy and practice of discourse.

## Observer and Participant in Discourse

In addition to being a student of discourse who profited from the teachings of Small and Wythe and who had obtained, read, and commonplaced books produced by leading theorists and practitioners of the classical and British/Continental periods, Jefferson followed a political and legal career that enabled him to observe and participate in rhetorical transactions at home and abroad. As a member of the Bar, Virginia's House of Burgesses and House of Delegates, and the Continental Congress; and as governor of Virginia, minister to France, secretary of state, vice president, and president, he gained firsthand knowledge of numerous forms of discourse in action. It was his good fortune, in sum, to be a major player in the formation of the American nation, and to be present in Paris as elements in that country struggled to enact a republican government at the onset of the French Revolution. From these rich personal experiences, he often was able to use the narrative approach to illustrate and emphasize his principles of discourse.

## Member of the American Philosophical Society

In 1780, Jefferson, then governor of Virginia, was elected as a member of the American Philosophical Society, generally recognized at the time as the most prestigious scholarly organization of its kind in America.[27] After serving in subsequent years as one of the society's counselors and vice presidents, in 1797 he was elected to the position of president, an office he held from 1797 to 1814 even though, during his tenure, he also performed his duties as vice president and president of the United States.[28] The society had as its goal "the improvement of useful knowledge more particularly what relates to this new world." This useful knowledge was broad in its scope, comprehending "the whole circle of arts, science, and discoveries especially in the natural world. . . ."[29]

So pivotal was Jefferson's position in the organization, according to Daniel J. Boorstin, that he functioned as the leader of a group of men who constituted the preeminent American philosophers of the age. These scholars, all of whom were devotees of the philosophy of republicanism, were described by Boorstin as "the Jeffersonian Circle." They included David Rittenhouse, the creator of a "planetarium which came to be considered the first mechanical wonder of the American world"; Dr. Benjamin Rush, a distinguished physician and signer of the Declaration of Independence; Benjamin Smith Barton, "the greatest American botanist of his age"; Joseph Priestley, a chemist who discovered oxygen; Charles Willson Peale, the celebrated artist and illustrator; and Thomas Paine, whose pamphlet *Common Sense* and *American Crisis* essays were the most effective works "in building Revolutionary morale."[30] To be the leader of such a circle for more than two decades was a tribute to the strength of Jefferson's image as a scholar of philosophy whose range of interests spanned the arts and sciences. Moreover, from time to time throughout this study we see how his frequent dialogues and correspondence with three members of this circle—Rush, Priestley, and Paine—helped him formulate and reinforce his ideas on rhetorical philosophy and virtue.

# Evolutionary Approach to the Study of Rhetoric

What did Jefferson have in mind when he spoke of the meaning of rhetoric, and what function did he believe this field of study may perform in society? To answer these questions, we must first recognize that Jefferson's love of books and thirst for knowledge in general made him an evolutionist and an eclectic. As an eclectic and pluralist, he drew his ideas from a wide variety of sources and then adapted them to the needs generated by a particular issue. As an evolutionist and a student of the Enlightenment, he saw the value of dynamic, developing changes of perceptions resulting from advances in the arts, humanities, and sciences. These new emphases in thought, he believed, must be taken into consideration when shaping one's new perspectives. But they should not be regarded as being necessarily in opposition to all of the conclusions reached in earlier ages. Often these advances, instead, may be viewed as important modifications or extensions of previous hypotheses. Let us see, then, how his faith in eclecticism and in the evolutionary approach to knowledge development helped forge his thinking on his philosophy of discourse.

Jefferson's fascination with the writings of the ancient scholars, and his familiarity with the Greek and Latin languages, led him naturally into the domain of neoclassicism—one of the prevailing rhetorical trends in the eighteenth century. From Aristotle he could learn that rhetoric is the art of discovering in a given situation "all of the available means of persuasion"; that the starting point of discourse is the occasion; and that persuasion consists of three forms of proof—personal, logical, and emotional. Cicero, moreover, explained to his readers that there are five major canons of rhetoric, each of which plays a significant part during a rhetorical exchange. They consist of the speaker's basic premises and supporting arguments; method of organizational structure and audience adaptation; language control and style; memory process; and delivery pattern. Cicero also upheld the notion that a rhetor should strive at all times to be an ideal communicator. Finally, Quintilian, the masterful summarizer of classical thought, impressed his students with his perception of rhetoric as "the science of speaking well," and his devotion to the ethical principle that to be a successful and responsible rhetor, one must be a good person.

Had Jefferson's intellectual growth stopped here, some might try to label him a neoclassicist. But this was not the case. Because he was an evolutionist who believed in the progressive movement of knowledge, he became fully aware of three other rhetorical trends emerging in Britain and on the Continent in the seventeenth and eighteenth centuries. One of these, called the psychological/philosophical or epistemological school of thought—led by such luminaries as Bacon, Locke, Hume, Lord Kames, and William Duncan—began to probe into the subject of discourse by studying the nature of man. Whereas Aristotle's starting point was the occasion, the epistemologists began with the audience, seeking to determine how the cognitive and affective elements of a person's mind responded to discourse. For them, reason and evidence were the central features of their thinking; so, too, was their belief that the mind was composed of a distinctive number of faculties, each of which must be understood if persuasion were to take place.

Speaking for the epistemologists as a whole, Bacon defined rhetoric as "the application of *reason* to the *imagination* for the better moving of the *will*." This conception of rhetoric said, in effect, that persuasion begins with the development of a logical base consisting of compelling reasoning and evidence, which is then reinforced by appeals to the imagination. This twofold discourse strategy then has the potential power to motivate the will in such a manner that a thoughtful decision on the part of the audience may be reached. Jefferson, as is evident in our discussion of his perspectives on argument in chapter 3, was impressed with this group of scholars because of their stress on philosophy and psychology as they relate to discourse.

A third dominating British/Continental rhetorical trend was the belletristic school, which defined discourse as an all-encompassing art that covers both oral and written forms of communication. This approach to the study of discourse became associated with the notion of politeness in the latter stages of the seventeenth century. At first, observes Lawrence Klein, "Politeness" was defined as "a vehicle for a kinetic and interactional model of human relations. . . ."[31] In the British Isles and in France, where the popular term *politesse* was used, considerable enthusiasm was shown for all aspects of interpersonal communication as a pleasurable and rewarding form of human behavior. Then with the publication of Lord Shaftesbury's influential volume *Characteristics of Men, Manners, Opinions, Times* in the first decade of the eighteenth century,[32] politeness expanded to include "modes" of discourse "more formal than social intercourse." Soon "expressions" such as "'polite learning,' 'polite arts,' and 'polite letters' . . . became an inscription of certain areas of intellectual and literary endeavor. . . ."[33]

With these developments, polite learning had become identified with belles lettres. This, in turn, meant that students of discourse no longer limited themselves to the study of the oral mode of communication. Now they also focused their attention on such forms as philosophical and historical writing, poetics, and criticism. This rhetorical trend, which remained popular throughout the eighteenth century, had an enormous appeal for Jefferson. He purchased a three-volume, 1714 edition of Shaftesbury's *Characteristics*, which he refused to include among the books he sold to the Library of Congress in 1814. Even more important, he applauded the writings of Hugh Blair, who was to become the leading representative of the belletristic school of thought. As Presbyterian minister of the famous Church of St. Giles and as professor of rhetoric and belles lettres at the University of Edinburgh, Blair began lecturing on rhetoric and polite literature in 1759. Then, in 1783, he published his *Lectures on Rhetoric and Belles Lettres*, which became the most popular textbook on discourse for the next one hundred years in the English-speaking world.[34] A three-volume edition of Blair's *Lectures*, published in 1788, was present in Jefferson's library.[35]

The organizational structure and educational philosophy that characterize the *Lectures* were attractive to Jefferson because they made it possible for a student to gain a thorough knowledge of rhetoric, literature, and criticism. The total of forty-seven lectures encompassed five broad subject areas. Five of the discourses dealt with taste, genius, beauty, sublimity, and criticism; four with the rise, progress, and structure of language; fourteen with the nature and elements of an effective style; three with organizational patterns and delivery; and nineteen with such various forms of discourse as public communication in popular assemblies, before the Bar, and in the pulpit, and writings on history, philosophy, poetry, and drama.

Jefferson's enthusiasm for the belletristic school, epitomized by its popular proponent Blair, prompted him to recommend the *Lectures* to others. To Robert Skipwith, who requested information on building a private library, to his relatives, and to fledgling lawyers, he suggested that they purchase or read diligently the *Lectures* to hone their rhetorical and critical skills. Jefferson's positive attitude toward Blair was contagious. On the eve of his departure to France in 1784, he announced his intention to fulfill a request from Madison: "I shall take care to get Blair's lectures for you as soon as published," he promised.[36]

The fourth and final major trend that influenced Jefferson's perspectives on the parameters of discourse was the growth and popularity of the elocutionary movement. These scholars, convinced that the canon of delivery had become a lost art in the modern age, sought to restore it to the high status that it had enjoyed in the theory and practice of Demosthenes and Cicero. In their public lectures and in their books, therefore, they instructed their audiences about the nature and importance of such discourse themes as vocal quality and inflection, force and projection, articulation and pronunciation, gestures and facial expression. Similarly, they argued that these elements, to reach their full potential, must be consistent with what the faculties of the mind—understanding, imagination, passions, and the will—dictate in a particular rhetorical situation.

Among the most popular and influential members of this movement were John Mason, John Walker, Thomas Sheridan—father of the well-known British playwright and parliamentary orator Richard Brinsley Sheridan—and John Rice. The writings of these four authors not only were included in Jefferson's library, but he also recommended them when giving instruction to students. In brief, he could not escape the fact that what he had seen in public discourse—especially the speeches of Patrick Henry—revealed the persuasive power of an effective delivery.

It was against the background of these rhetorical trends that Jefferson's evolutionary ideas of knowledge development came into play. As a result, when he used the term rhetoric, and when he put it into practice in his own discourse performances, he was not speaking of a truncated art that refers only to a single canon; nor was he alluding merely to the oral discourse genre associated with public speaking and oratory. He was thinking instead of an integrated art—one that combines all of the five canons and the written as well as the oral form. The word "rhetoric," he believed, focuses on all major types of oral and written discourse that have as their principal ends to create a close relationship between the rhetor and the listener or reader, to generate understanding and advance knowledge, to promote ethics and values, and to produce a desired reaction. Falling within this scope, he placed such discourse areas as public speaking and debate—both secular and religious, interpersonal communication and letter writing, poetics and criticism, historical and philosophical writing, parliamentary law, and journalism. In considering each of these discourse areas, he included the following representative rhetorical elements: the rhetor's modes of argumentation and proof; organization and adaptation of ideas; language usage and style; and, when appropriate, delivery patterns.

Jefferson, in brief, incorporated into his thinking the best elements of neoclassicism, the belletristic tradition, the epistemological school, and the elocutionary movement. It should be observed, however, that in blending these trends, he was more than an eclectic transmitter of the ideas of others. For, as we have seen, he was a close observer and participant of discourse in action. Consequently, his perspectives also were forged, to a large extent, by his own personal experiences and his political, cultural, social, and religious philosophy. Given these circumstances, it seems evident that as far as his philosophy of discourse was concerned, Jefferson was fulfilling his dream of becoming an "impresario of America" not only by introducing his fellow citizens "to the finest and most enlightened aspects of European culture," as Gordon Wood suggested; but, as our later discussions demonstrate, by acquainting them with virtue-centered principles of discourse emanating from American republicanism in which the people were the dominating force.

## Importance of Rhetoric in a Democratic Society

Because of its wide-ranging scope and owing to its enormous power to instruct and stimulate the people, discourse for Jefferson was a significant enterprise in a democratic society. It is through discourse, he wrote George Wythe in 1786, that knowledge is disseminated to the people and freedom and happiness are preserved.[37] Years later he explained to the French philosopher Destutt de Tracy that discourse was an effective tool for an executive to use in the development of governmental philosophy. After noting approvingly how discourse was employed during Washington's first administration, he recalled how it functioned during his own two terms as president. In doing so, he spoke feelingly of how participants with particular agendas and worldviews could reach a satisfactory solution that each could endorse with respect to a pressing problem. He put it this way: "We sometimes met under differences of opinion, but scarcely ever failed, by conversing and reasoning, so as to modify each other's ideas, as to produce an unanimous result."[38]

Throughout his adult life, Jefferson constantly reminded his cohorts, his family members, the students who sought advice about their educational futures, and many others that discourse could be used to combat prejudice, to help one's career, to give buoyancy to democratic principles, and to promote happiness and harmony in one's life. After explaining to John Adams, for example, the need for a rhetor to avoid extremes of big-

otry on the one hand and excessive enthusiasm on the other, he confidently asserted that "education and free discussion are the antidotes of
both."[39] Discourse, he further held, is especially valuable to those who
seek a career in law and politics. To them he said: "In a country and government like ours, eloquence is a powerful instrument, well worthy of the
special pursuit of our youth. . . ."[40] He often counseled his daughters to
use discourse in such a manner that their marriage bond would be
strengthened and their social relations improved. The rhetorical advice
he freely dispensed grew out of his abiding belief that "in a republican nation, whose citizens are to be led by reason and persuasion, and not by
force, the art of reasoning becomes of first importance."[41]

Given this strong commitment to the value of discourse, it is not surprising that Jefferson wanted this subject to become an essential part of
higher education, but occasionally in doing so he suggested that attending lectures was not always necessary. He made rhetoric an exception,
however, in a letter to his nephew Thomas Mann Randolph in 1787:
"You would do well," he advised, "to attend the public exercises in this
branch," and "do it with very particular diligence."[42]

Consistent with a practice that characterized his attempts to direct the
studies of those close to him, he contacted professors or administrators
whom he either knew personally or with whose work he was familiar, in
an effort to pave the way for a student's enrollment. He was aware, for instance, that John Witherspoon, who had migrated to America from Scotland and became a signer of the Declaration, was an administrator and a
celebrated professor of rhetoric at Princeton University in 1792. With
this thought in mind, Jefferson introduced to him by letter an incoming
Virginia student, Benet Taylor, expressing the hope that as part of Taylor's
preparation for the profession of law he could take a course in rhetoric
from Witherspoon.[43]

What Jefferson had to say about "General Schools" and the University
of Virginia as he wished it to become also revealed his compelling interest in discourse. In September 1814, he described his vision of "General
Schools" to his nephew Peter Carr. These schools, he wrote, should center their attention on useful sciences organized in three departments consisting of "Language," "Mathematics," and "Philosophy." Within the first
department, he observed, would be the following sub-areas: "1. Languages
and History, ancient and modern; 2. Grammar; 3. Belles Lettres; 4.
Rhetoric and Oratory. . . ." He then specified that "Belles Lettres," as he
conceived the term, includes "poetry and composition generally, and criticism. . . ."[44] Not to be overlooked in his treatment of discourse is that he

placed in the department of moral philosophy two other sub-areas that have an important bearing on discourse—"Ideology and Ethics."

Jefferson further held that college curricula, as was the case in "General Schools," should also make discourse theory a part of a student's program. As early as 1800, the year he was elected president, he wrote to his friend Dr. Joseph Priestley, the renowned scientist and author of *A Course of Lectures on Oratory and Criticism*, that he was contemplating the creation of a university in central Virginia that would highlight courses designed to meet the particular needs of a developing America. Among the subject areas to be stressed were "history, ethics, law, arts," and "fine arts."[45]

In the ensuing years, as Jefferson's vision for the university became increasingly clear, discourse became more prominent even though its placement within a department would vary from time to time. It is instructive to observe that in 1817, when the University of Virginia was still in its formative stage, the first offer of a professorship was tendered to a Dr. Knox of Baltimore. His teaching assignment would be instruction in "languages, belles lettres, rhetoric, history, and geography. . . ."[46] When Knox eventually turned down the offer, it was then extended to Dr. Thomas Cooper.

The preliminary university curriculum was again modified in the following year. Of the ten department areas listed, two were in the languages, five in the physical and biological sciences, one in government, one in law, and one in ideology. The latter had four sub-areas: "general Grammar, Ethics, Rhetoric," and "Belles Lettres and the fine arts."[47] Three months after this 1818 report was discussed and tentatively accepted, Jefferson, who was the rector, sought to persuade a promising scholar he had befriended, George Ticknor of Boston, to become a member of the faculty. He made his plea with the following appeal: "I pass over our professorship of Latin, Greek, and Hebrew, and that of modern languages, French, Italian, Spanish, German, and Anglo-Saxon, which, although the most lucrative, would be the most laborious, and notice that which you would splendidly fill, of Ideology, Ethics, Belles Lettres, and Fine Arts."[48]

Soon after the opening of the university, the proposed curriculum had undergone additional refinements. Rhetoric and belles lettres, though still occupying an important place in the program of study, were now placed "in the school of ancient languages," which also included ancient history and geography. Ethics, general grammar, and ideology, which for Jefferson were important aspects of rhetorical philosophy, were assigned to the school of moral philosophy.[49] In each of the patterns of course arrangements outlined here, rhetoric was positioned with other fields of study that shared a strong connection with ethics and virtue.

In retrospect, the vision Jefferson held of himself as a young man interested in taste and in the emerging thought of the Enlightenment, and the part that rhetoric would perform in elevating taste and promoting virtue, increased with each passing year. He spent more than six decades in creating a dynamic and relevant philosophy of discourse, and in observing its application in private settings and the public arena. To read his thousands of extant letters—many of which take the form of well-developed essays—and to review the curricula he devised at the University of Virginia is to discover his unmistakable emphasis on all dimensions of rhetoric. Unlike Aristotle, Cicero, and Quintilian in the classical period; or Hugh Blair, George Campbell, Lord Kames, and Joseph Priestley in the eighteenth-century British era, Jefferson did not write a textbook on the philosophy and practice of rhetoric. But his strong and continuing interest in this theme led him to follow the pattern of rhetorical instruction adopted by such authors as Plato, Francis Bacon, John Locke, David Hume, Adam Smith, James Boswell, and John Wesley—all of whom incorporated into their voluminous writings extensive insights on the central elements of rhetorical philosophy and their implementation in a rhetorical setting.[50]

In addition to being a philosopher of rhetoric and a critic, Jefferson also was an effective practitioner of the art of discourse. Merrill D. Peterson, among the most prominent Jefferson scholars of the twentieth century, wrote in his book *The Jefferson Image in the American Mind* that he was "a great rhetorician, one who lived on the spiritual capital of his words even more than on the tangible rewards of his work."[51] Later in his *Portable Thomas Jefferson*, Peterson again emphasized Jefferson's effectiveness in discourse by referring to him as "a superb rhetorician, in the ancient use of that term, interested in the communication of ideas rather than in beauties of expression."[52] We deal in detail with Jefferson's practice as a rhetor in part two of this study.

Notwithstanding the availability of a significant body of material that Jefferson discussed and put in writing regarding his ideas of rhetoric, his lifelong pursuit to apply these principles to his own performances in private and public settings, and his desire to use this subject as a force in the period of the American Enlightenment, no one to date has conducted a systematic study of this potentially enriching subject. Encouraged by the data we have discovered during the past decade, we have undertaken in the present volume to address the oversight by seeking to answer three questions. First, what did Jefferson say about the principles of rhetoric as they relate to the subject that defined his primary concern in life, that of virtue? Second, to what degree did his own practice conform to these principles? Third, in what manner did his philosophy and performance contribute fresh and innovative ideas? Answers to these questions, we feel, provide data showing the degree of success that Jefferson may have achieved in using discourse philosophy and practice as an essential educational and cultural instrument of the Enlightenment.

# Notes

1. Gordon S. Wood, "The Trials and Tribulations of Thomas Jefferson," in Peter S. Onuf, ed., *Jeffersonian Legacies* (Charlottesville: University Press of Virginia, 1993), 403–404.

2. "Autobiography," in Paul Leicester Ford, *The Writings of Thomas Jefferson*, 12 vols. (New York: Putnam, 1904–1905), 1: 5. (Hereafter, Ford.)

3. Duncan's work on logic, discussed in chapter 3, had a profound influence on Jefferson's philosophy of argument. See Wilbur Samuel Howell, "The Declaration of Independence and Eighteenth-Century Logic," *William and Mary Quarterly* 18 (October 1961): 463–84.

4. At the encouragement of Lord Kames [Henry Home], Adam Smith presented lectures on rhetoric and belles lettres in Edinburgh from 1748 through 1751. A few years later Hugh Blair began lecturing on the same subject at the University of Edinburgh.

5. *William and Mary Quarterly Historical Papers* (October 1894), 12n.

6. "Journal of the Meetings of William and Mary College, September 25th, 1760," in ibid., 130.

7. "Autobiography," in Ford, 1: 6.

8. President Lyon G. Tyler, Address before the American Antiquarian Society, Worcester, Mass., October 20, 1915, *William and Mary College Quarterly Historical Magazine*, 1st Series, 24 (April 1916): 222.

9. Ford, 2: 99.

10. Randolph, "Introduction to that Part of the History, Embracing the Revolution," *Virginia Magazine of History* 43 (1935): 122.

11. "Brief Autobiography of Governor Page," in William Maxwell, ed., *The Virginia Historical Register and Literary Notebook* (Richmond, 1850), 3: 147,150.

12. Ford, 1: 5–6.

13. Randolph, "Introduction," 122.

14. TJ to James Madison, July 26, 1780, in Julian P. Boyd, Charles T. Cullen, John Catanzariti, and Barbara Oberg, eds., *The Papers of Thomas Jefferson*, 28 vols. to date (Princeton: Princeton University Press, 1950–    ), 3: 507. (Hereafter, Boyd.)

15. Rutherford Goodwin, *A Brief and True Report Concerning Williamsburg*, 4th ed. (Williamsburg: A. Dietz, 1941), 176.

16. TJ to Ralph Izard, July 17, 1788, in Boyd, 13: 372.

17. TJ to Judge John Tyler, November 25, 1810, in Ford, 11: 159.

18. Ford, 1: 6.

19. See ibid., 1: 8.

20. See the following letters: TJ to Abigail Adams, August 22, 1813, in Lester J. Cappon, ed., *The Adams-Jefferson Letters*, 2 vols. (Chapel Hill: The University of North Carolina Press, 1959), 2: 367 (hereafter, Cappon); TJ to John Adams, June 10, 1815, in Andrew A. Lipscomb and Albert E. Bergh, eds., *The Writings of Thomas Jefferson*, 20 vols. (Washington, D.C.: The Thomas Jefferson Memorial Association, 1905), 14: 301 (hereafter, L&B); and TJ to John Adams, June 1, 1822, in Cappon, 2: 578.

21. As an example of the care he took, he wrote to the bookseller Thomas Payne from Paris on October 2, 1788 the following note: "When I name a particular edition of a book, send me that edition and no other. When I do not name the edition, never send a folio or quarto if there exists an 8 vo. or smaller edition. I like books of a handy size." Boyd, 13: 650.

22. His explanation was as follows: "I have been fifty years making it, and have spared no pains, opportunity or expense, to make it what it is. While residing in Paris, I devoted every afternoon I was disengaged, for a summer or two, in examining all the principal bookstores, turning over every book with my own hand, and putting by everything which related to America, and indeed whatever was rare and valuable in every science. Besides this, I had standing orders during the whole time I was in Europe, on its principal bookmarts, particularly Amsterdam, Frankfort, Madrid and London." TJ to Dr. Samuel H. Smith, September 21, 1814, in Ford, 11: 427–28. It should be noted that TJ continued to collect books following the sale of most of the holdings to the Library of Congress.

23. Most of Jefferson's Library books are listed in the following source: E. Millicent Sowerby, *Catalogue of the Library of Thomas Jefferson*, 5 vols. (Washington, D.C.: Library of Congress, 1952–1959). What makes this work so valuable are its thousands of listings and helpful editorial comments, including occasional important letters.

24. Of outstanding use to this study is Douglas L. Wilson's edition of Jefferson's *Literary Commonplace Book* (Princeton: Princeton University Press, 1989). (Hereafter, *LCB*.) In addition to this volume, see Gilbert Chinard, ed., *The Commonplace Book of Thomas Jefferson: A Repository of his Ideas on Government* (Baltimore: Johns Hopkins University Press, 1928); and Douglas L. Wilson, "Thomas Jefferson's Early Notebooks," *William and Mary Quarterly*, 3rd Series, 42 (October 1985): 433–52.

25. February 10, 1814, in L&B, 14: 85.

26. This work also contains an excellent introduction and a well developed section on "Registry of Authors."

27. Daniel J. Boorstin, *The Lost World of Thomas Jefferson* (Chicago: University of Chicago Press, 1948), gave this assessment of the society's home city of Philadelphia: "In the years between of the death of Franklin in 1790 and the end of Jefferson's presidency in 1809, the South showed no comparable intellectual metropolis. New England was on the intellectual periphery; those were dull days for Harvard College and for the theology which she represented. The American Academy of Arts and Sciences (the Boston counterpart of the Philosophical Society) founded by John Adams in 1780 never attained the stature of a rival. It surely was in the Jeffersonian spirit that the center of American action should be the center of thought" (11).

28. Jefferson's participation in and election to various offices in the society is outlined in the *Early Proceedings of the American Philosophical Society For the Promotion of Useful*

*Knowledge. From 1744–1838* (Philadelphia: Press of McCalla & Stavely, 1844). Also see Gilbert Chinard, "Jefferson and the American Philosophical Society," *Proceedings* 87 (1944): 263–76.

29. Charles Thomson to TJ, March 9, 1782, in Boyd, 6: 163.

30. Boorstin, *The Lost World of Thomas Jefferson*, 8–26.

31. Lawrence Klein, "The Third Earl of Shaftesbury and the Progress of Politeness," *Eighteenth Century Studies*, 18 (1984–85): 187.

32. Anthony Ashley Cooper, Earl of Shaftesbury was the author's official name. But he is generally referred to as Lord Shaftesbury or the Third Earl of Shaftesbury. His significant ideas on virtue are discussed in chapter 2.

33. Klein, "The Third Earl of Shaftesbury and the Progress of Politeness," 200–201.

34. Robert M. Schmitz has listed twenty-five separate editions produced in the British Isles between 1783 and 1853; and thirty-three American editions covering the period between 1784 and 1873. In addition, numerous translations and abridgments were published. Robert M. Schmitz, *Hugh Blair* (Morningside Heights, N.Y.: King's Crown Press, 1948), 148.

35. The best available edition of Blair's *Lectures* is Harold F. Harding's edited work published by the Southern Illinois University Press, 1965. It is a two-volume production.

36. See the following exchange of letters: Madison to TJ, February 11, 1784, in Boyd, 6: 537; and TJ to Madison, February 20, 1784, in Boyd, 6: 544.

37. TJ to George Wythe, August 13, 1786, in Boyd, 10: 244.

38. TJ to Destutt de Tracy, January 26, 1811, in Ford, 11: 184–85.

39. TJ to John Adams, August 1, 1816, in Cappon, 2: 484.

40. TJ to George W. Summers and John Garland, February 27, 1822, in L&B, 15: 353.

41. TJ to David Harding, April 20, 1824, in L&B, 16: 30.

42. TJ to Thomas Mann Randolph Jr., July 6, 1787, in Boyd, 11: 557.

43. TJ to John Witherspoon, January 12, 1792, in Boyd, 23: 40.

44. TJ to Peter Carr, September 7, 1814, in Merrill D. Peterson, *Writings* (New York: The Library of America, 1984), 1349. (Hereafter, *Writings*.)

45. TJ to Joseph Priestley, January 18, 1800, in ibid., 1071.

46. "An Extract of the Minutes of the Board of Visitors of the University of Virginia, during the Rectorship of Thomas Jefferson," in L&B, 17: 365–67.

47. "Aim and Curriculum, University of Virginia," August 1–4, 1818, in Saul K. Padover, ed., *The Complete Jefferson* (New York: Duell, Sloan, and Pearce, 1943), 1100.

48. TJ to George Ticknor, October 25, 1800, in George S. Hillard, ed., *Life, Letters, and Journals of George Ticknor*, 2 vols. (Boston: J. R. Osgood, 1876), 1: 303.

49. See Supplementary Manuscripts, Minutes of the Board of Visitors," April 17, 1824, in L&B, 19: 434; and October 5, 1824, in L&B, 19: 456.

50. In each of the following representative studies, the author examined the leading works of the scholars listed and gleaned from them what the writers said about discourse theory and practice. A similar pattern has been used in the present volume on Jefferson. See James L. Golden, "John Wesley on Rhetoric and Belles Lettres," *Speech Monographs* 28 (November 1961): 250–64; Golden, "James Boswell on Rhetoric and Belles Lettres," *Quarterly Journal of Speech* 50 (October 1964): 266–76; Golden, "Adam Smith as a Rhetorical Theorist and Literary Critic," *Costerus: Essays in English and American Language and Literature* 1 (Winter 1972): 89–113; and Golden, "Plato Revisited: A Theory of Discourse for All Seasons," in Robert J. Connors, Lisa S. Ede, and Andrea A. Lunsford,

eds., *Essays on Classical Rhetoric and Modern Discourse* (Carbondale: Southern Illinois University Press, 1984), 16–36.

51. Merrill D. Peterson, *The Jefferson Image in the American Mind* (New York: Oxford University Press, 1962), 444.

52. Merrill D. Peterson, ed., *The Portable Thomas Jefferson* (New York: Viking Penguin, 1975), xvii.

# CHAPTER TWO

~

# The Role of Virtue in Discourse

Since the fourth century, B.C., when Socrates and Plato devised their moral philosophical view of rhetoric and Aristotle described the major forms of rhetorical proof, students of discourse have given a prominent place to what they believed to be the persuasive power of virtue as a central element in all forms of communication. Among those strongly committed to this belief was Thomas Jefferson. The subject of virtue or morality, from which discourse derives its unique appeal, was a defining element in his worldview. As Paul A. Conkin has perceptively noted: "He spent a lifetime agonizing over the foundations of morality . . . and trying to find the types of intellectual authority needed to support moral conduct. . . ."[1]

Jefferson's compelling concern about the theme of virtue, with its unusually strong rhetorical implications, first found expression in the listings he included in his *Literary Commonplace Book.* Many of these recorded items, taken from the works of classical and modern scholars, were assembled in his Williamsburg days. Seventy extracts from the plays of the Greek dramatist Euripides, for example, were written down for the purpose of future recall. Most of these excerpts contain a moral message that has a poignant application to discourse. Similar value-laden lines are drawn from the writings of such favorite Jefferson authors as Homer, Shakespeare, Lord Bolingbroke, and Alexander Pope.

Of the many sources that profoundly influenced Jefferson's views on virtue and their relationship to discourse, four receive special attention in this chapter: (1) the basic tenets of the Epicureans and Stoics; (2) the ethical teachings of Jesus; (3) the moral emphases of the English epistemologists Bacon and Locke and the aesthetician Lord Shaftesbury; and (4) the doctrines of the moral philosophical school as seen in the writings of Francis Hutcheson and Lord Kames. Our purpose is to illustrate how

Jefferson, motivated by these perspectives and by his dialogues with his American contemporaries, reached the conclusion that a fundamental message of discourse, regardless of the rhetorical form that is used, is the subject of virtue.

In analyzing Jefferson's philosophy of virtue, we have found that he developed five major perspectives. The first, in dealing with the general nature of this theme, suggests that *the foundation of morality rests upon its being largely an inborn trait.* To emphasize this point, Jefferson asserted that the Creator of the universe, wishing us to function effectively in society, endowed us at birth with a "moral sense" that enables us to distinguish between right and wrong. This sense, in addition, is as real as the physical senses of "hearing, seeing," and "feeling"; and it is as vital to our well-being as a "leg or arm."[2]

More than two decades later, Jefferson continued his arguments in support of the idea that the roots of our moral attitudes and actions are in our basic nature. He complimented Thomas Law on his work, *Second Thoughts on Instinctive Impulses,* saying he agreed with Law in "the general existence of a moral instinct." He added: "I think it the brightest gem with which the human character is studded, and the want of it as more degrading than the most hideous of bodily deformities."[3]

Because virtue, thought Jefferson, is a natural endowment that is a part of human nature, it implies the presence of a conscience which should be obeyed when decisions are to be made. As a young student, he recorded in his *Literary Commonplace Book* Euripides' statement that one should have the courage to follow "the dictates of his heart." From this principle he never departed, often citing it as an "ought" proposition. Consequently, he advised his daughter Martha, who was frightened about predictions that the world would soon come to an end, to remain calm and hopeful. The way to meet this crisis, he said, was to pay close attention to your conscience. For this "internal Monitor" will show us the difference between right and wrong, and forthwith prepare us for any eventuality such as the predicted dissolution of the earth.[4]

Jefferson applied the same principle to moral actions that may be taken on the national and international levels. While disapproving of a young American boy's decision to side with the British during the Revolutionary War, for example, he nevertheless praised him for adhering to his conscience.[5] He similarly expressed the hope that Lafayette, who had been ordered to vote in a prescribed way in the French Assembly, would disregard the command and vote as his conscience dictated.[6]

In arguing that virtue was an innate and intuitive faculty, Jefferson was building on the ideas of Lord Shaftesbury, Francis Hutcheson, and Lord Kames.[7] Shaftesbury was generally regarded "as the founder of the 'moral sense school' of ethics," which upheld the notion that one's "moral sense is a potentiality with which all men have been endowed by Nature."[8] Even though this endowment may vary in strength from one person to another, Shaftesbury asserted that no one is "without a moral sense or natural affection"[9] that assists in determining whether an act or a thought is morally right or wrong.

A few decades later, Hutcheson expanded on and popularized Shaftesbury's ideas by noting that every person has a practical disposition toward what is good implanted in his nature which may be called a "moral sense." This natural human trait, in turn, creates a desire to promote happiness through friendship and love, and to enjoy the pleasures of "Beauty," "Order," and "Harmony."[10] Lord Kames echoed the sentiments of Shaftesbury and Hutcheson by also claiming that God has bestowed on us moral attributes at birth. Among these are natural feelings, sentiments, and inclinations; and a tendency to want to regulate our behavior in conformity with the dignity of our nature.[11]

Quite clearly, Jefferson stood in good company in articulating the premise that virtue was deeply embedded in the concept of a "moral sense." But Jefferson's firm belief in the power of nature to influence our moral inclinations and actions did not deter him from appreciating the significant part that nurture can also play in improving these traits. Often when he gave advice to others as they planned for their future, he recommended, in keeping with the ideas of Bacon, that they could sharpen their natural and moral sensibilities in three ways: exercise, reading, and reason. Exercise, he told Peter Carr, is as essential in the area of virtue as it is in the physical realm. A steady, well-disciplined program of exercise can help us produce a positive modification of our disposition and permit us to become a more grateful, generous, and loving person. Performing an act of service to others, he added, is a form of exercise that cannot help but reinforce our moral faculties and thereby enlarge our personal worth. This, of course, would then provide pleasure.[12]

Reading works that have an ethical message likewise is an effective method for improving our moral conduct and feelings. He found the writings of Epicurus, Xenephon's *Memorabilia*, the Socratic Dialogues, the philosophy of Cicero, and the novels of Laurence Sterne particularly useful.[13] As a result he urged Carr to take time to study them. Nor did

Jefferson neglect to follow his own advice. As we have seen, his own moral life was positively affected by what he had read. When he was seventy-six years of age, he could tell one correspondent that he never went to bed "without an hour, or half hour's previous reading of something moral, whereon to ruminate in the intervals of sleep."[14]

A third strategy recommended by Jefferson for directing our moral instincts so as to improve our conduct was to rely on reason. Conscious of Locke's strong emphasis on the potential power of reason to generate self-evident premises on moral issues,[15] Jefferson made use of this principle in showing how argumentative claims may strengthen one's sense of virtue. (How this is achieved is discussed in a later section of this chapter.)

A second major perspective advanced by Jefferson was his conviction that *a starting point for the achievement of virtue was the "pursuit of happiness."* When he included this celebrated phrase in the second paragraph of the Declaration of Independence, he was developing an idea, argues Adrienne Koch, that was "central to his philosophy of man and society, and in so doing he envisaged a dynamic balance between power and morals."[16]

As Jefferson reflected on the philosophical principles of the Greeks and of Cicero, on the moral teachings of Jesus, and on the closely reasoned arguments of Locke in his *Essay Concerning Human Understanding*, he found inspiration and support for his belief that to experience virtue one must reach a state of happiness. In a letter written to William Short in 1819, he praised Epicurus for devising a highly rational system of ethics. In the same letter, he included a syllabus containing the essence of Epicureanism, all of which, he felt, was worthy of emulation. The outline holds happiness to be "the aim of life," and virtue to be "its foundation." The syllabus further notes that Epictetus, a major spokesman for stoicism, shared Epicurus's idea that happiness is the desideratum of an enjoyable and productive life.[17] In sum, Jefferson appreciated the emphasis of the two Greek philosophers on self-reliance as a proper means of controlling our passions and promoting happiness and peace of mind in general. In the same vein, Jefferson applauded Cicero for his contention that a life of virtue in and of itself has the power to generate happiness regardless of the nature of the circumstances.[18]

Jefferson also found great inspiration in the moral philosophy of Jesus.[19] Late in life he was able to inform Charles Thomson that he had made "a wee-little book" that he called the *Philosophy of Jesus*. It consisted of passages containing the moral statements of Jesus, arranged in a structural pattern that made them easy to understand and to apply in a practical way to our daily lives. The doctrines of the "wee-little book," he boasted, confirm that he himself was "a real Christian" and not the "infidel" portrayed by the modern-day Platonists and "preachers of the gospel." He then asserted that if he had the time he "would add" to his book (which became known as *The Jefferson Bible*) "the Greek, Latin, and French texts, in columns side by side."[20]

The fundamental elements of Jesus' ethical teachings that constitute *The Jefferson Bible* represent the attitudes that we should have toward God, toward others, and toward ourselves. Because of God's infinite wisdom and exalted position in the universe, we should love, adore, and revere him with all our might. This first great commandment also instructs us how to show our appreciation to God by laying up our treasures in heaven rather than on earth.

Second, we should love our neighbors as ourselves. This second great commandment given by Jesus as a new mandate urges us to seek restitution from those we have wronged; to forgive those who have wronged us by turning our other cheek; to help the needy by giving alms; and to maintain a feeling of friendship and good will.

Finally, we should adopt an appropriate stance toward ourselves. This requirement suggests that at all times we should be humble and free from excessive pride. Most of all, to ensure that we will not be victimized by hypocrisy, we should strive to make our words reflect our innermost feelings. Those who abide by these teachings will, unlike the Scribes and Pharisees, be free from the charge of insincerity. In brief, they would be building their moral house on a rock, not on sand. It was against the background of the collection of New Testament verses, with their stress on the importance of assuming a proper attitude toward God, others, and ourselves that Jefferson, in his declining years, felt justified in making this bold claim: "Had the doctrines of Jesus been preached always as pure as they came from his lips, the whole civilized world would now have been Christian."[21] In making this claim, Jefferson was strongly suggesting that the person who successfully travels on the path to happiness is one who is genuinely sincere in his/her actions and utterances, and whose love for God and others represents a higher value than that of self-interest.[22]

That Jefferson received a strong emotional justification for his devotion to the phrase "the pursuit of happiness" from the moral principles of Jesus seems clear. But he still needed a strong logical underpinning that would elevate the concept to an intellectual plane. This he was able to discover in the epistemological thought of John Locke. In his *Essay Concerning*

*Human Understanding,* Locke not only used the words "pursuit of happiness" but also applied his philosophy of human nature to them. Describing happiness "as the utmost Pleasure we are capable of," he asserted that happiness alone *"moves desire"* because it promotes "what we call Good. . . ." By contrast, he added, that which produces "uneasiness" or "pain" is to be designated an "evil." He then set forth this high-probability premise: "I lay it for a certain ground, that every intelligent Being really seeks Happiness, which consists in the enjoyment of Pleasure, without any considerable mixture of uneasiness. . . ."[23] There can be little doubt that these sentiments were uppermost in Jefferson's mind as he wrote the second paragraph of the Declaration of Independence.

As a third perspective articulated by Jefferson on the issue of virtue, he argued that *for a person to experience happiness and for a democratic society to flourish there must be a meaningful and productive interaction between private and public good.* Private good, the first of these related elements, commanded the attention of both classical and modern scholars. The Epicureans, in particular, placed their greatest emphasis on this type of good, and, in doing so, instructed Jefferson regarding its nature and importance. Thus, when he was summarizing the characteristics of Epicureanism in his syllabus, Jefferson endorsed the idea that the soothing passion of "tranquillity" could not be experienced unless the mind was free from the "diseases" of "desire and fear." Finally, the syllabus listed the virtues of "prudence," "temperance," "fortitude," and "justice," along with their troubling counterparts of "folly," "desire," "fear," and "deceit."

The author who influenced Jefferson most on the issue of private good was probably Cicero who, along with Bacon, Locke, and Newton, became one of his significant intellectual heroes.[24] Cicero's most impressive and influential volumes on virtue were his *Tusculan Disputations* and *On Moral Duties.* Late in life, Jefferson thanked a Boston publisher for sending a gift of a new edition of Cicero's writings. "I happened at the time of their arrival," he said, "to be reading the 5th Book of Cicero's Tusculans, which I followed by that of his Offices (On Moral Duties), and concluded to lay aside the variorum edition, and to use yours, after which I might write more understandingly on the subject."[25]

Nor was the reading that Jefferson had undertaken on this occasion a casual examination of the book's contents. Indeed, it was sufficiently thorough for him to express his displeasure with the number of errors—"one for each 13 pages"—he had observed in the New York and Philadelphia editions."[26] Similarly, he had recorded many years earlier in his *Literary Commonplace Book* twenty-one excerpts from the *Tusculan Disputations.*

His understanding of the two Ciceronian volumes on virtue led him to recommend that they be read by those who opted for a career in which discourse was important.

What was it that Cicero said about private good and its relationship to virtue that helped form Jefferson's thought on this moral question? The answer may be found in the four cardinal virtues summarized in Plato's *The Republic* and embraced by the Greeks as a whole: Wisdom, Temperance, Courage, and, most of all, Justice. In setting forth his position on these elements of private good, Cicero noted that if we are wise, temperate, and courageous, the pursuit of justice, which leads to a "greatness of soul," will then be our goal. He further observed that justice maintains "the society of men, in rendering to each man his duty in respecting the sanctity of agreements." Also by encompassing the traits of "generosity," "kindness," "beneficence," and "equality," it emphasizes trust as its overriding concern. Moreover, if people are trustworthy, they are inclined both to engage in just acts, and, additionally, to do whatever is possible to prevent one from performing an unjust act against another. When viewed from this vantage point, justice transcends in significance the crucial virtue of wisdom. For, as Cicero put it, whereas wisdom "has no power to inspire trust" unless it is accompanied with justice, justice, on the other hand, "has enough influence of itself without wisdom." Thus "justice should be nurtured for its own sake."

Justice, added Cicero, is particularly advantageous in enhancing one's reputation because "it increases a man's dignity and self-eminence." To highlight this assertion, he alluded to the alleged quotation from Socrates which affirmed the sentiment that the "nearest path . . . to glory" that a man can follow is to try "to be the same person he wanted people to think he was."

Jefferson, finally, was intrigued by the Latin notion of decorum, which Cicero analyzed and recommended as a persuasive force that may be compared to glue that binds the four cardinal virtues into a unified whole. For when our manner and actions are marked by decorum, we strive "to see the truth in every situation and support it," and "to seek a balance and harmony in our body and soul that conforms to the realities of nature."

If we put the cardinal virtues into practice in our daily lives, Cicero and Jefferson believed, an important result will occur. For, by freeing us from feelings of grief, pain, and immoderate desires, these personal virtues not only will make us wise but also will render us happy. If, however, we fail to make them a part of our thoughts and actions, we run the risk of being motivated by selfish desires such as excessive ambition and self-love.

Notwithstanding the importance of private good as a contributing factor in producing happiness, its primary function, in Jefferson's opinion, is to serve the larger public good. It is for this reason he warmly accepted Cicero's contention that those who exemplify private virtue are useful to their country. In a memorable statement that was supported not only by Jefferson but by later students of virtue in Western thought, Cicero asserted: "Now let our wise man be considered as protecting the public; what can be more excellent than such a character?"

Francis Bacon also spoke for Jefferson when he said that true virtue cannot be fully achieved unless we embrace the public good. This higher level of good, according to Bacon, is other-centered owing to its devotion to duty and service rather than merely to the fulfillment of personal needs and contentment. In arguing this point, Bacon, like Jefferson in constructing his syllabus on Epicureanism, criticized Epicurus for his excessive preoccupation with private good and his lack of concern for public good. Public good, as viewed by Bacon and Jefferson, embraces private good, but goes beyond in range and scope. It is a good nurtured and sustained by charity or love. For whenever we have a feeling of love toward God, our fellow human beings, and our country, our mind is exalted in such a way that virtue is experienced to a larger degree than that which can be learned by studying numberless doctrines of morality.

Two other authors whose ideas on public good Jefferson shared were Lord Shaftesbury and Francis Hutcheson, both of whom warned that there must be an interaction, a harmony, and a consistency between private and public good. In language that Jefferson could embrace, Shaftesbury proclaimed: "Thus the wisdom of what rules, and is first and chief in Nature, has made it to be according to the private interest and good of everyone to work towards the general good, which if a creature ceases to promote, he is actually so far wanting to himself, and ceases to promote his own happiness and welfare."[27]

In extending the ideas of Shaftesbury, Hutcheson went beyond other writers in contributing to Jefferson's philosophy of the public good. Recognized by many authors as the leader of the British Enlightenment,[28] Hutcheson, according to Garry Wills in his volume *Inventing America*, had a greater impact on the construction of the Declaration of Independence than did Locke.[29] Although this claim has been widely disputed by other Jefferson scholars,[30] it is not our wish to enter into this dialogue. We are content in knowing, as our research has shown, that Hutcheson's contribution to Jefferson's thought, like that of Locke, was unmistakable. His two outstanding books on virtue—*An Inquiry into the Original of our*

*Ideas on Virtue,* and *Book One of a Short Introduction to Moral Philosophy*—were essential parts of Jefferson's library. A leader of the "moral sense" school of philosophy, Hutcheson maintained that virtue at its highest consists of benevolence in the service of the public good. Arguing that benevolence "is the Foundation of all the apprehended *Excellence in Social Virtues,*" he claimed that the quality of one's conduct is to be evaluated by the ethical standard that measures the degree of public good and happiness that flows from a particular moral action. Additionally, we honor a person's character not by any accidental acts "of compassion," "affection," or "gratitude" that are evident in a specific situation. Rather, we salute those who consistently demonstrate the quality of benevolence in their lives, emanating from a "moral sense" that guides them to place the interests of others first. So strong and demanding is this principle that we should be willing "to hazard our lives in any good Action which is of importance to the Public. . . ."[31]

Hutcheson made it clear, however, that an act in and of itself was not enough to qualify as virtue. One's motive must also come into play. Most of all, this means that one who performs an act based on "self-interest" or "self-love," even if justice is the end result, has not engaged in a virtuous deed, because benevolence was not the motivating factor. Thus by excluding "self-interest" and personal advantage from its domain, benevolence directs its full power toward the end of promoting the public good.[32]

As Jefferson analyzed this discussion of benevolence in the service of the public good, he could recall Cicero's penetrating analysis of the cardinal virtues as a model of personal conduct, as well as Jesus' stress on the need to love others while, at the same time, being humble in our attitude toward ourselves. This gave him the rationale for concluding that private good must have an integrating relationship with the public good, which meant that private good's duty was to be the foundation for and servant to the public welfare. In this way, benevolence on behalf of the larger society becomes a dynamic, virtuous force. This type of thinking set the stage for Jefferson and his colleagues, at the time of the Revolution, to articulate a political philosophy that was to make republicanism a centerpiece of their ideas on the public good.

In his volume, *The Creation of the American Republic, 1776–1787,*[33] Gordon Wood persuasively demonstrates how Americans in 1776 viewed the notion of public good as an indispensable element of a republican form of government. "No phrase except 'liberty'" he noted, "was invoked more often by the Revolutionaries than 'the public good.'"[34] For they had come to recognize that a republic, with its devotion to the welfare of the people, can only be sustained if the people were willing "to submerge their personal wants into the greater good of the whole"; indeed, "to surrender all, even their lives for the good of the state. . . ." This, of course, strongly suggested that each individual in a republic must not only be patriotic but live an exemplary life marked by "justice, benevolence and the social virtues." Public virtue, in short, was primarily the consequence of men's individual private virtues.[35]

The idea that there should be an integrative relationship between private and public good was an important part of Jefferson's philosophy of virtue. During the last phase of the formation of the American government, he told Madison that the only code of morality we should accept for men is that their actions when alone should coincide with those that are performed in a group. For one to argue, therefore, that he may be a rogue when acting collectively so long as he is an honest person when acting alone is to produce a negative reaction that says, in essence, that he is a rogue in both instances. How much better it would be, he noted in reflecting on the sentiments of Hutcheson, to have one hundred honest men work together for the public good.[36]

Jefferson strongly emphasized this call for consistency in later years. In explaining to Lafayette why he had made the difficult decision to accept the appointment as secretary of state, he suggested that he did so primarily after concluding that President Washington's "national and private ethics were the same. . . ."[37] In addition, he was convinced that no person holding public office should ever participate in a private enterprise that might increase his personal fortune.[38] This principle, requiring one to have a system of virtue that teaches the importance of maintaining consistency between private and public ethics, according to Jefferson, works both ways. If it is incumbent on us to act in public as in private, we should at the same time have the freedom to express personal sentiments in private even though we hold public office. Not to be able to do so, he observed to Washington, is to deprive us of independence of thought and go against our nature.[39]

A second guideline on this point, Jefferson argued, is the need for a similar system of ethics on the part of men and of nations. Both the people and the countries they represent should share the same characteristics of virtue. They should be "grateful," and "faithful to all engagements and under all circumstances"; and they should be "open and generous," promoting "in the long run even the interests of both. . . ." To put into action these virtues is to generate happiness as a reward.[40]

In 1776, the people and their leaders were united in the view that the public good—especially in a republic—was the ultimate concern in achieving virtue. But as the decade of the 1780s led to the creation of the U.S. Constitution, a new emphasis on the concept of public good, asserted Wood, began to take place. "Tyranny was now seen as the abuse of power by any branch of government, even, and for some especially, by the traditional representatives of the people."[41] No one became more aware of the possible danger of governmental tyranny than did Jefferson. He now saw the urgent need to balance an individual's needs with those of the government. He made these feelings known in a letter to James Monroe in 1782, when he said:

> If we are made in some degree for others, yet in a greater are we made for ourselves. It were contrary to feeling & indeed ridiculous to suppose that a man had less right in himself than one of his neighbors or indeed all of them put together. This would be slavery & not liberty which the bill of rights has made inviolable and for the preservation of which our government has been charged. Nothing could so completely divest us of that liberty as the establishment of the opinion that the state has a *perpetual* right to the services of all it's members. . . .[42]

Jefferson here was calling for an appropriate balance between private and public good—one in which each form of virtue supports the other.

Perhaps more than any other single factor, it was this principle of maintaining the need for individual and governmental morality that helped shape Jefferson's attitudes toward Alexander Hamilton. On one occasion, for instance, when he was present during a contentious conversation between Hamilton and John Adams "on the merits of the British Constitution," he witnessed a clash of ideas that had strong overtones. Years later, he described the episode to Benjamin Rush. Adams, he said, developed the claim that "if some of its defects and abuses were corrected, it would be the most perfect constitution of government ever devised by man." Rejecting this assertion, Hamilton vigorously argued that even "with its existing vices, it was the most perfect model of government that could be formed; and that the correction of its vices would render it an impracticable government."[43] This gave Jefferson an opportunity to make his own ethical position clear. "Mr. Adams," he noted, "was honest as a politician, as well as a man; Hamilton, honest as a man, but, as a politician, believing in the necessity of either force or corruption to govern men. . . ."[44]

The significance of Jefferson's description of Hamilton's value system as it relates to private and public good cannot easily be overemphasized. J. G. A. Pocock's influential *The Machiavellian Moment: Florentine Political Thought and the Atlantic Republican Tradition*, gives resonance to this premise.[45] In this insightful work, Pocock draws significant distinctions between the ethical philosophy expounded by Hamilton and that upheld by Jefferson. To set the stage for this comparative analysis, Pocock explains the fundamental differences between "Court Ideology" and "Country Ideology"—two philosophies of governmental virtue imported to the colonies from Great Britain in the eighteenth century.

To subscribe to the philosophy of "Court Ideology," according to Pocock, was to believe that "personal morality" was "private rather than public," and that it did not have "to be expressed in acts of civic morality or statesman-like virtue. . . ." It further stated "that men were by nature factious and interested beings"—moral faults that were not "fatal" because they could be "policed by a strong central executive. . . ." In other words, there was no need to have an integrative relationship between private and public good. By contrast, "Country Ideology" was "founded on a presumption of . . . an ethos of the civic life, in which the ego knew and loved itself in its relation to (the) common good. . . ." A true republic, therefore, would not be able to function properly or effectively if it were "perpetually threatened by corruption operating through private appetites and false consciousness." To adhere to this position is to maintain that a republic should be characterized by "a civic virtue" dedicated "to universal public good. . . ." This ideology, in short, brings private and public good together as two complementary parts.

Pocock proceeds to show that Hamilton and other Federalist leaders adopted important facets of the "Court Ideology" when they moved "away from virtue and toward interest," leading them to conclude "that the virtue of the individual was no longer a necessary foundation of free government. . . ." Jefferson and other Republican leaders, who were partial to the "Country Ideology," were gravely concerned by their perception that Hamilton's philosophy supported "a strong executive" who would have sufficient power to exert undue influence over the legislature, thereby disrupting the balance of power; promoted ideas and actions that were sympathetic toward a "parliamentary monarchy" and the "English constitution"; endorsed banking proposals in which "fundholders" would eventually "become a hereditary aristocracy"; and advocated "permanent military strength" in which he might be asked "to head that strength." "We can see, in the light of the scheme provided here," observes Pocock, "why it was necessary, both at the beginnings of the Jeffersonian perspective and as it took further shape, to reject Alexander Hamilton as a false prophet and even a kind of Antichrist; he looked east, not west, saw America as commercial empire rather than agrarian republic, and proclaimed that corruption was inescapable. . . ." There was no way that Jefferson's philosophy of virtue could accommodate itself to the view that corruption was inevitable in a republican form of government and that private good and public good do not need to be mutually supportive of each other.

Two important inferences that show the influence of Hutcheson on Jefferson's ideas may be drawn from the foregoing guidelines recommending consistency and balance between private and public ethics, and between a country and its citizens. First, an individual who has a benevolent attitude toward himself and others most likely would embrace the concept of consistency because of the contribution that this moral trait can make with respect to the public good. Second, whenever a country and its people have similarly high ethical standards based on the integrative relationship characterized by benevolence, the public good will be served.

*Reason and the affections*, Jefferson argued as a fourth perspective, *play a reciprocal role in promoting and sustaining virtue*. He spoke about each of these discourse elements separately, and also described the special relationship that exists between them as they do their work in advancing the cause of virtue. Conscious of Locke's emphasis on the potential power of reason to generate self-evident premises on moral issues, Jefferson made use of this principle in showing how argumentative claims may strengthen one's sense of virtue. The use of arguments, he said, that are pointed, yet simplified in nature, will aid us to reflect on what is right or wrong, just or unjust. He illustrated this concept in a letter to his grandson Francis Wayles Eppes: "When tempted to do anything in secret, ask yourself if you would do it in public. If you would not, be sure it is wrong."[46] In this type of reasoning process based upon self-reflection and the questioning of ourselves, Jefferson was arguing that it may be profitable to use the test of publicity or Locke's "Law of opinion or Reputation"[47] to ascertain the moral value of a feeling or an action. For if we are willing to make our innermost thoughts or private conduct known to others, it may be a good sign that we are standing on high moral ground.

Reasoning expressed in questioning form and addressed to ourselves became a favorite rhetorical device for Jefferson in his search for answers to moral issues. He made this clear in a letter to another grandson,

Thomas Jefferson Randolph, who was at the formative stage of his career. Drawing upon his personal experience, he said:

> From the circumstances of my position I was often thrown into the society of horse racers, card players, Foxhunters, scientific and professional men, and of dignified men; and many a time have I asked myself, in the enthusiastic moment of the death of a fox, the victory of a favorite horse, the issue of a question eloquently argued at the bar or in the great Council of the nation, well, which of these kinds of reputation should I prefer? That of a horse jockey? a foxhunter? an Orator? . . . Be assured my dear Jefferson, that these little returns into ourselves, this self-catechizing habit, is not trifling, nor useless, but leads to the prudent selection and steady pursuits of what is right.[48]

This was the type of insightful recommendation that was consistent with Bacon's belief that, on all matters of virtue, we should probe deeply into our mind for direction.

These ideas on the function that reason performs with respect to virtue were consonant with those expressed by the British epistemologists beginning with Bacon and Locke and extending through the writings of Hutcheson. But when he turned to the subject of affections, Jefferson, like many of his American contemporaries, drew heavily from Lord Shaftesbury's influential volume, *Characteristics*. This work described the power of "natural social affections" as they related to the theme of virtue. Included among these affections, or impulses as Shaftesbury sometimes labeled them, were such moral elements as enthusiasm, sympathy, good will, "the drive for preservation of the species," and "the various forms of a familial affection—parental, filial, conjugal, and sibling love—friendship, patriotism, and love of humanity."[49] Of these, the single most "essential element of virtue," according to Shaftesbury, was "enthusiasm." This "natural honest passion," he observed, "has properly nothing for its object but what is good. . . ."[50] It is, in short, an "enthusiasm for all that is true, good, and beautiful, the elevation of the soul above itself to more universal values, the living out the whole peculiar power of the individual by the devotion to something higher."[51] Shaftesbury illustrated this point with a reference to poets who, when under the inspiration of enthusiasm resulting from the stimulation of the faculty of imagination, often can experience the transcending presence of the divine.

There is also an aesthetic dimension to virtue as conceived by Shaftesbury. "Love of order, harmony, and proportion," he observed, stimulates "the elegant passion" of "beauty," which is so advantageous to virtue. . . ."[52]

Similarly, these social affections are also "fundamental" to "moral law and philosophical truth."[53]

Shaftesbury suggested that the social affections, with their power to stimulate the imagination and the passions, must be considered as essential aspects of virtue. But they cannot produce or nurture virtue in and of themselves unless they have an integrating relationship with reason, which has as its principal goal the generation of understanding. When reason and the affections, therefore, work in concert with each other, an orderly and harmonious result will occur. If this is not the case, however, the level of virtue will be diminished. Stanley Grean, a leading modern interpreter of Shaftesbury's moral and aesthetic philosophy, clarified this point: "Since the affections are the 'springs of action,' the rational mind would be immobilized without them. The relation between the affections and the intellect is reciprocal; an affectional imbalance may distort our reasoning, just as false reasoning may misdirect our impulses."[54]

Jefferson was well pleased with Shaftesbury's description of the reciprocal relationship between reason and the affections. With this perspective on virtue in his mind during his tenure in France, he developed his views on this discourse principle in a remarkable letter to Maria Cosway in the autumn of 1786. Jefferson had become infatuated with her while she was visiting in Paris from her home in England. He found it especially intriguing that she was an artist and a delightful conversationalist who shared his interests in aesthetics. When she had to return to London, Jefferson, then a widower, was saddened by her departure. In his effort to make certain that they would keep in close contact with each other, he wrote what Julian Boyd has described as "one of the notable love letters in the English language. . . ."[55]

What makes this communication rhetorically significant, however, was not Jefferson's expression of love toward Cosway, but his description of the distinction between the cognitive and affective nature of human beings. This letter, in brief, may be viewed as the exploration of a metaphor that delineates, from the perspective of virtue and faculty psychology, the characteristics of the "Head" and the "Heart." Consequently, it sheds light on what constitutes reasoning based on highly probable, well-documented premises so essential to the understanding on one hand, and appeals to the affections and sentiments, which arouse the imagination and the passions on the other.

The structure of the letter uses the dialogue format, in which the "Head" and the "Heart" take turns presenting their arguments. This was the type of discourse that Shaftesbury believed to be the best channel for discussing a philosophy of virtue.[56] With its interest in factual data and understanding, the "Head" argues the importance of making decisions and forming attitudes only after sufficient evidence has been carefully weighed. Any opinion, therefore, that appears to be "improbable" should be discarded. This type of reflective process, the "Head" continues, will discourage us from making unreasonable choices—even in the selecting and nurturing of friendships—that tend to promote a wish rather than to reach a sound and meaningful conclusion. This pathway, suggests the "Head," leads to pleasure and happiness—a state of mind free from pain.

In response, the "Heart" acknowledged the Head's supremacy in and jurisdiction over the area of science and in the use of diagrams, charts, and other forms of experimental data that have a special appeal to the faculty of understanding. But it is within the "Heart" that one's moral sense resides. It is here that "the feeling of sympathy, of benevolence, of gratitude, of justice, of love," and of "friendship" are found. It is the "Heart," moreover, that experiences the pleasures of beauty and sublimity so cherished by the imagination. Then, in its most pointed refutation, the "Heart" reminded the "Head" that if the American patriots had listened to their heads alone, they would have been inclined "to calculate and compare wealth and numbers. . . ." Fortunately, asserted the "Heart," "we supplied enthusiasm against wealth and numbers: we put our existence to the hazard, when the hazard seemed against us, and we saved our country: justifying at the same time the ways of Providence, whose precept is to do always what is right, and leave the issue to him."

Some scholars have argued that in this disputation the "Head" was the victor; others, with equal conviction, have declared the "Heart" the winner.[57] We have reached a different decision, for Jefferson, it would appear, had no intention to let one side prevail over the other.[58] Instead, there was harmony between the "Head" and the "Heart" in which each part of our dual nature needs guidance and encouragement from the other. It is not surprising, therefore, that Jefferson placed in the mouth of the "Heart" these closing lines of the dialogue:

> If you [the Head] can at any time furnish matter for their [my friends'] amusement, it will be the office of a good neighbor to do it. I will in like manner seize any occasion which may offer to do the like good turn for you with Condorcet, Rittenhouse, Madison, La Cretelle, or any of those worthy sons of science whom you so justly prize.[59]

There could be little doubt, therefore, that, in Jefferson's opinion, if virtue is to be properly nurtured through discourse, the elements of reasoning and the affections must be equal partners, both of which derive their strength from a reciprocal relationship with each other.[60]

Lee Quinby has used the dialogue between the "Head" and the "Heart" to show that Jefferson was committed to a moral philosophy that could be described as "The Virtue of Aesthetics and the Aesthetics of Virtue."[61] It is a philosophy, he argued, that recommends "a fusion of art and morals, whereby reflective beings are capable of discerning the path to virtue through aesthetic experience"; and which suggests that "the wisdom of sentiment" should be added "to the wisdom of rationality." The result of this process is the "conjoining" of "head and heart" for the purpose of producing a "dialectical unity." It is primarily in this way, he concludes, that through "the dialectic between sentiment and all of the mental faculties" a true virtue leading to "happiness" based on "tranquillity" can occur.[62]

The four perspectives on moral theory and conduct analyzed in the preceding discussion constitute the foundation upon which Jefferson constructed his philosophy of virtue. It was a social enterprise based on the principles of human nature, in which an innate moral sense helps us to distinguish between right and wrong, and creates in us a desire to interact with each other for the purpose of achieving and sustaining a state of happiness. Through these social relations, the discourse that takes place emphasizes the harmonious relationship and balance that should exist between private and public good, and between reason and the affections.

Jefferson's interpretation of virtue as a social phenomenon was consistent with the views of many of his contemporaries during the early stages of the American republic; and it was in keeping with the "politeness" movement launched in France and in the British Isles. Among the first Americans to reflect the influence of this movement were James Wilson and William White of Pennsylvania who, in 1768, developed a series of essays in which they defined the subject of "politeness" as "the natural and graceful expression of social virtues."[63] Twenty-three years later, in July 1791, the editor of the *New-York Magazine* published an essay "On Refinement of Manners," raising the question: "What does the idea of politeness or refinement among people suppose?" Immediately his answer was expressed in interrogative form. "Is it not this, that they cultivate intimate friendship; that they mutually sympathize with the misfortune of each other, and that a passionate glow of affection is promoted?"[64] Commenting on this trend, Gordon Wood stated that "promoting social affection was in fact the object of the civilizing process."[65] It would appear, in short, that Jefferson, like many of his cohorts, adopted a new or modern form of virtue that flowed, not "from the citizen's participation in politics," but from "the citizen's participation in society" by means of discourse.[66]

Jefferson's philosophy of modern virtue, with its commitment to republican values and to the power of communication to hold a society together, led him to a fifth claim, asserting that it is the primary duty of all forms of discourse to emphasize virtue as their principal subject matter. Here he sought to answer this question: In what way is the message of virtue presented through the various forms of discourse? In responding to this query, Jefferson turned once more to Hutcheson.

As he developed his views on this perspective, Hutcheson described how such rhetorical forms as conversation, oratory, poetry, drama, and historical writing fulfilled this task. The conversationalist, he said, carries out his duty by expressing candid ideas that are truthful in a courteous, pleasant, and, at times, humorous manner. It is this face-to-face dialogue that has the best chance to "promote friendliness and good will in society."

Because an orator's principal power is founded upon a "moral sense," such a rhetor becomes a successful proponent of virtue if the arguments and language he uses can stir the passions. What makes this claim so important, in the opinion of Hutcheson, is that "the Passions which the orator attempts to raise, are all found on moral Qualitys." This point may be illustrated by observing that, in defending a client, a lawyer must give the audience a positive impression of the "moral Qualitys of the Person accus'd." The same challenge faces a political orator in a deliberative setting whose primary task is to show how an act that is being advised or dissuaded will affect the public good.

When Hutcheson looked at a poetical or dramatic work, he again reminded us that the subject of virtue becomes a dominating factor. For a poem or a play to create a feeling of pleasure, he noted, the characters and actions depicted must be "distinctly represented as morally good. . . ." He gave the following explanation in support of this claim:

> The representing the Actions themselves, if the Representation be *judicious*, natural, and *lively*, will make us admire the *Good*, and detest *the Vitious*, the *Inhuman*, the *Treacherous*, and *Cruel*, by means of our *moral sense*, without any Reflections of the Poet, to guide our sentiments. . . .

As in the case of poetry and drama, historical writing also has a moral responsibility to exceed "bare narration."[67] Thus the success that the historian has "in representing *Manners*," the "Characters," and the actions that are under discussion, and then in relating these elements to the interests of the State, would determine the degree of pleasure and happiness that is produced on part of the reader.

Hutcheson, it seems evident, was suggesting that virtue is the crucial subject matter that must be present in all forms of discourse. This conclusion stemmed from his conviction that "where there is no virtue, there is nothing worth Desire or Contemplation."[68] A few decades earlier, Shaftesbury concluded his "Inquiry Concerning Virtue or Merit" with this graphic description, which both Hutcheson and Jefferson surely would have embraced:

> So that Virtue, which of all excellences and beauties is the chief and most amiable; that which is the prop and ornament of human affairs; which upholds communities, maintains union, friendship, and correspondence amongst men; that by which countries, as well as private families, flourish and are happy, and for want of which everything comely, conspicuous, great, and worthy, must perish and go to ruin; that single quality, thus beneficial to all society, and to mankind in general, is found equally a happiness and good to each creature in particular, and is that by which alone man can be happy, and without which he must be miserable.[69]

These sentiments, along with those of Hutcheson and other figures of the British Enlightenment, profoundly impressed Jefferson because they conformed closely to his own experiences and feelings as a father who loved his family, as a political leader who dedicated the prime years of his life to the service of his country, and as an educator who sought mightily to elevate the taste of all Americans by constructing a virtue-centered philosophy of discourse with the hope that he could put its principles into practice in his own communication transactions.

# Notes

1. Paul K. Conkin, "The Religious Pilgrimage of Thomas Jefferson," in *Jeffersonian Legacies*, 20, 24.
2. TJ to Peter Carr, August 10, 1787, in Boyd, 12: 15.
3. June 13, 1814, in *Writings*, 1338.
4. TJ to Martha Jefferson, December 11, 1783, in Boyd, 6: 380–81.
5. TJ to Katherine Sprowle Douglas, July 5, 1785, in Boyd, 8: 260.
6. TJ to George Washington, May 10, 1789, in Boyd, 15: 118–19.
7. Anthony Ashley Cooper, third Earl of Shaftesbury, was an English aesthetician whose works appeared in the early part of the eighteenth century; Francis Hutcheson and Lord Kames (Henry Home) were Scottish epistemologists whose writings were published several decades later.
8. See Stanley Grean, *Shaftesbury's Philosophy of Religion and Ethics: A Study in Enthusiasm* (Athens, Ohio: Ohio University Press, 1967), 199–201; and Grean, "Introduction"

to John M. Robertson, ed., Lord Shaftesbury's *Characteristics of Men, Manners, Opinions, Times* (Indianapolis: Bobbs-Merrill, 1964), xxxi. (Hereafter, *Characteristics*.) This book contains two volumes in one.

9. Grean, *Shaftesbury's Philosophy of Religion and Ethics*, 202.

10. *Characteristics*, 1: 279.

11. The references to Lord Kames in this study are taken from his three-volume work the *Elements of Criticism* (Edinburgh; A. Kincaid and J. Bell, 1762); and from *Essays on the Principles of Morality and Natural Religion* (1751; New York: Garland, 1976).

12. TJ to Peter Carr, August 10, 1787, in Boyd, 12: 15.

13. TJ to Peter Carr, August 19, 1785, in Peterson, *Portable Thomas Jefferson*, 382.

14. TJ to Dr. Vine Utley, March 21, 1819, in *Writings*, 1417.

15. See Locke's discussion "of Maxims," in John Locke, *An Essay Concerning Human Understanding* (Oxford: Clarendon Press, 1975), 591–608.

16. Adrienne Koch, *Power, Morals, and the Founding Fathers: Essays in the Interpretation of the American Enlightenment* (Ithaca: Cornell University Press, 1961), 23.

17. A copy of the Syllabus of the doctrines of Epicurus is printed in *Writings*, 1433. The full letter to Short, written on October 31, 1819, appears in ibid., 1430–33.

18. Cicero's argument as stated here is based on the following sources: C. D. Yonge, ed., Cicero's *Tusculan Disputations* (New York: Translation, n.d.). We have also relied heavily on the edition of Cicero's *De Officiis/On Duties* by Harry G. Edinger (Indianapolis: Bobbs-Merrill, 1974).

19. In answering the question of how "virtue" may "be a guide to the pursuit of happiness," Jefferson's answer, according to Koch, "moved beyond the ancient philosophers to the inspiration of Jesus, for he considered that the ancients failed to recognize the reality of love and the duties toward others." Koch, *Power, Morals, and the Founding Fathers*, 32. Our research, as the ensuing discussion suggests, supports Koch's conclusion.

20. TJ to Charles Thomson, January 1–9, 1816, in Ford 11: 488–99. *The Jefferson Bible*, ed. by E. Forrester Church, was published by Beacon Press in Boston in 1989. Jefferson's devotion to the teachings of Jesus was a significant dimension in helping him fulfill his goal of becoming a representative to the American people concerning the Enlightenment. Gordon Wood gives the following explanation showing the importance of this point: "His [Jefferson's] scissors-and-paste redoing of the New Testament in the early years of the nineteenth century stemmed from his desire to reconcile Christianity with the Enlightenment and at the same time answer all those critics who had said he was an enemy of all religion. Jefferson discovered that Jesus, with his prescription for each of us to love our neighbors as ourselves, actually spoke directly to the modern enlightened age. Jefferson's cut-up version of the New Testament offered a much needed morality of social harmony for a new republican society." Wood, "Trials and Tribulations of Thomas Jefferson," 407. Also of importance in studying *The Jefferson Bible* is the following source: Dickinson W. Adams and Ruth W. Lester, "The Philosophy of Jesus" and "The Life and Morals of Jesus," in *Jefferson's Extracts from the Gospels* (Princeton: Princeton University Press, 1983). (*The Papers of Thomas Jefferson*, second series.)

21. TJ to Benjamin Waterhouse, June 26, 1822, in Thomas Jefferson Randolph, ed., *The Memoirs, Correspondence and Private Papers of Thomas Jefferson*, 4 vols. (Charlottesville, 1829), 4: 349. (Hereafter, Randolph.)

22. This statement reflects Jefferson's response to Jesus' teachings, which he believed to be superior to those of the Epicureans and Stoics. In one of his eulogies of Jesus, he said: "It is the innocence of his character, the purity and sublimity of his moral precepts, the

eloquence of his inculcations, the beauty of the apologues in which he conveys them, that I so much admire." TJ to William Short, April 13, 1820, in Randolph, 4: 321.

23. See Locke's discussion on happiness, 258–79.

24. On several occasions, Jefferson referred to Bacon, Locke, and Newton as his great triumvirate of intellectual heroes. But he was similarly enthusiastic about the philosophical teachings of Cicero. The library he sold to the Library of Congress, for instance, contained 14 titles that constituted 39 volumes. In addition, the books he purchased on Cicero's works following the sale to Congress in 1815 included 17 titles arranged in 46 volumes. *LCB*, 160.

25. Cited in *LCB*, 160–61.

26. Ibid. Unless otherwise specified, Cicero's ideas on virtue discussed in the text are based upon his thoughts on this theme expressed in the *Tusculan Disputations* and *On Moral Duties*, sometimes entitled the *Offices*.

27. *Characteristics*, 1: 338.

28. See William Robert Scott, *Francis Hutcheson: His Life, Teaching and Position in the History of Philosophy* (New York: Augustus M. Kelley, 1966), 258.

29. The full title of the work is *Inventing America: Jefferson's Declaration of Independence* (Garden City, N.Y.: Doubleday, 1978). See his discussion on pp. 229–39.

30. Wood, "The Trials and Tribulations of Thomas Jefferson," 399–400.

31. Our discussion of Hutcheson's ideas on virtue is based primarily on the following edition: Francis Hutcheson, *An Inquiry into the Original of Our Ideas of Beauty and Virtue* (New York: Garland, 1971). This is a facsimile of the original work in the Yale University Library. The work was first published in 1725.

32. Adam Smith, *The Theory of Moral Sentiments*, gives Smith's assessment of his former teacher's philosophy of virtue: "But of all the patrons of this system (which makes virtue consist in benevolence), ancient or modern, the late Dr. Hutcheson was undoubtedly beyond all comparison, the most acute, the most distinct, the most philosophical, and what is of the greatest consequence of all, the soberest and most judicious." (1759–1790; Indianapolis: Liberty Classics, 1976), 477.

33. Gordon S. Wood, *The Creation of the American Republic, 1776–1787* (Chapel Hill: University of North Carolina Press, 1969; reprint, New York: Norton, 1972).

34. Ibid., 55.

35. Ibid., 68–69.

36. TJ to James Madison, August 28, 1789, in Boyd, 15: 367.

37. TJ to Marquis de Lafayette, April 2, 1790, in Boyd, 16: 293.

38. He expressed this view in a letter to an unidentified person on March 18, 1793, in L&B, 9: 44–45.

39. TJ to George Washington, June 19, 1786, in Ford, 8: 246–247.

40. TJ to Madame d'Enville, April 2, 1790, in *Writings*, 965.

41. Wood, *Creation of the American Republic*, 608.

42. *Writings*, May 20, 1782, 779.

43. TJ to Benjamin Rush, January 16, 1811, in ibid., 1235.

44. Ibid., 1236. Jefferson stated a similar view concerning Hamilton as reported in his *The Anas*. In this instance, he noted that "Hamilton was, indeed a singular character." To illustrate this point, he observed: "Of acute understanding, disinterested, honest, and honorable in all private transactions, amiable in society, and duly valuing virtue in private life, yet so bewitched and perverted by the British example, as to be under thorough

conviction that corruption was essential to the government of a nation. . . ." This document labeled *Anas*, which contains primary source material from Jefferson, appears in Randolph. The quotation cited here appears at 4: 451.

45. J. G. A. Pocock, *The Machiavellian Moment: Florentine Political Thought and the Atlantic Republican Tradition* (Princeton: Princeton University Press, 1975). Our discussion of Pocock's ideas which follows is based upon his analysis in portions of chapter XIV, "The Eighteenth-Century Debate: Virtue, Passion and Commerce," 462–505; and chapter XV, "The Americanization of Virtue: Corruption, Constitution and Frontier," 506–52.

46. TJ to Francis Wayles Eppes, May 21, 1816, in Edwin Morris Betts and James Adam Bear Jr., eds., *The Family Letters of Thomas Jefferson* (Charlottesville: University Press of Virginia, 1966), 415.

47. In his discussion of "Moral Relations," Locke analyzes three laws: "The Divine Law," the "Civil Law," and the "Law of Opinion or Reputation." See *An Essay Concerning Human Understanding*, 352–54.

48. TJ to Thomas Jefferson Randolph, November 24, 1808, in Betts and Bear, *Family Letters*, 363.

49. Green, *Shaftesbury's Philosophy of Religion and Ethics*, 153–54; and *Characteristics*, 1: 293.

50. *Characteristics*, 2: 170.

51. The author of this quotation is Wilhelm Windelband, from his work *A History of Philosophy* (1901). It is cited in Grean, "Introduction to *Characteristics*," xix. The emotion of "Enthusiasm" was so essential to Shaftesbury's philosophy of virtue that his opening section of *Characteristics* (5–39) is devoted to this theme; and, as we have noted, Grean includes the words "A Study of Enthusiasm" in his title on Shaftesbury's *Philosophy of Religion and Ethics*. It should further be noted that his views on this subject marked a significant departure from Locke's description of this concept. Locke regarded this emotion as a possible enemy of "Reason" and "Revelation." Locke, *An Essay Concerning Human Understanding*, 696–706.

52. *Characteristics*, 1: 279.

53. Grean, "Introduction," to Shaftesbury's *Characteristics*, xxxv. In making this claim, Grean is quoting Ernst Cassirer.

54. Grean, Shaftesbury's *Philosophy of Religion and Ethics*, 221.

55. TJ to Maria Cosway, October 12, 1786, in Boyd, 10: 443–54. The ensuing description of the dialogue is taken from this source. The Boyd quote appears on 453n.

56. *Characteristics*, 1: 51–54. In stating this view, Shaftesbury praised the ancients for their use of dialogue.

57. Boyd, for example, argues that the head was the predominant participant, while Garry Wills asserts that the heart won the debate. See Boyd, 10: 453n, and Wills, *Inventing America*, 276–77.

58. To find additional support for this claim, see Lee Quinby's essay, "Thomas Jefferson: The Virtue of Aesthetics and the Aesthetics of Virtue," *American Historical Review* 87 (April 1982): 338–39.

59. In his brief explanation at the close of the disputation, Jefferson noted: "I thought this a favorable proposition whereon to rest the issue of the dialogue." Boyd, 10: 52.

60. This is made more clear in chapters 3 and 4, which focus on Argumentation and the Rhetoric of Social Affections, respectively.

61. This essay by Quinby, in effect, makes the case that Jefferson's theory of discourse is a combination of rhetoric and belles lettres.

62. Quinby, "The Virtue of Aesthetics and the Aesthetics of Virtue," 338–55.

63. Stephen A. Conrad, "Polite Foundation: Citizenship and Common Sense in James Wilson's Republican Theory," *Supreme Court Review 1984* (1984): 361. This highly informative essay provides valuable insights on how the "politeness" movement contributed to the thinking of Wilson and White, and to other American leaders as well.

64. Vol. II, 406–7.

65. Gordon S. Wood, *The Radicalism of the American Revolution* (New York: Knopf, 1992), 217.

66. Ibid. Wood further noted: "It was society—the affairs of private social life—that bred politeness, sympathy, and the new domesticated virtue. Mingling in drawing rooms, clubs, and coffee houses—partaking of the innumerable interchanges of the daily comings and goings of modern life—created affection and fellow feeling. Some now argued that even commerce, that traditional enemy of classical virtue, was in fact a source of modern virtue. . . . The importance of this domestication of virtue for American culture can scarcely be exaggerated. . . ." Ibid., 217–18.

67. Hutcheson suggested that historical writing often loses its effectiveness because of its frequent reliance on narration that lacks the liveliness and vividness which are needed to arouse the affections as an important step in creating virtue.

68. *An Inquiry into the Original of Our Ideas of Beauty and Virtue*, 246. We feel that this statement captures the essence of the fifth perspective. The discussion of the forms of discourse and virtue appears in this edition, 242–64.

69. *Characteristics*, 1: 338.

# CHAPTER THREE

~

# Principles of Argumentation and the Generation of Understanding

After forming his ideas on virtue, Jefferson was prepared to apply his knowledge, experiences, and feelings to the task of developing a philosophy of discourse that would be morally and philosophically sound, and one that would be applicable for an emerging nation. In the tradition of the British epistemologists who were among the major forces in the Enlightenment movement, he concluded that his search for a philosophy of discourse would have to begin with human nature. Early in his probes, he wanted to discover the essential elements of argumentation because of their far-reaching significance in achieving virtue.

The thinkers who influenced him most as he began his quest were Bacon, Locke, Lord Bolingbroke, Hume, William Duncan, Thomas Reid, and Dugald Stewart. Given that Bacon and Locke were two of his scholarly heroes, it was only natural that he had in his library Bacon's *Advancement of Learning and Locke's Essay Concerning Human Understanding*. Jefferson's appreciation of Bolingbroke is evident from the number of excerpts from his writings appearing in the *Literary Commonplace Book*. In all, there are fifty-four entries totaling more than 10,000 words. This enormous sum comprises "nearly 40 percent of the contents of the [book]."[1] It is of special importance, moreover, that most of the Bolingbroke quotations deal with various aspects of reasoning and evidence. Although the majority of Jefferson's allusions to Hume refer to his *History of England,* there can be little doubt that he also felt the influence of Hume's philosophical and rhetorical essays. He not only occasionally recommended that they be read by others, but he often developed and emphasized arguments reflecting the elements of moral reasoning espoused by Hume. Similarly, William Duncan's *Elements of Logic,* doubtless introduced to him by Dr. William Small, was part of his library,[2] and had a profound effect on molding his argumentation theory and practice—particularly in writing the Declaration of Independence. As early as 1771, moreover, he included Reid's *Inquiry into the Human Mind* on his recommended reading list for Robert Skipwith.

Lastly, Dugald Stewart, who Jefferson met in France, was an occasional correspondent. Far more important, he sent a copy of his book *Elements of the Philosophy of the Mind* to Jefferson, eliciting this response:

> It is now 35 years since I had the great pleasure of becoming acquainted with you in Paris. . . . At a subsequent period you were so kind as to recall me to your recollection of the publication of your invaluable book on the Philosophy of the Mind, a copy of which you sent me, and I have been happy to see it become the text book of most of our colleges & academies and pass thro' several reimpressions in the U.S. . . .[3]

As Jefferson studied human nature for the purpose of developing his discourse of virtue, he came to the belief—shared by Bacon, Locke, and Hume—that the mind is composed of mental faculties, each of which serves a special function. Bacon argued that the mind consists of six faculties: Understanding, Reason, Imagination, Memory, Appetite, and the Will. Locke reduced the number to two: the Understanding and the Will. His justification for doing so, he noted, was that the mind has the power to *perceive* (Understanding) and to *prefer* (Will). Hume and his disciple George Campbell took a middle position between Bacon and Locke by suggesting that there were four faculties: Understanding, Imagination, Passions, and the Will. The stance taken by Jefferson reflected the influence of each of these epistemologists. The mind, he said, consists of the faculties of Memory, Reason (which he equated with Understanding), Imagination, and the Passions.

These faculties are an important part of the organization of this chapter, and of chapters 4 and 5 as well. For Jefferson was saying, along with earlier writers, that if persuasion leading to virtue in a rhetorical situation is to be accomplished, a rhetor must appeal to each of these faculties. What he had to say about the subject of argumentation, therefore, is our current focus because it is the element of discourse that utilizes memory and reason for the purpose of generating understanding and intended meaning. In chapter 4, we discuss the social affections and the stimulation of the imagination and the passions; and in chapter 5 we treat the theme channeling the message of virtue through language control and style.

# The Role of the Faculties of Memory and Reason or Understanding in Argumentation

Jefferson understood the first of these faculties—Memory—as the ability to store up knowledge in the mind and be able to recall and apply it at the appropriate time in a discourse situation. He did not use an elaborate memory system as recommended by Bacon,[4] but he did have three suggestions for improving this mental faculty. His first, and favorite advice for improving his own memory and that of the students he tutored was to maintain a commonplace book. If we record impressive passages from the works of celebrated authors, and notes from public lectures, and then learn to condense these materials in language that is clear, concise, and pithy, we will, he thought, have access to useful ideas needed to create arguments. Additionally, we will have adopted a means of improving our style.[5] He recommended, second, that persons wishing to strengthen their memory should adopt a regular program of exercise; and, third, that they should study languages. For this latter form of training "exercises our memory while that and no other faculty is yet matured. . . ."[6]

During the period between 1820 and 1825, Jefferson also used the faculty of memory as one of three category systems to arrange "A Catalogue of Books Forming the Body of a Library for the University of Virginia." This category included books under the area of "History," which was then subdivided into "Civil" and "Physical" histories. These subject areas, Jefferson believed, contained factual data that should be memorized and managed.

The second faculty of the mind that had an unusually strong appeal for Jefferson was reason, which he tended to combine with understanding. Throughout his long and distinguished public and private career, he maintained an enduring commitment to the utility and power of reason. With Cicero, he regarded this faculty as "the mistress and queen of the world," and a persuasive force that is the epitome of virtue.[7] In sharing this Ciceronian view, Jefferson could with confidence invite his political rival Hamilton to meet with him for a dialogue in which both men, consulting together, could present reasonable arguments for the purpose of adopting a workable plan "which was to save the Union."[8]

Jefferson's faith in reason as the road to understanding and virtue prompted him to stress the value of reflection as the first step in the argumentation process. It was desirable for him as president, therefore, to express gratitude to those citizens who provided him with valuable information that could stimulate his thinking before undertaking action on a difficult problem.[9]

In sharp contrast to the beliefs of a large number of Federalist leaders, Jefferson was thoroughly convinced that the people, on the whole, are capable of responding to and evaluating reasonable appeals. He made this principle a cornerstone of a brief address delivered to the citizens of Albemarle County in February 1790, on the eve of his departure to Washington to serve as secretary of state. Motivated by a sense of duty that caused him to accept the cabinet assignment, he asked his listeners to join with him in bowing "down to the general reason of the society." For, in the end, he concluded, their judgment on this principle of virtue would be sound.[10]

Whenever a person's freedom to use his or her faculty of reason was threatened, as in the case of proposals to censor books or newspapers, Jefferson voiced his strong dissent. In telling language that showed the depth of his feeling on this moral issue, he wrote to Dr. Benjamin Rush during the presidential campaign of 1800: "I have sworn upon the altar of God, eternal hostility against every form of tyranny over the mind of man."[11] So important was the faculty of reason to Jefferson's educational philosophy, it was the second area he used in grouping books in the University of Virginia Library. Under the general heading of "Philosophy," he subdivided reasoning into two parts, Mathematical and Moral. The latter category, which was identified with practical argumentation, included four of his favorite subjects: Ethics, Religion, Law, and Politics.[12]

On the basis of what has been said here about Jefferson's attitude toward reason, it is not surprising that he could enthusiastically concur with the following statement by Lord Kames:

"The pleasures of the understanding are suited to man as a rational and contemplative being; and they tend not a little to ennoble his nature."[13]

When argumentative appeals using the faculties of memory and reason are made, the rhetor has the organizational mechanism to produce a desired result. Observe, for example, how Jefferson attempted to use these two faculties in drawing comparisons among the white population and African Americans and Indians. The reasoning upholding his views appears in his *Notes on the State of Virginia*. The criterion he used was the relative strength of each group with respect to memory and reason. After comparing the qualities of their memory, he then discussed reason or understanding by employing the guidelines of comprehension and reflection.[14]

# The Elements of Argument

In his discussion of the elements of argument, Jefferson emphasized the four points of moral reasoning discussed by Hume and Campbell—experience, testimony, analogy, and calculation of probabilities. Because of his interest in human nature, the influential positions he held, and his extensive travels, he had an opportunity to see how experience functions in the accumulation of knowledge. What one sees and hears, he asserted, may make an indelible impression upon the senses.[15] It was experience, he told John Randolph, that taught him the "reasonableness of mutual sacrifices of opinion among those who are to act together for any common object. . . ."[16]

Late in life Jefferson put his ideas on experience together in a letter to John Adams. Echoing the philosophy of the epistemologists, he explained how meaningful knowledge enters the mind through the organs of the senses. He then expressed an impatience with those beliefs promulgating the notion of immaterialism. Existences that are immaterial in nature, he said, are "nothings." Since they have no connection with our senses and with reality, they are mere "hyperphysical and antiphysical" speculations. Although he was willing to admit, as did Duncan, that our senses may occasionally lead us into error, such a possibility is a rare occurrence.[17] What Jefferson had in mind in making these points is that experience constitutes a persuasive form of evidence.

When Jefferson analyzed the second element of argument, testimony, he shared the view of the epistemologists that to be effective, this form of proof must conform to reliable experience. To illustrate this premise, he alluded to the works of several classical historians and philosophers. We have no difficulty, he asserted, in accepting the description of an event by Livy or Siculous so long as the account was consistent with our own experience. But if they were to "tell us of calves speaking, of statues sweating blood, and other things against the course of nature," we must exclude these claims from history and consign them to the category of fables. The same doubt in our thinking occurs when a historian provides descriptions of a well-known figure that are strikingly incompatible with a significant body of evidence presented by respected scholars.

These perspectives on testimony constitute the basis of Jefferson's reservations about Plato who, he believed, did a disservice to his master teacher Socrates. By frequently placing childlike and shallow words or phrases in the mouth of Socrates, noted Jefferson, Plato presented an image of the pioneering Athenian philosopher that was in direct opposition to the perceptions held by "all antiquity." Thus the words of Socrates that are reported in the dialogues should be perceived as fanciful and unreliable testimony.[18]

The preceding discussion by Jefferson suggests that the following questions, which are still applicable in the contemporary period, serve as criteria for evaluating the worth of testimony:

(1) Does the testimony conform to known experience?
(2) Is it consistent with other knowledge that was acceptable at the time the testimony was given?
(3) Is it given by a reputable witness whose motives are pure?

One of the most interesting aspects of Jefferson's attitudes toward testimony pertains to question three, on the importance of citing reputable witnesses. Often he was inclined to demonstrate how his conclusions on a controversial issue were in line with those of celebrated scholars or influential political colleagues. The ensuing two statements are representative of this policy:

> I cannot reason otherwise: but I believe I am supported in my creed of materialism by Locke, Tracy and Stewart.[19]

> And I should really be alarmed at a difference of opinion with you (on the question of national improvement), and suspicious of my own, were it not that I have, as companions in sentiments, the Madisons, the Monroes, the Randolphs, the Macons, all good men and true, of primitive principles.[20]

As these quotations suggest, Jefferson held firmly to the idea that testimony given by trustworthy witnesses is more likely to be sound and persuasive.

On the third element, argument from analogy, Jefferson, like the epistemologists, recognized its relationship to experience and to testimony, and pointed out the need to draw comparisons that are reasonable and relevant. He demonstrated that this form of argument could be used effectively to delineate the similarities and differences between the following themes: Roman and American slavery; the social attitudes of Northerners and Southerners; the cultural characteristics of the French and English people; and the republican and monarchical forms of governance. Analogy, moreover, is a useful rhetorical strategy, he believed, for comparing men and women, the young and the old, the philosophies of Federalist and Republican newspapers; and the various forms of plant and animal life.

Jefferson's most instructive lesson on the use of analogy to develop an argument occurred on an excursion to southern France in 1787. When he arrived at the town of Tours, he decided to take time out to investigate a scientific problem that earlier had aroused his interest. It was a report Voltaire had included in his *Questions Encyclopediques* concerning the presence of shells "unconnected with animal bodies at the chateau of Monsignor de la Sauvagiere near Tours." This reported finding had been sent to Voltaire by Sauvagiere. As part of the query, Jefferson conversed with Monsignor Gentil, the commissariat in the region, who for years had collected and analyzed different types of shells. During the discussion, Gentil noted that he had received correspondence from Voltaire confirming the reliability of the published claim; had been told by a physician and scientist friend that the Sauvagiere-Voltaire assertion about the shells was true; and that his own findings also proved "that shells are a fruit of the earth, spontaneously produced. . . ."

As he listened to Gentil's argument in support of the unusual thesis that a shell may grow within the earth in the same way that it is created as part of animal life, Jefferson felt that all of the cited authorities, including the brilliant historian and philosopher Voltaire, had improperly used an analogy based on perceived relationships or associations that in reality did not exist. Consequently, when he later reported this incident in his description of the conversation with Gentil, he informed his readers of what he believed was the true analogy that should have been used:

> The bark of trees, the skin of fruits and animals, the feathers of birds receive their growth and nutriment from the internal circulation of a juice thro' the vessels of the individual they cover. We conclude from analogy that the shells of the testaceous tribe receive also their growth from a like internal circulation. If it be urged that this does not exclude the possibility of a like shell being produced by the passage of a fluid thro' the pores of a circumjacent body, whether of earth, stone, or water; I answer that it is not within the usual economy of nature to use two processes for one species of production.

Convinced that this analogy was buttressed by experience grounded in the law of nature, Jefferson concluded that either the hypothesis on shells advanced by Voltaire, Sauvagiere, and Gentil should be summarily rejected, or assent to the proposition must be withheld until "further and fuller observations" were provided.[21]

On the fourth element of reasoning, the calculation of probabilities, Jefferson was noticeably influenced by Bacon's concept of antitheta and by Hume's experimental system of weighing evidence, which, we saw, was employed by the "Head" in its debate with the "Heart." His faith in these methods of compiling and evaluating evidence before reaching a decision may again be observed in his 1787 letter to his nephew Peter Carr. The subject of the relevant section of the letter was religion. The argumentative pattern that Jefferson used, however, would apply to other questions as well.

Jefferson began with the premise that Carr was mature enough to develop his own personal philosophy about the existence and nature of God, and the degree of reliability of the biblical accounts set forth in the Old and New Testaments. He also made certain that what he planned to say was in no way meant to influence how his nephew would frame his own answers to the questions raised. His primary goal in this endeavor was to map out a strategy that Peter might follow.

The first step, said Jefferson, is to "fix reason firmly in her seat, and call to her tribunal every fact, every opinion." This would require the removal of all prejudices and other preconceived beliefs. Moreover, the task should be approached with the attitude of doubt even concerning "the existence of a god."

When next considering the authenticity of the Bible, Jefferson wrote, it is desirable to apply the same criteria of evidence that would be used in determining the validity of a historical text written by Livy or Tacitus. The measuring gauge here is the ascertainment of the relationship between the narrative and what the laws of nature have taught us. If the biblical story, as developed in the Book of Joshua, asserts that "the sun stood still several hours," this claim doubtless was a violation of the laws of nature. It may only be countered by the argument that the book was written under inspiration. But evidence for the presence of inspiration must be offered. Finally, in his references to the New Testament, Jefferson asked Carr to examine with an open mind whether or not it was probable that Jesus was born of the Virgin Mary, that he performed miracles, and that he arose from the dead. It would be helpful in this enterprise to read as many histories as possible about Christ.

Whatever decision Carr was to render (with respect to the existence of God and the reliability of the biblical stories that might be viewed as being incompatible with the physical laws of nature) would, in Jefferson's opinion, be acceptable provided the weight of evidence that was assembled and evaluated persuaded Carr to make the choice. If, after this weighing process of all the available proof is concluded, some critics find fault with the decision, Carr should take comfort in knowing that his own "reason is the only oracle given him by heaven," and that he was "answerable not for the rightness but uprightness of the decision."[22]

## Special Methods for Assessing the Strength, Soundness, and Relevance of an Argument

Jefferson's voluminous writings contain at least four special criteria for assessing the effectiveness of an argument. One of these requirements suggests that *an argumentative claim should epitomize the qualities of coherence or consistency.*[23] That is, all parts of the argument should be logically related or connected to one another, and remain consistent in its emphasis throughout. If this principle is violated, the argument will be significantly weakened.

Three episodes involving politics and religion illustrate Jefferson's concern for coherency and consistency. The first occurred in 1790, in correspondence he had with the lexicographer Noah Webster on the question of a state constitution. What stimulated the correspondence was an argument that Jefferson had advanced in the *Notes on the State of Virginia*. In this volume, Jefferson argued that a state constitution may be altered or replaced by a legislature. To buttress his contention, he showed how the majority of citizens in the various states have supported this principle. Webster responded in a series of letters, each stating that Jefferson was mistaken in advocating the notion that a constitution is alterable. But in making his point, he took a stand that seemed inconsistent with the philosophy he was expounding. Seizing upon this apparent inconsistency, Jefferson asserted: "An argument which is good to prove one thing, may become ridiculous when exhibited as intended to prove another thing."[24]

The second episode, which took place in 1816, related to an author's critique of Priestley's views on religion. After reading the essay, Jefferson wrote to Adams indicting the critique on the grounds that the arguments used were incoherent. The author, he noted, had taken passages from the Scriptures out of context and strung them together in a manner that pointed to the conclusion he had already reached. The end product was an argument in which the parts were not reasonably related.[25]

The final episode again dealt with the subject of religion. It was a theme that set traditional Christians apart from Unitarians and Jews. The question at issue was this: Is there one God or are there three Gods in one? Jefferson answered this query by arguing that to say "one is three, and three but one" is incomprehensible and unreasonable. For the para-dox contained in this question, he felt, could not help but produce a log-ical inconsistency. Then, realizing that such a bold assertion would be anathema to traditional Christians, he softened his tone by acknowledg-ing that those who believe in a triune God are honest people who have a right to their conviction.[26] This confession, however, did not alter his strongly held feeling that to be sound and relevant an argument must meet the test of coherence and consistency.

A second special requirement for assessing the strength of an argu-ment is *the test of fidelity in its use of evidence*. At issue here is the level of truth associated with the proof that is offered to support a claim. So con-cerned was Jefferson with this problem, that he warned us to be on guard against those speakers or writers who were inclined to draw "general conclusions from partial and equivocal observations"; who form opin-ions without adequate verification; and who appear to be motivated by excessive prejudices, uncontrolled passions, and party spirit. In each of these instances, the rhetors usually fail to confine themselves "to facts and well-rounded probabilities."[27] He put his ideas on fidelity succinctly in his *Notes on the State of Virginia*: "To justify a general conclusion, re-quires many observations, even where the subject may be submitted to the Anatomical Knife, to Optical glasses, to analysis by fire, or by sol-vents."[28] Only in this way may one approach the degree of truth needed for responsible discourse.

With these ideas on validity and reliability of evidence in mind, Jef-ferson delivered a "Special Message" to Congress on the Burr Conspir-acy on January 1, 1807. Even though he was convinced that Burr's guilt in leading an insurrection against the federal government in the south-west was "beyond question," he explained to his audience that there was not yet sufficient proof to convict him of treason. He gave this assess-ment of the evidence he had obtained to date, and of the limitations that were present:

> The mass of what I have received, in the course of these transactions, is vo-luminous, but little has been given under the sanction of an oath, so as to constitute formal and legal evidence. It is chiefly in the form of letters, of-ten containing such a mixture of rumors, conjectures, and suspicions, as render it difficult to sift out the real facts, and unadvisable to hazard more than general outlines, strengthened by concurrent information, or the par-ticular credibility of the relater. In this state of the evidence, delivered

sometimes too under the restriction of private confidence, neither safety nor justice will permit the exposing names. . . .[29]

At this point, Jefferson, in his desire to accumulate evidence that would pass the test of fidelity, announced that investigations by his informants would continue.

In stating that investigations by his informants would continue, however, Jefferson revealed a weakness in the administration's case against Burr. For not only, according to Leonard W. Levy, had the president earlier assumed Burr's guilt but indeed argued it even before formal investigative measures had gone into motion. Moreover, in asserting that he was indebted to "his informants," Jefferson was arguing that he, rather than a federal government attorney, was in charge of the investigation. On this crucial issue, Levy claims that "Jefferson did not turn the case over to the U. S. attorney, but acted himself as a prosecutor, superintending the gathering of evidence, locating witnesses, taking depositions, directing trial tactics, and shaping public opinion as if judge and juror for the nation."[30]

As a third special test, according to Jefferson, *an argument, whenever possible, should be initiated with self-evident premises and common sense principles as a foundation or starting point.* He was familiar with Locke's unusual claim that arguments on virtue, if developed properly by the use of appropriate definitions and supporting data, may reach the level of mathematical certainty.[31] In addition, he was aware of Duncan's argument that the concept of self-evidence may be derived from the intellectual process of intuition, which in its normal form is associated with demonstrative reasoning.[32] But Jefferson also believed, as did George Campbell, that there is a type of intuition that is a fundamental characteristic of moral reasoning. It is the intuition that deals with matters of fact rather than "abstract relations." And this is the kind of reasoning process that assists us in the "conduct and business of life." The following example used by Campbell illustrates how intuition may operate in the area of psychology: "I am certain that I see, and feel, and think, what I actually see, and feel, and think." Such an intuitive statement cannot be subjected to a mathematical analysis. It may, however, be consistent with the doctrine of "common sense," which is "an original source of knowledge common to all mankind."[33]

Notwithstanding that Jefferson made no references to Campbell in his writings, they both were directly and significantly influenced by Reid's notions on the principles of common sense. Campbell, for example, observed: "This doctrine hath lately, in our country, been set in the clearest light, and supported by invincible force of argument, by Dr. Reid, in his *Inquiry into the Human Mind.* . . ."[34] Jefferson also showed his indebtedness to Reid by asserting that common sense principles may help guide our "moral sense," dictate actions that should be taken on foreign policy, and provide a rationale for permitting a legislative body to alter a constitution.[35]

In his volume, first published in 1765, Reid described common sense as a defining characteristic of human nature. He noted:

> Such original and natural judgments are . . . a part of that furniture which nature hath given to the human understanding. . . . They are part of our constitution, and all the discoveries of our reason are grounded upon them. They make up what is called *the common sense of mankind*; and what is manifestly contrary to any of those first principles, is what we call *absurd*. The strength of them is *good sense*. . . .[36]

For Reid, therefore, common sense consists of the shared knowledge of mankind that emanates from our nature, which, in turn, is inspired by "the Almighty." It is, in short, an original principle of our being that enables us to recognize self-evident truths that no philosophy of metaphysics can successfully refute. Once a self-evident principle has been observed, and its importance fully appreciated, it then may be used as a basis to launch a chain of reasoning in support of a proposition.

In the end, Jefferson was not willing to go as far as Locke did in blurring the distinction between demonstrative and moral reasoning involving the issue of virtue. He chose instead to follow Duncan and Reid in their interpretations of intuition and its relationship to the rhetorical element of self-evidence. And he strongly endorsed Reid's conclusion that the argumentative concepts of self-evidence and common sense unite to form a persuasive bond crucial to moral reasoning. We see how this plays out in chapter 10 when we analyze Jefferson's arguments in his *Summary View of the Rights of British America* and in the Declaration of Independence.

A final goal for an argument to achieve, in Jefferson's opinion, is *the production of positive consequences*. One of these favorable consequences is to persuade. It is with this thought in mind that, on important questions not involving matters of personal relations, he could warmly endorse Locke's assertion that "every man has a commission to admonish, exhort, [and] convince another of error."[37] One of the rhetorical strategies he recommended for those who wish to become persuaders is to single out the most influential people in a community, and then present to them arguments that they, in turn, could pass on to others.[38]

In some situations, Jefferson believed, argumentation intended to persuade may require a rhetorical strategy based on organized collective action. A dramatic controversy that flared in Massachusetts in 1786–1787
presented such a need. Confronted with an unmanageable and growing
debt, the state legislature enacted a controversial new tax to solve or at
least to alleviate the problem. In the eyes of the people of western Massachusetts, who already nursed grievances against the government, this tax
imposed an unbearable and unjustifiable burden. They responded, therefore, with threats, including assembling and marching in the street to demand not only repeal of the tax but other measures for the relief of debtors.
Nor were these idle threats. Eventually, bands of armed citizens in western
Massachusetts invoked the right of armed resistance under the symbolic
leadership of Daniel Shays, a former captain in the Continental Army and
a hero of the Revolutionary War. These uprisings alarmed the political
leaders of Massachusetts; taken together with similar debtors' uprisings
from Virginia and the Carolinas north to the "independent republic of
Vermont," they attracted the attention of the nation as a whole.[39]

From Paris, Jefferson heard about the Shays' Rebellion and became
concerned about its implications. On the one hand, he believed the
event could be interpreted as an example of the people's right to protest;
on the other, it might suggest that it was further proof of "the weakness
of the executive authority. . . ."[40] But his feelings were allayed after receiving a letter from Adams, stating: "Don't be alarmed at the Turbulence
in New England . . . all will be well."[41] Adams's optimistic description of
the situation, it would appear, masked his true feelings as well as those of
his wife Abigail. Throughout the 1770s, Adams had praised the citizens
for their devotion to virtue. But he began to see an unmistakable change
in their attitude a decade later. Within a ten-year period, he felt the people had lost much of their moral fortitude. As they did so, their attitudes
toward him, especially during his tenure in Europe in the 1780s, had become negative. For this to happen to a man of "rectitude," as he perceived
himself, was a sign of a diminishing commitment to virtue. As a result,
the Shays Rebellion forced him to conclude "that virtue in America had
declined alarmingly, and that the people were apparently no longer able
to live peaceably under the gentle rule of government."[42]

To Abigail Adams the Shays' Rebellion was a threatening sign that put
democracy at risk. Deeply disturbed, she wrote to Jefferson, saying:

> With regard to the Tumults in my native state which you inquire about, I
> wish I could say that report had exaggerated them. It is too true Sir that

they have been carried to so alarming a Height as to stop the Courts of justice in several Counties. Ignorant, wrestless desperadoes, without conscience of principals, have led a deluded multitude to follow their standard,
under pretence of grievances which have no existence but by their imagi-
nations. . . .[43]

Within this context, Jefferson made several comments about the event
that have become a famous part of his legacy. He wrote to Abigail Adams
on December 21, 1786, that he "liked to see people awake and alert."[44]
On January 30, 1787, he sent a message to Madison, saying "that a little
rebellion now and then is a good thing. . . ."[45] Three weeks later he sent
a second letter to Abigail, who shortly before had described the episode
in a letter to him cited above. This time the language was direct and
pointed:

> The spirit of resistance to government is so valuable on certain occasions
> that I wish it to be always kept alive. It will often be exercised when wrong,
> but better so than not to be exercised at all. I like a little rebellion now and
> then. It is like a storm in the Atmosphere.[46]

In defending the legitimacy of a rebellion under certain circumstances,
Jefferson, it would appear, was not authorizing disorganized mob action
based on force. Such a method of producing change would be contrary to
his ideas on reason and the freedom of choice so necessary for the public
good. What he was advocating instead was the right of a group of people
to form a collectivity as a means of exerting pressure on the government
to accept change. His faith in the good sense of the people to engage in
this type of group persuasion on behalf of the public good was consistent
with one of the self-evident claims set forth in the Declaration of Independence. Additionally, it proved to be justified in light of subsequent developments that led to "much needed reforms."[47]

But, Jefferson thought, there is a more significant consequence than
producing persuasion. It is the use of argument for the purpose of creating knowledge. The rationale behind this belief, as observed earlier, is
that knowledge-generation moves in an evolutionary manner. An important conclusion may be drawn from this premise. It is the idea that appeals to tradition often are limited in their power and scope. This, of
course, would not apply to universal truths as expressed in self-evident
premises involving natural rights, for these are enduring values that transcend time and locale. But it does apply to many other matters in daily
life that must be responsive to scientific advances. Since science pushes
forward the frontiers of knowledge, it is unreasonable, Jefferson often as-

serted, for one to take the static and retrogressive approach that such knowledge is a dangerous innovation because it deviates from the findings and actions of our forefathers. Moreover, this tendency is also to be condemned because it is based upon the faulty premise that "the human mind is incapable of further advances." Let us revere our ancestors, he noted, for the conscientious, pioneering efforts they made in the development of our country. But this reverence must not function as a deterrent to an improvement of our society. He voiced this sentiment in a letter to Samuel Kercheval on July 12, 1816:

> Some men look at constitutions with sanctimonious reverence, and deem them like the arc of the covenant, too sacred to be touched. They ascribe to the men of the preceding age a wisdom more than human, and suppose what they did to be beyond amendment. I knew that age well; I belonged to it, and labored with it. It deserved well of its country. It was very like the present, but without the experience of the present. . . . Laws and institutions must go hand in hand with the progress of the human mind. As that becomes more developed, more enlightened, as new discoveries are made, new truths disclosed, and manners and opinions change with the change of circumstances, institutions must advance also, and keep pace with the times.[48]

Because of these considerations, one of the purposes of argument, therefore, is to go beyond tradition and, with the help of what an emerging science has discovered, create fresh and imaginative ideas that meet the challenge of the day.

It is ironic that Jefferson, whose words have perhaps been quoted more than those of any other Founding Father, would discourage the widespread practice of appealing to tradition. But, as we have seen, he did so because of his belief that a rhetor should use arguments designed to perform the epistemic function of advancing knowledge.

## Adapting an Argument to the Rhetorical Situation

The last points to be considered in our discussion of Jefferson's philosophy of argument are his views on audience analysis and adaptation. Whereas he believed with the epistemologists that a rhetor should be concerned with people in general and persons in particular, most of his comments on this subject focus largely on what communicators need to know about a specific group or individual. The first idea to be analyzed is the question of rhetorical exigencies and responses. This is followed by a treatment of what is important in adapting an argument to such themes as locale, nationality, age, gender, and the physical setting or rhetorical container.

## Rhetorical Exigencies and Responses[49]

The degree of urgency in connection with a problem in the rhetorical situation determines whether or not an argumentative response is required. In supporting this principle, Jefferson copied the following statement by Euripides into his *Literary Commonplace Book*: "There are occasions when silence would be better than speech; there are others when the reverse holds good."[50]

Jefferson developed the need for silence by recalling three types of situations in which a response is either unnecessary or undesirable. A person, first of all, should remain silent as long as he or she is consumed by anger. The rhetorical strategy to be used here is to wait until the anger has subsided or is under control.[51] We observe in chapter 4 how Andrew Jackson was rendered inarticulate because of his tendency to try to argue when in a state of anger.

Second, a rhetoric of silence should be adopted if one's argument in a given situation would needlessly hurt a revered person who is recognized as an outstanding leader. This principle prompted Jefferson to refuse to respond to a misleading charge made against him in a newspaper story. If he did not remain silent about the unfair personal attack, he would be placed in the position of putting an unfavorable interpretation on an action taken by George Washington. Since the two men had never had a "personal difference" with each other, he chose not to defend himself by offering a clarifying statement.[52]

Third, when the subject under discussion is of trivial importance, silence is the stance that should be taken. Jefferson used this precept to explain to a fellow legislator why he, as a member of the Virginia Assembly, would not participate in an inconsequential debate in which insignificant issues were being discussed. Not to follow this policy, he said, would serve only to prolong a debate that should be stopped or shortened.[53]

By contrast, he added, a response to a rhetorical situation is necessary when the issue before us is significant and relevant. This principle was put to the test when Washington, near the end of his first term, advised Jefferson that perhaps he would not seek re-election. At first, Jefferson decided to be silent because of his conviction that Washington was inclined to reflect thoroughly about any decision he was to make. Moreover, once he had reached a decision, Washington tended to look with disfavor on any attempt to persuade him to change his mind. But the strong uneasiness Jefferson experienced as he pondered the possible consequences that might ensue convinced him that the exigency was too powerful to be ignored. If Washington refused to run again, he concluded, it was highly probable that the Federalists would start a movement that might eventually lead to a monarchical form of government. Motivated by a sense of duty toward his country to promote the public good, he thus wrote to Washington describing his deep concern and his feeling that a second term was crucial:

> And this is the event at which I tremble, & to prevent which I consider your continuance at the head of affairs as of the last importance. The confidence of the whole union is centered in you. North and South will hang together, if they have you to hang on. . . .[54]

Jefferson's response on this occasion gave force to his conviction that when an exigency is sufficiently strong, an appropriate and relevant argument must be presented if the need is to be reduced or eliminated. To do otherwise would adversely affect the public good, which is so essential for the maintenance of virtue.

## Adaptation to Specific Groups and Their Characteristics

Jefferson had an interest in delineating the general characteristics of groups of people who are important to rhetors. One such group comprises those who live in a particular locale within America. His most instructive discussion of this aspect of audience analysis is contained in his September 1785 letter to General Chastellux. In this communication Jefferson presented broad generalizations highlighting what he thought were the dominating psychological and social traits of Northerners and Southerners. The list below shows how he compared these two groups, pointing out in a telling way both positive and negative aspects of each:

| Northerners | Southerners |
| --- | --- |
| Cool | Fiery |
| Sober | Voluptuary |
| Laborious | Indolent |
| Independent | Independent |
| Persevering | Unsteady |
| Jealous of their own liberties, and just to those of others | Zealous for their own liberties, but trampling on those of others |

| | |
|---|---|
| Interested | Generous |
| Chicaning | Candid |
| Superstitious and hypocritical in their religion | Without attachment or pretensions to any religion but that of the heart |

As one approaches the line that separates the North from the South, Jefferson added, the gradations "grow weaker and weaker." When we arrive at the state of Pennsylvania, we are in a locale that is marked by freedom "from the extremes both of vice and virtue."[55]

In the letter to Chastellux, Jefferson, conscious of the subject of virtue, urged the French traveler, who spent most of his time in America in the state of Virginia, to include arguments in his projected book about his experiences that pinpoint the vices of Virginians so "that they may amend them; for a malady of either body or mind once known is half-cured."[56]

Jefferson also wrote insightfully on the subject of *nationality* and what should be remembered by a communicator who plans to address the citizens of a particular country. Important here are his descriptions of the English, the French, white Americans, and Native Americans. He asserted that the English placed more stress on the faculty of reason or judgment than on that of imagination. But much of what he said about the English was uncomplimentary. He depicted them as admirers of "pomp," "wealth," and "nobility," and as being more prejudiced and less learned than was generally perceived.[57] Even more critical and penetrating was his comment that the peculiarity "of English education" is its emphasis on "drinking, horse-racing and boxing."[58]

The people of France, Jefferson noted, were most attentive to the faculty of imagination; and, perhaps because of their experiences during the turbulent times of the 1780s, French men, women, and children were obsessed with the subject of politics. He was further struck by their overall lack of prejudice, their freedom from drunkenness, the brilliant accomplishments of their men of letters, the high quality of their fine arts, and the politeness of the people as a whole. But he was very critical of the economic and social disparity between the masses and the upper class, the pervasive sexual immorality of the young and the old, and the ignorance of the public regarding the field of science.[59]

Jefferson's generalizations about white Americans included these portrayals: white Americans, like the English, put the faculty of reason on a higher plane than that of imagination; they also stress equality for all classes of people, take pride in domestic felicity, and value simplicity and chastity. But they should strive to improve their overall nature by giving more attention to the subject of fine arts, and by making a conscious effort to emulate the French in developing the ingratiating art of politeness.[60]

What Jefferson said about the need for white American rhetors to adapt their message to native Americans is memorable in its stress on conciliatory discourse, and on specific rules to follow in order to win their support for the governmental mission. Jefferson clearly and forcefully stated the rhetorical approach in a letter describing his instructions to Lewis and Clark as they planned for their famous western expedition in 1803. He told the two explorers to be conciliatory at all times in their manner and language; to make the peaceable intent of their journey evident; and to offer these benefits if the Indians cooperated with the mission: (1) the promoting of commercial intercourse; (2) the ascertaining of what objects and ideas are of most interest to them; (3) the arranging of visits by their chiefs to an appropriate government office, with all expenses paid; and (4) the offering of an education to any of their young people who would like the opportunity to gain more knowledge about "useful arts."[61] These rhetorical instructions exemplify Jefferson's strongly felt desire to establish a peaceful relationship between the government and the Indians; and, in addition, his interest in using the rhetorical strategy of adopting arguments suitable in fulfilling his goal.

The question of *age* was, for Jefferson, another relevant factor in the adaptation of an argument. As was the practice of Aristotle, Jefferson occasionally drew distinctions between the characteristics of the young and those who were advanced in years. Youth, he claimed, are inclined to have good memories, to be susceptible to deep impressions on the senses, to enjoy feelings of passion, and to be hopeful about the future. These traits make it possible for them to learn foreign languages, and desirable for them to read history because of the lessons this subject teaches about preparing for and evaluating the future.[62] On grave matters, however, youth are not likely to excel since they have not yet lived long enough to profit from experience.

When treating the nature of the elderly, Jefferson, as a young man, sanctioned Euripides' assertion that "the experience of old age can offer sager counsel than can youth."[63] He also recognized that the elderly have the capacity to display a sense of gravity when speaking on a serious issue.[64] When he himself became old, he trumpeted the virtue of tranquillity as "the old man's milk," and suggested the need to die "in the good will of all mankind." But he complained that the aging process diminishes the memory, which, like the physical body, steadily decays.[65] Similarly, for this age group, contemplation of the past provides more pleasure than re-flections about the future.

But, despite the elderly person's occasional memory lapses, inherent desire for peace and tranquillity, and tendency to center on the past rather than on the future, these general characteristics, Jefferson be-lieved, should not necessarily disqualify an aging person from holding a challenging public office. For many of these people possess virtues that function as a balancing force that frequently offsets any perceived physi-cal or psychological shortcoming. He explained this position in justifying his decision to appoint Samuel Bishop, a seventy-seven-year-old Repub-lican from Connecticut, to serve as collector of the port of New Haven. He spoke directly to the issue of age, which had become a point of criti-cism by the people of New Haven:

> It is objected, indeed, in the remonstrance, that he is 77 years of age; but at much more advanced age, our Franklin was the ornament of human na-ture. He may not be able to perform in person all the details of his office; but if he gives us the benefit of his understanding, his integrity, his watch-fulness, and takes care that all the details are well performed by himself or his necessary assistants, all public purposes will be answered.[66]

This argument strongly suggests that Jefferson saw the potential of an older person to have an understanding enriched by experience, and a sense of ethical responsibility toward the meaning of duty that only years of observation could have taught. Such a man, despite his age, could build upon his private good in order to create public good.

Jefferson's analysis of *gender* was consistent with the traditional conser-vative views of the majority of his contemporaries. Women, he felt, should not concern themselves with politics, or be appointed to public of-fice. They should, instead, remain in the home as guardians of family val-ues and as objects of love. With this principle of reciprocal relationship between parent and child uppermost in his mind, he told his daughter Mary Jefferson Eppes:

> . . .when I am to write on politics I shall address my letter to Mr. Eppes. To you I had rather indulge the effusions of happiness on yours, and feels in every other object but little interest. . . .[67]

To Jefferson this type of role for American women was far superior to what he had observed in Paris. There he witnessed with a critical eye the passion that French women demonstrated by their constant practice of expressing their opinions on politics.

Adaptation to an audience, concluded Jefferson, meant more than taking into consideration a listener's locale, nationality, age, and gender. It also has to deal with the degree of moral sense with which a listener or reader is endowed. In addressing such a person, the rhetor should construct arguments designed to strengthen a person's natural inclination to prefer good rather than evil. This type of person, for the most part, was representative of those young men whom Jefferson tried to help in their personal and public lives. But although the majority of people are blessed with an innate moral sense that steers them in the direction of what is right, there are those, according to Jefferson, who from early in life lack the propensity to move toward what is morally acceptable when developing beliefs and in choosing a course of action on an ethical issue. In such cases, a more vigorous intervention is required. Jefferson explained to Thomas Law how a rhetor might address this problem:

> When it [a moral sense] is wanting, we endeavor to supply the defect by education, by appeals to reason and calculation, by presenting to the being so unhappily conformed, other motives to do good and to eschew evil, such as the love, or the hatred, or rejection of those among whom he lives, and whose society is necessary to his happiness and even existence; demonstrations by sound calculation that honesty promotes interest in the long run; the rewards and penalties established by the laws; and ultimately the prospects of a future state of retribution for the evil as well as the good done while here. . . .

If these argumentative guidelines were followed, Jefferson concluded, they would "lead into a course of correct action all those whose disparity is not too profound."[68]

To recapitulate, Jefferson developed a philosophy of argumentation that was in the tradition of the British epistemologists. It was a system that drew its thrust from a knowledge of the nature of man, that recognized the distinction between demonstrative and moral reasoning, and that featured the importance of the rhetorical situation, including the audience, the occasion, and the setting. By reinforcing these discourse principles with stories drawn from his own experiences, he was able to demonstrate to potential rhetors how argumentation guided by a quest for virtue, culminating in appeals to the faculties of memory and understanding, constituted an important step for creating a moral imperative for action. But he also knew that genuine persuasion required reason to ally itself with the faculties of imagination and the passions so that a centerpiece of virtue—the social affections—could be aroused.

# Notes

1. *LCB*, 156.

2. On this point, Wilbur Samuel Howell notes: "Duncan's *Logick* . . . originally appeared as the first treatise of the second volume of Robert Dodsley's *The Preceptor* . . . Jefferson's library contained the second volume of Dodsley's *Preceptor* and thus also Duncan's *Logick*, although the latter fact has hitherto not been noticed. . . ." Howell, "Declaration," 470. For a confirmation of Howell's claim, see Sowerby, *Catalogue of the Library of Thomas Jefferson*, 1: 507.

3. TJ to Dugald Stewart, April 26, 1824, in *Writings*, 1487–88.

4. Bacon's system made use of four commonplaces and a commonplace book in which the materials were to be recorded by the rhetors themselves so that they could more easily be recalled.

5. Observe the letter to his grandson Thomas Jefferson Randolph, October 24, 1808, in Betts and Bear, *The Family Letters of Thomas Jefferson*, 353.

6. TJ to Thomas Mann Randolph, August 27, 1786, in Boyd, 10: 306.

7. *LCB*, 59–60.

8. *The Anas*, in Randolph, 4: 448. Although the face-to-face relationship between Hamilton and Jefferson almost always was marked by reasoned discourse, their well-documented ideological differences and personal and political rivalry helped shape the dynamics of the politics of the early republic.

9. See his letter to Wilson C. Nicholas, September 7, 1803, in ibid., 4: 3.

10. Peterson, *The Portable Thomas Jefferson*, 259–60. For similar judgments by Jefferson supporting his belief in reason as the desired method of governance, examine the following letters: TJ to George Mason, February 4, 1791, in *Writings*, 972; to Thomas Mann Randolph, January 7, 1793, in Ford, 7: 207; and to James Madison, February 5, 1799, in Randolph, 3: 416.

11. September 23, 1800, in Randolph, 3: 441. As many historians have noted, however, this unusually high standard of ethics often failed to be met during his two terms as president. In his 1963 volume *Jefferson & Civil Liberties: The Darker Side*, for example, Leonard Levy persuasively argues that in numerous instances (including the Burr conspiracy case and the embargo acts) Jefferson took administrative actions that violated the principles he had sought to uphold in the area of civil liberties. See Leonard Levy, *Jefferson & Civil Liberties: The Darker Side* (Cambridge: Harvard University Press, 1963; reprint, Chicago: Ivan R. Dee, 1989), 70–92 and 93–141.

12. Padover, *The Complete Jefferson*, 1093.

13. *Elements of Criticism*, II, 34.

14. William Peden, ed., *Notes on the State of Virginia* (New York and London: W. W. Norton, 1982), 139–43. Our goal in the discussion of African Americans in this chapter is to explain for illustrative purposes how he alluded to the faculties of memory and reason. In chapter 16, we show how TJ's conclusions on African Americans and slavery did not conform to his principles of reasoning.

15. TJ to John Page, May 1786, in *Writings*, 854.

16. TJ to John Randolph, December 1, 1803, in Randolph, 4: 11.

17. TJ to John Adams, August 15, 1820, in Cappon, 2: 567–69.

18. The foregoing arguments by Jefferson on testimony are found in his letter to William Short, August 4, 1820, in *Writings*, 1435–40.

19. TJ to John Adams, August 15, 1820, in Cappon, 2: 568.

20. TJ to Edward Livingston, April 4, 1824, in L&B, 14: 24.

21. "Notes of a Tour into the Southern Parts of France," in Boyd, 11: 460–62. In developing his argument, TJ used these words that were strikingly similar to the language used by Hume when he said: ". . . to command our belief, there should be such a suite of observations as that their untruth would be more extraordinary than the existence of the fact they affirm."

22. August 10, 1787, in Peterson, *Portable Thomas Jefferson*, 424–27.

23. We are indebted to Walter Fisher for his use of the terms "coherence," "consistency," and "fidelity" as criteria for evaluating arguments. We have found that Jefferson's first two evaluative criteria, including the use of the word "fidelity" which follows, are identical to those used by Fisher. See Walter Fisher, *Human Communication as Narration: Toward a Philosophy of Reason, Value, and Action* (Columbia: University of South Carolina Press, 1987).

24. The relevant documents to be evaluated here are the following: *Notes on the State of Virginia*, 121–25; Webster to TJ, October 1, 1790, in Boyd, 17: 598–99; TJ to Webster, December 4, 1790, in ibid., 18: 131–34; and Webster to TJ, December 12, 1790, in ibid., 18: 153–54.

25. TJ to John Adams, April 8, 1816, in Cappon 2: 468–69.

26. TJ to James Smith, December 8, 1822, in Randolph, 4: 360.

27. Examine the following letters for further information on these points: TJ to Peter Carr, August 10, 1787, in Boyd, 12: 15–17; to Nathaniel Cutting, July 24, 1788, in L&B, 7: 83; to Rev. James Madison, July 19, 1788, in Boyd, 13: 379; to Samuel Smith, August 22, 1798, in *Writings*, 1054; to John Smith, May 7, 1807, in L&B, 11: 204; and to James Monroe, March 10, 1808, in L&B, 12: 7.

28. Peden, *Notes*, 143.

29. *Writings*, 532.

30. Levy, *Jefferson & Civil Liberties*, 71.

31. Locke argued that he was "bold to think, that *Morality is capable of Demonstration*, as well as Mathematics: Since the precise real Essence of the Things moral words stand for, may be perfectly known; and so the Congruity, or Incongruity of the Things themselves, be certainly discovered, in which consists perfect Knowledge." *An Essay Concerning Human Understanding*, 516.

32. William Duncan, *The Elements of Logic* (1748; facsimile reprint, Menston, England: Scholar Press Limited, 1970), 178–80.

33. George Campbell, *The Philosophy of Rhetoric* (Boston: Charles Ewer, 1823), 65–69.

34. Ibid., 65n.

35. A case in point is Jefferson's letter to John Smith on May 7, 1807, in L&B, 11: 203–04.

36. Thomas Reid (Timothy Duggan, ed.), *An Inquiry into the Human Mind* (Chicago: University of Chicago Press, 1970), 268.

37. Gilbert Chinard, ed., *The Commonplace Book of Thomas Jefferson: A Repertory of His Ideas on Government* (Baltimore: Johns Hopkins University Press, 1926), 378.

38. TJ to James Monroe, February 11, 1799, in L&B, 10: 98.

39. An excellent brief summary of the rebellion may be found in Cappon, 1: 163–68.

40. Lawrence S. Kaplan, *Thomas Jefferson: Westward the Course of Empire* (Wilmington, Del: SR Books, 1999), 53.

41. Cappon, 1: 156.

42. John R. Howe Jr., *The Changing Political Thought of John Adams* (Princeton: Princeton University Press, 1965), 108. For similar views about Adams' changing attitudes toward the people in the 1780s, see John E. Ferling, *John Adams: A Life* (Knoxville: University Press of Tennessee, 1992); and Peter Shaw, *The Character of John Adams* (Chapel Hill: University of North Carolina Press, 1975. Published for the Institute of Early American History and Culture).

43. Cappon, 1: 168.

44. Ibid., 1: 159.

45. Boyd, 11: 93

46. Ibid., 11: 174. At the end of the letter, the editor gives an instructive explanation regarding the importance of the context in analyzing the significance of Jefferson's statements on rebellion, 175n.

47. Cappon, 1: 166.

48. *Writings*, 1401. Also see these letters: TJ to William Green Munford, June 18, 1799, in ibid., 1065–66; to Moses Robinson, March 23, 1801, in ibid., 1088; and to John Adams, June 15, 1813, in Cappon, 2: 333. Jefferson gently chided Adams for predicting that freedom of inquiry "will produce nothing more worthy of transmission to posterity than the principles, institutions, and systems of education received from their ancestors." Ibid., 2: 332.

49. Our use of these terms reflects the influence of Lloyd Bitzer, "The Rhetorical Situation," *Philosophy & Rhetoric*, 1 (January 1968): 1–15.

50. *LCB*, 69.

51. In a letter to Madison on January 30, 1787, Jefferson praised a mutual friend for his resolve to remain silent when he was experiencing "an excessive inflammability of temper. . . ." In Boyd, 11: 97.

52. TJ to James Madison, August 3, 1797, in L&B, 9: 413–14.

53. "Autobiography," in Ford, 1: 90.

54. TJ to Washington, May 23, 1792, in *Writings*, 988–89.

55. Boyd, 8: 468.

56. Ibid., 8: 469.

57. TJ to George Wythe, August 13, 1786, in Boyd, 10: 245.

58. TJ to John Bannister Jr., October 15, 1785, in Boyd, 8: 636.

59. TJ to Charles Bellini, September 30, 1785, in Boyd, 8: 568–69.

60. Ibid., 8: 569.

61. Jefferson summarized these instructions ten years after the launching of the expedition in a letter to Paul Allen, in April, 1813, in Padover, *Complete Jefferson*, 911–14. Although the instructions were influenced by governmental policy, they nevertheless also show, from a rhetorical point of view, how an argument should be adapted to Indian culture.

62. *Notes on the State of Virginia*, 147–48. It would appear that Jefferson put the desirability of studying languages and history while one is young into practice when instructing his children. Nathaniel Cutting, who was with Jefferson at the time of his return trip to America from France, recorded this description into his diary: "Arose about 6. Repair'd to the Breakfast Parlour . . . where I found Mr. Jefferson instructing his youngest daugh-

ter, Maria (who is about 11 years of age) in the Spanish Language. She was reading part of a chapter in the Spanish History of the Conquest of Mexico. . . ." In Boyd, 15: 497.

63. *LCB*, 71.

64. In a conversation with Daniel Webster, Jefferson recalled an incident when he, along with other youthful members of the House of Burgesses, asked a Mr. Nicholas—"a mature, grave and religious man"—to be the spokesman on behalf of a proposed Fast Day in the state of Virginia. It would not be appropriate, he felt, for a young member of the assembly to make the presentation. Fletcher Webster, ed., *The Writings and Speeches of Daniel Webster*, 18 vols. (Boston: Little, Brown, 1903), 17: 368–69.

65. TJ to Benjamin Rush, August 17, 1811, in L&B, 13: 75–76. Also see letters to Edward Rutledge, June 24, 1797, in L&B, 9: 411; to Dr. Waterhouse, July 19, 1822, in Randolph, 4: 353–354; and to James Smith, December 8, 1822, in ibid., 4: 361.

66. TJ to Elias Shipman and Others, a Committee of the Merchants of New Haven, July 12, 1801, in Peterson, *Portable Thomas Jefferson*, 297.

67. January 1, 1799, in Betts and Bear, *Family Letters*, 170.

68. TJ to Thomas Law, June 13, 1814, in *Writings*, 1338.

# CHAPTER FOUR

~

# Social Affections and the Stimulation
# of the Imagination and the Passions

According to Jefferson, argumentation based on sound and relevant reasoning focusing on the faculties of memory and understanding was an essential feature of virtue. But this emphasis, he also held, must be strengthened by appeals to the social affections in which the imagination and the passions are stimulated. When this takes place, the four faculties, working in unison, have the capacity to produce the highest level of virtue.

Like Shaftesbury and Hutcheson who preceded him, Jefferson knew that the arousal of the social affections was dependent, first of all, on the moral characteristics displayed by a speaker or writer; and, second, upon a rhetor's ability to stir the social affections in such a way that the audience members would experience a yearning for virtue. Shaftesbury struck a responsive chord in Jefferson when he wrote that a communicator who exhibits "the knowledge and practice of the social virtues, and the familiarity and favor of the moral graces" has "the character of the deserving artist" who is a "just favourite of the Muses." This statement permitted Shaftesbury to conclude with these oft-quoted words: " . . . the science of virtuosi and that of virtue itself become, in a manner, one and the same."[1] This happy condition is attained whenever rhetors show throughout their discourse that they are friends of virtue.

Because the virtuoso or the creator of discourse, whether the written or oral form, should be a representative of virtue, Jefferson confronted the challenge of determining the basic characteristics of a good person who wishes to inform or persuade. His compelling interest in this subject was evident when he began the development of his *Literary Commonplace Book.* Many of the listings he recorded were assembled in the 1760s during his stay in Williamsburg. Seventy extracts from the plays of the Greek dramatist Euripides, for instance, listed traits that characterize a good person. He drew similar telling passages from Cicero's *Tusculan Disputations* and *The Offices*—especially those dealing with the four cardinal virtues.

Moreover, Jefferson always was conscious of the ethical teachings of Jesus, which he so warmly praised; and he was aware of the three ethical laws in moral relations discussed by Locke: "The Divine Law"; "The Civil Law"; and "The Law of Opinion or Reputation."[2] With respect to "The Divine Law," his grandson Thomas Jefferson Randolph observed, Jefferson often turned to a biblical source that became one of his favorites— the fifteenth chapter of the Book of Psalms.[3] In this brief Old Testament chapter, consisting of five verses, King David, seeking the answer to the question what type of person is qualified to dwell in God's "holy hill," summarized (in verses 2–5) four essential elements of virtue:

(1) He that walketh uprightly, and worketh righteousness, and speaketh the truth in his heart.

(2) He that backbiteth not with his tongue, nor doeth evil to his neighbor, nor taketh up a reproach against his neighbor,

(3) In whose eyes a vile person is condemned, but he honoreth them who fear the Lord; he that sweareth to his own hurt, and changeth not;

(4) He that putteth not out his money to usury, nor taketh reward against the innocent. He that doeth these things shall never be moved.

The types of good persons described in these verses, it would appear, are those who engage in righteous thoughts and actions; who with sincerity speak the truth as they know it; who love God, their neighbors, and their friends, while hating all forms of evil; who avoid slanderous speech; and who refuse to take advantage of the poor and innocent, and of those who need to borrow money.

Jefferson was motivated to recommend this Psalm to aspiring young people because of its stress on the importance of virtuous speech and on the social affections. To fulfill these requirements, he argued, was to be well on the way to becoming an effective person and rhetor. Similarly, in taking the position that communicators, to be responsible as well as persuasive, should be intrinsically good persons, Jefferson supported a significant trend in Western rhetorical thought. It was a high-level stance endorsed by Plato as he described the noble lover in the *Phaedrus*; by Cicero in his analysis of the ideal orator in *De Oratore*; and by Quintilian in his belief, as observed in his *Institutio Oratoria*, that "no man can be an orator unless he is a good man." In the British period, Shaftesbury, Hutcheson, and George Campbell embraced a similar standard. Hugh Blair spoke for each of these epistemologists, as well as for Jefferson, when he made this observation in his suggestions for "Improvement in Eloquence":

> In the first place, what stands highest in the order of means, is personal character and disposition. In order to be a truly eloquent or persuasive speaker, nothing is more necessary than to be a virtuous man.[4]

But it was not enough, Jefferson believed, to be a good person who conformed to the moral criteria articulated by David in the fifteenth Psalm, or by Jesus in the Four Gospels of the New Testament. What was further required was a recognition by the audience that a communicator is a person of intelligence, of commendable character, and of good will. And this is to be determined by the rhetor's talent to display these constituent elements of discourse within the message itself and in the manner in which it is communicated. This thought was foremost in Jefferson's mind when, in 1824, he was trying to hire a faculty member from abroad for his emerging University of Virginia. By importing a British professor, he would be giving a further indication of his quest to bring American students in contact with Enlightenment philosophy. But he wanted to do so only on terms consistent with his own ethical philosophy. Thus in a letter to the Scottish philosopher and critic Dugald Stewart, he listed these requirements for the professorship:

> Besides the first degree of eminence in science, a professor with us must be of sober and correct morals and habits, having a talent of communicating his knowledge with facility, and of an accommodating and peaceable temper. The latter is all-important for the harmony of the institution.[5]

The thrust of this requirement for the professorial appointment was that instructors must exemplify three fundamental characteristics. They should, in the first instance, be inherently virtuous; second, they should have sufficient expertise in their academic field to construct a strong message with both an intellectual and moral emphasis; and, finally, they should have the discourse ability to epitomize their commitment to virtue to the audience in a persuasive manner.

# Perspectives on a Communicator's Ethical or Personal Proof

In keeping with the foregoing ideas, Jefferson developed three general perspectives on a communicator's ethical or personal proof and the fundamental part it performs in a rhetoric of virtue. First, he was convinced that the people as a whole, who constituted his audience during his presidency, were the reliable determiners of his motives and actions. It was they alone who had the power and insight to judge whether he was a good person competent in speaking.[6] With this philosophy, he could downplay negative assessments of his own character and motives by partisan critics.

Second, he believed that what an auditor knows about a communicator before a rhetorical episode occurs often will have an influence on the reception of a message. He often reminded his professional colleagues that this concept, described by Cicero and Quintilian as antecedent ethical proof, should be remembered as an important element in discourse. He thus told John Randolph in 1775: "If I affirm to you any facts, your knowledge of me will enable you to decide on their credibility. . . ."[7]

The third general characteristic associated with a rhetor's personal proof is the enormous rhetorical power it has the capacity to generate. This truth was entrenched in his mind during his Williamsburg days when reading the following statement from one of the works of Euripides: "For the same argument, when proceeding from those of no account has not the same force as when it is uttered from men of mark."[8] His faith in the convincing power of personal proof as described by Euripides remained a salient principle for him throughout his life. When he reminisced about colonial days in his conversation with Daniel Webster in 1824, he spoke of Lord Botetourt, who was sent from Great Britain to govern Virginia. Unlike his predecessors, Botetourt was perceived as an "honorable man" who was praised for "his character and integrity." When he spoke, therefore, the people of Virginia listened with respect. Because Botetourt, however, did not approve of the actions of the Virginia patriots in the early 1760s, his sudden death, asserted Jefferson, proved to be "a fortunate event for the cause of the Revolution." For had he lived, his arguments, deriving a strong boost from the force of his character and popularity, would have been a powerful deterrent against even the semblance of a revolt.[9]

If, as Jefferson maintained, a rhetor's task in the use of personal proof is to be a good person, and since this discourse requirement is highly prized by members of an audience, it is desirable for a speaker or writer to use communication strategies that enable a hearer or reader to perceive the ethical qualities that are in the messenger and in the message. Jefferson's ideas on how this might be accomplished fall under the headings of the laws of propriety and justice. These two laws were described by Lord Kames,[10] but they also reflect, in varying degrees, the beliefs of the classical rhetoricians and philosophers, and, most of all, of Jesus. If these laws were followed conscientiously, Jefferson came to believe, they would guide both communicators and audiences as they seek to occupy morally high ground when they make their rhetorical choices and evaluations.

## The Utilization of the Law of Propriety

This law, which is concerned with duties toward ourselves, requires, Jefferson believed, a rhetor to project an image of a person who is wise, courageous, and temperate. To be able to communicate moral principles and values successfully, we, first of all, must exemplify wisdom. This may be shown by having command of our subject matter and control of those impulses that might develop into harmful ambition and a tendency to exaggerate our importance. It follows, therefore, that if we appear to be overly ambitious and lack humility as we stand before an audience, we will be tempted to win approval by using tricks of speech and unsound principles in order to advance our cause. Such a demagogic practice is especially damaging when addressing a mob; consequently, it will be avoided by one who is wise.[11]

The cardinal virtue of wisdom had a high priority in Jefferson's thinking. He was convinced that the primary task of a political communicator was to educate the people. Because of this, he asserted, such a rhetor should have a "knowing head" and sound judgment as he conducts "a crusade against ignorance. . . ."[12]

Second, a communicator must, in all cases, be courageous and resolute in telling an audience to do what was ethically right rather than be content to present ideas that are morally weak and nonthreatening. Jefferson first encountered this principle of the importance of speaking to people, not necessarily as they were, but as they were capable of becoming, when studying a speech included in one of the historical works of Livy. In this speech, the orator Titus Quinctius felt compelled to criticize the Roman citizens for failing to do their duty while their enemies ravaged their lands and insulted their dignity:

> I know that there are other things more pleasant to hear; but even if my character did not prompt me to say what is true in preference to what is agreeable, necessity compels me. I could wish to give you pleasure, Quirites, but I had far sooner you should be saved, no matter what your feeling towards me is going to be.[13]

In this rhetorical episode, the speaker was willing to sacrifice his own reputation and popularity so long as it promoted the private good of the audience and the public good of Rome. It was the type of plea that Jefferson admired. Consequently, he not only incorporated this quotation into his *Literary Commonplace Book*, but consistently upheld its teaching as an "ought" proposition to be followed in discourse.

When considering the law of propriety, Jefferson saw the value of wisdom and courage as powerful virtues needed by rhetors at all times. But the virtue that seemed to concern him most was temperance because of its far-reaching potential to affect our well-being in a rhetorical situation. All too often, he had seen the negative results when one seemed incapable of controlling his or her emotions. The emotion that disturbed him most was anger. If you are angry, he advised his daughters, you will torment yourself and alienate those to whom you speak.[14] As a warmth of feeling begins to rise within us, therefore, we should take whatever steps are needed to suppress it.[15] Otherwise, we will not reach a state of happiness.

To Jefferson, anger is a greater threat to our rhetorical effectiveness in a public situation than it is in our private encounters. To illustrate this claim, he cited two telling stories. In commenting on debates in the French Assembly in the volatile year of 1789, he observed to Madison that the Noblesse were inept debaters because their anger rendered them inarticulate. Their lack of emotional control when trying to speak frequently made them appear to be "absolutely out of their senses" when constructing their arguments. By contrast, those who were "cool, temperate, and sagacious" were the ones with a positive rhetorical influence.[16]

The second narrative is found in Jefferson's description of Andrew Jackson as a political spokesman, recorded by Daniel Webster: "His passions are terrible. When I was President of the Senate he was a Senator; and he could never speak on account of his rashness of his feelings. I have seen him attempt it repeatedly, and as often choke with rage." Such a fault, combined with his disrespect "for laws or constitutions," concluded Jefferson, was enough to disqualify him from the office of the presidency.[17]

When speakers permit excessive anger to seize control of their emotions, they demonstrate an inability or an unwillingness to be temperate, and thereby violate the law of propriety. This belief led Jefferson to list this advice as his "tenth rule" of conduct: "When angry, count ten before you speak. If very angry, count a hundred."

One additional point with respect to the law of propriety was important to Jefferson. It was his belief, shared with Shaftesbury and Hutcheson, that the element of self-interest was counterproductive in the creation of virtue. This idea persuaded him that those participating in discourse, whether verbal or nonverbal in nature, should make certain that they were free from even the appearance of ambition or favoritism. Motivated by what he had observed as a participant on the regional and national scene, therefore, he knew that a person holding high office would jeopardize his position of influence if he communicated in a manner that showed partiality to a particular person or group. This problem, moreover, would be compounded, he felt, if the listener were a family member. He also was aware that political leaders—especially his opponents—were watching him closely to see how he as president discoursed on politics with his two sons-in-law who were members of Congress. To counter this fear, he weighed carefully each word he addressed to them on politics, making certain that they would not be privy to secret executive business. By limiting his remarks in their political discussions to historical issues only, he hoped to free himself of the charge of favoritism and attempting to have an unfair influence on Congress.[18]

Jefferson further believed that a similar policy of propriety should be adopted in nonverbal communication situations. This type of address, he thought, may consist of an act performed by virtue of one's position for the purpose of persuasion. The modern rhetorician Kenneth Burke described this nonverbal technique as administrative rhetoric. Jefferson experienced this sentiment when Governor James Sullivan of Massachusetts invited him to make a presidential tour to the northern states in the summer of 1807. In his response, he was reluctant to accept Sullivan's invitation, arguing that such a trip might be interpreted as an ambitious move based on self-interest designed to curry favor with the voters. Instead of producing the desired goal of conciliation, the act, he said, most likely would cause alienation:

> I confess that I am not reconciled to the idea of a chief magistrate parading himself through the several States as an object of public gaze, and in quest of an applause which, to be valuable, should be purely voluntary. I had rather acquire silent good-will by a faithful discharge of my duties, than owe expressions of to my putting myself in the way of receiving them.[19]

He ended his letter with the thought that he might consider such a trip in the future after he had become a private citizen.

## Employment of the Law of Justice

The law of justice, which stresses our duty obligations to others, focuses on the need for the rhetor to demonstrate values that promote harmony, identification, and good will. One of the ways to accomplish this goal, Jefferson believed, was to cherish and seek the social affection of friendship. When this rule is applied to discourse, the assumption that should be made is that the audience must be perceived as a friend who is seeking an answer to a problem. Evidence that Jefferson found inspiration in the writings of Euripides and Horace on this topic can be found in numerous quotations he included in his *Literary Commonplace Book*. These citations, which he strongly endorsed, contain maxims on the need to link friend to friend through the power of love, and warnings of the damage to our character and authority if an audience senses that communicators have an improper attitude toward their friends.[20]

A second method that rhetors may use to promote harmony and good will by showing respect for an audience is to reveal themselves as honest persons who were fully committed to truth-telling at all times. Jefferson, in his stay at Williamsburg, showed a strong interest in this value-laden discourse concept. During this period, he recorded statements from Homer and Euripides highlighting the principle that what one thinks or does in private must be matched by actions in public. Words and deeds, in short, should blend in such a manner that they possess a similar moral weight and share the element of consistency.[21]

As the years passed, Jefferson continued to emphasize strongly that a speaker, regardless of the circumstances, was never justified in lying to an audience. Not to obey this rule, he added, was to participate in the most useless and reprehensible vice that could be practiced. Moreover, whenever we betray a listener by expressing an untruth, we fail to show a loving concern for that auditor, and seriously diminish our own resolve to do what is right in the future.[22] By taking this uncompromising position on truth-telling and lying, he deviated sharply from a central aspect of Stoic philosophy represented by Quintilian. In his famous "good man theory" interpretation of ethical conduct, for example, Quintilian permitted an orator to tell a lie if it served the noble purpose of preserving the state or saving one's life. In such cases, he argued, the end justifies the means. Jefferson, on the other hand, stood with Jesus in asserting that there should be no exceptions.

When Jefferson spoke about duties of judges, he gave a different slant to the subject of honesty. Whereas in the instances cited above he dealt with dishonest claims that were consciously made, in the case of judges he sounded a different alarm. Here he warned us of the dangers to the public welfare if a well-intentioned judge unconsciously made a claim that was untrue. Although the judge's motives in such a situation may be pure, the falsehood that was unknowingly propounded was unfair to the audience; thus it must be perceived as a transgression of the law of justice.[23] The same principle would apply to other communicators as well.

To put Jefferson's ideas on lying and truth-telling in perspective, it is useful to point out his allegiance to the correspondence-to-truth theory of ethics. This doctrine adheres to the principle that a statement should be consonant with objective reality. That is, the argument presented should be capable of being supported by facts that may be verified by a competent and unbiased observer. If this cannot be done because a rhetor has deliberately distorted or misrepresented the data, a lie has taken place. If, by contrast, verification is impossible because the rhetor is unintentionally misled or carelessly mistaken, as in the case of a judge, there is an absence of truth-telling that still might produce irreparable harm to a person or society.

In sum, Jefferson's views on this important aspect of virtue were consistent with those developed by Locke and Reid. All three believed that an argument should use language in such a way that the rhetors' words should reflect their sincere feelings and intended meanings. Although the three men would admit, along with the current philosopher Stephen Toulmin, that failure to tell the truth was not always the same as telling a lie, they strongly held that communicators should possess the knowledge and care to avoid even the appearance of dishonesty or deception. When this goal is successfully implemented, we as rhetors have functioned in accordance with a fundamental principle of nature.

In the next place, Jefferson argued that the law of justice, with its audience-centered emphasis, teaches us that in a potentially contentious and divisive rhetorical situation, we should adopt the communication strategy of conciliation. One appealing technique to achieve this is based upon the premise that the winning of a person is more important than victory in argument. A reading of his letters to his daughters and grandchildren demonstrates the significance of this concept when one is engaged in interpersonal discourse involving a difficult question.

One of Jefferson's most memorable letters on this theme was addressed to his daughter Mary in 1798 in terms of familial affection. He advised her to use a communication pattern when dialoguing with her husband that was designed to bring them together, thereby promoting conjugal affection. This begins, he said, with the belief that love for each other should be the governing principle. The particular advice that followed suggests that a studious effort should be made to avoid cross-purposes and contradictions that were inclined to alienate. The practice of challenging each other on points that were relatively unimportant would, if continued over a long period of time, lead to painful hostilities. Rather than let this divisive result occur, it would be better to let a disagreement pass. When the issue at hand is very unimportant and tension between husband and wife is heightened, each participant should delay giving a response until strong feelings have subsided. These "little rules of prudence," noted Jefferson, were standards that should produce happiness in the long run.[24]

Letters to his grandchildren contained similar advice. Repeatedly, they were told to avoid disputes whenever feasible. By adopting a strategic policy of silence on trifling controversial matters, we improve our chances of demonstrating our love for others, which, in turn, would gain their respect. This conciliatory procedure, Jefferson stated, transcends any advantage that might be gained in winning an argument.[25]

If conciliatory discourse is valuable on the interpersonal level, it is equally worthwhile in a public setting. Jefferson took comfort in asserting this belief when recalling his relationship with Hamilton in a letter to Joel Barlow. Despite the fact that he and Hamilton had fundamental differences in their worldview, they never, while in the presence of each other, had "personal dissensions." This happened, he observed, because each "thought well of the other as a man. . . ."[26] But although this statement probably is true as it pertains to their interaction when they were together, it would not apply to their personal relationship in other types of rhetorical situations. In 1792, for example, Jefferson referred to Hamilton as baseborn and often used other personal uncomplimentary terms to describe him.

The person on the national stage Jefferson held up as the model for conciliatory discourse was Benjamin Franklin, who was universally recognized as "one of the most amiable" and beloved "men in society." What made him so popular, persuasive, and ingratiating was his persistent adherence to his vow "never to contradict anybody." And in those instances when he "was urged to announce an opinion, he did it rather by asking questions, as if for information, or by suggesting doubts."[27]

The use of good humor and politeness, said Jefferson, was a third persuasive strategy to be used to produce harmony and conciliation. Before discussing the nature of this argument with one of his grandsons in 1808, he drew an interesting distinction between these personality traits, even though he treated them as a single unit. Good humor, he noted, was primarily an inborn trait. Politeness, which has the same effect, is an artificial representation of good humor that may be developed through exercise. Rhetors who use good humor or politeness are willing to sacrifice some of their own wishes in a given setting in order to conciliate others. This self-sacrificing attitude, he suggested, was a small price to pay for the good will that might occur. Moreover, when a rhetor employs good humor as a response to a rude and belligerent attitude by another, the offending person would "be brought to his senses." In fact, there is a high probability that it would mortify and correct him "in the most salutary way by placing him at the feet of your good nature in the eyes of the company."[28]

From what has been said about Jefferson's ideas on conciliation, it is clear that he placed an unusually high premium on a speaker's duty to identify with and respect others. This duty, as we have noted, was a central feature of the law of justice. Jefferson reminded us, however, that no moral law, including justice, would ever condone an action or an attitude that goes against our conscience.[29] To perform an act or nurture a feeling that falls short of meeting this test is to commit an evil that is damaging to ourselves and to others.

In the preceding pages we have sought to show that Jefferson's description of a good person, which stemmed largely from his readings and personal experiences, in addition to his own nature, stressed the value of two moral laws—one of propriety and the other of justice. Rhetors who have good morals and who follow these laws in discourse, he believed, will be wise, courageous, and temperate as they fulfill their duties toward themselves; and they will seek friendship, practice honesty, and use conciliatory rhetorical strategies as they carry out their duties to others. Those who conform to these demanding standards when they speak will enhance their persuasive power, and produce a feeling of happiness and satisfaction in themselves. Similarly, this type of communicator often will be rewarded with challenging assignments when the occasion develops.[30]

The remaining subject to be discussed at this point pertains to discourse strategies that may be used by rhetors who are both intrinsically good persons and who are perceived as being virtuous by their audiences. In particular, our concern here deals with the arousal of the social affections by appeals to the imagination and the passions. To illustrate Jefferson's philosophy of discourse as it relates to this theme, we focus our attention on two narratives described by him, one analyzing an interpersonal communication event and the other consisting of a recreation of a parliamentary debate in the House of Commons. In the first instance, Jefferson was the principal rhetor; in the second, he served as a rhetorical critic of a performance by Lord Chatham.

The primary theme in the first narrative was friendship, considered by Jefferson, along with Shaftesbury and Hutcheson, as a powerful social affection that binds people together. The specific issue was the establishment, on June 19, 1783, of the Society of the Cincinnati by officers who fought in the Revolutionary War. The name of the organization was chosen in honor of the Roman ploughman and consul Cincinnatus, who left his farm to lead his country to victory in a battle for the republic's survival. Following this act of patriotism and heroism, he returned to his plough and to his consulship. As rules were being established for the society, provisions were made for the selection of honorary members who met certain criteria, primarily that of heredity. To add prestige and legitimacy to the group, George Washington was appointed as interim president general who would serve in this capacity until the society had its first official meeting in May 1784. But what appeared to be a natural and innocent development following the end of the war turned out to be a highly controversial issue that its opponents viewed as a threat to the public good and to the happiness of the American people at large.

A major precipitating factor in the generation of a protest movement was a pamphlet written by the South Carolina politician Aedanus Burke under the pen name Cassius: *Considerations on the Society or Order of Cincinnati; lately instituted by the Major-Generals, Brigadier-Generals, and other Officers of the American Army. Proving that it creates a Race of Hereditary Patricians, or Nobility. Interspersed with remarks on its Consequences to the Freedom and Happiness of the Republic.*[31] The title itself sounded an alarm among those who viewed the war as a victory for the democratic principle of equality for all the people, not for a select few.

No one was more emotionally disturbed by such a negative response than Washington. On April 18, 1784, he wrote to Jefferson asking him to study the matter and give his critical assessment. Included in the letter was "a copy of the proceedings of the society," important background material for his investigation.[32] What distressed Washington most was the apparent influence of Burke's arguments.

After analyzing written documents pertaining to the organization's purposes and goals, and holding interviews with interested parties, including members of Congress, Jefferson delivered his reaction in a letter dated April 16.[33] The principal claim he advanced centered on the relationship between discourse and friendship—a relationship, he said, that must be positive in nature. In a prefatory statement, he explained what he believed to be was the primary motivation for the creation of the society:

> When the army was about to be disbanded, and the officers to take final leave, perhaps never again to meet, it was natural for men who had accompanied each other through so many scenes of hardship, of difficulty and danger, who in a variety of instances must have been rendered mutually dear by those aids and good offices to which their situations had given occasion, it was natural I say for these to seize with fondness any propositions which promised to bring them together again at certain and regular periods. And this I take for granted was the origin and object of this institution.

But if perpetuating friendship among the Revolutionary comrades was the desired goal of the Society of the Cincinnati, it was clear to Jefferson that an opposite effect would be produced:

> I doubt . . . whether in it's execution it [the Society] would be found to answer the wishes of those who framed it, and to foster those friendships it was tended to preserve. The members would be brought together at their annual assemblies no longer to encounter a common enemy, but to encounter one another in debate and sentiment. Something I suppose is to be done at those meetings, and however unimportant, it will suffice to produce difference of opinion, contradiction and irritation. The way to make friends quarrel is to pit them in disputation under the public eye. An experience of near twenty years has taught me that few friendships stand this test; and that public assemblies where every one is free to speak and to act, are the most powerful looseners of the bonds of private friendship. I think therefore that this institution would fail of it's principal object, the perpetuation of the personal friendships contracted thro' war. . . .

It should not be concluded from this soundly conceived and convincing passage that Jefferson rejected outright the value of public debate. Experience had instructed him that debate was a vitally significant factor in parliamentary discussion. We may, however, draw these inferences from his remarks. First, debate as it is often practiced is not always an effective means of strengthening bonds between friends; second, when debate takes place, the advocates have a moral responsibility to adopt a rhetorical stance in which their opponents and members of the audience, whatever their perspective, should be treated as friends.

Along with the central argument on friendship, Jefferson suggested other potential dangers inherent in the society. It would, he added, run the risk of promoting dissension between civilians and the military, and between the American soldiers and foreign soldiers who had assisted them. But more important than these potential problems was the warning expressed by Burke, and echoed by certain delegates to Congress, which predicted that the society would create "a Race of Hereditary Patricians, or Nobility." On this point, Jefferson observed: "Experience has shewn that the hereditary branches of modern governments are the patrons of privilege and prerogative, and not of the rights of the people. . . ." Then, in responding to Washington's request for suggestions on what should be done "by the society at their next meeting," Jefferson, relying on interviews he had with members of Congress, gave this assessment: "If they should propose to modify it, so as to render it unobjectionable, I think this would not be effected without such a modification as would amount almost to annihilation; for such would it be to part with it's inheritability, it's organization, & it's assemblies."

Although Jefferson told Washington that these sentiments reflected the views of Congress, there could be little doubt he was stating his own philosophy of virtue. For, as noted in chapter 2, his preference for "Country Ideology" made it clear that a hereditary system of governance would lead to a form of aristocracy that constituted a grave threat to republicanism. Not surprisingly, therefore, he advised Washington: "I have wished to see you stand on ground separated from it" so that his well-earned reputation as a man who is revered would not be compromised.

Jefferson's letter, which combined strong reasoning with an emotional plea to the social affections, motivated Washington to incorporate some of the arguments into the confidential report he presented to the society a few weeks later. With deep conviction, Washington told the members that they must eliminate "every word, sentence, and clause which has a political tendency"; "discontinue the heredity part in all its connexions"; "admit no more honorary members"; and "abolish the General Meetings altogether, as unnecessary" and potentially divisive. On this latter demand for change, he quoted Jefferson directly, but without attributing the citation to him.[34] When some of these forcefully worded recommendations were challenged at a later session by delegates from New York and New Jersey, Washington vigorously defended his position in a lengthy speech. "With much warmth and agitation," one eyewitness observed, "he expressed himself on all the Parts of the Institution deemed exceptionable, and reiterated his determination to vacate his place in the Society, if it could not be accommodated to the feeling and pleasure of the Several States."[35]

The first narrative was a well-chosen example because of its emphasis on friendship, on duty, on the value of republican principles, and on the virtue of public good. What was most surprising about this incident was the discourse used by Washington, who has been described consistently by his contemporaries and by historians as an oral communicator who rarely spoke more than ten minutes at a time in public because of his natural diffidence and lack of animation. But on this occasion he spoke at length with a degree of enthusiasm recommended by Shaftesbury when discussing an issue of virtue. As a result, he both captivated and persuaded those who heard him. This changed persona and presentation may be attributed in part to Jefferson's remarkable letter.

So historically crucial was this episode involving the Society of the Cincinnati, with its emphasis on the possible formation of a hereditary aristocracy, that historian J. G. A. Pocock alluded to it as an illustration of a "Machiavellian Moment," "which suggests that the theses and antitheses of virtue and corruption continued to be of great importance in shaping American thought."[36]

The second narrative, which sheds further light on Jefferson's philosophy of social affections and the stimulation of the imagination and the passions, pertains to a brief speech delivered by the British orator and parliamentary leader, William Pitt, later Lord Chatham. Known as Chatham's Reply to Horace Walpole, this address, presented on March 6, 1741, was part of the House of Commons debate on a pending seamen's bill following a British declaration of war against Spain. The "bill was brought forward by Sir Charles Wager, in January 1741, conferring authority on Justices of the Peace to issue search-warrants, under which constables might enter private dwellings, either by day or by night—and if need be, might force the doors—for the purpose of discovering seamen, and pressing them into public service."[37] Earlier in the day, Pitt, outraged by this violation of human rights, gave a spirited attack:

> Sir, if you pass this law, you must, in my opinion, do with your seamen as they do with their galley-slaves in France—you must chain them to their ships, or chain them in couples when they are ashore . . . Shall we then for the sake of adding six or seven hundred, or even fourteen hundred seamen to his Majesty's Navy, expose our Constitution to so much danger, and every housekeeper in the Kingdom to the danger of being disturbed at all hours in the night?[38]

Seated in the audience as Pitt, then thirty-three years of age, expressed his strong opposition to the bill, was the veteran statesman Sir Horace

Walpole who supported the motion. When he, after several failed attempts, eventually gained the opportunity to be recognized, Walpole attacked Pitt with strongly worded invective designed to weaken his image
as a responsible speaker skilled in the art of discourse. With a spirit of sarcasm and ridicule, he faulted Pitt on two significant counts. First, he said,
Pitt was too young and inexperienced to have the privilege of addressing
his older colleagues on such a grave issue involving national security during time of war. For their richly earned status in life, enhanced by the
knowledge that only experience was able to provide, endows them with
"an indisputable Right to Deference and Superiority. . . ." Second, Walpole added, Pitt's youth has led him into the error of substituting
"pompous Diction and theatrical Emotions" for substantive arguments so
urgently needed in times of danger. This young orator would be wise,
therefore, to converse "more with those of his own Age," and permit his
seniors, with their superior knowledge and maturity, to conduct the business of the House of Commons.[39]

Walpole's attempt to denigrate Pitt's character, authority, and rhetorical performance produced a discourse situation that required a response.
Pitt, it would appear, was ready to confront this challenge by focusing on
the principal questions of age and theatrics that had been leveled against
him. His strategy in handling the issue of age was to use the argumentative device of turning the tables on his opponent. Merely because one
has "gray hairs," he asserted, does not guarantee that he is free from "ob-
stinacy" or "stupidity." In showing the seriousness of such a potential occurrence, Pitt declaimed, "Much more, sir, is he to be abhorred, who, as
he has advanced in age, has receded from virtue, and becomes more
wicked with less temptation; who prostitutes himself for money which
he cannot enjoy, and spends the remains of his life in the ruin of his
country."[40]

Pitt next turned to the charge that he was primarily an actor whose
histrionics—including his gestures, diction, and demeanor, and the use of
language presumably borrowed from others—constituted a "dissimulation" of his "real sentiments." He vigorously denied the charge, in a response filled with allusions to his personal philosophy of virtue:

> The heat that [has] offended them [my critics] is the ardor of conviction,
> and that zeal for the service of my country which neither hope nor fear
> shall influence me to suppress. I will not sit unconcerned while my liberty
> is invaded, nor look in silence upon public robbery. I will exert my en-
> deavors, at whatever hazard, to repeal the aggressor, and drag the thief to
> justice, whoever may partake of their plunder.

Pitt's initial speech and his reply to Walpole had an immediate and long-range effect. Chauncey Goodrich reported that as a result of Pitt's remarks, "all the clauses relating to searchwarrants were ultimately struck out of the bill."[41] Additionally, Jefferson, seventy-three years after the reply was presented, regarded the performance as "a model of eloquence" that should be read by all students interested in the subject of rhetoric as virtue. Describing the reply as "one of the severest which history has recorded," he urged Abraham Small to feature it in the proposed new edition of his *American Speaker*.[42]

Using his principles of virtue in general and his ideas on the social affections and the faculties of imagination and the passions in particular as his criteria for evaluation, Jefferson felt justified in classifying the speech as "a model of eloquence" and "one of the severest" addresses "which history has recorded." Pitt, he felt, had provided a strikingly vivid and disturbing picture of a bill that would treat seamen as "galley-slaves," deprive home owners of their legitimate rights, and adversely affect the public good by creating a dangerous threat to the Constitution. Similarly impressive to Jefferson was Pitt's masterly use of refutation and other argumentative strategies to reestablish his image as a good-man orator in the face of a withering personal and vindictive attack against his character, competence, and maturity. At the same time, Pitt's virtuoso performance had diminished the stature of his opponent, Sir Horace Walpole. In all, Pitt, in Jefferson's opinion, had demonstrated courage and conviction, had reaffirmed his faith in the need for an interactive relationship between private and public good, and displayed such a persuasive enthusiasm on behalf of human rights that his audience, as the vote on the bill indicated, left the parliamentary chamber with a renewed appreciation of the importance of virtue. It was, in brief, the type of moral philosophical discourse that Jefferson wanted American students to study and remember.

What we have observed in this study thus far is that Jefferson stood firmly in the tradition of the British epistemologists. With these thinkers (Bacon, Locke, Shaftesbury, Hutcheson, and Kames), all of whom were central figures of the Enlightenment, he had a strong appreciation for classical philosophy, history, literature, and rhetorical theory and practice; and both he and they expressed appreciation for the Bible. Moreover, he, like the epistemologists, became convinced that no philosophy of discourse could be sound, relevant, or complete unless it was grounded in human nature. This belief called for a need on the part of rhetors to obtain knowledge in the rapidly developing area of science and in the expanding field of the arts and humanities. As they made probes into these fields, they concluded that the human mind has both a cognitive and affective dimension consisting of well-delineated faculties, the most common of which are memory, understanding, imagination, passions, and the will. In subscribing to this psychological-rhetorical trend, Jefferson constructed his philosophy of argumentation based on memory and understanding or reason, and his perspectives on the social affections as they related to the imagination and the passions. All of these were necessary for the movement of the will. But Jefferson knew, as did the other epistemologists, that a fully developed philosophy of discourse not only must consist of a messenger, a message, and an audience, but also of a means to channel the message. These varied means that function as a channel include such subjects as a communicator's organizational pattern, language control, and, in the case of the oral genre, delivery. What Jefferson had to say about these discourse elements is the topic of our analysis in the ensuing pages.

# Notes

1. *Characteristics*, 1: 217.

2. "The Divine Law," according to Locke, "is the Law or Rule which God has set." It implies "rewards and punishments." "The Civil Law seeks to determine if men's actions constitute criminality or innocence. It also is involved with "rewards" and "punishments." "The Law of Opinion or Reputation" centers its attention on virtues and vices. Observes Locke: ". . . .the measure of what is every where called and esteemed *Vertue* and *Vice* is this approbation or dislike, praise or blame, which by a secret and tacit consent establishes itself in several Societies, Tribes, and Clubs of Men in the World. . . ." Locke, *An Essay Concerning Human Understanding*, 352–54.

3. Thomas Jefferson Randolph to Henry S. Randall, in Randall, *Life of Thomas Jefferson*, 3 vols. (New York, 1858), 3: 671.

4. Blair, *Lectures on Rhetoric and Belles Lettres*, 2: 238.

5. April 26, 1824, in *Writings*, 1489.

6. TJ to Thomas Jefferson Randolph, November 24, 1808, in Betts and Bear, *Family Letters*, 365. He expresses a similar sentiment in a letter to Martin Van Buren on June 29, 1804, in L&B, 16: 54–55.

7. TJ to John Randolph, August 25, 1775, in Boyd, 1: 242. For a similar argument, see TJ to Samuel Smith, August 22, 1798, in *Writings*, 1054.

8. LCB, 64.

9. "Memorandum on a Conversation with Thomas Jefferson," in Webster, ed., *Writings and Speeches of Daniel Webster*, 17: 369.

10. Kames argued that such virtues as "temperance," "modesty," and "firmness of mind" belong to the Law of Propriety. The traits of "fidelity," "gratitude," and forbearance, on

the other hand, are integral parts of the Law of Justice. See his *Elements of Criticism*, 3 vols. (Edinburgh: A. Kincaid and J. Bell, eds., 1762), Vol. 2.

11. See quotations from Euripides and Cicero included in *LCB*, 61, 64, 70, and 78.

12. Observe letters to Peter Carr and George Wythe, in *Writings*, 815, 859. Also note TJ to John Garland Jefferson, in Boyd, 19: 253.

13. *LCB*, 61–62.

14. He wrote this letter to Martha, asking her, in turn, to teach this truth to her sister Polly. April 7, 1787, in Boyd, 11: 278. Nothing appeared to motivate Jefferson more than to help his daughters experience happiness.

15. TJ to Francis Wayles Eppes, May 21, 1816, in Betts and Bear, *Family Letters*, 415.

16. TJ to James Madison, June 18, 1789, in Boyd, 15: 196.

17. Webster, "Memorandum on Conversation with Thomas Jefferson," in Webster, ed., *Writings and Speeches of Daniel Webster*, 17: 471.

18. TJ to John Randolph, December 1, 1803, in Ford, 10: 53–54.

19. June 19, 1807, in L&B, 11: 238–39.

20. Many of these quotations are from Euripides in *LCB*, 69–71, 73. On May 5, 1811, Jefferson wrote to Monroe, saying: "I know that the dissolutions of personal friendship are among the most painful occurrences in human life." Ford, 11: 206.

21. *LCB*, 67, 71, 77, 86. It is instructive to observe that the quotations in *LCB* on ethical proof remained as effective principles of Jefferson's philosophy of virtue.

22. Observe the following letters for Jefferson's detailed ideas on this point: TJ to Peter Carr, August 19, 1785, in Peterson, *Portable Thomas Jefferson*, 381; TJ to Thomas Mann Randolph Jr., November 25, 1785, in Boyd, 9: 60; TJ to John Garland Jefferson, October 11, 1791, in Boyd, 22: 210; TJ to Martha Jefferson, April 7, 1787, in Boyd, 11: 278; and TJ to John Melish, January 13, 1813, in Peterson, *Writings*, 1271.

23. "Autobiography," in Ford, 1: 122–23.

24. TJ to Mary Jefferson Eppes, January 7, 1798, in Betts and Bear, *Family Letters*, 151–52.

25. TJ to Ann Cary, Thomas Jefferson and Ellen Wayles Randolph, March 2, 1802, in *Writings*, 1102; TJ to Thomas Jefferson Randolph, November 24, 1808, in Betts and Bear, *Family Letters*, 364; and TJ to Francis Wayles Eppes, May 21, 1816, in ibid., 415.

26. January 24, 1810, in L&B, 12: 351.

27. TJ to Thomas Jefferson Randolph, November 24, 1808, in Betts and Bear, *Family Letters*, 364.

28. Ibid., 363. For a similar view, see TJ to Francis Wayles Eppes, May 21, 1816, in ibid., 415.

29. The supremacy of the conscience as a guideline to moral action was, as we have seen, a fundamental element in Jefferson's philosophy of personal proof.

30. Recall the letter to Dugald Stewart in which Jefferson described the type of professor he wished to hire.

31. Boyd, 7: 88n.

32. George Washington to TJ, April 8, 1784, in ibid., 7: 88.

33. TJ to George Washington, April 16, 1784, in ibid., 7: 105–108.

34. Ibid., 7: 109n. Washington, in quoting the words of TJ, said: " . . . it has been well observed. . . ."

35. Winthrop Sargent, ed., "A Journal of the General Meeting of the Cincinnati, in 1784," cited in ibid.

36. Pocock, *The Machiavellian Moment*, 527–28.

37. Chauncey A. Goodrich, ed., *Select British Eloquence* (New York: Harper & Brothers, Publishers, 1872), 79.

38. Ibid., 80–81.

39. Walpole's speech, along with that of Pitt and other debaters, is found in Donald C. Bryant, et al., eds., *An Historical Anthology of Select British Speeches* (New York: Ronald Press, 1967), 178–89.

40. This excerpt, along with others in Pitt's reply, is taken from Goodrich, 81–82.

41. Ibid., 81.

42. TJ to Abraham Small, May 20, 1814, in L&B, 14: 136–38.

# CHAPTER FIVE

~

# Channeling the Message

Jefferson's interest in aesthetics—including order, harmony, and beauty—which was evident in his treatment of virtue as the main subject matter of discourse and in his discussion of argumentation and the social affections—was similarly clear when he articulated his ideas on channeling the message. No discourse could fulfill its ultimate purpose, he held, unless it demonstrated a cohesive organizational pattern that fostered order; a language usage that exemplified simplicity, conciseness, and beauty; and a mode of delivery in an oral presentation that exuded clarity, conviction, and naturalness. When rhetors can meet these criteria of excellence, they significantly enhance their chances of assisting their audiences in their "pursuit of happiness." We launch our analysis of these topics with a consideration of the organizational structure of a message.

## The Rhetorical Canon of Organization

Jefferson's perspectives on the organization of a document, an essay, or a speech were primarily influenced by his love of systematic order, which he viewed as an important characteristic of virtue.[1] From his entry into politics until his closing days as a letter writer, he considered the structure of a message as a rhetorical canon that upholds the requirements of unity, coherence, and emphasis. This belief was evident, as noted previously, in the system he developed for arranging his books in his library, and in the grouping of fields of study in the curriculum he devised for the University of Virginia. In each case, he used a category of arrangement based on a classification system featuring related subjects and items.

As he was preparing for his mission to France in 1784 to renegotiate treaties with that country and with the Netherlands and Sweden, Jefferson sought to make it clear what the organizational pattern of a model treaty should be. Reflecting on "his work on the revisal of Virginia law in 1779,"[2] he suggested the need to place the various articles of a treaty under appropriate "classes." To illustrate this principle, he noted that different themes should be arranged under the following headings stated in outline form:

I. "Cases where both parties are in full Peace"
II. "Cases where one party is at war"
   A. "Rights of the Neutral party"
   B. "Rights of the Belligerent party"[3]

He offered this brief outline as a means of countering the faulty arrangement pattern that characterized previous treaties.

Jefferson's strong preference for a well-defined sequential order that promoted clarity of thought was one of the reasons why he was attracted to Hugh Blair's *Lectures on Rhetoric and Belles Lettres*. When John Minor was in the early stages of preparing for a career in law, Jefferson wrote to him that Minor should strive to improve his writing and speaking skills by "preparing orations on feigned cases." As these speeches are developed, moreover, they should follow "rigorously the disposition of Blair into Introduction, Narration & c."[4]

Blair was not content to limit the parts of a speech, as Aristotle had done, to a proem, a statement, an argument, and an epilogue. Nor was he willing to adhere to the five steps discussed by the Romans—exordium, narration, proof, refutation, and peroration. Instead, he used an expanded version of his own that he called "Conduct of the Discourse in All Its Parts." This structural plan included six major elements listed in chronological order: "Introduction," "Division," "Narration and Explication," "Argumentative Part," "Pathetic Part," and "Peroration."[5] What appealed to Jefferson was Blair's unified and coherent method, his progression based on the nature of the human mind, and his practical, concrete recommendations that pertained to each step.

# Language Control and Style

Sharing with representatives of the belletristic school of rhetorical thought a compelling interest in the question of how language and style should be used to transmit a message, Jefferson delved deeply and at times innovatively into the nature and utility of this canon of discourse. With strong conviction and a penchant for specific details, expressed in words and phrases designed to instruct and persuade, he discussed such broad topics as the basic principles of language and language as a foundation for the development of a philosophy of style.

## The Principles of Language

Jefferson set forth two general principles of language that, he felt, should be understood by students of discourse. *Language, first of all, should be viewed as a dynamic, developing process that stresses the value of change.* Positioned firmly on the side of "neology" and in opposition to "purism," he vigorously rejected the teachings of those scholars who resisted change in the field of language. Such a static approach, he noted, would render the English language fixed or stationary and rob it of its beauty, spontaneity, and power. In a celebrated letter addressed to the English linguist John Waldo in August 1813, he spoke enthusiastically about his partiality for the doctrine of neology because of its emphasis on the need to introduce new words in our idiom "without the authority of any dictionary." Then alluding to his favorite professional journal, the influential *Edinburgh Review*, he observed with regret the policy of some of its editors to "set their faces against the introduction of new words into the English language," and for their oft-expressed belief that American authors, if not properly challenged, would "adulterate it." It is unreasonable, he said in refutation, for such a large country, with varied climates, a rapidly expanding economy, and a developing interest in the arts and sciences to restrict the addition of new words into our vocabulary.

As he furthered his argument on behalf of neology, Jefferson commended the Athenians for incorporating the "Doric, the Ionian, the Aeolic, and other dialects" into the Greek language. Similarly, he praised the French language for its excellent use of neology, noting, for instance, that new words had been appropriately created to describe the "institution of parliamentary assemblies" brought about by the revolution of 1789. Additionally, he lauded the poetry of Robert Burns as an illustration of how the Scottish dialect he used enriched the beauty of the message he sought to convey. What was true in ancient Greece and Rome, in the history of France, and in eighteenth-century Scotland, Jefferson observed, should serve as representative examples of the power of neology to make a language more copious and appealing.[6]

Seven years later, Jefferson reaffirmed his commitment to the notion of neology in a letter to Adams. Again, he voiced his reservations about the prevailing tendency to regard dictionaries as the final arbiter of language usage:

> [Neology] is the only way to give to a language copiousness and euphony. Without it we would still be held to the vocabulary of Alfred or of Ulphilas; and held to their state of science also: for I am sure they had no words which could have conveyed the ideas of Oxigen, cotyledons, zoophytes, magnetism, electricity, hyaline, and thousands of others expressing ideas not then existing. . . .

In concluding his defense of language change, he offered this challenge to his British counterparts: "And if, in this process of sound neologisation, our transAtlantic brethren shall not choose to accompany us, we may furnish, after the Ionians, a second example of colonial dialect improving on it's primitive."[7] These letters to Waldo and Adams in support of the need for change as a means of modernizing a language suggest the presence in Jefferson's thought of a strong moral dimension that carries with it an implied duty on the part of a rhetor to enforce the principle of neology. The letters also lend credence to Joyce Appleby's claim that "Jefferson targeted the purist as the enemy of linguistic freedom."[8]

Jefferson advanced as a second principle the premise that *language study should be stimulated by the concepts of utility and pleasure*. This notion was uppermost in his mind when in 1818 he helped devise a language curriculum for the University of Virginia. The courses that he recommended for inclusion in the undergraduate program were Greek, Latin, Hebrew, Anglo-Saxon, French, Spanish, Italian, and German.[9] These classical and modern languages should be taught, he felt, because they are useful and provide pleasure.

As a classical student beginning in his early school years and remaining throughout his life, Jefferson believed strongly in the advantages that could be experienced by those who studied Greek and Latin. In almost every instance a person associated with a professional occupation, for example, could obtain information and competence that would be of practical value. The divine could have access to important translations "of the primary" biblical code; the moralist could gain insights into principles of ethics; the lawyer could obtain first-hand knowledge of civil law and the rules of justice; the physician could profit from studying the art of medicine in its earliest educated form, and come to appreciate the enduring power of these teachings; and the statesman could be informed about the arts and sciences, and learn how eloquence, ethics, democracy, and patriotism contributed to the welfare of the populace. The merchant alone, Jefferson asserted, had no real need to have proficiency in the classical languages.[10]

Combined with the practical worth of learning Greek and Latin is an aesthetic dimension that promotes pleasure. It was for this reason that Jefferson urged students of discourse to study specimens of classical eloquence and use them as models to be applied to the English language. This can only be done with maximum effect if one "reads the Latin and Greek authors in their original"—an enjoyable exercise that Jefferson called "a sublime luxury."[11]

In describing the aesthetic quality of the classical languages, Jefferson was not merely commenting on one's ability to read these works silently. He also had in mind the talent to articulate them orally, using the pronunciation that was practiced in the classical era. To be able to do this, he said, would permit us to appreciate "the sublime measure of Homer," and "the full sounding rhythm of Demosthenes. . . ."[12]

On a par with Greek and Latin as an important aspect of discourse was the Anglo-Saxon language. The degree of emphasis he placed on this subject elevated him to the level of pioneer in recognizing its significance as a foundation for the study of English. His first full statement containing his ideas on Anglo-Saxon appeared in his 1798 letter to the English scholar Herbert Croft.[13] In 1818, he expanded his thoughts in a document entitled: "An Essay Towards Facilitating Instruction in the Anglo-Saxon and Modern Dialects of the English Language For the Use of the University of Virginia."

Jefferson apparently had two purposes in this essay. First, he sought to describe four subject areas relating to the uniqueness of the Anglo-Saxon language: its alphabet, orthography, pronunciation, and grammar. In addition to this informative end, he also wanted to persuade his readers that there are two observable advantages to be derived from obtaining a working knowledge of the language. First is the edification it can provide for understanding the roots of the British legal system. Second, and perhaps more important for most students of discourse, is the foundation it creates upon which to build a philosophy of the English language. In developing this latter argument, he criticized George Hickes's *Institutiones Grammaticae Anglo-Saxonicae* and Samuel Johnson's *Dictionary* for their excessive dependence on Greek and Latin structures and derivations. It would have been more beneficial, he argued, if these authors had focused more on those characteristics of Anglo-Saxon that form the basis of contemporary English.

In the closing paragraphs of his essay, Jefferson predicted that those who know Anglo-Saxon would have the competence "to read Shakespeare and Milton with a superior degree of intelligence, heightened by the new and delicate shades of meaning developed [in] us by a knowledge of the original sense of the same works."[14]

Several months before his death, Jefferson continued to speak in superlative terms about the enormous benefits that could be obtained by those who mastered the basic elements of Anglo-Saxon. Upon learning, for instance, that a renewed taste for the language was being revived in England, he gave his unqualified support for this trend. If we are able to recover the county dialects and put them into print in a single volume, he claimed, we will make our present language more varied, copious, and emotive.[15]

Jefferson further held that European languages—particularly French and Spanish—were similarly valuable to students of discourse. French is important, he argued, because it contains the world's best collection of works in mathematics and in natural history and philosophy. From a practical standpoint, moreover, it "is the language of general intercourse, among nations. . . ."[16] The significance of Spanish stems from a different source. For it is the language that dominates large sections of the continents of North and South America. Further, many of the accounts of the early period of American history are written in Spanish. Such circumstances, therefore, require a public figure in America to be prepared to communicate, at least in a general way, through the channel of Spanish.

Less enthusiastic about Italian, Jefferson warned that to study this language along with French and Spanish would lead to confusion in conversational situations. The similarities are simply too striking.[17] The same is not the case, however, with respect to German. This language cannot be ignored because of its works in science and the arts, and because it emanates from the "same original stock" as does Anglo-Saxon. German, in short, "furnishes valuable illustrations for us."[18]

As Jefferson preached the virtues of language study, he was careful to note that one should study in the country where the language is spoken. This was the only way, he felt, that one could develop an ear for pronunciation and accent, become accomplished in the areas of rhythm and harmony, and speed up the building of a vocabulary. In urging students to go abroad for language study, he pointed out the desirability of living with a native family and speaking as often as possible with the women and children of the household.[19] This theory was proven by Jefferson's own experience in France, where his language skills constantly improved.

Except for his highly original treatment of Anglo-Saxon, Jefferson's discussion of classical and modern languages was consistent with traditional practices sanctioned by many of his contemporaries. When he turned to the dialects spoken by Indian tribes, however, he helped push forward the frontiers of knowledge. His lifelong preoccupation with native culture led him to spend years studying their language and in developing a comprehensive list of their vocabularies. Such knowledge, he believed, was particularly important to those who planned a career in politics.

Jefferson's letters are filled with references showing his desire to understand the various tribal languages and to accumulate information about their vocabularies. From Paris he wrote to Thomas Paine about his purchase of a volume entitled *Indian Vocabulary*.[20] Soon afterwards he expressed thanks to Madison for sending him a "pamphlet on the Mohican language. I endeavor to collect all the vocabularies I can, of the American Indians," he noted, "as of those of Asia, persuaded, that if they ever had a common parentage, it will appear in their languages."[21]

Not only did he become an expert on the language of the Creeks, but he attempted to learn all he could about the vocabulary of an obscure Indian tribe—the Unquachogs—that had but twenty total members. Despite the group's unusually small size, he believed it worthwhile to put together a list of 101 words from their vocabulary following his visit to their New York location in 1791.[22]

By 1800, the year he was to run successfully for president, he thought that the time had come to have his collection of native vocabularies published. An important incentive to do so was his fear of having his lists stolen or lost. But after some deliberation, he hesitated to do so, saying that he would like to gather additional information on "the great Southern languages, Cherokee, Creeks, Choctaw, Chickasaw."[23] This indecision to print his findings at this time eventually proved to be his greatest mistake as a scholar of languages. When Dr. Benjamin S. Barton wrote to him in 1809 requesting access to the Indian vocabularies he had collected, Jefferson told him the following story:

> I have now been thirty years availing myself of every possible opportunity of procuring Indian vocabularies to the same set of words: my opportunities were probably better than will ever occur again to any person having the same desire. I had collected about fifty, and had digested most of them in collateral columns, and meant to have printed them the last year of my stay in Washington. But not having yet digested Captain Lewis's collection, nor having leisure then to do it, I put it off till I should return home.

The whole, as well (as a) digest (of the) originals, were packed in a trunk of stationary, and sent round by water with about thirty other packages of my effects, from Washington, and while ascending (the) James river, this package, on account of its weight and presumed precious contents, was singled out and stolen. The thief being disappointed on opening it, threw into the river all its contents, of which he thought he could make no use. Among these were the whole of the vocabularies.[24]

All that remained of his vocabulary collection following this tragic incident were a few water-soaked fragments that floated to the banks of the river. The episode, however, did not weaken Jefferson's interest in Indian languages, which he thought could provide clues concerning the origin of the American Indians, and, additionally, give to a white American rhetor an important instrument for identifying with a tribal audience. It seems clear, therefore, that in urging the study of classical and modern languages as an important subject area, Jefferson showed an awareness of the significance of the virtues of wisdom and duty for those who wish to make discourse a pleasant enterprise and to use it as a means of serving the state.

## Language Principles as a Basis for Creating a Philosophy of Style in the English Language

The foregoing language principles, in Jefferson's opinion, constitute a foundation for building a theory of style in communication. For it is reasonable to assume, according to Jefferson, that the rhetor who embraces the change-oriented doctrine of neology and possesses a knowledge of classical and modern foreign languages, in addition to the native Anglo-Saxon tongue, will have the linguistic tools to forge an effective style. The basic elements of this style may be organized under the three headings widely used in eighteenth-century British rhetorical thought: the Doctrines of Usage, Perspicuity, and Sublimity. The doctrine of usage reached its zenith with the publication of George Campbell's *Philosophy of Rhetoric*. In one of his most famous discussions, Campbell suggested that an effective written or oral style should conform to the standards of reputable, national, and present usage.

In many respects, Campbell's standards were too rigid for Jefferson. To him, they were a form of purism inconsistent with the principle of neology. Notwithstanding this feeling, Jefferson, as a devoted student of classical and modern languages, believed that a speaker's or writer's style should meet the elementary tests of correctness and appropriateness. Most of his comments on correctness pertained to the subject of grammar because of its perceived impact on the reader and on the ethos or personal appeal of the rhetor.

One of his strongest statements against the use of incorrect grammar appeared in his 1816 letter to the publisher Joseph Milligan. Asked to revise a translation of Destutt de Tracy's book on political economy, and to write a preface for the work, Jefferson, after completing the task, complained about the grammatical errors that characterized the original translation. "The translator's orthography," he said, "will need correction, as you will find a multitude of words shamefully misspelt; and he seems to have had no idea of the use of stops; he uses the comma very commonly for a full stop; and as often the full stop, followed by a capital letter, for a comma." He added:

> Your copyist will, therefore, have to stop it properly quite through the work. Still, there will be places where it cannot be stopped correctly without reference to the original; for I observed many instances where a member of a sentence might be given either to the preceding or following one, grammatically, which would yet make the sense very different, and could, therefore, be rectified only by the original.[25]

In these critical remarks on the damaging effect of punctuation errors, Jefferson's major concern related to the issue of meaning. But he also believed that faulty spelling practices might diminish one's ethical appeal. This conviction prompted him to give the following advice to his daughter Martha:

> Take care that you never spell a word wrong. Always before you write a word consider how it is spelt, and if you do not remember it, turn to a dictionary. It produces great praise to a lady to spell well. . . .[26]

Jefferson joined ranks with those who wished to reform spelling. As we note later in this chapter, the rationale for the reform movement was a desire to bring spelling into conformity with pronunciation.

Jefferson's remarks to Martha regarding the importance of correct spelling were in marked contrast to his own practices. Often he would vary his spelling of a particular word, sometimes within the same sentence. He was consistent, however, in his tendencies to substitute the contraction "it's" for the possessive pronoun "its," and vice versa, and to begin a new sentence in a paragraph by using a small letter for the opening word. If these practices, along with the use of questionable punctuations, were inconsistent with his own advice, they were consonant with contemporary trends of the day.[27]

Far more significant were Jefferson's perspectives on appropriateness as an essential quality of usage. Motivated by his conviction that language symbols—as they are represented in words, phrases, and sentences—are fraught with meaning, he found it necessary for a rhetor to make a proper choice. He made this point poignant with several telling examples. One pertained to the popular use of puns and bon mots, or clever statements, that characterized the style of numerous French speakers in 1787. He felt this practice was highly inappropriate because of the intense gravity of the political situation. Although levity and ridicule may be acceptable stylistic strategies in certain instances, he thought, they are inclined to become a distraction when an issue of revolutionary importance is being discussed.[28]

A second instructive example was Jefferson's strongly worded response to the Senate's initial proposal involving the name to be used to describe the office of the presidency at the time of Washington's first inauguration. The proposal stated that he be called "His Highness George Washington, President of the United States and Protector of their Liberties." Such a pretentious label, Jefferson told Madison, "was the most superlatively ridiculous thing I ever heard of."[29] He repeated his concern a week later to William Carmichael. After commending the House of Representatives for insisting that the title be listed as "George Washington, President of the United States," he observed in the following words that have become a part of his legacy: "I hope the terms of Excellency, Honor, Worship, Esquire, for ever disappear from among us from that moment. I wish that of Mr. could follow them."[30] Jefferson's strong negative reaction to the symbols used on this occasion to address a person or label an office suggests forcefully his belief that hyperbolic language of this nature is inappropriate for a society dedicated to a republican philosophy based on virtue.

Another example dealing with appropriateness sheds light on the care that Jefferson gave to the type of phrasing that should be used in forming a balanced structure. To illustrate this point, he listed the following two statements, the first of which he attributed to one of the regicides of Charles I:

(1) Rebellion to tyrants is obedience to God.
(2) Rebellion against tyrants is obedience to God.[31]

By changing the syntax of sentence 1 to that of sentence 2, he said, "all the strength and beauty of the antithesis" has been lost. Because the first sentence, therefore, contains the balance needed for an effective struc-

tural contrast, it successfully meets the criterion of appropriateness required by the doctrine of usage.

A final consideration in his treatment of appropriateness in language
usage dealt with the issue of virtue directly. This point was evident in several references he made to his political opponent Chief Justice John Marshall, who he described as a "cunning" rhetor inclined to use "sophisms"
to twist the language by deliberately giving words a distorted meaning for
the purpose of advancing his own political and social agenda. For evidence in support of this claim, Jefferson alluded to passages in Marshall's
*Life of George Washington*, to Marshall's controversial opinion for the
Court in *Marbury v. Madison* (1803), and to his alteration of word meanings in order "to twist [Aaron] Burr's neck out of the halter of treason."[32]
These manipulative actions, he concluded, were gross violations of the
principle of appropriateness required in the use of language.

Jefferson's extensive readings in the classical and modern languages, including Anglo-Saxon, and his own experiences as a participant in and
observer of political discourse convinced him that the doctrine of perspicuity was an exceedingly significant factor in shaping a rhetor's style.
He liked the exemplification of clarity and conciseness in the writings of
Tacitus, Sallust, and Bolingbroke; and he was impressed with the attention given to the plain style by Bacon and Blair. These sources, in addition to many other writers in the classical and British periods, developed
ideas on perspicuity that strengthened Jefferson's natural inclination to
prefer speeches and essays that were short and pithy. His partiality for this
kind of simple style was grounded in the premise that all discourse should
be able to stimulate the faculty of understanding.

The two primary enemies of perspicuity, Jefferson came to recognize,
were the use of words whose meanings could easily be misinterpreted, and
reliance on needlessly repetitious and verbose language. When these two
stylistic problems occur in the area of political discourse where a legal issue is involved, the potential for misinterpretation of an intended meaning may produce consequences that are national or international in
scope. The following cases described by Jefferson are instructive. The first
instance appears in a letter to Adams that he wrote in 1777 concerning
an action taken by Congress on the question of commerce. The issue under consideration was whether Congress had been granted specific powers by a proviso in the Articles of Confederation to regulate the trade between the respective states. When it ultimately was concluded that
Congress by "implication" had not been granted such powers, Jefferson
was disturbed "that an article so important" was not "laid down in more

express terms . . . so as to exclude all possible doubt . . . that at some future day such a power should be assumed. . . ."[33]

The second instance took place during Jefferson's tenure as secretary of state. George Hammond, as a representative of the British government, announced to Jefferson that American vessels no longer would be permitted to transport their own goods to any of "the British European dominions." This letter informing the Americans that the new regulation would be strictly enforced contained the following words that the two men interpreted differently: "official communication," "official notification," "formal assurance," "personal conviction," and "private belief." In an attempt to clear up the confusion in the interpretation of these words, Jefferson reminded Hammond that "formal assurance" and "official assurance" do not represent the same meanings, whereas the words "personal conviction" and "private belief" are equivalent terms. The lesson that Jefferson was attempting to teach in this case is that ambiguities related to the meaning of words should, if possible, be cleared up so that rhetors and their audiences will have a shared interpretation. To underline this message, he noted that he was not "scrupulous about words when they are once explained. . . ."[34]

Still more troubling to Jefferson was the incomprehensibility that occurs when a speech or written document is filled with verbosity and numerous tautologies. This was a major problem, he thought, in legal discourse—especially as it relates to the wording of statutes. Far too often these statutes contain "parenthesis within parenthesis," an undue dependence on "saids," and "aforesaids," as well as "ands" and "ors." This practice of "saying everything over two or three times, so that nobody but we of the craft can untwist the diction, and find out what it means" was, to Jefferson, a direct violation of the doctrine of perspicuity that should be condemned.[35] From this premise it follows that his favorite rhetors were those who spoke in concise, pithy terms. For those orators who failed to do so, he had this warning:

> Amplification is the vice of modern oratory. It is an insult to an assembly of reasonable men, disgusting and revolting instead of persuading. Speeches measured by the hour, die with the hour.[36]

Jefferson's enthusiasm for a clear, pithy style, uncluttered by needless verbiage, did not deter him from warmly embracing the doctrine of sublimity in certain rhetorical situations. His grounding in the writings of the classical authors and in the works of the leading European poets and rhetorical scholars helped him to see the power of sublimity and beauty that emanates from appeals to the faculties of the imagination and pas-sion. Longinus, whose famous volume *On the Sublime* was introduced to European scholars in 1674, was a significant book in Jefferson's library. In that work, which had a profound effect on the belletristic school of thought, Longinus described five sources of the sublime: (1) "the com-mand of full blooded ideas"; (2) "the inspiration of vehement emotion"; (3) figures of speech; (4) figures of thought; and (5) "dignity and eleva-tion." Here Longinus was suggesting that when a communicator unites compelling ideas with powerful emotion and elevated phrases, he trans-ports the audience. So vital is this ability, he added, that one may redeem "all his mistakes by a single touch of sublimity and true excellence."[37]

But it was Hugh Blair who had perhaps the most lasting influence on Jefferson's attitudes toward sublimity. His emphasis on the grandeur and beauty of nature and on the magnanimity of the human spirit as demon-strated in a heroic act was instructive. Moreover, Blair's penchant for combining the best elements of perspicuity with those of sublimity con-formed to Jefferson's own standards. Both believed that sublimity in speaking and writing is characterized by simplicity, conciseness, and strength. And both shared the conviction that a genuinely sublime pas-sage is an expression of bold, pathetic thoughts phrased in language that is free from bombast, frigidity, and profusion, but, at the same time, is suf-ficiently effective to give a clear and moving impression of the person or object being described.[38]

Jefferson's ideas on sublimity and beauty may be seen more clearly by examining his descriptions of the three levels of style. His categories were similar to those developed by Cicero, Quintilian, and St. Augustine. The classical rhetoricians used the terms "plain," "medium," and "grand" to characterize the language options open to the rhetor. Jefferson's choice of similar words relied on the terms "familiar," "middling," and "elevated." The "plain" or "familiar" placed its emphasis on clarity and simplicity. In contrast, the "grand" or "elevated," while stressing the value of perspicu-ity, focused heavily on sublimity and beauty. In between was the "medium," or "middling" level. Jefferson illustrated his categories with the following clarifying statements: (1) letter writers and comic authors tend to use the "familiar" style; (2) historians most likely will use the "middling" style; and (3) orators and poets have the best opportunity to employ the "elevated" style.[39]

When to use a particular style depends upon the nature of the subject and the rhetorical situation. In the field of history, where the "middling" style is appropriate, he recommended the study of Tacitus, Sallust, and

Hume. For his models of excellence in poetry and oratory, he advised the reading of Homer's *Iliad* and *Odyssey*, Shakespeare's plays, Demosthenes' orations, and representative parliamentary speeches delivered in the House of Commons. In each of these cases that he cited, the rhetor had learned the art of channeling the message by utilizing a style that was suitable to the occasion at hand.

When discussing the stylistic trait of appropriateness, Jefferson felt that in some cases the propitious rhetorical strategy to use is to substitute actions for words. This becomes necessary, he argued, in those situations in which verbal symbols appear to be incapable of presenting a genuine, heartfelt sentiment or feeling. He experienced this conviction about the potential limitation of language in a letter to Washington before Jefferson's projected diplomatic trip to France following the end of the Revolutionary War. Filled with a sense of emotion and gratitude about the suffering Washington had endured in leading the American troops to victory, and aware that the two men would be unable to see each other for a long period of time, Jefferson said: "Were I to indulge myself in those warm effusions which this subject for ever prompts, they would wear an appearance of adulation very foreign to my nature; for such is become the prostitution of language that sincerity has no longer distinct terms in which to express her own truths." He then concluded his letter of appreciation by stating he would zealously seize any opportunity while abroad to perform whatever service that Washington might desire. This nonverbal action that rendered a service, Jefferson believed, would be more appropriate than a reliance on written symbols that would be, at best, an imprecise and exaggerated attempt to praise.[40] Such an effort, in short, would project an image of insincerity—a condition in opposition to the laws of justice and propriety.

On the topic of language and style, Jefferson, as we have seen thus far, recognized the value of perceiving language, in all of its myriad forms, as a dynamic rhetorical channel subject to the forces of change; and viewed style as a linguistic element featuring the doctrines of usage, perspicuity, and sublimity. The conclusion of the present section analyzes his recommendations for improving the English language in such a way that it would have a salutary effect on a rhetor's style.

The suggestions that Jefferson put forward were consistent with his ideas on neology which, he claimed, had made significant contributions to the enrichment of the Greek, Latin, and French languages. He convinced himself that if the copiousness of these tongues could be enhanced through neology, so, too, could that of English. Out of this belief came the following program for improvement. The first step included recognition of the need to adhere to a policy adopted by the Greeks of varying the terminations of every root so as to form new words from each of the parts of speech. Note, for example, what may be done with the root term "gener." From this root have come the nouns "generation," "gener-ator," "de-gener-acy," "gener-osity," and "generalship." The same principle using the identical root has worked with other parts of speech. The adjective "gener-ative," the verbs "gener-ate" and "gener-alize," the participle "gener-ating," and the adverb "gener-al-ly" further illustrate how a vocabulary may be enlarged by this method.

A second recommendation for improving the English language by making it more copious is "to compound every root and its family with every preposition, where both sense and sound would be in its favor." To exemplify this idea, he cited the possibilities inherent in the English root of the verb "to place." From this root, he observed, have already come the words "mis-place," "dis-place," and "re-place." To these words, which were currently a part of common usage, could be added such new words as these, each of which combines a root with a preposition: "after-place," "by-place," "for-place," "in-place," "under-place," "up-place," and "with-place."

In making these suggestions for rendering the English language more copious, Jefferson felt confident that such a policy based on neology would permit a rhetor to add "strength," "beauty," and "variety" to achieve a more elevated style. He knew, however, that such a radical change would be difficult because of the widespread proclivity to rely on dictionaries to determine the standards of usage and propriety. To counter this potential obstacle, he offered this advice:

> The example of good writers, the approbation of men of letters, the judgment of sound critics, and of none more than of the Edinburgh Reviewers, would give it a beginning, and once begun, its progress might be as rapid as it had been in France, where we see what a period of only twenty years has effected.[41]

Jefferson, it seems clear, harbored the thought of placing English on a par with Greek, Latin, and French so that it could offer a more copious channel for American rhetors.

## Voice Control and Bodily Activity

Unlike his thorough treatment of language and style, Jefferson did not provide a detailed account of his notions on delivery. What he did say, however, on the nature of this rhetorical channel was consistent with what he had read in the works of Cicero and Quintilian, and in the teachings of the British elocutionists. In his *Literary Commonplace Book*, he recorded this statement from Cicero's *Tusculan Disputations*: Speech "cannot take place without tongue and palate, or without a formed throat and chest and lungs in active working."[42]

His interest in the British elocutionary movement, which grew rapidly in the last half of the eighteenth century, was evident in the following books he had in his library—volumes that he freely recommended to others: John Mason, *Essays on Poetical and Prosaic Numbers, and Elocution* (1761); Thomas Sheridan, *A Rhetorical Grammar of the English Language* (1783), and *A Course of Lectures on Elocution* (1787); and John Walker, *A Critical Pronouncing Dictionary, and Expositor of the English Language* (1803).

Of these three authors, Sheridan was perhaps the most popular and influential. As he examined representative speakers of the period, Sheridan became discouraged with what he believed was a lack of competence in conveying their message either in a private or a public setting. Blaming rhetorical scholars, like Bacon, for their tendency to ignore or deemphasize the canon of delivery, Sheridan was determined, both in his public lectures and in his books, to demonstrate the importance of this rhetorical canon and to offer a scientific plan explaining its nature and a system of exercises that would help a speaker improve his or her voice control and bodily activity. By giving delivery a scientific base, and by relating the elements of the voice and of gestures to the four faculties of the mind, Sheridan could satisfy Jefferson's scholarly inclinations. Equally significant was Sheridan's announced goal of trying to improve the English language by seeking to establish a fixed, universal standard of pronunciation. As part of his attempt to accomplish this, he devised a method of visible markings to designate how a particular word should be articulated.[43]

It was against this background of Sheridan's ideas, and those of Mason and Walker as well, that Jefferson turned his attention to the vocal element of pronunciation. He had revealed his interest in this subject, as observed earlier, by trying to discover how Greek was pronounced in the classical era, and how Anglo-Saxon was uttered in its period of dominance. Nor did he ever forget the "vulgar and vicious" pronunciation used by Patrick Henry even though this fault often was overlooked "while he was speaking."[44]

The aspect of pronunciation that troubled him most was the inconsistency between spelling and pronunciation. He held, as did George

Bernard Shaw almost a century later, that steps should be undertaken to modify orthography so that the spelling and the sounds would be made consonant with each other. Not to do so, he said, was to perpetuate the condition of making the study of English too difficult for children and foreigners. His plan for improving spelling in order to upgrade pronunciation embraced such proposals as these:

(1) Eliminate the letter "d" from words like "bridge," "judge," "hedge," and "knowledge." This change would bring these words in line with "age," "cage," "sacrilege," and "privilege."
(2) "Drop the letter u in words of Latin derivation ending in our, and . . . write honor, candor, rigor. . . ."
(3) When pluralizing a noun ending in y and ey, only the letter "s" should be used.[45]

Although these possible reforms perhaps would win the support of the British elocutionists, Jefferson was realistic enough to believe that his plan would gain little sympathy from the purists.

Concurrent with Jefferson's interest in pronunciation was his belief in the persuasive power that may ensue from a speaker's appearance, vocal quality and diction, and bodily action. He made this point in a telling way in a letter to John Adams in 1812. His purpose was to give an eyewitness account of a speech he had heard when he was a boy. The speaker was a Cherokee Indian Chief and orator named Outassete who presented a farewell address on the eve of his departure to England to meet some of the members of Parliament and of the royal family. With "the moon in full splendor," Jefferson recalled, Outassete delivered an eloquent speech that ended in prayers for his own safety on the trip and for the welfare of members of his tribe while he was away. Of the presentation, Jefferson gave this moving description:

> His sounding voice, distinct articulation, animated action, and the solemn silence of his people at their several fires, filled me with awe and veneration, altho' I did not understand a word he uttered.[46]

The story of Outassete's memorable speech was a positive example of the rhetorical power that may be generated by a rhetor's voice control and bodily activity. If, however, this channel is misused, it will function, not as an arm of persuasion, but as a counterattraction that splits attention from the desired response. With this feeling in mind, Jefferson expressed his displeasure with those actors and actresses in France who speak with a "dreadful wheeze or rather whistle in respiration which resembles the agonizing struggles for breath in a dying person."[47]

Because channeling a message through the canons of organization, language control, and delivery constitute the last steps in a speech act, Jefferson gave to these subjects a high priority when instructing others. He had become convinced of the merits in the teachings of the educational philosophical rhetoricians of the classical period, and of the pedagogical programs created by the elocutionists and the belletristic scholars of the British era. A pivotal point in these rhetorical approaches was a stress on the practical value of training and exercises intended to improve a rhetor's facility in transmitting a message. Jefferson formed a plan of his own that will now be considered.

## Strategies for Improving One's Writing and Speaking Skills

In the late 1760s, shortly after he had begun his legal career, Jefferson received a letter from a young student, Bernard Moore, requesting information that might be used by one interested in the field of law. As was his general practice, he responded to the inquiry by outlining a detailed plan that included a recommended bibliography and a series of instructions. Fortunately for Jefferson scholars, the letter to Moore was misplaced. For almost a half century later when another student, John Minor, asked for a copy of the same letter, Jefferson not only found Moore's original written request, but now had an opportunity to update it with more recent materials and guidelines. The result was that part of this letter, written in 1814, represents the single most important statement we have found of Jefferson's ideas on improving one's writing and speaking skills. Although the specific profession under consideration at this time was law, the advice offered would apply equally well to all professions in which discourse is a major enterprise.

The final section of his "Program of Study," which was to be undertaken beginning with dusk and ending at bedtime, dealt with the topics of "Belles Lettres, Criticism, Rhetoric, and Oratory." With varying degrees of detail, Jefferson presented a series of recommendations.[48]

(1) When studying belles lettres, he noted, attention should be centered on all types of poetry, encompassing such forms as "epic, didactic, dramatic, pastoral," and "lyric." To experience "the full powers of the English language," one should read the works of Shakespeare with a de-

termination to understand and appreciate the propriety, beauty, and sublimity of his style.

(2) Among the works to be read in criticism are Lord Kames' *Elements of Criticism* and representative essays appearing in the *Edinburgh Review*.

(3) Rhetorical study should concentrate on John Mason's *Essays on Poetical and Prosaic Numbers, and Elocution*; Blair's *Lectures on Rhetoric and Belles Lettres*; and Sheridan's *Course of Lectures on Elocution*.

Under the concluding heading of "Oratory," Jefferson presented six exercises for the purpose of strengthening one's ability as a writer or speaker.

(1) A first step is to read any book of choice and then put into writing a critique of its style.

(2) This should be followed, second, by an effort to translate the style of the book, in successive order, into the "familiar," the "middling," and the "elevated" forms. By doing this, he thought, one may develop competence in the type of style needed for various rhetorical situations.

(3) In the third place, one should compose a series of short compositions or letters. As this is being done, careful attention should be given "to the correctness and elegance of your language."

(4) Fourth, it is desirable to study thoroughly the speeches of Demosthenes and Cicero. The points to be analyzed in this exercise are the nature of the organizational patterns; the levels of language, including the use of figures of speech and thought; and the persuasive quality of the cases and arguments.

(5) After examining samples of the leading orations of the classical period, one should next analyze models "of English eloquence," which may be found in such works as Abraham Small's *American Speaker* and Carey's *Criminal Recorder*.

(6) The final exercise is to prepare orations on a case that is feigned. This type of hypothetical situation, Jefferson believed, gives to the student an ideal opportunity to achieve proficiency in those canons of discourse which, when combined, constitute an effective channel for propelling a message. In the implementation of this exercise, the first step is to arrange the message with the organizational pattern discussed by Blair. Next, it is advisable to make certain that the language and style are suitable for the different parts of the oration, and that the arguments are appropriate for the imaginary audience and rhetorical setting that have been chosen. The procedure that now should be undertaken is to select another student in the neighborhood to serve as a partner in the exercise. One person would play the role of the prosecutor, and the other as the defense lawyer. To make this joint venture as realistic as possible, the prosecutor would make

the initial speech, the defense would offer a reply, and the prosecutor would return to give a closing response.[49]

As the presentations are delivered, the speaker should concentrate on his voice control and bodily activity. In fulfilling this function, care should be taken to speak, not from memory or from a manuscript, but from brief notes that characterize the extemporaneous mode. Similarly helpful in the exercise on delivery is to have a designated person present to "be considered as your judge."

Jefferson's ideas on channeling a message were, in part, a reflection of the dominant rhetorical trends that were present in the Classical and British/Continental eras. But it is also clear that his insights on ancient and modern languages, on the subject of neology, and on pedagogical theory and techniques as they pertain to writing and speaking skills were strongly influenced by his own taste and natural proclivities, and by what he had experienced as a lawyer, a diplomat, and a political leader.

# Notes

1. Boyd, 7: 463.
2. Ibid.
3. Ibid., 7: 465.
4. We have noted throughout the preceding chapters the admiration that Jefferson had for the teachings of Blair.
5. Blair, *Lectures on Rhetoric and Belles Lettres*, 2: 157–202.
6. To John Waldo, August 16, 1813, in *Writings*, 1295–1300.
7. To John Adams, August 15, 1820, in Cappon, 2: 566–67.
8. Wood, "Jefferson and His Complex Legacy," 6. On February 24, 1823, Jefferson wrote to Edward Everett: "Nor am I a friend to a scrupulous purism of style. I readily sacrifice the niceties of syntax to euphony and strength. It is by boldly neglecting the rigorisms of grammar, that Tacitus has made himself the strongest writer in the world." L&B, 15: 414–15.
9. "Report of the Commissioners for the University of Virginia," August 4, 1818, in *Writings*, 457–62.
10. To John Brazier, August 24, 1819, in *Writings*, 1424–25.
11. To Dr. Joseph Priestley, January 27, 1800, in Peterson, *Writings*, 1072.
12. To John Adams, March 21, 1819, in Cappon, 2: 538. Also see TJ to John Paradise, May 25, 1786, in Boyd, 9: 578; and TJ to Nathaniel Moore, September 22, 1819, in *Writings*, 1428–30.
13. TJ to Herbert Croft, October 30, 1798, in L&B, 18, 361–64.
14. The arguments summarized from the essay may be found in L&B, 18: 361–91.
15. To the Honorable J. Evelyn Denison, M.P., November 9, 1825, in *Writings*, 1502–1505. Jefferson, who was not known as being overly sympathetic to the English, actually believed that a joint effort between British and American scholars to promote a revival of Anglo-Saxon studies would tend to bring the two countries closer together.

16. TJ to Peter Carr, August 19, 1785, in *Writings*, 817; and "Report of the Commissioners for the University of Virginia," in id., 465.

17. TJ to Thomas Mann Randolph Jr., July 6, 1787, in Boyd, 11: 558.

18. "Report of the Commissioners for the University of Virginia," in *Writings*, 465.

19. TJ to Thomas Mann Randolph Jr., July 6, 1787, in Boyd, 11: 557.

20. October 2, 1788, in Boyd, 13: 651.

21. January 12, 1789, in L&B, 7: 267.

22. June 14, 1791, in Boyd, 20: 467–70.

23. TJ to Colonel Benjamin Hawkins, March 14, 1800, in L&B, 10: 161–62.

24. September 21, 1809, in *Writings*, 1212. Jefferson repeated the story of his loss in a letter to P. S. Du Ponceau, November 7, 1817, in L&B, 15: 150–53.

25. To Joseph Milligan, April 6, 1816, in L&B, 14: 457.

26. November 28, 1783, in Boyd, 6: 360.

27. See Merrill Peterson's editorial comments in *Writings*, 1546.

28. Observe the following two letters sent from France: TJ to Abigail Adams, February 22, 1787, in Cappon, 1: 173; and TJ to John Adams, ibid., 1: 194–95.

29. July 29, 1789, in Boyd, 15: 315.

30. August 9, 1789, in Boyd, 15: 336–37.

31. To Edward Everett, February 24, 1823, in L&B, 15: 415.

32. TJ to John Adams, January 24, 1814, in Cappon, 2: 423. Also note the following two letters: TJ to John Adams, August 10, 1815, in ibid., 2: 452–53; and TJ to Justice William Johnson, June 12, 1823, in *Writings*, 1474–75. Jefferson's unusually harsh criticism of John Marshall's *Life of Washington* doubtless was influenced in part by his disdain for the chief justice's political views. But his overall negative view of the work was shared by Daniel Boorstin who gave this scathing criticism in his *The Americans: The National Experience* (New York: Random House, 1965). Boorstin noted: "Soon after Washington's death, his nephew Bushrod Washington persuaded Chief Justice Marshall to undertake the official life. This enterprise was to have a shaping influence on American thinking about American history, not through its success but through its resounding failure. . . . When the first installment of Marshall's work finally reached subscribers in 1804, it quickly established the book as the publishing catastrophe of the age. The whole volume one, called "Introduction," was consumed by a pedantic account of colonial history beginning with Columbus; toward the end, there were two casual mentions of Washington. Dull, laborious, rambling, and second hand, the work lumbered into its third, fourth, and fifth volumes. . . ." (342) By contrast, James Thomas Flexner, a modern biographer of Washington, called the work "solid" and "factual." *George Washington: The Forge of Experience (1732–1775)*. (Boston: Little, Brown, 1965), 357.

33. December 17, 1777, in Cappon, 1: 8–9.

34. To George Hammond, February 16, 1793, in L&B, 9: 27–29. This letter was in response to earlier communications from Hammond.

35. See "Autobiography," in Ford, 1: 70; and his essay on a "Plan for Elementary Schools," in L&B, 17: 417–18. Jefferson not only was willing to criticize examples of prolix language, but often showed how the verbosity could be eliminated without affecting the meaning. A sample of this approach occurred during his work on a model treaty in 1784. In rewriting a passage of the original treaty, he reduced the number of words in one of the sentences from 117 to 71, thereby enhancing the clarity. See Boyd, 7: 464.

36. TJ to David Harding, April 20, 1824, in L&B, 16: 30.

37. *On the Sublime*, 8: 1.

38. See Lectures III and IV in Blair, *Lectures on Rhetoric and Belles Lettres*, 1: 36–79.

39. Ford, 11: 425n.

40. January 22, 1783, in Boyd, 6: 222–23.

41. The quotations on Jefferson's recommendations appear in his letter to John Waldo, August 16, 1813, in *Writings*, 1294–1300.

42. See *Tusculan Disputations*, 1.16.; and *LCB*, 57n.

43. Sheridan described elocution as "the just and graceful arrangement of the voice, countenance, and gesture in speaking." Sheridan, *A Course of Lectures on Elocution, 1762* (1762; Menston, England: Scholar Press, 1968), 19.

44. Daniel Webster, "Memorandum of Conversations with Thomas Jefferson," in Webster, ed., *Writings and Speeches of Daniel Webster*, 17: 367.

45. TJ to John Wilson, August 17, 1813, in Ford, 11: 309–22.

46. June 11, 1812, in Cappon, 2: 307.

47. TJ to William Short, March 29, 1787, in Boyd, 11: 254–55.

48. These recommendations are found in Ford, 11: 424–26.

49. Jefferson knew that hypothetical cases long had been a standard device in legal education and training. Indeed, "moot court" societies were long used by fledgling barristers in England and law students in America, both before and after the founding of formal law schools. Jefferson's recommendations, moreover, were consistent with the legal education that he had with George Wythe.

# CHAPTER SIX

~

# Private Discourse and Poetics

Despite the years he spent on the public stage, Jefferson was, to a large degree, a private person who had a compelling desire to engage in interpersonal discourse with his family, friends, and fellow politicians. In doing so, he believed that the substance of these informal exchanges of information and feelings should not appear in published form on the grounds that such an act would be a betrayal of personal confidences. The fear of possible publication of his personal sentiments, however, did not deter him from recognizing the need and potential power of private discourse, as manifested in conversation and letter writing. He thus established general guidelines for improving one's effectiveness in these two rhetorical genres.

## Private Discourse

### Conversational Communication

In his provocative and influential essay "On Moral Duties," Cicero expressed regret that no rhetorician had yet developed a science of conversation. He then proceeded to offer a few suggestions as a starting point to meet this need. Among his recommendations were the following: (1) focus on timely and worthy subjects such as politics, family affairs, or of the arts and sciences; (2) be aware of when and how long to speak; (3) adapt your remarks to the interests and understanding of those present; (4) maintain throughout the discussion an attitude of decorum, tact, self-control, and reasonableness; (5) when desirable, employ humor to liven the discussion; (6) channel your ideas through a clear, pleasant, and articulate vocal pattern; and (7) avoid the tendency to braggadocio.[1]

Jefferson, who was a careful and appreciative student of this work, did not, as was the case with other writers as well, try to fulfill Cicero's challenge for someone to write a science of conversation. Had he sought to do so, he would not have had the time to succeed. Nevertheless, like Cicero, he provided helpful insights on what constitutes productive conversation. Buttressed by the knowledge he had gained from reading the dialogues of the classical scholars, from studying the writings of Shaftesbury and Hutcheson, and from participating in and observing conversations in America and in Europe, he was able to discover its nature and importance, and determine what worked and should, therefore, be recommended. Our purpose here is to list and discuss briefly seven principles that he believed to be essential for achieving excellence in conversation.

*First, a participant in conversational discourse should be well informed about the subject and should understand the nature of argument and its relationship to virtue.* Only in this way can conversation lead to the sharing of information on matters of interest and significance, and to the development of solutions to problems that call for an urgent response designed to advance the cause of the public good and generate personal happiness. In addition, it should be remembered that a knowledgeable discussant alone understands the principles of human nature—including the existence of a moral sense; has a grasp of both private and public virtue; and has the capability to construct thoughtful, moral, and convincing arguments. It is this type of wise and sensitive person, according to Jefferson, who uses conversation to enlighten and persuade.

*Second, a conversationalist should earnestly embrace the goal of producing social cohesion and cementing personal relationships.* Jefferson's ideas on this premise were reinforced after he had studied Shaftesbury's description of his "interactional view of human behavior." It was both a rhetorical and a philosophical theory that gave a preeminent position to conversation as a means of bringing people together for the purpose of perpetuating social relationships. Tied in with the "politeness" movement, this theory made use of such concepts as "self-management," "self-presentation," "self-concern," "social competence," and "intersubjectivity."[2] But it was more than a "feel-good" approach, for it gave each participant an opportunity to reveal his or her true identity, and to show a concern for listeners by conveying knowledge and stimulating the social affections. For these reasons, Jefferson made this principle a centerpiece of his philosophy of conversational discourse.

*Third, a participant in a conversational situation should have the freedom to express his or her opinions with candor and commitment without fear of being unduly criticized for exerting this rhetorical privilege.* To illustrate this principle, Jefferson presented the example of a Christian minister who by virtue of his profession is constrained to speak on specified subjects when in the pulpit. These constraints, however, must be removed when the minister takes part in informal discussions outside the church. Since his "leisure time" is "his own, and his congregation" is "not obliged to listen to his conversation or to read his writings," he must be granted the freedom to state his views as an equal partner in conversation.[3]

During his five years in France, Jefferson deviated from this principle, as observed in an earlier chapter, by criticizing the French women's tendency to engage in political discussions—a practice, he noted, that was not acceptable in American society.[4] In his late retirement years, however, he was more than willing to grant full freedom to women to join fully in the discussion of all topics that may be raised in conversation. George Ticknor, a young Massachusetts scholar whom Jefferson greatly admired, gave this description of a dialogue that took place at Monticello:

> The ladies sat until about six, then retired, but returned with the tea-tray a little before seven, and spent the evening with the gentlemen; which was always pleasant, for they are obviously accustomed to join in the conversation, however high the topic may be. . . .[5]

Consistent with his ideas on personal proof, Jefferson articulated a fourth conversational principle: *Participants in a dialogue must at all times maintain an attitude of mutual respect for one another.* This was the rationale for the recommendations that he gave to his daughters so that they could strengthen their marital relations. Similarly, he always took pride in asserting that this was the operating premise upon which he and Alexander Hamilton developed their conversations, thereby creating an atmosphere of openness and cordiality rather than needless face-to-face confrontation.[6]

When disagreement does occur, Jefferson added, it should be handled with an attitude of good will. His conversation with the renowned scientist Comte de Buffon in France brought this principle into clear focus. When introducing the two men at a dinner party in France, a guest observed that Jefferson's *Notes on the State of Virginia* contained several refutations of Buffon's widely accepted conclusions that animal and human life was degraded and degenerate in the New World by comparison with the Old World. Rather than engage in a confrontational argument, Buffon, according to

Jefferson, "took down his last work, presented it to me, and said, 'When Mr. Jefferson shall have read this, he will be perfectly satisfied that I am right.'"[7] Notwithstanding the fact that Buffon had held firmly to his original position, Jefferson recalled the incident and the evening as a whole in a positive manner. Buffon, he asserted, was "a man of extraordinary power in conversation"—one who dialogued in an agreeable non-declamatory manner that exuded trust.

But if the pleasant encounter with Buffon on a touchy, controversial issue exemplified the advantages to be accrued from a dialogue motivated by mutual respect, Jefferson faulted several participants in another rhetorical episode that ended in a communication breakdown owing to a genuine lack of trust. At the urging of John Adams, the American representative in London in 1786, Jefferson, then stationed in Paris, was advised that the two men should arrange a conciliatory and informative conversation with the king and queen, and with the foreign secretary. The aim of the proposed sessions was to bring Britain and America closer together on a series of troubling issues. An opposite result occurred, in Jefferson's view, because of a noticeable lack of good faith on the part of the British leaders. On all points that were discussed, the king, queen, and foreign secretary, both in their verbal and nonverbal patterns, were "ungracious," "uncooperative, hostile, vague," evasive, and deliberately misleading. Overall, they made it clear that they had an "aversion to have anything to do with us."[8]

*Fifth, productive and rewarding conversation requires a discussant to be a good listener.* If a person is impatient, fidgety, or inattentive while another is speaking, the quality of the dialogue that ensues will be diminished. Additionally, this lack of interest by a participant may increase tension within the rhetorical situation because it sends a message of boredom or disrespect. This point was emphasized in the following description of the conversational practices of Madam Necker, the wife of the parliamentary leader in France in the late 1780s:

> Madam Necker was a very sincere and excellent woman, but she was not very pleasant in conversation, for she was subject to what in Virginia we call the 'Budge,' that is, she was very nervous and fidgety. She could rarely remain long in the same place or converse long on the same subject. I have known her to get up from [the] table five or six times in the course of the dinner, and walk up and down her saloon to compose herself.[9]

Madam Necker's conversational habits, it would appear, fell far short of Jefferson's requirement that an interlocutor in a dialogue must not only contribute ideas but also listen carefully to others while they speak.

*Sixth, a conversationalist must use an appropriate style and delivery.* In both a formal and informal dialogue, it is unacceptable to adopt an oratorical or declamatory pattern, or to use language that is artificial or ornate. When the subject is grave, as in the case of a significant political question, it is often desirable to use chaste language and an urgent delivery. Moreover, humor may be needed to defuse a tense situation. This principle echoes the views of Cicero.

Jefferson's frequent tendency to teach others by using the narrative technique has been evident in this and in preceding discussions. This discourse technique emerges again as we summarize his perspectives on the nature of an ideal conversational situation by a small group of people on a historic occasion. The setting was Paris during the early phase of the formation of a republican government. The Marquis de Lafayette, one of the leaders of this movement, informed Jefferson that he would like to bring a group of six to eight friends to a dinner at Jefferson's residence. This unusual request was granted. The group which appeared consisted of men with different opinions who wished to exchange ideas for the purpose of forming a coalition that might influence the direction the assembly should take. All the participants agreed in the beginning that they would speak frankly and without fear, and expressed a willingness to modify their views if arguments against their initial positions were sufficiently informative and persuasive.

At four o'clock the discussions began and continued until 10 P.M. During this six-hour period of intense dialogue, Jefferson, as he himself recalled,

> was a silent witness to a coolness and candor of argument unusual in the conflicts of political opinion; to a logical reasoning, and chaste eloquence, disfigured by no gaudy tinsel of rhetoric or declamation, and truly worthy of being placed in parallel with the finest dialogues of antiquity, as handed to us by Xenephon, by Plato and Cicero.[10]

Jefferson's strong enthusiasm regarding the quality of the event he had witnessed was doubtless enhanced by his belief that the participants had conformed to the principles he had long upheld about conversational discourse. The discussants used reasonable arguments that were modified in the end to reach agreement; they felt free to state their convictions without fear of offending others or placing themselves in jeopardy; they demonstrated an attitude of respect and fairness; they proved to be interested and sympathetic listeners; and they spoke freely, yet naturally, in a manner suitable to conversational discourse. In brief, they had, in the presence of Jefferson, succeeded in establishing social cohesion, in sharing important information, and in developing a rhetorical strategy designed to solve a problem fraught with danger to the nation and to themselves.[11]

*Seventh, conversation may be enhanced—especially in a dinner party setting—if care is taken in the choice of the number of guests and in the physical setting.* A host, for example, would be wise to invite between six and fourteen people who have similar interests, habits, and tastes, and who are compatible with one another. Then, when the dinner has ended and a new phase of conversation is ready to begin, it is frequently desirable to arrange the chairs in a circular fashion rather than to place them in parallel lines. Such an arrangement permits face-to-face rhetorical transactions and keeps the participants from breaking into smaller groups. What Jefferson most earnestly wished in making these suggestions and implementing them while he was in the White House was to create, whenever possible, a rhetorical situation in which dialogue could be improved and enjoyed.[12]

It would appear that conversational communication, as perceived by Jefferson, presents the participants with an opportunity to display a moral sense by sharing substantive, as well as informal, ideas on a wide range of topics; by establishing personal relations through the rhetorical element of identification or good will; and by following the rules of decorum in the use of language and voice control. To adhere to these principles is to strengthen social cohesion, to enlarge understanding, and to create an environment in which virtue is transmitted.

## Letter Writing

Of all the forms of communication that commanded the attention of Jefferson, letter writing perhaps was paramount. Because of the length of his life, the prominent positions he held, the far-reaching influence of his accomplishments, and the love he had for his family and friends, he spent thousands of hours in writing and in reading letters. He also had firmly etched in his mind the model of Cicero—one of his lifelong heroes whose career as a philosopher and practitioner paralleled his own. Included in his extensive library collection of Cicero's works, for example, were approximately "900 personal letters, mostly Cicero's own. . . ."[13] These combined experiences became the substance out of which Jefferson developed perspectives on the nature of this form of private discourse. Our present purpose is to highlight three of these principles that should give us an understanding of what Jefferson perceived as significant characteristics of letter writing.

*First, letter writing* (or epistolary communication as he often described it) *should be viewed as a form of conversation.* The notion that letter writing and other forms of written discourse had a strong affinity with conversation became a popular thesis in Britain and on the Continent in the seventeenth and eighteenth centuries. Lawrence Klein has observed that "as early as (John) Dryden, one finds conversation identified as one, perhaps the most important component of literary refinement." He quoted Dryden as saying: "The superiority of conversation in the present age, the growth of gallantry, the expansion of conversational freedom, and the greater accessibility of writers to conversation at the highest social levels had fertilized English literature."[14] This philosophical point of view became a central theme of the "politeness" movement represented by Shaftesbury, and was enthusiastically adopted by Jefferson.

While in France, Jefferson sat down at his desk and penned this line to Madison: "Seven o'clock, and retired to my fireside, I have determined to enter into conversation with you. . . ."[15] Later he told his granddaughter Cornelia that letter writing is a valuable exercise because it enables one "to converse with an absent friend, as if present."[16] With his treatment of letter writing as conversation, Jefferson would have been pleased with Moses Hadas's description of Cicero's letters to Atticus: "To read them is as tantalizing as to overhear one end of a telephone conversation. . . ."[17]

What makes this perspective so essential is that it places a responsibility upon the recipient of a letter. If letter writing is conversation, as Jefferson maintained, it is incumbent upon both parties to take part in the rhetorical exchange. Not to do so is to violate the law of propriety. It is for this reason (among others) that he kept a careful record of the letters he sent, and, in turn, reminded delinquent respondents—especially family members—that they often had failed to fulfill their duty to respond within a reasonable period of time. In sum, although Jefferson clearly believed that the best form of private discourse is face-to-face communication,[18] he concluded with enthusiasm that free exchanges of letters on matters of mutual interest enable the participants to carry on a perpetual dialogue with each other at home and abroad.

*Second, letter writing should be regarded as the development of an appropriate response to an identifiable need.* The key words in this claim are "need" and "appropriate." A need, in Jefferson's opinion, exists when one wishes to share information on a particular subject, such as a historical event or on a liberal art or science; to seek advice on a course of action that should be taken, such as a decision to be made or a proper educational program to be followed; to satisfy an urge to express his or her deeply felt sentiments with respect to an issue or person; or to promote a desire to establish or strengthen a bond between the author and the addressee.

Once the need has been identified, an appropriate response is to be constructed. The requirement of appropriateness, as Jefferson conceived it, is to be met by an adherence to the best elements of rhetoric. In this belief, he was supported by the impressive rhetorical characteristics that marked Cicero's letters; and by the Medieval and Renaissance practices, as recommended in a series of manuals, of applying classical discourse theories to the construction of letters.[19] What Jefferson wished to be included in letters was a rhetorical approach consistent with the ideas he advanced on argumentation, the social affections, and language control.

Not the least of these discourse elements, according to him, is the choice of a topic geared to the nature, knowledge, and interests of the person being addressed. In a letter from Paris in 1786, he described to his friend and former classmate John Page the types of themes that he would like to be included in letters to him. The subjects he mentioned were sufficiently applicable to anyone concerned about daily happenings, the activities of friends or acquaintances, and public affairs. In a perceptive statement which has universal significance, he noted:

> It is unfortunate that most people think the occurrences passing daily under the eyes, are either known to all the world, or not worth being known. They therefore do not give them place in their letters.[20]

His list of other subjects that should have a prominent place in letters included such topics as: "proceedings of our political bodies"; "progress of the public mind on interesting questions"; and "the casualties which happen among our friends." He then concluded with the statement that "whatever is interesting to yourself and family will always be anxiously received by me."[21]

After a suitable topic has been selected, care should be taken in developing the content, organization, and style in accordance with the subject and need. Here it is significant to note that the personal and logical proof offered in support of an argumentative position should be strong and relevant. This may only be achieved, Jefferson thought, if the author is guided by the principle that the content of a letter should always contain the truth.[22] Finally, the letter at all times should display a control of language that meets the test of the doctrine of usage.

In some special cases, Jefferson believed, an appropriate response may justifiably result in no correspondence at all between two individuals who share similar personal and public goals, and who for years had worked closely together. He explained this position to Martin Van Buren in 1824. Van Buren wanted to know if Jefferson and Washington had communicated with each other following the inauguration of John Adams in 1797. In replying to this query, Jefferson observed that during this period of the final two and one half years of Washington's life "both of us were too much oppressed with letter writing, to trouble, either the other, with a letter about nothing."[23] In viewing the dynamics of American politics in the late 1790s, however, Jefferson's claim is not altogether convincing. Perhaps the real reasons for the lack of correspondence between the first and third presidents, we feel, were these: first, after Jefferson left the cabinet in early 1794, he and Washington had no further communication because of Washington's feeling that Jefferson had betrayed his trust by leaving public life after persuading Washington to accept election to a second term; second, Jefferson believed that Washington was unduly influenced by Hamilton and the "monocrats"; and, third, Washington was unhappy over the role played by Jefferson in creating political parties.

The letter writer who fails to demonstrate effective rhetorical strategies in responding to a need, Jefferson believed, runs the risk of being perceived as one who lacks a strong mind or personality. Thus, in a letter to Madison, he criticized William Carmichael, the American representative in Madrid, because his letters revealed a man who was "vain and more attentive to ceremony and etiquette than we suppose men of sense should be." Moreover, the letters further suggest that while he possessed a "good understanding," he had a mind that was "not of the first order." In the same letter, he faulted another American leader—Robert Smith, who sought to replace John Adams as chargé d'affaires in England—arguing that his letters, like those of Carmichael, also show a mind that is similarly limited in its range and scope.[24]

To illustrate more specifically what Jefferson had in mind concerning the importance of responding to a need, let us examine briefly the relationship between letter writing and the challenge of promoting friendship. As one of the important social virtues, friendship is a powerful social affection. In his book *The Inner Jefferson: Portrait of a Grieving Optimist*, Andrew Burstein devotes a full chapter to the theme "Letter Writing and Friendship," in which he describes how Cicero, Pliny, and Petrarch, among others, laid the foundation for Jefferson's ideas on how epistolary communication may strengthen friendship bonds. Using Cicero's letters to Atticus, one of Cicero's closest friends, as a model to be emulated, Jefferson, according to Burstein, recommended that this type of letter should contain "self revelation and self cultivation," "benevolence," "learning," and "honesty" as a means of unlocking a friend's "heart." Of particular importance here is the fact that "Jefferson . . . saw friendship as a blessing built upon a universally appreciated moral foundations."[25]

*Third, letter writing that is private in nature must be treated as a personal statement that should not be published either by the author or the recipient.* When this concept is ignored, either by design or by accident, irreparable harm may occur. When he learned, therefore, that a letter he had sent to Dr. George Logan which contained disparaging remarks about recent French policies and atrocities committed by Napoleon appeared in newspapers throughout the country and abroad, he was deeply concerned. That he had grounds to feel betrayed seems clear. What was even more alarming to him was the strong negative reaction of France, the country with which he had for years developed strong ties. Under such conditions, he did not hesitate to let Logan know how he felt. "And do you not think that I had a right to decide," he said, "whether the sentiments I trusted to you were meant for the whole world? I am sure that on reflection you will perceive that I ought to have been consulted."[26]

On a more personal level involving friends, Jefferson held, a published letter that was meant to be private can produce troubling tensions that are also potentially harmful. This fact led him to remind Adams that both men had been hurt when letters they had written to others, which contained confidential observations on public men, were intercepted and published without their permission. This was often done out of a feeling of malice, he asserted, by those who wished "to make mischief."[27]

This strongly held conviction that a private communication should only be read by the person to whom it was addressed prompted him on occasion to devise a strategy to prevent those who work at the "post" from having an opportunity to examine it. "When you write what should be read by myself only," he told Edward Carrington in 1787, "you must be so good as to confide your letter to some passenger or officer of the packet. . . ."[28] This penchant for secrecy was not only owing to the harm that might be caused by publicizing a personal letter; it was also due to rhetorical considerations. For if a letter is to be published or to be made known to others by additional means, Jefferson felt, the types of arguments developed and the language employed would have to be modified so as to suit the larger audience.[29]

From the perspective of Jefferson, letter writing, in sum, is to be seen as a conversation between two people who have shared interests; and, as a form of communication requiring the use of appropriate rhetorical elements related to a particular need. Because, moreover, the correspondence is private in nature, the law of propriety is broken if the content of a personal letter is printed or otherwise publicized.

# Poetical Discourse

Jefferson's interest in poetics began to develop in earnest during his days as a student and young lawyer. It was in this period that he initiated the practice, as we have seen, of developing commonplace books that, he hoped, would serve to trigger his memory while engaged in a discourse situation. One of these unpublished works, now known as the *Literary Commonplace Book*, was largely completed by the time of his marriage in 1772.[30] In it may be found excerpts from the writings of the classical and British poets, playwrights, and novelists. These passages, all of which made an indelible impression on Jefferson's mind, helped set the direction his thinking would take in the formation of his perspectives on the three major aspects of poetics—poetry, drama, and fiction. Of these three rhetorical forms, poetry occupied the preeminent place.

## Poetry

To Jefferson, the study of poetry gave him an opportunity to offset what he perceived to be the negative aspects of the field of law. The practice of law, he told John Bernard, the British actor and author, "gave me the view of the dark side of humanity." By contrast, he added, poetry enables one to "gaze upon its bright side; and between the two extremes I have contrived through life to draw the due medium. . . ."[31]

His fascination for poetry was also rooted in the idea that what moves one toward the good is both desirable and pleasing. And this, he felt, is precisely what poetry seeks to do. Since the faculties of imagination and the passions and the concept of judgment are its primary motivating characteristics, poetical discourse at its highest displays knowledge of the human heart. Given this favorable attitude toward the potential power of poetry to generate understanding, to stimulate the imagination, to stir the passions, and to motivate the will, it is not surprising that Jefferson drew heavily upon the poets in assembling his *Literary Commonplace Book*: "Of the 407 entries, 339 are poetry, and of 41 authors represented, 35 are poets."[32]

In his evaluation of Classical and British poets, Jefferson shared the sentiments of most of his contemporaries. He trumpeted the virtues of Homer and Virgil as the leading Greek and Roman authors; and he recommended the reading of such poets as Anacreon, Quintus, Symrnaeus, Catullus, Horace, and Ovid. He likewise praised the works of Chaucer, Spencer, Milton, Dryden, and lesser writers. But his favorite English poets were Shakespeare and Pope, not only because of their power of language but because of their knowledge of the human spirit.[33] In his famous 1771 letter to Robert Skipwith, he suggested the importance of reading Homer and Virgil, along with the poems of at least eighteen British authors.[34]

Jefferson's most thorough statement on the rhetoric of poetry may be found in his essay-letter entitled "Thoughts on English Prosody." The inspiration for the "Thoughts" began with Marquis de Chastellux's visit to Monticello in 1782. During this visit, Chastellux—a member of the French Academy and a general in the French army that participated in the American Revolution—and Jefferson held several dialogues on the nature of English poetry. The two men had a polite but gentle disagreement regarding the principal characteristic of English prosody. As the discussions unfolded, Jefferson upheld the traditional view advanced by Samuel Johnson that the principal characteristic of English prosody, like that of its Greek counterpart, is quantity. Chastellux, on the other hand, argued that its distinguishing trait is accent.

Because the Monticello discussions ended in a friendly stalemate, Jefferson decided to put the issue aside. But while in France a few years later, he once again reflected on the topic as he took daily walks "in the Bois de Bologne."[35] Fortunately for him, he had brought to Paris his *Literary Commonplace Book*. He thus was able to consult his carefully chosen specimens of English poetry as a starting point for further investigation of the identifying characteristic of English prosody.[36] Fully convinced that his original position was sound, he approached his task with confidence. He soon discovered, however, that Chastellux, not he, had the stronger case. When he had finished putting his thoughts into writing, he forwarded his essay to Chastellux with these words:

> I began with the design of converting you to my opinion that the arrangement of long and short syllables into regular feet constituted the harmony of English verse. I ended by discovering that you were right in denying that proposition. . . . The next object was to find out the real circumstance which gives harmony to English poetry and laws to those who make it. I present you with the result.[37]

Jefferson began his argument with the contention that the pronunciation of Greek and Latin is based on the element of quantity.[38] He then acknowledged that the common practice of English scholars, as represented by Samuel Johnson, assumes that English prosody similarly relies on the dimension of quantity. But as Jefferson reexamined typical British poetry, he was forced to conclude, as did Chastellux, that accent is "the basis of English verse." Whenever a word with multiple syllables appears, he said, "there is some one syllable strongly distinguishable in pronunciation by its emphasis or accent." As Jefferson further developed his argument, he maintained that a poet's natural interest in rhythm and harmony leads to the use of a pause as a form of accent. This pause may be demonstrated by an emphatical word or phrase placed in a strategic position, or it may be seen as a marker for the conclusion of a particular verse. But regardless of what it represents, if used properly, a pause that signals an interval in the poet's thought will render the composition pleasing to the ear.

Jefferson next drew a comparison between a classical author's use of a poetical foot and an English scholar's use of the same linguistic device. The Greek language, he noted, permitted Homer "to compose in verse of six feet. . . . The English language, on the other hand, will not sustain a verse that is longer than five feet." Jefferson saw in this fact a distinct advantage for English poetry because by limiting a verse to a maximum of five feet, Shakespeare, Milton, and Pope, for example, were able to express their ideas in blank verse—"the most precious part of our poetry." Because blank verse, moreover, is not fettered by needless rhyme, it avoids the danger of constructing disturbing tautologies and childlike jingles, and prolongs our sense of taste for the beauty of poetical language.

Also contained in Jefferson's essay was a reference to the oral interpretation of poetry. Suggesting that an effective reading of literature depends largely on the use of a suitable accent, he commented on the widespread popularity of two performers. Samuel Foote, he noted, was able to command large sums of money for his "exquisite" reading of Milton's poetry; and David Garrick, by utilizing sonorous tones and an appealing accent or emphasis, was unmatched in his interpretation of Shakespeare's poems and plays.

In his assessment of this essay, Douglas L. Wilson commended Jefferson for his valuable insights on English prosody, and for the care he took in developing his arguments. But he described the work as a whole as being "marred" and "muddled" in its structure. We have no disagreement with the conclusion that Jefferson's analysis lacks strong unity, coherence, and emphasis; at the same time, however, our general reaction is positive for the following reasons. The essay represents Jefferson's most complete statement on a very important dimension of poetry; it shows his willingness to reexamine an earlier position by probing again into the samples of poetry compiled in his *Literary Commonplace Book*, and in other readings as well; it reveals a rewarding tendency on his part to modify his original views when arguments drawn from the re-analyzed data warrant it; and it depicts a scholar who was anxious to send his findings, along with congratulatory sentiments, to the person with whom he had originally disagreed. In sum, it would appear, in this instance Jefferson adhered closely to his own teachings on personal and logical proof as he sought to discover the true nature of English prosody.

## Dramatic Literature and Other Forms of Fiction[39]

Jefferson's interest in drama extended over a period of approximately forty years, from the decade of the 1760s through the end of his first term as president. Evidence of his attachment to this rhetorical form first manifested itself in the *Literary Commonplace Book*: at least one third of the entries are devoted to passages from plays. Of these, roughly one-half came from representative speeches in the works of Euripides.[40] His Account Book, moreover, lists a number of occasions in which he purchased tickets for plays that he and his friends attended. In the year 1770 alone, he was present at twelve plays; and following his election to a second term in 1804, he celebrated by purchasing four tickets to a play performed in Washington. During the years in between, while he was in France and a traveler on a journey throughout neighboring countries, he often went to plays and then occasionally evaluated the performances of the actors and actresses.[41]

Whereas in developing a philosophy of poetry Jefferson stressed the aesthetic and moral dimensions of this genre, when he commented on plays his principal concern was with the ethical and moral teachings that permeated the speeches and dialogues of a particular drama. This, as we saw in the chapter on social affections, was why he reacted so favorably to the moral messages emphasized by Euripides. Douglas Wilson has noted that Jefferson's attraction for "Euripides's penchant for apostrophe and moralizing speeches" also explained his positive attitude toward his favorite English dramatists. On this point, Wilson observed: "The declamatory nature of the drama readily lends itself to this mode, and the

English dramatists favored by Jefferson in the Commonplace Book—Shakespeare, Otway, Rowe, and Young—fully availed themselves of their opportunities. . . ."[42]

As a student of dramatic literature and of plays performed on the stage, therefore, Jefferson measured the worth of such a work by the quality of the philosophical and moral content that constituted its substance. In making this evaluation, he believed the best rhetorical channel that might be used to convey the ethical teachings is a speech. For this method of communication gives to the actor enough time to develop an effective argument.[43]

If we were to examine the *Literary Commonplace Book*, we would find only one brief passage drawn from a novel. In addition, if we study Jefferson's writings in the period following his presidency, we see little enthusiasm on his part regarding contemporary fiction as a whole. Notwithstanding this paucity of material, it is instructive to note that on several occasions he articulated a clear-cut and consistent philosophy of what he thought to be the essential elements of fiction.

The first of these sentiments appeared in his 1771 letter to Robert Skipwith.[44] Jefferson's principal argument was a defense of fiction based upon the premise that this rhetorical genre, in its most desirable form, seeks to persuade the reader to become more virtuous. His rationale for this claim may be expressed in the following categorical enthymeme:

Anything which promotes virtue is useful and pleasant.
Fiction promotes virtue.
Fiction, therefore, is useful and pleasant.

To illustrate this enthymeme, Jefferson observed that if a character in a fictional work performs acts of "charity" and "gratitude," the audience member will be inclined to pursue similar acts in his or her private and public life. Quite the contrary is true, however, if the main character in a book engages in a deed that is "atrocious" and "abhorrent." In such a case, the reader will become "disgusted with its deformity."

What makes a virtuous act persuasive, according to Jefferson, is an author's ability to appeal not only to the faculty of understanding but to those of the imagination and the passions. It is by means of these latter faculties that an emotion is aroused in such a way that the reader will experience the same feeling that the fictional character is portraying. Moreover, this shared sentiment may occur regardless of whether the described event is historically factual or fictitious. In developing this thesis,

Jefferson turned to a Shakespeare play and to a novelist he admired as examples in support of his case. He phrased his argument as follows:

> I appeal to every reader of feeling and sentiment whether the fictitious murder of Duncan by Macbeth . . . does not excite in him as great a horror of villainy, as the real one of Henry IV by Ravaillac as related by Davila? and whether the fidelity of Nelson and generosity of Blandford in Marmontel do not dilate his breast and elevate his sentiments as much as any similar incident which real history can furnish?

As he proceeded in his defense of fiction as a useful and rewarding art, Jefferson made the bold claim that one can learn more about the virtue of filial duty by reading *King Lear* "than by all the dry volumes of ethics, and divinity that ever were written. . . ."[45]

During the presidential campaign year of 1800, Jefferson noted that fiction still had an attraction for him. In a letter to the American novelist Charles Brockden Brown, he reaffirmed many of the ideas that he had communicated to Skipwith twenty-nine years earlier. He added: "Some of the most agreeable moments of my life have been spent in reading works of the imagination."[46]

At first glance, it appears that Jefferson radically changed his views on fiction in his postpresidential years. He opined to Nathaniel Burwell in 1818, for instance, that most contemporary novels are little more than "trash"; consequently, they do not merit study because they fail to depict reality. Additionally, by concentrating on "figments of fancy," they present the image of a "bloated imagination."[47] Even though he stated these strong reservations about current novels in general, he did not, even in the letter to Burwell, alter his central belief that a fictional work that becomes a useful vehicle of "sound morality" cannot be easily ignored. This is why, he said, one may receive important moral instruction by reading "Marmontel's new moral tales. . . ."[48]

Some Jefferson scholars, including Julian P. Boyd, have downplayed the significance of Jefferson's perspectives on fiction, arguing that his analysis merely tends to reflect "the views of English critics from Sir Philip Sidney to Addison and to Johnson. . . ."[49] It is our contention, however, that this assessment is only partly true. For Jefferson's deeply felt personal experiences were also a factor in causing him to believe strongly that a well-written fictional work has the power to modify our worldview, and thereby move us in the direction of the good life. Let us observe, for example, the influence that two novels had upon his thinking and action. The first was Laurence Sterne's *Tristram Shandy*.

In the days preceding the death of his young wife Martha, both he and Martha turned to the novel they had long admired as a means of helping them cope with her impending death. As they did so, they recalled and recorded these lines from *Tristram Shandy*:

> Time wastes too fast: every letter
> I trace tells me with what rapidity
> life follows my pen. The days and hours
> of it are flying over our heads like
> clouds of windy day never to return—
> more every thing presses on—and every
> time I kiss thy hand to bid adieu, every absence which
> follows it, are preludes to that eternal separation
> which we are shortly to make![50]

These lines, almost poetical in form, echo Jefferson's abiding belief that a work of fiction should strive to capture reality and point to worthy values that may provide comfort even in moments of deep sorrow. Not surprisingly, therefore, he frequently advised others to read *Tristram Shandy*, along with Sterne's other works.

A second novel that affected Jefferson's thinking was Cervantes' *Don Quixote*. Early in the 1780s, as he began to study the Spanish language in depth, he read this fictional work with considerable enthusiasm. In the ensuing years, he purchased copies for both of his "Monticello libraries," urged his daughters and others to study the story, and reread it himself.[51]

From the point of view of content and style, *Don Quixote* met those literary standards that Jefferson believed were necessary for achieving excellence and having a positive influence on one's life. The novel, in the first place, had a stimulating appeal to the faculty of imagination, but perhaps what appealed to Jefferson most about this witty and fanciful satire were the persuasive moral messages that were emphasized. When we analyze the primary events of the story and the dialogues between Don Quixote and his squire Sancho Panza, we discover four major themes that are worthy of emulation. First are the contests between man and "his environment," between a "protagonist" and his "setting," and between the "material" and "spiritual world."[52] Second is the importance of "independence" and "freedom." At one point in the journey Don Quixote summarizes this philosophy with these words: "Freedom, Sancho, is one of the most precious boons that the heavens bestow upon man. All the treasures hidden in land or sea cannot equal it."[53] To these virtues may be added a third—a sense of duty that demands the fulfillment of obligations and the honoring of pledges.[54] But the most powerful moral message of all may be the theme of death and reconciliation. This is a topic, as noted in the words drawn from *Tristram Shandy*, that provides sustenance for those whose lives would be changed by the death of a loved one in the family. The description of Don Quixote's courage in facing death became a story of victory of "spiritual restitution" over "physical dissolution," and of "reconciliation" over permanent separation.[55]

In summary, Jefferson viewed private discourse as a means of strengthening social relations, of enlarging our understanding on subjects that affect our personal and public lives, and of solving problems related to pressing needs. With this perspective entrenched in his mind, he gave us practical guidelines for effective conversation and letter writing reflecting his role as a student of rhetoric and as a participant in and observer of discourse in action during a pivotal period in American history. Through his power of description in relating an anecdote, moreover, he permits us to hear Buffon display his conversational skills and to witness a group of French republican leaders using interpersonal communication to design a discourse strategy to be used in the French Assembly at a crucial moment on the eve of the French Revolution. We also learn from him the importance of remembering that a personal letter is a private message that reveals, in part, the nature of one's mind.

Jefferson also set aside time to turn his attention to poetical discourse as a rhetorical form that gives a poet, a dramatist, and a novelist an opportunity to present a moral theme in an instructive, persuasive, and aesthetically pleasing manner. If a work failed to fulfill these ends, it was not, in his opinion, worthy of our consideration. If, however, a poem, a play, or a novel succeeded in developing a powerful moral lesson in language capable of stirring our imagination and influencing our will, we have much to gain by studying it carefully. Although Jefferson grew impatient with the average author's inability to achieve this high ideal, he took comfort in knowing that the great writers—including Homer, Euripides, Virgil, Shakespeare, Milton, Cervantes, Pope, and Swift—and even a lesser author like Sterne, gave us enduring models demonstrating that the noble ideal is possible.

# Notes

1. Moses Hadas, ed., *The Basic Works of Cicero* (New York: Modern Library, 1951), 50–52.

2. Lawrence Klein, "The Third Earl of Shaftesbury and the Progress of Politeness," *Eighteenth Century Studies*, 18 (1984–85): 186–214.

3. TJ to P. H. Wendover, March 13, 1815, in L&B, 14:282. According to the editors, this letter was endorsed but not sent.

4. Jefferson obviously made an exception for Abigail Adams, for the two corresponded freely on political themes.

5. G. S. Hilliard and Anna Eliot Ticknor, eds., *Life, Letters, and Journals of George Ticknor*, 2 vols. (Boston: Houghton Mifflin, 1909), 1: 36.

6. It should be observed that while this claim is apparently true, there is a considerable body of evidence to suggest that both men made disparaging remarks about each other when they spoke to Washington and to friends in Congress.

7. Webster, *The Writings and Speeches of Daniel Webster*, 17: 371.

8. "Autobiography," in Ford, 1: 97–98.

9. Webster, *The Writings and Speeches of Daniel Webster*, 17: 373.

10. "Autobiography," in Ford, 1: 154. It is difficult to accept Jefferson's description of being a "silent witness." Lawrence S. Kaplan, in his book on *Thomas Jefferson: Westward the Course of Empire*, portrays Jefferson as one who freely expressed his ideas on all occasions during his "European Years." 35–65.

11. Although TJ was sympathetic to the meeting, he was upon reflection concerned that he had been the host of the session while representing a neutral government. When he explained his misgivings to Count Montmorin on the next morning, he was told that no problem existed, and that it was hoped that he would "assist at such conferences in the future" because of his recognized ability to moderate "the warmer spirits," and promote "a wholesome and practicable reformation only." Ford, 1: 155.

12. The description of this principle was discussed in Margaret Bayard Smith, *The First Forty Years of Washington Society* (New York: Scribner's, 1906). Smith, the wife of the editor of the *National Intelligencer*, was a frequent visitor at Jefferson's dinner parties. See 383–91.

13. Hadas, *Basic Works of Cicero*, 397.

14. Klein, "Shaftesbury," 209–11.

15. TJ to Madison, October 28, 1785, in *Writings*, 840.

16. TJ to Cornelia Jefferson Randolph, December 26, 1808, in Betts and Bear, *Family Letters*, 373.

17. Hadas, ed., *Basic Works of Cicero*, 397.

18. He once told Adams "an hour of conversation would be worth a volume of letters." TJ to Adams, April 8, 1816, in *Writings*, 1381.

19. See James J. Murphy, tr., "Principles of Letter Writing," in Patricia Bizzell and Bruce Herzberg, eds., *The Rhetorical Tradition: Readings from Classical Times to the Present* (Boston: Bedford Books of St. Martin's Press, 1990), 425–26.

20. May 4, 1786, in *Writings*, 853.

21. Ibid.

22. TJ to John Adams, June 27, 1813, in Cappon, 2: 336.

23. June 29, 1824, in Randall, *Life of Thomas Jefferson*, 3: 613.

24. January 30, 1787, in Boyd, 11: 95, 97. On another occasion, he wrote to Thomas Mann Randolph, Sr., saying: "Your son Thomas, at Edinburgh has done me the favor to open a little correspondence with me. . . . I perceive by his letters that he has a good genius. . . ." August 11, 1787, in Boyd, 12: 21–22. Although the use of the word "genius" to describe his grandson may be a bit overdrawn, it does show the stress that Jefferson placed upon the quality of a letter.

25. Andrew Burstein, *The Inner Jefferson: Portrait of a Grieving Optimist* (Charlottesville: University Press of Virginia, 1995), 116–49.

26. May 19, 1816, in Ford, 11: 526–27.

27. TJ to Adams, June 27, 1813, in Cappon, 2: 336–37.

28. January 16, 1787, in *Writings*, 881.

29. In the letter to Logan cited above, Jefferson asserted: "It became necessary then to ask myself seriously whether I meant to enter as a political champion in the field of the newspapers? He who does this throws the gauntlet of challenge to everyone who will take it up. It behooves him then to weigh maturely every sentiment, every fact, every sentence and syllable he commits to paper, and to be certain that he is ready with reason, and testimony to maintain every title before the tribunal of the public." Ford, 11: 526.

30. *LCB*, 4.

31. John Bernard, *Retrospections of America* (New York: Harper & Brothers, 1887), 238.

32. *LCB*, 11.

33. Bernard, *Retrospections of America*, 238.

34. August 3, 1771, in Boyd, 1: 76–81.

35. Jefferson made this statement in the letter to Chastellux which accompanied his "Thoughts on English Prosody," in L&B, 18: 414.

36. On this point, Douglas L. Wilson, the editor of *LCB*, has observed: "That he would carry this Literary Commonplace Book with him to Paris at all is noteworthy and would seem to indicate his attachment to it; on the other hand, he may have had expressly in mind the project to prepare a demonstration of his prosodical arguments for the Marquis. In any case, Jefferson's reliance on the Literary Commonplace Book in working out his contentions in the essay on prosody is fully evident." *LCB*, 9–10.

37. L&B, 18: 414.

38. The discussion, which follows, is based on the "Thoughts on English Prosody," in L&B, 18: 415–51.

39. Although Jefferson at times viewed various forms of fictional writing as distinctive genres, he often discussed them as an integrated whole.

40. *LCB*, 12.

41. As a typical example, see the following letter to William Short, March 29, 1787, in Boyd, 11: 254–55.

42. *LCB*, 13.

43. Shakespeare, in particular, illustrated this principle in a number of his plays.

44. The Skipwith letter, in Boyd, 1: 76–81, is perhaps Jefferson's most thoroughly developed statement on the inherent values associated with well-written fiction.

45. Skipwith letter, in Boyd, 1: 77.

46. See *Maryland Quarterly*, I (1944), 2 & 68, cited in *LCB*, 11.

47. TJ to Nathaniel Burwell, March 14, 1818, in *Writings*, 1411.

48. Ibid., 1412.

49. Observe Julian Boyd's editorial comments in Boyd, 1: 81n.

50. This excerpt, along with explanatory comments, may be found in Boyd, 6: 196–97.

51. This opinion is expressed by Wilson, in *LCB*, 11.

52. Jean Descola, *A History of Spain* (New York: Knopf, 1963), 277.

53. Cited in Descola, *History of Spain*, 277.

54. Ibid.

55. For an excellent discussion of this point, see Ernst Robert Curtius, *European Literature and the Latin Middle Ages* (New York: Harper & Row, 1953), 558. In addition, see M. H. Abrams, *The Mirror and the Lamp: Romantic Theory and the Critical Tradition* (New York: Norton, 1958). Abrams makes the interesting argument that Cervantes' frequent descriptions of death and reconciliation paralleled his own philosophy of life. "Everywhere," he says, "the feeling of the author—even the innermost depths of his own intimate individuality—gleams through, visibly invisible. . . ." Abrams, *Mirror and the Lamp*, 241. This strong intellectual and emotional bond between a novelist and the protagonist on the central moral issues of a work is doubtless largely responsible for Jefferson's great attachment to *Don Quixote* and its author Cervantes.

# CHAPTER SEVEN

∼

# Political Communication

When Jefferson was elected to the Virginia House of Burgesses in 1769, he began a political career that was to last for four decades. By the time he became president in 1801, he not only had served in the House of Burgesses, in the Continental Congress on two occasions, and in the Virginia House of Delegates, but he also had held such offices as governor of Virginia, American minister to France, secretary of state, and vice president. Out of these experiences at home and abroad, he was able to create a vision of what he felt effective political communication should be. The basic essentials of this vision, we believe, can be seen by focusing our attention on his ideas pertaining to three important aspects of this discourse form: parliamentary procedure, legislative debate, and the role of the press in governmental affairs. As is shown below, he himself became a serious scholar in the first of these discourse forms; a practitioner, though somewhat reluctant at times, in the second; and a critic in the third. In all, to him, the field of political communication was an ideal forum in which to send a message of virtue to the people.

## Parliamentary Law as a
## Controlling Medium in Political Speaking

In the spring of 1766, while visiting the city of Annapolis, Jefferson attended a meeting of the Maryland Assembly. He brought with him on this occasion an appreciation of parliamentary law that he had gained from his mentor George Wythe, that, in turn, inspired him to develop commonplace readings on the subject. What he witnessed on this occasion, he wrote his friend John Page, was an astonishing lack of order, decorum, and awareness of how a meeting should be conducted. The members, he said, often were engaged in discourteous behavior and irrelevant "chit-chat" that produced a "great noise and hubbub" characteristic of the actions "you will usually observe at a publick meeting of the planters in Virginia. . . ." Moreover, three or four speakers "without rising from their seats" often spoke at the same time. When a motion was made, the presiding officer, instead of stating its wording to the delegates, merely asked the body to answer "yes sir" or "no sir" on any action that was being considered. These votes, noted Jefferson, were taken even though most of the participants did not know what was being proposed.[1]

Despite the negative practices he had observed in Annapolis, Jefferson's interest and training in parliamentary law continued to develop as he launched his political career in the late 1760s. From 1769 to 1775, he was a delegate to the House of Burgesses from Albemarle County. In this capacity, he served as a member of several important committees, and consequently had an opportunity to report their findings and recommendations to the body as a whole.[2] In 1775, as he ended this phase of his career, he asked John Randolph, who was preparing to migrate to England, if he would be willing to "dispose of some" of his collection of books on parliamentary procedures.[3]

Within one year after contacting Randolph, Jefferson, then a member of the Continental Congress, was appointed to a three-person committee "to Draw Up Rules of Procedure in Congress." It was his task to prepare the notes summarizing the findings and recommendations of the committee. On July 16, 1776, the report, after being discussed and amended, was approved. The sixteen provisions appearing in the revised document included rules governing such procedures as roll calls, the handling of motions, the division of questions, election to offices, and the general conduct of members during a session.[4] When the Congress adjourned and Jefferson returned to Virginia to continue his service to the Commonwealth, his reputation as a careful student of parliamentary law was on the rise.

Almost immediately, he had a chance to expand his knowledge of parliamentary discourse through his participation in the Virginia House of Delegates from 1776 through 1779. This period in which he "was a legislator in his own Commonwealth," according to Dumas Malone, "comprised his most creative period as a statesman during the American Revolution, and there was no part of his entire career that he afterwards looked back upon with greater satisfaction."[5]

In 1789, by the time that Jefferson was completing his five-year stay in France, he was being recognized in some quarters as an international authority in parliamentary law—especially as the system was practiced in America.[6] Aware of this, the French scholar François Soulés, who had just published a work entitled *The Parliamentary Pocket-Book*, wrote to Jefferson asking him to evaluate a criticism that he had received with respect to a particular rule he had recorded in his volume.[7]

In part because he was conscious of his growing reputation as an authority in parliamentary law as he returned to America, Jefferson felt uneasy about the practices in the House of Representatives and in the Senate as the new American government emerged in the 1790s. This concern deepened significantly when he was elected vice president in 1797. Convinced that the rules of procedure were consistently undergoing dramatic change, he became insecure about his forthcoming duty as presiding officer of the Senate. With few up-to-date books on the subject to guide him, he asked George Wythe to supply him with any notes on the topic that might be in his file.[8]

Vice President Jefferson's inaugural address to the Senate in 1797 revealed his lingering insecurity about his knowledge of all the rules, but contained a promise that he would follow a policy of justice and fairness to the best of his ability on any ruling he would make. In making this promise, he asserted:

> The rules which are to govern the proceedings of this House, so far as they shall depend on me for their application, shall be applied with the most rigorous and inflexible impartiality, regarding neither persons, their views, nor principles, and seeing only the abstract proposition subject to my decision. If, in forming that decision, I concur with some and differ from others, as must of necessity happen, I shall rely on the liberality and candor of those from whom I differ, to believe, that I do it on pure motives.[9]

With this statement, Jefferson had injected a premise in his remarks describing the powerful role that virtue must play in parliamentary discussions. The need for virtue, he made clear, must apply not only to a presiding officer but also to the members of the assembly, who might be inclined to equate a particular parliamentary ruling that goes against their wishes with a deliberate act of injustice based on political or selfish motives.

During this period of uneasiness concerning the need to have a well-developed system of rules for the Senate, which could also be applicable to the House, Jefferson was motivated to take on the primary responsibility to produce a handbook on the subject.[10] He had in his own file a list of rules and practices that he had assembled over a forty-year span, excerpted largely from six major European works. They included, for instance, ninety-seven listings from Henry Scobell's *Memorials of the Method and Manner of Proceedings in Parliament in Passing Bills*; ninety from George Petyt's *Lex Parliamentaria*; seventy from John Hatsell's *Precedents of Proceedings in the House of Commons*; sixty-nine from William Hakewill's *Modus tenendi Parliamentum, or the Old Manner of Holding Parliaments in England*; forty-five from Sir Edward Coke's *Institutes*; and twenty-nine from Anchitell Grey's *Debates of the House of Commons, from the Year 1667 to the Year 1694*.[11]

When these, along with other, sources are combined to form the Parliamentary Pocket-Book, they cover approximately 115 pages and 588 paragraphs in the modern scholarly edition by Wilbur Samuel Howell. The paragraphs are almost equally divided between "Procedural" and "Constitutional Matters."[12] What is more significant is that the Pocket-Book became a depository of information for Jefferson's influential *Manual of Parliamentary Practice: for the Use of the Senate of the United States*. Published in 1801, this work makes use of at least fifty different publications, and includes the Senate rules that had generally evolved and were generally accepted.[13]

In section I of the *Manual*, Jefferson spoke of the "importance of adhering to rules." He began his introduction by quoting a maxim often repeated by Arthur Onslow who, in his opinion, was "the ablest among the Speakers of the House of Commons." The maxim expressed the view that "nothing tended more to throw power into the hands of administration and those who acted with the majority, of the House of Commons, than a neglect of, or departure from the rules of proceeding. . . ."

After confirming the continuing relevance of Onslow's perspective, Jefferson warned of the dangers that would occur if a tyranny of the majority prevails. Parliamentary law, therefore, is a vitally significant political procedure that is necessary for protecting the rights of the minority. This would be the case, he added, even if a particular rule does not appear to be "rational." He then observed: "It is much more material that there should be a rule to go by, than what the rule is; that there may be an uniformity of proceeding in business, not subject to the caprice of the Speaker, or captiousness of the members."[14] By ensuring that all discussions are handled in an orderly, dignified, decent, and predictable manner, parliamentary law, concluded Jefferson, promotes the public good within a rhetorical setting permeated with an attitude of fairness and civility.

The *Manual* contains fifty-three different rules of procedure, often accompanied with multiple sources cited for each point.[15] These cover such traditional matters as regular and privileged motions, types of committees and methods of reporting, resolutions, elections, and quorums. One of these fifty-three rules, we feel, is worthy of special mention because of its emphasis on a member's conduct while addressing the chair on an issue. This rule requires a discussant to focus on the question at hand in a pertinent manner; to sit down when called to order until the challenge has been decided; and to avoid the use of "indecent" or "disorderly language," the tendency to mention another by name who is present, the practice of alluding to business being undertaken by the other branch of Congress, and the habit of wearing a hat upon entering the Senate chamber. With considerable specificity, this rule spells out the following requirement:

> No one is to disturb another in his speech by hissing, coughing, spitting, speaking or whispering to another; nor to pass between the Speaker and the speaking member, nor to go across the House; or to walk up and down it, or to take books or papers from the table, or write there.

These rules, assembled by Jefferson and supported by a wide variety of data and authorities, did more than offer guidelines for maintaining order and eliminating needless counterattractions. They also placed parliamentary law within the framework of a moral enterprise that nurtured respect for the institution and for one's colleagues.

Although Jefferson did not list the *Manual* as one of his original works,[16] his monumental effort in producing this volume was greeted with universal praise. Samuel Smith warmly commended it in a book review appearing in *The National Intelligencer and Washington Advertiser*.[17] Twenty-five years later, in his "Eulogy on Adams and Jefferson," Daniel Webster enthusiastically observed that the *Manual* "is now received as the general standard by which proceedings are regulated, not only in both houses of Congress, but in most of the other legislative bodies in the country. . . ."[18] The *Manual* lost none of its appeal or relevance in subsequent years. In 1988, Howell was able to report that "from 1801 to the present time, the *Manual* has received at least 143 editions."[19]

As we have seen, parliamentary procedure, to Jefferson, was a highly effective medium in the field of political discourse. He believed that its stress on the moral obligations and duties of the majority and on the rights of the minority ensures the achievement of justice, fairness, and impartiality in an assembly meeting. The rules governing behavior of participants, moreover, create an environment in which Cicero's integrating virtue of decorum becomes the prevailing moral principle. The reasoning process in such a rhetorical setting, he further believed, is strengthened, and personal relations are enhanced. Parliamentary procedure presents an opportunity, in sum, that has the capacity to produce actions designed to promote the welfare of the public community. These were the reasons why he was willing to invest so much time in writing two works for the purpose of teaching others how to use this communication form in a productive and rewarding manner.

## Legislative Discourse

Most of Jefferson's comments on legislative discourse center on the rhetorical form of debate. From his unique vantage point as a member of the House of Burgesses and the House of Delegates, as a representative of the Continental Congress, and as presiding officer of the United States Senate, he came to appreciate the elements of effective debate practices. In using these experiences to develop his ideas on this type of discourse medium, he gave major emphasis to the quality of reasoning as used by influential men of recognized virtue. In doing so, he praised in particular six men whose content, style, and impeccable characters placed them above most of their contemporaries in the use of arguments in a political assembly that led to action. These men were John Adams, George Mason, Peyton Randolph, Edmund Pendleton, George Wythe, and James Madison.

What the above rhetors had in common as debaters, noted Jefferson, was a power of intellect; a comprehensive knowledge of the subject matter under discussion; the ability to frame and organize an argument and to clothe it in language that was clear, concise, and chaste; and, to a greater or lesser degree, the talent to speak extemporaneously, which permitted them to engage freely in a give-and-take dialogue.[20] More important, as these men spoke, the audience, aware of their dedication to truth and to the public good through the years, was moved by their sense of dignity, decorum, and justice.[21] Consequently, therefore, these characteristics, on the whole, proved to be more suitable for everyday legislative discourse than the more flamboyant, oratorical style of Richard Henry Lee.[22]

To see in greater detail what, according to Jefferson, constitutes excellence in legislative discourse, we may turn to a telling example in his description of Edmund Pendleton as a debater. Calling him the "ablest man in debate" he had ever seen, Jefferson gave this portrait of Pendleton in action:

. . . he was cool, smooth, and persuasive; his language flowing, chaste & embellished; his conceptions quick, acute and full of resource; never vanquished; for if he lost the main battle, he returned upon you, and regained so much of it as to make it a drawn one, by dexterous manoeuvres, skirmishes in detail, and the recovery of small advantages which, little singly, were important altogether. You never knew when you were clear of him, but were harassed by his perseverance until the patience was worn down of all who had less of it than himself.[23]

Pendleton's performance as a debater, as may be seen by this brief analysis, was strengthened significantly by the power of his conception, the weight and phrasing of his arguments, the effectiveness of his rhetorical strategies and maneuvers, and his relentless persistence.

Jefferson also believed that Pendleton was an exemplar of virtue and a masterful user of personal proof: "he was one of the most virtuous & benevolent of men, the kindest friend, the most amiable & pleasant of companions, which ensured a favorable reception to whatever came from him. . . ."[24]

But if Pendleton was the type of speaker Jefferson wanted in the legislature, he shared with John Adams the following reservations about the kind of communicator who was not acceptable. Late in his life, when privately discussing the debates on the Declaration of Independence, Adams interrupted his chronological account to condemn those legislators who used a grandiloquent oratorical style in an effort to impress their colleagues with their talent for using "wit," "sarcasm," "repartee," or "satire." Drawing upon what he had read of the histories of Greece, Rome, England, and France, and upon what he had "observed at home, and abroad," Adams maintained "that Eloquence in Public Assemblies is not the surest road, to Fame and Preferment, at least unless it is used with great caution, but very rarely, and with great reserve." To illustrate this principle, he cited "the examples of Washington, Franklin and Jefferson," each of whom was inclined to prefer silence or reserve over "oratory."[25]

Given that Jefferson believed that debate was the fundamental characteristic of legislative discourse, he had three special concerns about how discussion should be conducted. These three potential problems pertained to the time allotted to debate, the size and shape of the chambers in which the discussions would take place, and the tendency on the part of some participants to monopolize or dominate the arguments.

On the question of time, he believed strongly that a protracted debate runs the risk of being needlessly repetitive, dull, and unproductive. To counter this eventuality, he himself sometimes adopted a policy of silence rather than take part in a discussion that he perceived to be excessively prolonged. It was only natural for him, therefore, to take considerable interest in learning that in the winter of 1810 the House of Representatives was in the process of finding a remedy to "the external protraction of debate by sitting up all night, or by the use of Previous Question."

It did not take Jefferson long to come up with a possible solution to this problem. Relying upon his experiences as a parliamentarian and his own proclivity to prefer short, concise speeches and to produce action, he outlined his suggestions in a letter to his son-in-law John Wayles Eppes, then serving in Congress. Rejecting the notions that congressional action on an issue should be speeded up by remaining in discussion throughout the night or by calling for the "Previous Question," he offered the following motion as a possible remedy to the problem:

> Resolved that at (VIII.) aclock in the evening (when-ever the house shall be in session at that hour) it shall be the duty of the speaker to declare that hour arrived, whereupon all debate shall cease.[26]

Jefferson next addressed the question of how action should proceed at the hour designated to stop debate. If it simply is debate on a main motion that is pending, he advised, discussion should be stopped and a vote be taken. If, on the other hand, a subsidiary motion such as an amendment, a postponement, or a laying on the table has been attached to it, these secondary motions should immediately be discharged, and a call for a vote on the main question be made. Although Jefferson's recommendation did not altogether conform to the accepted procedures on parliamentary law included in his *Manual*, it had the saving merit of demonstrating his conviction regarding the need to institute an action-oriented legislative policy that would help control, at least partially, unnecessary lengthy debates in a political assembly.

An additional factor in Jefferson's discussion of legislative discourse is the relating of an argument to the occasion and setting. Trained in the small, informal room that housed the debates in the House of Burgesses, he came to admire a chamber that encouraged informal discourse and made it easy for everyone present to be heard. With this background, he could not be enthusiastic about the debates in Paris on the eve of the French Revolution. It was impossible, he said, for 1,200 people in one room to have a well-organized, productive debate. This form of rhetorical setting could only produce an unmanageable exchange among the participants.[27]

Years later, as he wrote his *Autobiography*, he stated misgivings about the attempt of the "present Congress" to have debates with "one hundred and fifty lawyers" present, each of whom is tempted "to question everything, yield nothing, and talk by the hour?"[28] In developing these claims, Jefferson knew that it was not always possible to change the rhetorical setting for a legislative debate. But in pointing out the advantages associated with an inappropriate room and a limited number of discussants, he showed a sensitivity regarding the importance of this facet of argumentation.

The third concern that he felt should be addressed if the quality of legislative discourse were to improve was the discouraging practice on the part of some speakers to monopolize a debate. Here again he found himself in agreement with John Adams, his ally in supporting the Declaration of Independence. When writing his *Autobiography*, and reflecting on the Continental Congress debates during the period from April to July 1776, Adams asserted: "A public speaker who inserts himself, or is urged by others into the Conduct of Affairs, by daily Exertions, to justify his measures, and answer the objections of opponents, makes himself too familiar with the public, and unavoidably makes himself Ennemies."[29] Such an insight would have resonated with Jefferson. For it provided a rationale explaining why Adams, in following his own policy of knowing when and when not to speak on behalf of the Declaration in the weeks preceding its adoption, enhanced the persuasive power of his overall performance.[30] But similarly important, it was also an apt description of Jefferson's sense of decorum, which prompted him to take a negative view of any rhetor on an assembly floor to be unduly aggressive, inconsiderate, and talkative when advancing or defending a cause, however just that cause may be.

## The Role of Journalism in the Political Process

For Jefferson, political communication required more than a representative's knowledge and implementation of parliamentary law and an effectiveness in legislative debate. It also embraced the use of newspapers as a means of influencing governmental affairs in such a positive and moral way that the people will become educated and interested participants.

In his career as a public servant, and in his retirement years as well, Jefferson was both fascinated and repelled by the performance of the press as a communication medium. As might be expected, he was gratified by the way that newspapers disseminated the American message of independence during the Revolutionary War era. But he became disillusioned by what he often perceived as a lack of responsibility and honesty in the reporting and analysis of news in the 1790s and early 1800s. As his love-hate relationship with the press during this formative period became strikingly evident, he never wavered from a philosophy that he had developed in the 1770s concerning the proper role that newspapers should play in the political process.

This philosophy consisted of three principles that were integrally related. The first may be stated in this form: *The principal task of the press is to form an interactive and trustworthy relationship with the public for the purpose of serving as monitors or gatekeepers of the government's policies and actions, and for advancing learning and taste.* The primary motivation for this claim stemmed from his abiding faith that, because a government exists to serve the people, it is the function of a newspaper to provide data and interpretations that will produce an informed electorate. This type of partnership between the press and the public, he argued, empowers both the newspaper as a communication channel and the audience as a receiver of the message in such a manner that they will be in a position to be censors of the government.[31]

Using the preceding premise as a starting point, he proceeded to make this historically significant assertion about the worth of the press: "were it left to me to decide whether we should have a government without newspapers, or newspapers without a government, I should not hesitate a moment to prefer the latter."[32] For such a strong conclusion to be justified, thought Jefferson, it was necessary, first of all, for newspapers to be sufficiently available to penetrate all sections of a community; and, second, for the public to have the knowledge and desire to read critically what is printed. So strong was Jefferson's faith in the people that he repeatedly stated his confidence in their judgment to weigh carefully the strengths and shortcomings of any arguments presented to them.[33]

As an important figure in conveying principles of the Enlightenment to the citizens of an emerging nation, Jefferson was also convinced that the press could be an ideal channel to promote learning and taste on social issues that have political implications. Consequently, whenever he saw that the taste of Americans was being corrupted by those elements of the press that focused on unseemly and sensational events, he forcefully expressed his displeasure. It was repulsive, he noted in a letter to Abigail Adams, that London newspapers were too inclined to fill their pages with accounts of "assassinations," "suicides," "thefts," "robberies," and "slanders." But what was even worse, he added, these "horrors of which human nature is capable" of producing are then sometimes reprinted by "foolish" editors of American newspapers.[34] The papers he admired used their good offices to elevate their readers, and, in doing so, to enhance the public good.

Jefferson argued in his second principle that *to fulfill the challenges assigned to it in a democratic system, the press must be free to carry out its duties*. When he maintained that he had "sworn upon the altar of God, eternal hostility against every form of tyranny," he had in mind such issues as freedom of speech and freedom of the press. Described "as the foremost exponent in history of the necessity of a free speech,"[35] he took advantage of every communication opportunity to affirm that unless the press is free to do its work, it would not be possible to form an effective partnership with the people so that they in unison could be gatekeepers in evaluating the government.[36] This conviction was affirmed again and again in his letters; and it was highlighted in such public messages as the Kentucky Resolutions in 1798, and in his two inaugural addresses.

But Jefferson did more than make statements on behalf of the freedom of the press; he also took specific actions to support this principle. When Congress passed the Sedition Act in 1798, for example, he was alarmed that this oppressive law constituted a dangerous threat to all newspaper printers and editors who might dare to criticize the government, however justified they may be. To counter this act, he contributed money in support of Republican papers that were charged with sedition; then, when he became president, he discharged those who "were under the persecution of our enemies, without instituting any prosecutions in retaliation."[37]

In taking his stand on this issue, Jefferson was willing to admit that a number of newspapers often were guilty of excesses he believed to be unjust and immoral. This was particularly true of the attacks on his administration during his first term in office, he told his audience in the presentation of his second inaugural address. But even in those cases where the press had crossed the line of propriety, the federal government, he strongly held, had no right to intervene.[38]

If it is the duty of the government and of society to ensure the concept of a free press, at the same time, Jefferson noted, *it is incumbent upon the press to be truthful, and to present to the public alternative philosophical choices*. When a newspaper consistently seeks to report data and make claims that are both valid and reliable, he said during his sixth year as president, it should be regarded as "a noble institution, equally the friend of science & of civil liberty."[39] Four months later, he began a letter to John Norvell with these words: "To your request of my opinion of the manner in which a newspaper should be conducted, so as to be most useful, I should answer by restraining it to true facts & sound principles only."[40]

Whenever he reflected on the criterion of truth as it pertained to the press, he found it easy to fault the British newspapers. Referring to them as "those infamous fountains of falsehood," he accused their reporters of remaining in "their garret," instead of doing research, while they wrote their stories.[41] Such unscholarly and unethical practices, he observed, result in fabrications and other forms of misinformation.

What concerned Jefferson most about the British press was their persistent inaccurate characterization of what had happened during and following the Revolutionary War. One of the first assignments he undertook upon his arrival in France in the autumn of 1784, therefore, was to write a brief essay on the "Representations of the Affairs in America by British Newspapers," which he hoped to have published in the *Courier de l'Europe*. This reply was designed to inform Europeans that because they could not rely on the accounts of America in the British newspapers, they would be wise to discontinue their habit of copying material from these unreliable sources. We know from experience, he observed, that the British press made false claims about what had occurred on the battlefields in the war; and that now their newspapers, without even utilizing eyewitness materials from the American press, are giving an inaccurate picture concerning the so-called turmoil and unrest in the states. The problem with the British papers, he emphasized, is that they "have been under the influence of two ruling motives: 1. Deep-rooted hatred, springing from an unsuccessful attempt to injure; 2. a fear that their island will be depopulated by the emigration of it's inhabitants to America."[42]

It should be noted that Jefferson was equally severe in his indictment of American newspapers that failed to conform to the principle of truth. To John Norvell, he asserted: "It is a melancholy truth, that a suppression of the press could not more compleatly deprive the nation of it's benefits, than is done by it's abandoned prostitution to falsehood."[43] In this moment of discouragement, written in the middle of his second presidential term, he sardonically recommended to Norvell that

> Perhaps an editor might begin a reformation in some such way as this. Divide the paper into four chapters, heading the lst, Truths, 2d. Probabilities, 3d. Possibilities, 4th, Lies.[44]

These moments of malaise would soon pass, however, as he took refuge in his faith in the nature and power of the people. For it was they, he firmly believed, who in the end would separate falsehood from truth and licentiousness from fairness, as they rendered a critical judgment based on the virtues of justice and benevolence in the service of the public good.[45]

In addition to its emphasis on truth, Jefferson's third principle articulated the notion that the press should present alternative philosophical views on the question of politics. This did not mean that a particular newspaper would be required to take a neutral stance on all controversial issues, for such an approach would imply the lack of a governing political philosophy. What he had in mind in supporting this premise was that if the people had access to a Federalist paper with its clearly delineated philosophy, they should also have the right and privilege to read a Republican paper and then evaluate the worth of its philosophy. This would make it possible for the reader to compare both philosophies before rendering a political decision.

An opportunity for Republicans came in 1791 when Jefferson, now serving as secretary of state, sought to create a national Republican newspaper that might compete on equal terms with Hamilton's Federalist organ, the *Gazette of the United States*, edited by John Fenno. The man whom he and Madison persuaded to accept the editorship was Philip Freneau, a literary scholar and poet whose liberal writings were popular during the Revolutionary War. To make the offer attractive, Jefferson appointed him to the vacant position of Clerk for Foreign Languages in the office of the secretary of state at a salary of $250 a year. Just as important, he promised to provide him with letters, foreign intelligence and newspapers, "the publication of all proclamations & other public notices," including "the printing of the laws. . . ." Freneau also was informed that he could hold the two positions concurrently.[46] When Hamilton, then secretary of the treasury, heard of Jefferson's actions, he complained to President Washington that the State Department was using the newly organized paper for partisan political purposes.[47]

Jefferson felt justified in promoting the development of the *National Gazette* for three reasons. First, he held, Fenno's paper had not adequately supplied Washington with sufficient information on foreign affairs; second, Hamilton had been free to use his own organ to advance his economic policies; and, third, the American people needed and wanted another national newspaper that could give them an alternative philosophical choice.[48]

As plans for the launching of the *National Gazette* were being finalized, another publication event occurred that was to have a powerful influence on the relations between the Federalists and the Republicans. In late 1790, Edmund Burke's *Reflections on the Revolution in France* was published. A few months later, in the spring of 1791, Thomas Paine offered a refutation of Burke in his volume, *Rights of Man*. These controversial works, described by Julian Boyd as "two of the most notable political tracts in the English language,"[49] immediately placed American political leaders into opposing philosophical groups which Jefferson labeled as "Burkites" and "Painites."[50] This, in effect, was another way of saying that the schism between the Federalists (the "Burkites") and the Republicans (the "Painites") had widened.

Early in the controversy, the *Gazette of the United States* began publishing articles under the name Publicola that defended the arguments that Burke had made against the French Revolution. Thinking that the unidentified Publicola was John Adams, Jefferson concluded that the vice president was moving toward the heretical position that America should eventually adopt the British system of governance consisting of aristocrats and a monarchy. He expressed his concern about this trend toward Toryism in a letter to Jonathan B. Smith, with an enclosure of Paine's pamphlet. After stating that he was pleased "to find it will be reprinted here," he asserted "that something is at length to be publicly said against the political heresies which have sprung up among us."[51] Much to Jefferson's chagrin, the substance of the letter he had written to Smith was inserted in the preface of Paine's pamphlet. Because of the wording of his statement of praise for Paine's tract, it was clear to all discerning authorities that it could only have been written by the former American minister to France. This event had now significantly heightened the controversy.[52]

At once Publicola shifted his arguments away from Paine, and began to indict Jefferson for charging the "Burkites" with heresy.[53] But Jefferson was not without his defenders. The *National Gazette*, along with other Republican papers, pointed out the inherent dangers and weaknesses in Publicola's arguments. Even though Jefferson was told by some observers that John Quincy Adams, not his father, was Publicola, he continued to believe that the vice president's political philosophy and current feelings were being advanced in the columns.[54]

In helping to create the *National Gazette*, Jefferson had given the people an alternative philosophical choice. The Burke-Paine controversy, moreover, reinforced his confidence in the ability of the electorate to distinguish between the relative worth of competing views, and to recognize what was a reasonable probability as contrasted to a mere possibility. Although Adams won the election in 1796, he never fully recovered from the charge that he had developed sympathies for the British form of government.[55] It was clear to Jefferson that the ascendancy of the Republicans in the 1790s indicated that the people, after examining newspaper accounts, tended to side with the political philosophy that characterized the Republican press.[56]

As the decade of the 1790s progressed, Jefferson remained firm in his conviction that competing philosophies of the press should be upheld. Thus on May 15, 1791, he sent Thomas Mann Randolph a number of issues of Fenno's Federalist paper as well as copies of Bache's paper, the *Aurora*, that propounded the Republican position. This principle was even more evident in his communication in 1795 to professor Christoph Ebeling, a foreign scholar, who had asked him for advice in the preparation of his *Biography and History of North America*. On the question of press reliability, he gave this warning: "To form a just judgment of a country from it's newspapers the character of these papers should be known, in order that proper allowances & corrections must be used."[57] Following this brief lesson in informal reasoning, he presented this descriptive account:

> As in the commerce of human life, there are commodities adapted to every demand, so there are newspapers adapted to the Antirepublican palate, and others to the Republican. On the former class are the *Columbian Sentinel*, the Hartford newspaper, Webster's *Minerva*, Fenno's *Gazette of the U. S.*, Davies's Richmond paper & c. Of the latter are Adams's Boston paper, Greenleaf's of New York, Freneau's of New Jersey, Bache's of Philadelphia, [and] Pleasant's of Virginia & c.[58]

When presented with this balanced approach, Ebeling, in Jefferson's opinion, would be able to determine which arguments were sound and relevant, and which were overly partisan and unconvincing.

Jefferson's perspectives on the nature and influence of newspapers as a political communication medium were formed in keeping with his ideas on virtue. In exchange for their guaranteed freedom of expression, he wanted printers, editors, and columnists to be just, wise, temperate, and courageous in functioning as censors of the government in their role as representatives of the people. Although the press has a necessary and legitimate right to be partisan with respect to the advancing of a particular political philosophy, he maintained, it must do so by selecting significant and tasteful topics; by developing its stories and analyses in a sound, responsible, and ethical manner; and by never knowingly straying from the truth. Any newspaper that violates these rules by presenting unwarranted personal attacks, licentious claims, or false and misleading data, he concluded, has no moral justification in a democratic society.

Jefferson's standards for the press were rigorous and demanding, but they were, in his opinion, also achievable. With his encouragement and guidance, for example, his two favorite newspapers were established,[59] both of which successfully implemented his three principles. These highly influential media organs—the *National Intelligencer* and the *Richmond Enquirer*—were created in 1800 and 1804, respectively. His enthusiasm for and confidence in the editors and the approaches they used remained strong for the rest of his life. In the summer of 1819, he wrote to Adams that Samuel Smith of the *Intelligencer* and Thomas Ritchie of the *Enquirer* "cull what is good from every paper, as the bee from every flower. . . ."[60] When he reached the age of eighty in 1823, he suggested to William Short that the *Enquirer* was the best paper that had ever "been published in America."[61] The brief discussion of the philosophies and practices of these newspapers that follows provides a summary of Jefferson's attitudes toward what represents virtuous journalism practices.

When the *National Intelligencer* published its first issue on the eve of the presidential election of 1800 as a tri-weekly journal, Samuel Smith, who was to become a close friend of Jefferson, made it clear what the philosophy of the paper would be. As "the *first Paper* printed in Washington," he said, the goal of the *Intelligencer* is to "furnish the earliest and correct notices of" the "deliberations" taking place in Congress, and provide information on "national affairs" as they relate "to our internal and external situation." He then reminded his readers that because he was conscious of the power and duties of the press, "truth and truth only, shall be the guide of the Editor." If on any occasion, he added, something inaccurate were reported, the "error" would "be followed by a candid renunciation of it." For "the design of the *National Intelligencer* is to diffuse correct information through the whole extent of the union."[62]

The next issue, appearing three days later, was even more direct and specific in the outline of the philosophy to be delineated. After stating what would and would not be included in the paper, Smith asserted that while "the conduct of public men and the tendency of public measures will be freely examined, so, on the other, private character will remain inviolable; nor shall indelicate Ideas or expressions be admitted, however disguised by satire or enlivened by wit." All investigations that are to be discussed in the *Intelligencer*, he further noted, will be governed by "a desire to enlighten, not only by fact, but by reason"; and will be in conformity with the "general good" and the "general welfare."[63]

Whether or not Smith formed his philosophy from his frequent conversations with Jefferson cannot be known. What is clear, however, is that it was completely consistent with the three principles Jefferson had adopted for the press. That the implementation of this philosophy of virtue was the trademark of the *Intelligencer* in the years that followed was evidenced by the continuing interest and respect it generated.

To gain a grasp of the philosophy of the *Richmond Enquirer*, we examined the extant issues of its first year of publication in 1804, beginning with the month of May and extending through the November presidential election. What we found would have pleased Jefferson. Each issue contained sections on domestic affairs and foreign intelligence. The domestic category included such items as analyses of different laws of the United States, reprints of congressional debates as reported in the *National Intelligencer*, and related political matters. Because Jefferson was a candidate for re-election, and because the *Enquirer* was a Republican paper, Ritchie republished the texts of the Declaration of Independence and of *A Summary View of the Rights of British America*. Similarly, he recognized the anniversary of Jefferson's first election victory of 1800. But instead of taking a strong partisan stance pertaining to the 1804 contest, he was content to publish from time to time a list of Republican electors. Further proof of the *Enquirer's* restrained approach could be seen in the way that it covered the death and funeral of Alexander Hamilton. The great Federalist leader was praised as a man of exceptional talents, of persuasive eloquence, and of moral deportment. But the readers were advised not to embrace his Tory sentiments.

In the sections on foreign intelligence, the war between Great Britain and France received heavy emphasis. References to speeches in Parliament and to activities in France, especially to the deeds of Napoleon and his elevation to the position of emperor, were plentiful.

Jefferson would have responded approvingly, moreover, to the manner in which the *Enquirer* incorporated materials on history, literature, and culture. He could read, for instance, accounts of works that had appeared on the French Revolution, an analysis of a tract on Bacon's Rebellion (which was a part of the early history of Virginia), a biographical sketch of Edward Gibbon, and a review of John Marshall's *Life of George Washington*. He could also see a section on "English Literature," a review of a new life of Samuel Johnson, a study reporting anecdotes of Voltaire, and a description of Humboldt's travels in America. Finally, he would have the pleasure of reading essays and columns on culture dealing with topics that had long appealed to him. Among these were "Conditions of Women," "American Genius," "Forensic Eloquence," "The Illusions of Fancy" (Imagination), "On Politeness," and on "Practical Farming." In

all, the *Enquirer* and the *National Intelligencer* were representative anecdotes of Jefferson's moral ideal of what the press should be in a democratic
society.

Motivated by a strong moral sense, by a commitment to the philosophy
of republicanism, and by a belief in the power of discourse to enlighten
and persuade the public on matters of virtue and taste, Jefferson, as we
have seen, regarded political communication as an engine that could drive
a society. For this reason, he provided guidelines for rhetors to remember
when participating in parliamentary procedure, in legislative debates, and
in journalism. For these discourse channels, in their unique way, produce
rhetorical settings in which actions can be taken for the purpose of elevating the people and thus strengthening the government.

# Notes

1. TJ to John Page, May 25, 1766, in Boyd, 1: 19–20.
2. His participation is described in his "Autobiography," and is recorded in John
Pendleton Kennedy, ed., *Journals of the House of Burgesses* (Richmond, VA: 1907). See in
particular his role on Nov. 28 and Dec. 5, 1769; July 11, 1771; and June 15, 1775.
3. TJ to John Randolph, August 25, 1775, in Boyd, 1: 242–43.
4. "Report of the Committee to Draw up Rules of Procedure in Congress," July 10,
1776, Boyd, 1: 456–58.
5. Dumas Malone, *Jefferson The Virginian* (Boston: Little, Brown, 1948), 247.
6. Boyd, 1: 457n.
7. François Soulés to TJ, March 21, 1789, in Boyd, 14: 684.
8. TJ to George Wythe, January 22, 1797, in Ford, 7: 110.
9. *The Debates and Proceedings in the Congress of the United States; With an Appendix
Containing Important State Papers and Public Documents. Fourth Congress—Second Session,
Comprising the Period from December 5, 1796, to March 3, 1797*, 581.
10. See his letters to George Wythe, April 7, 1800 and April 10, 1800; and to Edmund
Pendleton, April 19, 1800. The substance of these letters appears in Wilbur Samuel Howell, ed., *Jefferson's Parliamentary Writings* (Princeton: Princeton University Press, 1988),
19–20.
11. We made these tabulations by examining his *Writings* in Howell.
12. Howell, *Jefferson's Parliamentary Writings*, 44.
13. The complete text of this work, along with that of the *Pocket-Book*, appear in Howell, *Jefferson's Parliamentary Writings*. Because Jefferson listed his source material, we were
able to make the count.
14. Jefferson's assertion that the existence of a rule is more important than its content
is surprising. Quite clearly, this would not be the case in contemporary parliamentary procedure.
15. The tendency to make such extensive use of supporting data shows Jefferson's concern for the need to rely on evidence, especially that which was a part of the British parliamentary system.

16. When John W. Campbell asked for permission to publish a complete edition of his writings, Jefferson, after listing several of his works, observed: "I do not mention the Parliamentary Manual, published for the use of the Senate of the United States, because it was a mere compilation, into which nothing entered of my own but the arrangement, and a few observations necessary to explain that and some of the cases. . . ." TJ to Campbell, September 3, 1809, in *Writings*, 1211. Our research indicates that this self-effacing statement, resulting from TJ's modesty, is off the mark. His input in many instances was original and creative.

17. *National Intelligencer*, April 13, 1801, 1.

18. "Eulogy on Adams and Jefferson," in B. F. Tefft, ed., *Speeches of Daniel Webster* (New York: A. L. Burt, n.d.), 227.

19. Howell, *Jefferson's Parliamentary Writings*, 38.

20. Jefferson wrote the following note to John Tyler on May 26, 1810: "You wish to see me again in the legislature, but this is impossible; my mind is now so dissolved in tranquillity, that it can never again encounter a contentious assembly; the habits of thinking and speaking off hand, after a disuse of five and twenty years, have given place to the slower process of the pen. . . ." In *Writings*, 1226.

21. A typical example of this is Jefferson's description of Wythe as a man "of exemplary virtue," "inflexible integrity," and "exact justice." He could thus be called "the Cato of his country. . . ." TJ to John Saunderson, August 31, 1820, in H. A. Washington, *The Writings of Thomas Jefferson*, 9 vols. (Washington, D.C.: Taylor & Maury, 1853) 1: 114. Another instance is provided in these words of praise for Madison: "With these consummate powers were united a pure and spotless virtue which no calumny has ever attempted to sully." "Autobiography," in Ford, 1: 66.

22. TJ to George A. Otis, December 25, 1820, in L&B, 18: 307.

23. "Autobiography," in Ford, 1: 59.

24. Ibid.

25. L. H. Butterfield, ed., *Diary and Autobiography of John Adams*, 4 vols. (New York: Atheneum, 1964), 3: 336.

26. January 17, 1810, in Charles T. Cullen, ed., *The Papers of Thomas Jefferson*, Second Series (Princeton: Princeton University Press, 1988). Reprinted in Howell, *Jefferson's Parliamentary Writings*, 29. See also L&B, 12: 343–44.

27. TJ to John Jay, August 5, 1789, in Boyd, 15: 334.

28. "Autobiography," in Ford, 1: 90–91.

29. Butterfield, *Diary and Autobiography of John Adams*, 3: 36.

30. Jefferson's unusually strong praise of Adams's performance in the debates on the Declaration of Independence is described in chapter 14 of this study.

31. TJ to George Washington, September 9, 1792, in *Writings*, 999. On this occasion, TJ reminded the president that "No government ought to be without censors. . . ." Ibid.

32. TJ to Edward C. Carrington, January 16, 1787, in L&B, 6: 58. Josephus Daniels described this statement as "the strongest utterance of faith in the power of a free, honest and liberty-loving press, made by man. . . ." Taken from his essay on "Jefferson's Contribution to a Free Press," in L&B. 18: i.

33. He presented these ideas in numerous letters covering a period of more than thirty years, and in both of his inaugural addresses.

34. September 25, 1785, in Cappon, 1: 70.

35. Frank L. Mott, *Jefferson and the Press* (Baton Rouge: Louisiana State University Press, 1943), 64–65. Leonard Levy, who claimed that Jefferson's views on freedom of the press lacked the depth he had shown in constructing a philosophy of religious freedom, suggested that Jefferson, like Blackstone, believed "that the press should be free in the English or common-law sense. . . ." This meant that it should be "free from censorship or licensing acts in advance of publication, but responsible for abuse of an unrestrained freedom to publish." *Jefferson & Civil Liberties*, 49. For a further analysis of Jefferson's ideas on a free press and liberty, see ibid., 44–56, and 171–72.

36. He told Judge John Tyler that the "most effectual" means of keeping the avenues of truth open "is the freedom of the press." For this reason, he added, the press is all too often "shut up by those who fear the investigation of their actions." TJ to John Tyler, June 28, 1804, in *Writings*, 1147.

37. TJ to Governor James Monroe, July 17, 1802, in L&B, 10: 334.

38. In his essay on "Jefferson's Contribution to a Free Press," Daniels concluded with these words of praise: "As the years shall pass . . . and, one by one the nations that sit in darkness come into the glorious light of freedom—freedom of conscience, freedom of speech, freedom to think and write and print—the majestic figure of Jefferson will loom up as the inspiring spirit who first breathed into the printing press . . . the breath of life, and made it responsive, sentient, virile, free. In this new life that dates from Jefferson, this free press has become the champion of the oppressed, the teacher of the young, the guide of the mature, the comfort of the aged, and the mightiest power for good that blesses and shall ever bless mankind." L&B, 18: xlvii–xlviii. Jefferson did believe, however, that state governments should have the right to exert some control over the press. Levy, *Jefferson & Civil Liberties*, 59.

39. TJ to Thomas Seymour, February 11, 1807, in Ford, 10: 369.

40. June 14, 1807, in Ford, 10: 417.

41. TJ to Francis Hopkinson, with Enclosure, August 1, 1787, in Boyd, 11: 657.

42. "Jefferson's Reply to the Representations of Affairs in America by British Newspapers" (Before 20 Nov., 1784), in Boyd, 7: 540–45. Although Jefferson inserted an introduction to this essay after his arguments had been developed in which he identified himself as an officer who had fought in the war, the reply was never published in the *Courier*. It did appear, however, in the *Leyden Gazette*—the paper Jefferson believed to be the best in Europe. It is surprising, that in identifying himself as a war veteran for the purpose of increasing the emotional impact of his argument, he did so while discussing the issue of truthfulness. Additionally, this violation was in opposition to his oft-repeated statements that he never sought to write a piece for a newspaper without signing his name.

43. June 14, 1807, in Ford, 10: 417.

44. Ibid., 418.

45. He stated his position on this point to John Tyler on June 28, 1804: "The firmness with which the people have withstood the late abuses of the press, the discernment they have manifested between truth and falsehood, show that they may safely be trusted to hear everything true and false and to form a correct judgment between them. . . ." L&B, 11: 203.

46. TJ to Madison, July 21, 1791, in Sowerby, *Catalogue of the Library of Thomas Jefferson*, 1: 270.

47. TJ reported Hamilton's attitude in a letter to Washington, September 9, 1792, in ibid., 1: 270–71.

48. Ibid.

49. Boyd, 20: 268.

50. TJ to Washington, May 8, 1791, in *Writings*, 977.

51. April 26, 1791, in Boyd, 20: 290.

52. Boyd noted: "The expressions of the Secretary of State more than the pamphlet itself, we may be sure, took precedence in the political gossip of the boarding houses, the taverns, and the Philadelphia dinner tables." 20: 274.

53. Ibid., 20: 270.

54. Boyd supported Jefferson's interpretation by saying that "John Adams found himself silently occupying the role of Burke, with John Quincy Adams as *Publicola* defending him and attacking Jefferson." Ibid. Despite this episode, Jefferson and Adams exchanged letters clarifying their positions and expressing their continuing friendship and respect for each other as persons of honor and dignity. See TJ to Adams, July 17, 1791, in Cappon, 1: 245–47; and Adams to Jefferson, July 29, 1791, ibid., 1: 247–50.

55. Ibid., 1: 283.

56. See his optimistic statements about the Republicans in his letter to Madison, February 5, 1799, in Randolph, 3: 416. Further confirmation of this claim may be seen in twenty-four years of Republican rule beginning with Jefferson's election in 1800 and extending through Monroe's second term. For an excellent analysis of politics and the press in the 1790s, see Michael Lienesch, "Thomas Jefferson and the American Democratic Experience: The origins of the Partisan Press, Popular Political Parties and Public Opinion," in Onuf, ed., *Jeffersonian Legacies*, 316–39.

57. "Notes on Prof. Ebeling's Letter of July 30, 1795," in Ford, 8: 205–11.

58. Ibid., 8: 210.

59. Mott, *Jefferson and the Press*, 48, 51.

60. July 9, 1819, in Cappon, 2: 543.

61. TJ to William Short, September 8, 1823, in Sowerby, *Catalogue of the Library of Thomas Jefferson*, 1: 279.

62. *National Intelligencer*, October 31, 1800.

63. Ibid.

# CHAPTER EIGHT

~

# Forms of Professional Discourse

In analyzing the nature of conversation and letter writing, and in describing parliamentary procedure and journalism as parts of political communication, Jefferson covered ground hitherto unexplored by many of his contemporaries. The freshness of his ideas was the result of his extensive readings and his own discourse experiences. Yet to be treated are his ideas on three special forms of discourse: philosophical/religious communication, legal advocacy, and historical writing. Completion of this examination concludes part 1 of this study, the purpose of which has been to summarize his principal views on his perspectives on the rhetoric of virtue.

## Philosophical Writing and Religious Discourse

A reading of Jefferson's writings—particularly his voluminous correspondence—indicates his lifelong interest in what he believed to be the related areas of philosophy and religion. He maintained this interest despite the fact that he was not a traditional philosopher, theologian, or recognized biblical scholar. He was too busy first as a lawyer, and second as a diplomat and political leader, to become an accomplished authority in the complex fields of philosophy and religion. This did not deter him, however, from producing insights about these forms of discourse that have enriched our understanding and appreciation. In chapter 1, for instance, we saw that he was comfortable in comparing the moral philosophy of Jesus with that expounded by the Epicureans and the Stoics; and we further noted that he shared with Cicero and the British epistemologists the thought that the relationship between a man and God must be marked by a feeling of reverence and love, and

159

a respectful attitude toward one's responsibilities associated with the concept of duty.

An additional point in support of Jefferson's tendency to see a relationship between philosophy and religion may also be cited. When in 1940 Walter Muelder and Lawrence Sears produced an edited volume entitled *The Development of American Philosophy: A Book of Readings*, they included three of Jefferson's letters as a means of highlighting representative samples of his philosophy.[1] The first letter, sent to Dr. Benjamin Rush in 1803, contains his syllabus comparing the relative merits of the moral teachings of Jesus with those of the Greek philosophers.[2] The second, addressed to John Adams in 1814, shows how Plato's dialogues have adversely affected the development of Christianity.[3] The third, written to Adams in 1823, is an attack on John Calvin and other theologians because of their presumably false interpretation of the nature of God and the universe.[4]

Although these two communication forms—philosophy and religion—are bound together by their shared interest in principles of morality and virtue, Jefferson was aware of several characteristics distinguishing them that are worth noting. We begin our probe by turning to several features of philosophical discourse.

## Philosophical Writing

Inspired by his basic interest in philosophy as a whole, by his extensive analyses of the ideas of the leading philosophers of the Western world, and by his experience as president of the American Philosophical Society for a number of years,[5] Jefferson believed that philosophical writing should deal with such important subjects as "the origin of mankind, the relations between the physical and moral faculties of man," and the "thinking faculty of man."[6] With such significant themes as its focal points of study, one is not justified to raise "a hue and cry against the sacred name of philosophy. . . ."[7]

The issue that troubled him most about philosophical writing was the quality of the author's reasoning and evidence in support of a claim. Good writers like M. de Sassure, he told John Rutledge, will refuse to assent to a conclusion unless sufficient evidence is provided. For a true philosophical premise must be grounded in fact, not fancy.[8] He further observed that a philosophical proposition that is "beyond finite comprehension" should be abandoned. This of course, he added, may be a matter of degree. To explain this point, he made this statement to Adams: "Were it necessary however to form an opinion, I confess I should, with Mr. Locke, prefer swallowing one incomprehensibility rather than two. . . ."[9]

The scholars whom Jefferson upheld as innovative and effective philosophical writers included such authors as Cicero, Bacon, Locke, and Hutcheson. He also admired the works of Dugald Stewart and Destutt de Tracy. In his opinion, these philosophers never failed to buttress their arguments with thoughtful analyses and compelling evidence. Nor did they rely on romantic fancy or whimsy instead of reality. Whereas these scholars met Jefferson's reasoning test, Plato fell far short of this standard in his dialogues. Jefferson felt dismay, for example, that tradition in general, and Cicero in particular, were inexplicably favorably disposed toward Plato.

Beyond his well-known objections to Plato's political philosophy, what was there in his dialogues that disturbed Jefferson? He answers this question in the 1814 letter to Adams, and in two letters to William Short.[10] His first major objection to Plato as a philosophical writer was his deficient reasoning process as demonstrated especially in his most famous dialogue, *The Republic*.[11] If we evaluate Plato by "the test of reason," according to Jefferson, it is necessary to conclude that he was a "genuine sophist" who led people into error "by the elegance of his diction." All too frequently he substituted "Whimsies" and "unintelligible jargon" for sound arguments, thereby "presenting the semblances of arguments which, half seen thro' a mist, can be defined neither in form or dimension." Such undesirable rhetorical tactics, moreover, would have been enough to relegate lesser-known authors to a state of oblivion.[12]

Jefferson's second objection to Plato's writings was their harmful effect on the reputation of Socrates. The schoolboy "paralogisms," "quibbles on words," and "sophisms" placed in Socrates' mouth had no relationship to the historical Socrates. They were merely "whimsies of Plato's own foggy brain. . . ."[13]

Third, and particularly troubling to Jefferson, was the adverse influence that Plato's philosophical works exerted on Christianity:

> . . . Plato's visions have furnished a basis for endless systems of mystical theology, and he is therefore all but adopted as a Christian saint. It is surely time for men to think for themselves, and to throw off the authority of names so artificially magnified. . . .[14]

In brief, by grafting Plato's mysticisms, incomprehensibilities, and ideas on immorality upon Christian doctrines, theologians by design, argued Jefferson, have deliberately used "indistinctness" to promote "everlasting controversy," which, they hoped, would "give employment for their order, and introduce it to profit, power, and preeminence." What is worse, he added, is that the practice of superimposing the philosophical writings of Plato upon Christianity is a direct affront to Jesus, who sought to present his ethical message in such a clear style that everyone could easily understand.[15]

Jefferson's critique of Plato was unusually harsh and poignant, and at variance with traditional interpretations. Similarly, it was perhaps influenced in large part by his own ideas on religion, as well as politics. But it also served to make the central point that philosophical writing has a moral obligation to feature significant themes, persuasive arguments, and mature language designed to promulgate wisdom and other facets of virtue.

## Religious Discourse

Jefferson's views on religion have been freely described and well documented. Some of these perspectives are noted in chapter 2 on virtue. In 1984, Charles B. Sanford produced a comprehensive study of this question, *The Religious Life of Thomas Jefferson*.[16] Our goal here, however, is not to rehash the findings of Sanford and other authors on Jefferson's enduring interest in religion, for that is not pertinent to the purpose of this chapter, which is to talk about the forms of professional discourse. The particular form now to be discussed is the issue of religious communication as perceived by Jefferson. He held a number of firm convictions on the subject of how religious instruction should be conveyed in written publications and from the pulpit.

His first concern dealt with what should be the primary theme of religious instruction. In discussing this point, he often began by noting what should not be taught. A sermon, for example, should, for the most part, avoid the use of nonreligious themes. One of the reasons for this belief was that a preacher is not adequately prepared to lecture "*from the pulpit* in Chemistry, in Medicine, in Law, in the Science and principles of Government, or on anything but Religion exclusively."[17]

Another rationale for this position, according to Jefferson, is that a preacher who uses the pulpit to discuss secular topics violates the central mission of the church. In most cases, a congregation, comprising members with a particular theological orientation, hires and remunerates a minister to fulfill his duties as a religious instructor. If this mandate is not observed, the conditions under which he most likely was employed have been disregarded, thus creating a breach of contract. In taking this ground, Jefferson was flexible enough to offer this caveat. It is acceptable for a preacher to urge the need for parishioners to "obey the laws of our country," to "assist our sick neighbors," and to "preserve our own health" because these premises, respectively, are not only political, sociological, and medical in nature; they also represent legitimate religious themes. Unless this is the case, however, arguments that focus on subjects which have no religious connection should be avoided in the pulpit. What is discussed by preachers in conversation and in letter writing, by contrast, should be free and open, because such communication has nothing to do with the pulpit.[18]

Second, Jefferson argued that a religious message that causes schisms by creating sects and promoting denominationalism produces far more harm than good. This was an extremely troubling issue for him, not only because of the disunity and societal disruptions that resulted from this practice but also because it so clearly constituted a rejection of the moral teachings of Jesus. He expressed his frustration with this problem in a letter to George Logan in 1816:

> When we see religion split into so many thousands of sects, and I may say Christianity itself divided into it's thousands also, who are disputing, anathematizing and where the laws permit burning and torturing one another for abstractions which no one of them understand, and which are indeed beyond the comprehension of the human mind, into which of the chambers of this Bedlam would a (torn) man wish to thrust himself.[19]

The presence of these sects within the Christian church was similarly responsible for his belief that denominationalism should be deemphasized or ignored in sermons and other types of religious instruction. In support of this assertion, he wrote to William Canby, a Quaker:

> An eloquent preacher of your religious society, Richard Motte, in a discourse of much emotion and pathos, is said to have exclaimed aloud to his congregation, that he did not believe there was a Quaker, Presbyterian, Methodist or Baptist in heaven, having paused to give his hearers time to stare and to wonder. He added, that in heaven, God knew no distinctions, but considered all good men as his children. I believe with the Quaker preacher, that he who steadily observes these moral precepts in which all religions concur will never be questioned at the gates of heaven, as to the dogmas in which they all differ. . . .[20]

That Jefferson was conscientious in his own life on the subject of denominationalism was clearly evident. While in Washington serving as president, he pledged financial support for building programs undertaken by Presbyterian, Episcopal, Methodist, and Baptist churches. He did the same in his years in Charlottesville.[21] And he took pride in asserting that four churches in his hometown worked together so closely that they took weekly turns in sharing the same building for their worship services.

Third, Jefferson held that religious communicators should not waste their time by delving into subject areas that transcend the laws of nature. He thus sought to discourage a ministerial acquaintance who requested a reaction to his researches into the question of whether it is possible to have "a transmigration of souls from one body to another in certain cases." Such speculation, he observed, was a useless exercise because we have no "means of physical knowledge of the country of spirits."[22] These representative examples reveal an intense feeling on Jefferson's part that specific creeds and metaphysical speculations are not the substance out of which religious messages should be created. It is a grave mistake, he concluded, for dogmatic theologians, with the help of Plato, to engage in this practice.[23] This type of rhetorical strategy, therefore, should be replaced by treating the one and only topic that all Christian instruction should emphasize—the moral teachings of Jesus.

A minister who focuses his attention on basic religious themes, and who places a spirit of ecumenism above an adherence to denominationalism or to sects, which are creatures of dogma, will then be in a position to meet Jefferson's standard for developing an appropriate sermon or treatise with Jesus' moral teachings as a centerpiece. To Jefferson, Jesus was a "benevolent and sublime Reformer" and the "best preacher who ever lived."[24] Not surprisingly, therefore, he could speak these words of praise to the Quaker minister William Canby: "Of all the systems of morality, ancient or modern, which have come under my observation, none appear to me so pure as that of Jesus. . . ."[25]

What made Jesus' teachings so impressive and enduringly valuable to Jefferson were the purity and simplicity of "the doctrines" of virtue, which were always clothed in sentiments and language that had as their controlling purpose to generate "the happiness of man." This happiness, moreover, will surely come if we follow Jesus' admonition that we be "just and good"; that we "love our neighbors as ourselves"; and that we "fear God."[26] These simply stated principles, if implemented in our private and public lives, will make it possible for us to become "honest and dutiful to society"; and this, in turn, will encourage others to judge us by our actions, as we judge a tree by its fruits. "For it is in our lives, and not from our words," Jefferson observed, "that our religion must be read."[27]

One of the strong motivations that Jefferson had for admiring Jesus' moral doctrines was his conviction that they contained universal principles of truth and sound reasoning that could apply to peoples of all religious faiths. Since they should be viewed as non-controversial, they have the power to produce unity rather than division, rapport instead of dissension. In short, he saw in them a means of elevating lives and improving society by bringing divergent groups together: Anglicans and Methodists, Presbyterians and Baptists, Protestants and Catholics, Unitarians and Trinitarians, and Christians and Muslims.[28] With such an all-embracing appeal, these teachings, not divisive dogmas, should be paramount in every sermon, homily, or religious document.

In this unit on philosophical writing and religious discourse, we have seen how virtue is the driving force behind these related rhetorical forms. Virtue in philosophical writing, as noted, consists of emphases on knowledge and wisdom in the development of argumentative positions on the powerful themes of the nature of man and the universe; and virtue in religious communication derives its principal thrust from the moral instructions of Jesus.

# Legal Discourse

Jefferson's three years of study as a student of law, his seven years of practice before the Bar, and his frequent applications of principles of jurisprudence throughout his political career and years of retirement gave him the background and interest to develop perspectives on legal discourse that he freely communicated to students who requested his advice. His ideas highlighted the overriding importance of knowledge, training, and experience, and the utilization of appropriate methods and means of acquiring these elements.

The first principle in his philosophy and practice of legal discourse dealt with *the need for an aspiring lawyer to adopt an effective educational program.* In developing his ideas on this principle, Jefferson held conflicting views on the value of an apprentice system that placed a student in the office of an experienced attorney. In 1769, for example, he observed that this traditional procedure—one that he himself had undergone—renders one vulnerable to the prejudices of the mentor, and encroaches on the time needed for reading.[29] Two decades afterwards, in 1790, he shifted his stance with these words of advice to another pupil: "It is a general practice to study the law in the office of some lawyer. This indeed gives the student the advantage of his instruction."[30]

But if Jefferson held varying beliefs on the value of the apprentice system, he maintained an enduring faith in the concept that to succeed in law a person must form and adhere to a thorough and well-designed reading program. "It is superiority of knowledge," he told John Garland Jefferson, "which can alone lift you above the heads of your competitors, and ensure your success." To achieve this end, he continued, it would be necessary to spend at least three years in reading a wide range of literature "before you think of commencing practice."[31]

Jefferson consistently advised law students to build a legal foundation by gaining a thorough knowledge in the fields of both science and the humanities. In his memorable 1814 letter to John Minor, which, in turn, was a revision of a letter to Bernard Moore written approximately fifty years earlier, he arranged the recommended reading list under six headings: Science, Philosophy and Religion, Law, Politics, History, and Discourse theory.[32]

Often in presenting advice on what to read in the liberal arts, he gave a rationale for the study of specific subjects. Languages and history, he said, serve as exercises to strengthen the faculty of memory. Mathematics, on the other hand, "gives exercise to our reason. . . ." Moreover, he asserted, "No inquisitive mind" can afford to be ignorant of "Astronomy, Natural Philosophy (or Physics), Natural History, Anatomy, Botany and Chemistry."[33]

Once the foundation had been laid in a broad range of the arts and sciences, the student should be ready for the study of law, in conjunction with such related subjects as Ethics, Religion, and various aspects of Communication and Criticism. Among the numerous legal volumes that should be probed thoroughly, the following, he noted, are of special value: Bracton's *De legibus Angliae*, Coke's *Institutes*, Matthew Bacon's *Abridgment of the Law*, and Blackstone's *Commentaries*.[34] These special works, along with other popular studies, cover such areas as Natural law, Common law, and Chancery.

In addition to supplying a reading list, Jefferson gave directions concerning where and when specific studies should be read and analyzed. Although he said it was "absolutely indifferent in what place" a person carries "on the reading," his generosity and willingness to help others often led him to invite students to come to Charlottesville, if possible, so that they could have access to the books in his own private library. This invitation was accompanied, however, with the caveat that the borrowed volumes must be returned promptly and then be carefully rearranged.

Jefferson was far more specific on the question of the time that one should set for particular readings. His most concrete suggestions pertaining to this issue appear in the Moore-Minor letters:

> Till VIII o'clock in the morning employ yourself in
> Physical studies, Ethics, Religion, natural and
> sectarian, and Natural law. . . .
> From VIII to XII. Read law.
> From XII to I. Read Politics.
> In the AFTERNOON. Read History.
> From Dark to Bed-time. Belles lettres, criticism,
> Rhetoric, oratory, to wit.[35]

Any spare time that might occur within these hours, he suggested, should be devoted to physical exercise and relaxation.

Jefferson's educational philosophical view of legal training centered heavily on the development of a rigid program consisting of extensive reading and critical thinking. But he also recognized that attending lectures on law presented by distinguished scholars was useful. For this reason, he urged Thomas Mann Randolph Sr. to have his son, then studying law in France, return to Virginia during his third year of training so that he could attend "Mr. Wythe's lectures."[36]

The well-trained lawyer visualized by Jefferson is a man who possesses a strong general background in all phases of knowledge and a specific grounding in the field of law. He may or may not have served as an apprentice in a law office, but he most likely would understand the leading historical and contemporary works, including significant precedent-setting decisions, that have marked the development of the legal profession. But one further dimension in the preparation of a lawyer, according to Jefferson, was the need for training in how to channel an argument in a pleasing and persuasive manner.

His suggestions for channeling an argument, as noted in chapter 5, called for specific discourse exercises to reinforce what was learned from readings in poetry and dramatic literature, from rhetorical treatises and oratorical compositions, and from works on criticism. Inspired by Blair's *Lectures on Rhetoric and Belles Lettres*, by Sheridan's and Mason's books on elocution, and by Kames's *Elements of Criticism*, Jefferson recommended that all students of law participate in such practices as studying samples of Classical, British, and American eloquence; writing orations on "feigned cases," and taking part in a debate with a fellow student in the presence of an observer who would serve as a critic. It followed naturally that he would strongly endorse the concept of a moot court that Wythe established in the College of Law at William and Mary. The recommendations summarized here stemmed from Jefferson's belief that when speaking before the Bar a lawyer must exemplify a clear, concise control of the message and of language usage, and possess an articulate delivery pattern that exudes a spirit of confidence.[37]

A second principle of legal discourse advocated by Jefferson was his conviction that *the issue of precedents constitutes the central feature in constructing a forensic argument*. His strongly held belief in this concept prompted him to state that any judicial decision rendered in the past that fails to qualify as a precedent would be of no value as a source to be studied or cited in a contemporary case. His arguments in support of this position are found in the preface of the *Reports of Cases Determined in the General Court of Virginia, From 1730, to 1740 and From 1768, to 1772*.[38] Compiled by Jefferson from a three-volume work in the possession of Attorney General John Randolph, these cases were carefully selected in accordance with their reliability as precedents. Those that Jefferson excluded from the *Reports* were not "worthy of preservation" because the judges of the court, "consisting of the King's Privy Counsellors only," were "chosen from among the gentlemen of the country for their wealth and standing, without any regard to legal knowledge. . . ." Consequently, "their decisions could never be quoted, either as adding to, or detracting from the weight of those of the English courts, on the same points."

By contrast, the cases that Jefferson included in the *Reports* were, in his view, useful "precedents" that could be studied with profit by students of law because "they established authoritatively the construction of our own enactments, and gave them the shape and meaning, under which our property has been ever since transmitted and is regulated to this day." Even if the decisions in some of these instances were formed on an incorrect principle of the law, Jefferson added, they still would have relevance as precedents because of the legitimacy and influence of the courts which had jurisdiction over the cases.[39]

A third and final principle of Jefferson's philosophy of legal discourse was his commitment to what he perceived to be *the value of constructing debate briefs when preparing a case*. This rhetorical procedure, he felt, would permit the lawyer to put in writing all of the essential arguments and supporting data that are required for the development of a prima facie case. The brief also would contain the potential refutation that might be offered by the opposing side. Similarly important, this practice would enable the advocate to arrange the materials in such a manner that the message would achieve unity, coherence, and emphasis.

In 1780 Jefferson wrote to William Short, advising him of the advantages to be accrued by constructing legal briefs. Contained in the letter were these words: "I send you by Col. Digges. . . Mr. Wythe's and my arguments in Bolling v. Bolling bound up together." By examining them, he noted, "It will enable you better to foresee your adversary's objections" and then "answer them." He then urged Short to use a "methodical and strict arrangement of your matter" because experience has shown that "the best arguments are lost without this."[40] (In a later chapter, we see how Jefferson relied heavily on the use of briefs during his years as a practicing lawyer.)

We have seen in the foregoing discussion that the type of legal discourse recommended by Jefferson was based on in-depth knowledge, both in the arts and sciences and in the nature and history of law. This acquired wisdom, moreover, when combined with a sense of justice and fairness, and then buttressed by the use of convincing rhetorical strategies, including a well-organized legal brief and compelling language control and delivery, place the advocate in a favorable position to present the best possible case that circumstances in a given situation may allow.

To see more clearly what Jefferson regarded as effective legal discourse, we now examine the murder trial of Eugene Aram which took place in England in 1759. Fifty-five years after Aram spoke in his own defense, Jefferson remembered reading his speech in vivid detail. As a result, when Abraham Small, who was planning a new edition of his edited volume the *American Speaker*, wrote to him asking for suggestions regarding possible discourses that might be included in the revised work, Jefferson gave this glowing recommendation of Aram's presentation:

> But the finest thing, in my opinion, which the English language has produced, is the defence of Eugene Aram, spoken by himself at the bar of the York Assizes, in 1759, on a charge of murder, and to be found in the *Annual Register*, of that date. . . . It had been upwards of fifty years since I read it, when the receipt of your letter induced me to look up a Ms. copy I had preserved, and on re-perusal at this age and distance of time, it loses nothing of its high station in my mind for classical style, close logic, and a strong representation.[41]

With Aram's speech fresh in his mind when he wrote to the young law student John Minor in August, Jefferson listed it as a sample of English

legal eloquence, describing it "as a model of logic, condensation of matter, and a classical purity of style." Because of the unusually strong praise
Jefferson used to describe Aram's speech of self-defense, and since he included the reading of it as a part of an exercise to study models of British
oratory, we feel it is appropriate to summarize it here by looking first at
the elements of the rhetorical situation, and then at the speech itself.

The alleged facts of the case, as reported in the *Annual Register* of
1759,[42] show that Daniel Clark, a shoemaker who recently had been mar-
ried, devised a strategy for presenting his wife to his neighbors at a social
gathering. To make the occasion more festive, Clark decided to borrow
plates and other valuable goods from his friends and acquaintances, without any intention to return the objects. He presumably chose as his ac-
complices in this fraudulent scheme Eugene Aram and Richard Houseman—a "flax-dresser." Shortly afterwards, Clark was pronounced missing,
and the borrowed goods were found on the properties of Aram and
Houseman. During the next several years, people in the area began to sus-
pect that Aram and Houseman were involved in the plot that led to the
disappearance of Clark. As a result, serious legal steps to solve the case
were taken up. This process was given a sense of urgency following the
discovery of what was believed to be the skeleton of Clark.

On August 3, 1759—almost fifteen years after the event had occurred—Aram and Houseman were officially charged with the crime. At
a hearing, Houseman asserted that he had seen Aram strike Clark several
times, causing his death. He then confessed that together the two men
dragged the body into a nearby cave. In support of this eyewitness account, the skull produced in court revealed a fracture on the left side.
When this evidence, along with other testimony accusing Aram, was presented before the bar, Aram was arraigned and charged with premeditated
murder. Meanwhile Houseman was acquitted, having agreed to serve as
the state's witness.

Aram had the type of rhetorical training and practice that permitted
him to construct a defense that would appeal to Jefferson. Throughout his
career, he was enamored with the subject of belles lettres and polite literature. This interest prompted him to become a close student of the
Greek, Latin, Hebrew, French, Arabic, and Celtic languages. His competence in these areas was on a sufficiently high level to qualify himself as
an usher or assistant teacher, and as a compiler of a lexicon of comparative literature containing approximately one thousand items. He was capable, as we can now see, to take advantage of his knowledge of discourse
in the speech that was prepared in writing for the court.

Aram's first argument was framed in terms of the good man as rhetor. "First, my Lord," he said, "the whole tenor of my conduct in life contradicts every particular of this indictment." He offered as proof of this claim that he had lived an exemplary life typified by industry and study, by freedom from greed, and by a disdain for luxury and accumulation of worldly possessions. To supplement this effort to persuade the audience that he was a person with an upright character, a praiseworthy temperament, and a love of knowledge, he sought to gain sympathy by a reference to his poor health. At the time of the alleged crime, he asserted, he often was confined to bed, and had such difficulty in walking that crutches were required. These were not the conditions, he noted, for one to engage in a criminal act as described in the arraignment.

Second, Aram contended, the disappearance of Clark did not necessarily mean he was dead. Indeed, it is quite probable he could be in hiding. To illustrate this claim, he cited the example of William Thompson, who, two years before, escaped from "double-ironed chains and had not yet been found despite the strictest possible search that could be undertaken." "If then," he inferred, "Thompson got off unseen, thro' all these difficulties, how very easy was it for Clark, when none of them opposed him?"

Aram next proceeded to the issue of the bones that had been discovered in a cave. His task here was to cast doubt on the claim that the fractured skull offered as evidence was that of Clark. Observe in the following passage how he dealt with the charge that the blows that Aram allegedly administered had produced a fractured skull.

> Here too is a human skull produced, which is fractured; but was this the cause, or was it the consequence, of death? . . . . If it was violence, was that violence before or after death? My Lord, in May 1732, the remains of William Lord Archbishop of this province were taken up, by permission, in this cathedral, and the bones of the skull were found broken: Yet certainly he died by no violence offered to him alive, that could occasion that fracture there.

To complete his refutation that the fractured skeleton belonged to Clark, Aram presented historical data to show how many tombs were ravaged or destroyed during the early days of the Reformation. Similar acts of destruction took place, he added, at nearby Knaresborough Castle which once served as a garrison of Parliament in time of military strife.

> All know it was vigorously besieged by the arms of the parliament: at which siege, in sallies, conflicts, flights, pursuits, many fell in all the places

round it; and where they fell were buried; for every place, my Lord, is bur-
ial earth in war; and many, questionless of these rest unknown, whose bodies futurity shall discover.

What Aram was arguing was that as all the earth around us, including
caves, contains the skeletons of those who have died, and as brutal acts
have been performed against the bodies of the dead throughout the centuries, it is only reasonable to assume that no positive identification of a
particular person can be made.

Content that he had fully answered the major charges rendered against
him, Aram, in the next-to-last paragraph of his address, tried to show that
the prosecution's case failed to reach the level of certainty needed for
conviction:

As to the circumstances that have been raked together; I have nothing to
observe; but that all circumstances whatsoever are precarious, and have
been but too frequently found lamentably fallible; even the strongest have
failed. They may rise to the utmost degree of probability; yet are they but
probability still. Why need I name to your Lordship the two Harrisons
recorded in Dr. Howel, who both suffered from circumstances, because of
the sudden disappearance of their lodger, who was in credit, had contracted
debts, borrowed money, and went off unseen, and returned again a great
many years after their execution? Why name the intricate affairs of Jacques
de Moulin, under King Charles II, related by a gentleman who was counsel for the crown? And why the unhappy Coleman, who suffered innocent,
tho' convicted upon positive evidence, and whose children perished for
want, because the world uncharitably believed the father guilty? Why
mention the perjury of Smith, incautiously admitted King's evidence; who
to screen himself, equally accused Faircloth and Loveday of the murder of
Dun; the first of whom in 1749, was executed at Winchester; and Loveday
was about to suffer at Reading, had not Smith been proved perjured, to the
satisfaction of the court, by the surgeon of the General hospital?

The concluding passage of the speech contained a summary of each of the
arguments Aram had presented, and a statement expressing his wish that
the presiding Lordship and members of the jury would make a decision
based upon "candour," "justice," and "humanity."

Jefferson's bold assertion that Aram's self-defense was "the finest
thing . . . which the English language had produced" was overdrawn.
But that the address may be regarded as a splendid example of English
eloquence seems unmistakable. It appears to have met the standards Jefferson had set (as discussed in chapters 2 through 4); and it conformed
to the three principles outlined in the present chapter on legal discourse.

Aram, as we saw, began his speech with a moving allusion to the moral precepts that had marked his life and to the state of his health at the time of the murder. Following this attempt to identify with his audience, he proceeded to the presentation of his arguments and supporting data. In doing this, he made effective use of cause-to-effect reasoning, of relevant historical examples that had the characteristics of precedents, and of refutational strategies. In general, all the elements of argumentation advocated by Jefferson—experience, testimony, analogy, and calculation of probabilities— were present; so, too, were the appeals to the affections. The conclusion combined a summary of all the major arguments with a climactic appeal calling for a just and fair verdict based on the evidence and the rules of law.

From Jefferson's perspective, another telling part of Aram's speech was his use of language. The words were carefully chosen symbols that were appropriate and perspicuous; the sentences included an excellent mixture of declarative and interrogative statements; and the overall style was copious. Because the language, moreover, was characterized by the frequent use of examples that were graphic in their descriptions, Aram successfully created what the late Chaim Perelman called "presence." In Jefferson's opinion, the overall style epitomized the kind of sublimity and elevation that legal eloquence at its highest demands. The content, structure, and style of the self-defense, it would appear, were the result of an address that grew out of a well-researched legal brief that made use of all the available means of persuasion. It was for these reasons, plus the address's brevity (only about two thousand words long), that Aram's presentation, according to Jefferson, represented a landmark case of what legal eloquence can become.

Although we concur with Jefferson's praiseworthy analysis of Aram's speech, it should be noted that it was an evaluation based on a legal defense as a work of art, such as a literary composition. What Jefferson did was to examine the quality of the content, the organizational structure, and the style of Aram's defense without any consideration of the outcome of the case. This approach led him to conclude that Aram's address constituted a model of legal eloquence that should be emulated. But when the concept of effect as seen in the decision is introduced, the judge of this speech would have to deal with the issues of guilt and innocence with respect to Aram's role in the murder. Had Jefferson read the full account of the trial in the *Annual Register* for the year 1759 (and it does not appear that he did), he would have become aware of these facts:

(1) Aram was found guilty of the murder of Clark, and sentenced to death.

(2) On the day following his sentence, Aram confessed to two clergy-men that he had murdered Clark.

(3) Aram's motive for doing so, he said, was his belief that Clark was having an affair with Aram's wife.

(4) The editor of the *Annual Register* asserted that Aram's guilt was "beyond all doubt."

(5) Prior to the date of his scheduled execution, Aram attempted, but failed, to commit suicide in his cell.

Because the five facts cited above are criteria that should be a part of the evaluation of Aram's legal defense, it is clear that he violated the principles of Jefferson's philosophy of virtue as discussed in chapter 2. By murdering Clark, however justified he perceived himself to be, Aram showed an attitude of hatred and revenge, rather than of love, toward his neighbor. Moreover, in denying in his speech that he had committed the unlawful act, he not only lied, but did so under oath. As a result, Aram, in defending himself, failed to achieve the level of private and public good.

We do not know for sure why Jefferson either accidentally overlooked or deliberately ignored the fact of Aram's guilt. What we do know from a letter he wrote to Abraham Small in 1814, recommending that Aram's address be incorporated into a new volume of speeches being prepared by Small, is that Jefferson's initial knowledge of Aram's rhetorical effort on this occasion came from a copy sent to him by a student. In this correspondence, there were no references to the decision rendered in the trial. Jefferson gave the following explanation: "I send you this copy which was taken for me by a school-boy, replete with errors of punctuation, or orthography, and sometimes substitutions of one word for another. It would be better to recur to the Annual Register itself for correctness, where also I think are stated the circumstances of the case. . . ."[43]

What Jefferson, perhaps unconsciously, taught us in this rhetorical episode involving legal discourse is that a speech viewed in isolation as a work of art will produce a different conclusion than one that also focuses on the decision that was rendered in a case.

# Historical Writing

While residing in Paris in the summer of 1786, Jefferson wrote to his grandson, giving him suggestions on readings he should undertake in preparation for his future professional career. When he turned to the discipline of history, he noted that it should be studied in the afternoon, using a chronological approach to show its evolutionary nature. One should begin reading in this area, he said, by examining the works of the Greek and Roman historians. This should then be followed by a careful perusal of Gibbon's *Decline and Fall of the Roman Empire*, which constitutes a useful transition to the study of English and American history.[44] In numerous other letters, he was more specific in identifying a group of influential authors and their works. Of particular relevance, he noted, were the writings of Herodotus and Thucydides in the Greek period; of Livy, Sallust, and Tacitus in the Roman era; and of such modern historians as Voltaire, Hume, and Robertson.[45]

Because the works of these historians, along with those of significant others, were a part of Jefferson's library,[46] he had easy access to them not only during his legal and political career but in his retirement years as well.[47] From these readings, combined with his own firsthand observations of events and people who helped bring them about, he forged a philosophy of historical writing that was consistent with his ideas on discourse. It was a philosophy, in short, that emphasized three rhetorical guidelines.

First, he asserted that *historical writing focuses on significant themes, events, and characters for the purpose of instructing and motivating readers on issues that promote personal and public good.* The affirmation of this principle was rooted in Jefferson's theory of moral philosophy and his admiration for the classical tradition. With considerable pleasure he could see how Herodotus and Thucydides had constructed their histories around powerful issues, episodes, and people. Instead of concentrating on minute details,[48] they opted to describe the nature, causes, and consequences of the Persian War and the Peloponnesian War, and their subsequent effects on the philosophy of democracy and the welfare of society.[49] A similar pattern, he also observed, was followed by Livy, Sallust, and Tacitus, who dealt with the grandeur of Rome.

What made these writers so appealing to Jefferson was their abiding faith in the belief that the principal task of historical writing is to convey the message of virtue. This conviction led them to conclude that it was their duty to provide examples of influential men who in leadership roles exemplified either ethically sound qualities and actions, or revealed traits that were morally reprehensible. The former, they argued, were worthy of emulation; the latter, by contrast, were fit only to be condemned by posterity.[50] It was primarily for this reason that he preferred reading the ancient historians. In

adhering to this practice, he confessed that the Roman period he loved often featured evil leaders such as Tarquin, Catiline, and Caligula. Fortunately,
however, when Livy, Sallust, and Tacitus delineated their lives, they were severely censured as evil men who should be consigned to infamy—a fate, he
anticipated, that would be experienced by King George III and Napoleon
when future historians accept the challenge to describe their character and
their deeds.[51]

The historical writer who, in Jefferson's opinion, most clearly recognized the importance of this first requirement of historical writing was
Tacitus. Describing him "as the first writer in the world without a single
exception," he praised his works as "a compound of history & morality
of which we have no other example. . . ."[52] Although this claim of Tacitus's superiority and uniqueness may be open to debate, the classical historians as a whole would endorse Jefferson's assessment of the unmistakable value that students would experience if they read historical works
containing a virtue-centered message on vitally significant subjects and
events:

> History by apprising (students) of the past will enable them to judge of the
> future; it will avail them of the experience of other times and other na-
> tions; it will qualify them as judges of the actions and designs of men; it will
> enable them to know ambition under every disguise it may assume; and
> knowing it, to defeat its views.[53]

Jefferson also was fully aware that the moral lesson historical writing
was obligated to teach could not be achieved unless *history relies on reasoning and evidence designed to produce truth*. He was impressed by the classical historians' emphasis on the need for truth and its relationship to
high-probability arguments utilizing persuasive evidence and inferences.
In each instance, beginning with Herodotus and concluding with Tacitus,
he was appreciative of the authors' claims that they had sought to use the
best available data, including reliable documents, testimonies, and personal eyewitness accounts to verify their claims.[54] Moreover, he liked the
way they discounted some purported evidence, especially that based on
myths, tradition, and obvious prejudices.[55]

Jefferson also had to be pleased with the conclusions drawn by two of
his favorite modern authors—Lord Bolingbroke and Hugh Blair. Among
many statements made by Bolingbroke on the need for historical accuracy
is the following claim that Jefferson copied into his *Literary Commonplace
Book*: ". . .Common sense requires that every thing proposed to the understanding should be accomplished with such proofs as the nature of it

can furnish."[56] Blair reached a similar conclusion: It is, he said, the office "of an Historian to record truth for the instruction of mankind."[57]

But far more important than any of these sources he had studied was Jefferson's own philosophy of argument, which gave a high priority to the use of factual data that could not be easily refuted. Historical writing, therefore, which contains errors, whether by accident or by design, must be corrected or, if not, be discarded as unreliable reading material.

Four instances show how strongly Jefferson was dedicated to this belief. The first two represented his attempts to collaborate, while living in Paris, with two French historians who, in writing segments on American history, asked him to respond to a series of queries concerning the accuracy of what they had already written and now planned to write.[58] Patiently and meticulously, Jefferson delivered responses shaped by documents, proceedings, and notes he had in his file; and, because many of the events were recent and indelibly imprinted upon his mind, he drew also upon his personal experiences and memory. His primary motivation in these collaborative endeavors was to make certain that Demeunier's essay and Soulés' history would be as accurate as possible in their portrayal of the past and present status of the United States as an emerging nation. As a result of his effort, numerous statements and claims were modified or deleted; and, in some cases, what Jefferson had written was inserted, causing an expansion of pages that went beyond the author's original intent.[59] Even so, he was not altogether content with the published versions because some factual errors remained.[60]

The third episode revealing the depth of Jefferson's concern for historical accuracy took place in France. As he read a book review in the *Journal de Paris* of a volume that dealt in part with the American Revolution, he was troubled, first of all, by the critic's attack on the reliability of contemporary historical accounts in general; and, second, by the strikingly erroneous claim that John Dickinson of Pennsylvania was primarily responsible for gaining the passage of the Declaration of Independence.[61] These two contentions created for Jefferson a rhetorical situation requiring an immediate response.

Almost at once, therefore, he sat down at his desk and addressed a letter to the editor pointing out in strongly worded language what he thought of the review. "If contemporary histories" are automatically presumed to be "false," he contended, "What will future compilations be?" For without the availability of eyewitness descriptions from those who participated in and observed important happenings, he argued, a historian in a later period would be at a great disadvantage in trying to recreate a scene.[62]

While making no direct allusion to the histories of Thucydides or Tacitus, he knew that these historical writers had bolstered the authenticity of their descriptions of events and of participants in their stories by incorporating into their narratives compelling evidence based upon what they had seen and heard in the scenes of action. In the same manner, Jefferson also felt qualified to draw upon his firsthand experiences to set the record straight on what happened during the debates on the Declaration of Independence. After explaining each major detail in the debate process and in the voting that ensued, he demonstrated the fallacy in the reviewer's claim that Dickinson was the principal force in securing the adoption of the Declaration. He phrased his refutation in these words: "In the evening of the 4th they (the debates) were finally closed, and the instrument approved by an unanimous vote and signed by every member, *except Mr. Dickinson.*"[63]

In the end, Jefferson decided not to forward his letter of protest to the editor. Whether or not this decision was the result of a subsiding anger or of a fear that he would be identified as a defensive respondent whose own great contribution to the Declaration had been ignored by the reviewer cannot be fully determined. That he wrote the letter and preserved it in his personal file, however, is further proof of his commitment to the proposition that historical writing is duty-bound to uphold the truth.[64]

The fourth and most compelling instance emphasizing Jefferson's strong commitment to the idea that historical writing demands the use of argumentation based on the standards of truth and objectivity occurred in his analysis of John Marshall's *History of George Washington*—a five-volume study that Marshall produced in the three-year period between 1804 and 1807. Jefferson's critique, appearing in *The Anas*, was written in 1815 or 1816. Much of the data he used in supporting his claims, however, came from the comprehensive notes he had taken while serving as secretary of state. It was during these formative years in establishing the American government that he worked closely with Washington, thus giving him the firsthand experience he needed to know and appreciate the president's overall political and ethical philosophy and the nature of his character and personality.

The evaluation began with the argument that Marshall had created a historical account that utilized inadequate proof to sustain his claims. Instead of making persuasive and responsible use of primary, authenticated source material from documents assembled by Washington, including handwritten statements by his own pen, Marshall, according to Jefferson, relied on raw, unexamined files that failed to distinguish between "suspicions and certainties, rumors and realities," and "facts and falsehoods"; as a result, he treated all of the information on Washington, his contemporaries, and relevant events as if each item in the files had equal historical significance and accuracy. "From such a congeries," added Jefferson, "history may be made to wear any hue, with which the passions of the compiler, royalist or republican, may chuse to taint it."

Jefferson's first claim, maintaining that Marshall's *History* did not represent truthfulness, was matched by a second damaging contention that pointed out the work's failure to be objective and fair. Unfortunately, in Jefferson's opinion, the "hue" that Marshall painted reflected an unmistakable Federalist bias that could be seen throughout the pages of each volume. It was a "hue" that cast a shadow over the arms "of the patriot warriors" whose heroic actions were motivated, not by their self-interest, but by the holy cause that propelled them in their battle for "human rights." When Marshall observed the political contest waged in the 1790s, his prejudices prevented him from seeing a great constitutional struggle grounded in principle in which two contenders to win the hearts and souls of the American people sought to determine whether the national government should be "republican" or "kingly" in nature. A reader of the *History*, Jefferson asserted,

> would suppose the republican party (who were in truth endeavoring to keep the government within the line of the Constitution, and prevent it's being monarchised in practice) were a mere set of grumblers, and disorganizers, satisfied with no government, without fixed principles of any, and, like a British parliamentary opposition, gaping after loaves and fishes, and ready to change principles, as well as position, at any time, with their adversaries.

Marshall's opus, concluded Jefferson, was a classic failure because it violated an essential requirement of historical writing—the need to use sound reasoning and evidence expressed with an attitude of fairness, and objectivity. He then speculated on what would have happened if Washington himself had written a history of the period using the same materials available to Marshall. Had he done so, "it would have been a conspicuous monument of the integrity of his mind, the soundness of his judgment, and it's powers of discernment between truth & falsehood; principles & pretensions."[65] In other words, it would have been a history inspired by virtue.

In taking such a firm stand on the need for accuracy and responsibility in the presentation of historical data, Jefferson became an ally of Cicero who in his *De Oratore* made the following claim phrased in interrogative form: "For who does not know history's first law to be that an author must not dare to tell anything but the truth?" But equally important, he was also in agreement with the next question Cicero asked: Who does not know "there must be no suggestion of partiality anywhere in his (the historian's) writings? Nor of malice?"[66] Both men knew that needless prejudice on the part of historical writers is an enemy of truth.

Notwithstanding the overriding importance of the first two elements of historical writing as discussed in the previous analysis, Jefferson became convinced that a third criterion must also be met if such an author were to obtain maximum effectiveness in his art. *It is necessary*, he therefore argued, *for a historical writer to channel the message of virtue through the use of a clear, coherent, and unified organizational pattern; and a plain, concise, and vivid style.*[67] The question of sequence for this type of discourse was easy to discern, since history requires a chronological order in which each story or event has a natural beginning, middle, and end. Thus Jefferson endorsed Hugh Blair's warning that if a historian neglects this organizational structure so that the narrative might be "rendered" more "agreeable," appropriate unity and coherence cannot be maintained.[68] The same negative result would occur if tangential remarks or needless digressions interrupt a description of an event.

But what concerned Jefferson most when a historical writer breaks the time sequence is the effect that such an action might have on an author's arguments in support of a particular position on a question. To illustrate this premise, he argued that Hume's *History of England* was significantly influenced by his decision to begin his multivolume study with a treatment of the Stuarts. Instead of moving forward at this point, Jefferson complained, Hume then went back to the Tudors, and then to "the Saxon and Norman periods. . . ." Such a violation of the chronological order, concluded Jefferson, was not only unwarranted but harmful.[69]

A historical writer's style was similarly important to Jefferson. Skill in the use of this rhetorical element, he thought, was a trademark of the classical historians. Because the Greek and Roman authors were both theorists and practitioners in the art of rhetoric,[70] they had the talent and training to infuse their stories with informative and moving appeals to the understanding and the imagination. As Jefferson reflected on the beauty and power of the Greek and Latin languages, he strongly urged the students he was advising to read the "original," not translated texts.[71] To do so, he said on a number of occasions, would be a "sublime luxury."[72] Moreover, it was the only way that one could fully appreciate the spirit of

Tacitus; and, without knowing this spirit, he noted, a reader would not be able to recognize "the solidity of his matter, his brevity, & his fondness for point & antithesis. . . ."[73] Nor would he sense Tacitus's ability to write in such a "delightful," "pithy" manner that he never omitted "a necessary word, nor uses an unnecessary one."[74]

When Jefferson relied on language usage as a criterion to measure the worth of several histories of Virginia, he found these writings to be deficient even though the content seemed to be acceptable. He faulted Captain John Smith's history for its use of a "barbarous and uncouth" style; and criticized William Stith's work for its "inelegant," and tasteless use of language.[75] He was even more severe in describing Marshall's *Life of Washington* as being "loose, vague," and "frothy."[76]

Since the primary challenge facing the historical writer, according to Jefferson, is to convey the message of virtue, such a rhetor might occasionally use a discourse strategy that goes beyond an effective organizational structure and style. One such technique was that employed by the classical historians—the incorporation of speeches in the narrative. First introduced by Thucydides, this method was designed to break the monotony of the historical narrative by permitting an orator, during a crucial moment involving a potential victory or defeat on the battlefield or in the political assembly, to bring his followers together and stir them with a powerful patriotic appeal. In explaining the use of this strategy of channeling a message, Thucydides observed:

> With reference to the speeches in this history, some were delivered before the war began, others while it was going on; some I heard myself, others I got from various quarters; it was in all cases difficult to carry them word for word in one's memory, so my habit has been to make the speakers say what was in my opinion demanded of them by the various occasions, of course adhering as closely as possible to the general sense of what they really said.[77]

As an admirer of Thucydides, and as a student of rhetoric, Jefferson could not help but be moved by Thucydides' remarkable re-creation of Pericles' famous Funeral Oration. In this celebrated address, described by John R. Finley as "probably the greatest short analysis of the strength of democracy" ever delivered,[78] Pericles began with a tribute to "our ancestors" for their "valour," and then praised the democratic form of government they adopted as an example of the creative genius of the Athenian people. With this emphasis on "equal justice to all," he said, Athens has opened its "city to the world," and has provided an example of how discussion and debate, instead of being "a stumbling block" to decision making on crucial issues, is "an indispensable preliminary to any wise action at all." He then praised the Athenian virtues of courage, generosity, liberality, optimism, justice, and steadfastness—moral characteristics that had instilled in the hearts of the people a willingness to die rather than submit to tyranny.[79] This galvanic appeal not only gave comfort to the parents of the dead soldiers who were being honored on this memorable occasion, but provided for later readers, such as Jefferson, an encouraging endorsement of his philosophy of republicanism.

Jefferson also found inspiration in the writings of Livy who, like Thucydides, was a devoted student of rhetoric.[80] He was impressed by Livy's talent to stir a reader's imagination and passions by his insertions of orations into a historical narrative. A classic illustration of this appears in Book III of Livy's history. The speaker in this instance, as we saw in an earlier context, was the Roman consul Titus Quinctius who was gravely concerned by the lackadaisical attitude displayed by the Romans who, when confronted by the enemy at the gates of their city, seemed content to prefer peace rather than justice and liberty. In his effort to persuade his fellow citizens to put aside their indifference and fight for their rights and survival, Titus Quinctius ignored his own self-interest and presented a moving appeal directed at the social affection of patriotic love for Rome.[81] Jefferson responded warmly to Livy's decision to incorporate this specimen of eloquence into his narrative account of a significant historical event. By taking this action, Jefferson felt, Livy had blended a powerful message of virtue based on the public good with an "elevated style" that reached the level of the sublime. Not surprisingly, therefore, he recorded this speech in his *Literary Commonplace Book* as a brilliant example of how a historical writer sought to lead his audience in their "pursuit of happiness."

As a general rule, Jefferson approved the use of speeches in a historical narrative as long as these addresses were not presented in the same way with respect to arguments and style; for to do this would result in undue monotony. One historian who used speeches as part of his narrative, and in doing so presented an interesting and comprehensive story, was the French author Carlo Guiseppo Guglielmo Botta in his history of the American Revolution.[82] But those historians, in Jefferson's opinion, who made the most persuasive use of orations as part of their narratives were Thucydides and the Roman authors Livy, Tacitus, and Sallust.[83]

When we reflect on Jefferson's perspectives on the forms of public oral and written discourse, we can see that he, like Blair, was convinced that historical writing, political communication, philosophical and religious discourse, and legal eloquence were important parts of rhetorical philosophy and practice. Moreover, both men, molded by what they had read and experienced, concluded correctly that all of these discourse forms were ideal communication media to transmit the message of virtue.

# Notes

1. The full source is as follows: *The Development of American Philosophy: A Book of Readings* (New York: Houghton Mifflin Company, 1940), 76–81.
2. April 21, 1803, *Writings*, 1122–1126.
3. July 5, 1814, in Cappon, 2: 430–34.
4. April 11, 1823, in ibid., 2: 591–94.
5. Jefferson was elected to the society in 1780. One year later, he was appointed to the position of counselor. From 1796 until 1815, he served as president of the society even though, during his tenure, he performed his duties as vice president and president of the United States. It should be noted that this society focused not only on traditional philosophy as being discussed here but also on such fields of study as anthropology and archaeology, all grouped under the term "natural philosophy."
6. See the following letters: Thomas Rodney to TJ, September 1790, in Boyd, 17: 548; TJ to Monsieur Cabanis, July 12, 1803, in L&B, 10: 404; and TJ to Adams, March 14, 1820, in Cappon, 2: 562.
7. TJ to Elbridge Gerry, January 26, 1799, in L&B, 10: 78.
8. TJ to John Rutledge Jr., September 9, 1788, in Boyd, 13: 594.
9. TJ to Adams, March 14, 1820, in Cappon, 2: 562.
10. TJ to William Short, October 31, 1819, in *Writings*, 1430–1431; and to Short, August 4, 1820, in ibid., 1436–1440.
11. TJ to Adams, July 5, 1814, in Cappon, 2: 432. Jefferson told Adams in this letter: "Having more leisure there (at Poplar Forest) than here (Monticello) for reading, I amused myself with reading seriously Plato's republic. I am wrong however, in calling it amusement, for it was the heaviest task work I ever went through. I had occasionally before taken up some of his other works, but scarcely ever had the patience to go through a whole dialogue." Ibid.
12. Ibid., 432–33.
13. Ibid., 433.
14. TJ to William Short, August 4, 1820, in *Writings*, 1436.
15. TJ to Adams, July 5, 1814, in Cappon, 2: 433.
16. Charles B. Sanford, *The Religious Life of Thomas Jefferson* (Charlottesville: University Press of Virginia, 1984, 1992). Another book on this theme that is similarly instructive is the following: Edwin S. Gaustad, *Sworn on the Alter of God: A Religious Biography of Thomas Jefferson* (Grand Rapids, Mich.: Eerdmans, 1996).
17. TJ to P. H . Wendover, March 13, 1815, in L&B, 14: 279–82.
18. Ibid.
19. November 12, 1816, in Ford, 12: 43.
20. September 18, 1813, in L&B, 13: 43.

21. See his Account Book listings for January and May 1805, and April 1806. Also, note the letter from Thomas Jefferson Randolph to Henry S. Randall, in Randall, 3: 672.

22. TJ to Reverend Isaac Story, December 5, 1801, in Washington, 4: 422.

23. Jefferson was extremely critical of the priests and theologians for what he perceived to be their harmful influence. "My opinion," he once said, "is that there would never have been an infidel, if there had never been a priest." TJ to Mrs. Harrison Smith, August 6, 1810, in L&B, 15: 60. On another occasion, he noted: "It is the speculations of crazy theologists which have made a Babel of a religion the most moral and sublime ever preached to man. . . ." To Ezra Stiles, June 25, 1819, in L&B, 15: 204. He also felt that much of the antagonism the priests had for him was owing to the role he had played in producing "the Act of Virginia for establishing religious freedom." Letter to Mrs. Smith cited above.

24. TJ to Ezra Stiles, June 25, 1819, in L&B, 15: 204. Also see letter to George Logan, November 12, 1816, in Ford, 12: 43.

25. September 18, 1813, in L&B, 13: 377–78.

26. TJ to George Logan, November 12, 1816, in Ford, 12: 43; to John Adams, January 11, 1817, in ibid., 48–49; and to Ezra Stiles cited above, n. 23.

27. TJ to Mrs. Harrison Smith, August 16, 1810, in L&B, 15: 60.

28. Jefferson wrote to Miles King in 1814, saying that people of different denominations upon entering the "gate" of heaven, will "leave those badges of schism behind, and find (themselves) united in those principles only in which God has united us all." September 26, 1814, in L&B, 14: 198. Moreover, he closed a letter to James Smith in 1822 with these words: "And with the assurance of all my good will to Unitarian and Trinitarian . . . accept for yourself that of my entire respect." December 8, 1822, in ibid., 15: 410.

29. To Thomas Turpin, February 5, 1769, in Boyd, 1: 3–25.

30. To John Garland Jefferson, June 11, 1790, in Boyd, 16: 480.

31. Ibid., 481–82.

32. Ford, 9: 480–81; and ibid., 480n to 485n.

33. TJ to Thomas Mann Randolph Jr., August 27, 1786, in *Writings*, 860–61.

34. See the following two letters: To Dr. Thomas Cooper, January 16, 1814, in L&B, 14: 54–63; and to Dabney Terrell, February 26, 1821, in ibid., 15: 318–22.

35. Minor-Moore letter, in Ford, 9: 481n–485n.

36. August 11, 1787, in Boyd, 12: 21.

37. In 1787, Jefferson wrote to Thomas Mann Randolph Jr., "I would therefore propose not only the study, but the practice of the law for some time, to possess yourself of the habit of public speaking." July 6, 1787, in Boyd, 11: 558. Six years later he gave this recommendation to Francis Eppes to pass on to his son, Jack: "The want of this habit (public speaking) has sometimes struck such a panic into a new orator as that he has never got over it. This too is the only method by which a student can discover his own powers, and decide for himself his future enterprizes." March 17, 1793, in Boyd, 25: 396.

38. This collection of cases, assembled and edited by Jefferson, was published three years after his death (Charlottesville: F. Carr, 1829).

39. In commenting on Jefferson's defense of precedents in his *Bolling v. Bolling* case, Edward Dumbauld noted that: "Jefferson bursts forth into an eloquent encomium in favor of *stare decisis*." *Thomas Jefferson and the Law* (Norman: University of Oklahoma Press, 1978), 102.

40. June 1, 1780, in Boyd, 15: 586. "The importance that TJ attached to the bound volume sent by Col. Digges," observes Boyd, "is understandable: no other legal brief of his except the Batture Case seems to have involved such a thorough and meticulous preparation." Ibid., 586n. Having examined carefully the two ensuing sources, we agree with Boyd's assessment: Bernard Schwartz, Barbara Wilcie Kern, and R. B. Bernstein, eds., *Thomas Jefferson and Bolling v. Bolling: Law and the Legal Profession in Revolutionary America* (San Marino, Calif., and New York: Henry E. Huntington Library and New York University School of Law, 1997); and Dumbauld, *Thomas Jefferson and the Law*, 94–120. The first of these two works is a lengthy volume, containing a thoroughly developed introduction, and the complete arguments of the opposing lawyers, George Wythe and Thomas Jefferson.

41. May 20, 1814, in L&B, 14: 137.

42. A description of the rhetorical situation, a transcript of Aram's speech, and the aftermath of the trial may be found in *The Annual Register, or a View of the History, Politics, and Literature of the Year 1759* (London, 1802), 351–62.

43. TJ to Abraham Small, 1814, L&B, 14: 137.

44. TJ to Thomas Mann Randolph Jr., August 27, 1786, in Boyd, 10: 305–309.

45. The following letters are representative: TJ to Robert Skipwith, August 3, 1771, in Boyd, 1: 78–79; TJ to Peter Carr, August 19, 1785, in L&B, 5: 84–85; and TJ to Thomas Elder, June 26, 1786, in Boyd, 10: 72.

46. Included in his library were these listings: A 1761 edition of Herodotus; four separate editions of Thucydides; three of Livy; four of Sallust; three of Julius Caesar; and two of Tacitus. Sowerby, *Catalogue of the Library of Thomas Jefferson*, 1.

47. Even after he sold most of his original library holdings to the Library of Congress, he continued throughout the following years to purchase additional works of the classical historians. For further information on Jefferson's library, see Douglas L. Wilson, *Jefferson's Books* (Charlottesville: Thomas Jefferson Memorial Foundation–Monticello Monograph Series, 1996).

48. Tacitus observed that his purpose was "not to relate at length every motion, but only such as were conspicuous for excellence or notorious for infamy." *Annals*, 3.65, in Moses Hadas, ed., *Complete Works of Tacitus* (New York: Modern Library, 1942).

49. In the opening statement of his work on the Persian Wars, Herodotus asserted: "These are the researches of Herodotus of Halicarnassus, which he publishes, in the hope of thereby preserving from decay the remembrance of what men have done, and of preventing the great and wonderful actions of the Greeks and the Barbarians from losing their need for glory; and withal to put on record what were their grounds of feud." F. R. B. Godolphin, ed., *The Persian Wars* (New York: Modern Library, 1942), 3. Edith Hamilton, moreover, has observed that Thucydides' "*History of the Peloponnesian War* is really a treatise on war, its causes and its effects." *The Greek Way* (New York: Modern Library, 1942), 186.

50. Tacitus put this point succinctly when he said: "This I regard as history's highest function, to let no worthy action be uncommemmorated, and to hold out the reprobation of posterity as a terror to evil words and deeds." *Annals*, 3.65.

51. TJ to William Duane, April 4, 1813, in L&B, 13: 230.

52. TJ to Anne Carey Bankhead, December 8, 1808, in Betts and Bear, *The Family Letters of Thomas Jefferson*, 370.

53. *Notes on the State of Virginia*, 148.

54. The following statement by Thucydides illustrates this point: "So little pains do the vulgar take in the investigation of truth, accepting readily the first story that comes to hand. On the whole, however, the conclusions I have drawn from the proofs quoted may, I believe, safely be relied on." *The Peloponnesian War*, Bk. I. 21.

55. Tacitus, who was Jefferson's favorite classical historian, made the following observation which TJ could endorse: "Hence my purpose is to relate a few facts about Augustus— more particularly his last acts, then the reign of Tiberius, and all which follows, without either bitterness or partiality, from any motives to which I am far removed." *Annals*, Bk. I. 1. This is an interesting statement in view of Tacitus' friendship with Augustus.

56. *LCB*, 51–52.

57. Blair, *Lectures on Rhetoric and Belles Lettres*, 2: 259.

58. For a list of those queries, along with an extensive background analysis, see Boyd's accounts: "Jefferson's Comments on François Soulés' *Histoire*, 10: 364–83; and "The Article on the United States" in the *Encyclopedie Methodique*, written by M. DeMeunier, in 10: 3–65.

59. TJ's contribution to the article was so extensive that the essay on Virginia consumed eighty-nine pages, more space than that which Demeunier had devoted to England, France, or Russia. Boyd, 10: 9. Much of the added material came from the *Notes on the State of Virginia*, see Ibid., 11.

60. These errors were owing largely to Demeunier's failure to submit the final copy of the manuscript to Jefferson. ibid., 10.

61. The letter appears in Ford, 5: 333–37; and in Boyd, 12: 61–64.

62. During the unfolding of this controversial episode, TJ wrote to Thomas Mann Randolph Jr., saying: "An author who writes of his own times, or of times near his own, presents in his own ideas and manner the best picture of the moment of which he writes." August 27, 1786, in Boyd, 10: 307.

63. Ford, 5: 337.

64. It should be pointed out that even though he signed the name "An American" as the author, he was aware that a number of the French literati knew that he was the creator of the Declaration of Independence.

65. *The Anas*, in Ford, 1: 165–67. Although it is fair to say that Jefferson's critique was influenced in part by his philosophy of republicanism, there is convincing evidence that others have held a similarly negative view about the weakness of Marshall's *History*. On July 3, 1813, Adams wrote to Jefferson saying: Marshall's work was "written to make money: and fashioned and finished, to sell high in the London Market." He then suggested that the *History* "is a Mausolaeum, 100 feet square at the base, and 200 feet high. It will be as durable, as the monuments of the Washington benevolent Societies." Cappon, 2: 349. Nor has it fared better in the modern period. Daniel Boorstin labeled the study a "resounding failure," one that is "dull, laborious, rambling, and second hand. . . ." *The Americans: The National Experience* (New York: Random House, 1965), 342. Similar negative comments on Marshall's *History* may be found in Joanne B. Freeman, "Slander, Poison, Whispers, and Fame: Jefferson's Anas' and Political Gossip in the Early Republic," *Journal of the Early Republic* 15 (spring 1995), 26–27, and 53–54.

66. *De Oratore*, II. xv. 62–63.

67. This rhetorical-centered criterion, he believed, was a trademark of the writings of the classical historians.

68. Blair, *Lectures on Rhetoric and Belles Lettres*, 2: 265.

69. TJ to William Duane, August 12, 1810, in *Writings*, 1228.

70. We have already observed Thucydides' re-creation of Pericles' Funeral Oration. In addition, Quintilian describes Livy's speeches as being "eloquent beyond description; so admirably adapted in all that is said both to the circumstances and the speaker; and as regards the emotions, especially the more pleasing of them, I may sum up by saying that no historian has ever depicted them to greater perfection." X. 1. 101–102. Finally, it may be observed that Tacitus wrote an influential "Dialogue on Oratory." See his *Complete Works*, 735–69.

71. Observe the letter to Peter Carr, August 19, 1785, in L&B, 5: 84.

72. TJ to Joseph Priestley, January 27, 1800, in *Writings*, 1072.

73. TJ to Charles Clay, May 1, 1813, in Sowerby, *Catalogue of the Library of Thomas Jefferson*, 1: 38.

74. TJ to Thomas Jefferson Randolph, December 7, 1808, in Betts and Bear, *The Family Letters of Thomas Jefferson*, 369.

75. *Notes on the State of Virginia*, 177.

76. TJ to John Adams, August 22, 1813, in Cappon, 2: 369.

77. *The Complete Writings of Thucydides*, 14.

78. Ibid., xiv.

79. Ibid., 102–109.

80. Quintilian noted that Livy wrote to his son urging him to "read Cicero, and Demosthenes and then such orators as most resembled them." *Institutio Oratoria*, X. 1. 39. As much as Jefferson admired Cicero as an essayist and philosopher, he did not appreciate his oratory.

81. B. O. Foster, tr, *Livy* 14 vols. (Cambridge: Harvard University Press, 1961), Bk. III. lxviii. 8.

82. TJ to John Adams, August 10, 1815, in Cappon, 2: 452.

83. TJ to John Wayles Eppes, January 17, 1810, in Ford, 11: 1–29.

# PART TWO

# Jefferson as Practitioner of the Rhetoric of Virtue

# CHAPTER NINE

~

# Conversationalist and Letter Writer

As the year of 1791 began, one of the leading political questions facing the new American government was "the French protest against the tonnage acts of 1789 and 1790 and its impact on the political contests that were dividing the government. . . ."[1] Among those leaders who had a special interest in this issue were Jefferson, then serving as secretary of state, and Madison, who was a congressman from Virginia. Convinced that the time had arrived for immediate action, Jefferson wrote to the man who had become his greatest political collaborator: "I shall see you at dinner, and be glad to exchange further thoughts on the subject, which is an important one."[2] Regrettably, as Boyd has stated, there is no record of what took place in that dialogue. But this incident does suggest that Jefferson was a man of words who relied on private discourse, in the form of conversation and letter writing, to deal with problems arising in the rhetorical situation. What strategies he used in each of these communication areas is the burden of this chapter.

## Conversational Discourse

Based in part on what Jefferson described in his own writings, and on what his contemporaries recorded in their written recollections, a picture emerges of his conversational experiences and practices. What we learn from these data is that he was remarkably successful in implementing his own ideas regarding the nature of effective conversation.

191

His first principle of effective conversational discourse, we may recall, is that a discussant should be well informed about the subject being considered and understand the nature of argument and its relationship to virtue. Jefferson was well equipped to fulfill this requirement because of his enriching personal experiences and penchant for reading. In his formative years in Williamsburg, he was a regular member of a group of four—that included Dr. William Small, George Wythe, and Governor Fauquier—who freely exchanged ideas on public and private issues of the day. It was a heady experience for a young man who had not yet launched his career to take part in discussions with three of the most respected persons in Virginia in the 1760s. "To the habitual conversations on these occasions," he later recalled, "I owed much instruction."[3]

Jefferson's conversational practices in subsequent years were marked by a thorough knowledge of general and specific topics. Those who participated in dialogues with him commented on his "infinite information" and "sound judgment" as he spoke on such wide-ranging themes as natural philosophy, politics, belles lettres, public affairs, American history, and moral questions.[4] In addition, they liked his versatility in balancing serious subjects with those that were light and entertaining. Daniel Webster explained the degree of impact which Jefferson's general knowledge had upon his contemporaries who sought to exchange ideas with him:

> . . . the extent of his acquirements, and, especially, the full store of revolutionary incidents which he possessed, and which he knew when and how to dispense rendered his abode in a high degree attractive to his admiring countrymen, while his public and scientific character drew toward him every intelligent and educated traveller from abroad. . . .[5]

This wealth of general information permitted Jefferson to speak authoritatively on a rich variety of specific topics in the arts and sciences. He was at home talking to Chastellux about the poems of Ossian; to Buffon about the nature of man and of lower animals; to Lafayette about emerging signs of republicanism in France; to Madison on preserving his notes of the Constitutional Convention's debates, and in mapping out rhetorical strategies to thwart what he saw as Hamilton's attempt to block the movement toward republicanism; to Benjamin Rush on the teachings of Jesus; and to a host of others in delineating the talents and characteristics of many of his prominent contemporaries.

After spending five days at Monticello in 1824, Webster listed several specific topics that commanded Jefferson's attention: "early anecdotes of revolutionary times"; "French society, politics, and literature such as they were when he was in France"; the developing University of Virginia; and "Greek" and "Anglo-Saxon" language, as well as "general literature."[6] Jefferson's expertise in these areas was well known to foreign travelers who visited him. Thus John Bernard, the English actor and author, observed that he "attempted to draw out his observations upon the period he had passed in France, where his official situation placed him in juxtaposition with the leading characters of the court, as well as most of the agents of the Revolution."[7]

Through Jefferson's effective use of informal reasoning and personal proof, he was able to transmit his ideas on virtue, which was the driving force in his discourse transactions. Bernard (who, like James Boswell, had the talent and memory to record comments he heard others utter in conversation), provided three examples revealing how his friend Jefferson when engaged in a dialogue could compress an argument into brief and concise terms.[8] When Bernard asked Jefferson to give his sentiments on Britain's decision to expatriate an aging Joseph Priestley, he responded:

> His antagonists think they have quenched his opinions by sending him to America, just as the pope imagined when he shut up Galileo in prison that he had compelled the world to stand still.

Jefferson was similarly precise and poignant in describing to Bernard that his strong attraction to science and literature was based on the positive effects they were capable of producing. In developing this argument, he said:

> I consider scientific knowledge to be that food which alone can enable the mental functions to acquire vigor and activity; but elegant literature as the wine that should invariably follow, because without it the mind would never rise to the full measure of its enjoyment, the power of sympathizing with itself, after sympathizing with Nature.

Even more telling were the words he used to compare the field of law with the subject of poetry. "I was bred," he noted, "to the law; that gave me a view of the dark side of humanity. Then I read poetry to qualify it with a gaze upon its bright side; and between the two extremes I have contrived through life to draw the due medium." After stating this philosophy of the golden mean, he added:

> And so, substituting history and biography for law, I would have every man form his own estimate of human nature, because it seems to me that precisely the same directing forces should subsist in the social as in the solar

system; there should be the same attractive or concentrating power in our hearts to draw us together qualifying the repelling impulse which we gain from our experience and reading.

These three arguments transcribed by Bernard feature a particular aspect of virtue as their underlying theme. The comments of the expatriation of Priestley represent support for the freedom of speech and research. The second claim that scientific knowledge and literature are intellectual companions, rather than two separate cultures of thought, demonstrates that these two fields of study, when joined together, strengthen the mind and produce pleasure. In stating, third, that poetry, history, biography, and law may unite through the power of argument in such a way that a high degree of probability may result in the social sphere, Jefferson was reaffirming his belief that practical reasoning is an important means of transmitting virtue in a persuasive and reliable manner.

There were other dimensions of Jefferson's use of informal reasoning in conversation that won the praise of eyewitnesses. Dr. Robley Dunglison, a University of Virginia professor and a respected physician, asserted that the data Jefferson offered in support of his claims were typically characterized by profundity, precision, and accuracy.[9] Additionally, Thomas Jefferson Randolph remembered with pleasure his grandfather's practice of utilizing anecdotes, of helping participants to resolve their differences on a contentious point, of providing information that was requested, and of inviting discussants who dialogued with him to feel free to scrutinize and evaluate "his own opinions."[10]

Another hallmark of Jefferson's conversational discourse was his constant awareness of the need to adjust his topics and arguments to the nature and background of each participant. As a result, he downplayed the subject of politics when speaking to his daughters. Moreover, when conversing with members of the literati, he often introduced the subjects of poetry, history, and philosophy. He was similarly adept in talking to mechanics, laborers, and farmers about their areas of interest. If these workers appeared to have a thorough grasp of their occupations, he "entered the information they gave, under appropriate heads, for reference, embodying thus a mass of facts upon the practical details of every-day life."[11]

Finally, he occasionally reserved an especially appealing method of reasoning for those "men of fertile and ingenious minds" who appeared to take pleasure in challenging particular propositions. To these persons, "he would sometimes suggest the opposite of the conclusion to which he desired them to come, then assent to the force of their objections, and thus lead them to convert themselves."[12]

Perhaps the most telling and memorable aspect of Jefferson's conversational discourse was the persuasive power of his personal proof. To most of those who knew and dialogued with him, he was perceived as a wise, fair, just, and benevolent man whose private and public life was marked by freedom from vice.[13] For the most part, therefore, they were inclined to agree with this assessment by Bernard: "His heart was warmed with a love for the whole human race; a *bonhomie* which fixed your attention the instant he spoke."[14]

As he conversed, Jefferson placed a premium on the virtue of decorum. This commitment to the importance of this personality trait led him, while stationed in Paris, to speak with directness and forthrightness at all times, avoiding even the appearance of subtleties, hidden agendas, or concealed goals. This cautious practice, he suggested, was, largely, responsible for his success in dealing with a normally suspicious Count de Vergennes.[15] It was also a sense of decorum that contributed to the friendly conversations he had with his political opponent Alexander Hamilton. In all, Jefferson's contemporaries, whether or not they agreed with his stands on particular issues, would likely endorse this testimonial by Dunglison: "I never heard from him a loose or indecorous speech. . . ."[16]

One of the important ways that Jefferson promoted good will in his rhetorical transactions was his ability to identify with each discussant. Partly owing to his own personality, and partly due to his own philosophy of discourse, he was able to establish a communication environment in which an attitude of mutual respect became evident. During his visit to Monticello, Chastellux was pleased to note that the initial phase of the first conversation he had with his host began with a coolness and restraint which soon turned to genuine warmth.[17]

In some instances, Jefferson initiated a conversation with a stranger that from beginning to end proved to be a case study of how identification may be produced. A graphic example of this occurred in December 1800 when Jefferson went to the home of Samuel Smith, a book publisher and editor of *The National Intelligencer and Washington Advertiser*, to deposit a copy of the just-completed manuscript of his Parliamentary *Manual*. Smith's wife gave this account of the event:

> I was one morning sitting alone in the parlour, when the Servant opened the door and showed in a gentleman who wished to see my husband. The usual frankness and care with which I met strangers, were somewhat checked by the dignified and reserved air of the present visitor; but the chilled feeling was only momentary, for after taking the chair I offered him in a free and easy manner, and carelessly throwing his arm on a table near

which he sat, he turned towards me in a countenance beaming with an expression of benevolence (and) with a manner and voice almost femininely
soft and gentle, entered into a conversation on the commonplace topics of
the day, from which, before I was conscious of it, he had drawn me into observations of a more personal and interesting nature. . . . I knew not who
he was (but he) put me perfectly at my ease; in truth so kind and conciliating were his looks and manners that I forgot he was not a friend of my
own, until on the opening of the door, Mr. Smith entered and introduced
the stranger to me as *Mr. Jefferson.* . . .[18]

Jefferson further created rapport by encouraging each participant in a
conversation to feel free to speak on any subject that arises with candor
and commitment, without fear of being unduly criticized for exerting this
rhetorical privilege.[19] This principle of freedom of expression grew out of
his belief that each person's sense of dignity and self-respect is of paramount importance in producing happiness.

Jefferson employed two other discourse strategies for the purpose of creating identification and generating good will. First, he strove to avoid
controversy, which might cause dissension and alienate a discussant. On
some occasions, he introduced another subject; at other times, in the tradition of Franklin, who was one of his models, he asked a series of questions leading to a shared conclusion instead of making frontal attacks in
the form of direct refutation.

Second, when the name of a contemporary person became the focus of
discussion, he consistently adhered to his resolve of speaking only of that
person's good qualities. This conciliatory gesture did not prevent him,
however, from criticizing an individual's views if they were perceived to
be adverse to "Republican institutions."[20] For one to do this, he firmly believed, was to cast aspersions on a political philosophy that draws its force
from its stated purpose of promoting the public good. He illustrated his
own practice with respect to this principle by describing a conversation
he held with President Washington at Mount Vernon on October 1,
1792. Early in this discussion, the president expressed his concern about
the current relationship between Jefferson and Hamilton. To mediate
these personal differences, Washington noted, was for him an urgent
challenge because of the significant contributions being made to the federal government by both cabinet members. He then alluded to one of Jefferson's major fears—a possible move by Federalists to substitute a monarchial form of government for the present republican system. There were
not, said Washington, "ten men in the United States whose opinions
were worth attention who entertained such a thought." To this claim,

Jefferson responded "there were many more than he imagined." For proof of this assertion, he reminded Washington of a dispute that occurred "at his own table a little before we left Philadelphia, between General Schuyler on the one side & Pinkney & myself on the other, wherein the former maintained the position that hereditary descent was as likely to produce good magistrates as election."

In providing further evidence of existing sympathies toward a monarchial system of governance, Jefferson argued "that tho' the people were sound, there were a numerous sect who had monarchy in contemplation," and that one of the principal leaders of this movement was "the Secretary of the Treasury." "I heard him say," he added, "that this constitution was a shilly shally thing of mere milk & water, which could not last, & was only good as a step to something better." But, he continued, this was not all; for it was Hamilton who "had endeavoured in the convention to make an English constitution of it"; and when that failed, he helped devise measures which "established corruption in the legislature, where there was a squadron devoted to the nod of the treasury, doing whatever he had directed. . . ." When Washington then suggested that it was only natural for members of a legislature in any government to act on occasion in a self-interested and dependent manner, Jefferson retorted: "There was a great difference between the little accidental schemes of self interest which would take place in every body of men & influence their votes, and a regular system for forming a corps of interested persons who should be steadily at the orders of the Treasury."[21]

This significant conversational episode was revealing in several important ways. It was a discourse event, first of all, that showed Jefferson's unmistakable devotion to republicanism with its emphasis on individual rights and privileges, and the happiness of the people in general. It also demonstrated his conviction that the public good would be threatened if one branch of government—in this case, the executive (Department of the Treasury)—seeks to gain control over another branch—the legislative. Additionally, it contains a strong indictment against a monarchial political philosophy because of its hereditary component. Finally, this rhetorical transaction reasserted Jefferson's belief that whereas Hamilton's private life may be commendable, he was all too willing to have the government on the public level to adopt an "end justifies the means" ethical philosophy. Such a notion, he concluded, constituted an enormous threat to republicanism and should, therefore, be rejected as an enemy of virtue.

That Jefferson was sincere in his belief that Hamilton was a potentially dangerous monarchist who represented a threat to republican government there could be little doubt. Modern scholars, however, generally agree that Jefferson greatly exaggerated this fear. Gerald Stourzh, for example, argues that Hamilton endorsed these three principles of republican government: first, it is a "government by the people"; second, it upholds "the rule of law"; and, third, it maintains that "virtue" is a fundamental principle. To emphasize this latter point, Stourzh alludes to this statement that Hamilton incorporated into Washington's Farewell Address: "T'is substantially true, that virtue or morality is a necessary spring of popular government— The rule indeed extends with more or less force to every species of Free Government." In addition, adds Stourzh, "on the day before he met Aaron Burr in his mortal duel," Hamilton noted that it was his "fervent wish" that the union will be preserved.[22]

In the early weeks of 1801, Jefferson provided additional instances depicting how he used conversational discourse to challenge those who presented ideas that he thought were incompatible with the principles of republicanism. The setting was fraught with controversy. In her essay "The Election of 1800: A Case Study in the Logic of Political Change," Joanne B. Freeman repeatedly uses the word "crisis" to describe the provocative political contest. It was a crisis, the author argued, that began in the 1790s, a period in which "it was difficult to distinguish friends from foes, and often impossible to predict what strange combinations of circumstances might alter a man's political loyalties or forge an alliance between former enemies." Following this turbulent decade, the campaign of 1800 took place, eventually reaching its "ultimate crisis," Freeman noted, with "the electoral tie between Thomas Jefferson and Aaron Burr."[23] Since later balloting placed Jefferson ahead but failed to give him the necessary majority, a group of Federalists sought to nullify the election results altogether by having the new president of the senate installed as temporary head of the government. Concerned about the serious political implications, which, in his opinion, had the potential to lead to civil conflict, Jefferson tried to remain neutral so that the people would be free and unencumbered to make the ultimate decision. This reluctance on Jefferson's part to intervene disturbed the Federalist gouverneur Morris and outgoing president John Adams, who had been an unsuccessful candidate for re-election.

As Jefferson left the Senate chamber one day, he came in contact with Morris who immediately initiated a conversation, in which he detailed the dire circumstances resulting from the lengthy stalemate. Morris proceeded to tell Jefferson "the reasons why the minority of states were so opposed" to his election. All you have to do to settle this conflict in your favor, he said, is to promise that you would not "turn all federalists out of office"; that you would not "put down the navy"; and that you would not "wipe off the public debt." In reacting to this demand, Jefferson said that it was his "duty to be passive & silent during the present scene." More important, he declared that he "should certainly make no terms, should never go into the office of President by capitulation, nor with (his) hands tied by any conditions which should hinder" him "from pursuing the measures which [he] should deem for the public good."

During the same period, Jefferson encountered Adams walking along Pennsylvania Avenue. Soon they began to speak about the pending crisis. As their dialogue unfolded, Jefferson advised Adams to veto the damaging proposal calling for the president of the Senate to be appointed to the presidency of the United States on a temporary basis. Disapproving of this recommendation, Adams gave the following nonverbal and verbal response:

> He grew warm in an instant, and said with a vehemence he had not used towards me before, "Sir, the event of the election is within your own power. You have only to say you will do justice to the public creditors, maintain the navy, and not disturb those holding offices, and the government will instantly be put into your hands. We know it is the wish of the people it should be so."

Sensing that these words from Adams were an ultimatum calling for him to accede to all of the Federalist demands if he wanted to become president, Jefferson spoke feelingly as he clothed his response in language that conformed to his philosophy of virtue:

> Mr. Adams, I know not what part of my conduct, in either public or private life, can have authorized a doubt of my fidelity to the public engagements. I say, however, I will not come into government by capitulation. I will not enter on it, but in perfect freedom to follow the dictates of my own judgment.[24]

At this juncture, Jefferson, satisfied he had made his point, introduced a new subject into the conversation.

These two dialogues with Morris and Adams, as reported by Jefferson, suggested that when the public good and the principles of republicanism were at stake, Jefferson believed that, as a conversationalist in this type of rhetorical situation, he had an obligation to follow his moral sense and conscience which placed a benevolent attitude to society on a higher ethical plane than that of personal ambition or welfare.

If it were possible to re-create a representative situation in which Jefferson used conversation to promote social cohesion and relations, we would be aware of several other features of his performance—his appearance, listening habits, and style of presentation. He would catch our attention, at the outset, by his overall size, demeanor, and pattern of dress. As we glance at him, we would see a tall, thin, "sandy-complexioned" man who was "six feet two-and-a half inches in height." When we moved closer, we would become aware of his peeling skin, resulting from undue "exposure to the sun."[25] Further, we would find that his countenance was "mild and pleasing," his behavior "cool and reserved," and his looks "kind and conciliating."[26] But we would be startled by his unconventional dress, which featured "sharp-toed boots," a "red plush waistcoat," "yarn stockings," and corduroy pants that seem "too small for his frame."[27]

As the conversation developed, we would be conscious of his tendency to encourage others to speak, and to listen attentively and patiently as they did so even if their comments included "artless details."[28] We would also take note that his language, while occasionally discursive, was simple, clear, and rendered "picturesque" by his effective use of "paradox" and "anecdotes," which were instructive and, at times, humorous and fanciful.[29] Finally, we would hear a voice that was soft and well modulated, and observe reluctance on his part to dominate the discussion by interrupting other participants.[30]

This power of conversation, which contemporaries so warmly admired, was evident both in the early stages and in the declining years of his life. John Adams recalled that though Jefferson was "a silent member in Congress" during the debates on the Declaration of Independence, "he was so prompt, frank, explicit, and decisive upon committees and in conversation . . . that he soon seized upon my heart; and upon this occasion I gave him my vote, and did all in my power to procure the votes of others. . . ."[31]

As the years passed, these conversational skills steadily increased. Fifty years after the event described by Adams had taken place, William Wirt gave this portrayal of what a visitor would see and hear when an aging Jefferson conversed with his guests:

And then came that charm of manner and conversation that passes all description—so cheerful—so unassuming—so free, and easy, and frank, and kind, and gay—that even the young and overawed and embarrassed visitor at once forgot his fears, and felt himself by the side of an old and familiar friend. There was no effort, no ambition in the conversation of the philosopher. It was as simple and unpretending as nature itself. And while in this easy manner he was pouring out instruction, like light from an inexhaustible solar fountain, he seemed continually to be asking, instead of giving information. The visitor felt himself lifted by the contact into a new and nobler region of thought, and became surprised at his own buoyancy and vigor. He could not, indeed, help being astounded, now and then, at those transcendent leaps of the mind, which he saw made without the slightest exertion, and the ease with which this wonderful man played with subjects which he had been in the habit of considering among the *argumenta crucis* of the intellect. And then there seemed to be no end to his knowledge. He was a thorough master of every subject that was touched. From the details of the humblest mechanic art, up to the highest summit of science, he was perfectly at his ease and everywhere at home.

Wirt concluded his vivid account with these words:

> Mr. Jefferson was wont to remark, that he never left the conversation of Dr. Franklin without carrying away with him something new and useful. How often, and how truly, has the same remark been made of him.[32]

In his *Life of Thomas Jefferson*, Randall describes a discourse event that graphically illustrates Wirt's claim that Jefferson, as a conversationalist, "was a thorough master of every subject that was touched, ranging from the humblest mechanic art, up to the highest summit of science." The event took place at Ford's tavern, located between Monticello and Poplar Forest. Upon arriving at the tavern, a popular "stopping place" for travelers, Jefferson was ushered into a room where a clergyman was sitting. Not recognizing who the new arrival was, the parson initiated a conversation on "the subject of certain mechanical operations which he had recently witnessed." Jefferson's enlightened inquiries and responses on this theme, the parson later recalled, convinced him that his discourse partner was an "engineer." When the subject next turned to agriculture, the information displayed by Jefferson led the parson to conclude that he "was a large farmer." Finally, when religion became the next topic of discussion, the parson was persuaded "that his companion was another clergyman." The latter statement was particularly revealing because when the parson later learned that he had been talking to President Jefferson, he exclaimed: "I tell you that was neither an atheist nor irreligious man—one of juster sentiments I never met with."[33]

The testimonials from eyewitnesses, both from Americans and Europeans, clearly indicate that Jefferson, as a conversationalist, conformed closely to the seven standards he believed to be essential for one who hopes to achieve excellence in this rhetorical form. He was well informed and understood how to use an argument to promote virtue; he was dedicated to the goal of producing social cohesion and cementing personal relationships; he encouraged others to speak freely on any issue that arises; he maintained an attitude of respect for others; he was a thoughtful listener; he used an appropriate style and delivery; and he understood the importance of the physical setting.

In the foregoing analysis, we have observed Jefferson as an accomplished conversationalist in social situations, in dialogues with both friends and strangers on a wide variety of subjects, and as a member of professional discussion groups where the goal of each person was to achieve consensus. In each of these communication settings, rarely were attempts made to keep the purpose and the content of the discussions secretive. There was, however, an exception to this practice that deserves to be considered as a concluding point on Jefferson in action as a conversationalist.

The rationale for this type of discourse could be seen in Jefferson's unpublished *The Anas*, "a collection of information or gossip about persons." While serving as secretary of state during Washington's first term, Jefferson began the practice of making "memorandums on loose scraps of paper, taken out of (his) pocket in the moment and laid by to be copied fair at leisure. . . ." When Jefferson heard in the early 1800s that John Marshall planned to write a biography of George Washington, he decided to have his notes "bound with the others by a binder who came into my cabinet, doing it under my own eye, and without the opportunity of reading a single paper." In 1818, Jefferson produced a "special compilation" of *The Anas*, and continued adding "material to that compilation before his death in 1826. . . ."[34] Although the content of *The Anas*, was meant to be secret, the record of these events, consisting largely of conversations Jefferson either held or observed, enabled him to recall what actually was said in a given rhetorical situation.[35]

# Letter Writing

In the early summer of 1822, Jefferson described to John Adams the difficult challenge he faced in trying to keep up with the demands on his time in letter writing. After examining his record book, he said:

> I happened to turn my letter-list some time ago, and a curiosity was excited to count those received in a single year. It was the year before the last. I found the number to be 1267, many of them requiring answers of elaborate research, and all to be answered with due attention and consideration. . . .[36]

The demands were especially heavy during his Washington years, in which he often was involved in epistolary communication beginning at sunrise and extending through the dinner hour.[37] Nor did this pressure ease in his retirement years. Altogether he became one of the most prolific correspondents in American history, writing and receiving approximately "forty thousand letters. . . ."[38]

## Letter Writing as Conversation

A careful analysis of Jefferson's letters leaves little doubt that when writing to family members, friends, and colleagues, he upheld his principle that this private rhetorical form should be viewed as conversation. Often he would begin a letter to an intimate person suggesting that he was in the mood to initiate a dialogue. Frequently he reminded his daughters of his desire to hear from them more often. In the autumn of 1775, while attending meetings in the Continental Congress in Philadelphia, he complained to his former classmate John Page that even though he had "set apart nearly one day in every week since I came here to write letters," he, in turn, "had never received the scrip of a pen from any mortal breathing. . . ."[39]

So that there could be no misunderstanding about his own faithfulness in fulfilling his responsibility in carrying on a dialogue through letter writing, he maintained a careful record of his entire correspondence. Consequently, when Francis Hopkins wrote, "I cannot at present lay my hands upon your last [letter] but recollect it was of an old date," Jefferson was fully prepared to respond with well-documented information. He pointed out after checking his "epistolary account," that he had written nine letters to Hopkinson between November 1784 and August 1786. During the same period, he had received ten in return. In listing the specific date of each letter sent and received, he noted that this disparity of one should hardly "justify a scold."[40]

Jefferson's correspondence with John Adams is an interesting case study of the conversational nature of letter writing between friends who, except for a few years, had an unusually strong sense of mutual respect for each other. The letters included in Cappon's two-volume edition, when tabulated, show that Jefferson wrote to Adams at least 135 times between 1777 and 1826—the year of their deaths. In addition, he communicated with Abigail on twenty-three occasions. During this forty-nine-year span, Adams sent 186 letters to Jefferson. Even though Adams wrote more often than Jefferson, especially in the fourteen years from 1812 to 1826, he was delighted with their correspondence and the conversation it maintained between them. In July 1813, Adams sought to alleviate Jefferson's concern about falling behind in his letters with these words of praise: "Never mind it, my dear Sir, if I write four letters to your one; your one is worth more than my four."[41] Five years later, he expressed further appreciation about the continuing dialogue. "While you live," he noted, "I seem to have a Bank at Monticello on which I can draw for a letter of Friendship and entertainment when I please."[42]

What subjects were discussed in this remarkable exchange between these two American Founding Fathers and friends? The whole range of arts and sciences became a part of their dialogue. They spoke of philosophy, history, belles lettres, education, religion, and theoretical aspects of government. Also included in their conversations were analyses of the strengths and weaknesses of the principal authors in the classical and modern eras. The only subjects that were taboo were any questions involving contentious issues in American politics. There were too many topics they agreed on, thought Jefferson; so why waste time concentrating on a subject that might be needlessly controversial?

Because Jefferson was dedicated to the idea that letter writing, at its most desirable level, is a conversation with loved ones or intimate friends and colleagues, he became increasingly burdened with correspondents, whose names he did not know, who constantly wrote to him requesting information on a variety of themes. This type of communication, he believed, not only sapped his energy in his declining years but failed to qualify as genuine conversation. He expressed his frustration to Rush, calling this problem an "obstacle to the delights of retirement. . . ."[43] In the end, however, his sense of virtue prevailed, and he painstakingly answered most of the letters he received because, as he noted, the requests were couched in the language of good will.[44]

## Letter Writing as the Development of an Appropriate Response to an Identifiable Need

The three major exigencies that Jefferson wished to address in his letters were the needs to inform, to persuade, and to give critical assessments of a person, a subject, or an event. To determine whether he met these challenges in an appropriate and effective manner is the concern of the remaining portion of this chapter.

His letters to Robert Skipwith in 1771, to Thomas Mann Randolph Jr. in 1786, and to Peter Carr and to John Minor in 1814 are typical examples of his effort to give instruction on educational training and planning to students in their formative years. What made the letter to Skipwith so significant was the enclosure for a list of books that should be obtained for his "Private Library." After prefacing his remarks with a discussion of the areas that were to be covered, he presented this list: seventy-seven books on the fine arts, seven on criticism of the fine arts, eight on politics and trade, fifteen on religion, three on law, twenty on ancient and modern history, thirteen on natural philosophy and natural history, and five on miscellaneous items. In all, these recommended listings totaled 148 separate works from classical and British/Continental scholars.[45]

When Jefferson gave advice to Thomas Mann Randolph Jr., who later would become his son-in-law, he offered the following educational plan for his legal training. Relying on a hierarchical system consisting of three steps arranged in a chronological order, he suggested that the study of language and mathematics should be the starting point. Once this foundation has been laid, the second step would consist of courses in the biological and physical sciences and readings in classical and modern history. The third phase would deal with the study of law and readings in the fine arts. As Jefferson outlined this program, he answered the following questions: (1) Which courses should be studied in America and which in Europe? (2) When should one attend lectures? (3) What instruction can be gained primarily by readings? Not to be neglected, concluded Jefferson, was a regular concentrated effort of exercise.[46]

The letter to Carr dealt with a proposed "System of Education" Jefferson had been asked to prepare by the trustees of a proposed academy or college to be established in central Virginia. Since he was unable to attend the meetings to discuss this report, he sent his recommendations to Carr, asking him to be his representative. This report, as explained in his letter, listed three levels of education that should be adopted: (1) elementary schools; (2) general schools; and (3) professional schools. The nature of each level was discussed, along with types of professorships that should be included in the general schools. One of these four recommended appointments was to be a professor of languages, history, belles lettres, rhetoric, and oratory. Another was designated as a professor of philosophy who was to be responsible for teaching ideology, ethics, law, and government.[47] These two multidisciplinary professorships, it seems clear, would offer an opportunity to students interested in discourse and its companion virtue.

Jefferson sent another important final letter focusing on advice concerning educational training in 1814 to John Minor, who planned to become a lawyer. This communication, as noted in chapter 5, was an expanded version of an earlier letter he had written to Bernard Moore in 1767. The extensive program of study recommended in this correspondence included an analysis of courses that should be taken, a list of books to be read, and a suggested time of study for each area. Minor was told to concentrate on "Physical Studies, Ethics, Religion, and Natural Law" before "VIII o'clock in the morning"; to focus on Law from "VIII to XII"; to read Politics from "XII to I"; to study History "in the afternoon"; and to center his attention on "Belles Lettres, Criticism, Rhetoric, and Oratory" from "Dark to Bed-time."[48]

These four informational letters contained specific and thorough details that were appropriate responses to a recognizable need. Moreover, as Jefferson had often said, they required hours of preparation and reflection on his part.

Three additional letters—one on the problems involving the workability of the Articles of Confederation, a second on archaeology and scientific developments, and a third on morals—offered further evidence of Jefferson's use of this rhetorical form to generate understanding.

In the first letter, written to Chastellux in 1784, several months after the French general and scholar had returned to Paris, Jefferson's purpose was to explain the present situation in America, which, he asserted, was at variance with the accounts being reported in Europe showing widespread "anarchy and opposition" to the American government. Strongly denying the existence of "anarchy" and major "opposition," he nevertheless acknowledged several concerns. These included lack of payment to members of the army as they were being disbanded after the war; slights shown to some of the state delegates at a meeting of their representatives; and a need for an adequate policy to cope with the issue of refugees. Reminding Chastellux that as a French general he had been a "witness to the total destruction of our commerce, devastation of our country, and absence of precious metals," Jefferson observed that steps were being undertaken "to avail ourselves of the productions of the earth." As this procedure continues, he concluded, it will go far toward increasing our money supply, which currently is the root of our principal need.[49] Whether Jefferson wrote this letter, as Boyd has conjectured, to prompt Chastellux to influence public opinion in France is not clear.[50] What seems certain, however, is that his commitment to accuracy in reporting was a driving force in moving him to set the record straight about conditions in America in early 1784.

In the second message, written in 1786 to Ezra Stiles, then president of Yale, Jefferson began his communication with the topic of archaeology as it pertained to the region between the Allegheny Mountains and the Atlantic Ocean. Observing that there were no artifacts suggesting that iron had been used by the "aboriginal inhabitants," he then cast doubt on the reliability of "the new discoveries which suppose regular fortifications of brickwork to have been in use among the Indians on the waters of the Ohio."

He next turned to the issue concerning the subject of early settlers on the North American continent, concluding that they may have migrated from "Eastern parts of Asia." But since there are radical differences in languages, it appears that the migrants did not come from any "common source."

In the final paragraphs of his letter to Stiles, Jefferson discussed recent scientific developments. He reported, for instance, that the "Abbe Rachon has applied the metal called platina"—which is incapable of rusting—"to the telescope." Additionally, he explained that "a new method of copying has been invented." He was so intrigued with this process that he took advantage of his presence in Paris and "called on the inventor" and asked for a demonstration. While there, he said, "I wrote a note on the plate, and in about three quarters of an hour he brought me an hundred copies as perfect as the imagination can conceive."[51] So pleased was Stiles with the contents of this letter that he wrote to Jefferson: "Your letter of Sept. 1786 contained so many curious Things in natural Knowledge that I not only took the Liberty to suffer a Copy or Extract to go into the public prints, but communicated it last Octo. to the newly formed Connecticut Society of Arts and Sciences. . . ."[52]

The third letter, on morality and virtue, set forth Jefferson's response to Thomas Law's new book *Second Thoughts and Instinctive Impulses*, which had been sent to him by the author. Praising the Creator for implanting in everyone a "moral sense" or conscience, Jefferson then refuted those who, he held, had mistakenly identified truth, the love of God, and taste as foundational elements of morality. The first two of these virtues, while important aspects of morality, he explained, are branches, not a foundation. The third—taste—is not a part of virtue at all. Most of all, Jefferson challenged the widespread notion that "self-interest," or "self-love" constitutes the foundation. Indeed, he stated, the contrary was true because this characteristic is the primary enemy of virtue. Jefferson ended his letter-essay by noting the important function that education, practical reasoning, and the social affections may perform in strengthening one's moral sense.[53]

Of all the exigencies confronting Jefferson that required a suitable response to provide information on a particular issue, none surpassed in importance a rhetorical situation that developed in 1799 while he was serving as vice president. The Federalists, contemplating a probable candidacy on Jefferson's part to seek the office of president in 1800, sought to undermine his credibility by describing his political beliefs as a threat to the tradition and stability of the federal government. Alarmed by the misrepresentations in the charges, Jefferson felt constrained to meet this challenge by writing a letter to his Republican colleague Elbridge Gerry explaining eleven major articles of his political faith.

Among the principal beliefs he set forth were these: a desire to preserve "our present federal constitution"; to guarantee "to the states the powers not yielded by them to the union"; to produce "possible savings of the public revenue" for the purpose of discharging "the national debt"; to maintain an adequate militia "for internal defence" and a "naval force" for protecting "our coasts and harbors"; to have a policy of "free commerce with all nations"; to uphold the principles of "freedom of religion" and "freedom of the press"; and to encourage "the progress of science in all its branches." Then, in a concluding statement designed to blunt the claim that, instead of remaining neutral, he had shown partiality toward France and its leader Napoleon in the war with England, he announced that "the first object" of his "heart" was his "own country"; for it is in America" that is "embarked" his "family," his "fortune," and his "own existence." Under these circumstances, he contended, his policy was to favor only those countries that would contribute significantly to America's welfare.[54]

This letter to Gerry was more than an attempt to set the record straight regarding his true beliefs on the essential issues of the day. It also contained vital data that were to become, in effect, the platform of the Republican Party in the forthcoming presidential campaign. Moreover, it further illustrates how Jefferson viewed letter writing as an effective method to convey information for the purpose of clarifying his deeply felt sentiments, which he was convinced the "great body" of Americans fully shared.

A second goal Jefferson emphasized in his letter writing was to use this discourse form as a means of persuasion. In an earlier context, we saw how he attempted to persuade his daughter Mary to be conscientious and careful in keeping up with her reading assignments, in studying Latin, and in practicing her spelling. His most important effort in seeking to persuade her to adopt a course of action was his letter on the need to promote harmony in marital relations. Beginning with the premise that "harmony in the marriage state is the very first object to be aimed at," he counseled her to avoid "little cross purposes," and to resist the temptation to find fault—especially on minor or inconsequential issues when company is present. If you follow these simple prudential rules, he urged, there will be communion and social cohesion rather than a spirit of alienation.[55]

Two letters Jefferson wrote in 1775 illustrate how he used direct persuasion to try to alter opinion, either of an individual or a nation in the field of international relations. In the spring of 1775, Jefferson became alarmed at the news of a disturbing event that had just occurred in Massachusetts. A clash between the king's troops and the residents of Boston led to the death of approximately five hundred British soldiers, including the Earl of Percy. Concerned that this episode would produce negative publicity in England and exacerbate the deteriorating situation in the American colonies, Jefferson decided to write to his former professor and respected friend Dr. William Small, arguing that the British government had been the real aggressor. Their mediator whose agreed-upon goal was to reduce tension by following a policy of reconciliation, he told Small, chose instead to present a series of incendiary speeches and declarations designed to intimidate the Americans, thus forcing them into submission. Such a contentious approach, he added, would cause an opposite effect because it ran counter to the basic principles of human nature. For the workings of human nature teach us that when a group of people are threatened, "whose sole crime has been the developing and asserting their rights," they are "more likely to be provoked, than frightened, by haughty deportment."

In an attempt to show American good will and a spirit of reasonableness, Jefferson next asserted that, had Lord Chatham's conciliatory bill been adopted, some type of accommodation could have been worked out with Congress. He concluded his argument with these words:

> But the dignity of Parliament, it seems, can brook no opposition to its power. Strange, that a set of men, who have made sale of their virtue to the Minister, should yet talk of retaining dignity![56]

We have no evidence of Small's response to Jefferson's argument, for at this time he was in a declining state of health, which soon led to his death. But it appeared to be the type of appeal that he would have appreciated because it made use of the principles of informal reasoning and moral philosophy that Small had taught and practiced during his tenure at the College of William and Mary, unless, of course, he disapproved of the American cause.

Jefferson wrote the second persuasive letter we have chosen for discussion to John Randolph in August 1775. Convinced that he no longer wanted to remain in America because of the rapidly increasing tensions with Britain, Randolph had recently made the decision to move to England. Jefferson viewed this move as an important opportunity in which he hoped to influence Randolph to try to alter public perceptions in Britain by describing prevailing conditions and attitudes in America.

In this communication to Randolph, he felt that Randolph should develop two arguments as soon as possible after his arrival. First, he urged, British leaders must be told, based upon Randolph's first-hand experiences, that they are wrong in claiming that opposition in America was limited to "a small faction." Second, he advised Randolph to refute the false notion that Americans "are cowards, and shall surrender at discretion to an armed force." To emphasize the significance of this point, he referred to the depth of his own feelings as being representative of American thought as a whole: "I am one of those, too, who, rather than submit to the rights of legislating for us, assumed by the British Parliament, and which late experience has shown they will so cruelly exercise, would lend my hand to sink the whole Island in the ocean." If you are willing to make these arguments, Jefferson concluded, you may change the disposition of the parliamentary leaders, which in the long run might "render service to the whole empire. . . ."[57]

In his messages to Small and Randolph, Jefferson believed it was his duty to argue on behalf of the public good. Although his first responsibility was to love and serve his own country, he sincerely believed that the welfare of Britain would also be enhanced if both countries were willing to have policies and attitudes based on accurate information, a spirit of justice, and an attitude of mutual respect.

We have seen thus far how Jefferson used letter writing both to inform and to persuade. But, at times, he also fulfilled another function in his letters, that of rhetorical criticism. These opportunities to be a critic often arose in the form of requests that he give his assessment of the character and discourse performance of a particular author or political leader. A typical occasion occurred in 1821 when Francis Eppes wrote to him asking for a comparison of Lord Bolingbroke and Thomas Paine.

Jefferson began his critique by pointing out their shared characteristics. Both men, he said, were devoted to truth-telling; both were "advocates for human liberty"; and both had the courage to challenge "the priests and Pharisees of their day." Besides these shared elements of virtue, the two authors also wrote with distinction, each emphasizing different elements of style. Paine, he felt, was unexcelled in utilizing an easy, familiar, and simple style that was "unassuming" in its word choice and sentence structure. In brief, he was able to elucidate his ideas in a perspicuous manner that reminded his readers of Benjamin Franklin. By contrast, Jefferson added, Bolingbroke, who had forged his style as a member of Parliament, presented his conceptions with a "bold" and "strong diction" that was "copious, polished, and commanding. . . ." In his writings and in his speeches, his "lofty, rhythmical, and full-flowing eloquence" was reminiscent of that used by Cicero. In praising the language usage of Paine and Bolingbroke, Jefferson noted that each was similarly effective—one as a master of the simple style, and the other as an exemplar of the sublime.[58]

Up to this point, our discussion of Jefferson as a letter writer has dealt with the magnitude of his correspondence and his attempts to use this discourse form as a means of conversation, and as a channel for informing or persuading a reader and offering a critical judgment of an author's use of the elements of style. Our next consideration is to pinpoint several rhetorical strategies that contributed significantly to the uniqueness and power of his letters.

One of these discourse techniques was his reliance on storytelling to make a point. In some instances, as in the autumn of 1785, while he was in France, he deliberately created a rhetorical situation that might produce an anecdote worth relating. The event took place near the town of Fontainebleau. In graphic terms, and with an emphasis on virtue, he gave this description to Madison:

> As soon as I had got clear of the town I fell in with a poor woman walking at the same rate with myself and going the same course. Wishing to know the condition of the laboring poor I entered into conversation with her, which I began by enquiries for the path which would lead me into the mountain: and thence proceeded to enquiries into her vocation, condition and circumstances. She told me she was a day laborer at 8 sous. or 4 d. sterling the day: that she had two children to maintain, and to pay a rent of 30 livres for her house (which would consume the hire of 75 days), that often she could get no employment and of course was without bread. As we had walked together near a mile and she had so far served me as a guide, I gave her, on parting, 24 sous. She burst into tears of gratitude which I could perceive was unfeigned because she was unable to utter a word. She had probably never before received so great an aid.

In closing the story, he suggested the principal meaning to be derived from this episode: "This little *attendrissement*, with the solitude of my walk, led me into a train of reflections on that unequal division of property which occasions the numberless instances of wretchedness which I had observed in this country and is to be observed all over Europe."[59]

Another representative anecdote illustrating a principle appears in a letter to Adams in 1812. Proud of the early and sustained contacts he had experienced with the Indians, and convinced that they often exhibited the power of eloquence, Jefferson gave this vivid description, as noted in an earlier context, of the impact of an Indian leader's use of nonverbal communication:

> I knew much the great Outassete [i.e., Outacity], the warrior and orator of the Cherokees. He was always the guest of my father, on his journeys to and from Williamsburg. I was in his camp when he made his great farewell oration to his people, the evening before his departure for England. The moon was in full splendor, and to her he seemed to address himself in his prayers for his own safety on the voyage, and that of his people during his absence. His sounding voice, distinct articulation, animated action, and the solemn silence of his people at their several fires, filled me with the awe and veneration, altho' I did not understand a word he uttered.[60]

As we can see from these two examples, Jefferson's use of the narrative paradigm in his letters was consistent with his practices in conversation.

A second important rhetorical strategy that often appeared in Jefferson's letters was the use of incisive arguments expressed in moving language when assessing the nature and thrust of a person he had known in an intimate way. Rarely, if ever, was this more evident than in a letter he wrote to Dr. Walter Jones, in 1814, describing his perceptions of George Washington. Jones had just written to Jefferson telling him of the daunting and difficult task he was about to face in delineating Washington's character and his role in the development of "the federal coalition." Your problems, Jefferson suggested, are not as "perilous" as you have imagined in your letter. He then proceeded to show how he himself would portray Washington if he were in Jones's position.

The first part of his now famous letter began with his treatment of the quality of Washington's mind. In a balanced overview, which included both strengths and limitations, he called Washington's mind "great and powerful," yet not of "the very first order." His penetration was "strong," although it was "not so acute as that of Newton, Bacon, or Locke." His mind, moreover, "was slow in operation, being little aided by invention or imagination." Nevertheless, he was able to draw sound conclusions after carefully examining the various recommendations presented to him by his staff. He was particularly outstanding in making battle plans, but had a tendency to falter in the field when a prepared strategy "was dislocated by sudden circumstances."

Following the depiction of Washington's mind and general thought processes, Jefferson turned to other elements of virtue that were essential parts of his character. What we learn about Washington in this analysis is that he was a courageous man "incapable of fear"; a just leader who scorned any form of bias or unfair partiality; and a generous person who freely bestowed gifts on others for projects he deemed useful. Above all, he strove mightily to adhere to the rules of prudence in conducting human affairs. Yet notwithstanding these positive traits, he had to rely on "reflection and resolution" to control his natural inclination to become excessively angry when he perceived a situation warranted it. Additionally, as "his heart was not warm in its affections," he used reason to calculate "every man's value, and gave him a solid esteem proportioned to it."

A picture of Washington's discourse characteristics also emerges from Jefferson's assessment. Possessing a pleasing stature and an "easy, erect and noble" deportment, he attracted attention as a commanding figure. When participating in a dialogue with friends, he was a competent and active conversationalist. In other rhetorical situations, however, he was far less effective. Indeed, "his colloquial talents were not above mediocrity" because of his lack of "copiousness of ideas" and "fluency of words." He was at his worst while speaking in public. When he was "called on for a sudden opinion," for example, "he was unready, short and embarrassed." As a communicator, Jefferson added, Washington's saving merit was a talent to write "readily" and in a diffuse, yet "easy and correct style." His extensive correspondence, therefore, constitutes one of his important legacies.

In this memorable portrait of Washington, Jefferson relied on the fundamental principles of his own philosophy of practical reasoning. His portrait was based not only on what he had observed himself but also on eyewitness accounts of Washington's decision-making processes by a group of officers who were with Washington during battle. By glancing at the conclusion of Jefferson's letter at this juncture, we see how he incorporated personal proof to reinforce his arguments.

"These are my opinions of General Washington," he confidently asserted, "which I would vouch at the judgment seat of God, having been formed on an acquaintance of thirty years." He then recounted how he had served with Washington in the Virginia legislature from 1769 to the Revolutionary War; how they had corresponded with each other during the war; and how they maintained a close relationship when he was in the cabinet as secretary of state. But Jefferson was not yet through in developing his conclusion. One major task was to be confronted with directness and forth-rightness. It was the major campaign launched by the "federal monarchists," following Jefferson's departure as secretary of state, to convince Washington that Jefferson was "a theorist, holding French principles of government, which would lead infallibly to licentiousness and anarchy." Washington, Jefferson confessed, was somewhat influenced by these claims because of his knowledge of Jefferson's "disapprobation of the British Treaty." But conscious of the rapport the two men were capable of establishing in conversation, and of his faith in Washington's sense of justice and fairness, Jefferson concluded his evaluation with these words:

> I never saw him afterwards, or these malignant insinuations should have been dissipated before his just judgment, as mists before the sun. I felt on his death, with my countrymen, that "verily a great man had fallen this day in Israel."[61]

This probing portrait, which combined the principles of a simple and sublime style featuring elements of virtue, is generally regarded as the single most important description of Washington's character and discourse practices.

In completing our discussion of Jefferson's use of rhetorical strategies in his letters, we have chosen to analyze his message to John Adams on October 12, 1823. Perhaps more than any other single communication episode associated with his name, this letter, epitomizing the concept of forgiveness, reveals the inner working of his mind and worldview as he engaged in the rhetoric of virtue.

To understand the full impact of this message, we need, first of all, to recreate the setting. It began in 1804 when Jefferson was seeking re-election as president. At that time, William Cunningham, "a distant relative of Adams," asked him to put in writing some of his ideas on Jefferson the man and political leader. So that he could be as forthright as possible in describing his feelings, Adams extracted from Cunningham the promise that the substance of the letter would not be published during his lifetime. Unfortunately, however, following Cunningham's death by suicide in the fall of 1823, his son, who was opposed to John Quincy Adams's expected plan to run for the presidency in 1824, published the letter as a means of harming the Adams family. John Quincy Adams referred to this mean-spirited, ill-advised publication as a "venomous business."[62]

Upon learning of the event by reading newspaper accounts, but not the letter itself, Jefferson was deeply disturbed because it violated his notion that private correspondence should never be published without the author's consent. Of still greater import to him was the possibility that a division might again arise between two men whose "friendship" was "coeval with our government. . . ." With these troubling thoughts in mind, he sat down at his desk to write a letter to put Adams's mind at ease and the whole incident in perspective. "The circumstances of the times, in which we have happened to live, and, the partiality of our friends, at a particular period," he noted, "placed us in a state of apparent opposition, which some might suppose to be personal also." Then alluding to their years of companionship, and to the frailties of human nature, he observed:

> And if there had been, at any time, a moment when we were off our guard, and in a temper to let the whispers of these people make us forget what we had known of each other for so many years, and years of so much trial, yet all men who have attended to the workings of the human mind, who have seen the false colours under which passion sometimes dresses the actions and motives of others, have seen also these passions subsiding with time and reflection, dissipating, like mists before the rising sun, and restoring to us the sight of all things in their true shape and colours.

Against the background of these soothing sentiments, Jefferson reached the climax of his remarks, which he expressed in sublime terms upholding the principle of benevolence:

> It would be strange indeed if, at our years, we were to go an age back to hunt up imaginary, or forgotten facts, to disturb the repose of affections so sweetening to the evening of our lives. Be assured, my dear sir, that I am incapable of receiving the slightest impression from the effort now made to plant thorns on the pillow of age, worth, and wisdom, and to sow tares between friends who have been such for near half a century. Beseeching you then not to suffer your mind to be disquieted by this wicked attempt to poison it's peace, and praying you to throw it by, among the things which have never happened, I add sincere assurances of my unabated, and constant attachment, friendship and respect.[63]

A short while later, as Adams was having breakfast with members of his family, Jefferson's letter arrived from the post office. "I know what the substance is before I open it," he said. After then affirming there were no secrets between these two friends, Adams directed one of the women to read it out loud. He then described to Jefferson the immediate response:

> When it was done, it was followed by an universal exclamation, The best letter that ever was written, and round it went through the whole table— How generous! How noble! how magnanimous! I said that it was just such

a letter as I expected, only it was infinitely better expressed. A universal cry that the letter ought to be printed. No, hold, certainly not without Mr. Jefferson's express leave.[64]

This memorable letter was a scintillating example of Jefferson's ability to put his philosophy of virtue into practice in a stressful personal relations situation. The message, with its appeal to the imagination and the passions; its emphasis on the social affections of love, friendship, and forgiveness; and its use of vivid and compelling language produced a galvanic response from the Adams family. With deep sincerity and spontaneous enthusiasm, they felt justified in exclaiming: "The best letter that ever was written. . . ."

This review of Jefferson's letter-writing methods has shown that his practice, like that which characterized his conversation, conformed closely to his philosophy. He successfully used this discourse form as a means of conducting a dialogue with a loved one or a respected associate. He also was effective in presenting an appropriate response to a pressing need. He did so by relying on carefully researched information and on his own personal experiences. Permeating his letters, moreover, were incisive arguments grounded in the principles of virtue, and clothed in simple, graphic language that occasionally produced a sublime effect. Finally, as Jefferson's eloquent message to Adams in 1823 clearly revealed, the most distinctive and persuasive feature marking the letters as a whole was the way they addressed the particular needs and interests of the reader. We agree, therefore, with Julian Boyd when he said that "TJ possessed in abundant measure one of the first attributes of the great letter writer: that of putting the need and desires of the recipient uppermost. . . ."[65]

# Notes

1. Boyd, 19: 544. For an excellent analysis of "Letter Writing and Friendship," see Andrew Burstein, *The Inner Jefferson* chap. 4, 116–49.

2. Boyd, 19: 544. In this volume, Boyd has an editorial section entitled: "The Great Collaborators."

3. "Autobiography," in Ford, 1: 6.

4. See comments from the following sources: G. K. Van Hogendorp to TJ, April 6, 1784, in Boyd, 7: 80 and 81; "Extract from the Diary of Nathaniel Cutting at the Havre and Cowes," September 28–October 12, 1789, in Boyd, 15: 498; Ticknor, *Life, Letters, and Journals of George Ticknor*, 1: 35; and Bernard, *Retrospections of America*, 233.

5. Webster's "Eulogy on Adams and Jefferson," in Tefft, *Speeches of Daniel Webster*, 228.

6. Webster to George Mason, December 29, 1824, in Webster, *Writings and Speeches*, 17: 361; and "Memorandum of Conversations with Thomas Jefferson," ibid., 366.

7. Bernard, 233.

8. The three ensuing quotations recorded by Bernard appear in *Retrospections of America*, 238–39.

9. "Dr. Dunglison's Recollections of Mr. Jefferson," in Randall, *Life of Jefferson*, 3: 670.

10. Thomas Jefferson Randolph to Henry S. Randall, in Randall, *Life of Jefferson*, 3: 673.

11. Ibid.

12. Ibid.

13. See Ticknor, *Life, Letters and Journals of George Ticknor*, 1: 35; Chastellux to TJ, December 27, 1784, in Boyd, 7: 586; "Dunglison's Recollections," in Randall, *Life of Jefferson*, 3: 670; and Webster's "Eulogy," in Tefft, *Speeches of Daniel Webster*, 228.

14. Bernard, *Retrospections of America*, 232.

15. "Autobiography," in Ford, 1: 99.

16. Randall, *Life of Jefferson*, 3: 670.

17. Chastellux, in Boyd, 7: 585–86.

18. Margaret Bayard Smith, *The First Forty Years of Washington Society*, ed. by Gaillard Hunt (New York: Scribner's, 1906), 6–7.

19. Thomas Jefferson Randolph to Randall, in Randall, *Life of Thomas Jefferson*, 3: 673.

20. Ibid.

21. "The Anas," in *Writings*, 680–82.

22. Gerald Stourzh, *Alexander Hamilton and the Idea of Republican Government* (Stanford: Stanford University Press, 1970), 1–8, and 38–75. For a similar view, see Karl-Friedrich Walling, *Republican Empire: Alexander Hamilton on War and Free Government* (Lawrence: University Press of Kansas, 1999).

23. *Yale Law Journal* 108 (1999), 1959–1994.

24. The conversations with Morris and Adams are described in *The Anas*, in *Writings*, 694–95. The more specific quotations of the Adams encounter appear in Jefferson's letter to Dr. Benjamin Rush, January 16, 1811, in ibid., 1237. Jefferson used a similar type of dialogue setting forth his principles of virtue in a meeting with Aaron Burr. Ford, 1: 311–12.

25. Ticknor, *Life, Letters, and Journals of George Ticknor*, 1: 34; and Henry Adams, *History of the United States of America During the First Administration of Thomas Jefferson* (New York: Antiquarian Press, 1962), 1: 185.

26. Chastellux, December 27, 1784, in Boyd, 7: 585; Van Hogendorp, in ibid., 80; and Smith, *The First Forty Years of Washington Society*, 7.

27. Adams, *History of the United States*, 1: 187–88. In commenting on Jefferson's unconventional dress, Ticknor observed: "There is breathing of national philosophy in Mr. Jefferson,—in his dress, his house, his conversation. His setness, for instance, in wearing very sharp toed shoes, corduroy small-clothes, and red plush waistcoat, which have been laughed at till he might perhaps wisely have dismissed them. . . ." In Ticknor, *Life, Letters and Journals of George Ticknor*, 1: 37. Apparently, Jefferson used plain, but conventional clothing while attending a diplomatic function in Paris. Thomas Shippen, who was an American student studying in France, gave this description of his host's appearance and demeanor: "I observed that although Mr. Jefferson was the plainest man in the room and the most destitute of ribbands (,) crosses and other insignia of rank that he was most courted and most attended to (even by the Courtiers themselves) of the whole Diplomatic corps. . . ." Cited in Boyd, 12: 504n.

28. See Smith, 7; and Randolph's letter to Randall, in Randall, 3: 673.

29. Ticknor, *Life, Letters, and Journals of George Ticknor*, 1: 35; and Bernard, *Retrospections of America*, 232. As we could see from the recorded excerpts of Jefferson's arguments in *Retrospections*, he made excellent use of vivid language, including figures of speech and thought. Also of importance is Bernard's observation that he "could fill pages" with "specimens of [Jefferson's] humor." After citing numerous examples to illustrate the extent this rhetorical element was used, Bernard summarized Jefferson's own description of his encounter with a Connecticut farmer shortly after he had been elected to his first term as president. With considerable pleasure, Jefferson told the story of a conversation he had with the farmer while both men were riding on their horses near the White House. Not recognizing the person with whom he was speaking, the farmer proudly said he had supported "John Adams, a real old New-Englander, after the manner of our forefathers, the Pilgrims of Plymouth Rock." He then suggested that he had heard "that this Thomas Jefferson is a very wasteful chap with our hard earned money, and you'll allow, mister, that that's unpatriotic upon principle." As they arrived at the gate of the White House, the farmer wanted to know who lived in this mansion which he suggested was as large as "Noah's Ark," and probably had as many as thirty rooms. When he was told it was the residence of the current president, the visitor from Connecticut asserted that this was further proof of Jefferson's tendency to waste "the people's money." Despite the criticism he had received from the stranger, Jefferson invited him into the White House for a tour—and offer he gladly accepted. But a moment later, when the startled farmer heard someone greet his conversational companion with the words, "Good-morning, [Mr.] president," he "turned and stared at Jefferson with a mixture of curiosity and alarm," and "in another instant . . . struck his spurs into his horse and was flying away like a whirlwind. . . ." *Retrospections*, 240–42. In interpreting the meaning of this story, Bernard suggested that Jefferson utilized this humorous anecdote in order to refute the opinions of those who were suspicious of his "character."

30. Examine Smith, 6–7; and Randall, 3: 673.

31. John Adams to Timothy Pickering, August 6, 1822, in *The Works of John Adams*, 10 vols. Ed. by Charles Francis Adams (Boston: Charles C. Little and James Brown, 1850), 2: 514.

32. L&B, 13: xlviii–xlix.

33. Randall, *Life of Jefferson*, 3: 345. In a footnote, Randall noted: "We have this [story] from one who had more than once heard it from the lips of the good 'parson' himself." Ibid., 345n.

34. This brief overview of the history of the "Anas" comes from Boyd, 22: x–xi, and 33–38.

35. In her essay "Slander, Poison, Whispers, and Fame: Jefferson's 'Anas' and Political Gossip in the Early Republic," published in 1995, Joanne B. Freeman provided a graphic portrait of a type of conversational communication that, despite its secretiveness and negative tone, was designed to promote a particular worldview. The Jefferson who emerges from the pages of Freeman's article fulfills three of her four rules governing gossip: He "avoided gossiping without proof"; he never revealed his "source without permission"; and he showed "no malice or motive when gossiping." He did, however, violate a fourth rule of etiquette, which states that "gossip should not be written." This was particularly evident in the history he compiled as a refutation of Marshall's *Life of Washington*. The Jefferson we also see is preoccupied with what he perceived to be Hamilton's monarchial ideas, chooses as his conversational partners those who share his republican philosophy, strives to protect his friends, and avoids the appearance of being a partisan combatant.

When Jefferson and his Republican colleagues, according to Freeman, engaged in "political gossip," some observers believed that this practice constituted an "immoral" and "dangerous behavior" which could unfairly destroy an opponent's reputation. Yet it was also viewed by those who participated in political gossip as "an ordinary event of the political drama" in the early republic. For it could be used "to form and reinforce alliances, devise political strategies, and shared goals." Finally, because gossip as practiced by Jefferson and other Republicans "allows us to view the world through a Republican lens, and offers us "a window into the heart of politics" in the crisis-filled atmosphere that marked the early republic, it must, argues Freeman, be regarded "as history." *Journal of the Early Republic* (spring 1995), vol. 15, no. 1, 25–57.

36. June 27, 1822, in Cappon, 2: 581.

37. TJ to Thomas Jefferson Randolph, December 30, 1809, in Betts and Bear, *The Family Letters of Thomas Jefferson*, 394–95.

38. Thomas Jefferson Randolph to Henry S. Randall, in Randall, *Life of Thomas Jefferson*, 3: 674.

39. TJ to John Page, October 31, 1775, in Boyd, 1: 251.

40. TJ to Francis Hopkinson, August 14, 1786, in Boyd, 10: 248–49.

41. John Adams to TJ, July 15, 1813, in Cappon, 2: 357.

42. John Adams to TJ, December 8, 1818, in Cappon, 2: 530.

43. TJ to Benjamin Rush, January 16, 1811, in *Writings*, 1234.

44. TJ to Benjamin Rush, ibid.; and TJ to John Adams, January 11, 1817, in Cappon, 2: 505.

45. TJ to Robert Skipwith, August 3, 1771, in Boyd, 1: 76–81.

46. TJ to Thomas Mann Randolph Jr., August 27, 1786, in *Writings*, 860–63.

47. TJ to Peter Carr, September 7, 1814, in ibid., 1346–1352.

48. TJ to John Minor, August 30, 1814, in Ford, 9: 480n–485n.

49. TJ to Chastellux, January 16, 1784, in Boyd, 6: 466–67.

50. Ibid., 467n.

51. TJ to Ezra Stiles, September 1, 1786, in *Writings*, 864–66.

52. Ezra Stiles to TJ, April 30, 1788, in Boyd, 13: 118. "TJ's letter of Sept. 1786 was printed in part in the *American Museum*, II (November 1787), 492–93, having doubtless been copied from the Public Prints to which Stiles communicated it." Ibid., 118n.

53. TJ to Thomas Law, June 13, 1814, in *Writings*, 1335–1339.

54. The letter to Gerry, written on January 26, 1799, is in ibid., 1055–62.

55. TJ to Mary Jefferson Eppes, January 7, 1798, in Betts and Bear, *The Family Letters of Thomas Jefferson*, 151–53.

56. TJ to Dr. William Small, May 7, 1775, in *Writings*, 747–48.

57. TJ to John Randolph, August 25, 1775, in ibid., 749–50.

58. TJ to Francis Eppes, January 19, 1821, in ibid., 1450–51.

59. TJ to James Madison, October 28, 1785, in ibid., 840–41.

60. TJ to John Adams, June 11, 1812, in Cappon, 2: 307.

61. TJ to Dr. Walter Jones, January 2, 1814, in *Writings*, 1318–21.

62. TJ to John Adams, October 12, 1823, in Cappon, 2: 600n.

63. Id., 599–601.

64. John Adams to TJ, November 10, 1823, in ibid., 601.

65. Boyd, 16: 28n.

# CHAPTER TEN

~

# Polemicist During
# the Revolutionary War Era

When writing his *Diary and Autobiography*, John Adams, recalling his days in the Continental Congress, gave this description of Jefferson as a public communicator:

> Mr. Jefferson had been now about a year a member of Congress, but had attended his Duty in the House but a very small part of the time and when there had never spoken in public: and during the whole time I satt with him in Congress, I never heard him utter three sentences together.

Later Adams extended his analysis of Jefferson the public speaker by explaining why he was sent to the Continental Congress to replace Richard Henry Lee as a delegate from Virginia. Lee, he said, "was not beloved by most of his colleagues," and "Mr. Jefferson was sett up to rival and supplant him." Everyone knew, Adams added, that "this could be done only by the Pen, for Mr. Jefferson could stand no competition with him or anyone else in the Elocution and public debate."[1]

The Adams portrait of Jefferson as a reluctant and ineffective orator who often preferred a rhetoric of silence instead of participation in a public assembly has, except in a few instances,[2] been the general consensus shared by most contemporary eyewitnesses and Jefferson scholars. This hesitancy to strive to become an orator in the tradition of Patrick Henry or of Richard Henry Lee was owing in part to his natural temperament and to his soft and gentle voice[3] which often could not be heard distinctly in a large auditorium.

But as a student of rhetoric and belles lettres, Jefferson, as we have observed, viewed discourse as being far more than oratory in the public assembly. It also includes, as both he and Adams recognized, eloquence of the pen. It is within this framework that we examine his efforts as a persuader in the public forum. We have chosen two of his most celebrated works for analysis in this chapter; they reveal him as an important polemicist before and during the Revolutionary War: *A Summary View of the Rights of British America* (1774) and the Declaration of Independence. We also consider briefly several addresses presented in 1775 that serve as connecting links between *A Summary View* and the Declaration.

Our goal in treating these discourses is not to try to cover the familiar ground so often discussed in depth by other scholars, but to answer two questions: (1) To what extent do these works conform to Jefferson's ideas on the rhetoric of virtue? (2) To what degree do they reflect his teachings on argumentation philosophy, on social affections, and on channeling a message? We approach these two questions as an integrated unit. Although our principal focus is on the salient features of each address, it is necessary in each case to recreate the rhetorical situation that gave rise to each discourse.

# A Summary View of the Rights of British America

## The Rhetorical Situation

Near the end of 1773, the East India Tea Company, with the approval of the British ministry, delivered large shipments of tea to Boston and to other ports in America. Objecting to the company's monopoly and what they considered to be high taxes on this product, many colonists were unwilling to accept the tea, and demanded that it be returned to England. In Boston, when this demand was denied by customs officials, a group of men, disguised as Indians, took action on December 18, 1773. They boarded the tea-carrying ships docked in Boston Harbor and deposited 342 chests of tea into the water. Outraged by this violation of private property rights, the British ministry, beginning in March 1774, initiated a series of laws designed to punish the citizens of Boston. These laws, called the Coercive Acts, produced at least four major results: (1) the charter of Massachusetts was radically altered; (2) the port of Boston was closed; (3) persons charged with capital crimes would be sent to England to stand trial; and (4) British soldiers would be sent to the Boston area so that they would be in a position to enforce the newly adopted laws.[4]

These actions aroused members of the opposition in Parliament who wanted a more conciliatory policy toward the colonies. On May 27, 1774, Lord Chatham gained the floor during a debate in the House of Lords. In his remarks of protest, he argued that it was unreasonable to punish all of the residents of Boston when the act of defiance was committed only by a few. After next suggesting that the destruction "of the tea was the effect of despair," he proceeded to say: "My Lords, I am an old man, and would advise the noble Lords in office to adopt a more gentle mode of governing America."[5] Despite Chatham's plea, the actions were upheld by a large majority, and the new rules were scheduled to go into effect on the first of June.

When word of the new British policy reached America in early May, consternation spread throughout the colonies. With the exception of Massachusetts itself, no colony of the country experienced a greater sense of urgency for an immediate forceful response than Virginia. On May 24, 1774, with Jefferson playing an active role, the House of Burgesses, convinced that the time had come for all of the colonies to act in unison, sought to lead the way by passing a resolution "designating a day of fasting and prayer." A preamble to the resolution expressed the hope "that the Minds of his Majesty and his Parliament may be inspired from above with Wisdom, Moderation, and Justice. . . ." Following this statement regarding the importance of three of the cardinal virtues, it then was recommended that on June 1 all members of the House assemble and shortly thereafter march to the church where they would hear prayers and a sermon "suitable to the Occasion."[6]

Three days later, when the House was again called into session, the members repeated their condemnation of the Boston port bills, and reaffirmed their belief "that an attack made on one of our sister colonies, to compel submission to arbitrary taxes, is an attack made on all British America, and threatens ruin to the rights of all, unless the united Wisdom of the whole be applied."[7]

Finally, Peyton Randolph, who was presiding chairman of the House of Burgesses, wrote to all members on May 31, reporting that he had received letters from Philadelphia and Boston depicting the serious consequences that the citizens of these cities would experience because of the British actions. The letter concluded with the announcement that the House would reconvene on August 1 to continue discussion of the crisis.[8]

During the period between Randolph's letter and the scheduled meeting on the first of August, Jefferson took two actions. First, early in July, as a representative to the House from Albemarle County, he coauthored a letter "to the Inhabitants of the Parish of St. Anne," requesting that they meet in their church on the 23rd of the month for the purpose of having "prayers and a sermon," expressing grave concern about the rapidly developing crisis, and asking God for guidance.[9]

Jefferson's second action was the preparation of an address to the House of Burgesses at their August meeting, with the desire that it might be adopted as "a petition to the King. . . ."[10] After he had completed his manuscript, and as the date of the session drew near, Jefferson set out for Williamsburg with several copies of the discourse, which he planned to propose in his "place as a member of the Convention of 1774."[11] But he fell ill with "dysentery on the road, and was unable to proceed."[12] To make certain, however, that the address be read to the Burgesses, he forwarded two copies of his remarks to Williamsburg—one to Peyton Randolph, the chairman, and the other to Patrick Henry, presumably because of his oratorical ability.[13]

According to Jefferson, Randolph informed the delegates that he had received an address from one of the members who was unable to be present because of a sudden illness. He then placed the manuscript on the table for anyone who wished to peruse it. Although no action was taken by the delegates who, in Jefferson's opinion, thought the arguments were too strong for the time,[14] the address was read aloud to a large group a short while later at the home of Peyton Randolph. Edmund Randolph, who was present at this gathering, recalled the response it generated: "I distinctly recollect the applause bestowed on most (of the resolutions), when they were read to a large company at the house of Peyton Randolph, to whom they were addressed."[15]

Some of Jefferson's friends concluded that the discourse should be published under the title: "A Summary View of the Rights of British America." Even though Jefferson had not given permission to have his address published, he nevertheless reported with some degree of satisfaction that the *Summary View* "found its way to England, was taken up by the opposition, interpolated a little by Mr. Burke, . . . and in that form ran rapidly through several editions."[16]

## The Content and Style of A *Summary View of the Rights of British America*

The opening statement of the introduction articulated the central idea of A *Summary View*. It stated that representatives of all the colonies, assembled in a "General Congress," hereby proclaim that the address, which will summarize the "united complaints of his majesty's subjects in America," be presented to the king. Its underlying premise was that the rights that were bestowed on the colonies and their inhabitants by "god and the laws" have been systematically violated. What is here being suggested, therefore, is not a request for special treatment, but a demand that America's natural rights be restored and perpetuated. His Majesty, moreover, should be reminded that the arguments now to be presented explaining our position are "penned in the language of truth."[17]

The body of the discourse contains three major claims which, in turn, are developed by multiple subordinate heads and supporting details. The first of these claims is based on a series of historical precedents grounded in experience and stated in the form of an analogy. This argument may be stated as follows: *Although the immigrants who settled in British America have consistently adhered to policies and practices comparable to those embraced by the Saxons who emigrated to Great Britain, the two groups have not been treated in a similar manner.*

To prove this contention, Jefferson asked the king to remember the history of the Saxons. These immigrants from northern Europe, he said, came to England, helped establish a renowned system of laws, and integrated themselves so completely in their new society that they and the natives became one people, the Anglo-Saxons. Similarly, there was no effort on the part of the countries from which they had come to exert any authority over them after they had migrated to another land. What mattered most in this historical precedent was the promotion of "public happiness."[18]

In further developing this experience-based argument from analogy, Jefferson drew a direct parallel to the English emigration to America. These bold adventurers, he noted, spilled their own blood "in acquiring lands for their settlement, their own fortunes expended in making their settlement effectual." As they risked their lives in this enterprise, they received some assistance from the British government in protecting them from their enemies. But this aid, while appreciated, appeared to be motivated not by a benevolent attitude toward the colonies but by the view that it would produce economic gains for England. Even more serious was the tendency of the mother country to disregard American laws even though they conformed to the Anglo-Saxon tradition. At no point, concluded Jefferson in summarizing his first claim, did the Americans have any intention to submit themselves "to the sovereignty of Great Britain." For to do so would be to sacrifice their "sacred and sovereign rights."

Convinced that he had successfully demonstrated through the simple rule of justice—which affirms the notion that people in the same essential category should be treated in an identical manner[19]—that British Americans did not receive the same consideration as that given to the Saxon immigrants who moved to England and their descendents, Jefferson was ready to be more specific in his second major claim: *The British Parliament, he argued, has treated the colonies in an unjust manner over a long period of time.*

This condition has been evident, in the first place, in cases in which they alone had a special interest. To see this more clearly, Jefferson continued, we may consider what has happened in the area of trade before the present era. In discussing this concept, Jefferson described free trade as a "natural right" of the colonists that, if "taken away or abridged," is an "unjust encroachment." Tracing the early modern history of trade regulations, he observed that before the mid-seventeenth century, Parliament prohibited the colonies from engaging in commerce "with all other parts of the world, except the island of Great Britain." Then in 1651, this practice was repealed, only to have this action reversed during the reign of Charles II.

These unjust, arbitrary acts regarding trade, continued Jefferson, were also strikingly present in our recent history. Besides the imposition of unfair duties on American exports and imports, the colonists have been permitted to have commerce in limited areas only; they have been restricted in the handling of surpluses of tobacco; they have been prohibited from making hats or furs for themselves; and they have been prevented from manufacturing iron products. Nor can it be overlooked that when iron is shipped to Great Britain, America is required to pay freight both to and from the island. Jefferson next emphasized the gravity of these arbitrary practices by offering the following disjunctive rhetorical syllogism:

> Either . . . justice is not the same thing in America as in Britain, or else
> The British parliament pays less regard to it here than there.

From this dilemma involving trade practices that deprived Americans of an opportunity to achieve public happiness through economic security, Jefferson drew these two inferences:

> . . . experience confirms the propriety of those political principles which exempt us from the jurisdiction of the British Parliament.
> The true ground on which we declare these acts void is that the British parliament has no right to exercise authority over us.

Thus far, we have observed that Jefferson used three of the elements of his philosophy of moral reasoning—arguments based on experience, on analogy, and on testimony, as seen in his citation of historical documents. He now was prepared to use the fourth element—the calculation of probabilities—as he attempted to show that Parliament not only had thwarted free trade but had repeatedly intermeddled "with the regulation of the internal affairs of the colonies." In addition to the grievances cited thus far, he presented the following litany of acts that Parliament had passed, each further diminishing the rights of the colonists: "An Act for levying certain duties"; the "Stamp Act"; an "Act for declaring the right of Parliament over the colonies"; an "Act suspending the legislature of New York"; and an "Act for granting duties on paper and tea." These grievances, combined with his earlier list, enabled him to declare:

> Single acts of tyranny may be ascribed to the accidental opinion of the day; but a series of oppressions, begun at a distinguished period, and pursued unalterably thro' every change of ministers, too plainly prove a deliberate, systematical plan of reducing us to slavery.

Although David Hume's Tory principles would have deterred him from endorsing Jefferson's arguments against Parliament, he most likely would have applauded his effort to construct an argument based on the weighing process of calculating probabilities.

These "tyrannical acts," Jefferson went on to say, stood in opposition to "the principles of common sense" he shared with Thomas Reid, and were in contrast with "the common feelings of human nature" upheld by Francis Hutcheson. It was also a violation of "common sense" and of a human being's nature that "160,000 tyrants" in Great Britain located several thousand miles away would be able to make slaves out of four million Americans, "every individual of whom is equal to every individual of them in virtue, in understanding, and in bodily strength." He brought the argument against Parliament to an end by recounting the injustices of the act to close Boston Harbor, and the decision to quarter British troops throughout sections of the Northeast.

Jefferson argued in his third claim that *His Majesty likewise has failed to fulfill his duties toward America.* The British Constitution has given to the king the power to veto a bill that has been passed by the "two branches of the legislature." Yet he has refused to exercise this right in British America. This was particularly evident with respect to the controversial subject of domestic slavery. It was Britain, asserted Jefferson, that introduced slaves in the colonies against the wishes of many British Americans. Yet whenever the colonies initiated steps "to exclude all further importations" of slaves "from Africa," his Majesty's "negative" defeated these proposals to eliminate an "infamous practice" that is an affront to the basic "rights of human nature."

We agree with those historians who have criticized Jefferson for suggesting that slavery was foisted on the Americans by the British. Among these critics were Joseph J. Ellis and Pauline Maier. In his *American Sphinx: The Character of Thomas Jefferson*, Ellis maintained that Jefferson's charge "made great polemic sense but historical and intellectual nonsense." For in blaming the British on the slavery issue, Jefferson was trying to absolve "slaveowners like himself from any responsibility or complicity in the establishment of an institution that was clearly at odds with the values on which the newly independent America was based."[20] While reaching a similar conclusion in her *American Scripture*, Maier used similarly strong language. Commenting on the long passage on the slave trade, the author asserted that Jefferson's use of such terms as "'prostituted,' 'murdering,' 'execrable,' and 'assemblage of horrors' . . . foundered in part because the image of King George personally 'captivating and carrying' innocent Africans into slavery was patently unbelievable."[21]

The second major criticism of the king stemmed from his refusal to "call another house of representatives" following the dissolution of "a previous one." Such neglect is a dereliction of duty because it violates even the most elementary principle of ethics rooted in our moral sense. Jefferson voiced his concern in words reflecting the views of John Locke:

> From the nature of things, every society must at all times possess within itself the sovereign powers of legislation. The feelings of human nature revolt against the supposition of a state so situated as that it may not in any emergency provide against dangers which perhaps threaten immediate ruin.

This fundamental moral principle of government, Jefferson observed, was upheld by our Saxon ancestors and by common law.

The final part of Jefferson's grievances against the king dealt with the arbitrary measures he sponsored that led to the use of English "armed forces, not made up of people here, nor raised by the authority of our laws." This has been done even though His Majesty has "no right" to do so. Moreover, these troops sent to our soil should be "liable to our laws," and be under civil authority rather than the military. The climax of this argument contained the observation that action taken "by force" can never produce a "right."

The conclusion of *A Summary View* makes use of appeals to the king that were more direct and personal. With language surprisingly bold and frank for the period in which he spoke, Jefferson declaimed:

Open your breast Sire, to liberal and expanded thought. Let not the name of George III be a blot on the page of history.
This, Sire, is the advice of your great American council, on the observance of which may perhaps depend your felicity and future fame, and the preservation of that harmony which alone can continue both to Great Britain and America the reciprocal advantages of their connection. Only aim to do your duty, and mankind will give you the credit where you fail.

In the conclusion, moreover, it seems clear how Jefferson used rhetoric to promote virtue. The ensuing statements—phrased in vivid language that goes beyond the "middling style" employed, for the most part, in the body of the discourse—use elevated words and thoughts that capture essential elements of his philosophy of virtue:

Let those flatter who fear: it is not an American art. To give praise where it is not due, might be well from the venal, but would ill beseem those who are asserting the rights of human nature.
The great principles of right and wrong are legible to every reader: to pursue them requires not the aid of many counsellors.
The god who gave us life, gave us liberty at the same time.

The overarching message Jefferson wished the king and leaders of Parliament to understand and appreciate was this: British Americans recognize the role that God plays in embedding a moral sense in human nature; they feel they have the natural ability to distinguish right from wrong; they are committed to the idea that honesty and courage are noble traits that should be a part of their daily lives; and their ardent wish is to have a government whose principal function is to promote happiness and the public good. Even though this latter goal had not been achieved because of oppressive measures enacted by Parliament and the king, "it is neither our wish nor our interest," acknowledged Jefferson, to "separate" at this time from Great Britain. Our "fervent prayer" instead, he added, is to have a policy of justice that establishes "fraternal love and harmony thro' the whole empire, and that (this) may continue to the latest ages of time. . . ." With these words he brought his first major public discourse to an end.

The impact of A *Summary View* was extensive in range and scope. The members of the Virginia delegation to the First Continental Congress, including Patrick Henry, took copies of the tract, or "instructions" as they viewed it, with them to Philadelphia.[22] Soon it was printed and distributed throughout the colonies. Meanwhile, after copies had been sent to England, "at least three British periodicals noticed the appearance of A

*Summary View* in their November 1774 issues. . . ."[23] When it became known that Jefferson was the author, he no longer was a relatively unknown legislator from Virginia; he had now become a major pamphleteer of the developing American Revolution.[24] By the time he arrived in Philadelphia as a delegate to the Second Continental Congress in June of 1775, he had become a celebrity. "Samuel Ward, a Rhode Island delegate, wrote Henry Ward on 22 June 1775: 'Yesterday the famous Mr. Jefferson a Delegate from Virginia in the Room of Mr. Randolph arrived, I have not been in Company with him yet, he looks like a very sensible, spirited, fine Fellow and by the Pamphlet which he wrote last summer he certainly is one.'"[25]

Jefferson scholars have given varied impressions of the content of *A Summary View*. Henry S. Randall, an early biographer, called the address "a declaration of independence nearly two years in advance of an adopted one."[26] Nathan Schachner described it as "an amazing document, blistering and revolutionary in content. . . ." He also noted that the author had covered new and provocative ground by attacking the king who hitherto had been regarded as being "above the battle."[27] Merrill Peterson suggested that this "6500 word paper" was "basically a wholesale repudiation of Parliament's authority over the Americans" which left "allegiance to a common King the only bond with the mother country."[28] More recently, Joseph Ellis extended the conclusions drawn by Peterson, arguing that Jefferson himself believed "his chief contribution was the constitutional argument that Parliament had no right *whatsoever* to exercise authority over the colonies." But, he added, it should be observed that Jefferson in his 1774 pamphlet was also beginning to focus on the monarchy "as the only remaining obstacle to the assertion of American independence." As a result, the indictments he made against the king in *A Summary View* prepared the way for a similar and more extensive attack appearing in the Declaration of Independence.[29]

Still other commentators, while recognizing the historical significance of *A Summary View*, singled out specific features in some of the argumentative claims which, in their opinion, contained either inaccurate or inappropriate interpretations. Alf J. Mapp Jr. complained that Jefferson addressed his "sovereign in a naively hortatory and pedagogic tone."[30] Garry Wills voiced concern over the references to the Boston Tea Party which, he believed, could not be supported by convincing data.[31] One of the more pointed criticisms came from Paul Finkelman, who questioned Jefferson's sincerity in his argument on the evils of the slave trade.[32] Ellis, moreover, found fault with Jefferson's first claim discussed above concerning the Saxons who had emigrated to Great Britain and formed a government worthy of emulation in the modern period. In accepting this traditional Whig interpretation of history, Jefferson, according to Ellis, was subscribing to a "romantic endorsement of a pristine past," or "an idyllic time and place" that never existed. This fabrication of history, he added, is nothing more than what is called the "Saxon Myth."[33]

The critics, in addition, focused on Jefferson's use of language in *A Summary View*. The discourse, observed Randall, "furnished a good number of *phrases* of the Revolution."[34] Mapp's view was divided on the merits of the style. "Some of its sentences," he said, "smack of the poster art of the pamphleteer and some are among the noblest written by any American of the eighteenth century."[35] Ellis cited one of Jefferson's typical claims to show that "The style . . . was simple and emphatic, with a dramatic flair that previewed certain passages in the Declaration of Independence."[36]

Our own concern in placing *A Summary View* in perspective is to determine whether Jefferson's claims met the standards he taught on the role of virtue in rhetoric and emphasized in his principles of argumentation and language control. We believe that his faith in the concept that the primary subject matter of rhetoric is virtue was largely upheld. The grievances he leveled against Parliament and the king, which occupied most of the space in the address, were based upon the perception that the two branches of government they represented had acted in an arbitrary manner that was unwise, intemperate, and unjust. Additionally, these leaders had consistently ignored that the Creator had endowed mankind with an unmistakable moral sense that provides insights with respect to what is right and wrong. In all, these grievances show that the colonists, instead of being treated as equal partners, had been relegated to slavery. Unless this lack of benevolence, this disregard for the public good, and this repeated violation of justice[37] were modified, there would be little chance, thought Jefferson, to have a harmonious relationship between America and Great Britain. Yet despite this apparent threat he was not at this point willing to give up hope that some type of reconciliation might be possible. Relying on his ideas on the social affections that taught the importance of identification, he asserted that America did not desire to separate from Great Britain. What it most urgently wished instead was to have a policy of mutual trust and respect.

We feel also that in most instances Jefferson put into practice his philosophy of argumentation and language control. As we have seen, he made persuasive use of the four elements of reasoning—experience, testimony, analogy, and the calculation of probabilities. Although his claims regarding the Boston Tea Party lacked strong supporting data,[38] and some of the charges against the king were overdrawn, he generally succeeded in fulfilling his introductory pledge that his arguments would be based on "truth." That the overall thrust of his case was also rooted in what he perceived to be the principles of common sense, there can be little question. The message, finally, relied on an organizational pattern that promoted unity, coherence, and emphasis, and on language that was clear, concise, and occasionally vivid and compelling. Because of this overall strength in word choice and arrangement, the style proved suitable to generate understanding, to stimulate the imagination, and to arouse the passions.

# The Declaration of Independence

In the months following the publication and distribution of A *Summary View*, the grievances that Jefferson had described not only were not addressed by Parliament and the king, but further acts of oppression were introduced. The heightened tensions resulting from the government's hostile responses caused alarm among those in Parliament who favored a policy of reconciliation. Not the least of these concerned leaders was a longtime sympathizer with the American cause—Lord Chatham. Armed with the knowledge he had obtained from consultations with Benjamin Franklin and from reading statements and proclamations from the First Continental Congress in Philadelphia, Chatham delivered two speeches in the House of Lords urging the use of conciliatory measures to dampen the conflict before it was too late.

On January 20, 1775, he argued in support of the proposition that troops should be removed from the Boston area as a gesture of British faith and good will. Parliament, he noted, must acknowledge that if the colonies are not granted the privilege of levying their own taxes, they are being denied the right of property. Then, turning to his fellow ministers who upheld the view that "the *Americans must not be heard*," he asserted: "*They have been condemned unheard.*" Those of us who have read the closely reasoned "papers transmitted to us from America," Chatham added, cannot help but conclude that the representatives in the Continental Congress at Philadelphia are men of "decency, firmness and wisdom" whose cause should be our "own." We have no reasonable alternative, therefore, but to institute policies affecting both them and us that are based on "justice," "dignity," and "prudence."[39] Parliament by a vote of 68 to 18 defeated the recommendation.

Eleven days later, after further consultation with Franklin, Chatham, still determined to do whatever was possible to solve the problem with America, introduced a bill for the creation of "an imperial union." The major features of the plan included three provisions: (1) The "Continental Congress" should "be made official and permanent"; (2) it should "be asked to make a voluntary grant for imperial purposes"; and (3) Parliament should "suspend the punitive acts."[40] This proposed bill, after a spirited debate, was rejected. Both of these presentations by Chatham, as will later be noted, made an impression on Jefferson.

Meanwhile, Lord North, Britain's Prime Minister, was developing a proposal he hoped might be satisfactory both to his government and to the American colonies. On February 20, North's plan was introduced to the House of Commons. The essence of this resolution was as follows: "whenever a colony, in addition to providing for its own government, should raise a fair proportion for the common defense, and place this sum at the disposal of Parliament, that colony should be exempted from all farther taxation, except such duties as might be necessary for the regulation of commerce."[41] The implications of this seemingly conciliatory measure were clear. By making it possible for Parliament to deal separately with each colony through a policy of rewards and punishments, the potential for generating animosity among the colonies toward one another would be unusually strong. It was, in effect, an attempt to weaken the united front that was beginning to characterize American responses to oppressive British actions—a fact that Edmund Burke fully realized and highlighted in his famous "Conciliation of America Speech" delivered in April.[42]

Lord North's proposal, along with military action in Massachusetts in the spring of 1775, provided the rhetorical setting for Jefferson to develop three persuasive public addresses that served as a vitally significant background to the writing of the Declaration of Independence.

## Prelude to the Declaration of Independence: Three Addresses by Jefferson in 1775

Two of these three important discourses were responses to Lord North's divisive proposal. The first, presented at the request of Peyton Randolph, was addressed to the Virginia House of Burgesses on June 10, 1775. Speaking in a spirit of moderation in the introduction, Jefferson observed "that next to the possession of liberty, we should consider" the desire for "Reconciliation the greatest of all human blessings." This conciliatory opening statement was followed by a brief discussion of six reasons why North's plan was unacceptable to the people of Virginia. Beginning each objection with the word "Because," he repeated a premise appearing in *A Summary View* that "the British Parliament has no right to intermeddle with the support of civil government in the Colonies."

In four of the remaining five claims, Jefferson argued that North's plan did not respond satisfactorily to the issues of taxation, trade, and the presence of British armed forces on American soil. He then developed the argument that the colonies were united in opposing a policy designed to weaken the cords that bind them. With strong language, he affirmed that these relationships would never be broken:

> We consider ourselves as bound in Honor as well as Interest to share our general Fate with our Sister colonies, and should hold ourselves base Deserters of that union, to which we have acceded, were we to agree on any Measures distinct and apart from them.

In general, Jefferson noted, the North proposal was far inferior to the conciliatory bills offered by Lord Chatham.

The conclusion of this public discourse reasserted that Parliament had consistently ignored the remonstrations of America; the king had refused to answer the colonists' supplications; and when appeals "to the native honor and justice" of the "British nation" had been made, "their efforts in our favour" have proved to be "ineffectual." In the face of these grievances that were being steadily intensified, "What," Jefferson asked, "remains to be done?" He found his answer in these words:

> That we commit our injuries to the even-handed justice of that being who doth no wrong, earnestly beseeching him to illuminate the Councils and prosper the endeavors of those to whom America hath confided her hopes; that thro' their wise direction we may again see reunited the blessings of Liberty, Property, and Union with *Great Britain*.[43]

Soon after the Virginia Resolutions, as written by Jefferson, were passed by a unanimous vote,[44] he journeyed to Philadelphia with the approved document in hand and reported the results to the Second Continental Congress. On July 22, he was appointed to a committee of four— the other members being Franklin, John Adams, and Richard Henry Lee—to prepare a draft expressing the opinion of Congress on North's

proposal. Because he had been the successful author of the Virginia Resolutions, he was given the same assignment by other committee members.

Not surprisingly, what he wrote contained similar arguments to those
advanced in the Virginia address. There were, however, several rhetorical
changes. This time, Jefferson enlarged the six arguments to ten, although
they covered essentially the same ground. The primary difference was
that several subordinate headings in the Virginia Resolutions were now
elevated to main contentions; and the arguments, like those made in A
Summary View, used more compelling speech details and language usage.
This was particularly noticeable in his tenth claim, which sought to refute North's attempt to "deceive" the "world" into believing that there
was nothing in dispute between America and Great Britain but the area
of "levying taxes."

When the world is made aware of these ensuing facts, they would come
to understand and appreciate the reasonableness of American appeals.
They would, for example, see clearly

> how inadequate to justice are these vaunted terms (laid down by Lord
> North). . . .
> the rapid and bold succession of injuries, which, during a course of eleven
> years, have been aimed at the Colonies. . . .
> the pacific and respectful expostulations, which, during that whole time,
> were the sole arms we opposed to them. . . .
> our complaints were either not heard at all, or were answered with new and
> accumulated injury. . . .
> (that) the Minister himself on an earlier occasion declared, 'that he would
> never treat with America, till he had brought her to his feet. . . .'
> the purpose (of the Ministry) has already in part been carried into execu-
> tion by their treatment of Boston, and burning of Charlestown. . . .
> the great armaments with which they have invaded us. . . .

When "laid together," said Jefferson, these cumulative data constituted
convincing proof that American leaders had been reasonable at every
stage in the smoldering controversy.[45] In sum, by using one of his favorite
arguments, the calculating or weighing of probabilities, and by phrasing
his claims in terms of virtue, he was persuaded that the world at large
would identify with the American cause. He also could take pleasure in
knowing that Congress adopted his resolutions on July 31.

Before Jefferson had concluded his discourse on Lord North's proposal,
he was busy preparing another address to be presented to Congress. It was
on the theme, the "Declaration of the Causes and Necessity for Taking up

Arms." A request for such a declaration was drawn up by Congress on June 23, two days after Jefferson had arrived in Philadelphia. Assigned to a committee with five other members, he was to collaborate with John Rutledge, William Livingston, Benjamin Franklin, John Jay, and John Dickinson. The final document that eventually was approved was coauthored by Jefferson and Dickinson. Because our purpose, however, is to see how Jefferson's mind and rhetorical practice were working during this pre-Declaration of Independence period, we first need to summarize the "Fair Copy" he wrote "for the committee." A number of the elements in this copy were incorporated into the final draft which Dickinson put together.[46]

The first part of Jefferson's "Fair Copy" reviewed again the steps that had been taken by Parliament in their persistent effort to exert "absolute" control over the colonies. Once this point had been made, he next asserted that the American cause was approved by "supreme reason," the rule of "justice," and by the example set by our forefathers who risked their lives and well-being as they came to this country to establish a society based on "civil and religious freedom."

While America has "reasoned" and "remonstrated with Parliament" to remove the policies that have enslaved its populace, continued Jefferson, British military forces brutally attacked Lexington and Concord, and burned and razed Charlestown—acts of perfidy that led to the killing of "great numbers of people." So that there would be no misunderstanding of American intent to protect itself with courage and resolve in view of such unwarranted attacks, Jefferson made this bold claim: "We do then most solemnly, before god and the world declare, that regardless of every consequence, at the risk of every stress, the arms we have been compelled to assume we will use with perseverance. . . ." Of importance in this address, as was the case with A Summary View and the two discourses on Lord North's plan for conciliation, was Jefferson's concluding expression of hope that the union between Great Britain and the colonies would not be fully broken. In stating this sentiment, he said: "we do further assure them (the members of Parliament) that we mean not in any wise to affect that union with them in which we have so long and happily lived, and which we wish so much to see again restored."[47]

In the spring and early summer of 1775, it is clear that Jefferson continued the rhetorical campaign he had begun the year before in A Summary View. Both in the Virginia assembly and in the Second Continental Congress, he was given assignments that gave him opportunities to reflect at length on the status of the American colonies as it pertained to the British government. His success in responding to these rhetorical challenges gave him a strong reputation as a polemicist whose knowledge of history and philosophy, and his ability to construct arguments and phrase them in a clear and compelling manner, ultimately led to his choice to become the author of a work that would be permanently associated with his name.

## The Declaration of Independence and the Discourse of Virtue

In the preceding overview of rhetorical events leading up to the Declaration of Independence, we have observed a steady progression of deteriorating relations between the colonies and Great Britain and a growing sense in America of impending crisis. In anticipating subsequent developments, historian John Hazelton observed that Jefferson's *A Summary View*, combined with the creation of the First Continental Congress in the same year, signaled *"the beginning of the American Union."*[48] The tumultuous events of 1774 were followed the next year by a series of events that further galvanized American sentiment. During this historically significant year, the battles of Lexington and Concord, the death of General Warren at Bunker Hill, the destruction of the community of Charlestown, and the inadequacy of Lord North's proposal helped to propel Jefferson on the American stage as a principal spokesman for the cause of the colonies. Similarly important, these developments influenced a continued shift in public opinion. As Hazelton noted, it became the first time that a number of the colonists were even willing to entertain independence as "a possibility."[49]

What seemed to give the idea of independence a significant thrust in the forum of public debate in early 1776 was the publication of Thomas Paine's *Common Sense*.[50] The influence of this pamphlet on the actual movement toward independence has been debated by historians, but the incendiary nature of its message is beyond dispute. Eric Foner, in his *Thomas Paine and Revolutionary America*, argued that *Common Sense* "transformed the terms of political debate" in America by attacking "hereditary rule," the English form of government, and a continuing plea for reconciliation with Great Britain. What was needed instead, Paine argued, was independence and a republican government. Written in plain, direct, and forceful language as well as a tone of "outrage," *Common Sense* had an "astonishing success." The pamphlet, observed Foner, "went through twenty-five editions and reached literally hundreds of thousands of readers in the single year of 1776."[51]

Paine's revolutionary message found a sympathetic audience in Virginia. On May 15, with 112 members present, the Virginia Convention passed this resolution: "RESOLVED unanimously, that the delegates appointed to represent this colony in General Congress be instructed to propose to that respectable body to declare the United Colonies free and independent states, absolved from all allegiance to, or dependence upon, the crown or parliament of Great Britain. . . ."[52] Within three weeks following the adoption of the resolution, the Virginia delegates at the Second Continental Congress carried out these instructions by introducing a motion stating that "Congress should declare that these United Colonies are & of right ought to be free & independent states. . . ."[53] With this action it had become clear that Virginia was to play a preeminent role in Congress in 1776.

During the discussion of the motion to separate from Great Britain, a five-person committee was appointed to draw up a document calling for independence: John Adams, Benjamin Franklin, Thomas Jefferson, Roger Sherman, and Robert R. Livingston. The first duty of the committee was to designate someone to serve as author. The two favorites for the assignment were Jefferson and Adams. The latter prevailed upon Jefferson to accept the challenge because of his reputation as an excellent writer and student of literature, because he was from the populous and powerful colony of Virginia, and because he had a non-controversial image.[54]

After agreeing to become the author, Jefferson decided to compose the work in the place where he was residing—a "new brick house" with three levels, located on Seventh and Market streets. Situated on the second floor, he sat at his desk in the parlor and, without the aid of notes or documents,[55] wrote "habitually" until the first draft was completed.[56] Jefferson's recollection that he had no source materials at his disposal to guide him as he composed the Declaration did not imply that his message was an impromptu discourse. For firmly engraved in his mind were the teachings of Cicero, Bacon, Locke, and the Scottish moral philosophers. He also, obviously, was fully aware of what he had written in A Summary View, in his two addresses opposing Lord North's proposal, and in his discourse in Congress supporting the use of arms by the colonies. Finally, Jefferson, according to Pauline Maier, was fully conscious of two other sources that stimulated his thinking as he sat down to write his drafts of the Declaration. "One was the draft preamble for the Virginia constitution that he had just finished and which was itself based upon the English Declaration of Rights; the other, a preliminary version of the Virginia Declaration of Rights, had been drafted for the convention sitting in Williamsburg by George Mason. . . ."[57] In each of these instances, either Jefferson or a colleague had covered themes and used historical data and language that would again be useful on this occasion.

When Jefferson had finished his "Rough Draft," he showed it to Adams and Franklin, the two committee members whose advice he cherished. He then made the changes they had recommended, along with several modifications of his own, and the committee submitted his second draft to Congress.[58] For the next several days an animated discussion, leading to the acceptance of several substantive amendments, culminated in the adoption of the Declaration of Independence as it is known today.

To examine Jefferson's creativity as a rhetor and his sense of virtue in fulfilling his duty as the author of the most important public discourse of his career, and arguably in American history, we need at the outset to summarize two major claims that were incorporated in the first two drafts but later deleted by members of the Continental Congress. The first of these claims dealt with the subject of slavery—a point he had discussed in *A Summary View*. In some of the strongest language he ever used in a public setting, he made this damaging charge against the king:

> He has incited treasonable insurrections of our fellow-citizens with the allurements of forfeiture & confiscation of our property. He has waged cruel war against human nature itself, violating it's most sacred rights of life and liberty in the persons of a distant people who never offended him, captivating & carrying them into slavery in another hemisphere or to incur miserable death in their transportation thither. This piratical warfare, the opprobrium of *infidel* powers, is the warfare of the *Christian* king of Great Britain. Determined to keep open a market where Men should be bought & sold, he has prostituted his negative for suppressing every legislative attempt to prohibit or to restrain this execrable commerce. And that this assemblage of horrors might want no fact of distinguished die, he is now exciting those very people to rise in arms among us, and to purchase that liberty of which he has deprived them, by murdering the people on whom he also obtruded them: thus paying off former crimes committed against the *Liberties* of one people, with crimes which he urges them to commit against the lives of another.[59]

In the first half of this two-pronged attack, Jefferson, as the preceding passage clearly reveals, indicted the king for promoting an "execrable" slave trade that was an offense against the liberty, justice, and dignity of the African people exported to America against their will. This contention was similar to the argument he had stressed in *A Summary View*. But Jefferson was not content to stop here. In the second half of the claim, he accused the king of arousing the slaves to such a fever pitch that they were willing to secure their rights by adopting a policy of insurrection in Virginia and other areas of the South. Apparently Jefferson felt justified in labeling the king as an enemy of the American people because of his unjust, unfair, and unchristian policies, which had produced division instead of harmony and public evil instead of public good.

When Congress later deleted this argument on the grounds that it would generate dissension among those Northerners who had endorsed (and in some cases had profited from) the slave trade in the past, and among those plantation owners in South Carolina, North Carolina, and Georgia who wanted to continue its practice,[60] Adams was disappointed. Jefferson's statement on the slave trade, he asserted, was on the side of right and justice. Moreover, it was an eloquent oratorical passage that was the high point of the first two drafts of the Declaration.[61] Some modern critics have been far less generous than Adams in evaluating the deleted argument on the slave trade. Merrill Peterson, for instance, gave this assessment of the decision by Congress to eliminate the passages on the slave trade:

> True, as Jefferson knew from Virginia experience, the Crown had suppressed legislative attempts to stop the importation of slaves. But the Virginians had been motivated perhaps less by humanitarian than by selfish considerations, such as protecting the value of their property in slaves and securing their communities from the dangers of an ever-increasing slave population.[62]

This critique, it should be noted, is in direct opposition to Jefferson's repeated testimony expressing his displeasure with all aspects of the adopted amendment.[63]

A second important deletion pertained to one of the sections focusing on the abuses of Parliament. It was in this portion of the first and second drafts that Jefferson reminded Parliament that America's decision to approve of the concept of "one common king" did not mean a submission to the rule of that legislative body—a political assembly that had permitted "their chief magistrate to send over not only souldiers of our common blood, but Scotch & foreign mercenaries to invade and destroy us." Jefferson continued his argument by asserting that these "unfeeling brethren" who regard "grandeur" and "freedom" to be "below their dignity" must be held "as we hold the rest of mankind enemies in war, in peace friends." Under such oppressive conditions, he suggested, the colonists had no moral recourse but to travel "the road to happiness & to glory . . . apart from them. . . ."[64]

Although Congress allowed other indictments against Parliament to remain in the final version, they thought this particular claim was too severe in its tone. Altogether, approximately one-fourth of the second draft which was debated on the floor between the first and fourth of July was deleted through amendments.[65] As this was being done, Jefferson remained silent, thinking that it was his duty to let others voice their opinions. But his nonverbal communication pattern indicated he was experiencing distress as some of his most deeply felt sentiments were being vigorously challenged. Aware of this, Franklin sought to allay the conflict by telling a story of John Thompson the hatter and his new sign.[66] Despite Jefferson's disappointment in the changes Congress made in the first draft he and the Committee of Five submitted, most commentators believe that the final document was superior. Carl Becker, for example, concluded that the revisions strengthened the Declaration.[67] Pauline Maier, in agreeing with Becker, rejected the arguments of those who believe that Jefferson's draft was "the document most worth studying and admiring. . . ."[68] Maier also reminded her readers that the final revision, in which Congress was a part, is what Americans have come to know as a "sacred" text in our country's history. We concur fully with the opinion of Becker and Maier. As we now begin our analysis of the Declaration, we turn to the document's content and style.

The opening sentence of the Declaration, consisting of seventy-one words, contains the rationale for the American action that was about to take place. Speaking directly to mankind as a whole, this statement asserts the premise that whenever one group of people, guided by the laws of Nature and of God, resolves to separate from another, with which it has been closely connected, it is necessary to explain the causes. What follows in the body of the document, therefore, are three main reasons for the decision to sever the ties that long have bound the colonies and Great Britain.

*The first cause requiring separation is based upon the philosophy of natural rights and the principles of virtue that constitute the essential nature of things.* In the most celebrated passage of all of his writings, Jefferson, in developing this claim, listed a series of self-evident premises which put in graphic form the essence of his political philosophy:

> We hold these truths to be self-evident, that all men are created equal, that they are endowed by their Creator with certain unalienable Rights, that among these are Life, Liberty, and the pursuit of Happiness, that to secure these rights, Governments are instituted among Men, deriving their just powers from the consent of the governed. That whenever any Form of

Government becomes destructive of these ends, it is the Right of the People to alter or to abolish it, and to institute new Government, laying its foundation on such principles and organizing its powers in such form, as to them shall seem most likely to effect their safety and Happiness.[69]

This brief passage, comprised of two sentences and 110 words, makes use of at least four self-evident premises that cannot easily be contested. They may be summarized as follows:

(1) "All men are created equal."
(2) God has endowed all people with the indisputable rights of "Life, Liberty, and the pursuit of Happiness."
(3) The purpose of governments is to recognize that their duty is to serve the governed.
(4) When any government fails to fulfill its responsibilities, the people have "the Right . . . to alter or abolish it" and "to institute" a "new Government."[70]

All of these statements in one way or another are intuitive, commonsense truths that give strength and reliance to the document as a whole. Moreover, it is worth noting that a rhetor who makes these claims needs to have the wisdom to understand human nature and to recognize the reciprocal relationships that exist between God and men, and between governments and their citizens. But this wisdom also has an alliance with the virtue of justice that combines duty and fairness, which are essential for the promotion of happiness.

The next paragraph, an extension of the preceding one, shows how prudence and experience build upon the notion of self-evidence for the purpose of giving further persuasive power to the philosophical argument. Using three sentences and 117 words, Jefferson states this contention in the following way:

Prudence, indeed, will dictate that Governments long established should not be changed for light and transient causes; and accordingly all experience hath shewn, that mankind are more disposed to suffer, while evils are sufferable, than to right themselves by abolishing the forms to which they are accustomed. But when a long train of abuses and usurpations, pursuing invariably the same Object evinces a design to reduce them under absolute Despotism, it is their right, it is their duty, to throw off such Government, and to provide new Guards for their future security. Such has been the patient sufferance of these Colonies; and such is now the necessity which constrains them to alter their former Systems of Government.

Telltale signs of Locke, Hume, and Hutcheson—all of whom influenced Jefferson's philosophy of argument—are visible in this claim. It was Locke who, in combination with his ideas on self-evidence, described the strength and relevance of constructing arguments grounded in first principles and in the essential nature of things.[71] It was Hume who, in extending the ideas of Locke, demonstrated how the generation of belief could be achieved through effective use of the calculation of probabilities. And it was Hutcheson who, motivated by his devotion to the public good, emphasized the point that a benevolent relationship must exist between those who govern and those who are governed. All these influences on Jefferson's philosophy of natural rights, of argument, and of virtue led him to reach the conclusion above that the past experiences and unfolding events now constrain the colonies "to alter their former systems of Government."

Jefferson knew, however, that two additional arguments must be developed before his discussion of the causes was complete. One of these would focus on the grievances produced by the king; the other with the responses to these wrongs by the colonists.

*The second cause for asserting independence, Jefferson argued, was that the king has repeatedly violated the endowed rights of the American people by adopting policies to exert tyrannical control over each of the colonies.* To prove this point, he announced that the facts he would now present would be addressed "to a candid world." He was confident that this type of universal audience[72] would be reasonable as they analyzed the charges against the king—grievances he had discussed in earlier discourses.

In describing the first cause for separation, Jefferson functioned as a philosopher interested in natural rights. This time, however, he fulfilled the role of a historian and an experienced political observer. Singling out eighteen specific wrongs, he presented the image of a noncaring king who had no intention to make Americans equal partners in the governing process.

The first three indictments were concerned with the king's practice of preventing laws to be passed which would promote the public good. The next three pertain to his unfriendly and provocative actions regarding the legislative bodies established in each colony. Charges 7 through 9 consider his policy of obstructing laws and the administration of justice. Eight of the remaining grievances accuse the king of using British armed forces, foreign mercenaries, and Indian tribes to endanger the lives and property of the American people. Not the least of these eight points that denied basic human rights and constitutional guarantees was item 14, which states: "He has abdicated Government here, by declaring us out of his Protection and waging war against us."

The thirteenth indictment, more so than the others, sought to create presence by listing a series of facts in the form of cumulative evidence to show how the constitutions of the individual states have been violated:

> He has combined with others to subject us to a jurisdiction foreign to our constitution, and unacknowledged by our laws; giving his Assent to their Acts of pretended Legislation: For Quartering large bodies of armed troops among us: For protecting them, by a mock Trial, from punishment for any Murders which they should commit on the Inhabitants of these States: For cutting off our Trade with all parts of the world: For imposing Taxes on us without our Consent: For depriving us in many cases of the benefits of Trial by Jury: For transporting us beyond Seas to be tried for pretended offences: For abolishing the free System of English laws in a neighbouring Province, establishing therein an Arbitrary government, and enlarging its Boundaries so as to render it at once an example and fit instrument for introducing the same absolute rule into these Colonies: For taking away our Charters, abolishing our most valuable Laws, and altering fundamentally the Forms of our Governments: For suspending our own Legislatures, and declaring themselves invested with power to legislate for us in all cases whatsoever.

This thirteenth complaint, with its nine supporting provisions, perhaps would have been more appropriate as a summary statement in the conclusion of the argument against the king. But despite its misplacement, it was an effective use of the weighing of evidence on an imaginary scale, as Hume had recommended.

*The third cause for asserting independence, according to Jefferson, was the persistent tendency of the king and other British leaders to ignore the pleas from the colonists.* Each time a major grievance had occurred, American representatives "petitioned for redress in the most humble terms." These petitions included references to early migration to America from England, statements protesting "unwarrantable jurisdiction" over the states, assertions that the two countries had a "common kindred," and appeals to the "native justice and magnanimity" of the British people. All of these remonstrations, Jefferson observed, were met with additional injuries.

Now that the three causes for separation had been explained, Jefferson moved to the conclusion. As he did so, he called upon "the Supreme Judge of the world" to recognize the "rectitude" of America's "intentions," and expressed the hope that the colonists would grant their approval and cooperation. He then declared "That these United Colonies are, and of

Right ought to be Free and Independent states. . . ." This declaration of freedom, he added, carries with it the "full Power to levy War, conclude Peace, contract Alliances, establish Commerce, and do all other Acts and Things which Independent States may of right do."

The question that now arises is this: How successful was Jefferson in conforming to his principles of argument and theory of virtue in constructing the Declaration of Independence? His awareness of the significance of this discourse can be seen, first of all, by noting the three audiences he wished to address. The three groups he hoped would lend their support to the message of independence were the colonists, the British government and people, and a "candid world" of thinking men and women who relied on reason. He thus needed to develop appeals that would stimulate the understanding, the imagination, the passions, and the will of the members of each target group.

What we also see from this analysis is that Jefferson's three claims depicting causes were developed in a soundly conceived and well-executed manner. By beginning with an argument rooted in the concept of natural rights,[73] he laid a solid foundation upon which the first cause for separation could be understood and felt. As he progressed to the next contention delineating a second cause, he confidently asserted that the facts he planned to submit would prove the serious nature of the grievances against the king. These facts, presented in 656 words out of a total of 1,281 for the full Declaration, embraced, as earlier observed, eighteen specific charges, many of which had appeared in A Summary View. It seems evident that in the presentation of these data, he handled his burden of proof.

The third cause, which described the numerous attempts by the colonists to instruct and warn the British—particularly the king—about the nature and impact of the wrongs bestowed on the Americans was a logical last step to demonstrate the need for independence. In detailing the remonstrations that had been patiently made by American leaders and then summarily ignored by the British over a number of years, Jefferson, according to Carl Becker, sought to demonstrate that the colonists had kept faith by not rushing "into rebellion," but were now confronted with such an oppressive situation that they must "either throw off the yoke or submit to be slaves."[74]

If the arguments and structure of the Declaration met the high standards upheld in Jefferson's philosophy of reasoning, so too did the appeals to virtue. The entire discussion centered its attention on moral principles. The introduction, the first cause emphasizing natural rights,[75] and the conclusion, setting forth the action that should be taken, discussed the positive aspects of virtue that had marked the beliefs and commitments of the colonists. By contrast, the grievances against the king and the rejected remonstrations of the Americans dealt with the troubling consequences resulting from actions that were immoral. In a more specific way, Jefferson alluded to "rights" seven times and "justice" four. In addition, he mentioned at least once such precepts of virtue as "duty," "equality," "prudence," "magnanimity," and "public good." What is more noteworthy was the stress he placed upon the reciprocal relationships between God and man, the government and the governed, and the people and each other. All of these virtues he singled out play a crucial role in generating the type of happiness Jefferson believed to be an endowed right of a free and independent people.

Because of the gravity of the subject matter, many of the words, phrases, and sentences used what Jefferson called the "middling style"— a style regarded as the appropriate linguistic vehicle for the historian and philosopher. Language on this level is marked by clarity, conciseness, and forcefulness in the tradition of Thomas Paine's *Common Sense*. There were, however, numerous instances when he employed a style that was "elevated" which he viewed as suitable to the orator and the poet. The following examples are representative:

> We hold these truths to be self-evident, that all men are created equal, that they are endowed by their Creator with certain unalienable Rights, that among these are Life, Liberty, and the pursuit of Happiness. . . .

> And for the support of this Declaration, with a firm reliance on the protection of divine Providence, we mutually pledge to each other our Lives, our Fortunes and our sacred Honor.

The first of these sentences achieves power that lifts the appeal to the level of the sublime because, as Longinus would have observed, it expresses great moral ideas in a vivid, compelling, and appropriate manner. The sentence, moreover, is drawn from the paragraph that Merrill Peterson portrays as "the most sacred writing of our history."[76] The second statement, which constitutes the concluding line of the Declaration, derives its strength from the theme of virtue that leads to a highly persuasive structural climax. In a moving periodic form, it begins by establishing the colonists' relationship to God and ends with a resolve that binds all Americans to a pledge of honor, even if it meant the loss of their lives and fortunes.

Two other sentences reveal how Jefferson, in describing the king, used incisive and penetrating language that opens the doors to the mind:

> He has plundered our seas, ravaged our Coasts, burnt our towns, and destroyed the Lives of our people.

> A Prince, whose character is thus marked by every act which may define a Tyrant, is unfit to be the ruler of a free people.

These vividly stated assertions, compressed in sentences that have an average length of twenty-one words,[77] let the reader see and feel the unjust acts, and grasp the meaning of what constitutes a tyrant. In all, we agree with Peterson's assessment that the language of the Declaration

> was bold yet elevated, plain and direct yet touched with philosophy, befitting a solemn appeal to the reason of mankind. In rhythmic strides from the first nobly turned phrase to the last, the argument inspired conviction in the cause of American freedom. . . .[78]

Jefferson's great triumph in 1776 gave him an immortal place in history. For the remaining years of his life, and in subsequent generations as well, July the Fourth became an annual day of celebration signaling a time for rededication to the importance of the ideas of "Life, Liberty, and the pursuit of Happiness." One of the highlights of these festive occasions was the oral reading of the Declaration. Samuel Harrison Smith, the editor of the *National Intelligencer*, described his experience at a dinner party where he was an oral interpreter on July 4, 1803:

> Yesterday was a day of joy to our citizens and of pride to our President. It is a day which you know he always enjoys. Before dinner, I had the honor of reading the declaration . . . tho' I did not have the ambition to be eloquent, yet I felt anxious to escape the implication of inability. As it happened, however, the reading went off very well, and I was complimented for the precision and spirit with which it was delivered, and I was pleased with learning that not a word was missed in the utmost parts of the room. . . .[79]

One of the most interesting aspects of the narrative account of this July Fourth event is that Smith, a journalist and specialist in written communication, was gratified by the oral dimension of his presentation. He demonstrated pride in saying that "the reading went off very well, and I was complimented for the precision and spirit with which it was delivered, and I was pleased with learning that not a word was missed in the utmost parts of the room. . . ." Jefferson too, despite his well-known reluctance to be a public performer, would have applauded Smith's successful presentation as an oral interpreter on this celebratory occasion. As we saw in chapter 5 on "Channeling the Message," Jefferson was familiar with and supportive of the teachings of leading scholars of the British elocutionary movement—men such as John Mason, John Rice, Thomas Sheridan, and John Walker—often urging young students to follow their instructions in order to improve their delivery.

Jefferson also recognized the relationship between the written and spoken word. No one has detected this aspect of Jefferson's discourse philosophy better than Jay Fliegelman in his book *Declaring Independence*.[80] Convincingly, he argues "that the Declaration was written to be read aloud," and this, in turn, "becomes a crucial clue to elements of its meaning." He then adds that as the "title suggests [his] concern is not just with the Declaration as artifact, but with 'declaring' as performance and with 'independence' as something that is rhetorically performed." Fliegelman illustrates this premise by describing Jefferson's "emphatical pauses" as they were noted with diacritical markings, in the tradition of the elocutionists, on his rough draft. In clarifying and emphasizing this point, Fliegelman drew this conclusion: "the reading marks on the rough draft of the Declaration speak eloquently of the pervasive social drama of personal expression in which Jefferson, his document, and his culture so fully participated, a drama at the heart of Revolutionary and early national culture."

With the widespread praise that Jefferson received during his lifetime for his greatest rhetorical effort, it is not surprising that he was troubled by the criticism of a few of his contemporaries who noted that the Declaration, despite its remarkable effect, lacked originality. When Richard Henry Lee said that it was essentially "copied from Locke's treatise on government,"[81] and John Adams asserted "there is not an idea in it but what had been hackneyed in Congress for two years,"[82] Jefferson felt led to respond in a series of letters. He reiterated to Madison in 1823 the claim that he "turned neither book nor pamphlet while writing it." It was not "any part of my charge," he added, "to invent new ideas altogether, and to offer no sentiment which had never been expressed before."[83] His real purpose, he later wrote to Doctor James Mease, was to articulate "the genuine effusion of the soul of our country at that time. . . ."[84]

Had Jefferson known about the continuing impact of his discourse through the ages, he would have been pleased. One of the most poignant analyses of the permanent relevance of the meaning of the Declaration was delivered by President-elect Abraham Lincoln in 1861. Standing before a large and enthusiastic audience in Independence Hall on February 22, and conscious of the growing crisis of disunion, he spoke these memorable words:

> all the political sentiments I entertain have been drawn . . . from the statements which originated, and were given to the world from this hall in which we stand. I have never had a feeling politically that did not spring from the sentiments embodied in the Declaration of Independence. . . . I have often inquired of myself, what great principle or idea it was that kept this Confederacy so long together. It was not the mere matter of the separation of the colonies from the mother land; but something in that Declaration giving liberty, not alone to the people of this country, but hope to the world for all future time. . . .[85]

Lincoln's words eloquently suggest that the Declaration was more than "the genuine effusion of the soul" of the colonies at the time it was written; for it also has become an ongoing, enduring expression of the American spirit.

What can we say in summary about this seminal work, associated with the name of Jefferson, which occupies such a formidable place in American history? The renowned historian Bernard Bailyn places the Declaration of Independence, along with *A Summary View*, in the pamphlet tradition which constitutes "the distinctive literature of the Revolution." It is a type of discourse, he further noted, that reveals "more clearly than any other single group of documents, the contemporary meaning of that transforming event." Bailyn next suggested that the principal substance of the Declaration consists of an "enumeration of conspiratorial efforts. . . ."[86] Nine years later, Norman K. Risjord argued that there were two major objectives of the Declaration. The first "was to convince the world that the colonies were in the right in separating themselves from Great Britain." The second was to seize "the occasion to set forth an ideological foundation for the new nation."[87]

One of the more interesting summary overviews of the Declaration is Pauline Maier's 1997 volume, *American Scripture*.[88] In this study, the author develops three major themes that deserve special mention. First, she argues persuasively that when the Second Continental Congress, consisting of sixty-five delegates, assembled in Philadelphia during the spring and summer of 1776, the members functioned as a national government. The task confronting them was "to take charge of a country at war . . ."— a daunting challenge they were to face until the conflict ended and the Articles of Confederation "were fully ratified."

In discussing a second significant subject, Maier maintains that the Declaration of Independence was not written by Jefferson alone, but was a collaborative effort, including participation by the Committee of Five and by Congress. Although Jefferson was designated to write the draft, he received important suggestions from Adams, Franklin, Roger Sherman, and Robert R. Livingston who were members of the drafting committee, and from a thoughtful Congress that amended some words and phrases, and excised sentences and paragraphs—especially the section on the slave trade. Maier concluded this argument by asserting that "what generations of Americans came to revere was not Jefferson's but Congress's Declaration, the work not of a single man, or even a committee, but of a larger body of men" who engaged in "group editing" of a text "that required cutting" more than it needed "extensive rewriting."

Although we concur with Maier's argument that both the drafting committee and Congress played an important role in the construction of the Declaration of Independence, we dissent from this claim which is also included in her overall analysis: "He [Jefferson] had forgotten, as has posterity, that a 'draftsman' is not an 'author' in the sense that a novelist, a poet, or a political essayist is." Rather than be viewed as the principal creator of a document that is recognized as "an authenticated expression of the American mind," Jefferson is relegated by Maier to the role of draftsman for Congress; thus the end result was largely their verbal act, not his.

The argument we wish to uphold is that Jefferson, far from being a mere "draftsman," has earned the right to be regarded as the author of the Declaration of Independence. We begin our refutation of Maier's claim by alluding to several statements developed by Boyd in volume 1 of *The Papers of Thomas Jefferson*:

(1) "The committee itself apparently made few changes, but Congress excised about a fourth of the text, including the famous passage concerning Negro slavery." [414] This contention suggests that Jefferson, in Boyd's view, was primarily responsible for much of the remaining three-fourths.

(2) "In all, there were eighty-six alterations, made at various stages by Jefferson, by Adams and Franklin, by the Committee of Five, and by Congress." [415] Of the eighty-six changes, therefore, Jefferson was responsible for an unspecified number of them.

(3) "It has long been noticed . . . that the preamble to the Virginia Constitution (which Jefferson wrote) and the charges against the Crown in the Declaration were very similar and in many cases identical in phraseology." [415] Our investigation of this assertion finds Boyd's statement to be true. The striking similarity, said Jef-

ferson in 1825, was to be expected since both documents have the same object, of justifying our separation from Great Britain. . . ." It was only natural, therefore, for both works to use "the same materials of justification. . . ." (Cited in ibid.)

Consistent with the arguments of Boyd were those advanced by David McCullough in his 2001 volume *John Adams*. In this work, McCullough reached these conclusions regarding Jefferson's authorship of the Declaration of Independence:

(1) Jefferson "borrowed heavily from his own previous writings. . . ."
(2) "What made Jefferson's work surpassing was the grace and eloquence of expression. Jefferson had done superbly and in minimum time. . . ."
(3) "Of more than eighty changes made in Jefferson's draft during the time Congress deliberated, most were minor and served to improve it."
(4) "But it was to be the eloquent lines of the second paragraph of the Declaration that would stand down the years, affecting the human spirit as neither Jefferson nor anyone could have foreseen. And however much was owed to the writings of others, as Jefferson acknowledged or to such editorial refinements as those contributed by Franklin or Adams, there were, when all was said or done, his lines. It was Jefferson who had written for all time."[89]

McCullough's position, it seems clear, was an endorsement of the stance taken by Boyd on the question of authorship of the Declaration.

To the foregoing arguments advanced by Boyd and McCullough, we add these claims. First, Jefferson doubtless was the author of *A Summary View of the Rights of British America*, and of the preamble to the Virginia constitution, two works from which he drew heavily in preparing the claims in the Declaration of Independence. Second, we have demonstrated that the final draft of the Declaration, which was approved by Congress, is rooted in Jefferson's principles of virtue as outlined in chapter 2 of this study. Third, the argumentative philosophy, the appeals to the social affections, and the use of language control, as seen in chapters 3 through 5, are remarkably similar to those same elements in *A Summary View* and the preamble to the Virginia constitution.

It is for the above reasons we feel that Jefferson's role in producing the Declaration meets the tests developed by Michel Foucault in his influential essay "What is an author?" Written in 1969, this study argues that "modern criticism in its desire to 'recover' the author from a work, employs devices strongly reminiscent of Christian exegesis," the critical evaluation of the scriptures. In making his point, Foucault referred to the criteria used by Saint Jerome in answering the question on what constitutes authorship of a particular text. Saint Jerome begins with the assumption that a presumed author has created a known body of work that can be used as a basis of comparison. With this as a starting point for analysis, Jerome argued, with Foucault's approval, that the text being examined must display a consistency in strength when contrasted with other recognized works of the author, thereby fulfilling the test of "a standard level of quality." Second, the text should feature a similar doctrine or political philosophy such as the sharing of "a certain field of conceptual or theoretical coherence." Third, the text should be written in a similar style, as it relates to word choice and phrases, thus resulting in "a stylistic uniformity."[90]

What we have sought to illustrate in this chapter is that, first, the Declaration of Independence, in drawing heavily from *A Summary View* and from the preamble to the Virginia constitution, possesses "a standard level of quality." Second, the Declaration shares with these two works "a certain field of conceptual or theoretical coherence." Third, these three texts have "a stylistic uniformity." Although we have focused primarily on three of Jefferson's works in making our comparison, we feel that additional analogies could be made in accordance with Foucault's claim: "Finally, the author is a particular source of expression who, in more or less finished forms, is manifested equally well and with similar validity, in a text, in letters, fragments, drafts, and so forth."

One final point, we believe, needs to be made in summarizing our argument on authorship. The fact that Jefferson was disappointed with many of the amendments produced by Congress in no way meant that the text that eventually passed did not represent his views. For it was he who helped keep the Declaration alive in the hearts of Americans during the early national period. Moreover, it was he who looked upon the revised Declaration as one of his three most important legacies. In all, we agree with the judgment of posterity that has designated Jefferson, not as a mere draftsman, but as the author of the Declaration of Independence.

But while we have differed with Maier on the issue of authorship, we recognize the significant merit of her study. Among her most interesting and informative themes is discussed in the closing section under the heading of the title of the book: *American Scripture*. Filled with fresh and innovative data, the narrative traces how the American people responded to the Declaration from the time it was signed and printed in July 1776 and through the generations that followed. Three important stages unfold, the first of which was characterized by an attitude of indifference on the part of the people from 1776 until 1790. Then, in stage two, beginning with the formation of political parties in the 1790s and proceeding through the early decades of the national experience, we are told how the Republicans and their descendants initiated a campaign stressing the importance of the Declaration and celebrating Jefferson's contribution to its creation. Finally, we see in stage three how Lincoln helped elevate the Declaration to the level of Scripture, an act of reverence that has persisted through the years.

During the period from 1774 through 1776, Jefferson as a polemicist used his principles of argumentation philosophy and language to conduct a rhetorical campaign to alert the colonists to the nature and harmful effects of the oppression they were experiencing. He then became an eloquent spokesperson for the creation of an independent government that would promote liberty, freedom, and justice. Only in this way, he argued, could America be a visible symbol of the meaning of public virtue and true democracy. Not content to limit his discourse appeals to the contemporary American audiences, he also spoke to a "candid world" or universal audience who were guided by reason and common sense. His unusual success in achieving his goal in the Revolutionary era paved the way for future national leadership roles and elevated him to a revered position among our Founding Fathers.

# Notes

1. *Diary and Autobiography of John Adams*, ed. by L. H. Butterfield, 4 vols. (New York: Atheneum, 1964), 2: 335–36.

2. Edmund Randolph, when describing the Spring Convention in Virginia in 1775, noted that "Jefferson was not silent. He argued closely, profoundly on the same side" as that being advanced by Henry. "Essay on the Revolutionary History of Virginia, 1774–1782," *Virginia Magazine of History and Biography*, 43 (1935): 223. We have been unable to find a more specific description of Jefferson's remarks on this occasion.

3. Margaret Bayard Smith described Jefferson's voice as "almost femininely soft and gentle. . . .", *The First Forty Years of Washington Society*, 6.

4. In commenting on the Boston Tea Party, Samuel Eliot Morison wrote: " . . . this comic stage-Indian business of the Boston Tea Party was important. It goaded John Bull into a showdown, which was exactly what Sam Adams and the other radical leaders wanted." *The Oxford History of the American People* (New York: Oxford University Press, 1965), 204.

5. Chatham's speech was printed in ibid., 126–28.

6. Boyd, 1: 106.

7. "Association of Members of the Late House of Burgesses," in ibid., 1: 107–108.

8. The letter appears in id., 1: 111.

9. The letter, written in cooperation with John Walker, is in ibid., 1: 116.

10. TJ to John W. Campbell, September 3, 1809, in *Writings*, 1210.

11. Ibid.

12. "Autobiography," in Ford, 1: 14–15. In commenting on Jefferson's explanation that illness prevented him from being present on this occasion, some writers have suggested that this was a typical "act of avoidance. . . ." Among those who expressed this view was Joseph J. Ellis, *American Sphinx*, 29. We have found no evidence to support this view.

13. Jefferson was pleased with the action taken by Randolph, but made this statement about Henry's eventual lack of action: "Whether Mr. Henry disapproved the ground taken, or was too lazy to read it (for he was the laziest man in reading I ever knew) I never learned; but he communicated it to nobody." "Autobiography," in Ford, 1: 15.

14. TJ to John W. Campbell, September 3, 1809, in *Writings*, 1210.

15. Edmund Randolph, "Essay on the Revolutionary History of Virginia," in *The Virginia Magazine of History and Biography*, 43 (1935): 216.

16. "Autobiography," in Ford, 1: 15.

17. All of the references to the content in *A Summary View* are taken from Boyd's version, 1: 121–35.

18. For Jefferson's views of history and the Saxon myth, see H. Trevor Colbourn, *The Lamp of Experience: Whig History and the Intellectual Origins of the American Revolution* (Chapel Hill: University of North Carolina Press for the Institute of Early American History and Culture, 1965; rev. ed., Indianapolis: Liberty Fund, 1998).

19. Chaim Perelman has discussed this concept. See Perelman and L. Olbrechts-Tyteca, *The New Rhetoric*, tr. by John Wilkinson and Purcell Weaver (Notre Dame: University of Notre Dame Press, 1971), 218–20.

20. Joseph J. Ellis, *American Sphinx: The Character of Thomas Jefferson* (New York: Knopf, 1997), 52.

21. Pauline Maier, *American Scripture* (New York: Knopf, 1997), 122.

22. "Appendix I: Historical and Bibliographical Notes on *A Summary View of the Rights of British America*, in Boyd, 1: 672–73. Joseph J. Ellis has pointed out, however, "The audience at whom Jefferson had actually aimed his instructions, the Virginia legislators, chose not to follow them, preferring to recommend that its delegates adopt a moderate posture toward Great Britain." *American Sphinx*, 29.

23. Boyd, 1: 676.

24. The following statements, which build on Jefferson's own description, are instructive: "Jefferson moved in one swift step to the forefront of the great pamphleteers of the Revolution. . . ." Nathan Schachner, *Thomas Jefferson: A Biography*, 2 vols. (New York: Appleton-Century Crofts, 1951), 1: 99. Another author has stated: "It was the publication of the *A Summary View* . . . together with its prompt republication elsewhere in the colonies, and then in London, that in a stroke transformed Jefferson from an eminent young lawyer and a highly regarded Virginia civic leader into a national and international voice during . . . the coming of the Revolution." Stephen A. Conrad, "Putting Rights Talk in Its Place: *The Summary View* Revisited," in *Jeffersonian Legacies*, 256.

25. Cited in Boyd, 1: 676.

26. Randall, *The Life of Thomas Jefferson*, 1: 98.

27. Schachner, *Thomas Jefferson: A Biography*, 1: 100, 102.

28. Peterson, "The Architect of Democracy," in *The World of Thomas Jefferson: A Guide for Teachers*. A Pamphlet sponsored by the Jefferson Commemoration Commission, the Council of Chief State School Officers, and the American Forum, 1994, at 2.

29. Ellis, *American Sphinx*, 31.

30. Alf J. Mapp Jr., *Thomas Jefferson: A Strange Case of Mistaken Identity* (Lanham, Md.: Madison Books, 1987), 87.

31. Garry Wills, *Inventing America: Jefferson's Declaration of Independence* (Garden City, N.Y.: Doubleday, 1976), 81.

32. Paul Finkelman, "Jefferson and Slavery," in *Jeffersonian Legacies*, 197.

33. *American Sphinx*, 32–35. For another insightful view on Jefferson and the "Saxon Myth," see H. Trevor Colbourn, *The Lamp of Experience: Whig History and the Intellectual Origins of the American Revolution* (Chapel Hill: University of North Carolina Press, 1965), chapter 8, especially 197–199, 220–225.

34. Randall, *Life of Thomas Jefferson*, 1: 188.

35. Mapp, *Thomas Jefferson: Strange Case of Mistaken Identity*, 86.

36. Ellis, *American Sphinx*, 30.

37. Conrad argues that in Jefferson's "hierarchy of values in the *Summary View* 'justice' ranks even higher than his concern over 'rights'. . . .", "Putting Rights Talk in Its Place: The Summary View Revisited," in *Jeffersonian Legacies*, 267.

38. Apparently Jefferson was misled on some of the particulars communicated to him by Samuel Adams. Ellis has given this evaluation of Jefferson's reference to the Boston Tea Party: " . . . perhaps Jefferson's version was itself a propagandistic manipulation, just as self-consciously orchestrated as the Tea Party itself." Ellis, *American Sphinx*, 34.

39. Goodrich, *Select British Eloquence*, 128–32.

40. Boyd, 1: 166n.

41. Goodrich, *Select British Eloquence*, 265.

42. Ibid., 288–89.

43. The address appears in Boyd, 1: 170–74.

44. Jefferson observed in his "Autobiography" that his manuscript was carried through the House. . . .a dash of cold water (was poured) on it here and there, enfeebling it somewhat, but finally with unanimity, or a vote approaching it. . . ." "Autobiography," in Ford, 1: 17.

45. "The Resolutions as Adopted by Congress" are reproduced in Boyd, 1: 230–33.

46. The final draft of this "Declaration of Causes," which Dickinson wrote, was produced by using Jefferson's "Fair Copy" as a starting point. Boyd notes that the finished product was "the result of a collaboration on the part of the two men. . . .", Boyd, 1: 190.

47. Jefferson's "Fair Copy" is reprinted in Boyd, 1: 199–203. "The Declaration as Adopted by Congress on July 6, 1775," appears in Boyd, 1: 213–18. It should also be noted that in addition to his discourses in 1775, Jefferson wrote two important letters pertaining to the deteriorating relations between the colonies and Great Britain. See the following: TJ to Dr. William Small, May 7, 1775, in Boyd, 1: 165–66; and To John Randolph, August 25, 1775, in ibid., 1: 240–43.

48. John H. Hazelton, *The Declaration of Independence: Its History* (New York: Dodd, Mead, 1906), 7.

49. Ibid., 33.

50. The actual influence of Paine's pamphlet on the emerging sentiment for independence has been debated by historians, but there is little doubt that, in the words of

Gordon Wood, it "touched off the argument that burned to the heart of the social is-sue." Gordon S. Wood, *The Creation of the American Republic, 1776–1787* (New York: Norton, 1969), 93–94.

51. Foner, *Thomas Paine and Revolutionary America* (New York: Oxford University Press, 1976), 71–106. Paine, it should be noted, was one of Jefferson's favorite writers be-cause of his excellence in style. Schachner alludes to Paine's use of "wing-tipped words. . . ." *Thomas Jefferson: A Biography,* 1: 117.

52. Boyd, 1: 291. Also see Hazelton's summary analysis of Paine's ideas, in *The Decla-ration of Independence: Its History,* 92.

53. Boyd, 1: 291n.

54. See *Diary and Autobiography of John Adams,* 3: 335–36; and *The Works of John Adams,* 2: 514–15.

55. Jefferson described his desk to his granddaughter Ellen Randolph Coolidge, No-vember 14, 1825, in Peterson, *Writings,* 1507–1508. He stated that he wanted her husband to have it as an historical artifact.

56. TJ to Doctor James Mease, September 26, 1825, in Ford, 12: 413–14.

57. Maier, *American Scripture,* 104.

58. See letter to Madison, August 30, 1823, in Ford, 12: 306–7.

59. Boyd, 1: 317–18.

60. "Autobiography," in Ford, 1: 33.

61. *The Works of John Adams,* 2: 515.

62. Merrill D. Peterson, *Thomas Jefferson and the New Nation: A Biography* (London: Oxford University Press, 1970), 91.

63. Observe Jefferson's "Notes of Proceedings in the Continental Congress," Boyd, 1: 315; and his "Autobiography," Ford, 1: 33.

64. Boyd, 1: 319.

65. Jefferson uses the "one-fourth" figure in his 1823 letter to Madison, in Ford, 12: 308–309. Boyd also asserts that "Congress excised about a fourth of the text. . . ." He fur-ther suggests "there were eighty-six alterations made at further stages by Jefferson, by Adams and Franklin, by the Committee of Five, and by Congress." Boyd, 1: 414.

66. Because of the relevance and humor in this story, we repeat it here in its entirety, using Jefferson's words to describe what Franklin said. "When I was a journeyman printer, one of my companions, an apprentice hatter, having served out his time, was about to open shop for himself. His first concern was to have a handsome sign-board, with a proper inscription. He composed it in these words, 'John Thompson, Hatter, makes and sells hats for ready money,' with a figure of a hat subjoined; but he thought he would submit it to his friends for their amendments. The first he showed it to thought the word 'Hatter' tau-tologous, because followed by the words 'makes hats,' which show he was a hatter. It was struck out. The next observed that the word 'makes' might as well be omitted, because his customers would not care who made the hats. If good and to their mind they would buy, by whomsoever made. He struck it out. A third said he thought the words 'for ready money' were useless, as it was not the custom of the place to sell on credit. Every one who purchased expected to pay. They were parted with, and the inscription now stood, 'John Thompson sells hats.' 'Sells hats!' says his next friend. Why nobody will expect you to give them away, what then is the use of that word? It was stricken out, and 'hats' followed it, the rather as there was one painted on the board. So the inscription was reduced ulti-mately to 'John Thompson' with the figure of a hat subjoined." L&B, 18: 169–70.

67. Becker, *The Declaration of Independence* (New York: Knopf, 1960), 209.

68. Maier, *American Scripture: Making the Declaration of Independence* (New York: Knopf, 1997), XVII.

69. All quotations are drawn from "The Declaration as Amended by the Committee and by Congress," Boyd, 1: 429–32.

70. After printing the argument beginning with the words, "We hold these truths to be self-evident. . . .", Maier notes: "This one long sentence, which was carefully worked over, asserted one right, the right of revolution, which was, after all, the right Americans were exercising in 1776." *American Scripture*, 135.

71. Locke noted: "The first therefore, and *highest degree of Probability*, is, when the general consent of all Men, in all ages, as far as it can be known, concurs with a man's constant and never-failing Experience in like cases, to confirm the Truth of any particular matter of fact attested by fair Witnesses: such are all the stated Constitutions and Properties of Bodies, and the regular proceedings of Causes and Effects in the ordinary course of Nature. This we call an Argument from the Nature of Things themselves." *An Essay Concerning Human Understanding*, 661.

72. Perelman and Olbrechts-Tyteca note that "Argumentation addressed to a universal audience must convince the reader that the reasons adduced are of a compelling character, that they are self-evident, and possess an absolute and timeless validity, independent of local or historical contingencies." *The New Rhetoric*, 32.

73. For an excellent discussion of Jefferson's commitment to the natural rights philosophy, see Becker, *Declaration of Independence*, 24–79. For an interesting and unique point of view, see a 1981 essay by John Phillip Reid who argues that the preamble to the Declaration is irrelevant, stressing instead the eloquent series of paragraphed charges indicting George III. In Reid's view, the indictment is the key part of the Declaration because it is the last official American statement in the constitutional argument with the former mother country. He further argues that the Declaration "was pure and simple, a legal document, claiming and executing a constitutional right." John Phillip Reid, "The Irrelevance of the Declaration," in Hendrik Hartog, ed., *Law in the American Revolution and the Revolution in the Law* (New York: New York University Press, 1981), 46–89. We applaud Reid for recognizing the importance of the legal and constitutional argument, but dissent from his claim that the preamble is irrelevant. As pointed out earlier in this chapter, Jefferson not only was speaking to the British people but also to the colonists and a "candid" world, both of whom would respond to ethical and emotional appeals, as well as to logical proof. What helped give the Declaration of Independence an enduring appeal, according to Jefferson scholar Merrill Peterson, is that the preamble to the Declaration constitutes "the most sacred writing of our history." Printed in booklet produced by the Thomas Jefferson Memorial Commission in honor of his 250th birthday.

74. Ibid., 15–16.

75. Observe how he used the terms "Laws of Nature" and "of Nature's God" in the opening statement.

76. An unpublished letter from Peterson to Roger G. Kennedy, May 4, 1994. Samuel Eliot Morison describes this statement in the following glowing terms: "These words are more revolutionary than anything written by Robespierre, Marx, or Lenin, more explosive than the atom, a continual challenge to ourselves, as well as an inspiration to the oppressed of all the world." *The Oxford History of the American People* (New York: Oxford University Press, 1965), 223.

77. The average length of all the sentences was more than fifty words. This was due in part to the number of compound sentences joined together by colons and semicolons.

78. Peterson, *The Portable Jefferson*, xviii. Schachner's enthusiasm was similarly positive regarding the style of the Declaration. "As literary art," he says, "as articulated structure and concatenated cadence, as a repository of magical and immortal phrases that burn in the mind and sing in the heart, the Declaration of Independence has no political peer." Schachner, *Thomas Jefferson: A Biography*, 1: 129. Becker voices a minority view as the following statement suggests: "With all its precision, its concise rapidity, its clarity, its subtle implications and engaging felicities, one misses a certain unsophisticated directness, a certain sense of impregnable solidity and massive strength, a certain effect of passion restrained and deep convictions held in reserve, which would have given to it that accent of perfect sincerity and that emotional content which belong to the grand manner." Becker, *Declaration of Independence*, 221–22.

79. Letter to Margaret Bayard Smith, July 5, 1803, in *The First Forty Years of Washington Society*, 38–39.

80. *Declaring Independence: Jefferson, Natural Language, and the Culture of Performance* (Stanford: Stanford University Press, 1993). See, in particular, 4, 25, and 196. Of further interest here is that the Thomas Jefferson Commemoration Commission in 1994 strongly recommended that on each July 4th, part of any celebration should include an oral reading of the Declaration.

81. Jefferson reports this in the letter to Madison on August 30, 1823, Ford, 12: 306–309. It should also be remarked that some of Jefferson's political critics, as late as 1822, argued that he was not the real author of the Declaration. See excerpts from several of these charges appearing in newspapers that are reprinted in Hazelton, *The Declaration of Independence: Its History*, 350–51.

82. Adams to Timothy Pickering, August 6, 1822, in *The Works of John Adams*, 2: 514. It does not appear, however, that Adams meant this to be a negative assessment since all of his other comments on the Declaration were supportive, including the deleted passage on the slave trade. Another point of interest is that in his August, 30, 1823, letter to Madison, Jefferson, who read Adams' statement, praised his colleague's oratorical performances during the floor debates on the Declaration.

83. Letter to Madison, August 30, 1823. In a letter to Henry Lee, Jefferson further noted: "Neither aiming at originality of principle or sentiment, nor yet copied from any particular and previous writing, it was intended to be an expression of the American mind, and to give to that expression the proper tone and spirit called for by the occasion." May 8, 1825, in Ford, 12: 409.

84. TJ to James Mease, September 26, 1825, in Ford, 12: 414. The ensuing quotation on this point, taken from the letter to Henry Lee, is also meaningful: "All its authority rests then on the harmonizing sentiments of the day, whether expressed in conversation, in letters, printed essays, or in the elementary books of public right, as Aristotle, Cicero, Locke, Sidney, & c."

85. "Speech in Independence Hall," February 22, 1861, in Roy B. Basler, ed., *The Collected Works of Abraham Lincoln*, 8 vols. (New Brunswick, N.J.: Rutgers University Press, 1953), 4: 240.

86. *The Ideological Origins of the American Revolution*, expanded ed. (Cambridge, Mass.: The Belknap Press of Harvard University Press, 1992), 8, 155.

87. Norman Risjord, *Jefferson's America, 1760–1815*. (Madison, Wis.: Madison House, 1991), 99.

88. Maier, *American Scripture*, 1–215.

89. David McCullogh, *John Adams* (New York: Simon & Schuster, 2001), 119–22, 134–36.

90. Michel Foucault, "What is an Author?" in Donald F. Bouchard ed., *Language, Counter-Memory: Selected Essays and Interviews*. (Ithaca: Cornell University Press, 1977), 113–38. In assessing the value of "Saint Jerome's four principles of authenticity, Foucault noted that they "define the critical modalities now used to display the function of the author." [129] The fourth principle by Saint Jerome and Foucault, which was not discussed in our analysis, was omitted because it did not apply. This principle reads as follows: ". . . those referring to events or historical figures subsequent to the death of the author (the author is thus a definite historical figure in which a series of events converge)." [128]

∼

# CHAPTER ELEVEN

# Select Public Addresses, 1781–1801

The national and international recognition that Jefferson received following the adoption of the Declaration of Independence led to his appointment or election to a number of influential diplomatic and political offices. This, in turn, placed him in a position in which it became necessary to deliver varied types of special occasional discourses. Although he felt more comfortable as a pamphleteer and a conversationalist than he did as an oral public communicator, he recognized that in fulfilling his official public speaking duties he had additional opportunities to show how his political philosophy and actions were formed and sustained by his principles of virtue. We have chosen for analysis a series of representative examples of his presentations during the twenty-year span from 1781 through 1801. The first half of our discussion focuses on several miscellaneous remarks, including a speech of greeting, three brief responses to speeches of welcome, and a farewell address upon his departure as presiding officer of the U.S. Senate. We next present an assessment of his celebrated First Inaugural Address.

## Samples of Special Forms of Discourse

### Speech of Greeting to Jean Baptiste Ducoigne, June 1781

Throughout his adult life, the study of Indian language and culture was a pleasurable experience for Jefferson. We already have observed his strong interest in the vocabularies of tribes, his speculations on the early history of native migration to America, and his recommendations to Lewis and Clark concerning methods of speech that would be appropriate for communicating with the Indians they encountered on their expedition to the

West. Later we see how, in his *Notes on the State of Virginia*, he used a speech by Logan to demonstrate the intellectual quality and rhetorical excellence of Native Americans. At this point in our discussion, we describe how Jefferson addressed the "half-breed" Jean Baptiste Ducoigne who was chief "of the dwindling Kaskaskia nation, from whose name was taken from that of the town of Ducoigne. . . ."[1]

The setting for this speech, the first that he ever delivered in praise of an Indian leader and his followers, was marked by a dangerous crisis in Virginia. Serving in his last days as governor of the state, Jefferson had viewed with concern the dual invasions of Virginia by Generals Charles Cornwallis and Benedict Arnold who, as a traitor, was now an officer in the British army. When Arnold's forces reached the outskirts of Richmond in late May, Jefferson and his government sought refuge in the Charlottesville area. It was during this brief stay that he made plans to entertain and honor Ducoigne. As part of the preparation for the occasion, he rushed a letter to Robert Scot asking him to produce a medal to present to his guest as a means of celebrating his past contributions to the American cause.[2]

Standing before Ducoigne and his Indian companions, and in the presence of legislators who had accompanied him to Charlottesville, Jefferson gave an impassioned speech that put into practice his elements of personal proof, and offered hope concerning the successful outcome of the Revolutionary War.[3] Filled with appeals designed to create identification, Jefferson's opening remarks included an expression of gratitude to Ducoigne for his "friendship," for naming one of his sons "Jefferson," for his help in assisting a Virginia garrison under attack from hostile Indian groups, and for the gift of beautifully designed skins that would permanently occupy a prominent place on the walls of his home, Monticello. Then in language more direct and poignant, he said: "We, like you, are Americans born in the same land, and having the same interests." He concluded his preliminary conciliatory statements with a solemn promise to continue embracing the "good old custom handed down by your ancestors" of smoking a peace pipe together as a sign of friendship toward each other.

Most of what Jefferson said in the body of the speech was related to the war still being fought on Virginia's soil. To provide a historical perspective, he described how the American "forefathers" had come from England, how those who remained behind used their power to enslave these colonists, and how the French and Spanish nations provided helpful support in the struggle for freedom and independence being undertaken by the settlers.

Jefferson was now set to address the question of whether or not Ducoigne and the members of his tribe should take up arms against the British. He answered by saying that unless the Kaskasians had been directly and ruthlessly harmed by the British, they should not waste their "blood in fighting our battles." Our wish for you instead as our "affectionate" friends, he noted, is that you will remain at peace and "multiply and be strong." He then spoke with confidence as he predicted that the thirteen states, though separate entities, functioned in unison as a single nation that would achieve ultimate victory. But although peace was close at hand, it seemed necessary to remind Ducoigne "that a nation at war cannot buy so many goods as when in peace." Thus if the help received from the states was limited until the conflict ended, Jefferson added, it would nevertheless be a fair "share of what little goods we can get." There was no reason to be discouraged, however, because England, with the world allied against her, "cannot hold out long."

In one of the most moving passages of the speech, Jefferson ended with a request that his message be transmitted to other interested tribes, that Ducoigne as a leader had the blessing of the state of Virginia, and that the longstanding friendship between the whites and the Indians would be strengthened in the future. He used the following graphic words to express these sentiments:

> This, brother, is what I had to say to you. Repeat it from me to all your people, and to your friends, the Kickapous, Piorias, Piankeshaws and Wyattanons. I will give you a commission to show them how much we esteem you. Hold fast the chain of friendship, which binds us together, keep it bright as the sun, and let them, you and us, live together in perpetual love.

This short peroration, using persuasive rhetorical strategies, was a fitting climax to an address, the purpose of which was to cement an enduring relationship between the government of Virginia and a friendly Native American chief.

Jefferson, in sum, strategically sprinkled throughout the discourse such terms of virtue as friendship, wisdom, justice, love, freedom, and rights. Additionally, we can see a difference of approach in these remarks when compared with that used in *A Summary View* and in the Declaration of Independence. The latter addresses, concerned about winning the approval of the universal as well as the immediate audience, presented a message of virtue by stressing the principles of argumentation and common sense. The speech to Ducoigne, by contrast, emphasized social affections by using conciliatory appeals and terms of identification. Jefferson addressed the Indian leader as "brother" eight times. Numerous sentiments, moreover, showed what white Americans had done and hoped to do for Ducoigne and his people in the future. The following examples illustrate this claim:

> If you will make known to me any just cause of complaint against them [the English], I will represent it to the great council at Philadelphia, and have justice done you.

> We . . . have often grieved for you.

> We wish to learn you all our arts and make you wise and wealthy.

> I will give you a commission to show them [the other Indian tribes who are our friends] how much we esteem you.

The warmth and camaraderie that permeate this speech of greeting to Docoigne were to become a pattern in future discourses presented to Indians by Jefferson during his presidency.[4] What made this particular presentation so memorable is that it was delivered a day or two before "the redcoats chased him [Jefferson] from Monticello."[5]

To provide a final perspective on the meaning and impact of Jefferson's brief speech to Ducoigne, we cite the following testimony from two distinguished scholars. After referring to the address as a "sympathetic response," Anthony F. C. Wallace noted:

> Jefferson's experience as a war governor was mellowing his perception of the Native Americans as enemies. No longer were they "merciless savages" from whom, at great price in blood and treasure, America's lands had been wrested by force. They were now, as he put it to du Coigne, some sort of brothers: "we, like you, are Americans, born in the same land, and having the same interests."[6]

In placing this speech within a broader context, however, Peter S. Onuf focused on the long-range limitations of Jefferson's Indian policy. "Despite the implied invitation to Ducoigne and other Indian leaders," Onuf argued, "Jefferson's generous assessment of the human potential of Indians did not lead to the construction of a durable multiracial, multicultural political order in the New World."[7] But although serious questions about the lasting legacy of his Indian policy may legitimately be raised, we feel that Jefferson's speech to Ducoigne upheld his basic principles of virtue.

# Jefferson's Replies to Speeches of Welcome in the Autumn of 1789

When Jefferson returned to Virginia in November 1789, after serving as America's minister in France for five years, he brought with him a letter that he had received from Washington a few weeks before suggesting that he would like to nominate him to be secretary of state.[8] This announcement, Jefferson later recalled, was disappointing news because of his desire to return to Paris and to an assignment he had come to admire and enjoy.[9] At the same time, he had decided that if Washington persisted in expressing a wish to have him serve in his cabinet, he would accept the position.

As his boat docked in Norfolk, he had not yet made any final decision. But because the people of Virginia had heard of the projected appointment, they assumed the offer would soon be made and accepted. A special committee had arranged for a welcoming ceremony on November 25 to congratulate Jefferson on his distinguished services to the state and to the nation. Included in the audience were a number of citizens from the Tidewater area who wanted to thank him for his successful efforts in promoting trade. Also present was the French minister to New York, whose task was to describe the event to an appreciative group of leaders in Paris, who felt indebted to the American representative who had become their friend.[10]

Immediately, Jefferson identified with the residents of Norfolk with these warm sentiments expressed in picturesque words. "I am happy," he said, "that circumstances have led my arrival to a place which I had seen before indeed in greater splendor, but which I now see rising like a Phoenix out of it's ashes to that importance to which the laws of nature destine it."[11] He next stated that with its beautiful geographical locale, its form of government, and the blessing of God, Norfolk would be able to provide the "happiness" and "prosperity" the people deserve.

The most important statement in this 166-word speech was the closing line in which he succinctly observed: "That my country should be served is the first wish of my heart: I should be doubly happy indeed were I to render it a service." The use of the word "country" in this instance might have referred to his native state of Virginia, but more than likely he was alluding to the nation as a whole. Whatever interpretation that is made of the intended meaning, however, it was clear that Jefferson was still committed to use his talents in the future as he had done in the past to help a government whose goal was to promote the powerful virtue he called the "public good."

Jefferson's next response to a welcome took place in Richmond in early December when he appeared before the Virginia House of Delegates. The welcoming remarks from the committee in charge have not survived. But apparently they contained a warm and friendly tribute to their native son for what he had accomplished both for Virginia and for the nation. He thanked them for their statements of gratitude, and then in a sentence featuring his philosophy of virtue as it related to a citizen's duty to serve the state, he noted: "I shall hope to merit a continuance of their goodness by obeying the impulse of a zeal of which public good is the first object, and public esteem the highest reward."[12]

It was easy for Jefferson to maintain a relaxed demeanor and attitude of decorum when speaking to the friendly audience at Norfolk and to the members of the House of Delegates, for these two groups seemed to be supportive of whatever decision he might render regarding his possible appointment as secretary of state. The situation was significantly different, however, when he spoke to the Virginia Senate. For this political body had grave reservations about the national government in general and about pending amendments to the Constitution then being debated. Aware of this negative perception, Jefferson wrote to William Short on December 14, 1789, giving his assessment of the senators' attitudes: "These (the amendments) have been accepted by our House of Delegates, but will probably not be so, entire, by the Senate, 7/8 of whom are antifederal." Even worse, Jefferson continued, those who, like Henry, oppose it "retain a good deal of malevolence towards the new government."[13]

It did not take Jefferson long to realize how accurate his assessment of the Anti-federal sentiment was in the Senate. Early in the welcoming speech, he heard the presenter state that "their satisfaction (today) would have been increased by this circumstance, if they could have hoped for the" continuing "Aid" of his "Counsel." Notwithstanding that they begrudgingly wished him well in his new assignment, Jefferson could not help but notice that the Senate already had concluded he would become secretary of state, and that they also preferred that he place the call of the state over that of the federal government. It was against this background that Jefferson delivered his brief 118-word response.

Always a communicator who wished to conform to decorum, Jefferson thanked the Senate for extending to him a warm welcome. But in describing the pleasurable feeling he experienced in being back in his "native country," he substituted the word "visit" for the term "return."[14]

What gave this change significance was that it sent the signal that perhaps his current stay in Virginia would be temporary. It further meant that he was one step away from giving Washington a positive answer to his offer.

Again, before closing his response, Jefferson downplayed the importance of his own contributions but reiterated his devotion "to the public service" and suggested that the only reward he hoped to receive was "approbation" from his fellow citizens. In this short speech, as in his earlier two responses since returning to Virginia, Jefferson reaffirmed his faith in the theme that public service for the public good, whether on the state or the national level, was a cherished feature of democracy.

## Farewell Speech to the Senate, February 28, 1801

For almost four years, while holding the office of vice president, Jefferson was the presiding officer of the Senate. Because of his strong interest in parliamentary law and in order and decorum in public debate, he enjoyed this role. Consequently, after being notified of his election to the presidency, he delivered a brief but telling farewell to a legislative body that had responded warmly to his leadership as presiding officer.

Thanking his audience for the respect they had shown to him, he suggested he had tried throughout his term as presiding officer to make a "conscientious endeavor to observe impartial justice, without regard to persons or subjects. . . ." If he had failed in making this attempt to be fair at all times evident, he added, it would be to him "a circumstance of the deepest regret." But if any decision in retrospect appeared to be wrong, it was his hope that it would be viewed as an honest error of judgment stemming from "the law of human nature" rather than from an unjust intent. Jefferson concluded his farewell by praising the senators for their "habits of order and decorum" as seen in their "calm and temperate discussions," and expressed the wish that the type of support he had received in the Senate would be duplicated by others in his tenure as president.[15]

This speech, consisting of only three-hundred words, was consistent with the rhetorical practice used in his other miscellaneous discourses, and with his preference for expressing moving convictions in short, concise terms. Motivated by a desire to identify with his audience, Jefferson, by standing squarely upon the principles of justice, fairness, and decorum, ably succeeded in associating his message with benevolence and the public good.

# First Inaugural Address

Jefferson's First Inaugural Address was a natural outgrowth of the rhetorical situation that unfolded in the 1790s. By the time he became secretary of state in 1790 and vice president in 1797, he had risen to prominence by authoring the Declaration of Independence; championing the Bill of Rights; and serving as a member of the House of Delegates, as a Virginia delegate to the Continental Congress, as governor of Virginia, and as United States minister to France. These experiences in domestic and international affairs gave him the background he needed to be a dominating force in the political arena—an opportunity that he reluctantly accepted. In assuming this role, moreover, he took advantage of his position, first of all, as secretary of state, and second, as vice president.

In the crucial formative years of our government during the period from 1791 to 1793, he contributed to "an American political experience," observes Michael Lienesch, in three important ways. He helped create a "free and partisan press," establish "a system of popular political parties," and demonstrate how "public opinion" could be "organized."[16] While performing these tasks, he wrote letters explaining the goals and aspirations of those who subscribed to republican ideology, and urged Madison to use his pen to answer such Federalist leaders as Hamilton. Two of these letters—one to Philip Mazzei in 1796 and the other to Elbridge Gerry in 1799—indicated his dedication to the Republican cause and his intent to do whatever was possible to stymie the efforts of the Federalists to maintain control of the federal government.

Jefferson wrote to Mazzei on April 24, 1796, advising him of the distressing changes occurring on the American political landscape. He expressed concern that the "noble love of liberty, & republican government" that had epitomized the sentiment of the Revolutionary War era was currently being undermined by "an Anglican monarchial, & aristocratical party" patterned closely after the British system. It would make one despair, he wrote, to observe how men "who" once "were Samsons in the field & Solomons in the council" have now "had their heads shorn by the harlot England." But despite this gloomy assessment, he took comfort in announcing that a vast majority of the citizens still "remain true in their republican principles. . . ."[17] The type of harsh attack included in Jefferson's April 1796 letter to Mazzei on Federalists who were sympathetic to England, along with his implied support for the French, were to be part of the fundamental dynamics of the Republican campaigns of both 1796 and 1800.

When Jefferson communicated with Elbridge Gerry on January 26, 1799, he was in command of a maturing Republican party that stood poised to challenge the Federalists for control of the national government. Buoyed by a rapidly developing public support, and convinced he would be a presidential candidate in 1800, he believed that the time had arrived to make another definitive statement about his political philosophy. In eleven clearly stated articles describing his political faith, he explained his position on states' rights, economic issues, military policies, trade and commerce, development of science, and freedom of religion and of the press. Then anticipating a repeat of the familiar charge that he was pro-French, he asserted that his "heart" belonged not to another nation but to his "own country."[18]

## Phase One of the 1800 Presidential Campaign: Jefferson versus Adams

The general nature of the first phase of this campaign, and indeed in others throughout the first half of the nineteenth century, was unlike that of modern presidential contests. Beyond the Electoral College peculiarities that were to prove pivotal to the outcome of this election, the candidates themselves performed only a limited role; so, too, did the voting public as a whole. In addition to the still extensive property qualifications for voting, no universal system existed for selecting electors; in ten of sixteen states, for example, they were selected by the state legislatures.[19] A campaign, in short, "was a series of local contests" held between May and the third of December, designated as "election days."[20]

That the candidates were, for the most part, behind-the-scenes participants in their own campaigns in no way meant that numerous arguments and slogans on behalf of a party or in opposition to it were not made. Newspapers and pamphlets, for example, became popular media for getting out the message. Newspapers throughout the spring, summer, and autumn of 1800 contained columns from the editors and guest authors, and letters from the public. Moreover, "the number of pamphlets issued by Jefferson's opponents and his friends undoubtedly passed one hundred and several of the more popular went through many printings."[21]

The use of surrogate speakers also was a prominent rhetorical strategy. Jefferson's Republican friends often fulfilled this function in an articulate and persuasive manner. Adams was less fortunate, because arrayed against him were both Republicans and Alexander Hamilton's faction of the Federalist Party, the latter preferring a candidate with stronger Federalist credentials.[22]

But there was another more telling reason for the schism between Adams and Hamilton. Adams broke decisively with Hamilton when he discovered that Hamilton was attempting to direct his own cabinet behind his back. Thereafter, Hamilton denounced Adams publicly in a pamphlet entitled *Letter from Alexander Hamilton, Concerning the Public Conduct and Character of John Adams, Esq. . . .*; the pamphlet further ruptured Federalist ranks by more openly pitting Hamiltonian or High Federalists against Adams Federalists.[23] As Republicans were fully aware, the now-public divisions in Federalist ranks surely would enhance their party's prospects to win the presidency.

In analyzing the first phase of the presidential election of 1800, a number of historians have focused their attention on two principal points: first was the minimal role played by the candidates in promoting their campaigns; and, second was a tendency of the supporters of the respective candidates to engage in personal and partisan attacks against their opponents. This practice of being negative may be noted in graphic form by examining the descriptive titles of two essays. "Politics and Libel, 1800" was the phrase used by Dumas Malone as a heading for one of the chapters in his volume *Jefferson and the Ordeal of Liberty*.[24] Moreover, Charles O. Lerche Jr. wrote an article for the *William and Mary Quarterly* using similarly strong language, entitling his study, "Jefferson and the Election of 1800: A Case Study in the Political Smear."[25]

Our own research supports the conclusions of Lerche and Malone concerning the partisan charges and excesses of the press coverage. Voluminous irresponsible attacks against Jefferson, for example, appeared in the Federalist organ *Gazette of the United States and Daily Advertiser* from August through November. Again and again, he was labeled an atheist or a French infidel who, if elected president, would threaten the very foundation of the Christian religion. Under the caption "The Grand Question stated," could be found these words:

> At the present solemn and momentous epoch, the only question to be asked by every American, laying his hand on his heart, is shall I continue in allegiance to GOD—AND A RELIGIOUS PRESIDENT; or impiously declare JEFFERSON—AND NO GOD!

This claim, which was a false charge concerning the tenets of Jefferson's religious faith, first was published in the September 17 issue, and then reprinted on October 8 and 11. In a variation of this theme, voters were given the choice of casting a ballot for God and a traditional religious person (Adams) or for a man (Jefferson) who allegedly believed in the pantheistic notion of multiple gods.[26] Accepting the misinterpretations of Jefferson's religious philosophy as an indisputable fact, not a few ministers warned their parishioners to hide their Bibles in the well if Jefferson won the election.[27]

Nor were these unjust charges of atheism the only personal attacks on Jefferson. Because of his letter to Mazzei in 1796, along with other statements and actions attributed to him, he was called an enemy of the British government, and an overly zealous supporter of the French Revolution whose presumed radical republican ideas caused him to become an anarchist or Jacobin interested in destroying the Constitution. Similarly, he was described as a coward who fled from Richmond in 1781 with remnants of the Virginia government because he was afraid of being captured by Benedict Arnold. What in some ways was even more extreme, and surprising, in light of Jefferson's scholarly achievements and skill as a polemicist, was the charge that he was intellectually and morally incapable of fulfilling the duties of the presidency.[28]

For their part, the Republicans also presented argumentative claims ranging from mild critiques of the Federalists to highly emotional and provocative counterattacks against their policies. William Duane, editor of the Republican journal *Aurora*, often matched the invective and sarcasm that were the trademarks of the campaign coverage in the *Gazette of the United States*. On one occasion, Duane ridiculed the attacks on Jefferson's religious philosophy and practice in these caustic terms: "It is proper, I think, that the subject should be well discussed, that we may find out whether CHRIST is a MONARCHIST, a REPUBLICAN, a JACOBIN—or WHAT!!"[29]

To offer what he saw as an alternative to the excessively partisan presses, and to let the nation's new capital—Washington, D.C.—have a strong voice in the area of politics and government, Samuel Harrison Smith launched the *National Intelligencer and Washington Advertiser* on October 31, 1800. He promised his readers in this initial issue that the "design" of this "*first Paper* printed in Washington" was "to *diffuse* correct information through the whole extent of the union." Several days later, he announced that it was his "firm determination, that nothing shall be admitted into the National Intelligencer, which shall wound national, or calumniate private character. . . ."[30] This was welcome news to Jefferson, who was to become a close friend and associate of Smith for the next eight years.

Phase one of the campaign of 1800, which had been marked by political "smear" and "libel," ended in early December. When the electoral votes were counted, Jefferson had defeated Adams by a margin of 73 to 65.

But rather than producing a clear-cut winner, the Electoral College vote, once counted, had ended as a tie between Jefferson and Aaron Burr, the presumed Republican vice presidential candidate; thus creating the nation's first disputed presidential election. Even though Burr was fully aware that he had been the party's intended vice presidential candidate, once the tie became clear he was within striking range of the presidency, he refused to withdraw. This tie vote—which had resulted from the nature of electoral voting prior to the Twelfth Amendment and perhaps from poor planning or a lack of communication on the part of Republicans—required the House of Representatives to render a final decision.[31]

## Phase Two of the Campaign of 1800: Jefferson versus Burr

One of the most interesting features of this second-stage campaign was the effect it had upon Federalists. Aware that they had lost control of the presidency and both the House and the Senate, they were confronted with the unhappy choice between two Republican candidates, each of whom would lead the country in a different direction than it had followed in its first twelve years under the Constitution. Political maneuvering designed to influence the vote in the House of Representatives began in late December and extended through much of February. As the pressures heightened, there were signs showing that a majority of the Federalists tended to lean toward Burr as the lesser of two evils.

When Hamilton became convinced of the strength of this developing sentiment for Burr, he initiated a frantic letter-writing campaign, arguing that Federalists had no choice but to support Jefferson. In making his case, Hamilton confessed he had compelling reasons for distrusting Jefferson because of his "fanaticism" in politics, his all too frequent opposition to past administration programs, his excessive perseverance in achieving his goals, and his occasional tendency to be a "hypocrite" who was not always "mindful of truth. . . ." But notwithstanding these faults, he added, Jefferson would support "a temporizing rather than a violent system," and "there is no fair reason to suppose him capable of being corrupted. . . ."

Hamilton's view of Burr's character and qualifications was decidedly negative. Drawing upon the firsthand knowledge that he had gained over a number of years, he described his fellow New Yorker as an "artful," "selfish," "profligate," and inordinately ambitious man who was without "probity" or "principle." Because the "public good" transcends in importance "every private consideration," concluded Hamilton, the Federalists must exert themselves to their "utmost to save our country from so great a calamity."[32]

While Hamilton was conducting his rhetorical campaign to block the election of Burr, Jefferson wrote letters to his friends describing his feelings and reporting on the progress of the balloting. After informing Monroe on February 15 that "four days of balloting have produced not a single change of vote," he reiterated his claim that he would not yield to those who wanted concessions from him in exchange for their support. "I have declared to them unequivocally," he said, "that I would not receive the government on capitulation, that I would not go into it with my hands tied."[33]

Partly because of the influence of Hamilton, and partly owing to the outpouring of popular support, Jefferson finally was elected by the House on the thirty-sixth ballot. He knew, however, that when the time came for him to deliver his inaugural address on March 4, his principal tasks were twofold: to set forth his promises of what he hoped to accomplish, and to develop ideas and rhetorical appeals that would bring a badly divided country together. His time for preparation would be short because of the long delay in learning the outcome of the election.

Both Republicans and Federalists had believed prior to the election of 1800 that it had the potential to be a major turning point for the young nation. This is a view traditionally shared by historians of the early republic, who have viewed this election from a variety of perspectives. Building upon the already impressive body of scholarship on this event is Joanne B. Freeman's 1999 article "The Election of 1800: A Study in the Logic of Political Change."[34] Although we do not feel that the Freeman study is a refutation of traditionally accepted views of the election of 1800, we are convinced that it is a significant addendum that contributes importantly to our knowledge of this memorable campaign. The author's emphasis differs from earlier analyses in several important respects. First, instead of stressing the nature and extent of personal attacks as a defining characteristic of the election, the role of honor in the campaign is highlighted. Second, the essay demonstrates the part that innovation played in the contest, including electioneering, a reliance on political caucuses, and a challenge to the Electoral College. Most of all, this study reveals how the early republic, faced with the possibility of a danger that could erupt into civil war, produced political change without threatening the stability of the Constitution. Especially with this last point in mind, we now proceed to a consideration of the inauguration of

Jefferson, the event that provided him with a forum for his most famous public address.

## The Rhetorical Setting

On March 4, there was considerable excitement in Washington as the city waited for its first presidential inauguration. During the midmorning hours of this historic day, which some observers, including Jefferson, regarded as a revolution in American politics, an artillery company from Alexandria discharged a volley of shots, much to the delight of the large numbers of citizens who had come from surrounding areas to witness the inaugural event.

At noon Jefferson, accompanied by some members of Congress and a group of "his fellow citizens," entered the Senate chamber where he was to deliver his address.[35] As he moved to the center of the auditorium, the audience stood to greet him. Seated on the platform were the recently appointed and confirmed chief justice John Marshall and the newly elected vice president Aaron Burr. Absent was John Adams, who was still chagrined and hurt by his disappointing defeat for reelection. He had departed earlier that morning for Massachusetts.[36] When the president-elect took his seat "with Aaron Burr on his right hand and John Marshall on his left, the assembled Senators," observed Henry Adams, "looked up at the three men who profoundly disliked and distrusted each other."[37]

It was not the kind of setting that Jefferson enjoyed, because of his lifelong preference for smaller, more informal rhetorical situations. Now he faced approximately one thousand auditors,[38] including senators, representatives, and other distinguished guests who had come together in a crowded room. But he was fully prepared. Before him was his carefully written manuscript, a copy of which he had deposited in the office of the *National Intelligencer* earlier that morning.

## Content and Structure of the Speech

In his opening words, Jefferson sought to allay the feelings of those who had constructed an image of him as a single-minded, fanatical leader whose radical political ideas represented a threat to the nation he had helped create. When he thought of the greatness, the magnitude, and the beauty of America, and then reflected on his own limited talents, he said, the challenges awaiting him were daunting if it were not for a Constitution that provided the "resources of wisdom" and "virtue." This immediate expression of devotion to and reliance on the Constitution was doubtless designed to answer the concerns of those who had repeatedly charged him during the campaign with being a French Jacobin who would threaten many of the document's most sacred principles. Then, directing his remarks to the senators and representatives in the audience, he made a unifying plea couched in vivid language: "I look with encouragement for the guidance and support which may enable us to steer with safety the vessel in which we are all embarked amidst the conflicting elements of a troubled world."[39]

This passage set the conciliatory tone that was to be maintained throughout the address. In keeping with this theme of reconciliation, the body of the discourse contained three main ideas, each of which drew its strength and thrust from his philosophy of social affections and other principles of virtue. The argument set forth in the first main contention took this form: *Since the difficult election we have just experienced has now been decided on constitutional, legal, and moral grounds, it behooves all Americans to unite for the "common good."* One of the ways this might be accomplished, he said, was to "bear in mind this sacred principle, that though the will of the majority is in all cases to prevail, that will to be rightful must be reasonable; that the minority possess their equal rights, which equal law must protect, and to violate would be oppression." These were comforting words to Federalists, who, after a vitriolic and dissension-filled campaign, were now in the minority. But they also were words of advice to the Republicans to remember that their responsibility as a major party was to be fair, considerate, and cooperative.

As Jefferson proceeded in his quest to have both his primary and his secondary audience "unite with one heart and one mind," he expressed the wish that all Americans should strive mightily to incorporate the elements of "harmony and affection" into their "social intercourse." At this point, he pushed aside the attacks upon his religious faith that were made during the campaign, and concentrated instead on the steps some states—especially Virginia—had taken to guarantee freedom of religion. He thus asserted that all citizens should abolish "political intolerance" as we have "banished from our land that religious intolerance under which mankind so long bled and suffered. . . ." This message, stated in optimistic terms, could not easily be overlooked by those who had falsely branded him as an atheist and enemy of God.

Jefferson's talent for developing a powerful argument in a short, pithy statement was strikingly evident when he next observed that "every difference of opinion is not a difference of principle." This was an effective springboard for him to leap to the next conclusion that put in bold relief his abiding faith in the power of identification between a speaker and the audience. In these frequently quoted lines, he asserted:

> We have called by different names brethren of the same principle. We are all Republicans, we are all Federalists.

This was a remarkable statement by one considered to be a persistent opponent of the policies of the first two administrations (of which he was a part), the major force behind the development of the Republican party, and the engine that powered a presumed political revolution in 1800. But the claim "we are all Republicans" and "all Federalists" was not surprising when we place these words in the context of his ideas on the social affections and on virtue. For these rhetorical goals, as previously noted, were central to his philosophy of discourse.

Now that he had established the need for unity, Jefferson was ready to demonstrate the advantages of such a policy. For his second argument, therefore, he developed this message: *If we become a truly united people, we will be able to enjoy together a number of blessings that may contribute to the happiness of the American people.* In a series of picturesque periodic clauses moving toward a structural climax, he articulated these sentiments:

> Kindly separated by nature and a wide ocean from the exterminating havoc of one quarter of the globe; too high-minded to endure the degradations of the others; possessing a chosen country, with room enough for our descendants to the thousandth and thousandth generation; entertaining a due sense of our equal right to the use of our own faculties, to the acquisitions of our own industry, to honor and confidence from our fellow-citizens, resulting not from birth, but from our actions and their sense of them; enlightened by a benign religion, professed, indeed, and practiced in various forms, yet all of them inculcating honesty, truth, temperance, gratitude, and the love of man; acknowledging and adoring an overruling Providence, which by all its dispensations proves that it delights in the happiness of man here and his greater happiness hereafter—with all these blessings, what more is necessary to make us a happy and prosperous people?

Here in a single paragraph filled with images of grandeur, Jefferson pictured a "chosen country" blessed with geographical size and beauty; an endowed people who had an "equal right" to develop their "own faculties," and who placed actions on a hierarchical scale of values above that of birth; a "benign religion" that upheld the virtues of "honesty, truth, temperance, gratitude, and the love of man"; and, most of all, a divine Providence whose loving concern was "the happiness of man."

The answer to the closing question of the paragraph—"What more is necessary to make us a happy and prosperous people?"—was stated in his third major premise. *All that remains for the happiness of Americans to be completely fulfilled, argued Jefferson, was to have a "wise and frugal Government" guided by a set of "essential principles."* These vital principles numbered fifteen in all. Seven emphasized basic human rights which citizens could expect from their government. The first of these, reaffirming a self-evident premise discussed in the Declaration of Independence, contended that all Americans should have "equal and exact justice" regardless of their particular "state or persuasion, religious or political." The other six principles assured them of the privilege of participating in elections with the understanding that a majority decision would prevail; of having "all abuses" settled "at the bar of public reason"; of being free to worship according to their conscience; of being able to receive information from a free press; and, if charged with a crime, of having a "trial" by jury "impartially selected."

The other eight "essential principles" dealt with states' rights and the federal government's policies with respect to foreign and domestic issues. Here the nation's role in avoiding "entangling alliances," in elevating "the civil over the military authority," and in promoting commerce, labor, and agriculture were outlined. Next, in a statement that was to win the approval of Hamilton and other Federalists, Jefferson promised that there would be "the honest payment of our debts and sacred preservation of the public faith." He concluded his argument with the following eloquent passage relating his principles of governance to past practices and to hopes and aspirations for the future:

> These principles form the bright constellation which has gone before us and guided our steps through an age of revolution and reformation. The wisdom of our sages and blood of our heroes have been devoted to their attainment. They should be the creed of our political faith, the text of civic instruction, the touchstone by which to try the services of those we trust; and should we wander from them in moments of error or of alarm, let us hasten to retrace our steps and to regain the road which alone leads to peace, liberty, and safety.

The conclusion to the First Inaugural Address relied extensively on soundly conceived arguments geared to the understanding, and appeals to the social affections that stirred the imagination and the passions. Jefferson forthrightly suggested that he did not expect the type of devotion and loving support that was tendered to George Washington, "our first and greatest revolutionary character." All that he could hope for, he noted, was for the people to have enough confidence in him "only as may give firmness and effect to the legal administration of your affairs." Again at this important juncture, he demonstrated humility by confessing that errors would be made as he strove to carry out his promises. But when these occur, he added, it should be remembered that the mistakes in judgment would never be "intentional." For he had but one goal as president, namely to do "all the good in [his] power . . . to be instrumental to the happiness and freedom of all." The closing lines of the address revealed his purpose to rely on the "good will" of the citizens and on the wisdom and guidance of "that Infinite Power which rules the destinies of the universe. . . ."

The content of the inaugural address had its roots in Jefferson's philosophy of virtue. Permeating the discourse from beginning to end was a stress on the reciprocal relationships between the citizens and their government, on the need for people to engage in harmonious and affectionate "social discourse" as they communed and worked with each other, and on a recognition of the dependence that individuals and the government must have upon an "adoring" Providence. If these relationships blend in an appropriate and productive manner they would, as both Hutcheson and Jefferson believed, place the virtue of benevolence in the service of the public good in order to promote happiness in society.

In communicating these principles of virtue, Jefferson used arguments based on reasonableness that featured self-evident premises, common-sense appeals, and experience. Similarly, because of his strong desire to woo his audience, and therefore remove the divisions that had been so prominent in the 1800 campaign, he strove to identify with his audience by highlighting the value of reconciliation. The combined rhetorical appeals succeeded in doing what Bacon had recommended and Jefferson had enthusiastically endorsed—a stirring of the imagination and the affections. It was these strategies, they both held, that had the capacity to strengthen the concept of virtue.

## Channeling the Message

Of the discourses we have examined, the inaugural address achieved the highest level of distinction in the language control and style. Relying almost exclusively on the "elevated" style he had suggested was suitable for oratory and poetry, Jefferson used figures of speech and thought which opened the doors to the mind. With him the auditors and readers could see a beautiful and spacious nation; a "vessel in which we are all embarked amidst the conflicting sentiments of a troubled world"; and the "bright constellation" of "essential principles" that "has gone before us and guided our steps through the age of revolution and reformation." The hearer or reader is also able to sense the beauty and variety of sentence structures that use both the simple and periodic forms; and a choice of words depicting clarity, conciseness, and force. Overall, the style, according to one eyewitness, was "chaste, appropriate, and eloquent. . . ."[40]

As the years went by, Jefferson's language usage in the address continued to win praise. Henry S. Randall proclaimed in 1858 that "the number of its phrases which have passed into popular axioms—which are constantly reproduced in political newspapers and addresses, and at the same time the most authoritative and most felicitous expressions of the ideas they embody—is astonishing, and perhaps unequalled in the instance of any similar production."[41]

But if the style was effective because it conformed to Jefferson's high standards for this canon of discourse, the same cannot be said for his delivery. The editor of the *National Intelligencer* may have been correct when he gave this description: "The manner in which it was delivered was plain, dignified, and unostentatious. . . ."[42] But Smith missed an essential point of delivery that his wife Margaret Bayard Smith observed—the problem of a weak voice that did not project. She noted in words often quoted or paraphrased, but generally without attribution, that "the speech was delivered in so low a tone that few heard it."[43] This failure to speak with sufficient force to be heard fell short of Jefferson's requirement for delivery.

For the next three or four weeks following the inaugural address, Jefferson continued his campaign to preach the doctrine of reconciliation. Convinced that it was "prudent" to allow sufficient "time for a perfect consolidation," he was pleased to assert on March 27 "that the great body of those called Federalists were real republicans as well as Federalists."[44] Concurrently, however, he told John Dickinson that he would never abandon "the principles of our revolution"; and boasted to Dr. Joseph Priestley that people "can no longer say there is nothing new under the sun."[45] Meanwhile he took comfort in responding to those who sent glowing accounts describing the favorable reaction to the discourse.[46]

That Jefferson's strategy of coming down on the side of unity and identification worked seems clear from the effect the address had on Federalists. On the morning of March 4, John Marshall wrote to General Charles C. Pinckney, stating the "hope that the public prosperity & happiness may sustain no diminution under democratic guidance." He then added a postscript at 4 o'clock, following the speech, in which he said: "It is in the general well judged & conciliatory. It is in direct terms giving the lie to the violent party declamation which has elected him, but it is strongly characteristic of his political theory."[47] This sentiment was echoed by James Bayard in a letter to Hamilton on March 8.[48] It is also significant to note that Hamilton, who had placed his standing among his Federalist compatriots in jeopardy by supporting Jefferson over Burr, was complimentary. On March 21, he wrote to the "Electors of New York," stating that Federalists should be able to support "the moderate views exhibited in the Presidential speech. . . ."[49]

There were a few reservations relating to the address. Some Republicans, fearful that they would not receive their fair share of presidential appointments, thought the conciliatory tone was too favorable to the Federalists. In addition, Henry Adams raised another issue about a particular portion of the speech. Jefferson was inconsistent, he argued, when he asserted on the one hand that the Republican victory had ushered in a revolution in 1800; and then proceeded to follow an evolutionary approach by extending many of the policies of the previous administrations.[50]

In general, however, the speech lost little of its appeal for Jefferson scholars and adherents in the twentieth century. A. A. Lipscomb and A. E. Bergh, for example, reported in the early 1900s that the "inaugural address is considered by many critics to be his masterpiece."[51] This perhaps was an overstatement because of the enduring influence and relevance of the Declaration of Independence. Nevertheless, tributes to the speech are ongoing in the modern era because of the power of the message and the elegance of the style. Describing an evening before John F. Kennedy was inaugurated in 1961, Arthur Schlesinger Jr. told this story:

> At eight o'clock [J. F. K.] and his wife went to the Inaugural Concert at Constitution Hall. An hour later they left at the intermission to go on to the Inaugural Gala at the Armory. . . . With the light on inside the car, he settled back to read Jefferson's First Inaugural, which had been printed in the concert program. When he finished, he shook his head and said wryly, "Better than mine."[52]

This was a telling statement from one whose own inaugural address has become an American classic; and it was further evidence that Jefferson, indeed, did write with an "eloquent pen."

# Notes

1. Boyd, 6: 63n–64n.

2. TJ to Robert Scot, May 30, 1781, in Boyd, 6: 43.

3. The speech appears in Boyd, 6: 60–63.

4. In commenting on the discourse, Boyd asserts: "And it sets forth most of the sympathetic and far-sighted views on the status and future of the Indian that were to be embodied in TJ's Indian policy as President." ibid., 63n.

5. Peterson, *The Portable Jefferson*, xxii.

6. Anthony F. C. Wallace, *Jefferson and the Indians: The Tragic Fate of the First Americans* (Cambridge, Mass.: The Belknap Press of Harvard University Press, 1999), 74.

7. *Jefferson's Empire: The Language of American Nationhood* (Charlottesville: University Press of Virginia, 2000), 19.

8. George Washington to TJ, October 13, 1789, in Boyd, 15: 519.

9. "Autobiography," in Ford, 1: 158.

10. Boyd, 15: 557n.

11. The speech appears in Boyd, 15: 556–57.

12. The speech is printed in Boyd, 16: 11.

13. December 14, 1789, in Boyd, 16: 26.

14. Boyd asserts that "the calculated choice of 'visit' instead of 'return' was TJ's response to the committee's indelicate attempt to elicit comment on Washington's offer." Boyd, 16: 13n.

15. The speech is reproduced in Ford (1896 edition), 7: 501.

16. Lienesch, "Thomas Jefferson and the American Democratic Experience: The Origins of the Partisan Press, Popular Political Parties, and Public Opinion," in Onuf, ed., *Jeffersonian Legacies*, 316–39.

17. *Writings*, 1035–37.

18. Ibid., 1055–62.

19. James Rogers Sharp, *American Politics in the Early Republic* (New Haven: Yale University Press, 1993), 243.

20. Dumas Malone, *Jefferson and the Ordeal of Liberty* (Boston: Little, Brown, 1962), 489.

21. Charles O. Lerche Jr., "Jefferson and the Election of 1800: A Case Study in the Political Smear," in *William and Mary Quarterly*, 3rd ser., 5 (October 1948), 471.

22. Sharp, *American Politics in the Early Republic*, 239. Adams's feeling against Hamilton was equally strong. ". . . he was reported to have said that he would sooner serve as Vice president under Jefferson than to be indebted to '*such a being* as Hamilton whom he did not hesitate to call a bastard. . . .'" Cited in Malone, *The Ordeal of Liberty*, 476.

23. Hamilton's letter-pamphlet, dated October 24, 1800, is reprinted in Harold C. Syrett, ed., *The Papers of Alexander Hamilton*, 27 vols. (New York: Columbia University Press, 1961–1981), 25: 186–234. The editor notes that "in the months immediately preceding the election . . . Hamilton made no secret of his preference for Pinckney over Adams. Adams, aware of Hamilton's attitude and intrigues, described him as a 'Hypocrite' and stated that he intended to maintain the 'same conduct towards him I always did, that is to keep him at a distance.'" [170]. See also Stanley Elkins and Eric McKitrick, *The Age of Federalism* (New York: Oxford University Press, 1993), 737–40.

24. This 24-page chapter provides an excellent account of the charges and counter-charges that dominated the 1800 campaign.

25. Lerche's description, which has frequently been cited, is especially valuable in analyzing the attacks appearing in newspapers and pamphlets both in the North and in the South.

26. The editor of the *Gazette of the United States* noted that the supporters of Jefferson "think it (is) of no consequence whether there are Twenty Gods or NO GOD. . . ." October 1, 1800.

27. Apparently, the ministers as a whole did not satisfy Jefferson's critics. A letter to the editor of the *Gazette* published this message to what the author perceived to be a "lukewarm Clergy:"

Reverend Sir, GOD AND A RELIGIOUS PRESIDENT
    OR JEFFERSON AND NO GOD

There is no mean between these two extremes, no place for neutrality; will a Christian Minister pause one moment to what side he will take? Will he forsake his RELIGION, and his SAVIOUR to take up with the World, and by his silence forward the election of an Infidel?

The letter was signed "NO INFIDEL." October 7, 1800. What makes the letter so ironic is the fact that Jefferson and Adams held similar views on religion. To suggest that Jefferson was an atheist is in direct contradiction of the facts. In our discussion of virtue in chapter 2, we saw how he warmly praised the teachings of Jesus, and in chapter 4 on the Social Affections how he greatly admired chapter 15 of Psalms. Also of interest on this point is the following information Martha Jefferson communicated to her daughter following the death of Mary in 1804: "My mother has told me that on the day of her sister's death, she left her father alone for some hours. He then sent for her, and she found him with the Bible in his hands." Randall, *The Life of Thomas Jefferson*, 3: 101–102. Although Randolph does not identify the author of the letter describing this event, we, after examining Jefferson's family tree, agree with Andrew Burstein's speculation that the letter was written by Martha's daughter Ellen Wayles Randolph Coolidge. *The Inner Jefferson*, 320 (chap. 7, footnote 3).

28. The charges mentioned in this paragraph, which often were repeated, may be found in the following issues of the *Gazette*: August 23, 29, 30; September 1, 3, 10, 13, 17; October 1, 2, 7, 9, 11, 13, 30; and November 1, 7, and 8.

29. *Aurora*, September 13, 1800, cited in the *Gazette*, October 1, 1800.

30. November 3, 1800.

31. Sharp, *American Politics in the Early Republic*, 247.

32. See the following letters: Hamilton to Gouverneur Morris, New York, December 26, 1800; and to James A. Bayard, December 27, 1800, and January 16, 1801, in Morton J. Frisch, ed., *Selected Writings and Speeches of Alexander Hamilton* (Washington and London: American Enterprise Institute for Public Policy Research, 1985), 458–65.

33. TJ to James Monroe, February 15, 1801, in Ford (1896 ed.), 7: 490–91.

34. Joanne B. Freeman, "The Election of 1800: A Study in the Logic of Political Change," *Yale Law Journal* 108 (1999): 1959–94.

35. *National Intelligencer and Washington Advertiser*, March 6, 1801.

36. Ibid. In commenting on Adams's departure before the inauguration of Jefferson, Henry Adams observed that "perhaps the late President was wise to retire from a stage

where everything was arranged to print a censure upon his principles, and where he would have seemed, in his successor's opinion, as little in place as George III would have appeared at the installation of President Washington." *A History of the United States of America During the First Administration of Thomas Jefferson* (New York: Antiquarian Press, 1962), 1: 191.

37. Ibid., 1: 196.

38. Margaret Bayard Smith, *The First Forty Years of Washington Society*, 26.

39. The edition of the address we have used is as follows: James D. Richardson, ed., *A Compilation of the Messages and Papers of the Presidents, 1789–1897*, 10 vols. (Washington, D.C.: Published by Authority of Congress, 1898), 1: 321–24.

40. *National Intelligencer*, March 6, 1801. Henry Adams was similarly enthusiastic about the style as the ensuing description shows: "Even as a literary work, it possessed a certain charm of style peculiar to Jefferson, a flavor of Virginia thought and manners, a Jeffersonian ideality calculated to please the ear of later generations. . . ." *A History of the United States of America*, 1: 199.

41. Randall, *Life of Thomas Jefferson*, 2: 633.

42. March 6, 1801.

43. *The First Forty Years of Washington Society*, 26. Henry Adams also noted that "Jefferson rose, and in a somewhat inaudible voice began his Inaugural Address." *History of the United States of America During the First Administration of Thomas Jefferson*, 1: 199.

44. See letters to James Monroe, March 7, 1801, in Ford, 9: 202–205; and to Henry Knox, March 27, 1801, in ibid., 9: 236.

45. March 21, 1801, in ibid., 9: 216–19.

46. Observe letter to Knox cited above, and to Doctor Benjamin Rush, March 24, 1801, in ibid., 9: 229–32.

47. Cited in Richard J. Hooker, "John Marshall on the Judiciary, the Republicans, and Jefferson, March 4, 1801," in *American Historical Review*, 53 (April 1948): 519–20.

48. Printed in Randall, *Life of Thomas Jefferson*, 2: 607.

49. "An Address to the Electors of the State of New York," March 21, 1801, in Harold C. Syrett, ed., *The Papers of Alexander Hamilton*, 27 vols. (New York: Columbia University Press, 1961–1987), 25: 366.

50. *A History of the United States of America*, 1: 200. At one point, Adams noted: "The Federalist newspapers never ceased laughing at the 'spasms' so suddenly converted into 'bilows,' and at the orthodoxy of Jefferson's Federalism; but perhaps his chief fault was to belittle the revolution which had taken place." Ibid.

51. L&B, 3: 316. In 1966, Robert T. Oliver and Eugene E. White asserted: Jefferson's speech, "noble in sentiment and phrased in language which was felicitous though more oratorical than the Declaration of Independence, was to become one of the two or three most memorable inaugurals." *Selected Speeches from American History* (Boston: Allyn and Bacon, 1966), 30.

52. Arthur Schlesinger Jr., *A Thousand Days* (Boston: Houghton Mifflin, 1965), 1. Of special interest in this quotation is that Jefferson's inaugural address "had been printed in the concert program."

# CHAPTER TWELVE

~

# Legal Advocate

We have seen how Jefferson functioned as a polemicist in the Revolutionary War era, and as a special occasional speaker in the period from the end of the war through his First Inaugural Address in 1801. This chapter, focusing on his performance as a public communicator, emphasizes his career as a legal advocate both in and out of the courtroom, and the effect that this interest and experience had on his participation in the political, educational, and social arenas.

We begin our analysis by turning to that phase of his professional career in which he was a practicing lawyer. After being tutored by George Wythe, reading extensively in law, and observing experienced Virginia advocates, including Patrick Henry, in action in a series of celebrated cases, Jefferson became ready to appear before the Bar of the General Court in 1767.[1] It was a profession that would command his attention for the next seven years. Some scholars have suggested that he was not fully committed to the practice of law because of his natural tendency to favor theory over practicum and his disinclination to engage in public speaking and debate.[2] Others have taken an opposing view, arguing that these seven years were an enjoyable and productive period in his life. Henry S. Randall asserted that Jefferson "loved his profession—keenly relished the study and practice of it—and continued both with unabated zeal, until the Colonial Courts were closed by the Revolution."[3] Sharing this assessment was Richard S. Morris who noted that Jefferson "was supremely happy in his work" and "valued all his life the knowledge which he obtained during these years of intensive study and reading. . . ."[4]

The documented evidence regarding Jefferson's legal practice is proof of his interest and success in functioning as a lawyer. His Case Book, for instance, contains a list of more than 900 cases he handled from 1767 through 1774.[5] He recorded in his Fee Book, moreover, the profits he earned each year. The figures for the period embracing the years from 1767 through 1772 were as follows: 293 pounds in 1767, 304 in 1768, 370 in 1769, 522 in 1770, 280 in 1771, and 349 in 1772.[6] Randall has estimated that his "average annual profits for his whole term of practice, reached three thousand dollars."[7] By 1771, Jefferson's reputation as a legal advocate had risen to such a high level that Robert Carter Nicholas sought to turn over his business to him—an offer that Jefferson refused to accept.[8]

Another gauge for determining the nature and scope of his practice is a consideration of the types of clients he served. Among them were well-known members of leading Virginia families—the Blands, Bollings, Burwells, Byrds, Carters, and Randolphs, and "several Royal Councillors of state, and other crown officers. . . ."[9] When these clients saw Jefferson perform his legal duties as an advocate, they were impressed with his emphasis on virtue, his respect for the jury system, his meticulous preparation in selecting and developing arguments, his talent for rebutting an opponent's claims, and his command of written language marked by clarity, conciseness, force, and precision.

What they did not see or hear, however, was a dynamic orator with a powerful delivery pattern in the tradition of his contemporary Patrick Henry. For his voice by nature, observed William Wirt, lacked the strength required in a large public assembly. Nevertheless, it "was all-sufficient for the purposes of judicial debate. . . ."[10] He thus was able to converse with ease and informality with the judges and jury.[11]

We have chosen three of Jefferson's cases for analysis so that we can see how he discovered the issues, constructed and supported his arguments, and incorporated into his appeals the principles of virtue that characterized the basic elements of his moral philosophy. The first case was *Howell v. Netherland*, argued in April 1770; the second was *Godwin et al. v. Lunan*, which occurred in October 1771; and the third was *Bolling v. Bolling* that took place in 1770 and 1771, but still remained in the hands of an arbitrator as late as 1772. Fortunately, the essential facts, along with Jefferson's extended legal briefs, in *Howell v. Netherland* and *Godwin et al. v. Lunan* were preserved by him and published in his *Reports of Cases in the General Court of Virginia*.[12] Even more important are the extant primary source materials that are available in *Bolling v. Bolling*, which recently have been published in book form.

## *Howell v. Netherland* (1770)

Samuel Howell, the plaintiff in this case, was the grandson of a mulatto woman whose mother was white and whose father was an African American. At the time of the grandmother's birth, a law that had been passed in Virginia in 1705 required her to be a servant until she reached the age of thirty-one. During the period of her servitude, she gave birth to a daughter, who by then was under the jurisdiction of a 1723 Virginia law, stating that the offspring of a mulatto must also be a servant until the age of thirty-one. When she, in turn, delivered her son Samuel, her master sought to require him to become a servant under the same terms. This meant that the 1723 law designed to impose servitude upon a mulatto's child was now being applied to a third-generation offspring. It was against the background of these events that Howell initiated a lawsuit, and asked Jefferson to represent him in the General Court.

It was evident from the beginning that, in preparing his case, Jefferson saw the need to combine legal arguments with those that centered on values and virtue. His first contention was that the purpose of the original act of 1705 "was to punish and deter women from that confusion of species, which the legislature seems to have considered as an evil, and not to oppress their innocent offspring." For this reason, therefore, a provision was introduced to protect the welfare of the child by granting power to "church wardens to choose out a proper master. . . ." Under these circumstances, he argued, if a master sought "to sell his ward" he would be violating a sacred covenant established by the church—an act that "would be a corruption of morals either by the wicked precept or example of the master, or of his family." It would be, moreover, a violation of the trust that was extended to the first mulatto.

At this juncture, Jefferson drew a distinction between a servant and a slave, and then reinforced this interpretation with a value-centered claim. A servant, he said, resembles an apprentice, not a slave; and since an apprentice cannot be "aliened" from his property and rights, any attempt to disregard this fact by a master should be condemned as an untrustworthy and dishonest action.

Jefferson made a second major argument on behalf of his client: "The plaintiff, being a mulatto of the third generation would not be detained in servitude under any law whatever. . . ." In support of this proposition, he developed two subordinate claims, the first of which was a strictly legal contention based on the wording in the acts of 1705 and 1723. The

1705 law, he reminded the jury, applied only to the grandmother; and the 1723 act expanded the coverage to include her children. To go beyond the second generation, therefore, was in direct opposition to the "common sense of mankind." Surely, he observed in commenting on this point, it should not be incumbent on him to prove that the word "'child' does not include the grandchild, great-grand child, great-great grandchild, & c. *in infinitum*."

But Jefferson, even in this early stage of his career, was not content to limit his argument to legal considerations alone. He thus introduced as his second subordinate contention a claim that was doubtless inspired by that part of his moral philosophy that conformed to the law of nature. He stated his position in strongly worded language:

> Under the law of nature, all men are born free, every one comes into the world with a right to his own person, which includes the liberty of moving and using it at his own will. This is what is called personal liberty, and is given him by the author of nature, because necessary for his own sustenance.

He then applied these principles of freedom, equality, and justice to the case at hand. "The reducing the mother to servitude," he asserted, "was a violation of the law of nature: surely then, the same law cannot prescribe a continuance of the violation to her issue [offspring], and that too without end, for if it extends to any, it must to every degree of descendants."

Jefferson was not yet through in developing his analysis of the law of nature. As he continued his discussion of this theme, he posed an argumentative dilemma. If this natural moral law, he said, demanded that Howell should be bound in servitude because his father was an African American, it should by the same token authorize his freedom because his mother was a free woman. Such a contradiction, he inferred, "proves it to be no law of nature."

The conclusion to Jefferson's presentation contained a summary of the legal issues in the case, and a conjecture stated in moral tones. "So that the position at first laid down," he observed, "is now proven, that the act of 1705, makes servants of the first mulatto, that of 1723, extends it to her children, but that it remains for some future legislation, if any shall be found wicked enough, to extend it to the grandchildren and other issue more remote, to the '*nati*': *natorum et qui nascentur ab illis*."

Jefferson's arguments did not persuade the General Court, for it sat in the midst of a slave-holding community. Edward Dumbauld noted that Jefferson's "eloquent and ingenious appeal to the law of nature, under which all men are born free, on behalf of a mulatto seeking release from servitude, fell on deaf ears." Moreover, Dumbauld added, "Wythe, for the defendant, was about to answer, but the court interrupted him and gave judgment in favor of his client."[13] Despite this humiliating defeat that Dumbauld believed to be "clearly correct," Jefferson's performance in this case was exemplary in a number of respects. It was consistent, for example, with his philosophy of reasoning and principles of law. His thorough analysis of acts passed by the Virginia Assembly, his call for the use of common sense, his posing of a logical dilemma, his carefully organized legal brief, and his language control were responsible discourse strategies. We are able to see, moreover, appeals to virtue that were to become a centerpiece of the Declaration of Independence six years later.

## Godwin et al. v. Lunan (1771)

In *Howell v. Netherland*, as we have just observed, the case focused principally on the interpretation and moral implications of the laws of 1705 and 1723 as they pertained to the status of a mulatto and her descendants. The case *Godwin et al. v. Lunan* dealt with the character and actions of a church minister and with the question of what person or group had the legal right to evaluate his performance and, if necessary, determine the nature of his punishment. The facts of the case appear in Jefferson's *Reports*.

In 1771, the "churchwardens and vestrymen of the upper parish in the county of Nansemond," as plaintiffs, "filed a libel in the General Court, as a court of ecclesiastical jurisdiction against the defendant" Patrick Lunan. The charges involving Lunan's personal immorality and dereliction of duty were as follows:

. . . he was of evil fame and profligate manners. . . .

. . . he was much addicted to drunkenness, in so much, as to be often drunk at church, and unable to go through divine service, or to baptize or marry those who attended for those purposes. . . .

. . . he officiated in ridiculous apparel unbecoming a priest. . . .

. . . he was a common disturber of the peace, and often quarrelling and fighting. . . .

. . . on the 10th of July 1767, and at other times, he exposed his private parts to view in public companies, and solicited Negro and other women to fornication and adultery with him. . . .

. . . he neglected the parochial duties of performing divine service, preaching and administering the sacrament of the Lord's supper. . . .

. . . he declared he did not believe in the revealed religion of Christ, and cared not of what religion he was [so long as] he got the tobacco, nor what became of the flock [so long as] he could get the fleece. . . .

Upon presenting these charges, "the libellants prayed that the said Patrick Lunan might be corrected, punished, and deprived, or otherwise, that right and justice might be administered." Responding to the plaintiffs' claims, the defendant countered with the argument that the bishop, not the General Court, should have jurisdiction of the case.

It was easy for Jefferson to agree to represent the plaintiffs because of his belief in the importance of personal morality, his conviction that the moral principles taught by Jesus had been grossly violated, and his strongly held opinion that a person's moral worth is to be measured by his actions. But none of these ideas became a part of his legal brief, which dealt exclusively with the issue of who had the legitimate power to decide what should be done with respect to the defendant.

Using Blackstone as an authority, Jefferson developed an elaborate argument showing, first of all, that there are three types of church organizations—the "*donatives, presentatives,* and *collatives.*" He then offered proof, second, demonstrating which of these types was applicable in the present case.

A donative church, explained Jefferson, is one that was "originally founded and endowed by the crown or lay subject, or perhaps by both. . . ." Its very existence, therefore, depended upon "the gift of the lay patron, whose deed of donation is an absolute investiture of the clerk, without presentation to the bishop or any other ceremony." Because the lay founder is the patron, he or she serves as the visitor—one empowered to evaluate the pastor and to determine what action should be taken when the situation seems to warrant it. Presentative churches are those that started out as donatives but lost this original status when they permitted bishops to encroach upon their right of approving nominees. Finally, added Jefferson, collatives from the beginning established the bishop as patron, giving him sole authority to function as the visitor.

Once Jefferson had presented his definitions, he moved to an analysis of this crucial question: Which of these three forms of churches did the plaintiffs represent? He answered this inquiry with the affirmation that they were members of a donative church, and as such possessed the rights and privileges that belong to a visitor. Their church is donative, he declared, because it was "founded by laymen" who, in turn, serve as the patron. Thus the church with its "lay foundation" is not "subject to presentation to the bishop."

Central to Jefferson's argument was his interpretation of the meaning of the concept of community as contrasted with his unfavorable perception of the authoritarian leadership role that the bishop presumably performs. "If we consider the community as made up of a King and People," he noted, "the King will then be the patron of our churches, it being a known branch of the royal prerogative, that where the King and his subjects are joint founders, the rights of patronage vest in the King." He next suggested that the same conclusion would be drawn if we examine the issue from a constitutional perspective: "If then our acts of Assembly, erecting cures of souls, and declaring that they shall be given to eccleciastics of a certain sect, have not said by whom the nomination shall be, it will follow that the King, who is to see the law executed, must nominate persons for that purpose."

Jefferson concluded his case with a reaffirmation of his belief that "our churches are donatives, because they wear the three characteristics of donatives." They were founded and sustained by laymen; they "are not subject to presentation to a bishop"; and they are maintained by gifts from the two patrons—the people and the king.

There were several distinguishing elements in Jefferson's arguments in this case. First, he used an exceptionally wide variety of source material to buttress his claims. Dozens of legal theorists and practitioners were cited. These included such seminal scholars as Lord Coke, Littleton, Blackstone, and Lord Holt. Similarly important was his use of at least five legal precedents, and his reference to three acts passed by the Virginia Assembly. Additionally, he cited Hume's *History of England*, alluded to specific actions of several kings, and described relevant events that happened at the College of William and Mary. Of significance also is that his argumentative claims and choice of language, as seen in his legal brief, fulfilled the basic requirements he had articulated in his standards for legal advocacy.

A second characteristic that permeated his presentation was the legal and political philosophy that seemed to dominate the message. By associating himself with the laity as the legitimate patrons of the church, he stood squarely on the moral foundation upon which his philosophy of republicanism rested. Power, he was saying, belongs to the people; and it is they, not the bishop, who should decide the fate of the cleric. From this faith in the people he never deviated.

A third defining element of this case was its effect on the judges. With respect to this rhetorical criterion, Jefferson's performance achieved its goal. For the court decided that the plaintiffs "possessed ecclesiastical jurisdiction, and that an ecclesiastical court then must proceed to censure or deprive the defendant, if there should be just cause."[14]

Finally, an indirect effect was implicit in the General Court's verdict in this case. That the church wardens and vestrymen were given the right and power to administer punishment to a clergyman whose private and public life were morally reprehensible in light of societal values meant that the standards Jefferson had set for a minister in his philosophy of pulpit eloquence would be upheld. And whenever this occurs, he firmly believed, the public good would be significantly enhanced.

## Bolling v. Bolling (1770–1771)

One of the most interesting and important cases in Jefferson's legal career was *Bolling v. Bolling*. It involved the influential family of Edward Bolling, a wealthy Virginia landowner who wrote his will on July 13, 1769, a year before his death. As we begin our analysis of this case, we wish to acknowledge our indebtedness to the following source that contains a thoroughly developed introduction and the arguments presented by the lawyers for the plaintiff and the defendant: Bernard Schwartz, Wilcie Kern, and R. B. Bernstein, eds., *Thomas Jefferson and Bolling v. Bolling: Law and the Legal Profession in Pre-revolutionary America*.[15] (Unless otherwise specified, all quoted material related to the case is drawn from this source.)

The participants in the case were as follows:

(1) Testator—Edward Bolling (died in 1770)
(2) Plaintiff—Archibald Bolling
(3) Defendant—Robert Bolling (executor of the will)
(4) Counsel
  a. George Wythe—for the plaintiff
  b. Thomas Jefferson—for the defendant

What adds to the interest in this case is that Jefferson's opponent, as it was in *Howell v. Nethernand*, was his revered former teacher.

Edward Bolling's will had several important provisions that became the substance of an eventual lawsuit between two brothers who became the principal legatees of their brother Edward's assets.

(1) "I give and bequeath to my brother Robert Bolling my plantation called and known by the name of the Buffalo lick on the North side of James's river for him and his heirs for ever, as also my negroes Will, Joe, Bristol, Ball, Sarah, and Cis, with the children belonging to Sarah and Cis, for the said Robert Bolling and his heirs for ever." (p. 166)

(2) "I give and bequeath to my brother Archibald Bolling my plantation called and known by the name of the Old town, as also my warehouses at the place called Pocahuntas, and my lots at Bermuda hundred, for him and his heirs for ever." (p. 166)

(3) "the rest of my estate, negroes, houses, clothes and other parts of my estate, not already given, I give and bequeath to my brother Archibald Bolling, for him and his heirs for ever." (p. 167)

(4) "it is my will and devise that my book be *given* up to my brother Robert, and that he *receive* all the debts due me, and *pay* all that I owe." (p. 241)

These provisions in the will, in turn, produced two main issues in the case.

(1) "whether the defendant [Robert Bolling] was entitled to the crops growing on the Buffalo Lick plantation at the time of the testator's death, or whether they should instead pass to the plaintiff [Archibald Bolling], the residuary legatee, as part of Edward's personal estate." (introduction, p. 87)

(2) "whether the gift to the defendant of the testator's 'Book' was a legacy to him of surplus amounts collected over the debts to be paid, or whether that surplus also was an undisposed part of the decedent's personal property and should pass under the residuary clause of the will to the plaintiff." (introduction, p. 87)

Both lawyers spent far more time on the first issue than on the second. Jefferson, for instance, devoted 105 pages to issue one and 68 to the second. We will adopt the same plan since the editors of *Bolling v. Bolling* correctly argue that the second arguments of Wythe and Jefferson "only repeat, elaborate, and refine the points already made." We further agree with their claim that "the analysis given of the first arguments should give the reader an adequate idea of Jefferson's and Wythe's forensic techniques" (introduction, p. 104).

To set the stage for our analysis of Jefferson's arguments, we cite several legal terms (defined in Webster's *Dictionary*) that are used often in the case:

(1) *Emblements* are "the products or profits of land which has been sold or planted."
(2) *Chattels* are "movable articles of property" or "any article of tangible property other than land."
(3) *Devise* is the assigning or transmitting of property.
(4) *Residuary* means "entitled to the residue of an estate."
(5) *Legatee* describes "one to whom a legacy is bequeathed."

Of the five terms, the concept of emblements deserves the greatest emphasis because it is the crucial term in the first argument of each counsel. Wythe's opening argument began with a reference to emblements. Since they are mere chattels, he said, they "are not a part of the inheritance," and thus cannot be passed "with land by a devise." He then gave a social appeal based on the instrumental nature of American law as it relates to the promotion of agriculture. He phrased this argument in these terms: "The law gives the emblements to the representative of the sower when he dies before they be reaped to encourage agriculture and they are as much his separate property and subject to the regulations which concern personal chattels as his cattle, household furniture, and the like."

Convinced that he could weaken Jefferson's case by anticipating the sources his opponent would most likely use, Wythe named many of the potential authorities and then discussed their limitations as witnesses. He next downplayed the significance of the "Book," saying that it "does not impart a gift of the debts, and is no more than the appointment of an executor."

Jefferson countered Wythe's arguments on emblements, noting that "formerly, emblements went with the land." At a later period, he asserted, "our laws have given them to the executor of the sower" provided that the "estate was rightful" which in this case, he argued, it was. Persuaded that he had dealt convincingly with the question of emblements, Jefferson was fully prepared to refute Wythe's attacks on his sources. His approach was direct and specific. His strategy was to list Wythe's objection to a particular authority he had cited, and then given a refutation. Here are three representative examples of Jefferson's method:

Wythe    1. *Objection*—"all the cases in Winch are supposed not to have been collected by him; because, in one of them, is an eulogy on himself, on occasion of his death." (p. 191)

TJ  Refutation—"we might as well endeavor to destroy the authority of the Pentateuch, by observing that all the chapters thereof were not written by Moses, because in one of them, Deut. XXXIV. 5–12, *is an eulogy on himself, on occasion of his death.* in both cases the passage, which could not be by the author himself, is easily and equally distinguishable." (p. 192)

Wythe  2. Objection—"Sir Geo[rge] Croke was then but 27. years of age." (p. 200)

TJ  Refutation—"far be it from me to detract from that superiority of wisdom to which years give title, because they bring it. the longer a man has lived, the more facts have come under his observation, and the more time he has had for reflection. but the understanding of Sir Geo[rge] Croke must have been of slow growth indeed, if at the age of 27. he was yet unable to apprehend a case so simplified as this, when canvassed among the judges and counsel in court, and again explained to him in conversation with Coke: besides if this part of his book be not authority because of his youth, say where-abouts he begins to be old enough, that at that place we may draw a line in the book. our law books do not inform us; they cite equally every part of his work. . . ." (p. 200)

Wythe  3. Objection—"Wentworth was a complier." (p. 207)

TJ  Refutation—"what are the authorities produced in support of the pl[aintiff]'s right? Swinburne a compiler; Blackstone a compiler, Broke a compiler, Perkins a compiler, and Viner a compiler." (pp. 207–208)

These three examples of objections and answers or refutations are instructive and compelling. The first makes use of analogy, one of Jefferson's four elements of reasoning. The second deals with the concept of age, an essential aspect of his philosophy of audience analysis and adaptation. It also reveals his talent for ridicule, a rhetorical talent he later admired in William Pitt the Elder, when he was accused by Horace Walpole of being too young to be taken seriously in Parliament. Moreover, it is ironic that Jefferson himself was 27 at the time the case was being debated. Finally, Jefferson was at his best defending authorities described as compilers. The list he presented enabled him to turn the tables on Wythe. These three instances displaying Jefferson's talent for refutation, when combined with numerous others he cited in defending his authorities, prompted Edward Dumbauld to give this assessment: "Jefferson's exhaustive analysis of the authorities regarding emblements at common law was successful to the extent that it persuaded opposing counsel to concede that at common law the crops not severed at the testator's death would pass with the land devised to the defendant."[16]

In his refutations, Jefferson was making effective use of common law principles and of *stare decisis* or precedents. This crucial legal concept, he believed, is a defining principle of common law. Let us observe how he introduced this vitally significant theme in his first argument on behalf of the defendant. He did so with a reference to Gibb's *Law of Evidence*, stating: "I know not whether any objection will be made of this. He [Gibbs] is like Wentworth, a compiler, but I have ever supposed him unquestionable authority." With this brief introductory statement, he delivered his great defense of *stare decisis*:

> And here I cannot express the anxiety I ever feel when an attempt is made to unhinge those principles, on which alone we depend for security in all the property we hold, and to set us again adrift in search for new. and by the time these are found, they will again be sent off after the old. when rules of property have been settled, on their faith we buy things, and call them our own. they should therefore be sacred, and not wantonly set aside when ingenuity can persuade us to believe they are unfit, or inconsonant with other decisions. we should not, under a momentary impression, demolish what has been the growth of ages. this deference to adjudged cases is enjoined by our laws. (p. 208)

On the next page of his argument, Jefferson quoted another authority on the issue of *stare decisis* who asserted that it "is now become a permanent rule, which it is not in the breast of any subsequent judge to alter or vary from, according to his private sentiments . . ." (p. 209).

An additional claim by Jefferson is worth noting. After listing Wythe's objection suggesting it might in some instances be viewed as unjust to "detain the lands from their owner," Jefferson responded with an argument, similar to that used by Wythe, that had social and instrumental value. "But this private injury," he observed, "is made to give way to public good, which is promoted by the encouragement of agriculture." In making this point, Jefferson was saying that in this instance, the public good was on a higher level of virtue than a private good.

There were several other dimensions of Jefferson's case that were consistent with his rhetoric of virtue. First, he assumed that the testator was a benevolent person who was completely fair and just. As he put it near the end of the first argument, Jefferson noted that "the testator in this instance seems to have extended his bounties to those two brothers, pretty nearly in equal degree." Second, Jefferson carefully defined the words "give" and "receive," and stressed the importance of context in order to determine the meaning of a word or phrase. Third, he explained that meaning is clearer if we could be present and observe the nonverbal, as well as the verbal, communication pattern of the testator when he prepares and signs the will. Similarly, the reader of the will and the arguments in support of the defendant's position cannot help but be impressed by the common law arguments he articulated, by the extensive evidence he cited, by the arguments he announced would be used in developing his case, and by his frequent outlines recapitulating what points he had stressed. Of special significance, moreover, was his reliance on a legal brief that Schwartz et al. described as "the most complete account in existence of the arguments made in a late eighteenth century case" (introduction, p. 1).

Although our discussion of this case has centered its primary attention on Jefferson, we admit that both lawyers achieved distinction in this case, and both graphically demonstrated "the caliber of the American bar on the eve of the struggle for independence" (introduction, p. 122). This sentiment was shared by Dumbauld when he said:

> The arguments of counsel in *Bolling v. Bolling* constitute a splendid specimen of the professional powers and proficiency of the Virginia bar in the years immediately preceding the American Revolution. Both Thomas Jefferson and his former preceptor George Wythe displayed enormous erudition and handled with skill and resourcefulness the pertinent legal materials relating to the novel, intricate, and difficult questions under consideration. Statutory provisions were scrutinized with thoroughness, the language of judicial decisions and authoritative treatises was analyzed with acute perceptivity. . . . In every respect their performance was worthy of renown, and added lustre to the high esteem in which both men were held by fellow lawyers and their countrymen.[17]

There are no records to show who won this case. But since Jefferson received 9.17 pounds instead of the promised sum of 5 pounds, Schwartz et al. conclude that it is "probable" that "he prevailed." We do know for sure, however, that the "case was still on the General Court's chancery docket in October 1772" (p. 123).

As we place this phase of Jefferson's legal career in perspective, we are confronted with this question: How effective was he as a young practicing lawyer? In one respect, his accomplishments, through no fault of his own, were limited. "Since the General Court docket," for instance, "was years in arrears," some of his cases which started in 1767 "were still awaiting trial when he quit the practice in 1774."[18] On the whole, however, his seven "years as a trial lawyer," observed Frank L. Dewey, were a productive part of his early work experiences:

> They honed his forensic and writing skills. They gave him a wide acquaintance with Virginians from all parts of the colony and among all classes. His encounters with the other members of the elite General Court convinced him that he was at least equal in intellect to any of them, including Edmund Pendleton and George Wythe.[19]

Of importance also was the success he achieved in using moral precepts in his legal arguments. His application of the law of nature in the Howell case to show that "all men are born free," and his defense of the laity as legitimate representatives of the people in *Godwin v. Lunan*, were based on his principles of fairness, justice, and republicanism—traits of virtue that have the potential to produce happiness.

## Legal Advocacy Outside the Courtroom

To complete our analysis of Jefferson as a legal advocate, we now turn to another significant facet of his career as a lawyer in action. That dimension pertains to his important contributions resulting from his application of the principles of law to a select group of professional areas, principally the fields of education, religion, and politics. In each of these disciplines, he used his knowledge of and experience in jurisprudential rhetoric to produce an immediate and long-range effect.

His letters of advice to a large number of law students, his production and dissemination of legal briefs,[20] his role in establishing a chair of law at the College of William and Mary, his published works on Parliamentary Procedure, and his *Reports of Cases Determined in the General Court of Virginia* were typical examples of how he enriched the education of future attorneys. Additionally, his campaign to promote religious independence by upholding the sacred concepts of freedom of thought and worship has become a pivotal dimension of his legacy as a legal scholar.

Similarly, his study and practice of law became effective discourse tools for strengthening his influence as a political leader.[21] In cooperation with his colleague and mentor George Wythe, Jefferson, with considerable aid from James Madison, helped break up the "law of entails" which unfairly fostered and nourished "a vicious aristocracy at the expense of the community"; and he assisted in the repeal of the "law of primogeniture," a "feudal contrivance to create and keep up an artificial inequality among men whom the Creator had made equal. . . ."[22] Altogether Jefferson and Wythe were primarily instrumental in securing passage of 126 bills. Jefferson's particular contribution to this remarkable achievement has been summarized in the introduction to *Thomas Jefferson and Bolling v. Bolling*:

> Almost all of the revisors' bills were drafted by Jefferson and Wythe, with by far the major share of the work being done by Jefferson. Of the 126 bills, 51 have been identified as being Jefferson's handiwork, and 7 as written by Wythe. That leaves 68 bills unaccounted for. Jefferson probably did the major work on them also. At any rate, the bills known to have been drafted by Jefferson include all the major substantive ones recommended by the revisors.[23]

In commenting on these outstanding achievements, William Wirt suggested that the three Virginians produced "a system of jurisprudence so comprehensive, profound, and beautiful, so perfectly, so happily adapted to the new state of things, that, if its authors had never done anything else, impartial history would have assigned them a place by the side of Solon and Lycurgus."[24]

For the purpose of observing more clearly the specific nature of Jefferson's discourse strategies when functioning as a legal advocate outside the courtroom, we have chosen three of his presentations for analysis. One of these efforts occurred before he had completed his legal training; the others took place following his decision in 1774 to discontinue his occupation as an advocate before the Bar. These three rhetorical episodes dealt with the following themes: Christianity and the common law, the Act for Establishing Religious Freedom in Virginia, and the Batture Case. We treat them in chronological order, using the principle of virtue as a major criterion for evaluation.

## Christianity and the Common Law

When Jefferson was a student of law in Williamsburg in 1764, he became fascinated with the subject of the relationship between religion and the history of the common law tradition. As he read *Coke upon Littleton* and other legal works, he copied excerpts on this topic into his commonplace book, along with personal reflections that his readings had stimulated.[25]

These explanatory comments included a brief but important essay, which he entitled, "Whether Christianity is a Part of the Common Law?" Later he incorporated this little treatise in the appendix of his *Reports of Cases Determined in the General Court of Virginia*.[26] Moreover, in 1814, a half-century after he had written the study, he forwarded a copy of it to Dr. Thomas Cooper and discussed its contents in a letter to John Adams.[27]

What troubled Jefferson as he argued against the widely held proposition that Christianity was a fundamental part of common law was the persistent tendency by numerous judges and scholars throughout history to misrepresent the facts relating to the issue. For him this was a moral problem stemming from intellectual dishonesty or indefensible carelessness. In support of this belief, he began his argument by citing the ensuing statement by a prominent chief justice named Prisot: "To such laws of the church as have warrant in ancient writing our law giveth credence; for it is the common law on which all laws are based; and also, Sir, we are obliged to recognize the law of the church, etc."

The foregoing assertion, written by Prisot in Law French, was, according to Jefferson, grossly misconstrued by Sir Heneage Finch in 1613 when his translation made use of this phrase: "To such laws of the church as have warrant in *holy scripture*, our law giveth credence. . . ." This inaccurate substitution of the words "holy scripture" for the terms "ancient writing" or "ancient scripture," became known as "Finch's Law." Jefferson attacked this faulty interpretation of Prisot's claim on the grounds that "the term *antient* scripture must then be understood as meaning the *Old Testament* in contradistinction to the *New*. . . ." Consequently, those who cite this passage "to prove that the scriptures, or *Christianity*, is a part of the common law" have placed themselves in an untenable argumentative position.

From this starting point based on a refutation of Finch's Law, Jefferson next provided a litany of subsequent authorities who, while paying tribute to Prisot, were actually reaffirming the misleading interpretation of Finch. These consisted of inferences drawn by Wingate in 1658 and Sheppard in 1675. So strong had "this doctrine become in 1728" that "in the case of King v. Woolston, the court would not suffer it to be debated." In the late 1760s, Jefferson added, Finch's Law found expression in Blackstone's repetition of the notion that "Christianity is part of the laws of England"; and Lord Mansfield's dictum that "the essential principles of revealed religion are part of the common law."

All of these legal theorists, in Jefferson's view, shared two primary faults in their practical reasoning on this issue: They permitted themselves to be duped by Finch's inadequate translation of Prisot; and they failed to gain a needed understanding of the common law tradition as it pertained to religion. A more serious ethical shortcoming was displayed by a multitude of judges who for decades had rendered decisions in an arbitrary and irresponsible fashion by giving precedence to imprecise and inaccurate interpretations of biblical teachings over that of historical data, legal precedents, legislative actions, and freedom of debate, all of which are essential to the promotion of the public good.[28]

Following his indictment of Finch's Law and its undue influence on later commentators, Jefferson drew upon history and his philosophy of reasoning to demonstrate why Christianity, notwithstanding his devotion to the moral teachings of Jesus, was not a part of common law. To prove this contention, he presented two claims. First, he noted that "the common law" is that system of law introduced by the Saxons "in the middle of the fifth century." By contrast, he maintained, "Christianity was not introduced till the seventh century," thereby creating a period of two centuries "during which the common law was in existence, and Christianity no part of it."

Second, argued Jefferson, that several highly significant writers opted to remain silent on this issue is further "cogent proof" that Christianity was never meant to be a part of common law. Among these authors was Sir Henry Bracton, believed by Jefferson and many of his contemporaries to be a major authority on "the whole body of common law." One of his most influential works was a comprehensive treatise on the nature of common law, supposedly written a short while after the appearance of the Magna Carta in 1215—an event "which divides the common and statute law." Bracton's omission of any reference to the inclusion of Christianity into the corpus of common law was significant because of his status as an eminent judicial theorist and his position as an ecclesiastic. He thus represented to Jefferson a persuasive reluctant witness.[29]

The preceding ideas, written around 1764, were far more than the musings of a fledgling law student who had not yet completed his legal training or qualified to practice before the bar. His rhetorical strategies on this occasion were to become a vital aspect of all of his future performances in legal cases. Historical evidence, judicial precedents, analysis of central issues, refutation of dissenting views, and a unified and coherent organizational pattern were mature trademarks of the essay. The most important rhetorical element, however, was the emphasis on virtue—a virtue epitomizing the need for honesty and thoroughness in scholarship, freedom of discussion on controversial questions, and an avoidance of any form of arbitrariness when reaching a judicial decision. These deeply held sentiments were maintained and nourished for the rest of Jefferson's life as seen in his inclusion of the essay in the *Reports*, his summary of its contents in the 1814 letters to Cooper and Adams, and in the letter to Edward Everett in 1824.[30] Moreover, his thinking on this subject in his formative years helped prepare him to deal with the issue of religious freedom in his native state.[31]

## Act for Establishing Religious Freedom in Virginia, 1786

The second rhetorical episode illustrating the nature and effectiveness of Jefferson's use of forensic discourse in a non-courtroom setting also falls under the category of religion. As he reviewed the history of religious policies and traditional restraints that marked Virginia customs, he was deeply alarmed with the degree of oppression that seemed to be dominant. For more than a century following the settlement of Jamestown, he wrote in his *Notes on Virginia*, the Anglican Church had exerted control over the parishioners, and, worst of all, had become inextricably a political arm of the state.[32] From this position of influence, it consistently discriminated against other religious groups, especially the Quakers. Similarly, it sought and received tax support for the purpose of maintaining and extending its privileged status, and adopted rules for punishment of disobedient congregants who failed to provide adequate financial help or who were charged with some form of heresy.

At the time of the American Revolution, Jefferson could also sense that while political and social ties with British traditions were almost universally being broken, one yet remained. A number of governmental leaders, adhering to the wishes of Governor Patrick Henry, gave impetus to the movement to maintain a close and direct relationship between the Anglican Church (renamed the Episcopal Church) and the Commonwealth of Virginia. In particular, they strongly urged that tax relief be continued, an action that would bind the church and the state. It was in response to these developments that Jefferson launched a campaign to establish an act for religious freedom. This culminated in the production of a draft statute that was presented to the legislature in 1779.

For the next several years, Jefferson's bill periodically was discussed by the legislators, but in each instance following debate, action was delayed. When no final decision had been made by the time of his departure to France in 1784, he asked Madison, then a member of the House of Delegates, to be in charge of its eventual passage. This was an assignment that

Madison happily undertook because of his own conviction that the moment for an act affirming the right of religious freedom had arrived.[33] Early in the winter of 1786, Jefferson's document, after being modified by several amendments, was adopted.[34] The act consists of two major parts—a value-centered preamble containing many of the principles of Jefferson's philosophy of virtue, and a statement of specific statutory commands.

The preamble sets forth the moral and intellectual elements that Jefferson believed to be essential for religious freedom. It begins with the affirmation that "Almighty God," the "holy author of our religion," has chosen to create "the mind free." This strongly suggests that any attempts to influence or coerce one's mind by "temporal punishments or civil incapacitations" is not only a "departure" from God's "plan" but would "beget habits of hypocrisy and meanness." Thus it is necessary to guard ourselves against the danger that legislators or ecclesiastical leaders, when convinced that their beliefs are infallible, might strive to impose their religious convictions "on others." Such destructive actions, he added, have led to the establishment and maintenance of "false religions over the greatest part of the world and through all time."

Because such a coercive practice, he continued, constitutes a "sinful and tyrannical" strategy that ignores the concepts of freedom of thought and religion, the state of Virginia has a duty to stand upon these eternal principles:

(1) A person should not be compelled "to furnish contributions of money for the propagation of opinions which he disbelieves. . . ."

(2) He should have "the comfortable liberty of giving his contributions to the particular pastor whose morals he would make his pattern, and whose powers he feels most persuasive to righteousness. . . ."

(3) As in the case of our "opinions in physics or geometry," our religious convictions should in no way affect our "civil rights," including the opportunity of holding "offices of trust and emolument. . . ."

These just principles, Jefferson asserted, are based on the notion of "natural right," which protects a person's God-given privilege of having a mind that is free and cherishes liberty. Moreover, these principles derive their persuasive ethical thrust from the nature and power of "truth," which "is great and will prevail if left to herself." For truth "is the proper and sufficient antagonist to error, and has nothing to fear from the conflict unless by human interposition disarmed of her natural weapons, free argument and debate; errors ceasing to be dangerous when it is permitted freely to contradict them."

Once he had concluded the preamble providing the moral philosophical foundation upon which the act for religious freedom would rest, Jefferson next moved to the specific provisions of statutory command that would complete the legislation's work. All persons, it stated, must be free to worship wherever they please, and to defend openly, with arguments they deem appropriate, "their opinions in matters of religion" without fear of losing their civil rights. The final statement, after noting that actions taken by the current assembly could not from a legal standpoint be binding on future assemblies, declared "that the rights hereby asserted are of the natural rights of mankind, and that if any act shall be hereafter passed to repeal the present or narrow its operation, such an act will be an infringement of natural right."

As the author of this historically significant act, Jefferson did not succeed in having all of the wording in the initial draft remain in the final document approved by the House of Delegates and the Senate. This was particularly evident in his original first sentence which said: "Well aware that the opinions and belief of men depend not on their own will, but follow involuntarily the evidence proposed to their minds; that Almighty God hath created the mind free, and manifested his supreme will that free it shall remain by making it altogether insusceptible of restraint. . . ."[35] By process of a Senate amendment, all of the preceding words were deleted but these: "(Whereas) Almighty God hath created the mind free." Legislators deleted the language in question because they were not prepared to write into law Jefferson's Lockean conception of how the human mind works. But although one very important passage representing fundamental Jeffersonian philosophy was excised, the legislature kept his ringing affirmation that Almighty God created the mind free.

Two other deletions in Jefferson's submitted draft also are worthy of note. They contain the words, "but to extend it (God's will) by its influence on reason alone"; and, "that the opinions of men are not the object of civil government, nor under its jurisdiction." The legislature made these substantive cuts for two reasons. The first cut was yet again a victim of the legislature's reluctance to endorse Jefferson's Lockean vision. The second cut was a bow to the idea that in some cases (e.g., libel, slander, and sedition) the legislature wanted to preserve its authority over the opinions of men. Any other amendment calling for deletion, such as the

elimination of the words "and abhors," were minor changes having no effect on the nature and persuasive force of the message.[36]

Few rhetorical efforts undertaken by Jefferson in his public and private
career placed a greater emphasis on his philosophy of virtue and the role
that discourse may play in its dissemination than this statute for religious
freedom. First, it was a message ordained by God for members of a community to exercise their free will in choosing their own religion, church,
pastor, and means of financial support. Second, it was a declaration endorsing the principle that since one's religious preference is a "natural
right" which must be preserved at all times, it should never be a factor
concerning one's election or appointment to an office; nor a condition affecting any aspect of citizenship.

When Jefferson turned to the subject of truth and its implications for
one's personal life and for society at large, he lifted his appeal to a still
higher level. He did so with an eloquent plea calling for complete moral
and intellectual emancipation from all unfair and unjust restraints designed to control one's mind. What makes truth so strong and positive,
he argued, is that its achievement is primarily the result of "free argument
and debate," which assesses the merits of opposing ideas as a means of determining and eliminating errors in thought and practice.

The foregoing claims, embracing approximately 730 words expressed in
a clear and moving style, were filled with Jefferson's symbols of virtue.
They stressed the value and power of personal and public good by paying
tribute to reason and to the importance of argumentation and debate as
a truth-finding enterprise. In a similar manner, they emphasized the need
for models of righteousness to serve as examples for the people to emulate, and the desirability of dissociating one's religious convictions from
the requirements listed for public office or other community rewards.

Both Jefferson and Madison recognized the importance of the passage
of the freedom of religion bill. With the passage of this act, observed
Thomas E. Buckley, "the decade-long struggle to redefine the relationship
between the government and religion in the commonwealth had reached
a new level of development." He then noted: "For Madison the enact-
ment of the bill was a complete political triumph, marred only slightly by
the amendments to the preamble."[37] Upon hearing that his revised document had been adopted, Jefferson, from his Paris residence, brushed
aside the legislature's deletions of a few of his most pointed references to
the supremacy of reason,[38] and took pride in his authorship of the Virginia Statute for Religious Freedom. The finished product, he concluded,

was a legitimate extension of the Declaration of Independence. Consequently, he came to view it as being on the same exalted level.[39] With this favorable reaction firmly entrenched in his thinking, he launched a campaign to have the document dispersed throughout Europe as a rhetorical specimen showing the advancement of freedom of thought and religion in Virginia.

His first step in arranging for its distribution was to have a four-page pamphlet of the text printed in Paris in 1786.[40] He then sent copies "to some foreign courts," to the *Encyclopedia*, and to a group of scholars whose writings had impressed him. In forwarding a copy of the pamphlet to the Count de Mirabeau, he expressed the hope that the esteemed French author and politician would "be able on some occasion to avail mankind of this example of emancipating human reason."[41]

Jefferson's campaign to disseminate the act proved to be effective. In August, he wrote to George Wythe: "The Ambassadors and ministers of the several nations of Europe resident at this Court have asked of me copies of it to send to their sovereigns, and it is inserted at full length in several books now in the press; among others in the new Encyclopedia." He then noted: "I think it will produce considerable good even in these countries where ignorance, superstition, poverty and oppression of body and mind in every form, are so firmly settled on the mass of the people, that their redemption from them can never be hoped."[42] As the year of 1786 drew to a close, he told Madison that the act had "been received with infinite approbation in Europe & propagated with enthusiasm." Because of widespread public interest, for example, the work "has been translated into French & Italian, has been sent to most of the courts of Europe, & has been the best evidence of the falsehood of those reports which stated us to be in anarchy."[43]

The following year he inserted a copy of the act in the appendix of the authoritative Stockdale edition of his *Notes on the State of Virginia*.[44] Nor did the satisfaction he experienced from reflecting on his role as the author of this seminal work diminish in later years. It seemed inevitable, therefore, that in 1826 he would have this achievement, along with that of his creation of the Declaration of Independence and the University of Virginia, inscribed as the epitaph on his tombstone.

## The Batture Case

The most famous example of how Jefferson applied his knowledge of law in a contentious forensic situation after he had discontinued his legal

practice was the Batture case. On October 30, 1803, after a series of negotiations carried out by American diplomats Robert R. Livingston and
James Monroe, France ceded the Louisiana Territory to the United
States. Almost immediately, a large number of settlers migrated to the
area, many of whom moved to the rapidly developing community of New
Orleans because of its location on the Mississippi. One of these immigrants was Edward Livingston, a citizen of New York who saw an opportunity to become a wealthy landowner and business leader in a city with
a promising future. Soon after his arrival, he purchased land overlooking
the river. In doing so, he was firmly convinced that the batture adjoining
his lots (the soil, stone, or other material that builds under water and may
or may not break the surface) had now become his personal property.

As part of his ambitious plan to develop the batture, he hired a group
of laborers in the summer of 1807 to begin work on constructing a canal,
and on making other changes to control the direction of the water flow.
This action triggered an alarm among the residents of New Orleans, who
for several years had used the river surrounding the batture for transport-
ing their goods, and the beach for docking their boats in season, and for
recreational activities. Consequently, on several occasions they came en
masse to the spot where the canal was to be created and attempted to
force Livingston's men to discontinue their efforts.[45] But Livingston persisted in ignoring their wishes, arguing that he was the legitimate owner
of the water and land where the canal was being dug; therefore, those
who intervened with his freedom of action were guilty of trespass.

Jefferson, then in the middle of his second presidential term, sent a federal marshal to the batture to protect what he perceived to be public
property. This was a perception shared by the U.S. attorney general, the
governor of the Louisiana Territory, and the leaders of New Orleans.[46]
Livingston, as might be anticipated, held an opposing view. His first step
in voicing his protest was to inform Secretary of State Madison that he
would "bring the authority of the court into array against that of the executive, and endeavor to obtain a forcible possession."[47] He next stated
his protest by expressing resentment at the use of unwarranted force by
the federal government.[48] Later, after Jefferson's tenure as president had
ended, Livingston initiated legal action against him, seeking "damages of
100,000 Dollars."[49] The writ was filed in 1810 in the Circuit Court of the
United States for the district of Virginia, located in Richmond, and soon
was highly publicized throughout the country.

From his home in Monticello, where he had retired to live out his life
in serenity, Jefferson was deeply disturbed to learn that a private citizen

would sue a former president who, while in office, had taken action based on his duty to uphold the rights of the people. From a more practical perspective, he was persuaded that if he were to lose the case his financial resources would be seriously depleted.[50] As a result, he hired a law firm including William Wirt as head and George Hay and Littleton W. Tazewell as partners.[51] The lawyers, in turn, asked Jefferson to prepare a legal brief that the counsel could use in his defense.

Not trusting his memory regarding all the essential facts of the case, Jefferson wrote to his associates and other informed persons who were involved in the proceedings, asking them to check their files for any relevant documents or other forms of evidence they might have in their offices that he could incorporate into his brief. Among those he contacted were President Madison, who had been secretary of state when the disputed actions occurred; Albert Gallatin, secretary of the treasury; Dr. William Eustis, secretary of war; and Caesar A. Rodney, the attorney general.[52] These men, along with the secretary of navy and other members of the Jefferson administration, not only had extensive data on the case, but had concurred with Jefferson's decision to treat the batture as public property.[53]

As these factual sources were being assembled, George Hay wrote to Jefferson on December 5, 1811, informing him that "the case had been thrown out of court for want of jurisdiction."[54] The ruling stated that a United States Circuit Court in Virginia did not have jurisdiction involving an issue that took place in Louisiana. On the surface, it appeared that the case had been permanently settled. From a strictly legal point of view, such an interpretation might be feasible. But Jefferson knew that if the lawsuit were decided in that way, without a defense by him, Livingston and the American people might falsely infer that he had "wished to get rid of the case in this way. . . ."[55] Consequently, he determined on an immediate strategy to counter possible negative publicity resulting from the court's decision: he had his own well-developed brief published and disseminated to members of Congress and to the general public.

His first action was to contact Ezra Sargeant, editor of the New York Division of his favorite journal—the *Edinburgh Review*. He began his letter, written on February 3, 1812, with a summary of the issues of and actions in the case, and then noted: "The correctness with which your edition of the Edinburgh Review is printed, and of the passages quoted in those languages [French, Spanish, Latin, and Greek], induces me to propose to you the publication of the case I speak of." He then suggested that if his request was agreeable to the editor he would like 250 copies for himself that could be distributed primarily to members of Congress, and added that "the printer would be at liberty to print as many more as he pleased for sale, but without any copyright, which I should not propose to have taken out."[56] One week later, Sargeant responded, agreeing to the publication in accordance with Jefferson's terms. The total cost for the 250 copies, he said, would be $130.[57]

A short while later, Jefferson forwarded a copy of the brief, often referred to as a pamphlet or proceeding, to Sargeant, with the hope that its readers would recognize that his actions in the Batture case were morally, politically, and legally justified.[58] The materials included in this personal defense represent, along with *Bolling v. Bolling*, one of the two most thoroughly developed forensic briefs ever undertaken by Jefferson. The finished document, which includes a two-page preface and ninety-seven pages of informational and argumentative materials, was printed in 1812.

Jefferson's greatest challenge in presenting his case was to find an appropriate method for organizing his considerable body of data in such a clear and convincing manner that the public could understand fully the ramifications of the subject and the nature of the arguments. To achieve this end, he used a modified version of the structural pattern recommended by Hugh Blair in his *Lectures on Rhetoric and Belles Lettres*. Blair's plan of arrangement, which Jefferson often urged prospective lawyers to use when channeling their message,[59] consisted of an introduction and division, a narration and explication, an argumentative section, and a pathetic part and peroration.[60] Blair considered each of these parts as discrete units, totaling seven steps. The peculiar nature of this rhetorical situation, Jefferson thought, caused him to reduce and combine the steps: (1) The introduction and division constituted his first unit. (2) This was followed by his second unit, consisting of a blending of narration, explication, and argument. (3) His concluding section combined the pathetic part with a peroration.

The two-page preface, or introduction, was written on February 25, 1812—approximately eighteen months after the manuscript itself had been completed.[61] Because of this significant variation in time, Jefferson had ample opportunity to think about the case and the rhetorical strategies he had used. The first concern he addressed related to the court's decision to cancel the suit on jurisdictional grounds. "My wish," he said in his opening words, "had rather been for a full investigation of the merits at the bar, that the public might learn, in that way, that their servants had done nothing but what the laws had authorised and required them to do."

He next apologized for the complexity of the brief, and explained why the organizational pattern he had opted to use was necessary in this instance:

> The question arising, being many and independent of each other, admitted not a methodical and luminous arrangement. Proceeding, therefore, in a course of narrative, I have met and discussed the points of law in the order in which events presented them; thus securing, as we go along, the ground we pass over, and leaving nothing adversary or doubtful behind. Hence the mixture of fact and law which will be observed through the whole.[62]

In the conclusion of the preface, Jefferson noted that "vouchers for the facts are regularly referred to." These would consist of the following points: "1. Affidavits taken and published on the part of the plaintiff, and of the city of New-Orleans, very deeply interested in the question. 2. Printed statements, by the counsel on each side, uncontradicted by the other, of facts under their joint observation and knowledge. 3. Records. 4. Notarial acts, and 5. Letters and reports of public functionaries filed in the office of the department of state." The use of this type of factual data was consistent with Jefferson's philosophy of argument.

Following the completion of this introductory statement, Jefferson turned to the most comprehensive section of the legal brief—the narration and explication of the documented data and the legal arguments derived from these sources. Here he detailed the historical background of Louisiana as it evolved in the eighteenth and early nineteenth centuries; the initial purchase of lots overlooking the Mississippi River in the batture region; and the long-standing public use of the river and the adjoining beach. In producing this narrative, he explained how the Roman, French, and Spanish laws that contributed to the establishment of rules regarding the ownership of the batture were still operative at the present time.

Jefferson, as he had observed, mixed argumentative claims with points in the narrative. The primary arguments he developed were these: (1) By tradition and the law, the batture was public, not private, property. (2) Because Livingston's purchase of the lots did not and could not give him the right to modify the water current in the batture, he committed an illegal and unjust act in trying to build a canal. (3) Moreover, his act of intrusion, if permitted to stand, would be detrimental to the people and to the city of New Orleans, as well as to the federal government. (4) The removal of the intrusion by the federal marshal and his posse was both necessary and justified.

Jefferson used testimony, historical documents, legal precedents, and causal reasoning, combined with appeals to experience, common sense, and the social affections, to substantiate his four claims. The following argument demonstrating the potentially harmful result of Livingston's aggression is an excellent specimen of Jefferson's cause-to-effect reasoning:

> The planned action by Livingston would take from the city and the nation what is their port in high water, and at low tide their Quai; to leave them not a spot where the upper craft can land or lie in safety; to turn the current of the river on the lower suburbs and plantations; to embank the whole of this extensive beach; to take off a fourth from the breadth of the river, and add equivalently to the rise of it's waters; to demolish thus the whole leveè, and sweep away the town and country in undistinguished ruin.

Upon completing this dire prediction, Jefferson observed that his judgment concerning the question of harm was not "a matter of theory alone, but of experience. . . ."

As he concluded the narrative-argumentative phase of his cause, Jefferson summarized each of the main claims and subordinate points he had developed, for the purpose of letting his counsel and the American people know what the facts of the case were and what had been established through reasoning and evidence. Now he was set to close his remarks with a moving and memorable plea to the imagination and the passions. He began by saying that if an executive, in fulfilling his duty as a leader of the nation, were to be sued for monetary damages whenever he rendered a decision or took action that was not fully approved, it would mean that only paupers could hold positions of responsibility, for they would have nothing to lose. Let it be remembered therefore, he said, that "the spirit of our law" endorses the principle that "He who does [his] duty honestly, and according to his best skill and judgment, stands acquitted before God and man." With this principle of personal virtue clearly affirmed, he declared that even if the plaintiff believed errors may have been committed by the government in its actions in Louisiana, he could not possibly have classified these supposed mistakes as being "corruption and malice." In a series of rhetorical questions energized by graphic language, he asserted:

> What? was it my malice or corruption which prompted the Governors and Cabildoes to keep these grounds clear of intrusion? Did my malice and corruption excite the people to rise, and stay the parricide hand uplifted to destroy their city, or the grand jury to present this violator of their laws? Was it my malice and corruption which penned the opinion of the Attorney General, and drew from him a confirmation, after two years of further consideration, and when I was retired from all public office? Was it my malice

or corruption which dictated the unanimous advice of the heads of departments, when officially called on for consultation and advice? Was it my malice and corruption which procured the immediate thanks of the two houses of legislature of the territory of Orleans, and a renewal of the same thanks for the same interference, in their late vote of February last? Has it been my malice and corruption which has induced the national legislature, through five successive sessions, to be deaf to the doleful Jeremiads of the plaintiff on his removal *from his estate* at New Orleans? Have all these opinions then been honest, and mine alone malicious and corrupt? Or has there been a general combination of all the public functionaries Spanish, French, and American, to oppress Mr. Livingston? No. They have done their duties, and his Declaration is a libel on all these functionaries.

This paragraph, filled with appeals to the imagination and the passions and containing a repetition of phrases and a recapitulation of factual data stated in the interrogative form, was followed by this concluding paragraph emphasizing the nature of reason and the appeal of the social affections:

It is not for me to enquire into the motives of the plaintiff in this action. I know that his understanding is of an order much too high to let him believe that he is to recover the value of the batture from me. To what indirect object he may squint with one eye, while the other looks at me, I do not pretend to say. But I do say, that if human reason is not mere illusion, and law a labyrinth without a clue, no error has been committed; and recurring to the tenor of a long life of public service, against the charges of malice and corruption I stand conscious and erect.

The two closing passages cited here are, both in content and language, among the most impressive examples of Jefferson's rhetoric of virtue in his extant works. In demonstrating in the first cited paragraph that his actions taken on the batture were strongly supported by the Governors and Cabildoes, the grand jury, the attorney general, the department heads of his administration, the two houses of the Orleans territorial legislature, and the United States Congress, he provided cumulative evidence that appealed to the understanding and stimulated the imagination and the passions. In sustaining his ideas on virtue, moreover, he also successfully integrated reason with the social affections (duty, love of country, faith in the people) and private good with public good. In the second passage, he paid tribute to the power and relevance of human reason and to the utility of the principles of law; and argued that an examination of his "long life of public service" would prove that he could never countenance any form of "malice and corruption." When he ended with the words that he stood "conscious and erect," Jefferson felt confident that he had upheld his principles of virtue by promoting the happiness of the people.

The Batture case was a significant and defining instance of the nature of Jefferson's role as a legal advocate. The decisive action he took in removing the intrusion and the discourse of virtue he used to defend it were the products of a moral and rhetorical philosophy that gave priority to the rights and the welfare of the people. His value-laden message, it seems clear, emanated from his belief that, because Livingston's intrusion was a dangerous act spawned by self-interest, it must be countered by another act deriving its strength from the spirit of duty and benevolence in the service of the public good. At the heart of Jefferson's plea was his attempt to prove that true virtue can exist only when one's private good works were in harmony with the public good. But this, he argued, was not the case with Livingston; for in placing his private wants in direct opposition to the community's welfare, he was motivated by self-interest, which Jefferson, along with Shaftesbury and Hutcheson, viewed as an enemy of virtue. By contrast, Jefferson sought to illustrate both in his deeds and in his words that he was a servant of the public will.

The thought process that led Jefferson to the foregoing conclusions produced in him a feeling of contentment blended with a sense of pride. These sentiments were strengthened as he received numerous accolades describing the persuasive qualities of the legal brief. William Wirt, head of his defense team, wrote:

> It is by far the best piece of grecian architecture that I have ever seen, either from ancient or modern times. I did not think it possible that such a subject could be so deeply and at the same time so airily treated—because I never had seen such an union of lightness and solidity, of beauty and power, in any investigation.[63]

Even more noteworthy was the response from John Adams. When Jefferson received in the mail from Adams a copy of his son's (John Quincy's) *Lectures on Rhetoric and Oratory*,[64] he wrote a letter praising the work and, in return, enclosed a copy of his brief on the Batture. "You may have enough left of your old taste for law reading," he said, "to cast an eye over some of the questions it discusses."[65] In his reply, Adams gave a glowing assessment of the arguments Jefferson had advanced. "You have," he noted, "brought up to the View of the Young Generation of Lawyers in our Country Tracts and Regions of Legal Information of which they never had dreamed: but which will become, every day more and more necessary for our Courts of Justice to investigate." He then added these words of frustration that echoed Jefferson's convictions: "Good God! Is a President of the United States to be subject to a private Action of every Individual?"[66] Adams's suggestion that the brief on the Batture case was a splendid model of discourse that could be studied with profit by the current generation of law students was a comforting thought to Jefferson, who, as observed earlier, long had aspired to be an effective representative spokesman of Enlightenment principles to his contemporaries.

The one negative criticism about the brief that was sent to Jefferson came from one of the members of his defense team who faulted the organizational structure. "I wish that in preparing this work for the press," noted Tazewell, "you had given a different arrangement to its parts. The chronological order of events which you have pursued," he added, "altho' generally the best where facts alone are the subjects to be discussed, yet by dividing often times weakens the effect of the general argument." But even in making this criticism, Tazewell praised the overall excellence of the manuscript.[67]

Jefferson's success in publishing the *Proceedings* has withstood the test of time. In his volume *Thomas Jefferson and the Law*, Edward Dumbauld praised Jefferson for developing "a prima facie case authorizing the removal of Livingston," and for arousing "extensive interest" in the case. Then, in evaluating the importance of this discourse event, he stated: "Just as the nation had profited from the earlier contest between Jefferson and Hamilton, receiving the benefits of each antagonist's contribution to the struggle, so did the people of New Orleans, standing at the gateway to a 'vast empire for liberty,' derive advantage from the vigorous controversy between Jefferson and Livingston."[68]

Less praiseworthy of the brief was Douglas L. Wilson in his essay "Jefferson and the Republic of Letters." In the last portion of this informative and provocative study, which deals with the Batture controversy, the author expresses strong reservations about some of the aspects of Jefferson's approach on this occasion because of his tendency to use "self-serving" and "self-justifying" arguments revealing him to be excessively emotional, defensive, and "thin-skinned." As a result, in his effort to go to the extreme to "exculpate himself," Jefferson gave the impression that he was "as much concerned for his image as for his record." Notwithstanding these critical comments, Wilson commended Jefferson's "dry wit and keen sense of irony," his use of descriptive and compelling passages that could not help but "gain the attention of his readers," and his effective allusion "to one of Shakespeare's most hilarious scenes to point up an inconsistency."[69]

Jefferson's legal advocacy, as we have seen, was a persuasive discourse enterprise that began in the 1760s and extended through his retirement years. His thorough and meticulous preparation, his skill in selecting and marshalling arguments, his talent for constructing briefs that could be used as models, and his determination to make principles of virtue his primary rhetorical concern contributed vitally to his success as a scholar and practitioner in the field of jurisprudence.

In his seven years at the Bar in the General Court of Virginia, Jefferson became a popular and productive lawyer whose legal services were sought and admired. Far more important, however, he then applied this training and experience throughout his political career to the task of promoting such universal moral concepts as freedom of the mind, liberty to make choices in the area of religion, and the right of all citizens to have a fair trial regardless of the charges brought against them. Whereas law, he once said, may often be required to deal with the dark side of human nature, it has within its power the saving merit of producing justice.

# Notes

1. "Autobiography," in Ford, 1: 6.

2. Among those who held this view was Dumas Malone, who said: "From the beginning [TJ] was probably more interested in the study of law than in practice." *Jefferson the Virginian*, 113.

3. Randall, *The Life of Thomas Jefferson*, 1: 47.

4. Morris, "Jefferson as a Lawyer," *Proceedings of the American Philosophical Society*, 87 (July 1943): 213.

5. Case Book and Fee Books (Huntington Library). Photocopies in the University of Virginia Library.

6. Ibid.

7. *The Life of Thomas Jefferson*, 1: 48.

8. Ibid., 1: 49.

9. Ibid., 1: 48.

10. Wirt, "Eulogy on Jefferson," in L&B, 13: xiii.

11. Madison observed that he had heard Jefferson "address a court, and that he did it fluently and well." Cited in Randall, *Life of Thomas Jefferson*, 1: 50. Edmund Randolph noted that when speaking before the general court, TJ "drew copiously from the depths of the law" and "spoke with ease, perspicuity, and elegance." "Introduction to that Part of the History, Embracing the Revolution," *Virginia Magazine of History and Biography*, 43 (1935): 123.

12. This work by Jefferson was published in Charlottesville by F. Carr in 1829—three years after his death. It covers the periods from 1730 to 1740 and from 1768 to 1772.

13. Edward Dumbauld, *Thomas Jefferson and the Law* (Norman: University of Oklahoma Press, 1978): 83–84.

14. *Reports of Cases in the General Court of Virginia*, 108. Also see Ford, 2: 16n.

15. Bernard Schwartz, Wilcie Kern, and R. B. Bernstein, eds., *Thomas Jefferson and Bolling v. Bolling: Law and the Legal Profession in Pre-revolutionary America* (San Marino, Calif., and New York: Henry E. Huntington Library and the New York University School of Law, 1997).

16. Dumbauld, *Thomas Jefferson and the Law*, 102.

17. Ibid., 119–20.

18. Frank L. Dewey, *Thomas Jefferson, Lawyer* (Charlottesville: University Press of Virginia, 1986), 7.

19. Ibid., 113.

20. See in particular the arguments he prepared on behalf of John Lyne, January 13, 1782, in Boyd, 6: 145–46; in the case of Mace Freeland, February 15, 1782, in ibid., 6: 151–58; and in the Case Concerning Insubordination of Esek Hopkins, August 12, 1783, in ibid., 15: 578–82.

21. Morris has asserted that his greatest contribution to American law were his "law reforms which, though confined to Virginia, have set the pattern of early law reform throughout the United States." "Jefferson as a Lawyer," 215.

22. Wirt, "Eulogy on Jefferson," L&B, 13: xxix. Ford gives this description of the Bill to Abolish Entails: "On October 12, 1776, leave was granted to introduce this bill, and Jefferson, Starke, and Bullitt were named a committee to draft it. Jefferson reported this draft October 14th. It was considered and amended in the Committee of the Whole on October 17th and 18th, was passed by the lower house on October 23d, and concurred in by the Senate, November 1st. It was the first great blow at the aristocratic or landed class of Virginia. . . ." See Ford (1893 edition), 2: 103n–104n; and Boyd, 1: 560–62.

23. Schwartz, et al., *Thomas Jefferson and Bolling v. Bolling*, 70.

24. Wirt, "Eulogy on Jefferson," in L&B, 13: xxx.

25. TJ to Dr. Thomas Cooper, February 10, 1814, in L&B, 14: 85.

26. This essay appears at ibid., 14: 137–42.

27. TJ to John Adams, January 24, 1814, in Cappon, 2: 423. For the letter to Cooper, see footnote 24 above.

28. Jefferson makes the indictment in the preface of the *Reports*, vi.

29. Throughout his career, Jefferson viewed Bracton as an eminent authority on common law, often recommending that his writings be studied by students of law.

30. October 15, 1824, in L&B, 16: 80–84.

31. Even though both John Quincy Adams and Justice Joseph Story challenged Jefferson's position in this essay, Edward Dumbauld said: "Yet the distinction upon which Jefferson was insisting between ecclesiastical law and common law, the distinction between church government and civil government is very clear and important. Its neglect leads only to confusion of thought." *Thomas Jefferson and the Law*, 79.

32. Jefferson, *Notes on the State of Virginia*, 157–58. In some "Random Notes on Religion," written in October 1776, Jefferson asserted that "The bishops" of the Anglican Church "were always mere tools of the Crown." Ford (1904 edition), 2: 260.

33. William M. Hutchison, William M. E. Rachal, Robert Allen Rutland, and J. C. A. Stagg, eds., *The Papers of James Madison*, Series I, 17 vols. (Chicago: University of Chicago Press, 1962–1975; Charlottesville: University Press of Virginia, 1977–), 8: 195.

34. Boyd, 2: 547n–553n, provides a thorough treatment of the nature of the amendments in the debate.

35. In Boyd's reprint of the act, the final version, along with italicized statements of Jefferson's original draft that contained deleted phrases and clauses, are included. Boyd, 2: 545–47. The deleted terminology stated here is consistent with the following observations Jefferson wrote in his 1776 "Notes on Religion": "No man has *power* to let another prescribe his faith. Faith is not faith with believing. No man can conform his faith to the dictates of another. The life & essence of religion consists in the internal persuasion of belief of the mind. External forms of worship, when against our belief are hypocrisy & impiety." Ford, 2: 265. By the same token, he added, "no man is by nature bound to any church." Ibid.

36. Boyd, 2: 547n–553n. What would have made a difference in the intent, according to Jefferson, was an amendment to prefix the name of "Jesus Christ" to the words "the author of our religion." TJ to George Ticknor, May 1817, in Ford, 12: 60. This possible addition was not acceptable to him because it would have excluded any non-Christian religion such as that of the Muslims and Hindus, from the protection of religious freedom.

37. *Church and State in Revolutionary Virginia, 1776–1787* (Charlottesville: University Press of Virginia, 1977), 163–64.

38. Malone, *Jefferson the Virginian*, 279.

39. Boyd, 2: 547n. Wirt gives this assessment of Jefferson's rhetoric of virtue on this occasion: "The preamble to the bill establishing religious freedom in Virginia, is one of the most morally sublime of human productions. By its great author it was always esteemed as one of his happiest efforts, and the measure itself one of his best services, as the short and modest epitaph left by him attests." "Eulogy," in L&B, 13: xxx.

40. William Peden, ed., *Notes on the State of Virginia*, 297n. The contents of the pamphlet appear in Peden's edition which we have repeatedly used when referring to the *Notes*.

41. August 20, 1786, in Ford, 5: 167–68. In an earlier letter to Marquis de St. Lambert, written on August 8, Jefferson thanked him for providing a translation of the act of the Virginia Assembly. Ibid., 5: 144–45.

42. August 13, 1786, in Boyd, 10: 244.

43. December 16, 1786, in Boyd, 10: 603–604.

44. *Notes*, 223–25. There are numerous versions of the act, including the one in the *Notes* which was approved by TJ. The versions we have examined, in addition to the one in the *Notes*, are as follows: Boyd, 2: 545–47; and William Waller Hening, ed., *The Statutes at Large; Being a Collection of the Laws of Virginia* (Richmond: George Cochran, 1823), 12: 84–86.

45. Jefferson's description of this event appears in his brief.

46. The Batture brief was printed under the following title: *The Proceedings of the Government of the United States, in maintaining the Public Right to the beach of the Mississippi Adjacent to New Orleans, Against the Intrusion of Edward Livingston.* Prepared for the use of Counsel by Thomas Jefferson. New York: Published by Ezra Sargeant (Printed by D. & G. Bruce, 1812). The manuscript we are using is from H. A. Washington, *The Writings of Thomas Jefferson*, 9 vols. (Washington, D.C.: Taylor & Maury, 1853), 8: 504–604. All references to the content and style of the brief are taken from this source. It is also important to observe that TJ himself supplied the translation of French, Spanish, Latin, and Greek documents. In most instances, he would list the foreign language paragraphs on one column and the English translations opposite on another.

47. TJ to Governor (of the Louisiana Territory) W. C. C. Claiborne, July 17, 1808, in L&B, 12: 98.

48. In his brief, TJ noted that the plaintiff wrote "a letter of lamentation to some member of the government, on the 27th of June, 1809."

49. This statement was made in a letter to Madison written on May 25, 1810. Ford, 11: 140. In the same letter, he expressed concern that Livingston in making his suit was perhaps motivated in part by his feeling that if an appeal were made, Chief Justice John Marshall probably would rule in his favor. On this troubling point, he asserted: "His (Marshall's) twistifications in the case of Marbury, in that of Burr, & the late Yazoo case show how dexterously he can reconcile law to his personal biases: and nobody seems to doubt that he is ready prepared to decide that Livingston's right to the Batture is unquestionable, and that I am bound to Day for it with my private fortune." Id., 11: 141.

50. In a letter to Albert Gallatin, written on September 27, 1810, TJ noted that he thought an appeal eventually would be needed "as my only chance of saving my fortune from entire wreck." But he proceeded to ask: "And to whom is my appeal? From the judge in Burr's case to himself and to the associate judges in the case of Marbury v. Madison." Ford, 11: 153. These letters to Madison and Gallatin reveal TJ's longstanding resentment toward Marshall whose decisions in *Marbury v. Madison* and in the Burr case he believed to be violations of the rule of justice. Quite clearly, he had difficulty in living up to his philosophy of social affections whenever his thoughts turned to Marshall.

51. On May 25, 1810, he wrote to Madison saying he had "engaged Wirt, Hay, and Wickam as counsel." Later he added Tazewell to his defense team. Ford, 11: 140.

52. The following request to Dr. Eustis was typical: "You will be so kind as to have selected such of those (papers) deposited in your office as may offer either useful information, or evidence on the subject, on my assurance that they will be faithfully and promptly returned. . . ." TJ to Eustis, May 30, 1810, L&B, 19: 174.

53. TJ often said, as the following remarks to Madison state, that he had the support of his associates regarding his actions on the Batture: "I believe that what I did was in harmony with the opinion of all the members of the administration, verbally expressed altho' not in writing." TJ to Madison, May 25, 1810, in Ford, 11: 141.

54. Reference to letter from George Hay to TJ, December 5, 1811, in Sowerby, *Catalogue of the Library of Thomas Jefferson*, 3: 404.

55. TJ to Hugh Nelson, December 28, 1811, in ibid. He repeated the same idea in numerous letters and in the preface of his brief.

56. TJ to Sargeant, February 3, 1812, in L&B, 13: 132–33.

57. Sargeant to TJ, February 10, 1812, in Sowerby, *Catalogue of the Library of Thomas Jefferson*, 3: 405.

58. On April 20, 1812, TJ wrote to Claiborne expressing the following justification: "My wish was that it [the case] should have been tried on it's merits, that the public might have seen thro' that medium that the transaction complained of was one of duty as well as of right." Sowerby, *Catalogue of the Library of Thomas Jefferson*, 3: 410.

59. As a typical example of this advice to law students, see TJ's 1814 letter to John Minor, in Ford (1898 edition), 9: 485n. As we begin our analysis of this brief, it is worth remembering that Jefferson also may be writing a defense pamphlet—a political genre in the early republic discussed by Joanne B. Freeman, "Slander, Poison, Whispers, an Fame: Jefferson's "Anas" and Political Gossip in the Early Republic," *Journal of the Early Republic*, 15 (1995): 25–57.

60. Blair discusses organization of ideas under the heading of "Conduct of the Discourse in All its Parts." Blair, 2: 156–202.

61. The body of the brief was completed on July 31, 1810, as dated in this volume. He did not feel it necessary to update the manuscript at the time of its publication.

62. Apparently TJ had feedback with respect to the organizational pattern he used. He felt it necessary, therefore, to justify the method he adopted. In a letter to Gallatin, written on September 27, 1810, he explained his choice: "I had only to state to my constituents a common transaction. This would naturally be by way of narrative or statements of the facts as they occur, and bringing forward the law arising on them and pointing to the Executive the course he was to pursue." He then noted: "I suppose it was self-respectful to present it as a history and explanation of what had taken place. It does not, indeed, in that form display the subject in one great whole; but it brings forward successively a number of questions, solving themselves as they arise, and leaving no one unexamined. . . ." TJ to Albert Gallatin, September 27, 1810, in Ford, 11: 152n–153n.

63. Wirt to TJ, April 15, 1812, in Sowerby, *Catalogue of the Library of Thomas Jefferson*, 3: 407.

64. John Quincy Adams's *Lectures on Rhetoric and Oratory*, 2 vols. (Cambridge: 1810) were first presented while he was Professor of Rhetoric and Belles Lettres at Harvard University. The work covers the range of rhetoric from the classical through the modern period.

65. TJ to John Adams, April 20, 1812, in Cappon, 2: 298.

66. Adams to TJ, May 1, 1812, in Cappon, 2: 301. TJ expressed similar feelings to William Wirt on the 12th of April, 1812: "A love of peace and tranquility, strengthened by age and a lassitude of business," he stated, "renders it extremely disquieting to me to be harassed by vexatious lawsuits by persons who have no earthly claim on me, in cases where I have been merely acting for others." Ford, 11: 227. Jefferson had to feel pleased, however, when he received this reaction from Adams written on May 3, 1812: "It is as masterly a pamphlet as ever I have read; and every way worthy of the mind that composed and the pen which committed it to writing. There is witt and fancy and delicate touches of satyr enough in it to make it entertaining while the profusion of learning, the close reasoning and accurate Criticism must have required a Patience of Investigation that at your Age is very uncommon. . . ." Cappon, 2: 302.

67. Tazewell to TJ, May 15, 1812, in Sowerby, *Catalogue of the Library of Thomas Jefferson*, 3: 409.

68. Dumbauld, *Thomas Jefferson and the Law*, 74. Of particular relevance here is Merrill Peterson's ensuing description of what happened to Livingston following the publication of Jefferson's briefs. "Livingston published his answer; and by sheer persistence he eventually obtained title to the batture, enabling him, at last, to close his account with the government in 1830. It is pleasing to record that he enjoyed a friendly correspondence with the Sage of Monticello before his death." Peterson, *Thomas Jefferson and the New Nation*, 947.

69. Wilson, in Onuf, ed., *Jeffersonian Legacies*, 70–73.

# CHAPTER THIRTEEN

~

# Historical Writer and Social Commentator

Although, as we learned in chapter 8, Jefferson greatly admired certain modern historians, his perspectives on historical writing perhaps were inspired most by the ancients. He strongly shared the views held by the best historians from the Classical period that, at least as far as is humanly possible, historical writing should be an accurate recording of events; that, as a literary art, historical writing should be clear, concise, and eloquent; and that historians should use significant events and individuals as examples for the presentation of moral messages both to the present and especially to future generations. Although the third of these criteria—which often results in the combining of historical writing and social commentary—generally is not embraced by modern historians, it fits well with Jefferson's rhetoric of virtue. Indeed, to Jefferson, historical writing was one of the most effective means of expressing virtue.

In his own published and unpublished historical writings and social commentary, Jefferson attempted to uphold the high standards maintained by the best Greek, Latin, and modern historians for style, accuracy, and message. This chapter shows how Jefferson's performance as a historical writer and social commentator both conformed to and, at times, deviated from these standards. We use his three criteria for historical writing, outlined in chapter 8, as the guideline for the discussion. First, Jefferson believed that this communication genre should focus on significant themes, events, and people for the purpose of instructing and motivating readers on issues that advance personal and public good. Second, Jefferson held that historical writing should rely on reasoning and evidence designed to produce the truth. Finally, Jefferson believed that it is necessary for a historical writer to channel the message of virtue through the use of a clear, coherent, and unified organizational pattern, and a plain, concise, and vivid style. Clearly, these standards were consistent with, and very likely patterned after, those maintained by the ancients.

Although several examples illustrate Jefferson as a practitioner of historical writing and social commentary, we have chosen two for discussion. First, we offer an analysis of Jefferson's only book, *Notes on the State of Virginia*, a truly remarkable, albeit controversial, volume. Though this analysis of his native state was far more than a historical overview, it provides what we think is a good example of Jefferson's commitment to the application of high scholarly standards to help search for the truth. The second part of this chapter describes and evaluates his narration of events in France on the eve of the French Revolution. It was fortunate for Jefferson, as it is for us, that he was an eyewitness to the beginning stages of his era's most dramatic event. As an astute observer of social dynamics and historical change, Jefferson provided for his readers a compelling analysis of this watershed moment in modern history. Whereas the relationship between his observing first-hand the unfolding revolution in France and his views on republican government have been widely discussed,[1] the significance of his Paris experience in relation to his philosophy and practice of historical writing and his broader views on virtue has yet to be fully explored.[2]

## Notes on the State of Virginia

The preparation of Jefferson's *Notes* began with a strategic request in 1780 from François de Barbé-Marbois, secretary of the French legation in Philadelphia. The French government, it appears, was anxious, in the words of Jefferson, "to obtain such statistical accounts of the different states of our Union, as might be useful for their information."[3] The significance of the project was enhanced by the location, size, and influence of the state of Virginia. Although Jefferson's work on his manuscript was interrupted by the tumultuous events of the first half of 1781, he was able to mail a completed draft to Marbois by December. Over the next several years, the scope of the *Notes* broadened as Jefferson revised them. It became, in the words of historian Merrill Peterson, "a vehicle for the interpretation of his country to himself."[4] The broad-based subject matter covered in this treatise, first published privately in 1785, consisted of a series of twenty-three queries to which Jefferson provided answers with analyses that utilized both informative data and persuasive claims. In addition to the basic part of the text, the volume eventually contained four appendixes of supporting data.

The left-hand column of the chart contains the wording he used for the topic or chapter headings he expressed in each query. In the right-hand column, we have listed what we feel are the modern fields of study or disciplines that the question most closely represents.

| Query | Field of Study |
|---|---|
| I. Boundaries of Virginia | Geography |
| II. Rivers | Geography |
| III. Seaports | Geography |
| IV. Mountains | Geography |
| V. Cascades | Geography |
| VI. Productions Mineral, Vegetable, Animal | |
|    A. Minerals | Geology |
|    B. Vegetables (Food, trees, plants) | Botany; Agriculture |
|    C. Animals (Brutes and humans) | Biology; Anthropology |
| VII. Climate | Geography; Meteorology |
| VIII. Population | Geography; Demography |
| IX. Military Force | Military Science |
| X. Marine Force | Military Science |
| XI. Aborigines | Anthropology |
| XII. Counties and Towns | Geography; Political Science |
| XIII. Constitution | Political Science; Jurisprudence or Law |
| XIV. Laws | Political Science; Law |
| XV. Colleges, Buildings, Roads | Education; Architecture; Civil Engineering |
| XVI. Proceedings as to Tories | Political Science; Law |
| XVII. Religion | Religion |
| XVIII. Manners | Sociology; Ethnography |
| XIX. Manufactures | Economics; Business |
| XX. Subjects of Commerce | Economics; Business |
| XXI. Weights, Measures, Money | Economics; Business |
| XXII. Public Revenue Expences | Economics; Business |
| XXIII. Histories; Memorials; State Papers | History; Political Science |

In all, at least twenty fields of study in the arts and sciences, many of which have multiple listings, are included. In addition to the basic part of the text (which embraces 196 pages), the volume has four appendixes containing 61 pages of essential supplementary data. They consist of a commentary from Charles Thomson, secretary of Congress; Jefferson's "Draught of a Fundamental Constitution for the Commonwealth of Virginia"; a copy of his "Act for Establishing Religious Freedom" in Virginia; and supporting documents on the murder of Logan's family.[5]

A careful examination of the *Notes* shows that Jefferson selected and developed information throughout to emphasize important, timely themes and subjects directly related to the advancement of personal and public good. For example, in Query XVIII he expressed in strong and direct terms his desire to rid Virginia, albeit gradually, of slavery, an institution he considered to be an unconscionable moral evil. Believing that slavery was destructive to the "morals" and "industry" of a society, Jefferson held that the institution created an atmosphere not at all conducive to the development of republican virtue.[6] Another issue addressed in the *Notes* that was of overriding importance to Jefferson in his search for the advancement of the public good was the Virginia constitution of 1776. To Jefferson, this constitution was among the greatest threats to republican government in his native state.[7] Later in this chapter, we discuss this subject within the context of Jefferson's application of basic principles of reasoning.

Further evidence of Jefferson's concern over his first criterion of historical writing can be found in his strongly held views regarding the distribution of the *Notes*, initially intended to be limited. Beyond his select French audience, Jefferson desired only a modest circulation in the United States. The targeted American audience, however, was to include students at the College of William and Mary. Jefferson believed that what he called the "rising generation"—essential to the process of continued positive change—could best benefit from the contents of his treatise. But, despite its potentially positive long-term impact, Jefferson feared that immediate publication and widespread distribution of the *Notes* could have negative implications. Perhaps the most telling indication of Jefferson's conviction that the *Notes* should promote public good was his decision to withhold publication of his manuscript until he could be assured, primarily by Madison, that his reflections on slavery and the Virginia constitution would not be a deterrent for advancing reforms in Virginia on these issues.

In a June 7, 1785, letter to the Marquis de Chastellux, Jefferson expressed his views on both the potential immediate harm and the almost certain long-term good that could result from the publication and distribution of his *Notes*. After informing Chastellux that he did not want the "strictures on slavery and on the constitution" made public until he could determine whether his views on these subjects "would do most harm or good," Jefferson declared:

> It is possible, that in my own country, these strictures might produce an irritation, which would indispose the people towards the two great objects I

have in view; that is, the emancipation of their slaves, and the settlement of their constitution on a firmer and more permanent basis. If I learn from thence, that they will not produce that effect, I have printed and reserved just copies enough to be able to give one to every young man at the College. It is to them I look, to the rising generation, and not to the one now in power, for these great reformations.[8]

Ten days later, he explained his position on the publication of his manuscript to fellow Virginian James Monroe:

I have taken measures to prevent it's publication. My reason is that I fear the terms in which I speak of slavery and of our constitution may produce an irritation which will revolt the minds of our countrymen against reformation in these two articles, and thus do more harm than good.[9]

An examination of the Notes and Jefferson's concerns over the impact of its publication reveals that he never lost sight of his first criterion for historical writing. Throughout the period in which the Notes were produced and distributed, Jefferson, it would appear, continually focused on significant themes and events that he felt had a strong potential for elevating virtue by strengthening the moral principles of personal and public good.

With the notable exception of his blatantly racist arguments in Query XIV on the intellectual and physical traits of African Americans, which we discuss in chapter 16, Jefferson demonstrated forcefully his commitment to the task of making certain that the Notes would feature compelling reasoning and evidence in his search for truth.[10] He took eight steps in the accumulation of evidence that would be reliable, meaningful, and persuasive:

(1) He drew upon his extensive note-taking materials that he had assembled throughout his career.
(2) He wrote to friends and other authorities requesting information and their opinions regarding some of the subject matter included in the unpublished notes.
(3) He freely quoted, when necessary, from the works of recognized scholars.
(4) He used knowledge he had gained from experience—his first component of reasoning.
(5) He incorporated charts, diagrams, and a map to summarize factual materials, thus giving them salience. (Indeed, maps, lists, and charts play an important role throughout the volume.)
(6) He constantly edited and expanded his study.
(7) He stressed the importance of accuracy in the published text.

(8) He initiated action to counter the potential negative influence of a planned unauthorized and inaccurate French translation of the *Notes*.

For the most part, Jefferson's use of evidence-gathering techniques was consistent with his second criterion for effective historical writing. But what about his methods of reasoning based on the factual data he had accumulated for the purpose of writing the *Notes*? In earlier chapters, we saw how he incorporated into the *Notes* strong arguments in the defense of religious freedom; in addition, chapter 14 shows how he used, in an impressive manner, the Logan speech to rebut the Comte de Buffon's claim that American natives were not on the intellectual or artistic level of their European counterparts. Our intent now is to examine briefly the quality of his reasoning on one of the highly controversial issues that he addressed in the *Notes*—the Virginia constitution of 1776.[11] Jefferson argued that this constitution, adopted while he was serving as a member of the Second Continental Congress and busy drafting the Declaration of Independence, was basically flawed. To Jefferson, the most striking of its numerous defects were certain unrepublican features that resulted in an unfair and unequal representation of the state's population. Among these defects were (in his words):

(1) The majority of the men in the state, who pay and fight for its support, are unrepresented in the legislature. . . .
(2) Among those who share the representation, the shares are very unequal.
(3) The senate is, by its constitution, too homogeneous with the house of delegates. Being chosen by the same electors, at the same time, and out of the same subjects, the choice falls of course on men of the same description.
(4) All the powers of government, legislative, executive, and judiciary, result to the legislative body. The concentrating these in the same hands is precisely the definition of despotic government.

To make the foregoing defects more cogent, Jefferson added, it is important to note:

(5) That the ordinary legislature may alter the constitution itself, and
(6) That the assembly exercises a power of determining the Quorum of their own body which may legislate for us.[12]

Not content to limit his argument to a discussion of the problem, Jefferson, with Madison's help, developed what he perceived to be a problem-solving solution. Known as the "Draught of a Fundamental Constitution for the Commonwealth of Virginia," this proposal first appeared in 1785 as an appendix to the privately printed first edition of the *Notes*.[13] Using the principles of constitutional and parliamentary law that he had mastered, Jefferson removed the defects of the 1776 constitution. Notwithstanding his reliance on the principles of reason and virtue he had articulated, he was unsuccessful in inspiring an immediate and widespread movement toward constitutional reform. Not until 1830 was the Virginia Constitution revised. His arguments on this occasion, however, remain as a splendid example of his reasoning process at its highest.

On the third criterion for effective historical writing—the need for a unified, coherent organizational pattern and a clear, vivid style—Jefferson in the *Notes* illustrated both strengths and weaknesses. The use of twenty-three queries—adapted from Marbois's original twenty-two—enabled him to cover considerable ground, but at the same time it led to an unevenness in emphasis and to an overlapping of ideas. He devoted 47 pages to Query VI and 20 each to Queries XIII, XIV, and XXIII; and only one sentence to III and two to X. The overlapping of themes also was evident. Although Query VI on the "Aborigines" dealt exclusively with Indians, when he defined some of their distinguishing traits and described Logan's oratory, he placed this material in the Query on "Productions Mineral, Vegetable and Animal." He adhered to a similar pattern of repetition of categories in his analysis of African Americans and slavery. It is important to observe, however, that in many of the discussions within a chapter the organizational structure permitted him to present a unified and coherent argument. This was especially true in Query XIII on the "Constitution."

Because the *Notes* began as a statistical overview and maintained certain characteristics of that type of survey throughout Jefferson's various revisions, the writing style cannot be considered consistently eloquent. But although Jefferson's language control in the *Notes*, as a general rule, conformed to the "middling" style he thought appropriate for this type of writing, numerous passages epitomized the high standards he stressed for excellence in style. Short, concise, and clear sentences consistently were evident in each of the queries. Moreover, many passages in the *Notes* provide succinct, yet valuable, insights into deeply held Jeffersonian principles. In describing his ideal citizen, Jefferson wrote this memorable passage in Query XIX:

> Those who labour in the earth are the chosen people of God, if ever he had
> a chosen people, whose breasts he has his peculiar deposit for substantial

and genuine virtue. It is the focus in which he keeps alive that sacred fire, which otherwise might escape from the face of the earth. Corruption of morals in the mass of cultivators is a phaenomenon of which no age nor nation has furnished an example.[14]

In his *Notes*, Jefferson at times achieved distinction in his use of imagery that opened the doors to the mind; for example, in describing the scenic views of Virginia, he reached the level of the sublime. In the following paragraph from Query IV, he takes his readers to the top of the Blue Ridge Mountains to share with him a picturesque scenic view:

> The passage of the Patowmac through the Blue ridge is perhaps one of the most stupendous scenes in nature. You stand on a very high point of land. On your right comes up the Shenandoah, having ranged along the foot of the mountain an hundred miles to seek a vent. On your left approaches the Patowmac, in quest of a passage also. In the moment of their junction they rush together against the mountain, rend it asunder, and pass off to the sea. The first glance of this scene hurries our senses into the opinion, that this earth has been created in time, that the mountains were formed first, that the rivers began to flow afterwards, that in this place particularly they have been dammed up by the Blue ridge of mountains, and have formed an ocean which filled the whole valley; that continuing to rise they have at length broken over at this spot, and have torn the mountain down from its summit to its base. The piles of rock on each hand, but particularly on the Shenandoah, the evident marks of their disrupture and avulsion from their beds by the most powerful agents of nature, corroborate the impression.[15]

In another striking passage, Jefferson was effusive in his praise in Query V for the beauty of the Natural Bridge, located in Rockbridge County:

> It is impossible for the emotions, arising from the sublime, to be felt beyond what they are here: so beautiful an arch, so elevated, so light, and springing, as it were, up to heaven, the rapture of the Spectator is really indiscribable![16]

Jefferson's moving images portraying Virginia as a magnificent state with awe-inspiring splendor entranced Maria Cosway who wrote to him words of ardent praise:

> I have been reading with great pleasure your description of America. . . . Oh how I wish My self in those delightful places! Those enchanted Grotto's! Those Magnificent Mountains(,) rivers, &c. &c.! Why am I not a Man that I could sett out immediatly and satisfy My Curiosity, indulge my sight with wonders![17]

The responses to the *Notes*, as an example of historical writing and so-cial commentary, were interesting and varied. Reactions from contempo-raries who had read either the privately printed manuscript or the pub-lished *Notes* generally were favorable. In particular, a number of observers liked the range of the content and the way it was presented. On April 26, 1789, an enthusiastic Francis Kinloch wrote: "You will not, I trust, sus-pect me of flattery, when I assure you, that I consider all America as infi-nitely obliged to you for such a publication, for you have not only done us credit with foreigners, but have excited a wish in every man's mind who reads you, to become acquainted with his own state, and to consider the same questions as addressed to himself."[18] On specific points, how-ever, reaction was divided. This was strikingly evident on the issue of slavery and the related problem of the mental and physical traits of black Americans. Whereas generations of Southerners embraced Jefferson's ar-guments on the divisive issue of the inherent inferiority of blacks, anti-slavery Northerners increasingly began to dispute and ultimately to assail them.[19]

The body of modern scholarship has been ambivalent on *Notes on Vir-ginia*. While the work has continued to receive praise as a significant scholarly and literary achievement noted for its wonderfully descriptive passages and penetrating social commentary—including Jefferson's most extensive condemnation in writing of the institution of slavery—in re-cent years his offensive views of African Americans expressed in Query XIV have come under increasing scrutiny. To many modern observers, it seems, *Notes on Virginia* has come to represent many of the deepest and most challenging complexities of the character of its author.

# Jefferson in France

As the American Minister to France who, in 1785, had succeeded the popular and influential Benjamin Franklin, Jefferson provided insightful historical narratives of the developing conditions leading to the French Revolution.[20] For the most part, his accounts of these dramatic events were included in approximately 100 letters written between 1787 and 1789 to various friends and other prominent individuals, including John Jay, James Madison, Thomas Paine, and John Adams. Many of these let-ters, which were specific and thorough in range and scope, contain narra-tives that are highly instructive, vivid, and compelling firsthand descrip-tions. When writing his "Autobiography" more than three decades later, and with copies of his original letters before him, Jefferson expanded on some of the ideas he had developed while present at the scene of action. When examined in their entirety, these narratives constitute an important specimen of American diplomatic history and reveal information on how Jefferson worked as a historical writer. One of the main purposes of this analysis is to see to what extent these accounts conformed to his three criteria for excellence in historical writing.

Although he understood that many in the United States cared little about European affairs, Jefferson took seriously his written descriptions, narratives, and commentaries as the main source of information for leaders at home. Early in the crisis, he presented to Edward Carrington a persuasive rationale for his decision to provide the American people with concrete data on developing events in France and surrounding countries:

> I often doubt whether I should trouble Congress or my friends with these details of European politicks. I know they do not excite that interest in America of which it is impossible for one to divest himself here. I know too that it is a maxim with us, and I think it a wise one, not to entangle ourselves with the affairs of Europe. Still, I think, we should know them. . . . Tho' I am persuaded therefore that these details are read by many with great indifference, yet I think it my duty to enter into them, and to run the risk of giving too much, rather than too little information.[21]

According to Merrill Peterson, "No American minister reported with such regularity to the government at home or with a keener eye to European affairs."[22]

In his accounts of the steady movement from a state of unrest to the onset of the Revolution, Jefferson informed his readers of numerous external and internal threats to the welfare of the French people. He observed that a potential European war, which inevitably would involve France, appeared to be a strong probability. Within the country itself, Jefferson noted, the government was being weakened by several factors:

(1) There was a lack of a fixed constitution and a declaration of rights.
(2) There was an alarming money shortage that had brought the nation to the edge of bankruptcy.
(3) An inadequate bread supply had caused considerable concern, posing the threat of riots.
(4) Frequent references were made to deteriorating relations between the king and parliament.

According to Jefferson, these negative conditions prompted thousands of people, almost on a daily basis, to assemble outside the parliament house to voice their concerns and to apply pressure on the king and the assembly leaders. "For some time," he wrote John Adams in August 1787, "mobs of 10; 20; 30,000 people collected daily, surrounded the parliament house, huzzaed the members, even entered the doors and examined into their conduct, took the horses out of the carriages of those who did well, and drew them home."[23] As the crisis worsened in the spring and summer of 1789, Jefferson's narratives vividly depicted the movement of increasing numbers of citizens into the streets to express their relentless demands for justice and equality.

In addition to describing the dangerous circumstances that were developing in France, Jefferson gave his readers a critical assessment of representative political characters who were exerting either a positive or a negative influence. Among his more interesting descriptions was the one of Lafayette included in his January 30, 1787, letter to Madison. Note how after generally praising Lafayette, he concluded with a less than favorable assessment of his desire for acclaim:

> [He] is a most valuable *auxiliary to me*. His *zeal* is unbounded, and his *weight* with those in *power great*. His *education* having been merely *military*, *commerce* was an unknown feild to him. But his good sense enabling him to comprehend perfectly whatever is *explained to him*, *his agency* has been very *efficacious*. He has a great deal of *sound genius*, is well *remarked* by the *king* and rising in *popularity*. He has nothing against *him but* the *suspicion of republican principles*. I think he will one day be of the *ministry*. His foible is a *canine appetite for popularity and fame*. But he will get above this.[24]

Whereas during the course of the mounting tensions he generally was free in his praise of his friend Lafayette, Jefferson's description of the Duke d'Orléans was markedly unfavorable because of his faulty moral standards and practices. In an August 28, 1789, letter to Madison, Jefferson described the Duke as "a man of moderate understanding, of no principle, absorbed in low vice, and incapable of abstracting himself from the filth of that to direct any thing else."[25] Jefferson was somewhat more sympathetic in his portrayal of the king, suggesting that he was a well-intentioned monarch who, because of his weak natural temperament, unwittingly permitted himself to be maneuvered by a dominating and corrupt queen. This tendency, he later wrote in his "Autobiography," ultimately was to lead to his downfall and death.[26]

Jefferson, both in letters from Paris and in later writings, offered numerous unflattering descriptions of Marie Antoinette, often including negative assessments of the role she played in the unfolding crisis of the late 1780s. As early as August 1787, he wrote Madison that she was "detested and an explosion of some sort is not impossible."[27] When reflecting on the Revolution years later in his "Autobiography," Jefferson reserved his harshest criticism for the queen, noting that she was

> proud, disdainful of restraint, indignant at all obstacles to her will, eager in the pursuit of pleasure, and firm enough to hold to her desires, or perish in their wreck. Her inordinate gambling and dissipations, with those of the Count d'Artois and others of her clique, had been a sensible item in the exhaustion of the treasury, which called into action the reforming hand of the nation; and her opposition to her inflexible perverseness, and dauntless spirit, led herself to the Guillotine, & drew the king on with her, and plunged the world into crimes & calamities which will forever stain the pages of modern history.

His indictment of Marie Antoinette continued with this remarkable observation: "I have ever believed that had there been no queen, there would have been no revolution."[28]

But while Jefferson was vivid in his descriptions of many of the key participants in the Revolution, some of his observations were less compelling. Among his least satisfying descriptions was that of Jacques Necker, who held the important and highly visible position of director general of finance. He describes how the people often saluted him as the saviour of the oppressed; how he was cool in his relations toward America; and how his influence in parliament began to wane in 1789. But we learn little about his personality, his style of leadership, or the strengths and flaws of his character. Even so, when balanced against the more numerous powerful images of the Revolution that Jefferson presented to his readers, shortcomings such as this do not detract significantly from the overall impact of his account.

When evaluating Jefferson's attempts to provide the kind of analysis of the unfolding crisis that would advance the public good, his September 6, 1789, letter to Madison deserves special consideration. Significantly, in this letter Jefferson advances for the first time what would become one of his most cherished principles: "that the earth belongs in usufruct to the living."[29] "This concept of political relativism," noted Julian Boyd, "was the one great addition to Jefferson's thought that emerged from his years of residence at the center of European intellectual ferment."[30] For the rest of his long life, this principle was to be a hallmark of Jefferson's ideas an law, government, and society. Bernard Bailyn offers a brief but cogent assessment: "This letter contains Jefferson's first full statement of his deceptively simple belief that the world belongs to the living and not to the dead, a notion that, as he came to apply it, had enormous political and social implications which he did not hesitate to draw."[31]

Viewed one way, his September 6 letter was an attempt by Jefferson to outline certain ideas for his fellow Virginian—based on his own first-hand observations of the crisis in France—that might assist in directing the new government in America. Specifically, Jefferson wrote that the basic principle outlined in the letter "would furnish matter for a fine pre-amble to our first law for appropriating the public revenue."[32] But in his discussion of the letter, Boyd posed a different interpretation of Jefferson's reasons for writing it. This letter addressed to Madison, Boyd argues, may well have been written as a message to revolutionary leaders in France. Boyd concludes that "Jefferson consciously . . . converted the text into the form of a letter to Madison primarily as a protective device." His rea-sons for doing so were as follows: "Already too much involved in the in-ternal affairs of the sovereign to whom he was accredited, Jefferson, in ad-vancing arguments subversive to that sovereigns's power, may have used this indirect method because a direct one was interdicted."[33] In other words, fearful that such a letter directly addressed to revolutionary lead-ers might be viewed by some in France as a violation of his proper diplo-matic functions, Jefferson was forced to cloak his sentiments in a letter to America. If this is indeed true, this letter becomes far more significant and perhaps stands as an even stronger example of Jefferson's concern that his observations advance the public good—in this case, that of the French people.

Whatever the purpose of his September 6, 1789, letter to Madison, Jef-ferson's accounts of the French Revolution were written with clear focus and unmistakable intent. When writing these narratives, Jefferson clearly sought to fulfill his first criterion of historical writing by providing in-structive insights into an event of enormous historical significance. In both his discussion of important themes and his description of key occur-rences and the characters who played central roles in them, Jefferson, it would appear, was guided by his perspectives on what constitutes personal and public good both for the French people and the American govern-ment he represented. We now turn our attention to his second criterion—the strategies he used in giving meaning to the developing events through the process of practical reasoning rooted in virtue.

When describing the unfolding crisis in France, Jefferson employed multiple argumentative strategies so that he could produce valid and re-liable evidence and reasoning in his quest for truth. Most important, in gathering and evaluating evidence he made every effort to discover or create primary source material based on eyewitness accounts. Obviously, he was greatly assisted in these efforts by his close proximity to key events. To understand these historically significant events more fully, and to report them accurately, as the crisis grew in force, Jefferson, in the tradition of Thucydides and Tacitus, placed himself at the scene of action, and became, when appropriate, both an observer and a participant observer. Thus he visited the Assembly of Notables, sought their opinion, entertained republican leaders in his residence, conversed with ambassadors at diplomatic functions, walked among the throngs at the Bastille, and drove his carriage through the mobs at Versailles.

Throughout his years in Paris, Jefferson was committed to the idea that every step possible should be taken to ensure the reliability of all data used in his narratives. When he could not be present at an event, he sought to gain access to primary data on specific happenings. In other words, he was careful to cite, whenever possible, reliable accounts from those who had witnessed, or even had participated in, key events. But in an atmosphere conducive to exaggeration, rumor, and misinterpretation, accurate information was at a premium. Explaining his concern over reporting only reliable information, he wrote to John Jay:

> On account of the multitude of falshoods always current here, under specious appearances, I am obliged to be slow of belief. But whenever a fact worth communicating, is so far authenticated as to be worthy of belief, I never fail to avail myself of the first safe opportunity of communicating it to you.[34]

When gathering and evaluating evidence, most of which consisted of primary source data, Jefferson constructed arguments based on his principles of moral reasoning and his philosophy of virtue. He relied on each of the four elements of moral reasoning outlined in chapter 3. The position he held, the location of his residence, his constant visits to hear legislative debates, his rides and walks along the streets during moments of increasing tension, his visits to Versailles, and his conversations with leaders all permitted him to develop numerous arguments based on the element of *experience*. After closely observing conditions in France for four to five years, for instance, he felt confident in making claims about the nature of the French people and the tensions that were giving way to revolution. Perhaps most important, by drawing upon experience Jefferson argued that public opinion in France in 1789 was the generator powering the revolution. More specifically, by drawing upon his legislative experience Jefferson could see in the spring and summer of 1789 that the parliamentary body comprising 1,200 members, with no rules of procedure to guide them, would be seriously hampered in their effort to have meaningful discussion and debate. Writing to Thomas Lee Shippen in March, Jefferson observed:

> The difficulties which now appear threatening to my mind are those which will result from the size of the assembly. 1200 persons, of any rank, and of any nation, assembled together would with difficulty be prevented from tumult, and confusion. But when they are to compose an assembly for which no rules of debate or proceeding have yet been formed, in whom no habits of order have been yet established, and to consist moreover of Frenchmen among whom there are always more speakers than listeners, I confess to you I apprehend some danger.[35]

With the lessons of experience firmly entrenched in his mind, Jefferson confidently claimed that what he had observed in France and in Europe as a whole strengthened his conviction that all forms of monarchy are vastly inferior to republicanism. "I was much an enemy to monarchy before I came to Europe," he wrote George Washington in 1788. "I am ten thousand times more so since I have seen what they are." Concluding his ringing endorsement of republican government, Jefferson wrote that there "is scarcely an evil known in these countries which may not be traced to their king as it's source, nor a good which is not derived from the small fibres of republicanism existing among them."[36]

Because of his presence on the scene as an observer and, in some cases, as a participant, Jefferson had less need to build arguments in his narratives on *testimony*. Even so, he made some use of this second element of moral reasoning. He cited, as we have seen, statements from leaders who had access to primary source materials, and who themselves had made news because of the positions of authority they held.

Arguments from *analogy* also appear frequently in his historical account. He noted that there was a parallel between what was happening in France and what had occurred during the American Revolution. Writing to Thomas Lee Shippen in March 1789, Jefferson confidently stated:

> the opposition to the revolution which is working has been miraculously small, and he who would predict it's failure from the little obstacles which have happened, would be about as good a prophet as he who from the loss of two or three little skirmishes on our part would have foretold our final failure in the American revolution.[37]

Beyond drawing relevant comparisons between what happened in the American Revolution and what was occurring in France, Jefferson also relied on analogical reasoning based almost solely on his observations and experiences in Europe. When drawing analogies between France and England, for example, Jefferson felt it necessary to conclude that what France was trying to do was superior to what was taking place in England.

Although Jefferson was constantly surprised at the rapid pace and increasingly radical nature of events unfolding in France between 1787 and 1789, he eventually was able to combine the evidence and reasoning that he had developed through the elements of experience, testimony, and analogy to conclude, through the process of the *calculation of probabilities*, that the French Revolution was justified, and that France, not England, deserved the gratitude of the American people. In August 1789, Jefferson wrote that the intolerable conditions in France before the Revolution, combined with the positive nature of the republican principles that were being espoused, made the French Revolution a powerful force for public good. When weighing the reasoning and evidence in defense of what the Revolution had accomplished against the repressive conditions that existed under monarchical rule, he felt justified in saying:

> I have so much confidence on the good sense of man, and his qualifications for self-government, that I am never afraid of the issue where reason is left free to exert her force; and I will agree to be stoned as a false prophet if all does not end well in this country. Nor will it end with this country. Hers is but the first chapter of the history of European liberty.[38]

Although Jefferson was influenced by his pro-French sentiments and his blind faith in republican change as a positive force, he nevertheless was largely successful in upholding his second criterion for historical writing— the use of reasoning and evidence designed to produce the truth.

The organizational structure of Jefferson's narrative and his use and critique of language and style were consistent with his recommendations for historical writing. The stories he told featured a unified and coherent message in which significant political and moral themes were emphasized. Unity and coherence in the narratives resulted from a reliance on the time sequence pattern. As was common practice in the eighteenth century, he often would begin where the last communication had ended. In a July 11, 1789, letter to Thomas Paine, Jefferson wrote: "Tho you have doubtless heard most of the proceedings of the States general since my last [letter], I will take up the narration where that left it, that you may be able to separate the true from the false accounts you have heard."[39] His practice of having duplicate copies of his letters enabled him to keep from cluttering his stories with needless repetitions. In short, the stories with their beginning, their middle, and their ending moved forward in a clear and cohesive manner until they reached a climax.

Contributing importantly to the high compulsion value of the narratives was Jefferson's clear and vivid language control that permitted his readers to experience a scene. In the early stages of his historical account, he took them into the Assembly so that they could get a feel for the speakers' propensity for wordplay. "The most remarkeable effect of this convention as yet," he wrote Abigail Adams on February 22, 1787, "is the number of puns and bon mots it has generated. I think were they all collected it would make a more voluminous work than the Encyclopedie."[40] During the period surrounding the turmoil at the Bastille in mid-July 1789, he demonstrated a talent for the use of concise, picturesque, and moving descriptions of the dynamic and volatile scene:

> This threw the States into a ferment and Paris into open insurrection. The people here attacked with stones a body of German cavalry and drove them off. On the 13th, they forced the prison of St. Lazare, released the prisoners and got some arms. The city committee resolved to embody 48,000 Bourgeois. They asked arms at the invalids and being refused the people forced the place and got here a large supply of arms. They then went to the Bastille and made the same demand. The Governor after hoisting a flag of truce and decaying a hundred or two within the outer drawbridge, hoisted the drawbridge and fired on them. The people without then forced the place, took and beheaded the Governor and Lt. Governor, and here compleated arming themselves. The same day they beheaded the Prevost des marchands, discovered in a treacherous correspondence against them.[41]

In addition to dramatic descriptions such as this, we also observe how Jefferson used figures of speech to give an additional impact to a point. Even more compelling was the way he delivered a powerful message in a terse, single sentence. "The cutting off heads is become so much a la mode," he wrote close friend Maria Cosway, "that one is apt to feel of a morning whether their own is on their shoulders."[42] And in perhaps his most memorable quotation from his Paris years, Jefferson wrote in 1787 that the "tree of liberty must be refreshed from time to time with the blood of patriots and tyrants."[43] Significantly, even though this statement was made in regard to the overall reaction to Shays' rebellion in western Massachusetts and to Jefferson's fear of anti-republican ideas spreading in America, his experiences as an observer of events unfolding in Europe doubtless influenced in large part both the sentiment and the language.[44]

During the period when Jefferson, as an eyewitness historical writer, was describing unfolding events in Paris and Versailles, the images of what he saw and heard penetrated deeply into his mind, reminding him of the dramatic story of the American Revolution. Drawing upon his own experiences, reliable accounts from various eyewitnesses and participants, and his ability with the written word, Jefferson vividly portrayed France as a country struggling to move from absolute monarchy to a republican form of government. On balance, these portrayals were timely, instructive, and compelling. But although his narratives describing what was happening were poignant and captivating, the inferential leaps he sometimes made in interpreting these events—both in letters written during the crisis and later in his "Autobiography"—were either exaggerated or misleading. His claims that there "is scarcely an evil known in these countries which may not be traced to their king as it's source," and "had there been no queen, there would have been no revolution," clearly were overstatements.[45] Moreover, some of his predictions proved to be overly optimistic or inaccurate. He predicted, for example, that the political revolution emerging in France would take place "without bloodshed"; wrote that the king ultimately would remain as the principal executive in a new government; and declared that he (Jefferson) would be willing "to be stoned as a false prophet if all does not end well in this country."[46] Obviously, all these comments and rosy projections missed the mark. In commenting on Jefferson's assessment of his own narratives of the early stages of the French Revolution, Joseph J. Ellis has observed: "Later in his life, probably when he was reviewing his correspondence in preparation to write his autobiography in 1821, Jefferson was somewhat embarrassed at his unrelieved optimism in the late 1780s."[47]

But Jefferson could not have realized at the time he left France in 1789 that the country he had come to love, despite the warning signs such as the riotous acts in the streets and the frequent beheadings, would soon be subjected to even more bloodshed and, ultimately, to the dictatorial reign of Napoleon Bonaparte. For Jefferson, the eternal republican optimist, his stay in Paris had strengthened his faith in the ability of the people to govern in such a manner that all the citizens may enjoy the benefits to be accrued from a virtuous society based on the public good. It was understandable, therefore, that Daniel Webster was able to say, following his visit to Monticello in 1824, that one of Jefferson's favorite discussion topics was the revolutionary period he had observed in the epochal days in France in the 1780s.[48] For our purposes, his observing firsthand these dramatic events had a great impact on his constantly evolving rhetorical philosophy. It made him aware again of the persuasive power of eyewitness accounts in the writing of history, and the role that language may play in appealing to one's understanding, imagination, and passions.

# Notes

1. Much attention, obviously, has been given to the significance of Jefferson's experiences in France—as well as to his attraction to French culture and ideas—in regard to his political philosophy and specific positions on key issues of international diplomacy. For a variety of views on this, see Gilbert Chinard, *Thomas Jefferson: The Apostle of Americanism* (Boston: Little, Brown, 1929), 215 ff.; Lawrence S. Kaplan, *Jefferson and France: An Essay on Politics and Political Ideas* (New Haven: Yale University Press, 1967); Dumas Malone, *Jefferson and the Rights of Man* (Boston: Little, Brown, 1951); Conor Cruise O'Brien, *The Long Affair: Thomas Jefferson and the French Revolution* (Chicago: University of Chicago Press, 1996); and Peterson, *Thomas Jefferson and the New Nation*, 297 ff.

2. Some attention has been given to Jefferson's contributions to two French scholarly undertakings while he resided in Europe. First, he made significant contributions, at Jean-Nicholas Demeunier's request, to selected entries in the *Encyclopédie méthodique*, particularly to the article on the United States. In this instance, Jefferson initially provided information as a response to a list of questions supplied by Demeunier; subsequently, he made further editorial contributions to a draft of the completed article. Second, Jefferson had a less satisfying relationship with François Soulés, as the French historian prepared revisions for a new edition of his history of the American Revolution, *Histoire des troubles de l'Amérique Anglaise*. Unlike Demeunier, however, Soulés was somewhat reluctant to automatically accept a great deal of Jefferson's extensive suggestions and commentary.

3. TJ, "Autobiography," published in *Writings*, 55.

4. Peterson, *Thomas Jefferson and the New Nation*, 248.

5. The "Act for Establishing Religious Freedom" in Virginia is discussed in chapter 12 on TJ as a "Legal Advocate"; while the murder of Logan's family and Logan's dramatic speech that followed are addressed extensively in chapter 14 on TJ as a "Critic of Orators and Oratory."

6. *Notes on the State of Virginia*, 162–63. In many respects, Jefferson's expressions on slavery in Query XVIII upheld his first criterion for historical writing. As we will see in chapter 16, however, many of the views on African Americans Jefferson advanced in the *Notes* were quite negative and disturbing in nature.

7. Ibid., 110–29.

8. TJ to Chastellux, June 7, 1785, in *Writings*, 799–800.

9. TJ to James Monroe, June 17, 1785, in *Writings*, 804–805.

10. Even on the question of racial inferiority, "Jefferson tried to apply the scientific methodology and the governing ideas of the eighteenth century Enlightenment. . . ." According to John Chester Miller: "In subjecting American blacks to scientific scrutiny, Jefferson sought to observe all the canons of eighteenth century science: to reach no definitive conclusions without factual data to support them and to keep an open, sceptical, and detached mind until all the evidence had been assembled. Jefferson regarded himself as an impartial, wholly objective observer who viewed 'the gradations in the races of animals with the eye of philosophy.' He prided himself upon his unremitting enmity to irrationalism, superstition, prejudice, and dogmatic authority—none of which, he said, entered in the slightest degree into the comparative study of whites and blacks he undertook in the *Notes on Virginia*." *The Wolf by the Ears: Thomas Jefferson and Slavery* (New York: The Free Press, 1977), 46.

11. The far more contentious problem—one that would haunt Jefferson throughout the last two centuries—was his discussion of slavery and the characteristics of African Americans. This issue is addressed in detail in chapter 16.

12. TJ, *Notes on the State of Virginia*, 118–29.

13. Jefferson also had this revised constitution included in the 1787 Stockdale edition of the *Notes*. *Notes on the State of Virginia*, 209–22.

14. *Notes on the State of Virginia*, Query XIX on "Manufactures," 164–65.

15. *Notes on the State of Virginia*, Query IV on "Mountains," 19.

16. *Notes on the State of Virginia*, Query V on "Cascades," 25.

17. Maria Cosway to TJ, February 15, 1787, in Boyd, 11: 149.

18. Francis Kinloch to TJ, April 26, 1789, in Boyd, 15: 71.

19. Perhaps the most direct assault against the incendiary Query XIV was written by David Walker three years after Jefferson's death. See Charles M. Wiltse, ed., *David Walker's Appeal, In Four Articles; Together With a Preamble, to the Coloured Citizens of the World, But In Particular, And Very Expressly, To Those of the United States of America* (New York: Hill and Wang, 1965).

20. In addition to the analyses of the influence of Jefferson's European experiences on his political philosophy, there are many more general studies of Jefferson's years in Paris. See William Howard Adams, *The Paris Years of Thomas Jefferson* (New Haven: Yale University Press, 1997); Edward Dumbauld, *Thomas Jefferson: American Tourist* (Norman: University of Oklahoma Press, 1946); Howard C. Rice Jr., *Thomas Jefferson's Paris* (Princeton: Princeton University Press, 1976); and George Green Shackelford, *Thomas Jefferson's Travels in Europe, 1784–89* (Baltimore: Johns Hopkins University Press, 1995). See also the volumes cited in note 1.

21. TJ to Edward Carrington, December 21, 1787, in Boyd, 12: 446–47.

22. Peterson, *Thomas Jefferson and the New Nation*, 332.

23. TJ to John Adams, August 30, 1787, in Boyd, 12: 67.

24. TJ to James Madison, January 30, 1787, in Boyd, 11: 95.

25. TJ to James Madison, August 28, 1789, in Boyd, 15: 366.

26. TJ, "Autobiography," in *Writings*, 92–94.

27. TJ to James Madison, August 2, 1787, in Boyd, 11: 664.

28. TJ, "Autobiography," in *Writings*, 92.

29. TJ to James Madison, September 6, 1789, in Boyd, 15: 392–97.

30. Boyd, 15: 384.

31. Bernard Bailyn, *Faces of Revolution: Personalities and Themes in the Struggle for American Independence* (New York: Knopf, 1990), 25.

32. TJ to James Madison, September 6, 1789, in Boyd, 15: 397.

33. Boyd, 15: 390.

34. TJ to John Jay, February 5, 1788, in Boyd, 12: 563–64.

35. TJ to Thomas Lee Shippen, March 11, 1789, in Boyd, 14: 639.

36. TJ to George Washington, May 2, 1788, in Boyd, 13: 128.

37. TJ to Thomas Lee Shippen, March 11, 1789, in Boyd, 14: 638.

38. *Writings*, 956–59.

39. TJ to Thomas Paine, July 11, 1789, in Boyd, 15: 266.

40. TJ to Abigail Adams, February 22, 1787, in Boyd, 11: 174.

41. TJ to Richard Price, July 17, 1789, in Boyd, 15: 280.

42. TJ to Maria Cosway, Paris, July 25, 1789, in Boyd, 15: 305.

43. TJ to William Stephens Smith, November 13, 1787, in Boyd, 12: 356.

44. In regard to this passage, Dumas Malone wrote: "what he was really emphasizing was the greater social peace of republican America than despotic Europe." *Jefferson and the Rights of Man*, 166. Earlier in his tenure as American Minister to France, Jefferson made the following observation about "the vaunted scene of Europe" to Charles Bellini: ". . . you are, perhaps, curious to know how this new scene has struck a savage of the mountains of America. Not advantageously, I assure you. I find the general fate of humanity here, most deplorable. The truth of Voltaire's observation, offers itself perpetually, that every man here must be either the hammer or the anvil." TJ to Charles Bellini, September 30, 1785, in *Writings*, 833.

45. See TJ to George Washington, May 2, 1788, in Boyd, 13: 128; and TJ, "Autobiography," published in *Writings*, 92.

46. TJ to Diodati, August 3, 1789, in *Writings*, 958.

47. Joseph J. Ellis, *American Sphinx: The Character of Thomas Jefferson* (New York: Knopf, 1997), 107.

48. See Daniel Webster, "Notes of Mr. Jefferson's Conversation 1824 at Monticello," 1825, in Charles M. Wiltse, et al., eds., *The Papers of Daniel Webster: Correspondence*, 7 vols. (Hanover, N.H: Dartmouth College by the University Press of New England, 1974–1986), 1: 371–78.

# CHAPTER FOURTEEN

~

# Critic of Orators and Oratory

On Christmas Day, 1820, Jefferson wrote to George Otis, assessing one of Virginia's most renowned colonial and Revolutionary War era orators: "Mr. [Richard Henry] Lee," he said, "was considered as an orator and eloquent, but not in that style which had much weight in such an assembly of men that Congress was. Frothy, flimsy, verbose, with a musical voice and chaste language, he was a good pioneer, but not an efficient reasoner. . . ."[1] Almost five years later, as he engaged in reminiscences with Daniel Webster who had come to visit him in Monticello, Jefferson offered a critique of the speaking style of Samuel Adams—a man he had come to admire as one of the most important patriots in the Revolutionary War period:

> For depth of purpose, zeal, sagacity, no man in Congress exceeded, if any equalled, Samuel Adams; and none did more than he to originate and sustain revolutionary measures in Congress. But he could not speak; he had a hesitating, grunting manner.[2]

These two episodes show that Jefferson often used his knowledge of rhetorical canons and principles, and, even more important, his experiences as an observer to evaluate the oratorical practices of his contemporaries.

Our purpose in this chapter is to look at samples of Jefferson's rhetorical criticism of several representative public communicators with whom he had worked in public assemblies or related gatherings, and of Logan whom he did not know. The first category of speakers includes two influential men whose reputations were enhanced by their skill as debaters. The second category consists of two speakers—Patrick Henry and Indian leader Logan—whom Jefferson regarded as eloquent orators capable of presenting sublime images that stimulated the imagination and the passions.

Before we analyze these samples of criticism, however, it is necessary to review briefly the principal sources that profoundly shaped Jefferson's ideas on how to assess the worth of a rhetorical production. The most influential of these sources, all of which had an important place in his library, were Longinus's *On the Sublime*, Lord Kames' *Elements of Criticism*, and Hugh Blair's *Lectures on Rhetoric and Belles Lettres*. One of the primary reasons these works interested Jefferson was their broad-based, enduring appeal. Not surprisingly, therefore, the rhetorical trends which were popular in the last half of the eighteenth and first quarter of the nineteenth centuries—classicism, rationalism, and romanticism—all found degrees of relevance in the teachings of Longinus, Kames, and Blair.

# The Roots of Jefferson's Ideas on Criticism

## Longinus's *On the Sublime*

Longinus's celebrated treatise, first published about 200 A.D., was relatively unknown to modern rhetoricians until a translation with a commentary by Boileau-Despreaux dramatically appeared in 1674. The impact of the publication was immediate and profound. French and English scholars developed a compelling interest in the potential that such criteria as taste, beauty, and sublimity had for the field of rhetorical criticism. Their imagination was stirred by Longinus's claim that the goal of sublime discourse "is not to persuade the audience but rather to transport them out of themselves." The way to use this potential, he noted, was to rely on five genuine sources of the sublime: (1) "the command of full blooded ideas"; (2) "the inspiration of vehement emotion"; (3) figures of thought; (4) figures of speech; and (5) "dignity and elevation." Here Longinus was suggesting that when a rhetor combines profound ideas with powerful emotion and nobility of phrase, he transports the audience to the highest possible level. So crucial is this ability, he asserted, that one may redeem "all his mistakes by a single touch of sublimity and true excellence."[3]

These ideas on the sublime helped form a solid foundation upon which to build and launch the belletristic movement. Moreover, for Jefferson, as we will later see, they gave him significant insights for understanding and appreciating the power of Henry's oratory and Logan's moving speech.

## Kames's *Elements of Criticism*

When Lord Kames wrote his *Elements* in 1762, he was well prepared to plow fresh ground in the area of the fine arts. He had become well ac-

quainted with the teachings of Longinus; he had been the principal inspiration for setting up a series of public lectures on rhetoric and belles
lettres to be delivered by Adam Smith in Edinburgh; and he had wisely
incorporated into his theory of criticism some of the salient ideas advanced by the epistemologists. What he had to say on rhetorical criticism, therefore, captured the attention of Jefferson.

Starting with the premise that there was a strong relationship between
taste and the moral sense, Kames drew these comparisons: Both of these
elements were "rooted in human nature"; both had as their goal to "discover what is right and what is wrong"; and both could be improved or
strengthened through exercise and reason. By connecting the dimension
of virtue to taste, Kames sought to elevate criticism to a level approaching that occupied by science. In doing this, he called for a form of argument based on the inductive, not the deductive method of reasoning.
When rendering an evaluation, therefore, a critic is constrained to use a
plan that ascends "gradually to principles, from facts and experiments, instead of beginning with the former, handled abstractly, and descending to
the latter." These ideas made it easy for Kames to conclude that "by
means of these principles, common to all men, a wonderful uniformity is
preserved among the emotions and feelings of different individuals. . . ."[4]
Judging from the samples that we analyze below, Jefferson as a critic reflected the influence of Kames's contentions that rhetorical criticism was
an argument-centered enterprise that makes use of reasons based on
virtue and concrete supporting data epitomizing the commonsense principles shared by humankind as a whole.[5]

## Blair's *Lectures on Rhetoric and Belles Lettres*

Where Longinus featured sublimity and Kames stressed the nature of taste
and its relationship to virtue, Blair succeeded in melding these concepts in
such a clear and thorough manner that George Saintsbury declared that
he "is to be very particularly commended for accepting to the full the important truth that 'Rhetoric' in modern terms really means 'Criticism.'"[6]
Defining taste as "the power of receiving pleasure from the beauties of nature and art," Blair concurred with Kames that this concept responds to
reason and exercise. He also reaffirmed the notion that taste at its highest
incorporates appeals to the understanding and to one's feelings as well.
Similarly, he argued, as did Kames, that a "true" taste must coincide "with
the general sentiments of men" and be based on sound reasoning.

Blair's pedagogical method of explaining rhetorical elements in clear,
concise, and vivid language enabled him to demonstrate how sublimity

and beauty—the two main sources of the pleasure of taste—may stir the imagination by rendering it possible for an observer to be moved by the vastness, power, and force of infinite space, the oceans, and heavens; by a magnanimous and heroic spirit; and by the expression of bold and pathetic thoughts in language that is precise and elevated. What made these principles so important to Blair was the role they play in criticism, which he defined as the application of reason and good sense to the pleasures of nature and art.[7] All of these points were illustrated by Blair's practice of critical evaluation of a work of a particular author.

When in 1784 Jefferson arrived in France, he was familiar with and devoted to the subject of taste. He saw in this concept a useful instrument for elevating the culture for the newly emerging American nation. For taste, he came to believe with Kames and Blair, was not merely applicable to the area of discourse. It also was a crucial facet of the fine arts in general. Consequently, when he received word from Madison that the first brick of the new state capitol building in Richmond would soon be laid, he sounded a warning that the fundamental challenge facing the citizens of Virginia was not the eventual cost of the project, but whether his architectural design would meet the standards of a "national good taste." In words approximating the language used by Kames in dedicating his book on *Elements* to the king, Jefferson said: "You see I am an enthusiast on the subject of the arts. But it is an enthusiasm of which I am not ashamed, as its object is to improve the taste of my countrymen, to increase their reputation, to reconcile to them the respect of the world, and procure them its praise."[8] One of the ways to accomplish this end, Jefferson thought, was to promote the practice of a type of discourse that might function as a model of a universally accepted taste.

# Reflections on Two Debaters: John Adams and James Madison

John Adams and James Madison shared one vitally significant rhetorical trait that impressed Jefferson. They were highly intelligent and well-informed leaders who were effective debaters in upholding republican principles during the formative years of the American nation. The arguments they used, moreover, met the standards required by an appropriate taste and a moral sense inspired by a benevolent spirit and dedicated to the promotion of the public good. Jefferson's perceptions of these political colleagues as speakers were influenced both by his philosophy of taste and criticism and by his observations of them in action in the political arena.

## John Adams

Jefferson first met Adams in the Second Continental Congress, then served with him abroad as a diplomat, and, finally, as his vice president. But his most vivid memory of Adams—one that remained permanently etched in his mind—was the unmatched influence he exerted on the floor of Congress during the debates on the Declaration of Independence. In 1787, he suggested to Madison that Adams as a speaker occasionally displayed "a degree of vanity" and irritability, but that these faults—the only shortcomings that could possibly be ascribed to him—were more than offset by the profundity of "his views" and the accuracy of "his judgment." He then concluded his brief analysis with these words: Adams "is so amiable that I pronounce you will love him if ever you become acquainted with him. He would be, as he was, a great man in *Congress*."[9]

As the years passed, Jefferson continued to praise Adams's performance in the debates on the Declaration, using such descriptive statements as these: He "was a powerful advocate on the floor of Congress"; "our main pillar in debate"; a "host in our councils"; and a supporter of the Declaration "with zeal and ability, fighting fearlessly for every word of it."[10] And, as noted previously, he argued against the deletion of Jefferson's attack on the slave trade. Near the end of Jefferson's life, he confided to Daniel Webster a more specific and penetrating insight into Adams's forensic skills: "John Adams was our Colossus on the floor. He was not graceful, nor elegant, nor remarkably fluent; but he came out occasionally, with a power of thought and expression that moved us from our seats."[11]

The preceding comments suggest that Adams's persuasive influence as a debater on the floor of Congress in 1776 was not, according to Jefferson, the result of a graceful manner, an elegant style, or a smooth delivery. Nor was it the result, as he told Madison in 1823, of the development of ideas hitherto unknown to his contemporaries. It was instead a natural outcome of the use of familiar, powerful, and virtuous themes responding to the exigencies of a rhetorical situation, "which, like the ceaseless action of gravity weighed on us by night and by day."[12] For this reason, Jefferson, aware of the relevance of the doctrines of taste and sublimity, could commend Adams for "a power of thought and expression that moved us from our seats."

# James Madison

Unlike Adams, who was the dominating rhetorical force in the debates on the Declaration, Madison, when serving in the Virginia Convention of 1776, initially was content to be an interested observer rather than an active participant. But within a short time this diffidence disappeared and, according to Jefferson, Madison began utilizing his talent as a debater in such a convincing way that he became "first of every assembly afterwards of which he" was "a member."[13]

What was it that Jefferson saw in Madison that caused him to believe his great friend and "collaborator" was an ideal debater? He answered this question clearly and decisively in his "Autobiography." First, he said, Madison "acquired a self-possession" and "extensive information" that buttressed "the rich resources of his luminous and discriminating mind. . . ." His second important speaking tendency was his practice of "never wandering from his subject into vain declamation. . . ." He chose instead to pursue his theme "closely, in language pure, classical, and copious, soothing always the feelings of his adversaries by civilities and softness of expression. . . ."[14]

These two all-encompassing rhetorical characteristics reveal Madison as a brilliant, knowledgeable debater who used sound, relevant, and clearly organized arguments channeled in elegant language and a pleasing conversational pattern of delivery. From Jefferson's perspective, therefore, Madison the debater had an understanding and appreciation of the value of rhetorical logic, of personal proof designed to ingratiate an audience, and of the plain, "middling," and "elevated" forms of style. He also knew that legislative debate, as a general rule, should not be thought of as an oratorical enterprise featuring declamatory techniques, but as a type of face-to-face communication requiring a mastery of the issues under discussion and an ability to disagree with an opponent in a congenial manner. These rhetorical attributes were evident in the debates in Virginia on the ratification of the Constitution. Commenting on this protracted rhetorical situation, Jefferson asserted that Madison "sustained the new constitution in all its parts, bearing off the palm against the logic of George Mason, and the fervid declamation of Mr. Henry."

As was his practice when involved in the process of rhetorical criticism, Jefferson also commented on a speaker's moral sense as it revealed itself not only in the debate but in the private and public life as well. In speaking of Madison, after having had a chance to assess his entire public career, Jefferson could render this claim about his values: "With [his] consummate powers were united a pure and spotless virtue which no calumny has ever attempted to sully." This statement has an increased impact when we note that it was made during Madison's retirement years.

Because of Madison's supremacy as a debater, Jefferson often asked him to rebut in writing the Federalist arguments of Hamilton and others on the grounds that he alone had the talent to do so. He likewise expressed appreciation to Madison for the significant contributions he made to the "National Convention of 1787," for what he helped accomplish in re-forming the acts and laws of Virginia, and in particular for his success in getting "the act of religious freedom" enacted into law by the Virginia As-sembly in 1786.[15] Here was a debater, in brief, who, Jefferson felt, spoke and wrote with a taste and beauty that exemplified the principles em-phasized by Kames and Blair.

# The Oratory of Patrick Henry and Logan

## Patrick Henry

When William Wirt was preparing his biography of Henry, he wrote sev-eral letters to Jefferson asking him to give critical impressions of the man and the orator who was regarded as a seminal leader and eloquent spokesman on behalf of the American Revolution. Two of Jefferson's de-tailed responses show the care he took in making certain that he had nec-essary supporting documents to reinforce his memory of speeches and events. On August, 14, 1814, for example, he said: "I have been laying under contribution my memory, my private papers, the printed records, gazettes and pamphlets in my possession, to answer the inquiries of your letter of July 27, and I will give you the result as correctly as I can."[16] In August of the following year, Jefferson again wrote to Wirt, this time re-fusing to grant him permission to quote some general comments he had made on an address delivered by Henry on a loan case. He explained his refusal by pointing out that he was not present when the address was given, nor did he know anything pertaining to it "but by hearsay from others."[17]

For modern historians and rhetorical critics, Jefferson has become a valuable source as an analyst of Henry because of his firsthand knowledge gained from experience at the scene of action, and because of his keen ob-servation techniques and note-taking practices derived from a finely honed sense of taste, beauty, and sublimity. What these authors have dis-covered is an unusually high degree of ambivalence on Jefferson's part whenever he described Henry.

Perhaps we can only understand Henry the orator fully by beginning with a discussion of what Jefferson perceived to be his principal weaknesses. These visible shortcomings, stemming largely from Henry's inadequate legal training and aversion to reading and study, Jefferson explained by vividly developed narratives reported in letters, conversations, and in his "Autobiography." In one of his stories, Jefferson told Wirt how the two men met for the first time, and sketched his impressions of Henry's social characteristics, conversational habits, and legal study. The period was late 1759 and early 1760 when Jefferson, not yet seventeen years of age, was on his way to enroll at the College of William and Mary. During the journey, he stopped off at Hanover, where he spent a fortnight in the company of Henry; together they participated in the "revelries of the neighborhood" and the Christmas season.

On this occasion, Jefferson asserted, Henry's "manners had something of a coarseness of the society he had frequented; his passion was fiddling, dancing and pleasantry. He excelled in the last, and attached everyone to him." But, he added, Henry made no effort to take part in serious conversation although he had an opportunity to do so because of the presence of a scientist who enjoyed engaging in dialogue. This reluctance to take advantage of a potentially rewarding rhetorical situation, according to Jefferson, prevented Henry from revealing the nature and quality of his mind and the extent of the information he had acquired. It was during this two-week period, moreover, that Henry confessed "he had read law not more than six weeks" before receiving his license to practice before the Bar.[18]

Jefferson remained constant in his belief that Henry neglected reading and study throughout his career. As a recognition of his popularity and influence as an orator, Henry received from Jefferson a copy of *A Summary View of the Rights of British America* for the purpose of using his talents to build on its arguments. But when he remained silent on the work, Jefferson felt motivated to offer this critical reflection in his "Autobiography": "Whether Mr. Henry disapproved the ground taken, or was too lazy to read it (for he was the laziest man in reading I ever knew) I never learned; but he communicated it to nobody."[19]

Perhaps the most telling account of Henry's reading habits and lack of general knowledge comes from Jefferson's conversation with Daniel Webster in 1824. After declaring that his Virginia colleague "was a man of very little knowledge of any sort" who "read nothing, and had no books," he related this story: "Returning one November from Albemarle court, [Henry] borrowed of me Hume's Essays, in two volumes, saying he should have leisure in the winter for reading. In the spring he returned them, and declared he had not been able to go further than twenty or thirty pages in the first volume." Upon completing his anecdote, Jefferson sought to give further emphasis to the point he was making on Henry's glaring lack of scholarly interests by suggesting that Wirt was wrong in claiming that Henry "read Plutarch every year. I doubt whether he ever read a volume of it in his life."[20]

This weakness spawned other faults that were similarly evident to Jefferson. "He wrote almost nothing," averred Jefferson, because "he could not write."[21] To support this critical judgment, Jefferson recalled an incident which occurred "in the first session of the lst [Continental] Congress which met in September 1774." Because of Henry's "splendid" oral eloquence in the early days of this session, he was asked to take the responsibility, as head of a designated committee, to draw up a "petition to the King. . . ." When it was reported, the draft of the petition proved to be "unsuccessful," and "was recommitted for amendment." To modify this poorly written petition, "John Dickinson was added to the committee & a new draught prepared by him was passed."[22]

Not only did Henry's lack of research and reflection weaken his writing effectiveness, observed Jefferson, but in some rhetorical settings led to the construction of arguments marked by poor logic and desultory arrangement patterns. This was strikingly evident when Henry served in the Continental Congress. "As soon as they [the Congress] came to specific matters, to sober reasoning and solid argumentation," Jefferson noted, Henry "had the good sense to perceive that his declamation however excellent in it's proper place, had no weight at all in such an assembly as that, of cool-headed, reflecting, judicious men."[23]

A final major criticism rendered against Henry was his extreme Anti-Federal position during the debates on the ratification of the Constitution. In this phase of his career, Jefferson believed, Henry had departed from many of his early republican principles. Moreover, Jefferson believed that Henry's vigorous opposition to the Constitution, however sincere, was a misuse of the oratorical talents he so ably had displayed in the Revolutionary War period. Despite his own reservations about some of the fundamental aspects of the new government, Jefferson could understand why Madison, despite vigorous opposition from Henry and others in their native state of Virginia, eventually won the day with his arguments in support of the Constitution.[24]

The foregoing discussion, based on Jefferson's critique, has portrayed Henry as a leader who read little, wrote poorly, failed to produce sound and relevant arguments in the Continental Congress, and stood on the wrong side of history in the debates on the Constitution. But these weaknesses as pointed out by Jefferson were only a part of the real image projected by Virginia's greatest orator. How could Jefferson, it may be asked, be so willing to present enthusiastically another side of Henry the orator? Quite clearly, the faults that have been highlighted dealt with ideas that were in direct opposition to his own philosophy of discourse and principles of virtue. For study, books, writing ability, and closely reasoned arguments in any rhetorical situation were highly prized by Jefferson as signs of an educated person and effective communicator. The primary explanation of his divided opinion may be found in the following statement, cited previously, from Longinus's *On the Sublime*: An orator may redeem "all his mistakes by a single touch of sublimity and true excellence."

Henry's reputation as a sublime orator received a strong boost in his famous Stamp Act Speech delivered in 1765. Jefferson, then a student of law under the tutelage of George Wythe, stood "at the door of the lobby of the House of Burgesses" in Williamsburg as Henry spoke. It was, in his opinion, a virtuoso performance that he would never forget. He told Wirt forty-nine years after the event that he still remembered "the cry of treason, the pause of Mr. Henry at the name of George the III, and the presence of mind with which he closed his sentence, and baffled the charge vociferated."[25] When he wrote his "Autobiography" six years later, he described Henry's presentation on this occasion with this frequently cited line: "He appeared to me to speak as Homer wrote. . . ."[26]

Jefferson recalled two other memorable instances in which Henry used arguments and language control to defeat a pending motion he thought was inappropriate and unjust. The first event occurred in the House of Burgesses in 1762, again while he was a William and Mary student. John Robinson, a delegate from Hanover County and the speaker and treasurer of the house, devised a plan to the legislature to have some of his private debts transferred to the public. Unwilling to have a plan adopted that was based on self-interest at the expense of the public good, "Mr. Henry," asserted Jefferson, "attacked the scheme . . . in that style of bold, grand and overwhelming eloquence, for which he became so justly celebrated afterwards." So persuasive was Henry's speech that "he carried with him all the members of the upper counties, and left a minority composed merely of aristocracy of the country."

The second discourse episode, which took place in the House of Burgesses on an unspecified date, likewise focused on an unjust and discriminatory issue. The motion before the House was a proposal to provide relief to a group of wealthy property owners by delaying the designated time in which they were to pay their "contracted debts." Convinced that the motivation behind the proposition was based on favoritism for the rich, Henry delivered a stinging rebuke, using words that were "indelibly impressed" on Jefferson's "memory" for decades to come. "Sir," said he, "is it proposed then to reclaim the spendthrift from his dissipation and extravagance, by filling his pockets with money!" These remarks, Jefferson recalled, "laid open with so much energy the spirit of favoritism on which the proposition was founded, and the abuses to which it would lead, that it was crushed in its birth."[27]

Jefferson also was privileged to be present as a delegate to the Virginia Convention, which began on March 20 and adjourned on March 27, 1775. It was during these sessions that Henry delivered his historic "Give Me Liberty or Death" speech. The address was in support of the resolution that the colony of Virginia be placed "into a posture of defence, and for preparing a plan of embodying and disciplining such a number of men as might be sufficient for that purpose."[28] Edmund Randolph, in his "Essay on the Revolutionary History of Virginia," gave this penetrating portrait of Henry's eloquent effort:

> It was Patrick Henry born in obscurity, poor, and without the advantages of literature, rousing the genius of his country, and binding a band of patriots together to hurl defiance at the tyranny of so formidable a nation as Great Britain. This enchantment was spontaneous obedience to the workings of the soul. When he uttered what commanded respect for himself, he solicited no admiring look from those, who surrounded him. If he had, he must have been abashed by meeting every eye fixed upon him. He paused, but he paused full of some rising eruption of eloquence. When he sat down, his sounds vibrated so loudly if not in the ears, at least in the memory of his audience, that no other member, not even his friend who was to second him was yet adventurous enough to interfere with that voice, which had so recently subdued and captivated.[29]

Not the least of those who were captivated was Jefferson. Stirred by Henry's rousing address, he ignored his natural inclination to remain silent during a contentious public debate, and, upon gaining the floor, proceeded to deliver a profound, warmly argued speech in support of the resolution.[30] After a period of fifty-four years had passed, Jefferson wrote to Adams stating that Henry's resolutions, "far short of independance, flew like lightning thro' every paper, and kindled both sides of the Atlantic. . . ."[31]

An overwhelming body of evidence derived from his own personal experience, as we have seen, persuaded Jefferson that Henry was a powerful
orator who had the power to mesmerize his audiences. These comments
by Jefferson typified his responses:

> Mr. Henry's talents as a popular orator . . . were great indeed; such as I
> never heard from any other man. But torrents of sublime eloquence from
> Mr. Henry . . . prevailed. His eloquence . . . was impressive and sublime,
> beyond what can be imagined. His powers over a jury were so irresistible
> that he received great fees for his services. . . .[32]

Several explanations may be offered to show why Jefferson was so inclined to use the word "sublime" as a descriptive term regarding Henry's
oratory. In this connection, it is instructive to observe that Jefferson's employment of this rhetorical element as a mode of criticism was strongly
emphasized when critiquing Henry's discourses in the three years preceding and during the Revolutionary War. For it was during this quest for
freedom and independence that a strong need existed for someone to
come forward who demonstrated a "command of full blooded ideas"—a
requirement listed by Longinus as the first source of the sublime. And it
was during this tumultuous period that the two men shared republican
principles that were reflected in their discourses.

Jefferson and his contemporaries could not help but be moved, therefore, when they heard the Stamp Act Speech and the "Give Me Liberty
or Death" address, for in both instances a noble idea calling for action on
behalf of the public good was under discussion. It was, they believed, the
road to happiness. Henry's mastery of the "full blooded" idea prompted
Jefferson to say to Webster: "He was as well-suited to the times as any
man ever was, and it is not now easy to say what we should have done
without Patrick Henry." He then added, in words that later caused some
discontent in Massachusetts, that Henry "was far before all in maintaining the spirit of the Revolution."[33]

There was a second compelling reason why Jefferson felt comfortable
in calling Henry a sublime orator. It was the way that Henry channeled
his message of discontent against British oppression. When under the influence of a passion for the cause which propelled him, he apparently
could transport himself and the audience through the power of his "poetical fancy," "sublime imagination," and "lofty and overwhelming diction. . . ."[34]

There was something magical also in Henry's physical presence and
manner in front of an audience. Possessing a "full size," a "free and manly

voice," and a penchant for following the rules of decorum, he identified with his audience notwithstanding his use of a "vulgar and vicious" pronunciation. Fortunately, this practice "was forgotten while he was speaking." In some cases, the listener became so entranced with Henry's appearance and power of delivery that the message itself was sometimes blurred or lost. Jefferson illustrated this idea by reference to his own experience: "When he had spoken, in opposition to my opinion, had produced a great effect, and I myself been highly delighted and moved, I have asked myself when he ceased: 'What the d--l has he said?'. . . . I could never answer the inquiry."[35]

On the surface, the foregoing episode would tend to support Garry Wills's claim that "Jefferson . . . thought Henry worked most of his wonders by pure music without logic."[36] This assessment, however, represents an incomplete analysis of what Jefferson believed about Henry's oratory. When he told the above story, it was highly likely that he was describing the enormous power emanating from Henry's unique delivery pattern. We have noticed, for example, that Jefferson knew exactly what Henry was saying in the Stamp Act Speech, in his attack on the proposal recommending special treatment for the landed gentry in paying their debts, and in his "Give Me Liberty or Death" address. Indeed, we may be able to assert with confidence that he believed that Henry's Revolutionary period speeches fulfilled the five requirements for the sublime: "a command of full blooded ideas," the "inspiration of a vehement emotion," and effective use of figures of speech and thought, and a "dignity and elevation" of style and sentiment. In accomplishing this end, Henry had illustrated an important element in Jefferson's philosophy of imagination.

Jefferson's critical evaluation of Henry as an orator has withstood the test of time for the past two centuries. The conclusions he drew, largely through the narrative paradigm, conformed to the concepts of taste shared by his contemporaries. Those who knew Henry and had heard him speak were conscious of his lack of scholarship, his paucity of literary and philosophical knowledge, and of his sparse training in the field of law. They also understood his tendency to break some general rules while debating.[37] At the same time, however, they recognized and appreciated his tremendous ability to use eloquence in tune with the prevailing sentiments of the revolutionary age in which he spoke. Finally, because of Jefferson's talent as an observer, his knowledge of the meaning of taste and sublimity, and his competence as a writer, a critic, and a storyteller, he was able to provide an enduring portrait of Henry in action on the public stage.[38]

# Logan

As Jefferson turned his attention to Logan, a Mingo war leader, he was confronted with a different type of rhetorical problem as a critic. He had seen Adams, Madison, Henry, and other contemporary political spokesmen in action in the public arena. As a result, what he had to say about their discourse practices was deeply rooted in his personal experiences, as well as in the philosophy of virtue he had developed from years of study. Moreover, his critiques of these colleagues have become an important part of our understanding of early American history. By contrast, however, it seems certain he had never heard of Logan until "Dunmore's War," or "Cresap's War," as it was sometimes called, began in the late spring and early summer of 1774 on what was then described as the western frontier. All of this changed, however, following his receipt of a copy of the speech that Logan had prepared for delivery at the peace treaty. Little did Jefferson realize that his criticism of this address would set in motion an animated dialogue, consisting of charges and countercharges, that would last for two centuries. The story of how this controversy unfolded and persisted is a remarkable event in the history of rhetorical criticism in America.

Jefferson's long-held interest in Indian affairs was heightened in 1774. As explorers and settlers from Virginia moved westward into the far reaches of Pennsylvania and into territories that later were to become parts of West Virginia and Ohio, tension between these citizens and the Indians who occupied the land steadily increased, often leading to skirmishes that grew into battles. In one of the raids led by white men, many members of the family of Logan were murdered. This, in turn, led to widescale confrontations between several Indian tribes and Virginia soldiers under the overall command of Lord Dunmore, who was then governor of the colony of Virginia. This major encounter, which lasted approximately six months, led to the surrender of the Indians, following their defeat in the Battle of Point Pleasant on October 10, 1774. Along with other leaders, Logan was asked to attend the peace treaty held at Camp Charlotte, but refused to do so. He did, however, send a brief speech which had been translated into English by General John Gibson, his brother-in-law with whom he had a close contact through the years.

When Jefferson received details of what had happened to Logan's family, of the signing of the peace treaty, and of the favorable response to Logan's speech which had been read at the gathering, he obtained a copy of the address, presumably from Lord Dunmore.[39] Several years later, while writing his *Notes on the State of Virginia*, he seized upon the opportunity to reprint and assess the speech as a means of answering the French naturalist Comte de Buffon, who had cast aspersions upon the intellectual and artistic talents of Native Americans. Nature, Buffon argued, belittled the "productions" on the American side of the Atlantic. In his famous *Natural History*, which Jefferson had carefully examined, Buffon, drawing upon travel books and conversations with reputed authorities, concluded that American "natives were and are still savages" who were vastly inferior to their counterparts in Europe. He explained this disparity by alleging that American traditions, the lack of variety and diversity in social educational pursuits, and the climate combined to produce an uninspiring and relatively static ambience for mental and cultural advancement. This negative assessment led Buffon to infer that native-born Americans—both the Indians and the families of immigrants who had settled in what he still would have considered to be the new world—had accomplished little in the arts and sciences. He worded this claim in these unfavorable terms:

> That the Americans are a new people seems indisputable, when we reflect on the smallness of their number, their ignorance, and the little progress the most civilized among them had made in the arts.[40]

Buffon's damaging two-pronged indictment had disparaged the mental, physical, and artistic limitations both of the American Indians and of the European immigrants who had migrated to the colonies. With respect to the latter group, the French author Guillaume François Raynal reinforced Buffon's argument with this assertion: "One must be astonished that America has not yet produced one good poet, one able mathematician, one man of genius in a single art or a single science."[41] To answer what he perceived to be Abbé Raynal's mistaken and unjust analysis, Jefferson, first of all, argued that it took centuries for the Greeks, Romans, French, and English to produce a Homer, a Virgil, a Racine, a Voltaire, a Shakespeare, and a Milton. By contrast, he noted, America, unlike these ancient civilizations and modern countries, is a young nation that needs far more time to develop poets of comparable genius. He then responded to Raynal's claim that America had not produced "one able mathematician, one man of genius in a single art or science," by warmly praising the accomplishments of George Washington as a military leader, Benjamin Franklin as a physicist, and David Rittenhouse as an astronomer.[42]

But Jefferson directed his strongest refutation during this rhetorical episode at Buffon for his stance on the Native Americans. His principal argument consisted of a description of Logan and his speech, which he described as a masterpiece of eloquence.[43] To prove this point, he reprinted an account of the discourse, which reads as follows:

> I appeal to any white man to say, if ever he entered Logan's cabin hungry, and he gave him not meat; if ever he came cold and naked, and he clothed him not. During the course of the last long and bloody war, Logan remained idle in his cabin, an advocate for peace. Such was my love for the whites, that my countrymen pointed as they passed, and said, "Logan is the friend of white men." I had even thought to have lived with you, but for the injuries of one man. Colonel Cresap, the last spring, in cold blood, and unprovoked, murdered all the relations of Logan, not sparing even my women and children. There runs not a drop of my blood in the veins of any living creature. This called on me for revenge. I have sought it: I have killed many: I have fully glutted my vengeance. For my country, I rejoice at the beams of peace. But do not harbour a thought that mine is the joy of fear. Logan never felt fear. He will not turn on his heel to save his life. Who is there to mourn for Logan?—Not one.[44]

Jefferson's evaluation of this speech, and his decision to include the analysis in his *Notes*, constitutes a landmark case in the history of American rhetorical criticism. The motivation that prompted the critique, the success he had in obtaining an authentic copy of the text, the amassing of materials to evaluate the reliability of Logan's claims, the application of the principles of virtue to analyze the message and style, and the painstaking approach used to answer his critics who charged he had been misled by Logan combine to demonstrate Jefferson's careful method as an informed critic of oratory and as a champion of the strong potential that American Indians possessed for achieving eloquence.

A first important step in examining Jefferson's performance as a rhetorical critic on this occasion is to ascertain the accuracy of the text he used for this analysis in the *Notes*. On January 20, 1775, a few weeks after Lord Dunmore had returned to Williamsburg from the frontier, the young James Madison wrote to his friend and college classmate William Bradford, stating: "I have not seen the following in print and it seems to be so just a specimen of Indian Eloquence and mistaken Valour that I think you will be pleased with it."[45] This significant version of Logan's address then was published by Bradford in his family's *Pennsylvania Journal* on February 1, 1775.[46] Although there is no evidence to show from whom Madison received his copy, we do know, argues Irving Brant, that it represents the first time the speech appeared in print.[47]

During this period, Jefferson, who made no references to Madison's text, recalled receiving his copy of the manuscript from Dunmore. Almost at once he wrote it down, along with factual details he had accumulated concerning the murder of Logan's family members, and inserted the data in his Account Book.[48] Since our task here is to determine at the outset the reliability of the speech Jefferson produced in the *Notes*, we have compared this text, first, with the one incorporated into the Account Book; and, second, with the version obtained by Madison.

We have found that except for several minor variations, the speech in the *Notes* was almost identical to that incorporated into the Account Book. These few substitutions in the *Notes* constitute the only changes that were made:

(1) "he" for "I" in sentence one.
(2) "love" for "affection" and "pointed" for "hooted" in sentence three.
(3) "murdered" for "cut off" and "and" for "or" in sentence five.
(4) "*living* creature" for "*human* creature" in sentence six.

Though slightly more extensive than the changes made in the Account Book version, the alterations included in the *Notes*, when contrasted with the Madison text, have little observable effect on the clarity of the meaning and the elegance of style. These changes may be summarized as follows:

| Madison's Copy | Copy in the Notes |
| --- | --- |
| "to *day*"[49] | "to *say*" |
| "*I* gave him" | "*he* gave him" |
| "*or* naked" | "*and* naked" |
| "*I gave him not clothing*" | "*he clothed him not*" |
| "*those of my own country*" | "*my countrymen*" |
| "*to live*" | "*to have lived*" |
| "*cut off*" | "*murdered*" |
| "*human* creature" | "*living* creature" |

From these comparisons, we may conclude with a high degree of probability that Jefferson's Account Book version of Logan's speech was the copy translated by Gibson and submitted to him by Dunmore.[50] We also are able to infer that the minor changes in the copy included in the *Notes* were introduced by Jefferson.[51] There can be little doubt, in sum, that at the time he printed the speech in the *Notes*, he had compelling reasons for assuming that it was a reliable text of what Logan had said.[52]

Before Jefferson could proceed to evaluate the speech and present his critique as a refutation of Buffon's argument that Native Americans were intellectually and artistically inferior to their European counterparts, he needed to discover the facts pertaining to the murder of Logan's family members. These he learned from reading newspaper accounts of events that had occurred on the frontier, and from numerous conversations he had with knowledgeable colleagues interested in the relations between the white men and the Indians. As a result, when he wrote down the speech in his Account Book early in 1775, he included in a preface a description of the specific details that played no small part in precipitating "Dunmore's War" and its aftermath.[53]

The story told by Jefferson—one he repeatedly affirmed was a commonly shared perspective by his contemporaries[54]—began with the statements: "In the spring of the year 1774, a robbery and murder was committed on an inhabitant of the frontier parts of Va by two Indians of the Shawanee nation." Instead of treating this incident as an isolated case, he added, "the neighboring whites were induced to punish it in a more summary way."[55] As the story continued, Jefferson, endorsing the views expressed by Logan in his speech, identified the American officer he, and many others, believed to be responsible for subsequent events that led to the death of Logan's family. In strongly worded terms, he asserted:

Colo(nel) Cresap, a man infamous for the many murders he has committed on those much injured people, collected a party of whites and proceeded down the river Kanhaway in quest of vengeance. Unhappily a canoe of women and children with one man only was seen coming from the opposite shore, unarmed, and expecting nothing less than an hostile attack from the whites. Cresap and his party concealed themselves on the bank of the river, and, the moment the canoe reached the shore, singled out their objects, and at one fire killed every person in it. This happened to be the family of Logan an Indian chief who had long and often distinguished himself as a friend of the whites. But this unworthy and cowardly return provoked his vengeance. He accordingly signalized himself in the war which ensued.[56]

The narration concluded with a brief description of how the Indians were defeated in a battle "fought on the banks of the Ohio," and how they "sued for peace."[57] With this development, the stage was now set for a treaty-signing ceremony that was to provide the rhetorical setting for the reading of Logan's speech.

In addition to his conviction that the factual details cited by Logan were correct, there was much in the speech that Jefferson admired. First of all, his preference for brevity and conciseness was satisfied with the fact that its length was only 197 words. Far more important was the nature of the arguments and style. From the beginning to the end, Logan used reasoning and language characterized by a blending of appeals to the understanding, the imagination, and the passions.

His first claim set forth the premise that his attitude through the years was marked by a feeling of benevolence toward the whites. In words that resembled the sentiments and language employed by St. Matthew in the New Testament, he declared: "I appeal to any white man to say, if ever he entered Logan's cabin hungry, and he gave him not meat; if ever he became cold and naked, and he clothed him not."[58] Then relying on the testimony of his comrades, he affirmed: "Such was my love for the whites, that my countrymen pointed as they passed, and said, 'Logan is the friend of white men.'" He concluded this argument with the words that before his personal tragedy, he "had even thought to have lived with you. . . ."[59]

It was against the background of the evidence he had shown to demonstrate his longstanding benevolent spirit toward the white man that Logan developed his second claim. Colonel (Captain)[60] Cresap and his men, he said, ignored the close relationship that Logan and the whites had enjoyed through the years, and wantonly and unjustly destroyed his family. He illustrated this point with graphic language designed to arouse the imagination and stir the passions of the audience. During "the last spring, in cold blood, and unprovoked," Cresap "murdered all the relations of Logan, not sparing even my women and children." The climax of this argument was phrased in these words: "There runs not a drop of my blood in the veins of any living creature."[61]

Logan asserted in his third claim that, although he had "glutted his vengeance" by murdering some whites in retaliation for the brutal massacre of his family, he was at heart a man of peace.[62] You must remember, he suggested, that "during the course of the last long and bloody war, Logan remained idle in his cabin, an advocate for peace." Before completing this argument, however, he wanted to make certain that his avowed yearning for peace would not be mistaken for fear. In fact, he asserted, "Logan never felt fear," nor would he "turn on his heel to save his life."

The speech ended with a poignant question and answer that showed the depth of his feeling of sadness resulting from the awesome tragedy he had experienced. "Who is there to mourn for Logan?—Not one."

Jefferson believed that Logan projected the image of a speaker who showed wisdom in the choice of arguments; justice in the moral statements he cited; temperance in asserting that he had a warm and moderate attitude toward the white men as a whole; and courage in his declarations against fear. He came through, in fine, as a practitioner of the four cardinal virtues articulated by the classical scholars. Moreover, his avowed benevolent spirit, as emphasized by Hutcheson and reaffirmed by Jefferson, was put into the service of the public good. These principles, as we have seen in previous discussions, were essential elements of Jefferson's philosophy of virtue.

When these carefully crafted arguments were channeled in language that was precise, vivid, and elevated, all of the faculties of the mind—the understanding, the imagination, the passions, and the will—were stimulated. The effect was a speech that fulfilled the requirements of taste, beauty, and sublimity. Nor could it be forgotten that this sample of eloquence came from an American Indian who was motivated by a desire to have himself and the members of his tribe maintain a familial bond with the whites. These factors gave to him and to his speech an exalted place in Jefferson's mind. "I may challenge the whole orations of Demosthenes and Cicero," he said, "and of any more eminent orator, if Europe has furnished more eminent to produce a single passage superior to the speech of Logan, a Mingo chief, to Lord Dunmore, when governor of this state."[63]

Jefferson's positive critique was consistent with the taste of other Americans, and of the British public as well. "It (the speech) flew through all the public papers of the continent," he noted, "and through the magazines and other periodical publications of Great Britain; and those who were boys at that day will now attest that the speech of Logan used to be given them as school exercise for repetition."[64]

For twenty-three years following its presentation at the peace treaty in October 1774, Logan's address, sometimes described as a "lament," continued to receive accolades. But then, while serving as vice president and primary spokesman for the Republican Party in 1797, Jefferson was surprised and disappointed to learn that some of his political opponents began to indict him for his active role in promoting and disseminating the speech. He was severely criticized in part for praising an address they believed could not have been written by a presumably uneducated Indian "savage." In taking this position, these critics suggested the speech was a forgery produced by Jefferson himself for the purpose of demonstrating to Buffon that he had erred in making disparaging remarks about the intellectual and artistic deficiencies of American natives. To this claim, Jefferson responded: "Whether Logan's or mine, it would still have been American." This claim was merely a preface to his declaration concerning the authenticity of the work. "But it is none of mine," he said; "and I yield it to whom it is due."[65]

The far more significant charge against Jefferson, in the eyes of the critics, was the allegation that he had endorsed a speech that contained false information regarding Captain Michael Cresap, the army officer who Logan had declared was the murderer of his family. To make matters worse, Jefferson had earlier referred to Cresap as "a man infamous for the many murders he has committed on those much injured people. . . ."

The most devastating attack leveled against Jefferson and Logan was that by Luther Martin, the first attorney general of the state of Maryland and the son-in-law of Michael Cresap. Ever since the *Notes* appeared in print, he was disturbed by what he perceived to be Logan's misinformed statements about the father of his wife and the grandfather of his children. At first, however, he was reluctant to comment publicly on the content of the speech and Jefferson's endorsement of it. But at the urging of the Cresap family, he launched a campaign a few months after his wife's death in 1796 to rebut the charges in the *Notes*.

His first major step was to write to James Fennell, a renowned British actor who was scheduled to present a program at College Hall in Philadelphia which included a selection on "The Story of Logan, the Mingo Chief." In this letter, dated March 30, 1797, Martin said: "You found that story and speech in Jefferson's Notes on Virginia; you found it related with such an air of authenticity, that it cannot be surprising that you should not suspect it to be *fiction*." He then explained that Jefferson, as a philosopher, had a hypothesis "to establish, or what is much the same thing, he had the hypothesis of Buffon to overthrow."[66]

The second phase of Martin's campaign to defend Cresap's actions on the western frontier in 1774 consisted of a series of eight letters between July 1797 and March 1798 that were published in *Porcupine's Gazette*, a Federalist organ. Martin addressed each of these letters to Jefferson and challenged him to offer documentary proof that Cresap was either directly or indirectly responsible for the murders and that the speech included in the *Notes* was authored by Logan. He next tauntingly asserted that no such proof could be found. What evidence was available, he noted, were indisputable facts showing that Cresap was not present at the scene of the crime; and that General John Gibson, Logan's so-called translator, was the actual author of the speech.

In these highly personalized letters, Martin affirmed that Cresap, instead of being an "infamous murderer," had risked his life on the frontier by protecting settlers from unwarranted raids. By contrast, he sarcastically pointed out, Jefferson was a proven coward who, while serving as governor of Virginia, fled from the state capital as the British invaded the state in the later stages of the Revolutionary War. Finally, in a vitriolic attack rebuking both Jefferson and Logan, Martin labeled the speech as an "unfounded story" based wholly on fiction, and described the "celebrated Mingo chief" as "an ignorant, insignificant, worthless savage, without merit and without consequence."[67]

After reading Martin's first letter, Jefferson was deeply troubled because of the overly personal and excessively "partisan" nature of its content.[68] At once he resolved to read none of the remaining letters which Martin had scheduled to follow, and announced to his friends a determination to continue his oft-stated policy of refusing to respond to his critics by engaging in a dialogue through the medium of the press.[69] Jefferson's refraining to read any of the additional seven letters Martin addressed to him in the *Porcupine's Gazette* not only revealed an undue sensitivity toward criticism but violated his principles of argumentation and the social affections that were essential parts of his rhetoric of virtue. Nevertheless, he still confronted a rhetorical situation that required a thoroughly documented response. Consequently, for the next several years, he wrote a number of letters to his friends and to others who had been in a position to know what happened, and he requested that they search their memories and their files and report to him their findings about the facts surrounding the murder and what part, if any, Cresap had played in the episode. He also wanted to know if they had any data on the role that Logan performed in composing the speech.[70]

The letters of inquiry contained his promise that whatever evidence they uncovered would be published in the next printing of the *Notes*. From these correspondents and from other interested parties, he received more than twenty letters, sworn documents, and certified reports, all of which—except for one to be discussed later—were published in the appendix of the next edition.[71] In these twenty-three pages of data, drawn largely from firsthand knowledge, there was a general consensus of these points. First, Logan did indeed compose the speech that he delivered before Lord Dunmore and other individuals present at the peace conference. Second, many of Logan's family members were murdered, as he asserted in his address. Third, even though he may not have been present when the Yellow Creek murders occurred, Cresap, through his numerous raids, often unprovoked and unduly forceful in nature, had set an example of human rights violations against the Shawanese and Mingoes that served as a pattern for his comrades to follow.[72]

These findings did not placate Jefferson's most extreme partisan opponents.[73] But he himself was fully satisfied that he had done his scholarly and moral duty by printing supporting documents in the appendix of the *Notes*. The episode, moreover, in no way diminished his appreciation for Logan's address. On May 20, 1814, he wrote to Abraham Small, an English compiler and editor of famous speeches, recommending Logan's presentation as a model of eloquence worthy to be studied by students of discourse.[74]

Although Jefferson's original critique and his later evidence incorporated into the appendix of the *Notes* were widely accepted by educators and the general public during the twenty-five years following his death, a new challenge to his conclusions was published in 1851. It was a "Discourse" presented by Brantz Mayer—a lawyer and antiquarian—to the Maryland Historical Society on May 9, 1851, entitled: *TAH-GAH-JUTE or LOGAN and CAPTAIN MICHAEL CRESAP.*[75] The precipitating factor that led to this discourse was Mayer's discovery of a hitherto unpublished letter by George Rogers Clark, written on June 17, 1798. It was produced at Jefferson's request, and, as designed, sent to Dr. Samuel Brown, who, in turn, forwarded a copy to be included in the next printing of the *Notes*. But in the end, it became the only item of evidence, sought by Jefferson, which never appeared with the other primary source material. To make certain that the letter would be made public, Mayer placed it in his volume.[76] One of the crucial points in this document was Clark's claim that he was with Cresap, many miles from Yellow Creek, when the massacre occurred.

Mayer immediately raised questions about Jefferson's wisdom in suppressing the letter because it created a gap in the Logan story, and also represented an important broken promise. But his greatest concern was with Jefferson's decision to heap praise on an Indian "savage" who, in his opinion, was both brutal and immoral. Most of all, he believed that Logan had been guilty of a libelous act by falsely blaming Cresap for masterminding the murders at Yellow Creek. He phrased his deeply felt sentiments on this issue in these words:

> Indian error and obstinacy converted this Maryland man (Cresap) into a brutal monster; but I have striven to restore him to his original and meritorious manhood. Imagination transformed the savage (Logan) into a romantic myth; yet it has been my task not only to reduce this myth to a

man, but to paint him degraded by cruelties and intemperance even beneath the scale of an aboriginal birthright.[77]

For decades after the lecture was delivered and then published, historians were inclined to support Mayer's findings that Cresap in no way caused or contributed to these murders, and questioned Jefferson's judgment and scholarship in suppressing Clark's letter. A typical example of this perspective is found in Lawrence C. Wroth's brief biographical sketch of Cresap in the *Dictionary of American Biography*. Commenting on Jefferson's stance on Cresap, he noted: "Unhappily for his case in modern eyes, he suppressed evidence . . . notably the letter in which Clark exonerated Cresap from the specific charge of the Yellow Creek Massacre. . . . The testimony, in general, points to Cresap's innocence in the Logan matter, and shows him to have been no more brutal in his dealings with the Indians than the normal actor in a scene in which men went day and night in fear of an appalling death."[78]

Two other twentieth-century works became an essential part of the dialogue on Logan's speech. The first was Irving Brant's *James Madison: The Virginia Revolutionist*, published in 1941. Brant focused on the claims advanced by Mayer in his work on Logan. To analyze Mayer's effort, he observed, is to see that his numerous "1774 citations and quotations" focus on all major "subjects save one—Cresap. It contains not one description of Cresap's conduct written before attacks on Jefferson began in 1797." But Brant's most significant conclusion was this: "It is therefore utterly immaterial whether Cresap or [Daniel] Greathouse led the party which slaughtered Logan's family; the fundamental guilt was where Jefferson placed it, and was deeper than Jefferson claimed. For Jefferson after collecting all the information he could, only insisted that Cresap by his earlier murders set the example which Greathouse followed."[79]

The second work, appearing in 1970, is Paul S. Clarkson's and R. Samuel Jett's *Luther Martin of Maryland* which devotes a chapter to "The Logan-Cresap Affair, 1797–1800." After their examination of Martin's charges, Logan's speech, and Jefferson's discussion in the *Notes*, these historians concluded that whereas Martin's central arguments were justifiable, the story recounted by Jefferson had three serious flaws: He had, along with Logan, falsely accused Cresap of the murders; the evidence he used throughout his analysis was biased and largely based on rumors and hearsay; and since the man he had eulogized as an eloquent orator lacked the language skills and intellectual capacity to construct the speech, the real author was General John Gibson, who had command of the Indian dialect spoken by the Shawanese and the Mingoes.[80]

In the face of these conflicting views on the Logan address, what meaningful conclusions may we draw concerning this case, and the quality of Jefferson's performance as a critic of the speech? To answer this question properly, we must address four problems that have been major issues in the controversy. They are as follows:

(1) Did Cresap lead the raid that culminated in the Yellow Creek Massacre?
(2) If Cresap was not present, did he either by an order require the act, or by example create an environment that inevitably led to the atrocity?
(3) Why did Jefferson not include Clark's letter in the appendix of the *Notes*?
(4) To what degree was Logan, rather than Gibson, the genuine author of the speech?

On the first question—whether Cresap was present at the scene leading the raid at Yellow Creek—contemporary opinion was divided. Not a few of the observers, as seen in our reading of Peter Force's *American Archives*, gave testimony claiming that he was the leader in charge of the murders. Supporting this perspective were several of the key witnesses cited in the appendix of the *Notes*. Jefferson captured the essence of this contemporary sentiment by noting: "Logan imputed the whole to Cresap in his War note and peace speech; the Indians generally imputed it to Cresap; Lord Dunmore and his officers imputed it to Cresap; the country, with one accord, imputed it to him. . . ."[81]

It is also essential to observe, however, that both the *American Archives* and the *Notes* provide vitally important information that Cresap was not present when the killings were committed. By far the most compelling evidence in defense of this position was offered by two witnesses whose credibility on this point cannot easily be challenged—generals George Rogers Clark and John Gibson. Clark's letter, as noted earlier, asserts that Cresap was with him far removed from Yellow Creek on the day of the murders. In addition, Gibson, who was both the translator of the speech and the father of a child born to Logan's murdered sister, categorically declared that Cresap was not present when the crime occurred.[82] We concur with this conclusion, which Jefferson himself later reached.[83]

The second query, which has two parts—one involving a possible command order and the other an example to be imitated—is more difficult to answer, because of the apparent dual nature of Cresap's character and the opposing perspectives that his actions generated in the minds of the interpreters. Dr. Samuel Brown noted the dilemma in a letter to Jefferson on September 4, 1798: "There were, then, in that, as in almost every other frontier, two parties," he said. "By the one Capt. Cresap was considered as a wanton violator of Treaties[,] as a man of a cruel & inhuman disposition; By the other he was esteem[ed] as an intrepid warrior & as a just avenger of savage barbarities."[84]

In considering the second query, we conclude from our analysis that there is no concrete evidence to prove that Cresap ever issued a specific order to his soldiers to attack Logan's family. But we do infer, along with Jefferson and Brant, that Cresap did set a powerful example in his Indian policies and actions that led, in part, to the Yellow Creek Massacre. A significant body of data reprinted in the *American Archives*, for instance, shows convincingly that Cresap and his comrade Daniel Greathouse not only hated the Indians on the frontier, but often and, at times, without sufficient cause engaged in atrocities against them.[85]

To read these narrations beginning in April 1774, and extending through the summer and autumn of the same year is to learn that Cresap and Greathouse often gave their Indian victims rum, causing them to get drunk, so that they could easily be tomahawked and scalped. We further learn that among those who were killed during one of the raids were Logan's sister and other close relatives. Nor were Cresap and Greathouse reluctant to boast that "they would kill and plunder all (the Indians) that were going up and down the river" near Yellow Creek.[86]

Despite Cresap's appointment as the official head of marauding parties whose task was to attack Indians along the Ohio River,[87] contemporary observers generally linked him with Greathouse. The ensuing account from Devereux Smith, a Pennsylvanian praised by Governor Penn for his activities on the frontier in the Pittsburgh area, puts in clear focus the perception held by his colleagues regarding Cresap:

> As Mr. Butler was under the necessity of sending people to assist in bringing his peltry from the *Shawanese* towns, he sent off another canoe on the 24th of April, in care of two *Indians*, who were well known to be good men, and two white men. On the 27th, about ninety miles from here, they were fired upon from shore, and both the Indians were killed, by Michael Cresap, and a party he had with him; they also scalped the Indians. Mr. Cresap then immediately followed the above mentioned *Shawanese* Chiefs some small distance lower down, where they were encamped, and fired upon them, killed one and wounded two more.[88]

It was at this point in the narrative that Smith showed a linkage between this episode and the Yellow Creek raid by Greathouse, and a similar linkage between Cresap and Greathouse. His account proceeded as
follows:

> About the same time, a party headed by one *Greathouse*, barbarously mur-
> dered and scalped nine *Indians* at the house of one *Baker*, near *Yellow Creek*,
> about fifty-five miles down the river. Owing to these cruelties committed
> by *Cresap* and *Greathouse*, the inhabitants of *Rackhoon* and *Wheeling* fled
> from the settlement, and are chiefly gone to Virginia.[89]

This was the type of persuasive testimony that led Jefferson to argue correctly that Cresap set an example of violence on the frontier which
Greathouse was motivated to emulate as a means of forcing the Indians
into submission.[90] We conclude, moreover, that from these contemporary
sources Wroth was not justified in whitewashing Cresap's actions.

With respect to the third question—the exclusion of the Clark letter
from the *Notes*—Jefferson's position as a critic was not defensible. For in
requesting information on Cresap's role in the murders of Logan's family,
he had promised each addressee that the data he received would be published in the next printing of the *Notes*. This promise was honored except
in the case of Clark. What is especially troubling in this instance is that
he had actually recommended to Brown that the general be approached.[91] Yet for an unexplained reason he had refused to publish
Clark's letter, even though he had a copy of it in his files.

What is surprising and unfortunate about Jefferson's decision to suppress the letter is that its contents do not basically refute the central
thrust of the claims made in the *Notes*. Clark's description of events, for
instance, draws these conclusions: (1) The text of the speech, along with
Jefferson's commentary, are "substantially true." (2) The ruthless tragedy
summarized in the appendix was even worse than Jefferson had detailed.
(3) Daniel Greathouse, not Cresap, was the agent of the atrocity. (4) It
was understandable that Cresap might be blamed for the deed because of
the raids he had undertaken as a commander a few days before the murder of Logan's relatives.[92] In brief, it is regrettable that the only written
comment Jefferson recorded on this disturbing suppression of evidence
was this vague reference in a letter to Brown. "Your brother has explained
to you what was thought best as to Genl. Clarke's deposition."[93]

The final problem that must be addressed pertains to the authorship
of the speech. The strongest position on this issue, as we observed, was
taken by Luther Martin and his biographers Clarkson and Jett, who

maintained that Logan was incapable of producing his celebrated text, and that it was ghosted by Gibson who had knowledge of the Indian dialect. One of the items produced by Clarkson and Jett was the first sentence of Logan's speech which reads: "I appeal to any white man to say, if ever he came cold and naked, and he clothed him not." In singling out this poetical statement, they argue that it is "a direct paraphrase of the New Testament Book St. Matthew, chapter 25, verses 35–36." That this claim is correct seems clear. But we feel that their contention is unsound and unpersuasive when they add these words: "However natural such language might be to a white man, it is highly improbable that it would flow from the lips of an illiterate, non-Christian Indian like Logan."[94]

The only way these authors could have reached that conclusion was by ignoring some of the critical data that Jefferson had assembled and recorded in the appendix of his *Notes*. In particular, they showed no knowledge of the "Declaration" of the Moravian missionary John Heckewelder. Following numerous conversations that he had held with Logan over the years, Heckewelder concluded that Logan was "a man of superior talents" whose overall ability as a communicator transcended that of typical Indians on the frontier. In his "Declaration," he also cited testimony from senior missionary David Zeisberger who, during his fifty years on the mission field, had an opportunity to observe Logan from the time he was a young boy until he reached manhood. Based upon these experiences, Zeisberger described the Mingo leader as "a man of quick comprehension, good judgment and talents"; and "doubted not in the least, that Logan had sent such a speech to Lord Dunmore on this occasion." Then, to give an air of finality to his claim, he said: "Expressions of that kind [used in the speech] were familiar to him. . . ."[95] It would appear that in these multiple, friendly contacts with these Christian missionaries, Logan would have become familiar with the often cited passage from St. Matthew.

It seems evident, moreover, that Logan's brief message to Cresap on July 21, 1774, two months after the murder of his family, was not the work of an "illiterate man." In this three-sentence statement, Logan pointedly asserted:

> Captain Cresap, what did you kill my people on Yellow Creek for? The white people killed my kin, at Conestoga, a great while ago; and I thought nothing of that. But you killed my kin again, on Yellow Creek, and took my Cousin Prisoner. Then I thought I must kill too; and I have been three times at war since; but the Indians are not angry: only myself.[96]

Called by Jefferson "Logan's war note speech," this message is clear, concise, and forceful. It further served as a harbinger of the speech he was to make at the peace treaty ceremony in late October. For in both instances, he pointed an accusing finger at Cresap as a man responsible for the Yellow Creek Massacre.

Following this accumulation of the evidence he had obtained, Jefferson summarized his findings regarding Logan's role as author of the text by citing a series of facts that built toward a climactic ending:

> Of the genuineness of that speech nothing need be said, it was known to the camp where it was delivered; it was given out by Lord Dunmore and his officers; it ran through the public papers of these states; was rehearsed as an exercise at schools; published in the papers and periodical works of Europe; and all this, a dozen years before it was copied into the notes on Virginia. In fine, general Gibson concludes the question for ever, by declaring that he received it from Logan's hand, delivered it to Lord Dunmore, translated it for him, and that the copy in the notes on Virginia is a faithful copy.[97]

This impressive list of factual data, illustrating the argumentative element of the calculation of probabilities, contains one error—the part where Jefferson states that Gibson "received it from Logan's hand. . . ." What Gibson actually said in his deposition was that Logan "delivered to him the speech, nearly as related by Mr. Jefferson. . . ."[98]

As we continue our analysis of the issue of authorship, it is useful to look once again at Gibson's overall role. If, as Clarkson and Jett argue, he ghosted the speech—an assertion contrary to his own vigorous claims that he was merely a translator of the speech he heard—why did he allow two points to remain in the address that he believed to be false? At the time the lament was being presented to him in the copse in the woods, he told Logan, according to his testimony in his deposition, that Michael Cresap was a captain, not a colonel, and that Greathouse, not Cresap, was the principal agent of the crime at Yellow Creek. Yet the two errors remained in the speech as it was read to Lord Dunmore and others present at the peace treaty.[99]

In retrospect, we conclude that Jefferson's historically significant critique of Logan's speech was a unique and informative part of his rhetoric of virtue. First of all, he felt it was his educational and moral duty to publish the address so that it could be studied and appreciated as a model of persuasive discourse revealing the artistic talent of an American Indian whose eloquence represented the intellectual potential inherent in his race. It was for this reason, as we have seen, that a copy of the text, along with evaluative comments, became a part of the *Notes on the State of Virginia.*

Second, he realized in this instance that the strong moral, cultural, and historical implications of a specimen of rhetorical criticism might necessitate an ensuing productive dialogue that, in turn, required participation by the original critic as well as his detractors. Consequently, when the integrity of his analysis was challenged on both factual and ethical grounds, he opted not to follow the policy of silence that he often practiced when attacked by his opponents or by other interested observers. Instead, he sought to gather comprehensive data from informed and responsible witnesses for the purpose of determining the degree of validity and reliability of his and Logan's charges against Cresap. Finally, although he never wavered from his original position concerning Cresap's heavy involvement in the controversial affair, Jefferson, confronted with contradictory evidence, modified his earlier assertion that Cresap was unquestionably present at the scene during the Yellow Creek Massacre. In all, except for his inexcusable suppression of Clark's letter and his decision to read only one of Martin's newspaper columns addressed to him, his arguments with respect to the Logan speech conformed closely to the essential features of his philosophy of virtue and practical reasoning.

What we have observed in this overview of Jefferson as a critic of public discourse was a commentator who looked upon rhetorical criticism as a communication enterprise that stresses the value of factual data and reasoning ability as crucial starting points for the critic. This was particularly true in his evaluations of Henry and Logan. In both instances, he found it necessary to use strong documentary evidence combined with knowledge based on experience. Also evident in his method of criticism was his application of the doctrine of taste and sublimity as criteria for assessing the immediate and long-range impact of a speaker's content, organizational pattern, and language control. This process of criticism led him to conclude that Adams and Madison were debaters who used convincing and relevant practical reasoning strategies to influence their contemporaries during the period of the struggle for independence and of the adoption of the Constitution respectively. Similarly, it demonstrated that Henry in the Revolutionary War era and Logan in his 1774 speech elevated oratory to the level of sublimity.

# Notes

1. December 25, 1820, in L&B, 18: 306.
2. *Writings and Speeches of Daniel Webster*, 17: 370.
3. *On the Sublime*, xxxvi. 1–2. Jefferson had a 1733 edition of this work published in Edinburgh.

4. *Elements of Criticism*, 3 vols. (Edinburgh: A. Kincaid & J. Bell, 1762), 1: 17, and 3: 373.

5. Kames observed: "We intuitively conceive a taste to be right or good if conformable to the common standard, and wrong or bad if disconformable. . . . Hence in all disputes, we find the parties, each of them equally, appealing constantly to the common sense of mankind as the ultimate rule or standard." 3: 358–59. In the introductory chapter of Book I, he made a direct connection between criticism and virtue. p. 11. Jefferson had a two-volume edition of the *Elements* published in 1765. On several occasions, he recommended this work, the first time in a letter to Skipwith in 1771. Jefferson may have had Kames in mind when he told Thomas Law in 1814 that some have argued that taste is a fundamental part of morality. But it "is not even a branch of morality. . . ." Later in the same letter he observed that "whatever constitutes the domain of criticism or taste," is "a faculty entirely distinct from the moral one." TJ to Thomas Law, June 13, 1814, in *Writings*, 1336. It is important to note, however, that in making this statement Jefferson was inconsistent. For we have found that principles of virtue were continually present in his own rhetorical criticism. If, therefore, in theory he did not accept Kames's view, it is clear that he did so in his practice.

6. *A History of Criticism and Literary Taste in Europe*, 3 vols. (New York: Dodd, Mead, 1902), 2: 462.

7. Harold Harding, ed., *Lectures on Rhetoric and Belles Lettres By Hugh Blair*, 2 vols. (Carbondale: Southern Illinois University Press, 1965), 1: 15–96.

8. TJ to James Madison, September 20, 1785, in *Writings*, 828–30.

9. January 30, 1787, in Boyd, 11: 94–95.

10. TJ to Madison, ibid., 94; to Dr. Benjamin Rush, January 16, 1811, in L&B, 13: 8; to Benjamin Waterhouse, January 31, 1819, in *Writings and Speeches of Daniel Webster*, 17: 115, 370–71; and to Madison, August 30, 1823, in Ford, 12: 308.

11. *Writings and Speeches of Daniel Webster*, 17: 371.

12. Ford, 12: 308.

13. "Autobiography," in Ford, 1: 66.

14. Ibid.

15. Ibid., 45; and "A Memorandum (Services to My Country)" [ca. 1800], in *Writings*, 702.

16. L&B, 14: 162.

17. August 5, 1815, in L&B, 14: 338–39. In an earlier letter, TJ told Wirt that he had planned to send him a description of "Mr. Henry's ravenous avarice, the only passion paramount to his love of popularity. The facts I have heard on that subject are not within my own knolege, & ought not to be hazarded but on better testimony than I possess. And if they are true, you have been in a much better situation than I was to have information on them." April 12, 1812, in Ford, 11: 228–30. In some instances, when the authorities TJ used had an impeccable reputation for being reliable and truthful, he felt comfortable in offering a criticism based on their testimony. A case in point related to Henry's embarrassing performance in the 1774 Continental Congress which will be discussed later. TJ on this occasion was reporting what he had been told by "Mr. Pendleton and Col. Harrison of our own delegation. . . ." Ford, 11: 231n.

18. TJ to William Wirt, August 5, 1815, in L&B, 14: 341.

19. "Autobiography," in Ford, 1: 15.

20. *Writings and Speeches of Daniel Webster*, 17: 367.

21. Ibid.

374 ~ Part Two: Chapter Fourteen

22. TJ to William Wirt, April 12, 1812, in Ford, 11: 231n. In this letter, TJ included a paper he had written for Wirt in 1810 or 1811, but did not send until he enclosed it in his April 12 letter. That is why it appears in Ford as an extended footnote. Years later, when discussing this incident with Daniel Webster, Jefferson described Henry's draft in these pointed terms: ". . . Congress heard it with amazement. It was miserably written, and good for nothing." *Writings and Speeches of Daniel Webster*, 17: 370.

23. Ibid., 232n.

24. Jefferson told Short on December 14, 1789 that Henry stood "higher in public estimation than he ever did," yet was "so often in the minority in the present assembly that he has quitted it, nevermore to return, unless an opportunity offers to overturn the new constitution. . . ." December 14, 1789, in Boyd, 16: 26. Despite TJ's overall negative response to Henry's discourse on the Constitution, he did acknowledge that Henry at times was highly persuasive: Debate on the Constitution was "another of the great occasions on which (Henry) exhibited examples of eloquence such as probably had never been exceeded. . . ." Ford, 11: 234n. Yet despite these statements, Jefferson was at best ambivalent about the proposed Constitution. Indeed, he was claimed by both Federalists and anti-Federalists in 1787–88. He found the tussle over him embarrassing, especially when people quoted private letters he wrote as public statements of his views on the Constitution.

25. TJ to Wirt, August 14, 1814, in L&B, 14: 164. He provided more details of this event in the April 12, 1812 letter and enclosure. After discussing the debate on the last "and strongest resolution" which "was carried but by a single vote," TJ noted: "I was then but a student and was listening at the door of the lobby (for as yet there was no gallery) when Peyton Randolph, after the vote, came out of the house and said, as he entered the lobby, 'By god I would have given 500 guineas for a single vote,' for as this would have divided the house, the vote of Robinson, the speaker, would have rejected the resolution." Ford, 11: 229n.

26. "Autobiography," in Ford, 1: 8.

27. The first instance described here is discussed in Ford, 11: 229n; the second in TJ's letter to Wirt, August 14, 1814, in L&B, 14: 164.

28. *The Virginia Gazette* stated the resolution as follows: "*Resolved*, therefore, that the colony be immediately put into a posture of defence. . . ." Three of the members who were appointed to "a committee to prepare a plan for the embodying, arming, and disciplining such a number of men as may be sufficient for that purpose" were Henry, Washington, and Jefferson. This resolution was made on March 22. See the April 1775 issue. An excellent factual treatment of the Convention appears in Peter Force, ed., *American Archives*, 4th Ser., 2: 165–72. The total number of delegates as listed in Force were 121.

29. Edmund Randolph, "Essay on the Revolutionary History of Virginia, 1774–1782," in *The Virginia Magazine of History and Biography*, 43 (1935): 222.

30. Ibid., 223.

31. July 9, 1819, in Cappon, 2: 543.

32. These quotations appear in the following sources: Ford, 11: 228n–234n; TJ's account in Wirt, *The Life and Character of Patrick Henry* (Philadelphia: Porter & Coates, 1832), 77; "Autobiography," Ford, 1: 8; and *Writings and Speeches of Daniel Webster*, 17: 367.

33. *Writings and Speeches of Daniel Webster*, 17: 367.

34. "Autobiography," in Ford, 1: 59.

35. *Writings and Speeches of Daniel Webster*, 17: 367.

36. Garry Wills, *Inventing America: Jefferson's Declaration of Independence* (Garden City, N.Y.: Doubleday, 1976), 10.

37. "Edmund Randolph's Essay on the Revolutionary History of Virginia (1774–1782)," *The Virginia Magazine of History*, 43 (1935). Published under the Auspices of 'The Virginians' of the City of New York. By the Virginia Historical Society. Lee House, Richmond, Va., 1935, 223.

38. It is interesting to note that Jefferson earnestly wished to maintain a cordial relationship with Henry despite their differences in the 1790s. In 1795, he wrote to Archibald Stuart, saying: "With respect to the gentleman whom we expected to see there (Henry of Bedford Court), satisfy him if you please that there is no remain of disagreeable sentiment towards him on my part. I was once sincerely affectioned towards him and it accords with my philosophy to encourage the tranquillizing passions. . . ." April 18, 1795, in Ford, 8: 168.

39. TJ stated on several occasions that he thought he received the copy from Dunmore, but he could not be fully certain.

40. George Louis LeClerck, Count of Buffon, *Buffon's Natural History, Containing a Theory of the Earth, a General History of Man, of the Brute Creation, and of Vegetables, Minerals, &c.*, 10 vols. (London: H. D. Symonds, 1810), 4: 332–33. For a full discussion of North and South American natives, see *ibid.*, 307–52. Buffon, who TJ met and dined with in Paris, died in 1788. Throughout the *Notes*, we find many references to his views on animal and plant life.

41. *Notes on the State of Virginia*, 64. Raynal's statement which TJ quotes appears in *Histoire Philosophique et Poltique Des Etablissemens et du Commerce des Europeens dans les deux Indes* (1780). For further details on TJ's attitudes toward Raynal, see Sowerby, *Catalogue of the Library of Thomas Jefferson*, 1: 214–15.

42. *Notes*, 64.

43. Ibid., 62.

44. Ibid., 63.

45. *Papers of James Madison*, 1: 136.

46. Early in March, Bradford gave this reaction to the Logan speech sent by Madison. "I thank you for Logan's speech. I admire the nervous & untutor'd eloquence of it. . . . The last sentence is particularly pathetic & expressive; it raises a crowd of Ideas & at one stroke sets in a strong light the Barbarity of Cressop, the sufferings of Logan and his contempt of death. I thought it a pity that so fine a specimen of 'Indian Eloquence & mistaken Valour' (as you justly call it) should languish in obscurity and therefore gave a copy of it to my brother who inserted it in his paper; from which it has been transcribed into the others & has given the highest satisfaction to all that can admire & relish the simple Beauties of nature. I need make no apology for publishing what I suppose must be public your way, tho you say you have not seen it in print." *Madison Papers*, 1: 138. Among the newspaper versions of the speech TJ had in his files was the *Virginia Gazette* dated February 4, 1775.

47. Irving Brant, *James Madison*, 6 vols. (Indianapolis: Bobbs-Merrill, 1941–1961), I: *The Virginia Revolutionist, 1751–1780* (1941), 281.

48. The Account Books we used are located in the University of Virginia Library. The books are arranged according to years. The one being used here is under the heading of 1775.

49. The editors of *The Papers of James Madison* note that "JM's word was 'day,' but he probably meant to write 'say' as in the 4 February 1775 *Virginia Gazette* . . . version." 1: 137n. The word 'say' also appears in TJ's copy in the *Notes on the State of Virginia*.

50. Jefferson observed: "I copied, verbatim, the narrative I had taken down in 1774, and the speech as it had been given us in a better translation by Lord Dunmore." *Notes on the State of Virginia*, 227. General Gibson, who had translated the speech, concurred with TJ's assessment. Ibid., 228.

51. TJ noted that he supplied "only two or three verbal variations of no importance." Ibid.

52. This conclusion was confirmed by a number of the documents included in the appendix of the *Notes*. Later we will see as the issue of authenticity again arose that additional arguments and counterarguments were presented.

53. David I. Bushnell Jr., "The Virginia Frontier in History—1778," in *The Virginia Magazine of History and Biography*, 23 (April 1915): 115n.

54. TJ expressed this view with force when he said: "I repeated what thousands had done before, on as good authority as we have for most of the facts we learn through life, and such as, to this moment, I have seen no reason to doubt." *Notes*, 227.

55. Account Book, 1775; and *Notes*, 62.

56. Account Book, 1775.

57. Ibid.

58. The St. Matthew's passage alluded to here is chapter 25, verses 35–36.

59. The following statement by Richard White tends to support the commonly held view that Logan was justified in claiming a friendship with whites: "The villagers at Yellow Creek consorted regularly with a small settlement of Virginians living just across the line." Richard White, *The Middle Ground: Indians, Empires, and Republics in the Great Lakes Region, 1650–1815* (Cambridge: Cambridge University Press, 1995), 358.

60. The rank should have been "captain."

61. These words were not altogether true; some of his family members survived.

62. As the following sources suggest, Logan's act of revenge consisted of thirteen killings on his part, the same number of the family members murdered by the whites: "Extract of a Letter Received at Philadelphia," June 19, 1774, in Force, ed., *American Archives*, 1: 429; Arthur St. Clair to Governour Penn, June 22, 1774, in ibid., 475; and John Montgomery to Governour Penn, June 30, 1774, in ibid., 546.

63. *Notes*, 62.

64. TJ to Governor Henry, of Maryland, December 31, 1797, in ibid., 227. Although TJ did not provide specific sources concerning the publication of the speech, there is a considerable body of evidence to support his claim. Apart from appearing in the *Pennsylvania Journal* and *Virginia Gazette*, cited above, the oration was printed in the *Pennsylvania Ledger*, February 11, 1775; the *Rivingston's New York Gazetter*, February 16, 1775; and *The New York Gazette*, February 20, 1775. The speech also was included in the works of Diderot under the title of "Frontieres De Virginie," March 10, 1775. J. Assezat Et Maurice Tourneux, eds., *Oeuvres Completes De Diderot*, 20 vols. (Paris, 1876). Reprinted by Kraus Reprint, 1966), 17: 503–504. Approximately six weeks later, it appeared in the *Gazette de France*, April 21, 1775. Moreover, Stevens Thompson Mason testified that he studied the speech as a schoolboy. *Notes*, Appendix, 245.

65. *Notes*, 230. TJ would have been pleased to learn that the speech would later be included in McGuffey's Readers during the period from 1837 through 1879. Stanley W. Lindberg, *The Annotated McGuffey: Selections from the McGuffey Eclectic Readers, 1836–1920* (New York: Van Nostrand Reinhold, 1976), 248.

66. Paul S. Clarkson and R. Samuel Jett, "The Logan-Cresap Affair, 1797–1800," in *Luther Martin of Maryland* (Baltimore: Johns Hopkins University Press, 1970), 179–80.

67. The analysis of Martin's letters is based upon our examination of the following issues of *Porcupine's Gazette* located in the Library of Congress: July 17 and December 11, 1797; January 13 and 20, 1798; and February 3 and March 3, 1798.

68. TJ told James Lewis Jr. that Martin's style contained so much abuse and invective that it was obvious "that his object was not merely truth, but to gratify party passions. . . ." May 9, 1798, in Ford, 8: 416. He then proceeded to state: "Party passions are indeed high. Nobody has more reason to know it than myself. I receive daily bitter proofs of it from people who never saw me, nor know anything of me but through Porcupine and Fenno." Ibid., 416–17.

69. See letters to John Page, January 1, 1798, in Ford, 8: 353; and to Mann Page on the following day. Ibid., 353–54.

70. Among the letters he wrote are TJ to Peregrine Fitzhugh, June 4, 1797, in Ford, 8: 298–302; TJ to John Page, Jan. 1, 1798, in ibid., 8: 352–53; TJ to Dr. Samuel Brown, March 25 [, 1798], in ibid., 8: 390–91; TJ to Harry Innes, June 20, 1799, in ibid., 9: 71–73; and TJ to [Harry] Innes, January 23, 1800, in ibid., 9: 99–102. Other letters and declarations appear in *Notes*, 226–58.

71. This edition was entitled *Jefferson's Notes on the State of Virginia With Appendixes—Complete* (Baltimore: W. Pechin, 1800). Hereafter cited as *Notes–Complete*. It should be pointed out, however, that the appendix in the Peden *Notes* is almost identical to that used in this volume. One important difference is the use of John Sappington's full letter in the 1800 volume. Apparently Clarkson and Jett ignored this change, and thus criticized TJ for the shortened version in the Peden volume.

72. After evaluating the documents he had received, TJ drew the conclusions cited here, which he developed under the heading: "From this testimony the following historical statement results." *Notes–Complete*, 47–50.

73. Among those bitter opponents was Luther Martin whom TJ later described as an "unprincipled & impudent federal bulldog. . . ." TJ to DeWitt Clinton, June 19, 1807, in Ford, 10: 403. This is the kind of language TJ occasionally used to describe a political enemy.

74. May 20, 1814, in L&B, 14: 138.

75. The "Discourse" was published in 1851. Sixteen years later, Mayer expanded the Discourse delivered to the Maryland Historical Society, providing more historical and political background material. But the central arguments remained the same. The book carried the same titles *TAH-GAH-JUTE* (Albany: Joel Munsell, 1867). In both of these works, the author felt it was desirable to list Logan's name as part of the title. The English equivalent of *TAH-GAH-JUTE* is "Short Dress."

76. The letter is reproduced in the "Discourse," 72–75, and in the book, 149–56.

77. Discourse, 69. A similarly strong conclusion appears in the book, 142–43.

78. Lawrence C. Wroth, "Michael Cresap," in Dumas Malone, ed., *Dictionary of American Biography*, xx vols. (New York: Scribner's, 1930–19–), 4: 538.

79. Brant, *Madison: Virginia Revolutionist*, 288–90. After a careful analysis of the "Discourse" and the book, in which we examined all of the footnote references, we concur with Brant's conclusion that Mayer does not utilize the contemporary sources that show a highly unfavorable side to Cresap. On the whole, therefore, we feel that the author did not successfully fulfill his promise to present a balanced view.

80. *Luther Martin of Maryland*, 171–88.

81. *Notes–Complete*, 50.

82. Ibid., p. 36.

83. This is explained in the analysis of the data he obtained. Here he acknowledged that Greathouse was the apparent leader of the raiding party at Yellow Creek. But, as will be seen later, he strongly believed that Cresap had set the example.

84. Samuel Brown to TJ, September 4, 1798, in Sowerby, *Catalogue of the Library of Thomas Jefferson*, 309–310. These contrasting views are particularly evident when we compare the perceptions of the Pennsylvania soldiers and settlers in the Pittsburgh area with those of the Virginians under the command of Lord Dunmore. Of importance here is the longstanding dispute between the two commonwealths regarding jurisdictional rights. The Pennsylvanians were so friendly toward the Indian cause that Logan and other Indians announced that they would never attack the Pennsylvanians. See *American Archives*, I, April through October, 1774. For unqualified support of Dunmore's actions, see the *Virginia Gazette*, April through December 1774, and January 1775.

85. *American Archives*, I, April through December 1774. The editor was Peter Force.

86. "Extract of a Letter from David Zeisberger, Missionary at Schonbrunn," May 24, 1774, in *American Archives*, 1: 285; Arthur St. Clair to Governour Penn, May 29, 1774, in ibid., 1: 287; Devereux Smith to Dr. Smith, June 10, 1774, in ibid., 1: 468; and "Extract of a Letter received at Phila., Fort Pitt, June 19, 1774," in ibid., 1: 429.

87. Clark's letter explains how Cresap was placed in charge of the parties who engaged in raids against the Indians. Lecture, 72–73.

88. *American Archives*, 1: 468.

89. Ibid.

90. This was made clear by TJ in his summary analysis in *Notes–Complete*, 47–50.

91. TJ to Dr. Samuel Brown, March 25, 1798, in Sowerby, *Catalogue of the Library of Thomas Jefferson*, 3: 309.

92. Mayer's Discourse, 72–75; and his book in 1867, 149–59. This letter also appears in condensed form in Sowerby, *Catalogue of the Library of Thomas Jefferson*, 3: 310.

93. TJ to Samuel Brown, May 10, 1800, in Sowerby, *Catalogue of the Library of Thomas Jefferson*, 3: 314. This would suggest that TJ communicated his opinion on this issue orally.

94. *Luther Martin of Maryland*, 187.

95. *Notes*, 250.

96. This is an important message because it is the only other extant written statement authored by Logan. Innes gives this brief background of how and where the letter was obtained: "In 1774 I lived in Fincastle county, now divided into Washington, Montgomery and part of Wythe. Being intimate in Col. Preston's family, I happened in July to be at his house, when an Express was sent to him as the County Lieut. requesting a guard of the militia to be ordered out for protection of the inhabitants residing low down on the north fork of Holston river. The Express brought with him a War Club, and a note which was left tied to it at the house of one Robertson whose family were cut off by the Indians, and gave rise for the application to Col. Preston, of which the following is a copy, then taken by me in my memorandum book." *Notes*, 232. We have found no source that attempts to question the authenticity of this Logan message.

97. *Notes–Complete*, 49.

98. Ibid., 35–36.

99. Ibid. One of the most compelling analyses we have encountered with respect to the authenticity of this speech was developed by Theodore Roosevelt in 1889. After examining the Jefferson Papers and other primary source documents in the Library of Congress,

Roosevelt presented two major reasons for upholding the authenticity of the text appearing in the *Notes on the State of Virginia*, and then refuted the five claims articulated by the negative side. His two affirmative contentions were these: (1) "Gibson's statement," and (2) "The statement of George Rogers Clark." These two reliable witnesses, he asserted, were men of noble character who were appointed to prestigious positions of leadership by George Washington, and, most of all, were eyewitnesses to the treaty signing event. Moreover, he noted, there were other testimonies corroborating their accounts. By contrast, Roosevelt added, those challenging the validity of the speech relied on "hearsay" evidence and "discredited" and "silly" arguments. At the end of his analysis, he reached this conclusion: "There is probably very little additional evidence to be obtained, on one side or the other; it is all in, and Logan's speech can be unhesitatingly pronounced authentic." *The Winning of the West*, 4 vols. (New York: Putnam's, 1889–1896), 1: 349–53. Quoting Roosevelt, along with an extensive number of documents, Ray Sandefur similarly affirmed that the speech as TJ recorded it was "authentic." "Logan's Oration—How Authentic?" *Quarterly Journal of Speech*, 46 (1960): 289–96.

# CHAPTER FIFTEEN

~

# Critic of Non-Oratorical
# Forms of Public Address

If Patrick Henry, Logan, and other orators commanded Jefferson's attention as a rhetorical critic, so too did a group of authors who were poets, political commentators, and historians. In this chapter, we focus on four case studies that provide a portrait of Jefferson the critic in action as he strove to assess the worth of non-oratorical forms of discourse. These works were James Macpherson's *Poems of Ossian*; Montesquieu's *Spirit of Laws*, Destutt de Tracy's *Commentary and Review* of Montesquieu's celebrated work; and David Hume's *History of England*. Jefferson's analyses of these four rhetorical productions, we feel, illustrate how he sought to apply his philosophy of discourse to poetical, political, and historical studies.

## The Ossianic Poems

On August 3, 1771, Jefferson recommended to his neighbor and friend Robert Skipwith that he include in his "Private Library" a copy of "Ossian with (Hugh) Blair's criticisms."[1] Fifty-two years later, on November 4, 1823, he suggested to the Marquis de Lafayette that the poems of Ossian were "equal to the best morsels of antiquity."[2] During the period between these two communications, despite the fact that the Ossianic poems proved to be fraudulent, Jefferson was unwavering in his view that the poetry of the primitive Scottish Highlander author, as "translated" by James Macpherson in 1762, was a brilliantly conceived and executed rhetorical masterpiece featuring strength of sentiment and specificity in style.

Jefferson's enthusiasm for the poems had reached such a high level by 1773 that he wrote to James Macpherson's brother Charles, whom he had met in America a few months before, requesting that he obtain copies of the originals and additional related materials on the poetry. He prefaced his remarks with these words of praise for the translator and for Ossian:

> I understood you were related to the gentleman of your name Mr. James Macpherson to whom the world is so much indebted for the collection, arrangement and elegant translation, of Ossian's poems. These pieces have been, and will I think during my life continue to be to me, the source of daily and exalted pleasure. The tender, and the sublime emotions of the mind were never before so finely wrought up by human hand. I am not ashamed to own that I think this rude bard of the North the greatest Poet that has ever existed.

Following this effusive evaluation were specific instructions for reproducing a copy of the originals "in a fair, round, hand, on fine paper, with a good margin, bound in parchment as elegantly as possible, lettered on the back and marbled or gilt on the edges of the leaves." Jefferson concluded by noting that the cost of honoring his request should not be an obstacle since "the glow of one warm thought is to me worth more than money."[3]

Jefferson's continuing favorable response to the poems was similarly evident in conversational situations. When, for instance, the Marquis de Chastellux visited Monticello in 1782, one of the highlights of his stay was a discussion that was held on Ossian. Chastellux, whose literary accomplishments enabled him to gain membership in the prestigious French Academy, recalled his impressions of the event:

> I recall with pleasure that as we were conversing one evening over a "bowl of punch," after Mrs. Jefferson had retired, we happened to speak of the poetry of *Ossian*. It was a spark of electricity which passed rapidly from one to the other; we recalled the passages of those sublime poems, which had particularly struck us, and we recited them for the benefit of my traveling companions, who fortunately knew English well, and could appreciate them, even though they had never read the poems. Soon the book was called for, to share in our "toasts": it was brought forth and placed beside the bowl of punch. And before we realized it, book and bowl had carried us far into the night.[4]

When a new edition of the poems was produced in 1785, which again included a reprint of Blair's *Dissertation*, Jefferson added a copy to his library.[5] Soon he was urging his nephew Peter Carr to read Ossian for the purpose of helping "to form your style";[6] and telling his daughter Mary that her recent letter "was, as Ossian says, or would say, like the bright beams of the moon on the desolate heath."[7] Nor did the feeling of ecstasy he experienced when reading the Ossianic poems diminish during his tenure as president. He purchased another edition of the poems in 1802, which was bound for him in 1803. Moreover, on June 30, 1807, he received another two-volume publication of the work "bound in calf."[8]

There is other compelling evidence revealing Jefferson's highly favorable attitude toward the Ossianic poems. Early in the 1770s, he began recording excerpts into his *Literary Commonplace Book* from at least seven different Ossianic poems—Fingal (5 listings), Carthon and Darthula (2), and Carric-thura, Conlath & Cuthona, Lathman, and Temora (1 each). These passages, to which he frequently referred, embraced a total of 1,250 words. Additionally, before departing from France in 1789, he placed in the back of his personal copy of Gibbon's *Decline and Fall of the Roman Empire* a 56-word quotation from Ossian's "Carthon."[9] He even considered the possibility of inscribing a few lines from the poetry on the tombstone of his brother-in-law Dabney Carr.[10] Jefferson, in brief, not only remained an enthusiastic admirer of these poems throughout his lifetime but did what he could to inspire a similar feeling regarding their worth to others.

What was there in these poems that led Jefferson to take the extreme position that Ossian was "the greatest poet who has ever existed?" First and foremost, it would appear, he had fallen under the influence of Hugh Blair, the celebrated professor of rhetoric and belles lettres at the University of Edinburgh and influential minister of the church of St. Giles. From time to time throughout this study, we have seen how Jefferson's ideas on different aspects of discourse were shaped in part by Blair's *Lectures on Rhetoric and Belles Lettres*, first published in 1783. But twenty years before this work appeared in print, Blair had written his widely acclaimed *Critical Dissertation on the Poems of Ossian*.[11] This production made Blair famous in Britain and on the Continent. Because the *Dissertation* was included in almost every edition of the *Poems of Ossian*, Blair soon was recognized as a leading critic who was largely responsible for the popularity of Ossian.[12] On this point, we should recall that Jefferson's first recorded reference to Ossian was the 1771 letter to Skipwith in which he recommended the reading of "Ossian with Blair's Criticism."

The arguments that Blair advanced in the *Dissertation* struck a responsive chord in Jefferson's thinking.[13] Beginning with the premise that the Ossian manuscripts were the work of the Scottish Highlander poet who presumably lived during the third or fourth century, A.D., Blair then placed the poetry within the sphere of the epic genre. This meant, he suggested, that by their very nature, the poems had as their principal function to transmit moral instruction to the readers. He next proceeded to demon-strate how the primitive Scottish poet successfully fulfilled this task. Every hero who played an important role in the unfolding drama of Fingal's life and exploits, Blair argued, exemplified the cardinal virtues honored in Western culture. They were depicted as being just, wise, courageous, and temperate.

Jefferson doubtless was particularly impressed by Blair's description of the main protagonist Fingal and of his son Ossian, the poet. Blair's dis-cussion illustrates both the traits of character associated with Fingal and the principles of virtue that Jefferson believed to be essential as guidelines in one's daily life—especially in the area of discourse:

[Fingal possessed] all the qualities that can ennoble human nature; that can either make us admire the hero, or love the man.

He is not only unconquerable in war, but he makes his people happy by his wisdom in the days of peace.

He is merciful to his foes; full of affection to his children. . . .

[He is] full of concern about his friends; and never mentions Agandecca, his first love, without the utmost tenderness.

He is the universal protector of the distressed. . . .

Jefferson, moreover, would have liked the portrait that Blair drew of Os-sian as a man: "Ossian's own character, the old man, the hero and the bard, all in one, presents to us, through the whole work, a most re-spectable and venerable figure, which we always contemplate with plea-sure."

The reading of Blair's descriptions and of the poems themselves rein-forced Jefferson's own belief that Fingal—the primary hero of the epic story—was a benevolent leader who placed the welfare of his people above his own comfort and safety; and who understood the meaning of establishing needed priorities in personal and public relationships. Simi-larly, the character of Fingal's son Ossian highlighted anew that an older person's sense of virtue and commitment to aesthetic pleasures need not diminish with age.

In addition, Blair's contention that the noble sentiments voiced by Os-sian, clothed in the language of pathos and buttressed by the extensive use of figures of speech and thought, elevated the poems to the level of sublimity also was consistent with Jefferson's own feelings and philosophy of discourse. Not surprisingly, therefore, when Blair compared Ossian's effort favorably, in almost every respect, with the epic poetry of Homer and Virgil, Jefferson willingly accepted his judgment.

Another element that influenced Blair's critical assessment was his feeling of pride in realizing that a primitive epic poet from his native Scotland had produced poetry in the tradition of Homer and Virgil. This was particularly remarkable, he thought, given that this uneducated Celtic poetwarrior perhaps had no knowledge at all of what had occurred in Greek and Roman antiquity. Again Jefferson shared these sentiments, in part because of his family heritage and in part owing to his long-standing interest in the nature and history of language development. The Ossianic poems, in sum, gave further proof to the notion that nature has a powerful influence on the formation of a poet.

It is difficult to overestimate Jefferson's indebtedness to Blair with respect to the poems of Ossian. A majority of the fourteen quoted passages included in the *Literary Commonplace Book* were either direct or indirect citations in the *Dissertation*. Similarly, the quotation from Ossian that Jefferson had placed in his copy of *The Decline and Fall of the Roman Empire* was featured by Blair in his *Lectures on Rhetoric and Belles Lettres*—a publication with which Jefferson was very familiar.[14]

Based upon the galvanic response in many quarters to the *Critical Dissertation on the Poems of Ossian*, it appeared that Blair and Jefferson were in good company in expressing their devotion to the Ossianic poems. In a series of letters sent by David Hume from Paris to his close friend Blair in the mid-1760s, the philosopher and historian gave a graphic picture of how the *Dissertation* had gained the favor of numerous European luminaries. Elizabeth Montagu, the French public official A. R. J. Turgot, the Duc de Nivernois (who had served as French ambassador to Berlin and Rome), and William Pulteney, the first earl of Bath (to name but a representative few) had become "zealous partizans" of Ossian. In addition, the *Gazette litteraire* of Paris published a 20-page review of the second edition, calling the *Dissertation* an "excellent critique." "All the literati of my Friends, who understand English," concluded Hume, "think your Dissertation one of the finest Performances in our language."[15]

The *Poems of Ossian*, it seems clear, owed much of their enormous popularity to Blair's *Dissertation*.[16] Disregarding the powerful role that Blair had played behind the scenes in having the poetry published[17] and then in helping its dissemination by extolling its worth, Macpherson expressed pleasure with the favorable public reception his production had generated. In his preface to the fourth edition, published in 1773, he observed: "All

the polite nations of Europe have transferred [the poems] into their respective languages; and they speak of him [Macpherson] who brought
them to light, in terms that might flatter the vanity of one fond of fame."[18]
Four years later, he could take pride in what the scientist and rhetorician
Joseph Priestley, who later became a friend and confidant of Jefferson, had
to say about Ossian in his *Course of Lectures on Oratory and Criticism*. The
"simple and sublime Ossian," Priestley noted, has a significant effect on
the imagination because of his brilliant use of similes utilizing such objects
of nature as the "woods," "clouds," "mists," "tempests," "rocks," and "sun."
Following the lead of Blair, Priestley placed "Ossian the ancient Gallic
poet" on the level of "Homer and the very ancient Greek poets," all of
whom displayed an innate genius that enabled them to create sublime poetry notwithstanding the fact "they had no beauties of composition to
copy after. . . ."[19]

The *Poems of Ossian* made Macpherson and Blair international celebri-
ties and gave Jefferson years of aesthetic pleasure as he repeatedly read
and recited passages that inspired and uplifted him, and then used the
work as a favorite theme in his letters and conversations. Unfortunately,
there was a dark side to this rhetorical event that subsequently rendered
Macpherson vulnerable to the charge that he was a literary fraud, that diminished Blair's stature as a critic, and that placed Jefferson in the untenable position of failing to apply adequately his own principles of reasoning and theory of poetry regarding the critical question of
authenticity.

One of the first commentators to sense the dangers emanating from
this issue and the possible adverse impact it might eventually have upon
his native land of Scotland and upon the long-term reputation of Blair
was Hume. Although he greatly admired the quality of the *Dissertation*
and most earnestly wished to believe in the reliability of the poems, he
was deeply troubled that several eminent scholars he respected had expressed to him grave reservations concerning their authenticity.

To counter this growing suspicion, Hume outlined a plan for Blair to
follow when writing the next edition of the *Dissertation*, which, in turn,
would again be included in additional publications of the *Poems of Ossian*. The proofs that should be presented as part of an appendix, advised
Hume, "must not be arguments, but testimonies." The evidence, moreover, must come from multiple sources. "Let these persons," he added,
"be acquainted with the Gaelic; let them compare the original and the
translation; and let them testify to the fidelity of the latter."[20] At this
point in his recommendation, Hume sounded a warning: "it will not be

sufficient that a Highland gentleman or clergyman say or write to you that he has heard such poems." To supplement this advice, Hume related the ensuing story:

> I was told by [Edmund] Burke, a very ingenious Irish gentleman, the author of a tract On the Sublime and Beautiful that on the first publication of Macpherson's book, all the Irish cried out, *we know all these poems, we have always heard them from our infancy*. But when he asked more particular questions, he could never learn, or could repeat the original of any one paragraph of the pretended translation. This generality then, must be carefully guarded against, as being of no authority.[21]

Blair sought to follow this advice, and then, thinking he had done so, wrote to Hume claiming that the letters and testimonials he had received from the Highlands and printed in the appendix of the second edition of the *Dissertation* had "silenced all Infidelity and even scepticism concerning Fingal. . . ." He even boasted that he had received word that the "Barbarian Samuel Johnson," who had questioned the validity of the poems of Ossian, had been "converted." Then with an unusually high degree of confidence, he observed: "you may assure all France, that they are genuine antical Highland poems. . . ."[22]

But Blair was seriously mistaken in feeling that he had successfully carried out Hume's suggestions and in believing that his critics would be silenced by his newly discovered data. What he had received as a result of his investigation was "an incoherent mass of evidence"; and even these data were later suppressed by Macpherson.[23]

Within the next few years, the critics, though less numerous than the supporters, began to strengthen their attacks against the poems. Leading the way in this rhetorical campaign was Samuel Johnson, the noted literary critic, whom Blair had mistakenly labeled a "convert." Soon after he had met Blair in 1763, and unaware of his authorship of the *Dissertation* that had just been published, Johnson denounced the poems as a fraud. When Blair in responding raised the question of whether a modern author could have written such poetry, Johnson sarcastically replied: "Yes, Sir, many men, many women, and many children."[24]

A decade later, while touring the Hebrides with Boswell, Johnson explained what he believed Macpherson had done in constructing his fraudulent work. He "has found," he said, "names and stories, and phrases—nay passages in old songs—and with them has compounded his own compositions, and so made what he gives to the world, as the translation of an ancient poem. . . ."[25] When Macpherson attempted to intimidate

Johnson by demanding a retraction of many of his public statements, he received this curt and pointed response: "What would you have me retract? I thought your book an imposture; I think it an imposture still. For this opinion I have given my reasons to the publick, which I here dare you to refute."[26] In 1782, seven years after Johnson wrote to Macpherson, the *London Magazine*, after examining a wide variety of evidence, endorsed Johnson's claim that the Ossianic poems were a "forgery."[27]

In the late 1790s, the Scottish Highlands Society, determined to get at the truth of the Ossianic controversy, began a thorough investigation. As part of their research, the society requested Blair to give a full account of all the actions he had taken in promoting the publication of the poems and forward copies of the data he had in his files with respect to their authenticity. On December 20, 1797, Blair wrote to the society reaffirming his faith in the lasting contribution that the *Poems of Ossian* had made to "taste and literature" and expressing the hope that his part in helping them to be introduced to the public would be viewed as one of his permanent legacies.[28]

When the society completed its report in 1805, five years after Blair's death, it concluded that the poems were indeed fraudulent. In the same year, Malcolm Laing, the most prominent authority on the controversy, published a new edition of the work. In his preface, he asserted that Macpherson's "historical dissertations," as well as "many of his notes, are rejected, as full of falsehood. . . ." He also observed that his motivation for not including a reprint of Blair's *Dissertation* was the result of his wish not to dishonor "his memory."[29]

This review of the history of the Ossian controversy is of importance in analyzing Jefferson's performance as a critic of a significant poetical episode. What appears beyond dispute was a noticeable failure on his part to apply adequately his own discourse philosophy. Unlike his thoughtful and penetrating analyses of the oratory of Patrick Henry and Logan, on this occasion he did not use his principles of reasoning and evidence satisfactorily to uphold his claim regarding authorship. He had an opportunity to follow a similar course of action at the time of his correspondence with Charles Macpherson, who had written to his brother about Jefferson's wish to gain access to the supposed original manuscripts. But Jefferson was unexplainably gullible in accepting James Macpherson's feeble excuse for turning Jefferson down. The denial took this form:

> I should be glad to accommodate any friend of yours; especially one of Mr. Jefferson's taste and character. But I cannot, having refused them to so

many, give a copy of the Gaelic poems with any decency out of my hands. The labour, besides, would be great. I know of none, that could copy them. My manner and my spelling differ from others: And I have the vanity to think, that I am in the right.[30]

Such an unconvincing explanation should have been enough to raise doubts in Jefferson's mind.

Motivated by Blair's *Dissertation* and inspired by the emphasis on virtue that permeated the poems, Jefferson, in this landmark instance involving his role as a critic, seemed content to ignore a major literary controversy of which he doubtless was aware[31] and continue to believe that Ossian was an authentic, original primitive poet who drew his strength and forged his eloquence from nature. It was a classic case of substituting sentiment for reason. Fortunately, he became a more effective critic when he evaluated a work on Montesquieu's *Spirit of Laws*.

## Montesquieu's *Spirit of Laws* and Destutt de Tracy's *Commentary and Review*

Another important specimen of Jefferson's rhetorical criticism of non-oratorical forms was his treatment of Montesquieu's *Spirit of Laws* and Destutt de Tracy's *Commentary and Review* of this highly influential work. Montesquieu's comprehensive sociopolitical study, which he conceived in 1734, published in 1748, and revised and expanded in 1757, drew its source material and basic arguments from the author's commonplace book, consisting of classical and modern readings, and from his personal experiences and observations derived from his native France and travels throughout Europe. Tracy, who (like Montesquieu) was a French political philosopher, produced his *Commentary and Review* in 1811. These two publications gave Jefferson an opportunity to hone his skills as a critic and, in doing so, to strengthen his commitment to the belief that the subject of virtue is and should be the defining feature of a democratic society.

### The Spirit of Laws

What made Montesquieu's study so appealing to European and American leaders in the last half of the eighteenth century and the early part of the nineteenth was the subject matter he covered and the research methodology he used to present his thesis.[32] Convinced that by their very nature social phenomena could be analyzed from a scientific perspective,

Montesquieu developed principles and conclusions based on experimental data and the power of reason.[33]

A major thesis that permeated his study was this: The laws that govern a society should be determined by the form of government that has been adopted, and by the prevailing social and geographical forces—such as the location, education, religion, culture, climate, soil, population, and territorial size—of a political community. As analyses of these subjects unfolded, the pages within his three-volume opus teemed with discussions of a wide variety of topics, including crime and punishment, marriage and divorce, liberty and equality, popular sovereignty and taxation, slavery and free labor, commerce and trade, and church and state. Even the theme of suicide, with its moral implications, received attention.

Montesquieu's persistent devotion to order and to a clearly marked classification system led him to draw on and modify the traditional Aristotelean classification of three forms of government—monarchy, aristocracy, and democracy. Montesquieu's three categories included a republic, a monarchy, and a despotic government. A republic, he argued, emphasizes virtue as its defining trait; communication and education as the rhetorical channels for transmitting it; and the importance of patriotism that fosters the citizens' love for their native land and its laws. Personal ambition in a republic, he added, should always be subordinated to the public good among the populace if it becomes excessive or if the territory in which it operates is too large. Montesquieu's views on a republic were both similar to and different from Aristotle's description of an ideal democracy. Both stressed the importance of virtue as a governing principle in the lives of the people and in the performance of the state. But, unlike Aristotle, Montesquieu favored a populace and a territory that had limited size.

A monarchy and a despotic government are the second and third forms delineated by Montesquieu. The distinguishing quality of honor, he held, is the central feature of a monarchy. This activating principle is capable of producing "glorious acts" that might eventually lead to virtue even if the acts were the result of dishonest intentions. Such a practice, he was willing to admit, was inappropriate for a republic whose commitment to virtue does not permit an "end justifies the means" ethical philosophy. On balance, Montesquieu viewed both a republic and a monarchy in a positive light although a monarchy supported the notions of luxury and of a hierarchy that moves from the upper class downward. But his attitude toward a despotic government was decidedly negative because of its central purpose of generating fear, which, in turn, produces an attitude of obsequious obedience.

Montesquieu further recognized that the three branches of government that are essential parts of a republic and a monarchy—the executive, legislative, and judicial branches—must at all times be separate powers. Of these branches, the judicial, he maintained, should be the weakest. Although he learned much about a monarchical type of government by examining firsthand the practice in France, his travels to London, where he saw Parliament in action, the judicial system function, and the king perform his duties, convinced him that the British government was an ideal model to emulate.

Finally, much to the displeasure of the Christian leaders then in power, Montesquieu was an unmistakable relativist.[34] Rather than make claims that universal moral principles should apply to all people regardless of the conditions in which they lived, he opted instead for the relativistic position that the question of determining the overall moral value of a particular law depended on the specific political, social, and cultural factors that are operative in a community at a given period of time. His philosophy of relativism, moreover, was responsible for his assertion that the Catholic religion was more suitable for a monarchy, and the Protestant for a republic.

*The Spirit of Laws* was viewed as a monumental philosophical achievement by American political spokesmen throughout the late eighteenth century, particularly during the period of the creation of the American republican system of government. Various leaders cited arguments and illustrations appearing in the work for the purpose of discussing their own positions on a particularly compelling issue. One such issue was Montesquieu's claim that a republic to be effective should be small in size. Those who argued for strengthening the general government—including, ultimately, Hamilton and Madison in their essays in *The Federalist*—were forced either to distinguish Montesquieu's arguments on this principle as not applicable to America or to challenge them directly. Another difficult issue for the Americans during this period was this: Did Montesquieu's belief in "a doctrine of the separation of powers" mean that he also favored a system of "checks and balances"? W. B. Gwyn, in his *Meaning of the Separation of Powers*, argues that a definitive answer to this query is difficult to ascertain.[35] But despite this ambiguity on a central issue and their reservations pertaining to the optimal size of a republic, both Hamilton and Madison, for instance, alluded, either favorably or with reservations, to several of Montesquieu's key principles in the development of their essays in *The Federalist*. Often when citing his writings, they referred to the author as "the celebrated Montesquieu."[36]

From this brief background sketch of *The Spirit of Laws*, the following question arises: How did Jefferson respond to the basic contentions articulated by Montesquieu? Jefferson as a critic was strongly supportive of numerous sections of *The Spirit of Laws* during his formative years. It was in this period that he gave a prominent place to Montesquieu in his own *Commonplace Book*. Indeed, the twenty-eight pages containing excerpts from the French author, according to Gilbert Chinard, embrace more space than that devoted "to any other single writer."[37]

These cited pages, generally recorded in French with occasional summarized translations by Jefferson, focused on such themes as democratic government, love of country, equality and frugality, justice and punishment involving crimes, corruption of democracies, the federative system and extent of territory, the definition of liberty, the effect of climate and soil on legislation and on slavery, religious and civil laws, and population and its control. Chinard has noted:

> Everywhere in the *Spirit of Laws*, he [Jefferson] found illustrations of the theory which he maintained all his life that laws and constitutions are variable and changing and must be altered in accordance with climate, local conditions, and new circumstances. He even went one step further than Montesquieu in his relativism, when he proclaimed that a generation had no right to bind by laws the following generation.[38]

The excerpts further show that at the time they were recorded in the 1770s, they "corresponded to something which he already felt to be true," and "awakened" in him "some consonant echo in his mind." This conclusion, argues Chinard, "is proved beyond any doubt by the *Commonplace Book*."[39]

When in late 1789 Jefferson returned to America from France, he brought with him a changing attitude toward *The Spirit of Laws* which was to continue in the future. He could still applaud the ideas that a republic is inspired and guided by virtue; that its government is composed of the executive, legislative, and judicial branches; that separation of powers must be maintained; that popular sovereignty is a binding force designed to increase the participation and power of the people; that the freedom of speech and religion, along with the separation of church and state, should be guaranteed; and that laws and constitutions are properly influenced by the conditioning forces that prevail at any specified period in history.

But there were several vital provisions in *The Spirit of Laws*, Jefferson now believed, that failed to conform to the proven tests of experimental social science and of reason. One of these faulty provisions was the claim that a republic to be effective must be confined to a small territory. He thus told François d'Ivernois in 1795 that "experience" has "exploded" the myth "that small states alone are fitted to be republics."[40] Six years later, while serving as president, he commented to Nathaniel Miles that it is a "falsehood" to claim "that a republic can be preserved only in a small territory. The reverse is the truth."[41] The Lewis and Clark expedition, which he conceived, authorized, and planned in 1803, and the Louisiana Purchase, which he fostered and brought to fruition in the same year, were but two examples confirming his faith in the idea that a republic did not have to be limited in size. But in taking this position, Jefferson nevertheless concurred with Montesquieu that because a republic is motivated by a desire to promote peace and moderation, it should be disinclined to wage a war of conquest to expand its territory.

An additional changing perception developed by Jefferson with respect to *The Spirit of Laws* was his view of Montesquieu's claim that when a government condones the practice of "extreme equality" it renders itself vulnerable to a corruption of the democratic process. In refuting this claim, Jefferson argued that the moral value of equality—one of the cornerstones of his republican philosophy—can rarely, if ever, become so excessive that it would constitute a threat to democracy. This possibility should only be a concern, he noted, if "magistrates who had been entrusted with some powers by the people, attempted to usurpate more extensive powers."[42]

Similarly, Jefferson became disturbed by Montesquieu's affirmation that the British method of governance was a model of excellence that demonstrated how a monarch, a parliament, and a judicial system could work together in such a harmonious way that the dominating principle of honor could ultimately lead to virtue. This claim, made in 1748 and repeated in subsequent editions in 1757 and 1767, was, in Jefferson's opinion, little more than an exaggerated form of Anglomania that could not be justified in light of England's later actions against America. Furthermore, in Jefferson's view, the element of honor valued by a monarchy condones personal ambition and an "ends justifies means" philosophy—two characteristics he believed to be incompatible with the public good.

Jefferson continued his criticism of *The Spirit of Laws* following the completion of his second term as president. After noting in 1810 and 1811 that the book contained numerous theoretical and practical truths and sound principles, he faulted it for using "inconsistencies, apocryphal facts and false references." In brief, he affirmed that because it must be considered as "a book of paradoxes," it did not fulfill the requirements of sound and relevant reasoning.[43] Some of these reservations about Montesquieu's classic volume were not shared by most other major contemporary observers,[44] but they successfully prepared Jefferson for the critical task he would now undertake, that of becoming an analyst and a promoter of Destutt de Tracy's *Commentary and Review*.

## Tracy's *Commentary and Review of Montesquieu's Spirit of Laws*

During Jefferson's tenure as president of the American Philosophical Society, he communicated from time to time with Destutt de Tracy on matters of mutual philosophical interest. In February 1806, for instance, he thanked his friend for sending a copy of his recently published volume *Idéologie*, and announcing that the society had elected him as a member.[45] Subsequently, he asserted that Tracy was "the ablest writer living, on abstract subjects."[46] Not surprisingly, therefore, he was elated when he received a draft in 1809 of a proposed book-length manuscript entitled *A Commentary and Review of Montesquieu's Spirit of Laws*. It revealed, in brief, those of Montesquieu's claims that deserved continued support and those that should be rejected or modified because of a lack of relevance when applied to societal changes that had occurred since 1767.

In his critique, Tracy developed three major claims, all of which Jefferson approved. First, he argued, as did Montesquieu, that a government should fulfill two primary requirements: It should take actions that conform to the leading principles emanating from the developing field of social science; and it should rely on sound reasoning based on self-evident premises and a clear understanding. Among the self-evident premises he listed were these: (1) "Justice and injustice," contrary to what Montesquieu had suggested, "had an existence before any law." (2) "Knowledge [is] essentially united with justice, equality, and sound morality." (3) "We can ascertain and explain what is right or wrong, only according to our right and wrong comprehension of it."[47]

His second, and most important, claim was that government in its ideal form is a representative democracy—a designation he preferred to that of a republic. Since such a government, he noted, is founded on "enlightened reason," it is an example of "nature in a perfect state." What gives it perfection is a recognition that the will and welfare of the people, from whom all power should flow, must be a predominant concern. To implement this goal in a fair and just manner, "legislative power should be exercised by delegates freely elected for a limited term and from all parts of a nation. . . ."

In making this point, he again departed from Montesquieu by asserting that a representative democracy may exist "over a great extent of territory."

To reach the level of perfection that Tracy's ideal government sought, it should perform four duties. The first of these was the need to respect "truth" and reject "error and prejudice" by propagating "accurate and solid knowledge of all kinds. . . ." It should make certain, second, that religion is not "taught by authority" and that "the best moral doctrine" be inculcated by "the most enlightened persons of the time. . . ." Third, communication and education, rather than "direct and violent means," should be the method of establishing democracies. Last, it should make certain that "individual liberty and the liberty of the press" be permanently maintained as cornerstones of the democratic process.

Tracy's first two claims on *The Spirit of Laws* contained a mixture of positive comments in support of several essential conclusions, modifying interpretations of other points, and outright refutations of several aspects of the author's thesis and supporting arguments. His third claim, however, consisted of a strong frontal attack on Montesquieu's ideas about monarchy. A monarchy, with its emphasis on a king or queen as the executive, Tracy maintained, places excessive power in the hands of a single leader, thereby reducing the authority of the legislature and the judiciary. Similarly, by using a hierarchical pattern based on heredity, the kings, queens, and nobility are too far removed from public sentiment. In addition, by substituting the ambiguously defined notion of honor for the concept of virtue, a monarchy rests on lower moral ground than that occupied by a representative democracy.

Tracy was particularly unimpressed with Montesquieu's praise of the British government as a worthy model deserving replication. History has shown, he said, that the English constitution has not guaranteed an adequate separation of powers or a proper system of checks and balances. Nor has it provided for a satisfactory democratic means of altering its provisions. Consequently, on at least six or seven occasions, necessary change resulted, not from debate or inquiry, but from an insurrection.

If the British constitution, featuring a monarchy, failed to ensure a suitable means for the distribution of powers, what country, Tracy asked, meets this important challenge? He answered this inquiry with the ensuing argument that represented Jefferson's thinking:

> I would . . . claim this honor for the United States of America, the constitution of which determines what should be done when the executive, or when the legislature, or when both together, go beyond their legislative

powers, or are in opposition to each other; and when it becomes necessary to change the constitution of a state, or of the confederation itself.

Jefferson's function as a rhetorical critic came into full bloom as he evaluated and sought to disseminate the *Commentary*. In a series of letters to the publisher William Duane, he suggested that it would be a profitable "enterprize" for a publisher such as he to print the study. He then gave this positive assessment. The work, first of all, avoided the common practice of many critics who tended to focus on "words and sentences" in their analyses. Instead of relying on this "nibbling" type of criticism, Tracy, he observed, wisely examined *The Spirit of Laws* "by taking a book at a time, considering its general scope, & proceeding to confirm or confute it." This process enabled him to substitute "true for false principles." But there was a second and more compelling reason for Jefferson's enthusiasm for the *Commentary*. It was the emphasis that it had placed on virtue, which he stated as follows: The work, he asserted, "everywhere maintains the preeminence of Representative government, by shewing that its foundations are laid in reason, in right, and in general good." Thus it was, in his opinion, a manifesto of "republicanism."[48]

Jefferson's strongly worded and highly favorable critique of Tracy's manuscript was a major contributing factor in Duane's decision to publish the *Commentary*. Once this was determined, Jefferson's role as a critic took on broader dimensions. Concerned that Tracy's ideas and his unique use of the French language might lose some of their intended meaning and force during the process of translation into English, he volunteered to serve as a critic and, when necessary, a reviser of the pages submitted by the translator Duane had selected.[49] He was fully confident of assuming this task because of his knowledge of French, and of his long-standing familiarity with Tracy's republican philosophy and clear, concise style.

To prepare the way for the translation, Jefferson himself decided to translate Tracy's discussion of a large portion of Montesquieu's Second Book. By doing this, he thought, both Duane and the translator would have a clearer idea of how to proceed. When Jefferson began later to evaluate parts of the translator's work, he not only corrected the grammatical errors in the text but pointed out needed changes in word choice and "forms of expression" in the translation so that the completed manuscript would conform more closely to the personality and style that Tracy had demonstrated when writing in French.[50]

As the work progressed, Jefferson's tone of criticism concerning the quality of the translated pages became increasingly sharp. He complained to Duane of the haste that seemed evident—a haste that led to the use of incomplete sentences, "false syntax," a "want of perspicuity," and occasionally "a suspected mistranslation." So serious were these problems, he suggested, that "a change of translator" might be considered. He then concluded with this statement of concern: "It would be a subject of much regret that a work so distinguished for perspicuity, and a critical choice of words, should appear disadvantageously exactly in these particulars; and the more as there will be no original to recur to for correction or explanation."[51]

One additional challenge confronted Jefferson before the publication of the *Commentary* could be put in final form. Circumstances beyond his control gave him the responsibility of writing the preface. With Napoleon in power, Tracy's brand of republicanism was no longer in tune with the direction that the present French government had taken. As a result, he had fled his homeland, and now felt constrained to conceal his name as the author. In honoring his request for anonymity, Jefferson wrote the preface, developing ideas and using language he believed consistent with what he thought Tracy would have said.

Speaking, therefore, as if he were the author of the *Commentary*, he identified himself in the beginning as "a Frenchman by birth and education" who was an early supporter of the revolution" of 1789, but who later found it necessary to leave "the tyrannies of the monster Robespierre" and seek "safety, freedom, and hospitality" elsewhere. His principal occupations now, he noted, were "reading and contemplation," primarily "on those subjects which concern the condition of man."[52]

The second part of the preface contained a brief analysis of *The Spirit of Laws*, using sentiments he had expressed in his earlier critiques of Montesquieu, and which also reflected the current feelings of Tracy. "I have admired Montesquieu," he affirmed, for "his vivid imagination, his extensive reading, and the dextrous use of it." But, he added, "I have not been blind to his paradoxes, his inconsistencies, and whimsical combinations." If, therefore, such a historically important book as *The Spirit of Laws*, with its numerous truths and "powerful influence on the opinions of society," could have its errors corrected or eliminated, such an action would doubtless enhance the public good. It is this goal that the *Commentary* has sought to achieve.

The preface concluded with a statement of regret that the author was unable to write the book in English—the language of the American audience to whom the *Commentary* was directed. But it offered the promise that since the translator was "skilled in both languages," the original manuscript would be made available to any American citizen who wished to examine it.

Soon after the *Commentary* appeared in print in 1811, Jefferson wrote to Tracy commending him for producing a study which had "a depth of thought, precision of idea, of language and of logic, which will force conviction into every mind." Then calling it "the most precious gift the present age has received," he voiced the hope that the *Commentary* would become "the political rudiment of the young, and the manual of our older citizens. . . ."[53]

During the next six years, Jefferson, taking on the role of promoter and disseminator of the volume, sent copies to such friends as Thomas Cooper, Dupont de Nemours, Albert Gallatin, the Marquis de Lafayette, and John Adams.[54] He also encouraged the editor of the *Edinburgh Review* to publish an analysis of the book. In distributing these copies, and in recommending that the book be reviewed in his favorite journal, the message he wished to convey was clear. The *Commentary*, he suggested, could be read for amusement as well as instruction by American citizens interested in government and politics. Moreover, it would have a special value as a textbook in American colleges and universities.

Jefferson's unusually active participation in evaluating and disseminating the *Commentary*, along with Tracy's decision to maintain his anonymity as long as possible, helped create the impression in the minds of several American and French leaders that he was the real author of the work. This mistaken perception produced a rhetorical exigency that called for an immediate and effective response. In a series of letters, he testified that he not only did not write the *Commentary* but was incapable of doing so had he tried.[55]

In these related communication episodes of Jefferson as critic, we have seen his strategies unfold. His analysis of *The Spirit of Laws* indicated a tendency on his part to single out both the positive and negative elements of a popular and influential work. After identifying these factors, he then argued that the strengths should continue to be recognized and appreciated, and the weaknesses be modified or suppressed. This critical approach, defined in debate terms, may be classified as a repairs case. It was precisely this method of rhetorical criticism as argument that he regarded as being present in Tracy's *Commentary and Review*.

When Jefferson probed deeply into the *Commentary and Review*, his enthusiasm for the solution that Tracy had offered caused him to perform numerous roles that raised his criticism to a higher level. He became an analyst, an editor, a translator, and a persuasive advocate. As was the case in the previous discourse events described in this volume, he was motivated primarily by his dedication to the concept of virtue. He thus saw in the effort of Tracy a salutary emphasis on a type of republicanism that stressed the value of benevolence on behalf of the public good. The study, in sum, represented to him a noble act of cleansing and purifying *The Spirit of Laws* by questioning those conclusions from Montesquieu that had placed a monarchical form of government on a par with that of a republic; upheld the notion that a republic should be limited in size; stated a concern about the potential dangers of excessive equality; and adhered to a reasoning process that produced inconsistencies and paradoxes. In short, it was a book that fully endorsed Jefferson's own republican philosophy, moral sentiments, and the American system of government that he most earnestly wished to be formulated and implemented. If Jefferson had become overly zealous in praising Tracy's *Commentary and Review*, he had no dissonance in taking this stance because, in his opinion, he was speaking in defense of an improved, albeit sanitized version of *The Spirit of Laws*, and of a closely reasoned document grounded in the sacred tradition of republican virtue.

In her volume *Liberalism and Republicanism in the Historical Imagination*, Joyce Appleby asks, "What is Still American in Jefferson's Political Philosophy?"[56] She answers with a poignant and constructive analysis of Jefferson's perspectives on Montesquieu's *Spirit of Laws* and Tracy's *Commentary and Review*. Convinced that this incident was an important case study of Jefferson's philosophy of virtue as it pertains to republicanism, she makes it clear why Jefferson was so enthusiastic about Tracy's critique. "For Jefferson," Appleby argues, "the Review of Montesquieu became a new weapon in his old war against pernicious ideas." It was a war against "Montesquieu's veneration of ancient wisdom," his sympathy toward a government "led by monarchs and aristocrats," his belief that a republic makes "virtue consist in voluntary privations" and "self-denials," and his conviction that republics should remain small in size. By contrast, Tracy eulogized the future rather than the past, argued that a policy calling for privations and austerity was a roadblock to happiness, emphasized the notion that a republic should not be limited in size, and held that the balance of power structure described in the United States Constitution was vastly superior to the British monarchical system.

The *Commentary and Review*, in essence, was a confirmation of Jefferson's ideas that for him had enduring value. Among these was his boundless optimism about a future based upon the concept of "Americanism" which had no place for aristocracy. As he looked out upon his native country with its expanding territory and resources, Jefferson, "more than any other figure of his generation" (observes Appleby) "integrated a program of economic development and policy for nation-building into a radical moral theory." Appleby's perceptive generalizations were made possible, in part, because of Jefferson's highly effective performance as a critic of Montesquieu's *Spirit of Laws* and his recognition of the historical significance of Tracy's *Commentary and Review*.[57] Jefferson, however, was a far less effective critic in his analysis of David Hume's *History of England* and John Baxter's *A New and Impartial History of England*. Unfortunately, this instance—in which he sought to apply his principles of discourse to historical writing—has become the most widely known of our examples of Jefferson as a critic of non-oratorical forms.

## Hume's *History of England* and Baxter's *A New and Impartial History of England*

In establishing a background for his critique of Hume's highly influential *History*, it is instructive to note the great emphasis that Jefferson placed on English history, law, customs, and traditions. Throughout his career, Jefferson emphasized the need for future American leaders to have a thorough knowledge of English history and English historical works. "Our laws, language, religion, politics and manners are so deeply laid in English foundations," he wrote in 1810, "that we shall never cease to consider their history as a part of ours, and to study ours in that as its origin."[58] Often in recommending books for the building of a personal library, he included works on British history. In his frequently cited August 3, 1771, letter to Robert Skipwith, for example, he listed three such volumes as important contributions to an understanding of America's heritage: Hume's *History of England*, Clarendon's *History of the Rebellion*, and Robertson's *History of Scotland*.[59] Independence from Britain did not lessen his appreciation of the significance of British history. His August 10, 1787, letter to Peter Carr listed fourteen books that should be read in "English" history, including Hume's *History of England* and Robertson's *History of Scotland*.[60] In the declining years of his life, he still was interested in recommending readings on English history. He cited six volumes, for example, in his letter to George Washington Lewis, on October 25, 1825.[61]

Despite these recommendations, for much of his life Jefferson struggled to find a single volume, or set of volumes, in English history that met all his standards for historical writing. "There is," he wrote John Norvell in

1807, "no general history of that country which can be recommended."[62] Quite naturally, the one study that interested and troubled him most was Hume's widely read *History of England*. Because of its enormous popularity and what he considered to be its blatant anti-republican bias, Jefferson spent a great deal of time and effort in formulating his critique of Hume's *History*, and in recommending remedies for its negative impact on readers. As was his practice with all historical works, when evaluating the strengths and weaknesses of Hume's study, Jefferson, as outlined in chapter 7, used three criteria. First, historical writing should focus on significant themes, events, and characters for the purpose of instructing and motivating readers on issues that promote personal and public good. Second, this discourse form should rely on reasoning and evidence designed to produce truth. Third, a historical writer must channel the message of virtue through the use of a clear, coherent, and unified organizational pattern; and a plain, concise, and vivid style. Our research suggests that the conclusions Jefferson reached in using the three criteria for excellence in historical writing to evaluate Hume's *History* reveal a mixed result, with the weaknesses of the *History of England* outweighing the strengths.

## Hume's *History of England*

Not only, according to Jefferson, did Hume fail to meet the first standard for excellence in historical writing—the promotion of personal and public good—he did irreparable harm to this concept by challenging the traditional Whig interpretation of the English constitution. Jefferson, along with many other leaders of the early American republic, strongly upheld the view that the early Saxons had created in Britain a constitution that gave primacy to the people rather than to the monarch. Throughout his life, Jefferson maintained his belief in what has been called the "whig myth" pertaining to the presumed existence of a Saxon constitution.[63] In a letter written in his later years to George Washington Lewis, Jefferson showed his enduring commitment to the whig perspective on the supposed ancient constitution:

> The battle of Hastings, indeed, was lost, but the natural rights of the nation were not staked on the event of a single battle. Their will to recover the Saxon constitution continued unabated, and was at the bottom of all the unsuccessful insurrections which succeeded in subsequent times.[64]

Whereas Jefferson believed in the myth of the Saxon constitution, Hume sought in his *History* to rebut this claim. "Throughout the six volumes of

*History*," wrote Constance Noble Stockton, "one of Hume's continuing purposes is the refutation of the whig myth of the 'ancient constitution.'"[65] To Jefferson, Hume's challenging of this myth would have been a prime example of his history's Tory bias.

In addition to Hume's campaign in his *History* to rebut the traditional Whig position on the alleged Saxon constitution, he, in Jefferson's opinion, consistently promulgated other Tory principles that endangered a republican form of government. He did so, Jefferson argued, by interspersing claims that elevated the monarch and denigrated the people. Especially troubling was Hume's treatment of the early Stuart monarchs. During his formative years, Jefferson listed in his *Commonplace Book* eight anti-republican claims made by Hume. Among these statements were: "It is seldom that the people gain any thing by revolutions, in government"; and, "Government is instituted in order to restrain the fury and injustice of the people."[66] Two of the pro-Tory sentiments included in the *Commonplace Book* were cited in Jefferson's 1824 letter to the English radical, Major John Cartwright. These Humean assertions are listed below, along with Jefferson's strong reaction to them:

| *Hume* | *Jefferson* |
|---|---|
| During the reign of the Stuarts, "it was the people who encroached upon the sovereign, not the sovereign who attempted, as is pretended, to usurp upon the people." | This claim by "Hume, the great apostle of Toryism," "supposes the Norman usurpations to be rights in his successors." |
| "The commons established a principle, which is noble in itself, and seems specious, but is belied by all history and experience, *that the people are the origin of all just power*." | "And where else will this degenerate son of science, this traitor to his fellow men, find the origin of *just* powers, if not in the majority of the society? Will it be in the minority? Or in an individual of that minority?"[67] |

In a series of letters beginning during his tenure as president and extending through the year before his death, Jefferson openly attacked Hume's *History* because of what he believed to be its dangerous Tory bias. Writing to Horatio Spafford in 1814, Jefferson stated that the *History*, along with Blackstone's *Commentaries*, had "done more towards the suppression of the liberties of man, than all the millions of men in arms of Bonaparte and the millions of human lives with the sacrifice of which he will stand loaded before the judgment seat of his Maker."[68] So, also, he wrote to John Adams in 1816: "This single book [Hume's History] has done more to sap the free principles of the English constitution than the largest standing army of which their patriots have been jealous." To give further support to his claim that Hume gave an unjustified Tory slant to his History, Jefferson observed: "He even boasts, in his life written by himself, that of the numerous alterations suggested by the readers of his work, he had never adopted one proposed by a Whig."[69]

In fairness to Hume, we note that he consistently maintained that he sought to make his History an objective and balanced work. "The first quality of an historian," Hume wrote William Mure in 1754, "is to be true and impartial."[70] Attempting to explain why his work would be considered less than objective by some readers, he wrote:

> the truth is, there is so much reason to blame, and praise, alternately, king and parliament, that I am afraid the mixture of both, in my composition, being so equal, may pass sometimes for an affectation, and not the result of judgment and evidence.[71]

Had Jefferson been presented with an opportunity to read Hume's claims of neutrality, he would have remained unconvinced. For he was firm in his conviction that the History had violated the first major requirement of excellence in historical writing—the need to promote personal and public good.

As the years progressed, Jefferson also came to believe that Hume's History fell short in conforming to his second criterion of excellence demanded by historical writing—a reliance on reasoning and evidence designed to produce factual truths. Throughout much of his career, his critique of Hume's historical opus centered on what he perceived to be its biased interpretation, which downplayed or ignored opposing data. The following two statements illustrating this point were representative. Hume regarded, Jefferson wrote John Adams, "the arbitrary proceedings of the English kings, as true evidences of the constitution, and glided over its Whig principles as the unfounded pretensions of factious demagogues."[72] Writing to Mathew Carey in 1818, Jefferson declared: "Their [the Stuarts'] good deeds were displayed their bad ones disguised or explained away, or altogether suppressed. . . ."[73]

After reading George Brodie's History of the British Empire, published in 1822, Jefferson became emboldened and delivered this strongly worded sentiment indicting Hume: "For [his] purpose he [Hume] suppressed truths, advanced falsehoods, forged authorities, and falsified records. All this is proved on him unanswerably by Brodie."[74] In his four-volume study, Brodie consistently cites paragraphs from the History, showing how Hume was providing false data and criticizing him for not having access to needed firsthand sources. Our reading of Hume and Brodie suggests that Jefferson's claim that Brodie's arguments were unanswerable cannot be defended—especially when we use his own theory of reasoning as the criterion for evaluation.

When Jefferson turned to the third standard to be used in assessing a historical production, he criticized Hume's organizational structure but warmly praised his style and language control. By writing backwards instead of using a chronological pattern that moves forward, Hume, said Jefferson, was encouraged to produce a biased interpretation of people and events. In an 1810 letter to William Duane, Jefferson wrote:

> It was unfortunate that he first took up the history of the Stuarts, became their apologist, and advocated all their enormities. To support his work, when done, he went back to the Tudors, and so selected and arranged the materials of their history as to present their arbitrary acts only, as the genuine samples of the constitutional power of the crown, and, still writing backwards, he then reverted to the early history, and wrote the Saxon and Norman periods with the same perverted view.[75]

Until the end of his life, Jefferson continued to believe that Hume's faulty organizational pattern had a negative impact on what could have been an outstanding historical study. One year before he died, he offered the following assessment:

> Hume's [History], were it faithful, would be the finest piece of history which has ever been written by man. Its unfortunate bias may be partly ascribed to the accident of his having written backwards.[76]

But if Jefferson was critical of Hume's organizational structure because of its undue influence on the question of bias, he had nothing but praise for the author's brilliant writing style. He viewed Hume as one of the finest writers in contemporary times. "Every one knows," Jefferson wrote in his 1810 letter to William Duane, that "judicious matter and charms of style have rendered Hume's history the manual of every student. I remember well the enthusiasm with which I devoured it when young. . . ."[77] But Jefferson's praise for Hume's History rarely was not qualified. Statements such as the following clearly indicate his ambivalence:

The charms of it's stile and selection of it's matter, had it but candor and freedom from political bias, would make it the most perfect sample of fine history which has ever flowed from the pen of man; not meaning to except even the most approved models of antiquity.[78]

Because of Hume's virtue in language control, Jefferson was gravely concerned about the Tory sympathies expressed in the *History*. "The charms of his style and matter," he wrote in 1822, "have made tories of all England, and doubtful republicans here."[79] He especially was concerned about the persuasive power of the work whenever young students comprised the primary audience. When he himself was a youthful student, Jefferson was so captivated by Hume's moving style that he needed considerable "research and reflection" to "eradicate the poison it [the *History*] had instilled into my mind."[80]

Jefferson doubtless would have held that his critique of Hume's *History* was consistent with his criteria for excellence in historical writing in several important respects. He recognized that Hume, in giving politics a major emphasis in his work, was able to focus on significant themes, events, and characters. Jefferson believed that he was on strong argumentative ground in demonstrating that, because the *History* tilted toward the Tory side, it occasionally suppressed opposing data, thereby adversely affecting personal and public good. He was equally confident in reasoning that Hume's decision to move backwards in time not only deprived the narrative of achieving unity, coherence, and continuity, but contributed to an emphasis or perspective that lacked balance. Finally, in assessing the fundamental dangers of Hume's *History*, Jefferson made a strong case for the potential power of language and style to interest, captivate, and persuade a reader to adopt a particular stance.

In several key areas, however, Jefferson's critical analysis failed to meet the discourse standards he had upheld when describing the rhetorical canons and his own criteria for historical writing. He provided inadequate data in support of his claim that the Saxons had created a definite constitution. He was unjustified in accusing Hume, a philosopher-historian, of deliberately falsifying evidence.[81] He permitted his republican bias to cause him to exaggerate the presumed evil influence resulting from the *History*. He violated his own principles of language by using such question begging-terms as these to describe Hume, "this degenerate son of science, this traitor to his fellow man. . . ." Jefferson's criticism of Hume's *History*, as developed in the preceding first major point, gave him an incentive to offer solutions to the problem. In doing so, as we now show, his performance as a critic in this episode would be in even greater opposition to some of the principles of discourse and virtue he so earnestly had practiced and recommended to others.

## Proposed Remedy: Baxter's A New and Impartial History of England

In his search for a remedy that would protect readers—especially college or university students—from the harmful effects of Hume's *History*, Jefferson offered two solutions. First, he argued, we may "reprint Hume with the text entire, and in collateral columns, or in Notes, place the Antidotes of it's disguises, it's misrepresentations, it's concealments, it's sophisms, and ironies." This method, he believed, would confront readers with "authentic truths from Fox, Ludlow, McCaulay, Rapin and other honest writers." In prescribing this "antidote," Jefferson acknowledged that such an undertaking "would make a work of great volume, and would require for it's execution profound judgment and learning in English history."[82] Although this approach, in our opinion, would have been extremely difficult to implement, it nevertheless would be consonant with Jefferson's philosophy of argument and criticism.

The second potential solution, noted Jefferson, would be to substitute John Baxter's *A New and Impartial History of England* (1796) for Hume's work. In retrospect, Jefferson's acceptance and promotion of this obscure volume are bewildering, and deserve closer inspection here. "All in all," wrote historian Arthur Bestor, "Jefferson's effort to popularize Baxter must be regarded as one of his very few lapses—perhaps his only real lapse—from strict scholarly integrity."[83] Although we consider Jefferson's acceptance of Ossian to be another lapse in his own standards of scholarship, we agree that his promotion of Baxter raises much more troubling issues.

Any discussion of this episode must begin with an acknowledgment that Jefferson's attraction to Baxter's history was sincere. In fact, not until after he read Baxter did Jefferson begin his campaign against Hume.[84] Jefferson made his case for the substitution of Baxter for Hume in letters to publishers and friends. He provided this description and rationale in a communication to editor and publisher William Duane on August 12, 1810, writing that Baxter, a republican and a member of the London Corresponding Society,

> has taken Hume's work, corrected in the text his misrepresentations, supplied the truths which he suppressed, and yet has given the mass of the

work in Hume's own words. And it is wonderful how little interpolation has been necessary to make it a sound history, and to justify what should have been its title, to wit, "Hume's history of England abridged and rendered faithful to fact and principle."[85]

In presenting a similar recommendation to another publisher, Mathew Carey, on November 22, 1818, he was more specific and thorough, writing that Baxter

> gives you the text of Hume, purely and verbally, till he comes to some misrepresentation or omission, some sophism or sarcasm, meant to pervert the truth; he then alters the text silently, makes it what truth and candor say it should be, and resumes the original text again, as soon as it becomes innocent, without having warned you of your rescue from misguidance. And these corrections are so cautiously introduced that you are rarely sensible of the momentary change of your guide. You go on reading true history as if Hume himself had given it.[86]

Still reflecting on Baxter's *New Impartial History* a few months before he died, Jefferson wrote to George Washington Lewis, a University of Virginia faculty member:

> But there is a history, by Baxter, in which, abridging somewhat by leaving out some entire incidents as less interesting now than when Hume wrote, he has given the rest in the identical words of Hume, except that when he comes to a fact falsified, he states it truly, and when to a suppression of truth, he supplies it, never otherwise changing a word.[87]

When Jefferson learned that the only copy of Baxter's volume in America, as far as he could determine, was the one he brought to America—and eventually sold to the Library of Congress—he began a campaign to have the *New and Impartial History* reprinted.[88] Such a reprinting, he wrote Mathew Carey, would allow it to be placed "in the hands of our students" as "an elementary history" for the purpose of preventing a continuing erosion of "their affections to the republican principles of their own country and it's constitution."[89]

Jefferson's decision to commend and promote Baxter's *New and Impartial History*, and then to recommend its adoption as a replacement for Hume's work, was an indefensible rhetorical act that violated his standards for reasoning and evidence, for historical writing, and for virtue. He was, in effect, endorsing a publication that, despite the relatively flexible scholarly standards of his age, was a specimen of outright plagiarism. Both productions focused on the same events and themes—the constitution, the monarchs, the parliament, and the people. Thus both may be classified as political history. More important, when we compared sample pages of Baxter's effort with that of Hume, we found that in most instances Baxter had either used identical wording in his narratives or a closely paraphrased description. Surprisingly, Jefferson himself lauded this "editic expurgation" because it contained, as he put it, an almost verbatim account of Hume's language.[90] Moreover, Jefferson could not help but be aware of the dishonesty Baxter displayed in his lengthy preface. He acknowledged his indebtedness to thirteen different authors including such luminaries as Blackstone, Edmund Burke, Thomas Hardy, William Pitt, and Addison. Yet despite his plagiarizing of Hume, he did not have the moral fortitude to mention him in the preface. When Baxter later alludes to him in the body of the text, it is for the purpose of replacing a particular description by Hume with a republican interpretation.

Second, apart from the issue of plagiarism, Jefferson was giving his approval to a publication that was deficient in other areas of scholarship as well. He knew that the *New Impartial History* was an abridged version of Hume's *History* that omitted numerous specific details. Jefferson himself acknowledged the omissions in his November 22, 1818, letter to Mathew Carey:

> It is unfortunate . . . that Baxter has also abridged the work; not by alterations of text but by omitting wholly such transactions and incidents as he supposed had become less interesting to ordinary readers than they were in Hume's day . . . for those who aim at a thoro' knolege of that history, it would have been more desirable to have the entire work corrected in the same way.[91]

In counting the number of words on sample pages of each text, we have observed that Jefferson was correct in saying that the abridged volume was approximately one-half of that used by Hume.[92] Significantly, the approximately 50 percent reduction dealt only with Baxter's abridgment of Hume, whose *History* ended with the year 1688. Baxter sought to extend his work to 1796, well into the reign of George III.

Similarly important, even while defending *A New and Impartial History* Jefferson was forced to admit that Baxter, when expressing his own ideas as he had to do in the section that extended the history from 1688 to 1796, was an undistinguished writer who was unable to meet the standard of style required for historical writing. In a letter to Duane, Jefferson wrote:

I cannot say that his amendments are either in matter or manner in the fine style of Hume. Yet they are often unperceived, and occupy so little of the whole work as not to depreciate it.[93]

It is disappointing, further, to observe that during his regrettable campaign to have an American publisher reprint Baxter's history, Jefferson used arguments based on rationalizations to explain why he thought that British book editors had refused to produce a second edition. "This work is so unpopular, so distasteful to the present Tory palates and principles of England," he wrote to Duane, "that I believe it has never reached a second edition."[94] Expressing similar sentiments to Thomas W. White a decade later, Jefferson wrote that Baxter's history "was too republican for the meridian of England, and therefore never went there beyond the Original edition. . . ."[95] It is significant to note that despite Jefferson's campaign to persuade no fewer than three American publishers to reprint the work, none of the people he contacted was willing to do so.

Jefferson is to be faulted as a critic of Baxter's *New and Impartial History* for a variety of reasons. First, he was overly supportive of a plagiarized work that violated the most elementary principles of virtue. His efforts to have the work published in America indicated that he was willing, in the words of one historian, "to be a party to intellectual deception."[96] Second, he was too forgiving of Baxter's shoddy scholarship practices that did not conform to the high standards he set for excellence in historical writing. As one historian bluntly remarked, "Baxter's method, as Jefferson described it, was one to make a scholar's hair stand on end."[97] Finally, Jefferson accepted and approved Baxter's claim that he had written an "Impartial History," notwithstanding its unmistakable republican bias. In short, Jefferson's quality of criticism on Hume and Baxter was far inferior to the analysis he developed in analyzing the works of Montesquieu and Destutt de Tracy.

But despite this, in recommending Baxter's work as a substitute for Hume's *History* in American colleges, Jefferson was not, as some scholars have argued, advocating a form of censorship. For he made no effort to have the book banned.[98] On this point, Douglas L. Wilson has argued: "The ill-fated efforts to promote Baxter's book were not aimed at supplanting Hume's history or preventing people from reading it, but they were certainly politically motivated." One of the reasons for Wilson's belief, as noted above, was his conviction that "the most interesting and most neglected aspect of this entire affair is Jefferson's admiration for Hume's history of England."[99]

With this assessment we would agree, because, whereas Jefferson found it easy to criticize Hume and endorse Baxter, his preference was not to have an abridged version of the *History of England*, a work that, except for its Tory bias, was a major scholarly achievement. Jefferson's first choice was to have the complete text accompanied by extensive critical comments of the points he thought were unfair or inaccurate. But since this seemed impractical, he opted for his second choice—the abridged and adulterated version. And this, we believe, was a major fault in his critical assessment of Hume as a historical writer.

As a rhetorical critic of the foregoing major political, philosophical, and literary works, Jefferson, as noted, was at times perceptive and persuasive, and, on other occasions, guilty of ignoring data that were contrary to his views or of permitting excessive bias to affect adversely his reasoning. His analyses of Montesquieu's *Spirit of Laws* and Tracy's *Commentary and Review* were exemplary models showing how rhetorical criticism, as a form of argument, may be used to enhance the reader's understanding of and appreciation for a particular study. But, on the other hand, what he wrote about the Ossianic poems and Hume's *History of England* were vivid examples demonstrating what happens when sentiment is substituted for reason or bias for objectivity.

# Notes

1. August 3, 1771, in Boyd, 1: 78. Blair wrote A *Critical Dissertation on the Poems of Ossian*, published in 1763, which was included in Macpherson's *Poems of Ossian*.

2. November 4, 1823, in Randolph, *The Memoirs, Correspondence and Private Papers of Thomas Jefferson*, 4: 385. On December 26, 1825, Jefferson's granddaughter Ellen Randolph Coolidge, aware of his continuing interest in Ossian, wrote to him saying: "Mr. (John) Adams might say with Ossian, 'the sons of feeble men shall behold me and admire the stature of the chiefs of old. . . .'" Betts and Bear, *Family Letters of Thomas Jefferson*, 465.

3. February 25, 1773, in Boyd, 1: 96–97.

4. Marquis de Chastellux, *Travels in North America in the Years 1780, 1781, and 1782*, 2 vols., Howard C. Rice Jr., ed. (Chapel Hill: University of North Carolina Press, 1963), 2: 392.

5. This two-volume edition, published in London by W. Strahan and T. Cadell in 1784, contains not only the poems but three dissertations entitled as follows: "A Dissertation concerning the Aera of Ossian, A Dissertation concerning the Poems of Ossian, and A Critical Dissertation on the Poems of Ossian, the Son of Fingal. By Hugh Blair."

6. TJ to Peter Carr, August 19, 1785, in Peterson, *Portable Jefferson*, 382.

7. TJ to Mary Jefferson Eppes, February 7, 1799, in Betts and Bear, *Family Letters of Thomas Jefferson*, 173.

8. Sowerby, *Catalogue of the Library of Thomas Jefferson*, 4: 464. Wilson in the *Literary Commonplace Book* notes: "as President, he was still purchasing Ossian's poems to give away. . . ." *LCB*, 173.

9. Sowerby, *Catalogue of the Library of Thomas Jefferson*, 1: 47. Sowerby suggests that the version of the passage "differs slightly from the printed one, and may have been quoted from memory." Ibid. We have found that the quotation is almost identical to that published in Malcolm Laing's edition of the poems. *The Poems of Ossian, Containing the Poetical Works of James Macpherson*, 2 vols. (Edinburgh: James Ballantyne, 1805). Reprinted by AMS Press. 1: 322.

10. *LCB*, 172.

11. This volume was followed by a second edition in 1765.

12. It is of interest to note that the listing of the poems in Jefferson's library was under the caption: "Ossian by Blair." Sowerby, *Catalogue of the Library of Thomas Jefferson*, 4: 464. Also see Robert M. Schmitz, *Hugh Blair* (Morningside Heights, N.Y.: King's Crown Press, 1948), 4.

13. The editions we have consulted on the *Dissertation* are from the following sources which contain full reprints: James Macpherson, tr., *The Poems of Ossian*, 2 vols. (London: W. Strahan and T. Cadell, 1785), 283–435; and *The Poems of Ossian* (Boston: Phillips, Sampson & Company, 1854), 88–180. The first listing here was in Jefferson's library, the date of which is sometimes listed as 1784–1785.

14. Harold F. Harding, ed., *Lectures on Rhetoric and Belles Lettres by Hugh Blair*, 2 vols. (Carbondale: Southern Illinois University Press, 1965), 2: 380. In this work, Blair has a number of references to Ossian which are used for illustrative purposes.

15. Hume to Blair, October 6, 1763, in J. Y. T. Greig, ed., *The Letters of David Hume*, 2 vols. (Oxford: Clarendon Press, 1932), 1: 404; and August 23, 1765, 1: 516.

16. On September 19, 1763, Hume told Blair: "You have a just and laudable zeal for the credit of these poems . . . the child is, in a manner, become yours by adoption, as Macpherson has totally abandoned all care of it." Ibid., 1: 400–401. By affirming that Macpherson has "abandoned all care of it," Hume was thinking of Macpherson's failure to let anyone see the supposed original manuscripts.

17. On June 23, 1760, Blair wrote Lord Hailes: "I intended to have waited on you this day (but was hindered by some accident) that we might have had some conversation about any scheme that can be fallen upon, for encouraging Mr. Macpherson to apply himself to the making a further collection of Earse poetry, and particularly for recovering *our epic*. As the specimens are so highly relished, don't you think, that a pretty considerable collection, might be made for bearing his expences." Cited in Laing, *The Poems of Ossian, Containing the Poetical Works of James McPherson*, xvi–xvii. Also observe Schmitz, *Hugh Blair*, 43.

18. The preface was reprinted in Laing, *The Poems of Ossian, Containing the Poetical Works of James McPherson*, I. The quotation appears on lxvi. Instead of voicing appreciation for all Blair had done, the ungracious Macpherson complained about his use of "translator" to describe the role he as editor had performed.

19. Vincent Bevilacqua and Richard Murphy, eds., *A Course of Lectures on Oratory and Criticism* (Carbondale: Southern Illinois University Press, 1965), 161, 173, 177–78, and 227.

20. Hume to Blair, September 19, 1763, in Greig, *The Letters of David Hume*, 1: 399. Blair himself admitted he did not have knowledge of the Gaelic language.

21. Ibid., 1: 400. On October 6, Hume wrote a letter reinforcing his recommendation. He further noted that when he had informed Macpherson of his action in writing to Blair with suggestions for obtaining evidence with respect to the authenticity of the poems, Macpherson "flew into a passion. . . ." Ibid., 1: 404.

22. Blair to Hume, July 1, 1765, in Greig, *The Letters of David Hume*, 1: 516n.

23. Laing, *The Poems of Ossian, Containing the Poetical Works of James Macpherson*, 1: xxiii.

24. James Boswell, *The Life of Samuel Johnson*, 2 vols. (London: J. M. Dent & Sons, 1946), 1: 245.

25. Boswell, *Tour to the Hebrides with Samuel Johnson* (New York: Literary Guild, 1936), 206.

26. This letter, written in 1775, appears in *The Life of Samuel Johnson*, 1: 516. Johnson spoke for many of Macpherson's critics when he said during the Tour to the Hebrides in 1773: "Let Mr. Macpherson deposit the MS in one of the colleges at Aberdeen where there are people who can judge, and if the professors certify the authenticity, then there will be an end of the controversy." p. 67. These strong criticisms caused dissonance with Boswell who observed in his *London Journal*, 1763: "My blood still thrilled with pleasure. I breakfasted with Macpherson (on May 20), who read me some of the Highlands Poems in the original." (New York: McGraw-Hill, 1950), 264. Eventually, Johnson's campaign against the authenticity of the poems seriously shook Boswell's confidence in them.

27. "The Ossian Controversy Stated," *London Magazine*, 51 (1782): 511–12.

28. Cited in Schmitz, *Hugh Blair*, 127.

29. Laing, *The Poems of Ossian, Containing the Poetical Works of James Macpherson*, 1: viii.

30. James Macpherson to Charles MacPherson, August 7, 1773, in Boyd, 1: 100.

31. Wilson has observed: "Even in old age, when their (The Poems of Ossian) pretensions to be ancient had been thoroughly exposed, Jefferson clung to his high estimate of the poems." *LCB*, 173. Our research supports the idea of the exposure of fraud which had been widely circulated. We are convinced that even if Jefferson had not known about Hume's reservations or Johnson's bitter attacks, he most likely was aware of the *London Magazine* report, Laing's edition of the poems, and the published findings of the Scottish Highlands Society. It is further instructive to note that in 1786, his nephew Peter Carr wrote the following memo to him which expressed the belief of most of the critics of the poems: "You also advise me to read the works of Ossian, which I have done and should be more pleased with them if there were more variety." Carr to TJ, December 30, 1786, in Boyd, 10: 648. Samuel Johnson had drawn a similar conclusion in 1770 when developing his arguments against the authenticity of the poems, when he told Boswell: "The poem of Fingal was a mere unconnected rhapsody, a tiresome repetition of the same images. . . ." *The Life of Samuel Johnson*, 1: 393.

32. The two primary sources we have used for our summary descriptions of Montesquieu's ideas are as follows: *The Spirit of Laws*, tr. from the French of M. de Secondat, Baron de Montesquieu, 2 vols. The Fourth Edition (London and Edinburgh, 1768); and David Wallace Carrithers, ed., *The Spirit of Laws by Montesquieu* (Berkeley: University of California Press, 1977).

33. In his preface, Montesquieu noted: "I have laid down the first principles, and have found that the particular cases follow naturally from them; that the histories of all nations are only consequences of them; and that every particular law is connected with another law, or depends on some other of a more general extent." He then added: "I have not drawn my principles from my prejudices, but from the nature of things." Two twentieth-century authors asserted that Montesquieu was "the first man to attempt a 'scientific' approach to political theory. . . ." David D. Van Tassel and Robert W. McAhren, eds., *European Origins of American Thought* (Chicago: Rand McNally, 1969), 95.

34. For an excellent discussion of Montesquieu's philosophy of relativism, see Carrithers, 34–40.

35. W. B. Gwyn, *The Meaning of the Separation of Powers* (New Orleans: Tulane Studies in Political Science, IX, 1965), 100–128.

36. See, in particular, Hamilton's arguments in Numbers 9 and 78, and Madison's claims in Numbers 10, 14, 43, and 47 of the Federalist Papers. Jacob E. Cooke, ed., *The Federalist* (Middletown, Conn.: Wesleyan University Press, 1961). These essays show that both Hamilton and Madison supported Montesquieu's ideas on the three branches of government and on the need for a doctrine of separation of powers. But they argued, either directly or indirectly, that a republic, despite Montesquieu's reservations, may function effectively in a country that has a large geographical area and population.

37. Gilbert Chinard, ed., *The Commonplace Book of Thomas Jefferson: A Repertory of His Ideas on Government* (Baltimore: Johns Hopkins Press, 1926), 31.

38. Ibid., 37. When Chinard observed that Jefferson went "one step further than Montesquieu in his relativism," he doubtless was referring to Jefferson's famous letter to Madison in 1789 dealing with the theme that "The Earth Belongs to the Living."

39. Ibid., 38.

40. TJ to Francois d'Ivernois, February 6, 1795, in Chinard, *Commonplace Book of Thomas Jefferson*, 267n. Jefferson was mistaken in telling d'Ivernois that "experience" has "exploded" the myth "that small states alone are fitted to be republics." As Douglass Adair has pointed out, the opposite is true. Basing his remarks on an extensive investigation by Madison on this question, Adair asserted: "Madison's reading underlined a further point. Never in all the history of the world had it been possible to organize a republican state in a territory as vast as America; never in the past had it been possible to frame a popular government for a population of such heterogeneous elements as those inhabiting the United States. As he discovered in his books, and as Alexander Hamilton was later to argue in the Convention, all political theorists agreed that a stable republic promoting the general welfare of a varied population could be established only in a small country. Stable empires of vast extent had been organized in the past, but they had all been held together from above by the power of a king." Trevor Colbourn, ed., *Fame and the Founding Fathers: Essays of Douglass Adair* (New York: Norton, 1974; reprint, Indianapolis: Liberty Fund, 1998), 192.

41. TJ to Nathaniel Miles, March 1801, in ibid. Chinard noted that Montesquieu's argument on the size of a republic was perhaps the principal reason for "Jefferson's hostility" toward *The Spirit of Laws*. Ibid.

42. Ibid., 266n.

43. TJ to William Duane, August 12, 1810, in Chinard, *Jefferson et Les Ideologues* (Baltimore: Johns Hopkins Press, 1925), 54.

44. Spurlin argues that "Jefferson was the principal and almost only real detractor of Montesquieu in America." Spurlin, *Montesquieu in America*, 241. But, as we have seen, in *The Federalist*, both Madison and Hamilton, while endorsing some of Montesquieu's key premises, took issue with other parts of his philosophy, particularly on the issue concerning the size of a republic.

45. TJ to Destutt de Tracy, February 14, 1806, in Chinard, *Jefferson et Les Ideologues*, 41.

46. TJ to Francis W. Gilmer, June 7, 1816, in Randolph, 4: 278.

47. For our analysis of Tracy's ideas we have used *A Commentary and Review of Montesquieu's Spirit of Laws* (Philadelphia: William Duane, 1811). This is the same edition that was a part of Jefferson's library.

48. TJ to William Duane, August 12, 1810, in *Jefferson et Les Ideologues*, 54–55.

49. Ibid., 55.

50. TJ to William Duane, October 25, 1810, in *ibid.*, 61.

51. TJ to William Duane, January 18, 1811, in *ibid.*, 63.

52. The preface appears on p. ix of the *Commentary*.

53. TJ to Destutt de Tracy, January 26, 1811, in Chinard, *Jefferson et Les Ideologues*, 74–75.

54. Important excerpts of these letters appear in Sowerby, *Catalogue of the Library of Thomas Jefferson*, 3: 9–11.

55. See the following letters appearing in ibid.: D. B. Warden to TJ, November 1, 1812; Thomas Cooper to TJ, November 8, 1813; TJ to Destutt de Tracy, November 28, 1813; and TJ to Dupont de Nemours, November 29, 1813.

56. (Cambridge: Harvard University Press, 1992). The discussion that follows is based upon pp. 291–319.

57. For further insights on the works of Montesquieu and Tracy, see David N. Mayer, *The Constitutional Thought of Thomas Jefferson* (Charlottesville: University Press of Virginia, 1994), 135–41.

58. TJ to William Duane, August 12, 1810, in *Writings*, 1228.

59. TJ to Robert Skipwith, August 3, 1771, in *Writings*, 745.

60. TJ to Peter Carr, August 10, 1787, in *Writings*, 905.

61. L&B, 16: 125.

62. TJ to John Norvell, June 14, 1807, in *Writings*, 1176.

63. See Trevor Colbourn, *The Lamp of Experience: Whig History and the Intellectual Origins of the American Revolution* (Chapel Hill: University of North Carolina Press for the Institute of Early American History and Culture, 1965; new edition, Indianapolis: Liberty Fund, 1998), 193 ff., particularly 216–25.

64. October 25, 1825, in L&B, 16: 127. See also TJ to Major John Cartwright, June 5, 1824, in L&B, 16: 43.

65. Constance Noble Stockton, "Hume—Historian of the English Constitution," *Eighteenth-Century Studies*, 4 (spring 1971): 277–93.

66. Chinard, ed., *Commonplace Book of Thomas Jefferson*, 374–76.

67. TJ to John Cartwright, June 5, 1824, in L&B, 16: 44.

68. TJ to Horatio G. Spafford, March 17, 1814, in L&B, 14: 120.

69. TJ to John Adams, November 25, 1816, in L&B, 15: 87.

70. Hume to William Mure, 1754, in John Hill Burton, *Life and Correspondence of David Hume*, 2 vols. (New York: Burt Franklin, 1967), 1: 409.

71. Hume to James Oswald, June 28, 1753, in Burton, 1: 381.

72. TJ to John Adams, November 25, 1816, in L&B, 15: 87.

73. TJ to Mathew Carey, November 22, 1818, in Sowerby, *Catalogue of the Library of Thomas Jefferson*, 1: 176.

74. TJ to George Washington Lewis, October 25, 1825, in L&B, 16: 125–26.

75. TJ to William Duane, August 12, 1810, in *Writings*, 1228.

76. TJ to George Washington Lewis, October 25, 1825, in L&B, 16: 125.

77. TJ to William Duane, August 12, 1810, in *Writings*, 1228.

78. TJ to Mathew Carey, November 22, 1818, in Sowerby, *Catalogue of the Library of Thomas Jefferson*, 1: 176.

79. TJ to Messrs. George W. Summers and John B. Garland, February 27, 1822, in L&B, 15: 353.

80. TJ to William Duane, August 12, 1810, in *Writings*, 1228.

81. Recall that Jefferson was significantly influenced by Hume's philosophy of reasoning in his philosophical essays. This is noted in chapter 3.

82. TJ to Mathew Carey, November 22, 1818, in Sowerby, *Catalogue of the Library of Thomas Jefferson*, 1: 177.

83. Arthur Bestor, "Thomas Jefferson and the Freedom of Books," published in *Three Presidents and Their Books* (Urbana: University of Illinois Press, 1955), 19.

84. See Douglas L. Wilson, "Jefferson vs. Hume," *The William and Mary Quarterly*, 3rd Series, 46 (January 1989): 49–70.

85. TJ to William Duane, August 12, 1810, in *Writings*, 1229.

86. TJ to Mathew Carey, November 22, 1818, in Sowerby, *Catalogue of the Library of Thomas Jefferson*, 1: 177.

87. TJ to George Washington Lewis, October 25, 1825, in L&B, 16: 128.

88. In his August 12, 1810, letter to William Duane, Jefferson wrote: "I have often inquired for it in our book shops, but never could find a copy in them, and I think it possible the one I imported may be the only one in America." TJ to William Duane, August 12, 1810, in *Writings*, 1229. The three publishers Jefferson tried to convince to reprint Baxter's history were William Duane (1810), Mathew Carey (1818), and Thomas W. White (1820).

89. TJ to Mathew Carey, November 22, 1818, in Sowerby, *Catalogue of the Library of Thomas Jefferson*, 1: 177. See also TJ to Mathew Carey, July 31, 1820, ibid., 178; and TJ to Thomas W. White, Feb. 5, 1820, Dec. 11, 1823, and Jan. 7, 1824, ibid., 1: 178–179. See also TJ to William Duane, August 12, 1810, in *Writings* 1229.

90. See TJ to William Duane, Sept. 16, 1810, in Sowerby, *Catalogue of the Library of Thomas Jefferson*, 1: 175. See also TJ to [George Washington Lewis], October 25, 1825, in L&B, 16: 128.

91. TJ to Mathew Carey, November 22, 1818, in Sowerby, *Catalogue of the Library of Thomas Jefferson*, 1: 177.

92. Hume employed an estimated 1,192,500 words, while Baxter's number was about 575,190. This meant that the abridged version represented a reduction of 52 percent.

93. TJ to William Duane, August 12, 1810, in *Writings*, 1229.

94. Ibid.

95. TJ to Thomas W. White, February 5, 1820, in Sowerby, *Catalogue of the Library of Thomas Jefferson*, 1: 178.

96. Levy, *Jefferson & Civil Liberties*, 144–45.

97. Bestor, "Jefferson and Books," 18.

98. Leonard Levy takes a more critical position on the issue of TJ and censorship in this episode. See Levy, *Jefferson & Civil Liberties*, 142–57.

99. See Wilson, "Jefferson vs. Hume," 66–69.

# CHAPTER SIXTEEN

~

# Jefferson, African Americans, and Slavery

On April 22, 1820, Jefferson, greatly disturbed by the developing Missouri slavery crisis, wrote to John Holmes expressing his grave concern. This "momentous question, like a fire bell in the night," he said, "awakened and filled me with terror. I considered it at once as the knell of the Union." Later in the same letter, he observed that "we have the wolf by the ears, and we can neither hold him, nor safely let him go. Justice is in one scale, and self-preservation in the other."[1] These two oft-quoted metaphors graphically described a polarized rhetorical situation that had existed throughout Jefferson's life and represented the greatest single challenge that his philosophy and practice of the rhetoric of virtue ever encountered.

The unusually strong link between Jefferson and slavery, widely discussed by his contemporaries, has been the subject of extensive historical analysis. In recent years, interest in this vitally significant aspect of Jefferson's life has increased greatly. At a DNA press conference held at the International Center for Jefferson Studies on November 1, 1998, Daniel P. Jordan, president of the Thomas Jefferson Memorial Foundation, made these comments:

> Slavery and race are uncomfortable subjects for many Americans—but they are in the mainstream of our interpretation at Monticello today precisely because they are part of the Monticello story. The Foundation has long believed that you cannot understand Thomas Jefferson without understanding slavery, and you cannot understand Monticello without understanding the African-American community.[2]

Because of slavery's historical significance, and its relationship with Jefferson's philosophy of discourse as analyzed in part 1 of this volume, we have chosen to make this theme our focus in our last regular chapter. Our specific purpose is to analyze, first, his verbal communication messages consisting of arguments and appeals he used on this subject during chronological stages in his life. We next present a treatment of his symbolic actions, or nonverbal communication messages, which took the form of administrative rhetoric, as discussed in chapter 4. Included in this analysis is a historiographical overview of the issue, along with an application of Jefferson's philosophy of reasoning, and of the model of argument devised by the English logician Stephen Toulmin. This organizational structure, we believe, enables us to understand more fully how Jefferson's actions either conformed to or deviated from the words he used as he sought to cope with an unusually provocative and explosive problem that proved to be one of his greatest moral challenges.

# Verbal Discourse

## Progressive Arguments, 1769–1776

During the seven-year period from 1769 through 1776, Jefferson expressed what might be considered progressive views on this controversial social and political issue. As a recently elected member of the House of Burgesses in 1769, for example, he initiated a behind-the-scenes campaign to have the legislature consider adopting a policy that would lead to the possible emancipation of slaves.[3] He approached Colonel Richard Bland, a distinguished and respected senior member of the House, and urged him to introduce a motion that would make emancipation a workable option for slave-owners. When this was done, Jefferson seconded the motion. He soon learned, however, that such an action was viewed as being dangerously liberal for this period in Virginia history. Although Jefferson was spared criticism for his perceived youthful indiscretion, his friend and ally Bland "was denounced as an enemy of his country, & was treated with the greatest indecorum."[4]

One year later, in *Howell v. Netherland*, Jefferson, as we saw in chapter 12, continued to advance what for the time were progressive ideas on slavery. His arguments in this case, moreover, contained even broader implications regarding the condition of African Americans. After developing the legal argument that a third-generation mulatto could "not be detained in servitude under any law whatever," he proceeded to a moral argument rooted in human nature which maintained that "all men are born free" and, therefore, possess a "personal liberty" granting them the basic right to ensure their own "sustenance." Although, as we have seen, Jefferson lost this case, what he argued on this occasion was consistent with the principles of his rhetoric of virtue.

The arguments used in 1769 and 1770 prepared Jefferson for the role he was to play in producing A Summary View of the Rights of British America in 1774, and the first two drafts of the Declaration of Independence. These two addresses taken together, as noted in chapter 11, criticized the king and Parliament for introducing slaves into the colonies, for overruling serious attempts by the Americans "to exclude all further importations of slaves from Africa," and for violating the "sacred rights of life and liberty in persons of a distant people. . . ." Such inhumane actions, he proclaimed, not only condoned an "execrable commerce" in which men were "bought and sold," but also set the stage for possible insurrections against slaveowners. Although Jefferson's decision to blame the king for instituting slavery in Virginia was a "dubious notion," according to Grant McColley,[5] and despite the fact his antislavery arguments were deleted from the final draft of the Declaration of Independence, Jefferson could return to Virginia in the summer of 1776 comforted by the knowledge that he had earned the praise of John Adams and at least a few other Northerners.[6]

## A Period of Mixed Messages on Slavery in the 1780s

Before he went to France in late 1784, Jefferson was the author of two major messages, both of which focused in part on the subject of African Americans and slavery. The first was the draft legislation he wrote that became known as the "Ordinance of 1784"; the other was his Notes on the State of Virginia.

The arguments Jefferson presented in the "Ordinance" were in the progressive tradition that he had helped formulate in A Summary View and in the Declaration. Following the adoption of the "Act of Cession of 1783," in which Virginia ceded its "Territory North-Westward of the River Ohio" to the national government, Jefferson was assigned the task of drafting a report to his four-person committee and then to the Confederation Congress. The purpose of the report was to devise a plan for a temporary government that could be used in the areas to be formed from the territory.

Of importance in our discussion here was Resolution 5, which appeared both in the first report and in the revised one that the Confederation Congress adopted. It read as follows: "That after the year 1800 of the Christian era, there shall be neither slavery nor involuntary servitude in any of the said states, otherwise than in punishment of crimes, whereof the party shall have been duly convicted to have been personally guilty." An amendment to delete this proviso was passed with a one-vote margin because a delegate from New Jersey, who was ill, could not be present to cast his ballot.[7] A disappointed Jefferson later observed: "Thus we see the fate of millions unborn hanging on the tongue of one man, and heaven was silent in that awful moment."[8] But his courageous effort on this occasion did not go unnoticed. In 1830, Daniel Webster, in his famous debate with South Carolina Senator Robert Hayne, recreated the scene describing Jefferson's support of the proviso[9]; and, on August 23, 1852, Charles Sumner wrote to Edward Coles, saying: "To Jefferson belongs the honor of the first effort to prohibit slavery in the territories. . . ."[10] In sum, in this crucial debate on the antislavery proviso in the Ordinance of 1784, Jefferson was continuing the campaign on this issue that he had initiated in his A Summary View and the Declaration of Independence.

The second major Jefferson document in the 1780s was his Notes on the State of Virginia. In chapter 13 we gave an overview of this volume as a sample of historical writing and social commentary. Our goal here is to analyze a specific part of this work—the author's ideas on what he perceived to be the evils of slavery and the slave trade, his reflections on the physical and mental characteristics of African Americans, and his proposed emancipation and colonization plan.

The most devastating critique in Jefferson's writings against the institution of slavery appears in Query XVIII on "Manners."[11] Although this brief section of the Notes covers only two pages, it is filled with poignant and persuasive statements on the adverse political, social, and educational effects emanating from this practice.

In his first contention, Jefferson detailed the negative impact of slavery on "manners," "morals," and "education." The relationship "between master and slave," he said, often consists of a "perpetual exercise of the most boisterous passions," revealing "unremitting despotism," and "degrading submissions. . . ." To make matters worse, "our children see this, and learn to imitate it . . . for man is an imitative animal." When parents become excessively angry causing a loss of self-control when dealing with their slaves, they not only will set a bad example in front of their children, but will corrupt their own social affections, which should promote love, temperance, and justice. Jefferson emphasized the gravity of this point: "The man must be a prodigy who can retain his manners and morals undepraved by such circumstances." He next asserted that statesmen who permit "one half of the citizens . . . to trample on the rights of the other" will transform themselves "into despots" who have lost their "morals," and the slaves into "enemies" who no longer love their country.

A second argument contained claims that were religious in nature. Remember, he warned, that because the "liberties" we cherish are a "gift" from "God," we should "tremble" for our "country" when we "reflect that God is just; that his justice cannot sleep forever. . . ." He then gave this warning: If God is moved to "wrath" by our unjust actions against other human beings, a "supernatural interference" may occur. Jefferson's two principal antislavery contentions in Query XVIII were telling examples of how a Virginia plantation owner could set aside personal interests and come down forcefully against a social and political institution that prevailed throughout much of the United States, especially in the South, in the 1780s. It proved, moreover, that in this difficult instance Jefferson had relied on sound moral arguments. Regrettably, although Jefferson's arguments were morally sound, he, like most of his Virginia colleagues, often failed to translate his antislavery expressions into action. As Grant McColley put it: "the antislavery pronouncements of Virginia's statesmen were so rarely accompanied by any positive efforts against slavery as to cast doubt on their sincerity, and when initiative against slavery was proposed by others they normally resisted it."[12]

The objectivity and soundness of reason that marked the discussion of Query XVIII on "manners" was not present in the analysis of African Americans and slavery that constituted part of Query XIV on the subject of "Laws."[13] Unfortunately, it was in this section of the *Notes* that Jefferson moved into a controversial political and social area fraught with danger to his reputation as a champion of republican virtue. Convinced that his experience as a Southerner and as a plantation owner gave him firsthand knowledge of the physical, moral, and mental characteristics of blacks, he chose to compare these traits with those of whites. In doing so, he concluded that in most respects blacks were inferior to whites. He began by noting the disadvantage of their color, suggesting that whiteness was superior from both a physiological and a visual perspective.

Jefferson proceeded to a discussion of the faculties of memory, imagination, and reason. After conceding that blacks were equal in memory, he asserted that in imagination they "are dull, tasteless, and anomalous. . . ." This deficiency, he declared, rendered them incapable of "sublime oratory" or of "poetry."[14] In the area of reason, he argued, blacks are "much inferior, as I think one could scarcely be found capable of tracing and comprehending the investigations of Euclid. . . ."

His strong opinions cited above, backed by speculation and pseudo-science, led him to reach this disturbing conclusion: "I advance it there-fore as a suspicion only, that the blacks, whether originally a distinct race, or made distinct by the time and circumstances, are inferior to the whites in the endowments of both body and mind." In no other instance did he conclude an argument on such an important and volatile subject with these words: "I advance it therefore as a suspicion only. . . ."[15] In al-most every other case involving such an important issue, Jefferson drew on the basic principles of his philosophy of practical reasoning before es-tablishing a claim. His use of tentative words—a strategy he defended when criticized on the issue—does not lessen the damage he caused to the dignity of African Americans. Moreover, by "expressing 'suspicions' of the inferiority of blacks," one historian has noted, "Jefferson consid-erably weakened the impact of his appeal for freedom for the slaves."[16]

What is troubling to us in this instance was Jefferson's failure to apply his principles of argument and virtue in drawing his conclusions. He said in Query XIV that "to justify a general conclusion, requires many obser-vations, even where the subject may be submitted to the Anatomical knife, to Optical glasses, to analysis by fire, or by solvents." Yet he did not make use of convincing experience or testimony—two of his most im-portant elements of reasoning. Moreover, he made ineffective use of anal-ogy. By claiming that Roman slaves were superior to American slaves, even though the latter lived in more debilitating conditions, he was downplaying the importance of environment and elevating the power of nature without justification.

In brief, Jefferson's lack of scientific data based upon experience, his ig-noring of persuasive testimony, and his faulty use of analogy made it highly unlikely that he could reach a conclusion based upon the calcula-tion of probabilities. This failure to use his elements of reasoning on this occasion adversely affected his philosophy of virtue, his views on the re-quirements of historical writing, and, of course, his Declaration of Inde-pendence. In no way was this vintage Jefferson.

What is difficult for an observer to understand is how Jefferson the rhetor could elevate his discourse to such a high level in *Howell v. Nether-land*, in *A Summary View* and the Declaration of Independence, in the Ordinance of 1784, and in Query XVIII of the *Notes*, and then in Query XIV lower it to a point of unreasonableness that fell far below the re-quirements of his rhetoric of virtue. One possible interpretation of this inconsistency might have been his fear of the increasing pro-slavery sen-timent in Virginia; another was the strong dissonance he may have been experiencing that led to an inner turmoil resulting in ambivalent feelings. Whatever the cause, he set in motion serious counterattacks that have continued to the present day.

Jefferson's belief that blacks were not on an intellectual and physical par with whites contributed in part to the solution that he recommended for solving the slavery issue. It was a two-pronged plan that combined emancipation with colonization or expatriation.[17] Because of the large number of slaves in the United States, the time period for putting the process into effect would have to be gradual. The emancipation proposal discussed in Query XIV included the following provisions: (1) Whenever the bill is taken up by the legislature, slaves should remain with their parents until they reached "a certain age, then be brought up, at the public expence, to tillage, arts or sciences, according to their geniusses. . . ."; (2) the age requirement for women would be eighteen and for men twenty-one; (3) "they should be colonized to such place as the circumstances of the time should render most proper; and, (4) they should be sent "out with arms. . . ."

The foregoing plan for freeing slaves, it would appear, contained provisions that were costly, impracticable, and unreasonable. Even as he offered his solution, he expressed doubts about its ultimate effectiveness. "This unfortunate difference of color, and perhaps of faculty," he said, "is a powerful obstacle to the emancipation of these people." He then drew another comparison with the Romans. For them, he pointed out, "emancipation required one effort. The slave, when made free, might mix with, without staining the blood of his master. But with us a second is necessary. When freed, he is to be removed beyond the reach of mixture." This claim would be remembered in a negative way in the years ahead.

In the remaining years of the 1780s, Jefferson wrote two letters that provide instructive perspectives on his thinking about slavery and emancipation while he was in France. The first, addressed to the English scholar Richard Price in the summer of 1785, has special significance for students of rhetoric because of the insights given on the subject of audience analysis and adaptation. Price had written to Jefferson asking him how his pamphlet favoring emancipation was being received in America. Jefferson responded by predicting the possible impact the pamphlet would have in particular sections of the country.

There would be little support, he noted, south of the Chesapeake Bay. "From the mouth to the head of the Chesapeak," on the other hand, the recommendations made in the pamphlet would be approved in "theory" but a majority of the citizens would not be inclined to put the ideas into practice because they lacked "the courage to divest their families of a property. . . ." But there was a good chance that the character and influence of the minority in this geographical area were so strong that these residents might have the persuasive power to prevail against the majority in the end. The next location he discussed was the territory north of the Chesapeake. In commenting on this part of the east coast, Jefferson asserted with confidence that Price's work would generate a favorable reaction in this area because it contained only a few slaves.

When he next referred to his home state of Virginia, he spoke with optimism and enthusiasm about his hopes for the future with respect to the slavery question. What was interesting about Virginia, he observed, is that we may see a "spectacle of justice in conflict with avarice and oppression. . . ." The good news, however, about this tension is that it has produced this result: "The sacred side is gaining daily recruits from the influx into office of young men grown and growing up." So encouraged was he by this positive trend that he saw it as an example of the extension of the American Revolution. These young people, he declared, "have sucked in the principles of liberty as it were with their mother's milk, and it is to them I look with anxiety to turn the fate of this question."

To illustrate more graphically what the young people were capable of accomplishing, Jefferson alluded to what was happening at his alma mater—the College of William and Mary. Following a recent revision of the curriculum, he noted, students from around the state came to Williamsburg to prepare "for public life." There they are able to study under the tutelage of George Wythe, a knowledgeable and "virtuous" man "whose sentiments on the subject of slavery are unequivocal. . . ." At this point, Jefferson offered this advice to Price: "I am satisfied if you could resolve to address an exhortation to those young men, with all that eloquence of which you are a master, that it's influence on the future decision of this important question would be great, perhaps decisive."[18]

The letter by Jefferson is a splendid example of his rhetoric of virtue in action. Throughout, he emphasized such elements of virtue as justice, liberty, and human rights. The organizational structure of the arguments adhered to a well-conceived and executed need-solution format. The content of the letter, moreover, showed the author's knowledge of how different audiences in particular regions of America probably would react to the discussion of a highly controversial subject. Similarly, it revealed Jefferson's talent for using language that was clear, forceful, and vivid. Finally, in the history of Jefferson's use of arguments on behalf of emancipating slaves, this letter of optimism concerning his faith in the young people of Virginia, written in his early days in Paris, stands as a memorable moment in his rhetorical career.

In January 1789, in the final year of his diplomatic assignment in Paris, Jefferson obviously was still mindful of the problem of slavery in America. He wrote to Dr. Edward Bancroft that experiments that have been made show that giving "liberty to, or rather, to abandon persons whose habits have been formed in slavery is like abandoning children." He recalled that Quakers in Virginia who placed "their slaves on their lands as tenants" were often disappointed with the results. They had to be observed closely to make certain they performed needed tasks; and when they did not fulfill their duties properly, they were whipped. All too often, he added, "these slaves chose to steal from their neighbors rather than work; they became nuisances and in most instances were reduced to slavery again." At the close of the letter, Jefferson pleaded with Bancroft not to make "use of this imperfect information (unless in common conversation.)"[19] This communication, it would appear, suggests strongly that Jefferson, during his assignment abroad, had strengthened his belief that a major debilitating effect of slavery was its harmful effect "on a man's moral sense." But it also showed that Jefferson seemed afraid that his views, if known by the public, would create further dissension on an issue that was becoming increasingly controversial.

## Stance Taken as a Federal Government Servant, 1790–1809

Jefferson described the years between 1790 and 1809 as a period in which he felt out of touch with public sentiment on slavery in Virginia.[20] Nevertheless, as secretary of state, vice president, and president, he occasionally developed arguments that threw additional light on his attitudes toward African Americans and slavery. In 1791, for example, he expressed the hope that the governor of Spanish Florida would "execute with good faith the orders of his Sovereign to prevent the future reception within his province of slaves flying from the United States."[21]

In the same year, Jefferson exchanged letters with Benjamin Banneker, an African American scientist who had felt the pangs of racial discrimination. The correspondence began with a letter from Banneker, who asserted that his people had "long laboured under the abuse and censure of the world," "had been viewed with contempt, and had been perceived as brutes rather than humans." Such a condition, he noted, was indefensible since all men were created by "one Universal Father" who is a stranger to partiality and injustice. He then praised Jefferson for uttering these words to counter the tyranny of Great Britain: "We hold these truths to be self-evident, that all men are created equal, and that they are endowed by their creator with certain unalienable rights, that among these are life, liberty, and the pursuit of happiness."

Without specifically mentioning *Notes on the State of Virginia*, Banneker proceeded to a consideration of the arguments in this work, suggesting that the inferences that Jefferson had drawn about blacks were inconsistent with his earlier high ideals expressed in the Declaration. He then invited Jefferson to join with him in an effort to combat slavery and prejudice.

As a reminder to Jefferson that blacks are capable of engaging in scientific investigations, Banneker enclosed in his letter a copy of the Almanac he had developed "for the succeeding year." This astronomical gift, he said, is the result of my "unbounded desire to become acquainted with the secrets of nature. . . ."[22]

Banneker's letter, filled with both praise and criticism, was not the type of message Jefferson could easily ignore. Within days, he gave a response that appeared to soften the stance he had taken in the *Notes*. "Nobody wishes more than I do," he observed, "to see such proofs as you exhibit, that nature has given to our black brethren, talents equal to those of other colours of men, and that the appearance of a want of them is owing merely to the degraded condition of their existence both in Africa & America." It was his sincere hope, Jefferson added, that an effective system would be put in place designed to elevate the "body and mind" of blacks.

The letter concluded with a gesture of good will, in which Jefferson announced he had forwarded the Almanac to Monsieur de Condorcet, a member of the Philanthropic Society and secretary of the Academy of Sciences in Paris. This action was taken, he noted, to demonstrate that people "of colour had a right for their justification against the doubts which have been entertained of them."[23]

The exchange of letters between Jefferson and Banneker is important because it shows how Jefferson, in these letters, struggled mightily to take an enlightened and consistent position on the issue of race relations and slavery in America. As Boyd has persuasively argued, the author of the Declaration of Independence sincerely believed "that slavery was a violation of the natural rights of man and hoped for its abolition." At the same time, however, it appeared that he was equally committed to the contradictory idea that whites and freed slaves could not live in harmony with each other. Holding these conflicting principles as a starting point, Jefferson reached the conclusion that "emancipation must be accompanied by colonization of the freed slaves beyond the limits of the United States."[24] The letters further demonstrate that while Jefferson was never convinced that blacks were on the same intellectual and physical level as whites, he nevertheless pleased Banneker by stating his willingness to let science render a final decision on this vexing issue.

When Jefferson spoke of African Americans and slavery while serving as vice president and president during his first term, he had two major interests and concerns. First, he concentrated on the subjects of emancipation and colonization as a possible solution; second, he felt that if some type of meaningful action were not taken, a destructive insurrectionary movement might occur. To him, any proposed solution would be difficult because it would be almost impossible to satisfy the three groups who dominated public opinion on slavery: (1) those who were strongly committed to emancipation and colonization; (2) those who held that slavery was a legitimate institution that could not be modified if we tried; and (3) those who believed that slavery was a moral wrong.

On the whole, Jefferson tended to side with those who urged adoption of an emancipation and colonization plan they believed to be fair and just—one that was least likely to generate excessive passions and prejudices. In taking this position, he told Virginia governor James Monroe that the states, not the national government, should explore the possibility of choosing the West Indies as a home for freed slaves. If this did not work out, Africa should be considered as a second option.[25] The group that represented the greatest threat to peace and tranquility, according to Jefferson, were those who held firmly to the notion that the issue was a moral one. To hold this conviction, he said, is to reject compromise; and this rigidity, in turn, could be catastrophic. He thus informed St. George Tucker that the revolutionary storm sweeping around the globe may stir up an "insurrection" similar to that which took place in Santo Domingo. As a result, "if something is not done, & soon done, we shall be the murderers of our own children."[26]

These rhetorical episodes, in sum, were a battle between justice on one side and self-preservation on the other—or between an argument based on circumstance and one relying on principle. Because Jefferson's fear of insurrection took precedence over what was morally right, his reasoning on slavery during this phase of his leadership role fell far short of the well-articulated philosophy of private and public virtue that was an essential part of his rhetoric of virtue.

Several discourse events occurred during Jefferson's second term as president in which he functioned as a progressive in some instances and as a reactionary in others when he stated his views or took action regarding blacks and slavery. Consider, for example, what he said in his "Sixth Annual Message" on December 2, 1806:

> I congratulate you, fellow citizens, on the approach of the period at which you may interpose your authority constitutionally to withdraw the citizens of the United States from all further participation in those violations of human rights which have been so long continued on the unoffending inhabitants of Africa, and which the morality, the reputation, and the best interests of our country have long been eager to proscribe. Although no law you may pass can take prohibitory effect till the first day of the year 1808, yet the intervening period is not too long to prevent by timely notice expeditions which can not be completed before that day.[27]

These words constituted a clearly stated declaration reminding the members of Congress that they had the constitutional authority to take action that would prevent future "violations of human rights" so long practiced against the innocent "inhabitants of Africa. . . ." This statement was then given further urgency with the claim that such action was consistent with our "morality," our "reputation," and our country's heartfelt desire to be fair and just. Perhaps no other statement he delivered as president went this far in addressing the issue of slavery and, in particular, the African slave trade.

But if Jefferson could take a progressive stance in proposing an end to the international slave trade, he seemed unable or unwilling to alter his negative views on the intellectual and physical qualities of blacks. At the same time that he produced his "Sixth Annual Message" to Congress, he was still denigrating the innate talents of blacks. Sir Augustus John Foster, an Englishman who met with Jefferson at some point between 1805 and 1807, summarized some of the president's remarks. Jefferson told Foster that, while Banneker could produce almanacs, his letters often "were very childish and trivial"; and that "Negroes" seemingly do not have the "foresight" to make proper use of "blankets." But what bothered Foster most was Jefferson's assertion that members of the "Negro race" are "as inferior to the rest of mankind as the mule is to the horse"; and that the "English hobby" of persevering "in endeavouring to abolish trade" was rendering "the Negroes' fate more miserable. . . ." Foster alluded to these observations as proof of Jefferson's "prejudices."[28]

The issues raised in the letters from and to Banneker in 1791, and in the interview with Foster, were still very much alive in the closing months of Jefferson's second term as president. Prominent blacks continued expressing their concern about the arguments developed in Query XIV of the *Notes*. In August 1808, Bishop Henry Gregoire, a black religious leader, wrote to Jefferson for the purpose of refuting his claim that African Americans have far less mental and physical assets than do whites. He buttressed his claims by sending a copy of a recent book entitled *Literature of Negroes*. Jefferson's response to the volume was similar to that he had given to Banneker seventeen years earlier. "Be assured," he said, "that no person living wishes more sincerely than I do, to see a complete refutation of the doubts I myself entertained and expressed on the grade of understanding allotted to them by nature, and to find that in this respect they are on a par with ourselves." As he had done in his letter to Banneker, Jefferson again observed that what he had said in the *Notes* was stated in a tentative manner and with a great deal of "hesitation." But he covered fresh ground when he offered this additional justification: "My doubts were the result of a personal observation on the limited sphere of my own State, where the opportunities for the development of their genius were not favorable, and those of exercising it still less so."[29]

It is important to note how Jefferson's words to Gregoire and Banneker were markedly different in tone than those on the same topic written to Joel Barlow in 1809. His politeness had now been replaced by pointed criticisms revealing an increased sensitivity about the attacks on the arguments that he had advanced in the *Notes*. He ridiculed Gregoire for his tendency to round up every example he could find demonstrating the talents and accomplishments of blacks without offering specific supporting data as proof, and identifying the degree of "mixture" in the blood of each. His comments on Banneker were even more severe. Not only did he claim that the Almanac was created with the assistance of the white scholars George Ellicot and his cousin Andrew Ellicot, but he also observed that the letter he had received from Banneker in 1791 revealed "a mind of very common stature indeed."[30]

The letters to Banneker, Condorcet, Gregoire, and Barlow show clearly the nature of Jefferson's internal struggle and dissonance which he experienced from 1791 through 1809. He could not understand why his critics failed to recognize that his arguments in the *Notes* included a qualifier or reservation that his conclusions were based on "suspicion" only. Nor could he understand why they seemingly did not know, as he felt he did, that the mixture of white blood with that of blacks would increase the latters' intellectual and physical capacity. Most of all, he did not seem to appreciate the damaging emotional impact that his stance in the *Notes* had upon the well-being of blacks in general. But there were also several positive conclusions that may be drawn from what he said in some of the letters we have cited. First, he had demonstrated an increased awareness of the influence that environment may play in a system of slavery. Second, he appeared to be sincere in his wish that future scientific studies might prove that the intellectual and physical traits of African Americans have been underestimated.

## Positions Taken on Slavery during his Retirement Years, 1809–1826

It was exceedingly difficult for Jefferson to remain silent on the rapidly developing slavery crisis during his retirement years. From time to time, for instance, letter writers would send him recently published books and pamphlets with the hope he would give a specific response. For the most part, he was willing to state his position on the slavery question and give a recommendation with the caveat that young persons, not the elderly, should lead the campaign for change because they "can follow it up, and bear it through to its consummation." The need for "those unfortunate beings," as well as for "ourselves," he said, is to eliminate "our present condition of moral and political reprobation."[31] The problem, moreover, was aggravated because those who had been reared in a slave environment were, like children, incapable of taking care of themselves. As a result, concluded Jefferson, many slaves have become "pests in society for their idleness, and depredations to which this leads them."[32]

What is remarkable about Jefferson's arguments in support of a solution to the problem is that they did not go beyond the ideas discussed in the *Notes* in the 1780s. "The only practicable plan I could ever devise," he told David Barry in 1815, "is stated under the 14th quaere of the *Notes on Virginia*, and it is still the one most sound in my judgment."[33] A similar sentiment appears in his communication to Jared Sparks in 1824. Again he reasserted his belief that what he had "sketched in the *Notes*" was the most practicable and workable solution. But, in this case, he reiterated the points he had made forty-five years earlier. They included the following provisions: (1) Emancipate the "after-born"; (2) Leave "them on due compensation, with their mother, until their services are worth their maintenance"; and (3) Put "them to industrious occupations, until a proper age for deportation."[34]

When we review Jefferson's solution in its entirety, we see, as noted earlier, that his plan consisted of two steps: emancipation and colonization. Because there were 1.5 million slaves in the 1820s, according to his estimate, the fulfillment of the recommended plan had to be gradual. The locale for the projected colonization, he thought, should be either on the west coast of Africa, preferably in Sierra Leone, or in the West Indies. But his solution, as discussed in the *Notes*, would not achieve the practicality he had hoped. It simply was too costly, unworkable, and lacked sufficient public appeal. To counter this condition, Jefferson introduced two additional supporting claims that might make his plan more palatable. The first was an attempt to prove the advantages that it would have for the people of Africa or the West Indies. If the slaves were sent to Africa, he noted, they would be in a position to take their knowledge of "all the useful arts" back "to the country of their origin," and thereby be able to teach the natives "the seeds of civilization. . . ."[35] Notwithstanding that this was at odds with Jefferson's occasional description of the devastating effect that slavery had upon the culture and maturity of American blacks, it was positive in the sense that a former slave might become a teacher.

A second argument, designed to jump-start his emancipation-colonization plan, was to make it voluntary at the outset. In this suggestion, presented to Dr. Thomas Humphreys in 1817, Jefferson offered this claim: "Perhaps the proposition now on the carpet at Washington to provide an establishment on the coast of Africa for the voluntary emigrations of people of color, may be the corner stone of this future edifice."[36]

In section one of this discussion of Jefferson's use of verbal communication, we have sought to demonstrate how his arguments on African Americans and slavery were progressive at times and conservative bordering on reactionary on other occasions. His progressive arguments were numerous, as seen in *A Summary View*, the first two drafts of the Declaration, the Ordinance of 1784, Query XVIII of the *Notes*, and his message to Congress in 1806. But the power and appeal of these presentations largely were neutralized by his arguments in Query XIV of the *Notes*, in his interview with Sir John Foster, and his letter to Joel Barlow criticizing Benjamin Banneker and Bishop Gregoire. By his persistence in questioning the mental and physical capacity of blacks, and by giving his support to an emancipation-expatriation plan that was impractical and static, he stood on the wrong side of history.

As we turn to part two of this chapter, it is of significance to mention one other argument that was a vital element of Jefferson's verbal communication pattern on African Americans and slavery, and one that rendered him vulnerable in the area of administrative rhetoric. It was his strong attack against the practice of miscegenation. We first saw a reference to this contentious point in the *Notes* when he said that if the slaves are set free, they should "be removed beyond the reach of mixture." Later he spoke forthrightly and emphatically on this issue in his letter to Edward Coles in 1814. The "amalgamation" of blacks with whites, he asserted, "produces a degradation to which no lover of his country, no lover of excellence in the human character can innocently consent."[37] He stated this perspective in similarly strong language in 1826, a few months before his death, to William Short: "I consider that [the plan] of expatriation to the governments of West Indies . . . as entirely practicable, and greatly preferable to the mixture of colour here. To this I have great aversion. . . ."[38] The enormous significance of these views on miscegenation becomes clear in our ensuing analysis of Jefferson's nonverbal discourse on blacks and slavery.

# Nonverbal Communication or Administrative Rhetoric

## The Nature of Administrative Rhetoric

Soon after beginning his second term as president, Jefferson received a letter from Thomas Brannagan of Philadelphia asking him to purchase a recently published antislavery book entitled *Avenia; or a Tragical Poem on the Oppression of the Human.* Troubled by this seemingly innocent request, Jefferson immediately wrote to his friend Dr. George Logan stating his concern and asking him to intervene on what appeared to be a "small" and insignificant issue. After admitting that the theme of the volume dealt with a "holy" cause, and praising Brannagan for the warm and ingratiating sentiments he had expressed, Jefferson announced that he had "most carefully avoided every public act or manifestation on that subject." Consequently, he was reluctant even to answer the letter for fear that this act alone would prove to be controversial and unsettling, thereby resulting in a possible "lessening" of "confidence & good will" among many of his friends and supporters in slaveholding areas. It was for this reason he asked Logan to meet with Brannagan and explain why his request had to be denied.[39]

Two years later, in the summer of 1807, Governor James Sullivan of Massachusetts, as we discussed in chapter 4, invited Jefferson to make a tour through the New England states. In his letter of response to this friendly request, the president rejected the invitation because such a visit, he believed, might be interpreted as a means of ingratiating himself with the people of the North.

These two instances illustrate what the twentieth-century scholar Kenneth Burke called "administrative rhetoric."[40] This form of discourse suggests that when a person in a leadership position performs an act that has symbolic meaning, a message is being conveyed. It works both in a positive and in a negative way. Whether an administrator takes a specific action in a given instance, or refuses to perform a particular act even though asked or expected to do so, nonverbal communication occurs. Jefferson feared that if he had subscribed to the book recommended by Brannagan, this act would have been construed by his supporters as a public sign of his endorsement of a piece of antislavery literature. By the same token, he also equated a presidential tour as an overt effort to curry favor with the voters of New England. When he offered to make such a trip after he left office, he felt secure in the belief that the meaning of such an act would be understood.

That Jefferson was the administrator of a large plantation whose operations were built on slave labor gave him numerous opportunities to engage in nonverbal discourse. As a result, what he did and failed to do as head of his plantation proved to be a greater challenge to his rhetoric of virtue than any obstacle that had ever confronted him when participating in verbal communication situations involving African Americans and slavery.

In the first section of this chapter, we saw how Jefferson described in vivid detail the harmful effects of slavery, the need to abolish the slave trade, and the necessity to prevent the practice of slavery in the Northwest Territory. Yet, in spite of these pronouncements, he, unlike George Washington and John Randolph,[41] felt motivated to use his administrative power to free only a handful of his slaves. This became a particularly vexing problem for him because of his authorship of the Declaration of Independence. When Benjamin Banneker reminded him in 1791 that the words in the Declaration must apply to all of God's children, he was expressing the feeling that all slaves should be emancipated. Failure to do so was to communicate the message that blacks were not covered by the self-evident clause that "all men are created equal. . . ." Some Jefferson scholars have argued that, while Jefferson maintained slaves on his plantation, he nevertheless was a compassionate master.[42] But there is also a body of convincing evidence to show that a large number of the Monticello slaves would have preferred their freedom.[43]

It is against this background that we now turn to a consideration of one of the most important episodes in Jefferson's political and social career—

the Sally Hemings controversy. If, as Daniel Jordan said, we cannot understand Jefferson unless we realize how slavery was an integral part of Monticello life, we also cannot appreciate fully the nature of Jefferson's discourse practices on the institution of slavery until we examine what this event represents from the perspective of administrative rhetoric.

## The Sally Hemings Affair: A Case Study of Administrative Rhetoric

The person who was primarily responsible for breaking the story of a possible sexual relationship between Jefferson and Sally Hemings was James T. Callender, a Scotsman by birth who was forced to leave Britain following a series of articles and pamphlets he had written criticizing the crown. He settled in Philadelphia in the 1790s before moving to Richmond where he became a newspaper reporter. After identifying with the Federalists shortly after his arrival in America, Callender shifted his political support to Jefferson during the 1800 presidential campaign. In June of that year, he was found guilty of violating the Sedition Act of 1798, and was sentenced to prison for nine months and assessed a fine of $200. Upon his release, he urged newly elected President Jefferson to appoint him to the position of postmaster of Richmond. When this request was turned down on the grounds that he lacked the qualifications for the office, Callender felt betrayed by the man he had admired and actively supported.[44]

Partly because he had viewed Callender as a legitimate refugee, and in part because he believed he had been imprisoned by an unjust law, Jefferson sought to help him. He sent his aide Captain Lewis to meet with him, to present a gift of $50 to be applied to his fine, and to offer the hope that additional financial assistance might be available in the future. This gesture was rebuffed by Callender, prompting Jefferson to give this description of the meeting with Lewis: "He (Callender) intimated that he was in possession of things which he could and would make use of in a certain case; that he received the 50 D. not as a charity but a due, in fact as hush money. . . ."[45]

Sixteen months later, Callender, now an implacable enemy of the president, decided to publish his charges. They appeared on September 1, 1802 in a recently created newspaper, the *Richmond Recorder, or Lady's and Gentleman's Miscellany.* The charges and the language were specific and explosive. "It is well known," he wrote, "that the man, *whom it delighteth the people to honor*, for many years past has kept, as his concubine, one of his own slaves. Her name is Sally." His first argument in support of this belief was based on signs that led to his claim that Sally's oldest son, Tom, had "features" resembling "those of the president himself." Then, after observing that Jefferson had set a bad example for his two daughters by taking Sally with them to France, he asserted that if this intimate relationship with his slave had been known by the public, Jefferson would not have won the election in 1800. As he approached the conclusion of his column, Callender made these claims: (1) "By this wench Sally, our president has had several children." (2) "There is not an individual in Charlottesville who does not believe this story, and not a few know it." (3) "The American Venus is said to officiate, as housekeeper at Monticello."[46]

Callender's incendiary claims, relying on a mixture of circumstantial evidence and other forms of insufficient proof, and phrased in embellished and sarcastic language, titillated the fancy of the Federalists but were denounced by Jefferson's admirers and friends. Samuel Smith, the editor of the *National Intelligencer*, refused to print the story. To Smith and other Jefferson allies, Callender was a "scoundrel" and a "wretch"—a vengeful man whose flawed character was testimony against his claims designed to tarnish the reputation of the president.[47]

But many others, troubled by the thought that questionable moral practices might be taking place at Monticello, were willing to check out for themselves what Callender had written. Federalist newspapers throughout the country reprinted the assault on Jefferson and on his Republican allies who had defended him. Significantly, the story initiated in Richmond in the autumn of 1802, as Charles A. Jellison put it, "has echoed down the years. . . ." It "was used by British visitors to denigrate American democratic society in the 1830s, by abolitionists in the period around the Civil War, and by blacks in the late 1950s as part of the early civil rights campaign."[48]

If, as Jellison asserted, Callender's charges were still widely circulating in the 1950s, a century and a half after they appeared in print, we confront this question: What enabled the allegations to endure over such a long period of time? To a large degree, the answer to this query, we feel, is that it was a significant event filled with symbolic meaning. For, to believe, as some did, that the author of the Declaration of Independence had used his role as administrator of his plantation to make Sally Hemings his mistress, fathering one or more of her children, meant that this act resulting from his position of power as master was a visible and telling violation of what he had taught and advocated throughout his life. From the moral standpoint, it was startling and unreasonable, they thought, that he could have a sexual relationship with his slave after arguing that blacks were mentally and physically inferior to whites, and that because of this condition they should be expatriated following emancipation.

Callender's charges against Jefferson received scholarly attention from Winthrop D. Jordan in his comprehensive and pioneering volume *White Over Black*, published in 1968. Using statistical data and effect-to-cause reasoning, Jordan drew these conclusions:

> The entire Hemings family seems to have received favored treatment. . . . All the slaves freed by Jefferson were Hemingses, and none of Sally's children were retained in slavery as adults. She bore five, from 1795 to 1808; and though he was away from Monticello a total of roughly two-thirds of this period, Jefferson was at home nine months prior to each birth. Her first child was conceived following Jefferson's retirement as Secretary of State. . . . Three others were conceived during Jefferson's summer vacations and the remaining child was born nine months after his brief return to Monticello for the funeral of his daughter.[49]

Jordan's fresh and timely method of selecting data to form the basis for his insightful arguments proved to be a model for future studies on Jefferson and Hemings, many of which made use of the nine-month theory and the issue of favoritism toward the Hemings children. But before these studies are analyzed, it is useful to examine how a group of Jefferson scholars, aware of the continuing interest in the Sally Hemings affair—both before and after Jordan's study—felt that the time had come to respond to the rhetorical situation created by Callender and enthusiastically publicized by Federalists, antebellum abolitionists, and more than a few individuals in the twentieth century.

One of the first to do so was Merrill Peterson in his study *The Jefferson Image in the American Mind*, published in 1960. Convinced that the miscegenation charge against Jefferson relied "upon the flimsy basis of oral tradition" and anecdotal data, and that "paternity" in this case would "probably never be proven," Peterson suggested that the Sally Hemings "legend" derived its impetus from "three factors." First of all, it was politically motivated; second, the social and economic impact of "the institution of slavery," with which Jefferson was associated, was more relevant for him than for any of the other Founding Fathers; and, third, his personal life, marked by the early death of his wife and by his "interest in Negroes," made him an ideal target for his critics because of his status as a widower and a plantation owner. But in contrast to these allegations, asserted Peterson, there is a significant amount of evidence to suggest that the "domestic life" of Jefferson was sufficient to prove his innocence. His refutation was highlighted with this claim: "The legend survives, although no serious student of Jefferson has ever declared his belief in it."[50]

Nor had Peterson changed his mind on the controversy when he wrote his 1970 work *Thomas Jefferson and the New Nation*. Again referring to the so-called affair as a "legend," he noted that the evidence used to corroborate Jefferson's reputed involvement with the "African Venus" was "highly circumstantial" and inconclusive. Moreover, for a person of Jefferson's "character," a "miscegenous" affair would be inconceivable, because such "a mixture of the races, such a ruthless exploitation of the master-slave relationship, revolted his whole being." He then observed that while it "is of no historical importance . . . but the best guess is that Sally's children were fathered by Peter Carr. . . ."[51]

Also in 1970, Peterson's distinguished colleague Dumas Malone reached a similar conclusion in his publication of *Jefferson The President, First Term*, the fourth volume of a six-volume biography. Malone gave three reasons for rejecting the Callender–Federalist–abolitionist arguments on Jefferson's supposed sexual relationship with Sally Hemings. First, Callender, the initiator of the story, was a "vengeful" and "unscrupulous man" who was motivated by "bitter partisanship." Second, the charges could not "be proved and certain of the alleged facts were obviously erroneous." Third, for Jefferson to have committed such acts would have been inconsistent with his "character" and his "moral standards."[52] Of these three arguments of refutation, the last was the most telling and persuasive to Jefferson's admirers.

William W. Freehling, writing in the *American Historical Review* two years after the claims advanced by Peterson and Malone in 1970, drew this conclusion on what he called "the notorious case of Sally Hemings": "Those who enjoy guessing whether Jefferson sired Sally's many offspring can safely be left to their own speculations. The evidence is wildly circumstantial and the issue of dubious importance. Of greater significance is the way Jefferson and his contemporaries handled the ugly controversy." They failed to face the "embarrassing" problem directly because of the fear that "interracial sex would ruin anyone's reputation." It was better, they concluded, to adopt the rhetorical strategy of silence rather "than blurt out the full horror of America's nightmare."[53] In short, according to Freehling, the failure to use discourse properly about the allegations was more important than the allegations themselves.

In 1974, two years after Freehling's article appeared, a previously unpublished essay by Douglass Adair was included in Trevor Colbourn's edited volume on *Fame and the Founding Fathers: Essays of Douglass Adair*. Entitled "The Jefferson Scandal," the study summarized the arguments, both pro and con, about Jefferson's alleged involvement with Sally Hemings. Adair began with a discussion of Jefferson's role in the controversy, suggesting that Callender's allegations were written in a spirit of "revenge," and that as a witness he was "reckless with the truth." He then quoted Julian Boyd as asserting in 1954 that he knew "no single historian" who supported Callender's claim that Jefferson was the father of Sally Hemings's children.

Convinced that it was "possible to prove that Jefferson was innocent of Callender's charges," Adair presented reasons in support of this belief. First, he noted that Jefferson's Farm Book, known for its accuracy and specificity, did not list anyone as the father of Sally's children. Second, when the testimonies of the two most important witnesses in the case, Madison Hemings and Thomas Jefferson Randolph (a grandson), are analyzed, what Randolph had to say, argues Adair, is more reliable. Because Madison's testimony given in his interview with the *Pike County Republican* in Ohio on March 13, 1873 was based almost exclusively on what he had learned from his mother, because it lacks credibility owing to her false claim that she was pregnant upon her return from France in 1789, because a number of other claims she made were filled with "internal inconsistencies," and because she had a tendency to "overdramatize" her relationship with Jefferson, what she is alleged to have told Madison must be viewed as "untrustworthy."

By contrast, according to Adair, Randolph's claims asserting Jefferson's innocence must be taken seriously. For over the years, he was in a position to observe closely the actions of Jefferson and those of Sally Hemings. Often he occupied a bedroom near his grandfather's room, the door of which was always unlocked, without seeing or hearing any suspicious activity. More important, because Jefferson was "chaste and pure on sexual matters" and "as immaculate a man as God ever created," he was incapable of engaging in the immoral practices cited by Callender. Most of all, Randolph's strong faith in Jefferson's innocence was shared by an unimpeachable authority, Edmund Bacon, the overseer of the Monticello plantation from 1806 to 1822, and whose arguments, asserted Adair, were more believable than those articulated by Madison Hemings.

Adair next developed two additional claims in his defense of Jefferson. First, he maintained that the father of Madison Hemings's offspring was Peter Carr, Jefferson's favorite nephew, who had a love relationship with Sally Hemings for approximately fifteen years. In the second place, Jefferson's character, known and loved by Americans for two centuries, would not permit acts that were immoral. He affirmed this conviction in these words:

> All in all, Sally's story and the Jefferson she asks us to believe in, if credited as true, would require us not merely to change some shadings in his portrait but literally to reverse the picture of him as an honorable man, painted both by his contemporaries who knew him well and by the multitude of later scholars who have studied with care every stage in his career. The personality of the man who figures in Sally Hemings's pathetic story simply cannot be assimilated to his known character of the real Thomas Jefferson.[54]

Adair's essay on Jefferson, which he had hoped to revise, contained insights that placed him in the vanguard of mid-twentieth-century scholars who sought to probe into the Jefferson-Hemings story. Annette Gordon-Reed regards "Adair's interpretation," despite its flaws, as being "instructive" because it "makes the deepest and most thoughtful attempt to analyze the Jefferson-Hemings controversy." Similarly, she added, Adair "was virtually alone among his generation in perceiving that in order to come to grips with the story, one has to come to grips with Sally Hemings."[55] Notwithstanding this positive assessment by Gordon-Reed, it is to be regretted that Adair made a number of strong claims that lacked sufficient proof. This was particularly evident in his unproved assertion that Peter Carr, after a presumed love affair, was the father of Sally Hemings's children. Nor was Adair's argument convincing in trying to show that Sally and her son Madison were unreliable witnesses who developed inconsistent arguments and who exaggerated their so-called close bond with their master. Finally, Adair may have been mistaken when he alleged that Sally did not tell the truth when she asserted that she was pregnant upon her return to Virginia from France.

By rejecting the Sally Hemings story with the rationale that it was inconsistent with Jefferson's character and based upon circumstantial evidence, Peterson, Malone, Freehling, and Adair represented the majority sentiment of Jefferson scholars, and many others as well, in the 1960s and 1970s. They were united in the view that the sexual liaison could never be proven beyond a reasonable doubt. But this widely accepted perspective was challenged in a significant way in 1974, as it had been done by Jordan in 1968, with the publication of Fawn Brodie's biography, *Thomas Jefferson: An Intimate History*. This controversial study, relying on contemporary testimony and featuring bold and imaginative claims, was an attempt to debunk much of the traditional research. Among Brodie's principal claims were these: (1) Sally was treated "with special consideration" in Paris. (2) A deliberate attempt was made to keep the relationship secret by omitting her name from the Farm Book, and by refusing to make "specific denials" either "in public or in private." (3) Jefferson was at Monticello nine months before Eston Hemings was born. (4) Both Madison Hemings and Israel Jefferson testified that Sally was the mistress of their master at Monticello.

Brodie made two additional claims, both psychological in nature, which caused a strong negative reaction from more traditional scholars.[56] The first inferred that when Jefferson, in his letters and journals describing the countryside of Holland, France, and Germany in the spring of 1788, used the word "mulatto" eight times, it was a sign of his "preoccupation" with Sally Hemings. The second psychological claim, consisting of a similarly bold inferential leap, was phrased as follows: "If the story of the Sally Hemings liaison be true, and I believe it is, it represents not a scandalous debauchery with an innocent slave victim, as the Federalists and later the abolitionists insisted, but rather a serious passion that brought Jefferson and the slave woman much happiness over a period lasting thirty-eight years."[57] More than a few traditional scholars seized upon these latter two claims for failing to meet the requirements of responsible historical scholarship; and they dismissed the earlier contentions of Brodie because, in their opinion, they did not rise above the level of circumstantial evidence.[58]

But notwithstanding the strong reservations expressed by other Jefferson biographers concerning her study, Fawn Brodie is to be commended for challenging traditional views on the Jefferson-Hemings controversy. Annette Gordon-Reed, for instance, defended Brodie for a "revisionist spirit" that led her to make use of psychobiographical data in her analysis that claimed "the Hemings story is true." Moreover, she pointed out that An Intimate History "was well received by the public."[59]

The scholarly debate over the alleged intimate relationship between Jefferson and Sally Hemings was renewed in earnest with the 1993 volume Jeffersonian Legacies. This study, published in honor of the 250th anniversary of Jefferson's birth, contains four essays that give varying degrees of emphasis on the issue. A joint effort by Scot A. French and Edward L. Ayers provides a useful summary of recent literature on the question.[60] The essay by Gordon Wood not only summarizes some of the recent research but includes several critical assessments of the problem, the most important of which is the following claim: "But whether the Hemings relationship was true or not, there is no denying that Jefferson presided over a household in which miscegenation was taking place, a miscegenation that he believed was morally repugnant."[61]

More recently, in 1997, two other books were published that addressed the issue. One was authored by law professor Annette Gordon-Reed and the other by historian Joseph Ellis. Gordon-Reed's volume, *Thomas Jefferson and Sally Hemings: An American Controversy*, faults the traditionalists for failing to deal objectively with Brodie's study, and for refusing even to consider the possibility that the alleged sexual relationship might have occurred. Why, she further asked, have these scholars provided us with detailed information on the life and personality of Maria Cosway and, at the same time, made no legitimate attempt to probe into the life of Sally Hemings? If we did undertake such a probe, she suggested, there is a reasonable probability that untapped sources could be discovered.

Although Gordon-Reed was not willing to draw the conclusion that Jefferson was the father of Sally Hemings's children, she, like Brodie, listed several assertions that might tend to support this probability. Four of these include testimony from contemporary witnesses—James Callender, Madison Hemings, Israel Jefferson, and John Hartwell Cocke.[62] Two others cited the Jordan argument that Jefferson was present at Monticello nine months before *each child* was born, and that he gave preferential treatment to all of them.[63]

What gives Gordon-Reed's volume a special perspective is the author's background as a law professor, specializing in the law of evidence, at the New York Law School. She acknowledged her debt to Winthrop Jordan and to Fawn Brodie, and her book is a careful scholarly analysis not only of the evidence, but of the rhetorical posture of the Jefferson scholars and historians who previously had dismissed the Hemings version of events; she analyzes their assumptions in a perceptive critique. This was made particularly clear when she asserted that many historians, when confronted with new and compelling writings on the Jefferson-Hemings case, tend to "shift the focus from the content of these primary sources to the personalities of the individuals who produced them." In this highly negative manner, ad personam attacks are substituted "for analysis," as was evident in their treatment of James Callender.[64] But Gordon-Reed's influence went beyond this type of challenge because of her use of crosschecking of oral tradition among Hemings descendants against documentary evidence to which they had no direct access, such as Jefferson's own papers and reminiscences and contemporary accounts of other white planters and their neighbors.

The appearance of Gordon-Reed's volume in 1997 was followed in the same year by Joseph Ellis's *American Sphinx: The Character of Thomas Jefferson.* In the body of this work, Ellis quotes a reference from the Federalist *Port Folio* which alludes to Hemings as "Sally the Sable." This derogatory reference, he said, "was a casual insertion of the most sensational accusation made against Jefferson, a charge of sexual (and in its own day racial) impropriety that became the equivalent of a tin can tied to Jefferson's reputation that would rattle through the ages and the pages of the history books."[65] Later, in an appendix to the study, he included a four-page "Note on the Sally Hemings Scandal," in which he stated that "after five years mulling over the huge cache of evidence that does exist on the thought and character of the historical Jefferson, I have concluded that the likelihood of a liaison with Sally Hemings is remote." He did suggest, however, that his opinion could change if the Thomas Jefferson Memorial Foundation decided "to exhume the remains and do DNA testing on Jefferson as well as some of his alleged progeny. . . ."[66]

It is clear that as the year of 1997 came to a close, scholarly opinion concerning the Sally Hemings affair was divided. Many Jefferson scholars continued to believe that Jefferson's character, moral standards, and teachings in general made it unlikely he could have participated in a miscegenous relationship with one of his slaves. But relying on circumstantial evidence, eyewitness testimony, and an oral tradition spawned by the descendants of Sally Hemings, an increasing number of historians were keeping the issue alive. As pressure began to build for a resolution of the problem, as seen in the renewed interest in Brodie and in the volume by Gordon-Reed, a decision was made to conduct DNA testing. Only by combining the pioneering work of Gordon-Reed and others with a scientific method such as DNA testing, some believed, could a conclusion be reached that rose above the level of reasonable doubt. If such persuasive proof could be established, then we would know that Jefferson, in this instance, had engaged in an administrative communication act that was in direct violation of the rhetoric of virtue that epitomized most of his private and public life.

The test results, as reported in the scientific journal *Nature,* in its November 5, 1998 issue, explained the procedure that was used and the conclusions reached. "Because most of the Y chromosome is passed unchanged from father to son, apart from occasional mutations," the authors noted, "DNA analysis of the Y chromosome can reveal whether or not individuals are likely to be male-line relatives." With this as a controlling scientific principle, the method and findings were explained as follows:

We therefore analyzed DNA from the Y chromosomes: of five male-line descendants of two sons of the president's paternal uncle, Field Jefferson; five male-line descendants of two sons of Thomas Woodson; one male-line descendant of Eston Hemings Jefferson; and three male-line descendants of three sons of John Carr, grandfather of Samuel and Peter Carr.

There were important reasons for including in the study the descendants of Thomas Woodson and John Carr. Woodson had stated repeatedly that he was the son of Jefferson—a claim accepted by his family in succeeding generations; and Jefferson's daughter and grandchildren, along with numerous historians, believed that either Samuel or Peter Carr, the nephews of Jefferson who spent considerable time at Monticello, was the probable father of the Hemings children.[67]

When the statistical data were interpreted, the following conclusion was drawn: "The simplest and most probable explanations for our molecular findings are that Thomas Jefferson, rather than one of the Carr brothers, was the father of Eston Hemings Jefferson, and that Thomas Woodson was not Thomas Jefferson's son." This "molecular evidence" further shows that it "is at least 100 times more likely if the president was the father of Eston Hemings Jefferson than if someone unrelated was the father." To put it another way, "the probability of such a match arising by chance is . . . less than 1%." As soon as these results were forwarded to media organizations throughout the United States, major newspapers, including the *New York Times* and the *Washington Post*, featured the story on their front pages.[68]

The preceding discussion of the historical debate over the subject of Jefferson's relationship with Sally Hemings raises two questions. First, what inferences may be drawn concerning Jefferson's actions played in the relationship; second, what is the significance of this relationship as it relates to Jefferson's philosophy of the rhetoric of virtue? To answer the first question, which seeks to determine whether there is sufficient evidence to conclude beyond a reasonable doubt that Jefferson was the father of one or more of the Hemings children, we wish to use as our criteria of evaluation Jefferson's perspectives on argumentation as analyzed in chapter 3; and Stephen Toulmin's highly influential volume *The Uses of Argument*. Jefferson's view, as noted, included four elements of reasoning: experience, testimony, analogy,[69] and calculation of probabilities. It also contained four special criteria for assessing the strength of an argument: coherence and consistency, fidelity in the use of evidence, the occasional use of self-evident principles as a starting point, and the production of positive consequences.

When we consider the element of experience, which functions as a means of accumulating knowledge based upon an arousal of the sensory organs, we are able to assess the value of the evidentiary materials used in support of a claim. We know through experience, for example, that DNA testing—a successful scientific method of investigation—is often used to obtain genetic material in legal cases. We also know that when the participants in a scientific study are recognized as well-trained experts in their field, the reliability and validity of the results will be increased. This was the case in the present DNA experiment. The chairman of the study who traveled throughout the country gathering genetic data was Eugene A. Foster, a retired pathologist from the University of Virginia. Other members of the team were as follows: two professors of genetics from the University of Leicester; one professor of human genetics from Leiden University; and two faculty members from Oxford University—one in statistics and the other in biochemistry. This impressive group of scholars from four renowned universities, in short, used the element of experience in conducting their study.

Jefferson's second element of argument—testimony—also played a prominent part in providing answers to the first query. Madison Hemings (Sally's son born in 1805) and Israel Jefferson (born in 1797), both of whom were slaves and household servants in the home at Monticello, testified in interviews published in the *Pike County* (Ohio) *Republican* in 1873 that Sally Hemings was their master's "concubine."[70] This eyewitness testimony, presented forty-seven years after Jefferson's death, was discounted by some traditional historians who felt that a diminished memory may have affected their account.[71] But what the two ex-slaves had recalled was, as we have observed, strongly supported by the DNA test.[72] Thus, their other claims—not directly provable (except by DNA testing)—have increased credibility as well.

Eric S. Lander, who is at the Whitehead Institute for Biomedical Research at the Department of Biology at the Massachusetts Institute of Technology, and Joseph J. Ellis, a professor of history at Mount Holyoke College (and author of *American Sphinx*), wrote a companion essay that appeared, along with Foster's report, in the journal *Nature*. After examining the strength of the arguments created from experience and testimony with the results generated by the DNA experiment, these authors drew the following conclusion: "Together with the circumstantial evidence, it seems to seal the case that Jefferson was Eston Hemings' father."

In an effort to obtain additional data on the foregoing elements of reasoning—experience and testimony—we conducted two tape-recorded interviews in Charlottesville, Virginia, on May 13, 1999. The first was with Eugene A. Foster, chairman of the DNA committee; and the second was with Daniel P. Jordan, president of the Thomas Jefferson Memorial Foundation. Our primary purpose was to ascertain their views concerning the soundness of the DNA study.

Both Foster and Jordan agreed, first of all, that the DNA report was scientifically sound with respect to the research design and the methodology. This claim, suggested Foster, was supported because neither he nor the journal *Nature* had received any serious challenges from researchers concerning the reliability and validity of the study. In concurring with Foster's assessment on this point, Jordan was similarly forthright and specific. The Thomas Jefferson Memorial Foundation, he noted, had created a staff committee whose goal was to develop an independent study of its own on the relationship between Jefferson and Sally Hemings. Although this investigation at the time of the interview had not yet been completed, the committee had already contacted scientists from Yale University, the University of California at Berkeley, the University of Virginia, the Massachusetts Institute of Technology, and Cold Springs Harbor Laboratory (where Dr. Watson did pioneering research on DNA). With universal agreement, these scientists affirmed that the Foster study was scientifically valid. Foster and Jordan further agreed that the DNA report did not and could not claim with "absolute certainty" that Jefferson was the father of Eston Hemings.

But Foster did conclude that his study had shown that "it is more probable than not" Jefferson was the parent of Eston. He then proceeded to point out that when his scientific data are combined with the historical data, we are able to make such claims as these: "It is highly probable"; "it is much more probable than not"; and "it is very, very likely" Jefferson had a sexual relationship with Sally Hemings that led to the birth of Eston.[73] Jordan, on the other hand, hesitated to make a probability claim on the subject until his committee, some members of whom were scientists and experts in oral history, completed their investigation. In the meantime, he said, any researcher dealing with this question has a right and duty to suggest that the "weight of evidence" based upon his or her research points toward a particular conclusion.

Eight months after the interview with Daniel Jordan was held, the Thomas Jefferson Memorial Foundation Committee delivered its report at a press conference at Monticello. After meeting ten times between December 1998 and April 1999, after evaluating Foster's DNA study, and after examining a large body of documentary evidence and secondary sources, the members of the research committee reached these conclusions: (1) "Dr. Foster's study was conducted in a manner that meets the standards of the scientific community, and its scientific results are valid." (2) "The DNA study, combined with multiple strands of currently available documentary and statistical evidence, indicates a high probability that Thomas Jefferson fathered Eston Hemings, and that he most likely was the father of all six of Sally Hemings' children appearing in Jefferson's records." In assessing the soundness and persuasive strength of the research committee's conclusions, Daniel Jordan presented this argument: "I concur with the committee's findings. Although paternity cannot be established with absolute certainty, our evaluation of the best evidence available suggests the strong likelihood that Thomas Jefferson and Sally Hemings had a relationship over time that led to the birth of one, and perhaps all, of the known children of Sally Hemings."[74]

The "weight of evidence" criterion outlined by Jordan in his interview with us in the spring of 1999 constitutes what Jefferson, like Hume who preceded him, described as the fourth element of reasoning—the calculation of probabilities. As we have earlier noted, rhetors, in applying this argumentative principle, measure the strength and relevance of propositions based on experience, testimony, and analogy (when appropriate). If these elements, in turn, meet the test of coherence, consistency, and fidelity—and we believe in this case they have—a meaningful probability level may be established. What we have sought to demonstrate is that Jefferson's philosophy of argumentation, aided by DNA testing and supplementary historical data, leads to the conclusion voiced by Eugene Foster that "it is very, very likely Jefferson was the father of Eston Hemings."

Stephen Toulmin, an English philosopher and rhetorician who has held professorships at the University of Chicago and Northwestern University, developed a model of argumentation that, like that of Jefferson, is based upon informal or practical reasoning rather than upon formal logic. What makes his model unique is that it consists of six clearly delineated elements or steps, the most essential of which are Data, Qualifier, and Claim. Data represent the factual materials the arguer has to go on as a starting point. The Qualifier consists of the degree of probability the Data permit the rhetor to use. The Claim is the conclusion authorized by the strength of the Data and the Qualifier. Schematically, these three steps may be diagrammed as follows:

Data_____Qualifier_____Claim

Given that arguments in practical reasoning, according to Toulmin, can never achieve "absolute certainty" as in the case of formal logic, three additional elements may be needed when a Claim is or perhaps will be challenged. The first of these he labels as Warrant; the second is defined as Backing for the Warrant; and the third he calls Reservation. The Warrant and its Backing he describes as "general, hypothetical statements, which can act as bridges, and authorise the sort of step to which our particular argument commits." The phrasing of the Warrant usually begins with the word Since. The Reservation is a highly significant last step because it specifies under what circumstances the Claim might not meet the criteria of reasonableness, relevance, soundness, strength, and appropriateness. The Reservation generally is introduced with the opening word Unless.

When the six steps or elements of the Toulmin Model are combined, the layout of the argument would take this form:

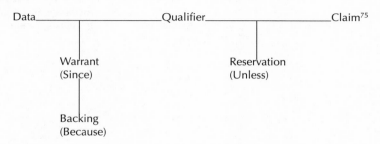

The ensuing chart, containing arguments under each of the above six elements in the Toulmin process, shows how the rhetor may move from Data to Claim on the issue of whether or not Jefferson was probably the father of Eston Hemings:

| Data | Qualifier | Claim |
|---|---|---|
| **Historical Evidence** | | |
| 1. Presence of TJ at Monticello 9 months before the conception of Sally Hemings's children | It is highly probable or There is a strong likelihood | That Thomas Jefferson was the father of Eston Hemings |
| 2. Preferential treatment of the Hemings children in TJ's Will | Warrant (Since) 1. The historical data are based upon | Reservation (Unless) 1. Future DNA studies generate results which |

*continued*

*Historical Evidence (continued)*

| | | |
|---|---|---|
| 3. Testimony by Madison Hemings that his mother was TJ's "concubine" | documentary sources.<br><br>2. The DNA results were developed by accomplished scholars with national and international reputations. | supercede the findings of the Foster Report<br><br>2. Hitherto undiscovered historical data on the issue are found which may alter the Claim |

*Scientific Evidence*

| | | |
|---|---|---|
| DNA results establishing a 99% probability level that TJ was the father of Eston Hemings | Backing<br>(Because)<br>1. The testimony of Madison Hemings, according to Dr. Eugene Foster, is important historical evidence.<br>2. Distinguished experts in the field of Genetics have affirmed the validity and reliability of the DNA study.<br>3. The Thomas Jefferson Memorial Foundation Committee (1/26/00) supported the findings of the DNA study. | 3. Future advances in the science of DNA theory and procedures lead to a re-evaluation of Foster's study which, in turn, produces different results concerning the methodology used and the conclusions reached. |

What we have observed in the foregoing discussion is that, by applying Jefferson's principles of argument and then by using the elements of the Toulmin Model, we have reached the same conclusion with respect to this question: "Was Jefferson the father of Eston Hemings?" The only major difference between the two procedures is Toulmin's use of a Reservation step, which enables a rhetor and the audience to become aware of a possible rhetorical situation that might occur in the future that could influence the long-range validity of the Claim. Despite the important Reservations we have listed, however, we feel that, given the evidence that is currently available, it is reasonable at this time to assume that Jefferson took part in a sexual relationship with Sally Hemings, culminating in the birth of Eston Hemings and perhaps her other children.[76] This conclusion, of course, would have to be modified if one or more of the Reservations eventually become a reality.

Since we have concluded it is highly probable that Jefferson was the father of Eston Hemings, our next task is to discuss the significance of his possible use of his position as administrator of Monticello to engage in a miscegenous master-slave relationship that led to the conception and birth of a son and perhaps other children. Several historians, addressing this problem before the DNA testing procedure was used, described in compelling language what it would mean if it could be proven that Jefferson had participated in sexual liaisons with one of his slaves. If such a possibility ever occurred, we earlier learned from Merrill Peterson, it would be "a ruthless exploitation of the master-slave relationship," causing a revulsion of "the whole being." Far more pointed and provocative were the following words of John Chester Miller:

> To give credence to the Sally Hemings story is, in effect, to question the authenticity of Jefferson's faith in freedom, the rights of man, and the innate controlling faculty of reason and the sense of right and wrong. It is to infer that there were no principles to which he was inviolably committed, that what he acclaimed as morality was no more than a rhetorical facade for self-indulgence, and that he was always prepared to make exceptions in his own case when it suited his purpose.

Even if we were willing to accept the premise that Jefferson "was deeply in love with Sally Hemings," continued Miller, "the case" would not be essentially altered. For "love does not sanctify such an egregious violation of his own principles and preachments and the shifts and dodges, the paltry artifices, to which he was compelled to resort in order to fool the American people."[77]

A more sympathetic view was articulated by Lander and Ellis in their commentary on the DNA results. "Now, with impeccable timing," they observed, "Jefferson reappears to remind us of a truth that should be self-evident. Our heroes—and especially presidents—are not gods or saints, but flesh-and-blood humans, with all of the frailties and imperfections that this entails."

Our strategy in responding to the question of significance is to evaluate Jefferson's administrative rhetorical act by applying the discourse perspectives he espoused in chapters 2 through 4 dealing with these themes: the role of virtue in discourse; the principles of argumentation and the generation of understanding; and the social affections and the stimulation of the imagination and the passions.

It is quite clear that Jefferson's sexual relationship with Sally Hemings could not possibly conform to his belief that all persons are endowed with a "moral sense" at birth that helps them to distinguish between right and wrong, and follow a path in life that promotes the "pursuit of happiness." Additionally, the role he played in this story was in direct contrast to his conviction that there must be a productive interaction between private and public good. Instead of making a reciprocal relationship between these two forms of good, as he had recommended to others, he did whatever he could to conceal his private actions in this case.

Similarly, he also clearly disregarded what he had said about argumentation and the generation of understanding. Reason, to him, was an intellectual gift that was a guiding light pointing the way toward truth. Yet, after learning of the charges Callender made against him in 1802—charges that were reinforced and embellished by the Federalists—he pushed them aside and presumably became the parent of Eston Hemings six years later, while he was still president. His teachings would not permit him to condone such unreasonable and reckless behavior in others whom he sought to advise. Nor can we overlook that on at least three occasions he condemned miscegenation as an immoral practice that threatened the stability of the republican form of government and society that he had helped to create. Rarely in any of his speeches, writings, and nonverbal discourse practices have we seen a more telling example illustrating how his philosophy of argumentation was so completely ignored.

Finally, in the Sally Hemings case, he, as a rhetor, did not adhere to what he had taught about the social affections and the stimulation of the imagination and the passions. He did not, for instance, make proper use of the "Law of Propriety," which is concerned with duties toward ourselves as reflected in the cardinal virtues of justice, wisdom, temperance, and courage. It was not just, wise, or temperate to have such a sexual relationship when, although his position of power allowed for it, his preachments condemned it. And he seemingly lacked the courage to talk or write about the problem.

He was similarly negligent in effectuating his ideas on the "Law of Justice," which stresses our duty obligations to others. He demonstrated the social affections of love and friendship in all of his actions involving his communication with his daughters Martha and Mary, but there is evidence to suggest that Eston Hemings and the other children of Sally did not receive comparable affection. At the same time, however, these children, it would appear, were treated with more consideration than were the other slaves,[78] thus violating the "Law of Justice," which frowns upon even the appearance of favoritism. A more disturbing factor was the adverse effect of Jefferson's liaisons upon family relations. For it would appear that he was engaging in questionable sexual activity in a home where his legitimate daughters and grandchildren often resided. This, in turn, placed them on the defensive as they later attempted to deny the story.[79]

Jefferson's attitudes toward African Americans and slavery have often been depicted in terms such as "ambivalent," "tortuous," and "hypocritical."[80] Our analysis of his verbal and nonverbal communication strategies lends further credence to the appropriateness of these troubling labels. His ambivalence was visibly evident in his *Notes on the State of Virginia*. In Query XIV, as we have observed, he asserted that African Americans were, by nature, inferior to whites both in their mental capacity and in their physical attributes. But then, in Query XVIII, he delivered a devastating attack on the evils of slavery. This conflict illustrates how he found it easy in his discourses on African Americans and slavery to express ideas that at times were progressive, and on other occasions conservative or even reactionary.

The issue of slavery, moreover, was a "tortuous" one for him when he realized in the last decade of his life that he and other members of his generation no longer had the power or the will to develop a workable solution to a problem that, like a "fire bell in the night," would not go away. He thus cried out for help from the young and visionary men of Virginia, who he believed represented the best hope for the future.

More regrettable, as far as Jefferson's rhetoric of virtue is concerned, is the claim that he was "hypocritical" on the problem of slavery. This charge, as we have attempted to show, is not without merit. That he "very likely" fathered at least one of Sally Hemings's children is a mockery of his stated belief that miscegenation was a morally reprehensible practice in an enlightened republican society. By participating in this administrative rhetorical act, therefore, he conveyed the symbolic meaning that his actions were a refutation of his words. This glaring inconsistency suggested a possible lack of sincerity when articulating his position on the most divisive issue of his time.

# Notes

1. TJ to John Holmes, April 22, 1820, in Ford, 12, 158–59.
2. Memo of Daniel P. Jordan, president of the Thomas Jefferson Memorial Foundation, November 1, 1998.
3. "Autobiography," in *Writings*, 5.
4. TJ to Edward Coles, August 25, 1814, in Ford, 11: 417.

5. Grant McColley, *Slavery in Jeffersonian Virginia* (Champaign-Urbana: University of Illinois Press, 1964), 116.

6. Paul Finkelman takes a decidedly unsympathetic view toward Jefferson's antislavery stance during this period. Commenting on the Bland proposal, he said: "Whether or not Jefferson took the initiative in 1769—and it seems likely that he exaggerated his role in retrospect just as he exaggerated the libertarian nature of the proposal—this was the last time while he held office in Virginia that he stuck out his neck on the issue of slavery. The lesson Jefferson learned in 1769 was to avoid discussions of slavery that might lead to unpleasant confrontations with his colleagues. However troubled he may have been by slavery, Jefferson would let others work for amelioration or reform." *Slavery and the Founders: Race and Liberty in the Age of Jefferson* (Armonk, N.Y.: M. E. Sharpe, 1996), 113. Since we are dealing with Jefferson's verbal arguments, we feel that his rhetoric during this period was progressive, for, as we have shown, he did "stick out his neck on the issue of slavery" both in his *A Summary View of the Rights of British America* and in the first two drafts of the Declaration.

7. Boyd, 6: 612n. For an extensive discussion of "The Virginia Cession of Territory Northwest of the Ohio" and the "Plan of Government of the Western Territory," see ibid., 6: 571–617.

8. Cited in Peterson, *Thomas Jefferson and the New Nation* 283.

9. "Second Speech on Foote's Resolution—Second Reply to Hayne," January 26 and 27, 1830, in Wayland Maxfield Parish and Marie Hochmuth, eds., *American Speeches* (New York: Longman's, Green, 1954), 179 and 19–93.

10. Boyd, 6: 612n.

11. William Peden, ed., *Notes on the State of Virginia* (New York: Norton, 1954 and 1982), 162–63. The Norton edition of the *Notes* is a photo-offset reprint of the Peden edition as originally published. Chapel Hill: University of North Carolina Press for the Institute of Early American History and Culture, 1955.

12. McColley, *Slavery in Jeffersonian Virginia*, 124.

13. Ibid., 130–49.

14. When Jefferson made this claim, he was comparing African Americans with Indians. Sublimity to him was represented by the speech of Logan, analyzed in chapter 14. We feel, however, that Jefferson was too harsh in his criticism of the poems of Phyllis Wheatley who, at the age of eight in 1761, was forced to leave Africa to become a slave in the household of John Wheatley of Boston. "The compositions published under her name," observed Jefferson, "are below the dignity of criticism." *Notes*, 140. By contrast, James L. Golden and Richard Rieke, in their volume *The Rhetoric of Black Americans*, spoke favorably of her poetry. The philosophy of ethnology, they said, "found eloquent expression in the poetry of Wheatley." In a poem dedicated *To the Right Honorable William, Earl of Dartmouth* in 1773, for example, "she spoke sorrowfully of her past and expressed the hope that other members of her race would not experience the pain of separation and tyranny." They then added this description: "A similar compassionate plea in another poem, entitled *On Being Brought from Africa to America*, challenged her readers to perceive the intrinsic worth of black Americans." (Columbus, Ohio: Charles Merrill, 1971), 52–53.

15. Some critics of the *Notes on the State of Virginia* complained "that Jefferson's 'suspicions' bore a closer resemblance to dogmatic assertions of fact than to hypotheses awaiting scientific verification." Miller, *Wolf by the Ears*, 56.

16. Ibid., 57.

17. See *Notes*, 137–38 and 143.

18. TJ to Richard Price, August 7, 1785, in Boyd, 8: 356–57.

19. January 26, 1789, in Ford, 5: 447–48.

20. TJ to Edward Coles, August 25, 1814, in Ford, 11: 417.

21. TJ to the governor of Georgia (William Telfair), March 26, 1791, in Ford, 6: 226.

22. Benjamin Banneker to TJ, August 19, 1791. Printed in a pamphlet entitled, *Copy of a Letter from Benjamin Banneker to the Secretary of State, With His Answer* (Philadelphia: Daniel Lawrence, 1792), 3–10.

23. TJ to Benjamin Banneker, August 30, 1791, in Ford, 6: 309–10. On the same day, TJ wrote to the Marquis de Condorcet commending Banneker for his Almanac, calling it a tribute to the Negro race. Ibid., 311.

24. August 19, 1791, Boyd, 22: 52n–54n.

25. TJ to James Monroe, November 24, 1801, in *Writings*, 1096–1099.

26. TJ to St. George Tucker, August 28, 1797, in Ford, 8: 335.

27. James D. Richardson, ed., *A Compilation of the Messages and Papers of the Presidents, 1789–1902* (Washington, D.C.: Bureau of National Literature and Art, 1905), 1: 408.

28. Sir Augustus John Foster, *Jeffersonian America: Notes on the United States of America Collected in the Years 1805–6–7 and 11–12* (San Marino, Calif.: Huntington Library, 1954), 148–49. Edited with an introduction by Richard Beale Davis.

29. TJ to Henri Gregoire, February 25, 1809, in *Writings*, 1202.

30. TJ to Joel Barlow, October 8, 1809, in Ford, 11: 120–21.

31. TJ to Edward Coles, August 25, 1814, in Ford, 11: 416–20.

32. Ibid.

33. TJ to David Barry, May 1, 1815, in Ford, 11: 470.

34. TJ to Jared Sparks, February 4, 1824, in Ford, 12: 334–39.

35. TJ to John Lynch, January 21, 1811, in Ford, 11: 178.

36. TJ to Doctor Thomas Humphreys, February 8, 1817, in Ford, 12: 53–54.

37. TJ to Edward Coles, August 25, 1814, in Ford, 11: 418.

38. January 18, 1826, in Ford, 12: 434.

39. TJ to George Logan, May 11, 1805, in Ford, 10: 141–42.

40. *Language as Symbolic Action* (Berkeley: University of California Press, 1966), 301–302; and *A Grammar of Motives and A Rhetoric of Motives* (Cleveland, Ohio, 1962), 682–90.

41. William W. Freehling observed: "By freeing their slaves George Washington and John Randolph lived up to Revolutionary ideals. These men, however, were exceptions." "The Founding Fathers and Slavery," *American Historical Review*, 77 (February 1972), 85. A revised version of this article appears in William W. Freehling, *The Reinterpretation of American History* (New York: Oxford University Press, 1994).

42. See Miller's chapter on "Jefferson as a Slavemaster," in *Wolf by the Ears*, 104–109.

43. Consider, for example, Madison Hemings's testimony reported in his "Memoirs." In this 1873 report, he noted: "But during that time (while she was in Paris) my mother became Mr. Jefferson's concubine, and when he was called back home she was *enciente* by him. He desired to bring my mother back to Virginia with him but she demurred. She was just beginning to understand the French language well, and in France she was free, while if she returned to Virginia she would be re-enslaved. So she refused to return with him. To induce her to do so he promised her extraordinary privileges, and made a solemn

pledge that her children should be freed at the age of twenty-one years. In consequence of his promise, on which she implicitly relied, she returned with him to Virginia." Annette Gordon-Reed, *Thomas Jefferson and Sally Hemings: An American Controversy* (Charlottesville: University Press of Virginia, 1997), 246. Even more important is the following statement of Gordon Wood: ". . . as recent historians have emphasized (Jefferson) . . . hunted down fugitives in much the same way his fellow Virginia planters did. . . ." "The Trials and Tribulations of Thomas Jefferson." *Jeffersonian Legacies*, 397.

44. To Callender, according to Michael Durey, "Jefferson was his father figure. . . ." *"With the Hammer of Truth": James Thompson Callender and America's National Heroes* (Charlottesville: University Press of Virginia, 1990), 143–45.

45. TJ to James Monroe, May 29, 1801, in Worthington Chauncey Ford, ed., *Thomas Jefferson and James Thompson Callender* (Brooklyn, N.Y.: Historical Print Club, 1897), 88–89.

46. *Richmond Recorder, or Lady's and Gentleman's Miscellany*, September 1, 1802, 1–2.

47. Smith declared that he would not "disgrace the columns of a Paper that entertains a respect for decency and truth, by republishing the infamous calumnies and vulgarities of a man who has forfeited every pretension to character, or refutations of falsehoods which may recoil on those who propagate them, but cannot impair the well earned esteem in which the first talents and virtues of the nation are held." Cited in Malone, *Jefferson The President, First Term, 1801–1805* (Boston: Little, Brown, 1970), 215. In his *Richmond Recorder* column, Callender ridiculed Smith for being a "censor." For the use of the descriptive terms "scoundrel" and "wretch," see the following studies: Charles Jellison, "That Scoundrel Callender," *Virginia Magazine of History and Biography*, 67 (1959); and Madison's letter to TJ, June 1, 1801, in Worthington Ford, p. 39. But Durey reminds us that "contrary to the opinion of Jefferson's admirers, Callender was not an incorrigible liar. His interpretations of facts frequently were strained and exaggerated, but there is little, if any evidence of his purposeful invention of stories or falsification of facts." *"With the Hammer of Truth,"* 160.

48. Durey, *"With the Hammer of Truth,"* 157.

49. Winthrop Jordan, *White Over Black: American Attitudes Toward the Negro, 1550–1812* (Chapel Hill: University of North Carolina Press, 1968), 465–66. For a fuller discussion of the issue, see *ibid.*, 461–69. Of further interest here is the following essay by Fraser D. Newman: "Coincidence or Causal Connection: The Relationship between Thomas Jefferson's Visits to Monticello and Sally Hemings's Conceptions," *William and Mary Quarterly*, LVII, No. 1 (January 2000). At the close of this empirical study, the author states: "Serious doubt about the existence and duration of the relationship and about Jefferson's paternity of his six children can no longer be reasonably sustained," 210.

50. Peterson, *Jefferson Image in the American Mind*, 183–87.

51. Peterson, *Thomas Jefferson and the New Nation*, 706–707.

52. Dumas Malone, *Jefferson the President: First Term, 1801–1805* (Boston: Little, Brown, 1970), 214–15.

53. *American Historical Review*, 77 (February 1972), 85.

54. Douglass Adair, "The Jefferson Scandals," reprinted in Trevor Colbourn, ed., *Fame and the Founding Fathers: Essays of Douglass Adair* (New York: Norton, 1974; reprint ed., Indianapolis: Liberty Fund, 1998), 227–73.

55. Annette Gordon-Reed, "Engaging Jefferson: Blacks and the Founding Fathers," in the *William and Mary Quarterly*, LVII (January 2000), 179.

56. Fawn Brodie, *Thomas Jefferson: An Intimate History* (New York: Norton, 1974), 293–318.

57. Ibid., 17.

58. In their essay on Jefferson and the slavery issue, Scot A. French and Edward L. Ayers observe that Brodie's volume "received favorable reviews in many publications, infuriating Malone and other Jefferson scholars, who considered its evidence inconclusive, its methodology questionable, and its thesis implausible." "The Strange Case of Thomas Jefferson: Race and Slavery in American Memory, 1943–1993," in *Jeffersonian Legacies*, 429.

59. Annette Gordon-Reed, "The Memories of a Few Negroes," in Jan Ellen Lewis and Peter S. Onuf, eds., *Sally Hemings & Thomas Jefferson: History, Memory, and Civic Culture* (Charlottesville: University Press of Virginia, 1999), 239–240.

60. Ibid., 418–56.

61. Gordon S. Wood, "The Trials and Tribulations of Thomas Jefferson," in *Jeffersonian Legacies*, 398.

62. Gordon-Reed, *Thomas Jefferson and Sally Hemings: An American Controversy*, 211–16.

63. Ibid., 216.

64. In evaluating Callender's charges against Jefferson, recent scholars have begun to reinterpret traditional views of his reliability as a witness. Annette Gordon-Reed has argued that instead of dismissing Callender as a "drunk," a "liar," and a "loathsome" character whose words lacked credibility, we should remember that he was "right about Alexander Hamilton's affair with Mrs. Reynolds"; he also was on target when he described "Jefferson's attempted seduction of the wife of his friend John Walker"; and he was correct in alleging "that Jefferson had encouraged his [Callender's] literary efforts against members of the Federalist party." Gordon-Reed, *Thomas Jefferson and Sally Hemings: An American Controversy*, 76. Other recent commentators have agreed that Callender should not be viewed as a "liar." "Of all the information published by Callender on the Sally affair, only one suggesting that her daughter was in service, can be proved to be incorrect." And even "in this instance, Callender specifically warned that it might not be true." Durey, *"With the Hammer of Truth,"* 159. Similarly, his article "James Callender and Social Knowledge of Interracial Sex in Antebellum Virginia," Joshua D. Rothman concurred with Durey when he said: "To brand Callender reckless in his journalistic style regarding Jefferson and Hemings . . . is to overstate the case. He was purposely sensationalistic. . . . But with respect to facts he presented, his tone was more cautious and variable. . . . James Callender was a lot of things, but he was not usually a liar. . . . Callender's attacks were by and large true. . . ." Joshua D. Rothman, in Lewis and Onuf, eds., *Sally Hemings & Thomas Jefferson: History, Memory, and Culture* (Charlottesville: University Press of Virginia, 1999), 89.

65. Ellis, *American Sphinx*, 217.

66. Ibid., 304–305.

67. See the letter from Ellen Randolph Coolidge to Joseph Coolidge, Edgehill, October 24, 1858, in Gordon-Reed, *Thomas Jefferson and Sally Hemings: An American Controversy*, 258–60.

68. The *Washington Post* carried these stories between November 1 and 7, 1998: Leef Smith, "Tests Link Jefferson," Nov. 1, A 1 and 16; Michael E. Ruane, "Rumors of an Affair Put on Public Display: Jefferson Scandal has Parallels in Today's," ibid.; Leef Smith, "Much Ado at Monticello: Tourists, Guides Ponder Jefferson and Genetics. Jefferson

Foundation Considers its Next Step," Nov. 2, C 1 and 7; Edwin M. Yoder Jr., "DNA and Deeper Inquiry," Nov. 4, A 25; and Ken Ringle, "The Secret Heart of Mr. Jefferson," Nov. 7, C 1 and 5. In addition, these four articles appeared in the *New York Times* on Nov. 1 and 2: Dinitia Smith and Nicholas Wade, "DNA Test Finds Evidence of Jefferson Child by Slave," Nov. 1, A 1 and 24; Brent Staples, "Jefferson and Sally Hemings, Together at Last?", Nov. 2, A 26; William Saffire, "Sallygate," Nov. 2, A 27; and Orlando Patterson, "Jefferson the Contradiction," ibid.

69. Although the argument from Analogy plays some part in comparing Jefferson's situation to that of President Clinton, we do not feel that it helps provide evidence to prove the reliability and validity of the DNA Study.

70. See Memoirs of Madison Hemings and Israel Jefferson, in Gordon-Reed, *Thomas Jefferson and Sally Hemings: An American Controversy*, 245–53.

71. Dumas Malone and his research assistant Steven Hochman argued that the Hemings testimony was an unreliable "piece of propaganda. . . ." French and Ayers, "The Strange Career of Thomas Jefferson," in *Jeffersonian Legacies*, 435.

72. It should be pointed out that early in January 1999, a group of Jefferson scholars and admirers met in Washington, D.C., for the purpose of challenging the results of the DNA Test. "They suggested that at least eight other Jeffersons could have sired the children of Sally Hemings." The group of candidates included "Jefferson's cousin George Jefferson, Jr., Jefferson's brother Randolph or one of Randolph's five sons. . . ." In response to this claim, Laura Garwin, *Nature*'s North American Editor, affirmed that "the study still stands." In addition, historian Joseph Ellis asserted that "If you want to argue Thomas Jefferson is not the father (of Eston Hemings), you now have a tough case to make. . . . You have to be on a crusade to rescue Thomas Jefferson to not believe it." *Washington Post*, January 6, 1999, A6 and 7. As we have attempted to demonstrate, we feel that Jefferson's own philosophy of reasoning, reinforced by the DNA results, make it incumbent upon us to conclude with a high degree of probability that Jefferson was the father of Eston Hemings.

73. In a telephone conversation with Dr. Eugene Foster on August 9, 2001, he reaffirmed his continuing faith in the validity and reliability of the arguments he advanced in the DNA study, and in our interview with him held in Charlottesville on May 13, 1999.

74. A copy of the written report of the research committee was sent to us by the Thomas Jefferson Memorial Foundation, along with Daniel Jordan's response, shortly after they were made public on January 26, 2000.

75. Our discussion of Toulmin's Model of Argument is based upon the following sources: *The Uses of Argument* (Cambridge: Cambridge University Press, 1964); Toulmin, "Logic and the Criticism of Arguments," printed in James L. Golden, et al., *The Rhetoric of Western Thought*, 6th edition (Dubuque, Iowa: Kendall/Hunt, 1997), 221–30; Interviews with Toulmin by James L. Golden; and Wayne E. Brockriede and Douglas Ehninger, "Toulmin on Argument: An Interpretation and Application," *Quarterly Journal of Speech*, 46 (February 1960), 44–53.

76. The probability level we are supporting here is advanced by both Joseph Ellis and Gordon Wood. In his article on "Jefferson: Post DNA," in the *William and Mary Quarterly*, LVII (January 2000), Ellis argues that "the new scholarly consensus is that Jefferson and Hemings were sexual partners." He then adds this claim: "To say that Jefferson's paternity of several Hemings children is proven 'beyond a reasonable doubt' sounds about right." (126) Wood expresses a similar sentiment in the following words: "So accepting of the

sexual relationship are most historians now that it will be difficult for any future scholarly cautionary notes to get heard." "The Ghosts of Monticello," in Lewis and Onuf, eds., *Sally Hemings & Thomas Jefferson: History, Memory, and Civic Culture*, 27. For a contrary opinion on the alleged relationship between Jefferson and Sally Hemings, see the "Jefferson-Hemings Scholars Commission Report on the Jefferson-Hemings Matter." Chaired by Robert F. Turner of the University of Virginia, the commission of thirteen national scholars presented its findings to the Thomas Jefferson Heritage Society on April 12, 2001. In the executive summary of the commission report, the following major conclusions were reached: "The question of whether Thomas Jefferson fathered one or more children by the slave Sally Hemings is an issue about which honorable people can and do disagree. After a careful review of all of the evidence, the commission agrees unanimously that the allegation is by no means proven; and we find it regrettable that public confusion about the 1998 DNA testing and other evidence has misled many people . . . our individual conclusions range from serious skepticism about the charge to a conviction that is almost certainly false."

After a thorough analysis of the commission study, we feel that the arguments and evidence presented in support of the foregoing conclusions set forth in the commission report are less convincing than those advanced in the Foster DNA study, in the Thomas Jefferson Memorial Foundation Committee report, in the claims made by Joseph Ellis and Gordon Wood in the early part of note 76, and in our application of Jefferson's principles of argument and in our use of the Toulmin Model. Of special significance, moreover, is Dr. Foster's statement made to us on August 9, 2001, that despite the criticisms made concerning the DNA testing, he still believed firmly in the validity and reliability of the DNA findings. In sum, what we have maintained in our text is that the DNA study, in combination with the historical data discussed, lead us to the highly probable claim that Jefferson was the father of Eston Hemings. They also increase the possibility that Jefferson may also have been the parent of one or more of the other Hemings children.

77. Miller, *Wolf by the Ears*, 176.

78. Jefferson's "Will" shows clearly the degree of preferential treatment given to the Hemings family. Betty Hemings had twelve children including Sally and John. The "Will" specified that John Hemings would be given his freedom "at the end of one year after" TJ's "death." It also stated that John would receive "the services of his two apprentices Madison and Eston Hemings, until their respective ages of twenty-one years, at which period respectively," they would be set free. Finally, he freed two other servants—Burwell and Joe Fosset—descendants of Betty Hemings, and, therefore, relatives of Sally. "Jefferson's Will," in Ford, 12: 478–83. For the "Hemings Family" Genealogical Table, see James A. Bear Jr., ed., *Jefferson at Monticello* (Charlottesville: University Press of Virginia, 1967). The table follows p. 24. Commenting on the terms of the "Will," Miller noted: "Betty Hemings and her quadroon children received favored treatment. Instead of being put to work in the fields, they were trained as household servants and artisans. Moreover, most of them, with the notable exception of Sally, were freed during Jefferson's lifetime or by his will." Miller, *Wolf by the Ears*, 162.

79. This was especially evident in the letter from Ellen Randolph Coolidge to Joseph Coolidge, October 24, 1858, in Gordon-Reed, *Thomas Jefferson and Sally Hemings: An American Controversy*, 258–60.

80. Consider the following quotations: "The ideological stance of Jefferson and other Founding Fathers on slavery . . . was profoundly ambivalent" (Freehling, 84); "Jefferson

was the crucial figure in American history both for slavery and for abolition. . . . [He] remained an ambivalent figure, a confusion of opposite policies" (Peterson, *The Jefferson Image in the American Mind*, 188); ". . . Jefferson's opinion [on race] was also a product of frivolous and tortuous reasoning, of preconception, prejudice, ignorance, contradiction, and bewildering confusion of principles" (Peterson, *Thomas Jefferson and the New Nation*, 262); and, "How can his [Jefferson's] frequent assertions that his conscience was clear and that his enemies did him a cruel and wholly unmerited injustice be reconciled with the Jefferson of the Sally Hemings story—unless, of course, Jefferson is set down as a practitioner of pharisaical holiness who loved to preach to others what he himself did not practice?" (Miller, *Wolf by the Ears*, 176)

# Postscript

~

I have sworn upon the altar of god, eternal hostility against every form of tyranny over the mind of man.

—TJ to Dr. Benjamin Rush, September 23, 1800

On July 6, 1826, two days after Jefferson's death, Madison wrote these words in remembrance of his great friend and political ally:

> we are more than consoled for the loss, by the gain to him; and by the assurance that he lives and will live in the memory and gratitude of the wise & good, as a luminary of science, as a votary of liberty, as a model of patriotism, and as a benefactor of humankind. In these characters, I have known him, and not less in the virtues & charms of social life, for a period of fifty years, during which there has not been an interruption or diminution of mutual confidence and cordial friendship, for a single moment in a single instance.[1]

Jefferson would have been pleased with these sentiments because of their emphasis on virtue—a virtue that stressed the value of learning, liberty, patriotism, friendship, social charm, and, most of all, service to the people. The subject of virtue, we have attempted to show, was the medium that he used and wanted others to use in generating value-laden messages to elevate society and strengthen the American government.

The Jefferson who has emerged from these pages performed two vital roles in his rhetoric of virtue; he was both a teacher and a preacher. He was not a teacher in the traditional sense, for he never received an appointment from a school board; he never delivered lectures or moderated discussions in a classroom setting; nor did he follow the example of Aristotle, Quintilian, Kames, Campbell, and Priestley by writing a textbook on rhetoric that could be used by college students or the general public. He opted instead to duplicate the strategy used by Bacon, Locke, and Hume, all of whom sprinkled their influential perspectives on rhetorical principles throughout their voluminous writings. What we have found is that Jefferson gave his instruction to the many students who consistently sought his advice as they prepared to train for their professional careers. Many of these teachings were developed in the informative and persuasive letters he wrote, in his conversations, in his *Notes on the State of Virginia*, and in the vast library holdings that he generously made available for research purposes. Moreover, when he functioned as a teacher, he addressed not only his interested primary audience but posterity as well. What becomes visible when we cull material from all the documents he preserved and from reading the impressions of his contemporaries is a rhetoric of virtue, with the exception of a few notable deviations, that is unified, coherent, and enduring in its relevance.

In preparation of his role as teacher, Jefferson became, in Merrill Peterson's opinion, an "olympian humanist."[2] This, we feel, is an accurate description because Jefferson was in every sense a Renaissance man. Proficient in the history of the Western world, in classical and modern languages, in politics and law, in philosophy and religion, in architecture and agriculture, and in ancient and British/Continental rhetorical theory, he was a persuasive force in championing the study of liberal arts and sciences in the Age of Enlightenment. Like Cicero and Blair, moreover, he had rewarding opportunities to be an observer and a participant in historically significant rhetorical situations. The lessons he learned from these firsthand experiences were passed on to those whom he sought to instruct.

As a teacher, Jefferson's "olympian humanism" also found convincing expression in his commitment to an evolutionary approach to the concept of knowledge generation. Although he remained devoted to many aspects of the classical tradition, the quest of knowledge, he believed, must include works produced in the modern era. For this reason, he could never accept Jonathan Swift's arguments in his essay on "The Battle of the Books," in which the neoclassical author concluded that such luminaries as Bacon, Descartes, Locke, and Boyle were easily defeated by Plato, Aristotle, and Horace.[3] To argue in this fashion, Jefferson held, would lead to a static conclusion.

Possessing a dynamic evolutionary philosophy of education, Jefferson as a teacher adopted two discourse strategies as part of his pedagogical method. In some instances, for example, he blended the best ideas of the ancients with the most insightful perspectives set forth by the moderns.

This was evident in chapter 2 when he fused the doctrines of virtue by Epicurus, Epictetus, Cicero, and Jesus with those of Bacon, Locke, Shaftesbury, Kames, and Hutcheson. It was also observable in chapter 4 when he integrated Cicero's views on the social affections with those of Shaftesbury and Hutcheson. The same pattern of instruction appears in chapter 5 on channeling the message. He developed ideas on style that were consistent with the teachings of the leading figures of the classical era; yet he likewise made use of the doctrines of the elocutionists when describing the canon of delivery.

The second discourse strategy he used in keeping with his evolutionary emphasis was the occasional tendency to stress, almost exclusively, the ideas advanced by modern scholars. This practice was strikingly apparent in his discussion of argumentation and in the partiality he showed concerning the combining of belles lettres with rhetorical philosophy. He was not attracted, for instance, to Aristotle's system of argumentation because of its preoccupation with enthymematic reasoning or artistic proof. He turned instead, as noted in chapter 3, to the British epistemologists because of the way they probed into the mysteries of human nature and featured the significance of scientific information and other forms of evidence in the development of their perspectives on practical reasoning. These probes, as pointed out, made him familiar with Bacon's fallacies of the idols, Hume's notions on faculty psychology and the four elements of moral reasoning, Locke's and Duncan's views on self-evident premises, and Reid's doctrine of common sense. All of these emphases he digested and then made them a vital part of his philosophy of argumentation.

Jefferson also, as an instructor of discourse philosophy, deviated from the Greek and Roman tradition of focusing primarily on the oral mode of rhetoric, in particular the oratorical model. He shared with Shaftesbury and Blair, as we have noted throughout this study, the belief that rhetoric embraces the written as well as the oral genre, and it includes private as well as public discourse. Moreover, another important aspect of his philosophy was the discourse element of criticism because of its reliance on argument. In brief, rhetoric, as Jefferson conceived it, encompassed all types of communication. This is why he discussed such varied forms as poetics, conversation, letter writing, political discourse, historical writing, legal advocacy, and journalism. All of these forms, he concluded, have as their principal duty the celebration of virtue.

We have observed in the preceding summary that Jefferson's moral philosophical principles of rhetoric as he taught them conformed closely to his strongly held conviction that knowledge generation is neither a static nor a revolutionary educational enterprise. Rather it progresses in an orderly and productive manner. As it advances, the best of tradition remains and then is joined with developing trends that make use of new discoveries and interpretations.

Jefferson's method of teaching consisted primarily of specific recommendations he presented in letters and essays, and in highlighting relevant sections from performances of rhetors he had studied or had observed in action. He could thus illustrate a point on effective historical writing by alluding to a specimen from the works of Thucydides, Livy, or Tacitus. For an illustration of moving poetry, he could cite a passage from Homer or Shakespeare; and if he wanted to make a reference on virtue, he could advise his students to study the philosophical essays of Cicero, Bacon, Shaftesbury, or Hutcheson. Because of his vast personal experiences, moreover, he often gave poignant descriptions of his contemporaries. Washington, for him, was a great leader whose sensitive, virtuous character offset any limitations he had in his rhetorical practices; Franklin was an incomparable conversationalist whose ingratiating manner enabled him to diffuse a controversy with grace and charm; Adams, Madison, and Pendleton were convincing legislative debaters who habitually moved their listeners to their political positions; and Henry was an orator whose sense of urgency and power of delivery and presence lifted his eloquence to the level of sublimity. These pen portraits, along with many others written in a similar vein, were a fulfillment of Jefferson's desire to furnish contemporary eyewitness accounts that would stimulate the understanding, imagination, and passions of his students. Moreover, after these pen portraits appeared in print, they proved to be of value to future scholars.

Another favorite method of instruction was the use of the narrative paradigm. By telling a story of an event he had witnessed, he could take his readers to the House of Burgesses and let them become members of Henry's audience during the Stamp Act Speech; to the Second Continental Congress in Philadelphia in 1776 and let them hear the debates on the Declaration of Independence; to his Paris residence on the eve of the French Revolution and let them observe the dialogues of Lafayette and his colleagues as they planned their strategy for democratizing France; and to private conversational encounters with Washington, Adams, and Hamilton dealing with the future of an emerging American nation. What made these stories so instructive and engrossing was the power of description that marked his control of language.

Jefferson the teacher reached the zenith of his influence with the establishment of the University of Virginia. Included in his vision of what the nature of higher education should be was his insistence that the subjects of rhetoric and virtue should become permanent fields of study in the university curriculum. That he was enormously proud of his devotion to teaching and education is shown by his desire to have the words "Father of the University of Virginia" inscribed on his tombstone so that this accomplishment could be remembered as a tribute to the lasting importance of knowledge.

But Jefferson was more than a teacher in developing his perspectives on the rhetoric of virtue. He was also a preacher who early in his career recognized that language has a sermonic dimension. In his 1962 lecture "Language is Sermonic," Richard Weaver explained how a rhetor may assume the role of a minister:

> As rhetoric confronts us with choices involving values, the rhetorician is a preacher to us, noble if he tries to direct our passions toward noble ends, and base if he uses our passion to confuse and degrade us. Since all utterance influences us in one way or the other of these directions, it is important that the direction be the right one, and it is better if this lay preacher is a master of his art.[4]

From what we have discovered in this study, it is clear that Jefferson made an intense effort "to direct our passions toward noble ends," and, for the most part, he proved to be a "master of his art." Whenever he participated in conversation or sat down at his desk to write a letter, he always was mindful of the need to use these related forms of private discourse to preach the value of virtue. Because he "was the very model of an eighteenth-century gentleman" who possessed "perfect self-control and serenity of spirit," he could through his informal dialogues and correspondence communicate knowledge and taste "in a new enlightened society. . . ."[5] A letter received by Jefferson requesting information on a particular historical event or the nature of a scientific theory, for example, did not go unanswered; nor did it lead to a brief, general reply. Instead, it often sent him to his files or to his bookshelves, and, in some cases, to his friends and acquaintances who might provide data. The result was an informed response designed to enhance the level of understanding of the correspondent and to promote the virtue of benevolence.

The moral earnestness that Jefferson displayed in his conversational discourse and letter writing was similarly evident in his public addresses. When he wrote A Summary View of the Rights of British America and the Declaration of Independence, for instance, the subject of virtue was the text. These two sermonic messages depicted in graphic detail how the

American people no longer were willing to stand idly by as the king and the Parliament adopted and enforced policies depriving them of their sacred rights of freedom, liberty, equality, and justice. Virtue again was the text developed in his First Inaugural Address. In this innovative, groundbreaking inaugural, he showed how the soothing element of good will or identification could become a rhetorical strategy for arousing the social affections and promoting the public good. Long after the speech had ended, audience members and subsequent readers remembered his claim that all of those assembled on this occasion were both Republicans and Federalists committed to the moral proposition that the majority must at all times protect the rights of the minority.

Virtue again was the prevailing theme when he functioned as a legal advocate both in the courtroom and in the legislative assembly. His 1770 defense of Howell, a third-generation mulatto, contained, as we have noted, these memorable words: "Under the law of nature, all men are born free, every one comes into the world with the right to his own person, which includes the liberty of moving and using it at his own will." Protecting "the natural rights of mankind" was also a part of the sermonic message he wanted to uphold in his lengthy, successful campaign to produce an act for religious freedom in his native state.

Although Jefferson never would have used the word "preacher" to describe his role as a champion of personal and public virtue, he nevertheless functioned as a minister by using arguments and language that were sermonic in nature. Because he had "sworn upon the altar of god, eternal hostility against every form of tyranny over the mind of man," it was inevitable that he would want posterity to remember that he was the "Author of the Declaration of Independence" and "Of the Statute of Virginia for religious freedom. . . ."

We address two further questions in this postscript: (1) To what extent did Jefferson's discourse practice conform to his philosophy? (2) To what degree did his ideas and practices contribute to our knowledge of the rhetoric of virtue?

With respect to the first of these queries, we have found that in most instances Jefferson, in his verbal communication performances, succeeded ably in putting his rhetorical principles into practice. As a conversationalist and letter writer, a polemicist during the Revolutionary War period, as a special occasional speaker, as a legal advocate, and as a critic of oratory and orators, he rarely deviated from his principles. With virtue ever present as a dominant theme, he made this subject poignant and persuasive by using strong reasoning and evidence, effective appeals to the social affections, and clear, concise, and vivid language. Moreover, his messages came alive through the use of examples, illustrations, and story-telling.

There were, however, several compelling instances in which the level of his argument did not meet the logical tests he had emphasized in his philosophy of practical reasoning. This was evident in his unfavorable critique of Plato's philosophical writings on the grounds that they were juvenile in substance and style, and gave an inaccurate description of Socrates. Second, his persistent devotion to the poems of Ossian, despite compelling proof showing they were fraudulent, was in direct violation of his own teachings on the fallacies of reasoning. Third, his support of Baxter's *History*, which was a condensed and plagiarized version of Hume's *History of England* with all pro-Tory sentiments removed, fell far short of the standards of scholarship he had articulated for historical writing. In each of these cases, his reasoning was significantly weakened by a personal bias—a bias against Plato for his non-republican principles and religious views; a bias in favor of Ossian's poems because of Hugh Blair's unyielding faith in their authenticity; and a bias against Hume's *History* because of its pro-Tory emphasis. What made the criticism of this latter work so startling was Jefferson's claim that the brilliance of Hume's writing style was so powerful it would increase the gullibility of the readers. This conclusion was hardly consistent with his oft-repeated faith in the judgment of the people.

Jefferson was both successful and unsuccessful in effectuating his standards for delivery. In private discourse and in the courtroom, he spoke with the sincerity, ease, and fluency that were appropriate for the subject matter and the physical setting. This was not the case, however, when addressing a large audience, such as that assembled in the Senate Chamber for his Inaugural Address. His voice was too weak and his manner too reserved for him to generate appropriate projection, often causing audience members to strain to hear what he was saying.

But none of the foregoing shortcomings compares in magnitude with the argumentative stance Jefferson took on the explosive political and social issues of African Americans and slavery. The quality of his reasoning, for example, was significantly diminished when he drew a comparison between whites and blacks on the question of the mental and physical characteristics of the two races. Both in his *Notes* and in subsequent letters and dialogues, he claimed, without adequate proof, that African Americans were genetically inferior in their intelligence and in their physical attributes. This type of reasoning, which was inconsistent with his philosophy, set the stage for strong counterattacks, not the least of which came from David Walker in his 1829 *Appeal*.[6]

Far more disconcerting with respect to the reputation of Jefferson as an advocate of virtue was his use of administrative rhetoric, as noted in chapter 16, that conveyed a troubling symbolic message regarding his sincerity and consistency on the issue of black Americans and slavery. He described the evils of slavery; yet he maintained slaves on his Monticello plantation.[7] He attacked what he called the immoral practice of miscegenation; yet it is very probable he had a miscegenous affair with Sally Hemings. Moreover, his philosophy of virtue upheld the notion that people in the same essential category should be treated in the same way; yet he demonstrated an attitude of partiality toward the children of Sally Hemings by treating them with a consideration not extended to the other slaves while not affording them the affection he showed the children of his marriage. These actions, which were a form of nonverbal communication, could not help but produce a negative reaction from many critics who saw a conflict between words and deeds. Five years before the recent DNA test results were published, Gordon Wood observed: "It is in fact his views on black Americans and slavery that have made Jefferson most vulnerable to modern censure."[8]

If we use the argumentative criterion of calculation of probabilities to summarize the overall degree to which Jefferson's rhetorical practice was consonant with his philosophy, we may infer that he succeeded in the subject matter covered in six of the eight chapters included in part 2 of this study. By contrast, in two other chapters his performance fell short— chapter 15, which revealed him as a critic of non-oratorical forms, and chapter 16, dealing with his ideas and practices on African Americans and slavery. It should be pointed out, however, that our discussion in chapter 15 suggests that Jefferson was partially successful. Although his criticism was deficient in his evaluation of the Ossianic poems and of Hume's *History of England*, he nevertheless wrote a splendid critique of Montesquieu's *Spirit of Laws* and Destutt de Tracy's *Commentary and Review*. The situation was different, however, in chapter 16. Notwithstanding that in his verbal communication practices Jefferson often pointed out the evils of slavery, urged the abolition of the foreign slave trade, and advocated the exclusion of slavery in the territory ceded by Virginia to the national government, he was on the wrong side of history for two important reasons. First, his argumentation on the genetic inferiority of blacks was unsound and harmful; second, his administrative rhetorical acts involving the Sally Hemings controversy were indefensible and immoral because they grossly violated his philosophy of virtue and deviated from generally accepted standards of modern civilization.

The second question we wish to answer pertains to the nature of the contribution that Jefferson's rhetoric of virtue has made to knowledge. He was an evolutionist and eclectic who gleaned helpful rhetorical insights from classical scholars, the British/Continental epistemologists, and the belletristic school of thought. By doing so, he played a fundamental part in helping his countrymen gain knowledge and inspiration which were key educational components in the Age of Enlightenment. But he was far more than a borrower who distilled ideas from others. To bring his influence and originality into clearer focus, therefore, we single out five distinctive features of his rhetoric of virtue that gave his ideas uniqueness and relevance.

*The first distinguishing characteristic of his perspectives on rhetoric was the degree that they were formed both in his extensive personal library and in a social setting and public arena.* The result was a happy blending of rhetorical philosophy and practice. Of those rhetorical scholars who preceded him, none perhaps could have matched his comprehensive library holdings; and only Cicero, a political leader, a critic, and a student of religion, could equal Jefferson's interests and achievements. And like his classical hero, Jefferson could draw upon his varied practical experiences to refine, discard, or replace a concept that only had theoretical value. Both men, moreover, were aided by an eloquence of the pen that enabled them to speak to future generations.

*Second, Jefferson recognized that discourse at its highest emphasizes virtue as its principal subject matter.* Not even Plato, with his stress on ideal forms and noble lovers, went further than Jefferson in developing this theme. Nor did Hugh Blair or George Campbell, both of whom were celebrated preachers and educators. What set Jefferson apart from his predecessors and contemporaries on this issue was not a difference in attitude toward the significance of virtue in discourse, but in the degree of emphasis that should be placed on it. The central mission of every form of rhetoric, he noted (as shown in part 1 of this volume), was to communicate virtue. In addition, he made this mission the cornerstone of his oral and written messages. He embraced, in short, a moral philosophical view of discourse that guided and sustained him throughout his life.

*Third, Jefferson's rhetoric of virtue contained instructive and innovative explorations in the area of language.* His early mastery of Greek and Latin, for example, gave him direct access to the writings of classical historians, philosophers, poets, dramatists, legal scholars, and rhetoricians. This mastery, in turn, prompted him to urge his advisees to read these works in the original. Only in this way, he believed, could one appreciate fully Cicero's philosophical and rhetorical essays, and, at the same time, condemn his ornate flamboyant oratorical style.

Jefferson also delved deeply into the Anglo-Saxon language, which he found necessary in the study of law and in discovering many of the roots of Modern English. Similarly, as shown in chapter 5 on channeling the message, he sought to build a native American vocabulary so that more information could be obtained about the early Indians' migration to America. Additionally, he felt, this research could be a useful tool for addressing members of an Indian tribe in a conversation or a formal address.

His most important contribution to the study of language was his support of the notion of neology. In his treatment of this subject, he argued that new words must be created and incorporated into our vocabulary, and obsolete ones eliminated. This was the method, he concluded, that was necessary for making the study of English a dynamic educational enterprise. This forward-looking view regarding language development was consistent with his belief that knowledge generation progresses along an evolutionary plane.

*Fourth, Jefferson's philosophy of rhetorical theory and practice enlarged the understanding of his contemporaries in three important forms of address: Private discourse, political communication, and rhetorical criticism.* In private discourse, first of all, he supplied helpful hints on how conversationalists may achieve excellence in a dialogue. This may be done, he said, by being reasonable and attentive, and by displaying the ingratiating traits of civility, politeness, self-control, and decorum. He then reinforced these suggestions by faithfully adhering to them in his own face-to-face encounters. He was even more instructive and persuasive when it came to letter writing. By sending at least 20,000 carefully constructed letters and receiving a comparable number himself, he became one of the most dedicated and proficient epistolary communicators in American history. It was, as we observed, an art form that not only teaches but entertains and persuades. For these reasons, he strongly believed that a letter writer should be well informed on the subject to be discussed, should understand the importance of adaptation, and should be aware that this rhetorical form takes on the characteristics of a conversation. It should not be forgotten, he further noted, that letter writing reveals the quality of one's mind.

Jefferson's influence on the theory and practice of political communication also has been enduring. Although American legislators were familiar with the basics of parliamentary law—as could be seen in the Continental and Confederation congresses, the Constitutional Convention, the state ratifying conventions, and the First Federal Congress—improvements in the form of refinements and amplifications were needed. Jefferson met this challenge by putting together a set of rules that became a model of governance for years to come. This thoroughly researched and carefully presented treatise was completed while he was vice president and presiding officer of the Senate during John Adams's administration. These rules, along with his two publications on parliamentary procedure, ensured that the American political process would not be marked by the kind of disorder that he had witnessed in the Maryland Assembly in 1766 or in France in the late 1780s.

What Jefferson did in making the press a crucial force in political communication was similarly noteworthy. He was a pioneer in laying the foundation for defining the role of the press in a democratic society by coming down strong on the side of freedom of expression, and on the responsibility of the newspaper editors to use this guaranteed freedom by being truthful, fair, and just in their presentation and analysis of news.[9] It was against this background need for balance that in 1792 he helped launch the *National Gazette*, a Republican organ that could compete equally in the marketplace of ideas with the nationalist Federalist paper, the *Gazette of the United States*.

In addition to his contributions to private discourse and political communication, Jefferson left a valuable legacy in the area of rhetorical criticism. Persuaded that this communication form belonged to the genre of argument, he demonstrated the need for a critic to understand the principles of taste and to use a convincing reasoning and evidence process when rendering a judgment on a rhetor's performance. He taught us, therefore, the importance of knowing Latin when assessing the style of Livy and Tacitus, and of having an in-depth knowledge of French when analyzing the works of Montesquieu and Destutt de Tracy. Critics likewise should be aware, he said, that when they attempt to evaluate a rhetorical episode they themselves have observed, it is unwise to trust their memory, for this mental faculty fades with time. The way to handle this problem, he asserted, was to keep a commonplace book and specific, thorough notes that may be consulted later. This was the policy he followed, for instance, when he responded to William Wirt's request that he give his impressions of Patrick Henry as an orator. And when he did not have adequate primary source material to support a particular critical judgment, as in the case of the Logan speech, he sought aid from his contemporaries who had firsthand information. The works of Jefferson, in brief, contain multiple well-documented descriptions of the rhetorical strengths and shortcomings of his contemporaries that have become rich source material for historians and communication scholars.

*Finally, Jefferson created and implemented a rhetoric of virtue that enabled him to introduce to the American people "the finest and most enlightened aspects of European culture"; then, after Americanizing these ideas, he used his discourse to influence Europeans as well as his own countrymen.* During the years leading up to Independence, he drew upon his republican philosophy and his principles of virtue, which resonated in the colonies, to create *A Summary View of the Rights of British America* and the Declaration of Independence. Both of these works, as earlier noted, had a significant impact on France and generated a favorable response from other parts of European society.

Similarly, the persuasive power of Jefferson's brand of Americanism was strikingly evident in his Paris days from 1784 through 1789. It was at this time his *Notes on the State of Virginia* (1787), containing arguments refuting some of the ideas advanced by Buffon in his *Natural History*, was published. The most memorable of these critiques was his analysis of Logan's celebrated peace-treaty speech to show that Buffon neither understood nor appreciated the potential that native Americans possessed to achieve eloquence. The tenure in France likewise gave Jefferson an opportunity to show how European countries might emulate the Virginians by adopting acts ensuring religious freedom; and it presented to him a chance to instruct the artist Maria Cosway on the reciprocal relationships between the "Head" and the "Heart"—a dialogue that alluded to the American Revolution as an example of the power of both of these dimensions of human nature, working in concert with each other, to produce an act of virtue that has had an enduring value.

Again, in his retirement years, Jefferson, in one of his most important performances as a rhetorical critic, evaluated Montesquieu's *Spirit of Laws* and Destutt de Tracy's *Commentary and Review*. Relying on his knowledge of the French language and on his philosophy of criticism, he balanced the weaknesses against the strengths of Montesquieu's major premises, and then demonstrated how Tracy's *Commentary* provided not only a document that substantially improved the *Spirit of Laws*, but one that all Americans and the citizens of other democratic nations should embrace. In all, Jefferson did more than construct a rhetoric of virtue that would elevate the taste and communication competence of his fellow Americans. For, as we have attempted to demonstrate, he also sought to apply his principles and practices of discourse for the purpose of influencing European political and social thought in such a way that an American form of republicanism and a rhetoric of virtue could flourish abroad. In a conversation he had with John Bernard, Jefferson used the following metaphorical language to summarize what he had in mind when reflecting on this fifth distinguishing feature of his rhetoric of virtue: "America, the child of the Old World, appears destined to become its teacher. Like the heart in the human system, it has received and sent back purified the diseased opinions of England and France."[10]

Jefferson, we suggest, constructed a virtue-centered philosophy of rhetoric that enabled him to transmit the basic elements of the Enlightenment to the American people, and, at the same time, helped the citizens to put these Enlightenment and discourse principles into practice as members of a republican society. Although he failed in some important instances to conform to his own teachings, especially on the subject of African Americans and slavery, he nevertheless left an enduring legacy emanating from a rhetorical philosophy that has withstood the test of time. It was a philosophy grounded in virtue and in the evolutionary concept of knowledge generation. Moreover, it was a philosophy that led to the creation of an influential pamphlet on the rights of British Americans, of a historically significant Declaration of Independence, and of a memorable First Inaugural Address. These representative accomplishments were possible because of his strong commitment to the power of discourse as a persuasive instrument, his extensive reading and note taking, his eloquence of the pen, and his pivotal role as a participant observer in the making of history. As students of discourse and history, we are pleased that he set aside time to use his talent to formulate and implement a rhetoric of virtue that shows what communication is capable of becoming.

# Notes

1. James Madison to N. P. Trist, July 6, 1826, in Gaillard Hunt, ed., *The Writings of James Madison*, 9 vols. (New York: Putnam's, 1910), 9: 247–48.

2. "Afterword," in Onuf, ed., *Jeffersonian Legacies*, 459.

3. Sir Walter Scott, ed., *The Works of Jonathon Swift*, 19 vols. (Boston: Houghton Mifflin, 1883), 10: 221–25.

4. Richard L. Johannesen, Rennard Strickland, and Ralph T. Eubanks, eds., *Language Is Sermonic: Richard M. Weaver and the Nature of Rhetoric* (Baton Rouge: Louisiana State University Press, 1970), 225. Chaim Perelman and L. Olbrechts-Tyteca, *New Rhetoric* (Notre Dame: University of Notre Dame Press, 1969), 75, speak

of the relationship between ethics and rhetoric: "But in the fields of law, politics, and philosophy, values intervene as a basis for argument at all stages of development." Ibid.

5. Gordon S. Wood, "The Trials and Tribulations of Thomas Jefferson," in *Jeffersonian Legacies*, 402–407.

6. In one of the articles included in his Appeal, entitled, "Our Wretchedness in Consequence of Slavery," David Walker singles out Jefferson nine times for criticism. He was particularly concerned with the arguments included in the *Notes on the State of Virginia* in which it was argued that blacks were inferior. *Walker's Appeal, in Four Articles, Together with a Preamble to the Colored Citizens of the World, but in Particular, and very Expressly to those of the United States of America* (Boston: D. Walker, 1830), 9–21.

7. In alluding to Jefferson's decision to remain a slaveholder, Boyd asserted that Jefferson "experienced increasing difficulty in reconciling his ownership of slaves with his libertarian political principles." This was especially evident when he failed to find a meaningful answer to this troubling question: were "the equalitarian ideals of the Declaration of Independence" meant to be applied "to all members of American society or to whites only?" Boyd, 22: 54n. This inconsistency was the basis for the concern expressed by Banneker in the early 1790s. Jefferson, in sum, created a moral dilemma from which he seemingly could not extricate himself.

8. Wood, "The Trials and Tribulations of Thomas Jefferson," in *Jeffersonian Legacies*, 386.

9. Although Jefferson as a political leader did not always put into practice his teachings on the need for a free press, what he had to say when discussing the philosophy and significance of this theme was both relevant and sound.

10. Bernard, *Retrospections of America*, 234.

# APPENDIX

~

# Thomas Jefferson's Scrapbooks

After we had completed the manuscript included for this volume, we read a column in the *Washington Post* entitled "Scrapbooks Believed to Be Work of Jefferson." This article, written by Lee Smith on September 30, 1999, advanced the thesis "that four Scrapbooks previously regarded as the work of Thomas Jefferson's grandchildren were actually compiled by the nation's third President." This conclusion was drawn by Robert Mac-Donald, a professor of history at the United States Military Academy, following extensive research at the University of Virginia.

In responding to MacDonald's findings, two important Jefferson scholars not only supported his thesis but pointed out the significance of the discovery. James Horn, Saunders director of the International Center for Jeffersonian Studies at Monticello, noted: "It conforms to everything we know about the aspects of his character." Similarly, Dan Jordan, president of the Thomas Jefferson Memorial Foundation, called the scrapbooks "a major find" because of the additional revelations they provide about Jefferson's personality and his wide-ranging intellectual interests.[1]

After reading the *Washington Post* story, we felt constrained to examine the four scrapbooks to see if the content appeared to us to be the work of Jefferson, and if they contributed in any way to the arguments we developed in our study. We located the first three scrapbooks in the Rare Book Collection at the Alderman Library of the University of Virginia. Because of the considerable interest the scrapbooks had generated, the fourth volume was placed on display at the visitor's center at Monticello. In order to accommodate us, officials temporarily moved this volume to the Research Center for Jefferson Studies located in the new Peter Jefferson building so that we could have access to it.

After a careful perusal of each page of the four scrapbooks, we learned, as did the other scholars previously cited, that the materials did indeed constitute additional Jefferson commonplace books consisting of newspaper clippings and other sources dealing with such forms of discourse as political, religious, and legal, expressed in both poetical verses and prose— with poetry being the dominant mode of channeling the message. Our note taking focused on representative samples of each of these communication forms. This procedure was then supplemented by research on those items that we believed to have high compulsion value on the subject of Jefferson's philosophy of the rhetoric of virtue.

Our analysis reinforces the claims articulated by MacDonald, Jordan, and Horn concerning the authenticity and importance of the scrapbooks. It is for this reason we have opted to include this essay as an appendix. In doing so, we develop the premise that these four commonplace scrapbooks, taken as a whole, are a compilation of data showing Jefferson's commitment to virtue. Although this commitment is expressed most often in a serious way, we will observe that he was, on occasion, attracted to humorous rhetorical specimens, including songs, parodies, and ballads.

The plan we have adopted in this addendum consists of two parts. First of all, we examine the clippings that consist of direct appeals to virtue in general and to virtue in particular. Second, we center our attention on those materials that fall under the headings of forms of discourse as discussed by Jefferson.

## Virtue as a Dominant Theme of the Scrapbooks

### Appeals to Virtue in General

We have selected three poems to illustrate typical emphases on virtue in general. The first, "An Apostrophe to Virtue," contains ten lines that begin with these words:

> Hail radiant Virtue! friend to humankind—
> Bright "emanation of the eternal mind!"
> To thee we owe, Whate'er becomes us best,
> Meekness in pain, and calmness when Opprest.

The second, entitled "Virtue Praised," is a sonnet that starts with this verse:

> Would you the bloom of youth should last?
> 'Tis Virtue that must bind it fast,

> And easy carriage, wholly free
> From sour reserve, or levity.

The third, labeled "More Lovely Virtue in a Lovely Form," depicts how virtue may be enhanced when beauty is present. "What is beauty?" the poet asks. It is, he said, "a flower" and a "rainbow of the sky." These little poems portray the centrality of virtue in our lives and in discourse.

## Appeals to Virtue in Particular

Far more numerous and persuasive were the scrapbook clippings that focus on particular virtues which take the form of social affections as discussed in chapters 2 and 4. In an essay sent to members of the "Republican Society," parents were told that the soothing affection of *happiness*, which is largely "the result of a virtuous conduct," often will feature "a decency of manners" and a "felicitous" state of mind.

The social affection of *benevolence*, which inspired both Francis Hutcheson and Jefferson, also found a place among the clippings both in verse and in prose form. In a poem embracing twenty lines, the author noted that "Benevolence was formed to save," and "to pluck the thorns that bar the way to heaven." Additionally, a paragraph on "Cursory Thoughts" argued that those who "render services . . . to their fellowmen" would fill their mind with "sweet sensations."

In various poems, the ingratiating affection of *friendship* was praised as the "Queen of earthly joys" and "harmony of souls" which has the power to "cheer the heart" and "wipe the tear from sorrow's eye." To be deprived of friendship, one writer observed, reduces "human life" to a "wretched void" and "a desert of despair."

The nature and impact of one's *conscience*, which was, to Jefferson, a person's guide along the pathway to virtue, found expression in this verse:

> A Quiet Conscience in the breast,
> Has only peace, has only rest;
> The music and the mirth of Kings
> Are out of tune, unless she sings.

These traits suggest why Jefferson believed strongly that one's conscience should always be obeyed.

Poems and prose selections highlighting *beauty* and *sublimity* are similarly included in the scrapbooks because of their influence on stirring the imagination. Especially appealing is a poem titled "Moral and Natural Beauty," and a vivid description of a sublime panoramic view seen by a traveler "on an excursion from Baltimore, by way of Berkeley Springs through Friend's Cove, over Dunning's Mountain to Bedford, PA in the summer of 1807." The scene portrayed in this vignette was reminiscent of some of the sublime passages in Jefferson's *Notes on the State of Virginia*.

Perhaps the most motivating and sentimental of all of the social affections, in Jefferson's opinion, was the emotion of *love*. It was this passion that marked the relationship with his wife and his daughters Martha and Mary. In 1799, as we saw in chapter 3, he wrote to Mary: "To you I had rather indulge the effusions of the heart which tenderly loves you, which builds its happiness on yours, and feels in every other object but of little interest." Not surprisingly, therefore, the clippings contain several poems addressed to a beloved girl named Mary. The one that was most graphic, forceful, and relevant to Jefferson, we feel, is a poem by Robert Burns with the title "To Mary in Heaven." Jefferson long had admired Burns for his penetrating insights, his beautiful language, and his mastery of the written Scottish dialect. From the thirty-one lines in this poem, we have chosen the ensuing five to illustrate the moving sentiment Burns wished to convey:

> My Mary from my soul was torn. . . .
> My Mary, departed Shade!
> Where is thy place of blissful rest?
> See'st thou thy lover lowly laid?
> Hears't thou the groans that rend his breast?

It is no wonder that this poem was incorporated into the scrapbooks, for Jefferson's daughter had died during his presidency.[2]

A second poem, "Love and Reason," describes what might occur if one of these affections excludes the other as a partner. In this instance, love, by neglecting reason, "expired on Reason's breast!" When inserting this poem into his scrapbooks, Jefferson, it would appear, most likely recalled his letter to Maria Cosway on the "Head" and the "Heart."

In still another poem, an "Ode from Anacreon," we see a different dimension of Jefferson's attitude toward love. Why, the question might be asked, would this ode, numbered XXI, be included when it ends with these lines:

> Then hence with all your sober thinking!
> Since Nature's holy law is drinking;
> I'll make the laws of nature mine,
> And pledge the universe in wine!

The answer for its inclusion, we believe, may be found in an earlier verse which reads:

Observe when mother's earth is dry,
She drinks the droppings of the sky;
And then the dewy Cordial gives
To every thirsty plant that lives.

The poem in its entirety describes the love of nature as seen in the sublimity of the sun, the moon, the earth, the ocean, and the rain.[3]

Among the other poems, essays, and maxims stressed in the scrapbooks are verses on the virtues of prudence, humility, sympathy, wisdom, knowledge, hope, contentment, constancy in death, and the dignity of man. All of these, in combination with the items discussed earlier, are positive social affections that uphold the values related to private and public virtue. But there are examples of the enemies of virtue that also are a part of the scrapbooks. Chief among these are undisciplined "ambition," "affectation," "deceit," "indolence," "insolence," "presumptuous pride," "habitual swearing," and, most of all, "slander." Here are a few select sentences depicting the unsavory nature of some of these enemies of virtue:

*Ambition*—Whenever selfish, ambitious and persecuting men, propose terms of accommodation to those whom they have attempted to crush, either they are afraid of their own weakness or they seek an advantage by stratagem.

*Deceit*—Dissimulation in youth is the forerunner of perfidy in old age. . . . Deceit discovers a little mind which stoops to temporary expedients. Without rising to comprehensive views of conduct, it betrays a dastardly spirit.

*Indolence*—There is nothing more conducive to vice and irregularities than the love of idleness.

*Insolence*—Insolence is always joined with meanness.

*Slander*—Slander, the worst poison ever, finds an early entrance in ignoble minds.

Fortunately for the reader, Jefferson, in compiling his scrapbooks, chose to stress another emotion or social affection—the subject of humor. He often said, as pointed out in our study, that humor could be used as an effective rhetorical strategy for counteracting unwarranted personal attacks. Moreover, he enjoyed reporting humorous stories as told by Franklin, and in relating incidents that reflected on himself. We are not surprised, therefore, when we see clippings on such themes as these: "Three Things a Good Wife Should be Like and Three Things She should not be like"; "Charm for Ennui—A Matrimonial Ballad"; "A Squint at the Ladies"; "Paine and the Devil: A Dialogue"; "Snuff"; "Address to my Segar"; and "The Bachelor's Soliloquy."

Considering the fact that the clippings were assembled almost two centuries ago, two poems in particular would have created a favorable response. The first was "The Old Maid's Prayer," comprised of ten lines. The initial and closing lines are as follows:

> Propitious heaven, O! lend me an ear,
> Give a kind answer to my prayer. . . .
> My prayer is short so grant it then,
> 'Tis but a word, give me a man.

Apparently Jefferson did not believe that such a theme would be inappropriate in a society that eulogized marriage and conjugal love.

Similarly topical was a poem making fun of Napoleon, then emperor of France. Entitled "Bonaparte in Stilts" or "Fortune's Frolic," the poem begins with this verse:

> When "Robin Rough-head," from the plough
> Became a Lord—the Lord knows how—
> The farce he acted had less fun,
> Than that at Paris going on. . . .

The last two lines reach this climax:

> The laughing world he's all surprised,
> And "Fortune's Frolic" realised.

This type of humor ridiculing one of the most powerful political leaders in the world expressed Jefferson's feelings about the anti-republican policies implemented by Napoleon. But because of his position as president, and his love for the French people he had known while serving in France, Jefferson would not state his negative attitudes toward Napoleon in public.[4] He felt safe, however, in having this poem appear in the scrapbooks.

We conclude the first half of this survey of the important role that the theme of virtue plays in the scrapbooks in general and in particular with a reference to a critique of an essay based on William Cowper's "Facetious History of John Gilpin." Cowper, like Burns, was a pre-Romantic poet[5] steeped in the literature of moral values. The author of this item pulled out these lines from Cowper's work and used them as a springboard for his observation: "He hung a bottle on each side, to keep the balance true." With this starting point as a foundation, he then said:

> It is an eternal truth, which no artifice can elude and no sophistry pervert, that to maintain an exact equilibrium between right and wrong, good and evil, pleasure and pain, is the only means to acquire and preserve our virtue, our happiness and our health. This position will universally apply in all cases whatsoever. . . .

Jefferson would have enthusiastically embraced this tribute to virtue.

We have observed in the preceding critique of items in the scrapbooks that Jefferson was inclined to preserve messages designed to move the reader or hearer in the direction of private and public good, and that he relied heavily on the medium of poetry as a major means of transmitting moral ideas. Yet to be considered is how other rhetorical forms (conversation, letter writing, historical narration, political communication, religious exhortations, and legal advocacy) also were popular methods of conveying the nature and power of virtue. How representative scrapbook-items perform this task is our next consideration.

# Application of the Principles of Virtue through the Special Forms of Discourse

## Conversation and Letter Writing

Sprinkled throughout the scrapbooks are several dialogues which both Shaftesbury and Jefferson believed to be the ideal rhetorical form for communicating virtue. One of these, to which we have already alluded, was a piece titled "Thomas Paine and the Devil."

Jefferson's compelling interest in domestic happiness and conjugal love, and his faith in the power of conversation to cement family relationships, prompted him to insert this maxim written by Samuel Johnson: "Marriage should be considered as the most solemn league of perpetual friendship; a state from which artifice and concealment are to be banished forever; and in which every act of dissimulation is a breach of faith." Not to follow this advice, Jefferson thought, is to engage in dishonest communication based on deception which, as Johnson noted, would break the bonds of friendship and violate the marriage oath.

Of particular interest was a five-verse poem entitled "Conversation," written by a Miss Moore. The sentiment expressed in this poem consists of a tribute to a form of discourse that, according to Jefferson, has enormous potential to promote the arousal of the social affections by bringing participants together as they seek to expand their knowledge in a productive atmosphere. The first and last verses catch the essence of the poem:

> Hail conversation, heavenly fair,
> Thou bliss of life, and balm of care!
> Call forth the long forgotten knowledge
> Of school, of travel, and of college!
>
> But 'tis thy commerce, conversation,
> Must give it use by circulation.
> That noblest commerce of mankind,
> Where precious Merchandise is Mind!

Jefferson himself could take pleasure in knowing that he gave this "noblest commerce of mankind" the type of "circulation" that was needed for strengthening the social affections.

Samples of letter writing are similarly a part of the scrapbooks. We may observe, for instance, how the two ensuing letters are concerned with disturbing conditions that represent unhappy relationships, illustrating what Jefferson would describe as enemies of virtue:

> Letter from a Deserted Wife to a Faithless Husband,
> Written in England a Few Years Since
>
> A Copy of a Letter from a Young Lady to her Seducer

By inserting letters that detail the acts of an adulterous husband and a seducer of a young woman, Jefferson was illustrating what might happen when mutual love, sympathy, and respect are not present in a relationship or a chance encounter.

## Historical Writing

Among the items on historical writing assembled in the scrapbooks were multiple stories about Indians; a book on "The Discoveries of Captain Lewis"; "A Picture Gallery: of Tacitus' narrative on the Soldiers of the Rebel Legions"; and a preview of a forthcoming book to be titled the "History and Character of the Ancient Music of Ireland." All of these stories fell within the range of Jefferson's love of history—a discourse form he thought was ideal for communicating virtue. It was only natural for him, therefore, to learn as much as he could about the culture and vocabulary of Indians. It is similarly understandable why he was excited about a volume on "The Discoveries of Captain Lewis," for it was he who had selected and prepared Lewis for his famous expedition that resulted in opening up the West and in advancing the cause of science. It also was understandable that he would be attracted to the works of Tacitus because of the author's high moral standards, his power of narration, and his mastery of language which enabled the Roman historian to become, in Jefferson's opinion, one of the truly great writers of all time. Finally, the book on ancient Irish music would appeal to him for two reasons: First, throughout his lifetime he spent many leisure hours playing music; and, second, he was aware that a number of critics had suggested a possible connection between ancient Irish ballads and the Ossianic poems.

## Political Communication

Of all the virtues that interested Jefferson throughout his life, few transcended in importance the philosophy of republicanism, because of its concerns for the rights of the people. Republicanism, he believed, gave the citizens the greatest promise in their quest for happiness. So strong was his faith in this philosophy of government, as we saw in chapter 6, that he took advantage of every opportunity which arose in a conversational situation to uphold its value system. With such pro-republican sentiments as these, Jefferson made certain that the following passage from the *National Intelligencer* would be included in the scrapbooks:

> It is a fact which cannot have escaped the notice of literary men, that most of the works which have been written in Europe on morals, lay down principles, which in their application inevitably tend to convince the mind of the preference of republican to all other descriptions of political institutions.

The *Intelligencer* went on to say: "Indeed we believe it to be an incontrovertible fact that science, physical or moral, but particularly the latter, wherever it diffuses its light, makes men in principle republican. . . ." Doubtless, such a conclusion was consistent with Jefferson's thinking.

Another significant aspect of Jefferson's philosophy of republicanism was his opposition to a monarchical system of government, like that of Great Britain, which placed a high premium on privileged classes who achieved their positions by virtue of their birth. When he saw the following proverb, therefore, he knew it belonged in his scrapbooks:

> Let high birth triumph! What can be more great?
> Nothing—but merit—in low estate.

This proverb extolling "merit," while denigrating "high birth," took on additional meaning when Jefferson realized that the author was Edward Young (1683–1765), a poet, satirist, and cleric who he, like many of his contemporaries, had come to appreciate.[6]

Discovered among the clippings, moreover, were remarks addressed to the Whigs, two letters written by Thomas Paine which were directed "To the Citizens of the United States," and an essay on "Toryism." There were, in addition, two items focusing on what Jefferson had said two decades earlier about the liberty of the press, and what he had observed to Congress on the slavery issue at the end of 1806.[7]

Political discourse, as seen in the scrapbooks, was strikingly evident during July Fourth celebrations, and following Jefferson's two presidential election victories. Odes and songs were produced for the occasions, and both the Declaration of Independence and the two inaugural addresses were reprinted. The audiences could join in the singing of a song entitled "The People's Friend," and one described as "The Land of Love and Liberty," set to the tune of "Rule Britannia."

But perhaps the form of discourse which delighted Jefferson most were the toasts. At Liberty Hall in Cincinnati on July Fourth, 1806, this toast was read: "Thomas Jefferson, President of the United States—The firm supporter of the rights of man; the Philosopher, the Statesman and the Philanthropist: who justly merits our grateful appreciation, and whose integrity and virtue will live in the remembrance of a free and enlightened People, when calumniators are buried in oblivion." Another toast, delivered on July 4, 1807, noted in part: "his influence depends not on hereditary right, or musty precedent; but on his personal merit and progressive improvement of man."

In celebration of his election to a second term, he was praised for a margin of victory of 162 votes to 14. And in a toast, he was saluted with these words of praise in Windsor, Vermont: "Thomas Jefferson—the Scholar, the Statesman, the Patriot, and the Philospher." To his supporters, the president was an "impregnable rock against which the poisoned arrows of calumny have been hurled, but have fallen harmless at his feet." The theme of these toasts, which was repeated in the various states during his presidency, suggests that Jefferson's political enemies had little hesitation in indicting him for his anti-Federalist stances. But the theme also demonstrated his capacity to handle his detractors with a degree of equanimity consistent with his views on the social affections.

On the whole, it would appear that Jefferson went to great lengths to preserve political materials that were highly complimentary to him and to his achievements. He felt justified in accumulating these praiseworthy messages, however, because their central focus was on attributes epitomizing principles of virtue. In addition, it should be noted, he was willing to include data that were critical of him and his policies. This was evident, first of all, in his decision to save several pieces on the embargo—one of the most controversial issues during his second term as president.

A more compelling example showing his open-mindedness with respect to the scrapbooks was his inclusion of a message addressed to him from a concerned citizen named Beri Hesdin. The letter, clipped from a newspaper, began with this verse from the Old Testament: "Oh, that I were made judge in the land, that every man who hath my suit, or cause, might come unto Me, and I would do him Justice!"[8] Then, in a taunting manner, Hesdin sarcastically asserted: "What think you of this, Mr. Jefferson? But as you are unacquainted with the old fashioned book, from which it is taken . . . common politeness urges an introduction." He proceeded to point out that the citation came from Absalom, the third son of King David, who was seeking to placate the people who were suffering from "the bondage of government, and the encircling arm of law." But these noble-sounding words calling for justice on behalf of the people, observed Hesdin, were both insincere and demagogic for at the time they were uttered, Absalom was devising a plot to overthrow his father and place himself on the throne.

The example of Absalom then was applied to the Republicans who, like the insincere prince, posed as the friend of the people. Yet they rarely have been seen on the streets in support of their unfortunate brethren "who have been grievously oppressed by the land tax, alien law and sedition act!" What makes the insertion of this passage so interesting is that it runs counter to Jefferson's reputation of being unduly sensitive to criticism of Republicans.

## Religious Discourse

When Jefferson turned to items containing religious messages, the subject of sermon topics caught his attention. We have selected several examples illustrating his devotion to the moral teachings of Jesus and their influence on society. One of these selections was grounded in a theme drawn from the Sermon on the Mount, in which Jesus urged his hearers "to pluck the beam out of (their) own eyes" before examining the mote in another's eye.

A second sermon illustrated Jesus' second great commandment—
"Love thy neighbor as thyself"—with these words: "Happy is that man
who is free from envy, who wishes for and rejoices in his neighbor's prosperity, being content with his own condition, & delighted at the good
fortune of those around him. . . ." In a similar vein, a third message noted
that we need to think "justly of men, wisely of virtue, and humanely of
ourselves." A fourth religious theme that was developed in another presentation drew this conclusion: "As Christianity exhibits the most enrap-
turing motives to the practice of virtue, so it urges the most tremendous
considerations to deter from vice."

We suggested in our chapter on religious discourse that Jefferson believed a minister should emphasize almost exclusively moral principles
such as those taught by Jesus. This is the rationale he may have used,
therefore, to preserve a piece labled "Reflections." In this instance, the
author condemned ministers who were overly inclined to fill their sermons with ideas cited from Aristotle, Quintilian, and Longinus, and from
the speeches of Cicero to show their knowledge of classical literature.
When they do so, he added, the parishioners would frequently be unaware that they "were listening to a minister of the Christian religion." It
was concluded that preachers who follow this practice "are only ambitious of the character of elegant rhetoricians, and connosieurs in variety
of style; now flying on the unfeathered wings of high sounding words. . . ."
The fact that Jefferson's rhetorical philosophy was influenced in part by
Cicero, Quintilian, and Longinus did not prevent him from agreeing with
the author's claim that a preacher's primary duty in constructing a sermon
is to rely on religious and/or moral themes designed to appeal to the understanding and to stir the social affections.

Since we have repeatedly sought to demonstrate that the quest for
virtue was, for Jefferson, the significant guiding principle in his life, we
were impressed with two other listings on religious discourse. The first
was a critique of an English clergyman, Dr. Archibald Maclaine, who for
forty-eight years served as minister of the English Church in The Hague.
When he died, the English newspapers described "A Funeral Oration" in
which Maclaine was eulogized "for his great piety and learning." Such a
tribute to Maclaine was rejected outright by the author of the column appearing in an American newspaper. The article accused Maclaine of using his office as a divine for political purposes by instilling into his listeners "all the pernicious principles of the English cabinet." Even more
disconcerting were his practices of securing "court favor for himself and
his children"; and of "gambling, drinking," "wenching," and "swearing."

Indeed, so reprehensible were his actions "that his company . . . was shunned by every man and woman in the Hague, who had the smallest regard for their own reputation."[9]

The second clipping on insincerity and hypocrisy was stated in a poem entitled "On Going to Church." The question addressed by the poet was why do we attend church? Among the answers offered were these: to take a "walk" or to "laugh and talk"; to "meet a lover" or a "friend," and "to learn the parson's name" so that we can "wound his fame." The last two lines then read:

> Many go there to dose and nod—
> But few go there to worship God.

Before we conclude this section on religious rhetoric, it is important to observe that there were occasional statements in a few of the items we have discussed which would not be consistent with Jefferson's thinking. They include references to Jesus as "the lamb of God, which taketh away the sins of the world," and as "our blessed Redeemer." Nor would he accept the premise that the task of "A Gospel Christian" is to inculcate "the plain, simple and obvious doctrine of 'CHRIST, AND HIM CRUCIFIED.'" For the same reason, he could not endorse the words appearing in "A Hymn for Easter" which he also placed in the scrapbooks. His decision to keep such items, however, was consistent with the open-minded policy he followed in later years when creating his "Syllabus" and his "Bible."[10] But one of his beliefs remained constant, and that was his enduring faith in the moral perspectives of Jesus.

## Legal Advocacy

Our primary concern in this section on legal advocacy is with two documents that became a part of the scrapbooks. The first, which was taken from the *Aurora*, is a portion of an "Address to Lawyers by an Eminent Quaker Minister in 1656." The lawyers were told to forget their own personal welfare and to develop arguments grounded in truth and justice. This end should be achieved without experiencing feelings of envy or a desire for revenge. They were further advised to be willing to defend "the poor against the rich" when the situation demanded it, and to strive hard not to offer remedies which may be "worse than the disease." Quite clearly, this brief message, marked by appeals to virtue, could not help but resonate with Jefferson.

The second example of legal communication was a speech delivered before the Lord Chief Justice in Ireland on May 16, 1802, by the celebrated lawyer and parliamentary leader John Philpot Curran. Almost immediately, the speech was reprinted in its entirety in pamphlet form in Richmond, Virginia.[11] It represents, in our opinion, the single most valuable material included in the four scrapbooks because of its thoroughness and clear focus on what Jefferson believed about virtue as it relates to jurisprudential discourse.[12]

The principals in the litigation were John Hevey, the plaintiff, and Major Charles Henry Sirr, the defendant. The central issue was "On an Action for Assault or False Imprisonment." Curran represented Hevey, a brewer, who had sued Sirr for 5,000 pounds in damages because of his unjustified arrest and imprisonment, and the unfair treatment he had received during his weeks of incarceration. The case was unique in that there was a need for two distinct steps in the narration of the facts describing what had taken place.

Curran began his narration in phase one by going back to the year 1798. At that time, Sirr was an insignificant "town-major" whose influence in Dublin was negligible. Suddenly, he was invested with enormous police powers that gave him absolute authority over the citizens of Dublin and the surrounding area. "With this gentleman's extraordinary elevation," argued Curran, "began the story of the sufferings and ruin of the plaintiff."

The precipitating factor that created Sirr's animus toward Hevey was the latter's testimony against a prosecution witness in a trial involving a man accused of an offence against the state. The witness was described by Hevey, his former employer, "as a man of infamous character." On the basis of this damaging testimony, the witness was dismissed and the prisoner set free. A few days later, an angry Sirr met Hevey on the street and accused him of interfering "in his business, and swore by God he would teach him" not "to meddle with his people." On the next evening, Hevey was attacked in a "lonely alley" by unidentified authorities who charged him with treason against Major Sirr. As a result, he was promptly sent to the "Castle Yard called the provost"—a prison commonly known as "a mansion of misery." There he was placed under the supervision of Major Sandys, a friend and confidant of Sirr, and remained unnoticed for seven weeks. Not even his family members knew where he was or what had occurred.

While in prison, Hevey had his horse confiscated and turned over to Sandys for his personal use. This was being done, observed Sandys, because "you are to be sent down tomorrow to Kilkenny, to be tried for your life; you will most certainly be hanged. . . ."

Fortunately for Hevey, Lord Cornwallis, upon reading an account of the proceedings, concluded that Hevey had been unjustly treated, and thus signed an order releasing him from prison at once. As a free man, Hevey brought an action against Sandys.[13] At this point in the narration of phase one, Curran stated that he was discussing "a system of concerted vengeance and oppression." Sandys and Sirr, he claimed, "acted in concert." He then made this telling argument:

> I see Major Sandys in Court; (thus I want him to know) I can prove the facts beyond the possibility of denial. If he does not dare to appear . . . as I have called upon him, I prove it by his not daring to appear. If he does not venture to come forward, I will prove it by his own oath, or if he ventures to deny a syllable that I have stated, I will prove it by irrefragable evidence that his denial was false or perjured.[14]

With the conclusion of this strongly worded argument, phase one of the narration ended.

The second phase detailing the facts in the case began with Curran's reference to a volatile incident that occurred three years later. While Hevey and Sirr were seated in two different places in a public coffee house, the former was notified that Sirr had just asserted that Hevey "ought to have been hanged." Upon hearing this, Hevey approached Sirr and called him "a slanderous scoundrel." Hevey was immediately grabbed by Sirr's men and sent to the Castle guard where "he was flung into a room," 12 by 13 feet in size. Shortly afterwards, Major Sandys, speaking in a condescending and threatening manner, gave this warning to Hevey: "Your crime is your insolence to Major Sirr; however, he disdains to trample upon you—you may appease him by proper and contrite submission, but unless you do so, you shall rot where you are."

Under strong pressure from his family, Hevey, observed Curran, signed "a submission dictated by Sandys." He had, in short, released "his claim to the common rights of a humane creature, by humbling himself to the brutal arrogance of a pampered slave." At the close of his narration in phase two, Curran summarized the arguments he had made and the conclusions to be drawn from them. He was now ready to turn to the question of the damages that should be given to Hevey.

After suggesting that "the full amount of the damages laid in the declaration" (5,000 pounds) should be awarded, "either as a compensation for the injury of the plaintiff, or as a punishment for the savage barbarity of the defendant," he gave two reasons why this action should be taken. First, he said, Ireland is under the dominion of England; and, second, because there is no freedom of the press in Ireland, England is unaware of "the thousand instances of atrocity which we have witnessed, as hideous as the present. . . ." These conditions make it imperative, therefore, that a verdict will be rendered that will attract attention throughout Great Britain. The strategy required to achieve this goal, continued Curran, was to follow the example of Homer who, when portraying great historical events, chose to exemplify rather than describe. To illustrate the significance of this rhetorical approach, Curran observed:

> I am therefore anxious that our *masters* should have one authenticated example of the treatment which our unhappy country suffers under the sanction of their authority; it will put a strong question to their humanity, if they have any—to their prudence if their pride will let them listen to it; or, at least, to that anxiety for reputation, to that pretension to the imaginary virtues of mildness and mercy. . . .

What Curran was arguing, in the tradition of Homer, is that a vivid representative anecdote has the power to appeal to the understanding and to arouse the imagination.[15]

Almost every aspect of the case had meaning for Jefferson. In the first place, Curran, like his American counterpart, was a lover of the classics and of history, literature, jurisprudence, and Whig principles. Moreover, both placed their faith in the people, fought against governmental tyranny, and recognized the value of rhetoric as a means of producing and sustaining virtue. But it was the message in the oration itself that inspired Jefferson most because of the emphasis placed on private and public good. At the heart of the case was the subject of human rights and justice. Similarly, the arguments in the brief also dealt with such enemies of virtue as anger, hatred, revenge, suppression of a free press, and governmental tyranny. There could be little doubt that Jefferson relived in his own mind the problems facing the colonies during the period from 1774 through 1776 as he read of the conditions in Ireland and the indifference in England concerning them in the four-year period between 1798 and 1802. Jefferson, moreover, would have shared with Curran a feeling of consternation and disgust at the ruthless actions of Majors Sirr and Sandys as they sought to dehumanize Hevey. Finally, he, like Curran, would have been deeply disappointed in learning that the court, under the influence of the loyalists, was motivated to reduce the fine to a mere 150 pounds.[16]

In 1804, two years after the trial had ended, Curran published a book titled *Forensic Eloquence* which contained a reprint of his oration on *Hevey v. Major Sirr*.[17] As proof of Jefferson's continuing interest in this case and in Curran's forensic career, he purchased a copy of *Forensic Eloquence*, and on February 15, 1805, had it bound for his library.[18]

The scrapbooks, as we have attempted to show, are a revealing portrait of Jefferson's devotion to the subject of virtue during his two terms as president. There are, of course, other materials compiled in the four volumes, including messages on agriculture, science, and the mechanical arts. But the pervasive theme of private and public virtue, from our perspective, constitutes the dominant thrust.

We are indebted to the researchers responsible for this "major find," and to the libraries at the University of Virginia and at the Research Center for Jefferson Studies for making the materials so readily available to us. Together, they have given us an important opportunity to have access to data that reinforce the thesis developed in *Thomas Jefferson and the Rhetoric of Virtue*.

# Notes

1. *Washington Post*, September 30, 1999, A9. In a telephone interview on October 14, 1999, with Christine Coalwell, Gilder Fellow for Monticello and a colleague of James Horn, we were given these opinions: (1) The *Post* story was accurate in its facts and in its interpretations; (2) The scrapbooks are actually commonplace books similar to the others produced by Jefferson; (3) Jefferson occasionally wrote brief comments on the clippings, such as the words "very fine" on one of the poems; (4) he sometimes corrected faulty spelling in the messages; and (5) he alluded at one point to the organizational plan that was adopted for compiling the materials.

2. Burns's poem "To Mary in Heaven" is printed in *An Anthology of Romanticism* as an example of the "Pre-Romantic Movement," in Ernest Bernbaum, ed., *Anthology of Romanticism* (New York: Ronald Press, 1948), 91–92.

3. We found Anacreon's poem in Thomas Moore, *Odes of Anacreon* (Philadelphia: Hugh Maxwell, 1804). The listing in the scrapbooks is marked number XXI in Moore's edition, 115–117. This work was first published in London in 1800 and was a part of TJ's library. Sowerby notes that "the work copied in the *Literary Commonplace Book* over his name was not actually by Anacreon," but "it was thought to be his work in the 18th century and was so regarded by Jefferson, whose great library contained a number of editions and translations of this early Greek poet." Sowerby, *The Catalogue of the Library of Thomas Jefferson*, vol. 5.

4. See TJ's letter to Dr. George Logan, May 19, 1816, in Ford, 11: 527. This letter is discussed in chapter 16 of our text.

5. See *Anthology of Romanticism*, 3, 4. Other favorite writers of TJ are included; among them are Shaftesbury and James MacPherson.

6. TJ recorded approximately 30 citations from Young in his *Literary Commonplace Book*. He also classified Young as a "great" poet.

7. This reference was taken from TJ's "Sixth Annual Message to Congress," December 2, 1806. This speech was discussed in chapter 16 of our volume.

8. This verse from the Old Testament is found in 2 Samuel 15:4.

9. Maclaine's private immorality as a preacher most likely would have stimulated Jefferson's memory of the case of *Godwin et al. v. Lunan* (1771), as analyzed in chapter 12 of our book.

10. See E. Forrester Church, "Introduction" to *The Jefferson Bible*, 27.

11. (Richmond, Va.: Pleasants, 1802). This is the copy appearing in the scrapbooks.

12. The Richmond edition occupies 14 lengthy pages. This has the same wording as that included in *Forensic Eloquence*.

13. This suit was successful. The decision of the court required Sandys to return Hevey's horse and to pay for the costs of the suit.

14. We can conclude from this argument that Sandys was present during Sirr's trial, but apparently he refused to be a formal witness.

15. The subject of a representative anecdote was discussed in chapter 16. But the scholar we quoted as the initiator of the naming of this rhetorical concept was the twentieth-century rhetorician Kenneth Burke. Although TJ did not use this term, he put the concept into practice. We are indebted to Curran for his use of the Homer example.

16. A footnote in *Forensic Eloquence* features this statement which epitomized Curran's feelings about the limited award: "The jury being very loyally inclined, gave to Mr. Hevey by their verdict, for all his insults, losses and sufferings, *one hundred and fifty pounds*" (321).

17. *Forensic Eloquence*. The full description in the title is as follows: *Sketches of Trials in Ireland for High Treason, etc. including the Speeches of Mr. Curran at length: accompanied by certain papers illustrating the history and present state of that country* (Baltimore: G. Douglas, 1804).

18. Sowerby, *Catalogue of the Library of Thomas Jefferson*, vol. 5:30.

# Name Index

~

# Subject Index

~

Account Book (Jefferson), 128, 359, 360

Act of Cession (1783), 419

*Adams, John, Diary and Autobiography of*, 221; Jefferson "could stand no competition with [other political leaders] in the Elocution and public debate," 221

*Advancement of Learning* (Bacon), 8, 47

African Americans and slavery: comparison of blacks with Indians, 50; comparison of blacks with whites, 50, 421–23; comparison of Roman and American slavery, 52, 422; Britain blamed for introducing slaves in the colonies against the wishes of many British Americans, 227, 239; slavery, a moral evil not conducive to republican virtue, 324; recommendation of a delay in the publication of the *Notes on the State of Virginia* because of views expressed on slavery, 324–25; slavery issue a "fire bell in the night" and a "knell of the Union," 417; "all men are born free," thus possessing a "personal liberty," 419;

involuntary servitude to be phased out after 1800, 419–20; negative impact of slavery on "manners," "morals," and "education," 420, 421; blacks incapable of "sublime oratory" or of "poetry," 421–22; letters to and from Benjamin Banneker noted that slavery had a debilitating effect on a man's "moral sense," 425–26; TJ sent Banneker's *Almanac* to the French scholar Condorcet, 426; TJ acknowledged that "slavery was a violation of the natural rights of man," 423, 426; emancipation and colonization plan, 420, 423, 427, 431; TJ defended his views by asserting that he advanced his premises as a "suspicion only," 422; administrative rhetoric or nonverbal communication, 432–34; Sally Hemings affair as a case study in administrative rhetoric, 434–51; DNA test leads to the conclusion that it is highly probable that Jefferson was the father of Eston Hemings, 442–46; application of the Toulmin model of argument to the DNA test

# About the Authors

~

**James L. Golden** received his B.A. from George Washington University in 1947, his M.A. from The Ohio State University in 1948, and his Ph.D. from the University of Florida in 1953. He spent seventeen years as a faculty member at such colleges as the University of Maryland, University of Richmond, Pasadena College, Muskingum College, and Illinois State University. He then joined the Department of Communication (now called Journalism and Communication) at The Ohio State University in 1966, where he remained until his retirement in December 1987. While at Ohio State, he also served as a visiting professor for one quarter at Shaw University and for two quarters at Dartmouth College. Following his retirement, he became a visiting professor at Emerson College for two years.

As a teacher and researcher, he focused primarily on rhetoric, public discourse, and political communication. He has published more than sixty articles in regional, national, and international journals, and has co-authored five books, the most important of which is *The Rhetoric of Western Thought*, now in its seventh edition. In addition, he has presented lectures throughout the United States, at the Universities of Lisbon and London, and at conferences in Belgium and France. Many of these publications and lectures deal with the theories of such classic scholars as Cicero and Quintilian as well as British authors John Locke, David Hume, Lord Kames, and Hugh Blair—all of whom had a profound influence on the rhetorical thought and practice of Thomas Jefferson.

He was a recipient of the Distinguished College Teaching Award sponsored by the Communication Association of Ohio in 1973, and was awarded the Distinguished Alumni Teaching Award by The Ohio State

University in 1982. For twelve years, he was Parliamentarian of The Ohio State University Senate. In 1986 a book was published entitled *Rhetorical Studies Honoring James L. Golden,* and in 1993 he was appointed as a member of the Thomas Jefferson Commemoration Commission Honoring His 250th Anniversary.

**Alan L. Golden** received his B.A. from the University of Richmond in 1978, his M.A. from the same institution in 1981, and his Ph.D. from The Ohio State University in 1990. His major emphasis for each degree was American history. His doctoral dissertation focused on "The Secession Crisis in Virginia: A Critical Study of Argument." An important background chapter in the study deals with the subject of "Jefferson Republicanism and the Emerging Concept of States Rights."

Before obtaining his last degree, he was an archivist for the Virginia Historical Society from 1979–1984, the acting curator for the Edgar Allan Poe Museum from 1980–1985, and a research archivist at the Virginia State Library and Archives from 1984–1985. During the period from 1989–1992, he served as an adjunct faculty member in history at J. Sargeant Reynolds Community College, Mary Baldwin College, Virginia Commonwealth University, and the University of Richmond. In 1992 he became an assistant professor of history at Lock Haven University, and in 1998 he was promoted to associate professor. Of the twelve courses he taught, ten were in American history, ranging from a course on colonial America to one on American political history.

Among his publications, two deal with aspects of Jefferson's political career. The first, entitled "Thomas Jefferson's Perspectives as an Instrument of Political Communication," appeared in the *American Behavioral Scientist* in 1993. The second, "Dialogue and Disagreement in Washington's First Cabinet," was published in the *Journal of Contemporary Thought* in 2000. Jefferson also was a theme in Professor Golden's numerous conference presentations before historical groups. These themes include Jefferson's views on education, his arguments in the Batture Case, and his notions on republican virtue and Hume's *History of England.* Finally, at the time of his death in the fall of 2001, he had begun work as coauthor of a projected volume on "Logan's Lament: An Ethnohistorical Analysis." This work in progress was inspired by Jefferson's celebrated critique of the famous Mingo leader's peace treaty speech in 1774.